TEST PREP SERIES

GRE®
VERBAL PRACTICE QUESTIONS
2025-2026

> 2 Full Verbal Tests

> Realistic GRE-Style Questions

> Detailed Answer Explanations

> In-Depth Focus on All Question Types

Scan the QR Code to access Online Resources
bit.ly/GRE-VPQ

GRE® Verbal Practice Questions
First Edition

Copyright © 2025, by Vibrant Publishers LLC, USA. All rights reserved. No part of this publication may be reproduced or distributed in any form or by any means, or stored in a database or retrieval system, without the prior permission of the publisher.

Published by Vibrant Publishers LLC, USA, **www.vibrantpublishers.com**

Paperback ISBN 13 : 978-1-63651-441-3

Ebook ISBN 13: 978-1-63651-495-6

Library of Congress Control Number: 2025939626

This publication is designed to provide accurate and authoritative information regarding the subject matter covered. The Author has made every effort in the preparation of this book to ensure the accuracy of the information. However, information in this book is sold without warranty, either expressed or implied. The Author or the Publisher will not be liable for any damages caused or alleged to be caused either directly or indirectly by this book.

All trademarks and registered trademarks mentioned in this publication are the property of their respective owners. These trademarks are used for editorial and educational purposes only, without intent to infringe upon any trademark rights. This publication is independent and has not been authorized, endorsed, or approved by any trademark owner.

Vibrant Publishers' books are available at special quantity discounts for sales promotions, or for use in corporate training programs. For more information, please write to **bulkorders@vibrantpublishers.com**

Please email feedback/corrections (technical, grammatical, or spelling) to **spellerrors@vibrantpublishers.com**

Vibrant publishes in a variety of print and electronic formats and by print-on-demand. Some material included with standard print versions of this book may not be included in e-books or in print-on-demand. To access the complete catalog of Vibrant Publishers, visit **www.vibrantpublishers.com**

GRE® is the registered trademark of the Educational Testing Service (ETS) which neither sponsors nor endorses this product.

GRE® Books in Test Prep Series

GRE® QUANTITATIVE PRACTICE QUESTIONS

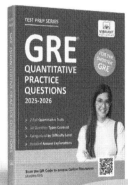

Paperback ISBN:
978-1-63651-440-6

PRACTICE TESTS FOR THE GRE®

Paperback ISBN:
978-1-63651-439-0

GRE® WORDS IN CONTEXT: THE COMPLETE LIST

Paperback ISBN:
978-1-63651-206-8

GRE® MASTER WORDLIST: 1535 WORDS FOR VERBAL MASTERY

Paperback ISBN:
978-1-63651-196-2

For more practice, visit www.vibrantpublishers.com

Dear Test Taker

Thank you for choosing GRE® Verbal Practice Questions by Vibrant Publishers. We are truly honored to support you in this significant stage of your academic and professional journey. Preparing for the GRE is both a challenge and an opportunity—one that demands not just hard work but also the right guidance and resources. At Vibrant Publishers, we aim to be that reliable support system by creating books that are:

- **Content-rich** – Covers key GRE topics in a way that's clear, practical, and easy to absorb
- **Concise** – Designed to focus on what really matters, without unnecessary distractions
- **Approachable** – Written in a clear, accessible manner to ease your learning process
- **Strategic** – Built to mirror the test format and sharpen your skills for the actual GRE

How This Book Supports Your Success:

- Helps you identify strengths and areas for improvement
- Builds the confidence you need to tackle challenging questions
- Trains you to manage time effectively under test conditions
- Encourages a step-by-step approach to mastering verbal reasoning

Tips for Getting the Most Out of This Book:

✓ Set a regular practice schedule and stick to it

✓ Take notes and track recurring errors or patterns

✓ Use the answer explanations as learning tools—not just to check accuracy

✓ Stay patient and persistent—progress comes with consistent effort

We also recognize that every learner's journey is unique. If you have questions, feedback, or suggestions as you work through this book, we warmly invite you to connect with us. Your input helps us create better resources for all learners.

Email us anytime at reachus@vibrantpublishers.com

As you take on this challenge, we hope this book proves to be a valuable companion and that your preparation opens doors to exciting new academic and professional opportunities.

Wishing you focus, clarity, and success on your GRE journey!

Warm regards,
The Vibrant Publishers Team

Table of Contents

	How to Use This Book	vii
	Focused Book Plan	xii
Chapter 1	Overview of the GRE General Test	1
Chapter 2	Introduction to Verbal Reasoning	13
Chapter 3	Reading Comprehension	17

Introduction to Reading Comprehension 18

Practice Set 1: Arts and Humanities 27

Practice Set 1: Answer Key 38

Practice Set 1: Answers & Explanations 39

Practice Set 2: Biological Sciences 49

Practice Set 2: Answer Key 60

Practice Set 2: Answers & Explanations 61

Practice Set 3: Business 73

Practice Set 3: Answer Key 86

Practice Set 3: Answers & Explanations 87

Practice Set 4: Everyday Topics 98

Practice Set 4: Answer Key 112

Practice Set 4: Answers & Explanations 113

Practice Set 5: Physical Sciences 125

Practice Set 5: Answer Key 136

Practice Set 5: Answers & Explanations 137

Practice Set 6: Social Sciences 148

Practice Set 6: Answer Key 160

Practice Set 6: Answers & Explanations 161

Chapter 4   Text Completion   173

Introduction to Text Completion   174

Practice Set 1: One Blank   179

Practice Set 1: Answer Key   186

Practice Set 1: Answers & Explanations   187

Practice Set 2: Two Blanks   204

Practice Set 2: Answer Key   212

Practice Set 2: Answers & Explanations   213

Practice Set 3: Three Blanks   229

Practice Set 3: Answer Key   238

Practice Set 3: Answers & Explanations   239

Chapter 5   Sentence Equivalence   253

Introduction to Sentence Equivalence   254

Practice Questions   258

Answer Key   280

Answers & Explanations   282

Chapter 6   Practice Test #1   313

Section 1   314

Section 2 (Easy)   317

Section 2 (Hard)   321

Answer Key   324

Answers & Explanations   325

Chapter 7   Practice Test #2   335

Section 1   336

Section 2 (Easy)   338

Section 2 (Hard)   341

Answer Key   345

Answers & Explanations   346

How to Use This Book

GRE® Verbal Practice Questions is your complete guide to mastering the Verbal Reasoning section of the GRE. Whether you're starting your preparation or refining your skills for test day, this book provides the right blend of foundational knowledge, smart strategies, and realistic practice to help you succeed.

1. Why This Book?

This book is carefully designed to replicate the real GRE in terms of structure, content, and difficulty level.

You can use this book in two effective ways:

- **Option 1:** Begin with a targeted practice on individual question types.
- **Option 2:** Start with a full test to identify your strengths and weaknesses, then zero in on areas that need improvement.

2. Understand the Test Before You Start

Before jumping into practice questions, it's crucial to:

- Review the **GRE General Test structure** and understand where Verbal Reasoning fits.
- Learn about the **three key question types:**
  - ❑ Reading Comprehension
  - ❑ Text Completion
  - ❑ Sentence Equivalence
- Read the **strategies and tips** in the section to build a strong foundation and avoid common pitfalls.

3. Practice by Question Type and Topic

Each question type is broken down into manageable, focused sections. Since Reading Comprehension accounts for about half of all Verbal questions, we've provided a diverse range of reading passages categorized by subject:

- Arts and Humanities
- Biological Sciences
- Business
- Everyday Topics
- Physical Sciences
- Social Sciences

This topic-based approach ensures you're exposed to a wide variety of content styles and subjects, just like on the real test. Each practice question includes a **detailed answer explanation,** helping you understand the reasoning behind each answer and learn from your mistakes.

After mastering individual question types, put your skills to the test with two full verbal practice tests.

For more practice, visit www.vibrantpublishers.com

4. Simulate Real Testing Conditions

Taking practice tests is most effective when you simulate the actual test environment. This not only helps you become familiar with the test format but also builds focus that is required for the real exam.

How to Create a Test-Like Environment?

- **Follow the official timing:** Stick to the time limits for each section. Use a timer to practice pacing yourself.
- **Avoid distractions:** Put away your phone, turn off notifications, and choose a quiet place where you won't be interrupted

The Verbal practice tests in this book are made up of 3 modules instead of 2 to give you an adaptive test experience **on paper**. It will look like this:

- Section 1 (mix of easy, medium, and hard questions)
- Section 2 (easier questions)
- Section 2 (harder questions)

Attempt Section 1 and note down the number of answers you get right. If you get less than 7 questions right, move to Section 2 (Easy) and if you get 7 or more questions right, move to Section 2 (Hard).

5. Review Your Performance Thoroughly

The most valuable part of your preparation lies in analyzing your results.

Steps to Review Your Test:

- **Check your answers:** Use the answer key to score your test. Note both correct and incorrect responses.
- **Understand mistakes:** For every incorrect answer, refer to the detailed explanations in this book. Identify whether the mistake was due to a lack of knowledge, a misinterpretation of the question, or a timing issue for the tests.
- **Revisit challenging questions:** Redo the questions you answered incorrectly without looking at the solutions. This helps reinforce your learning.
- **Identify patterns:** Look for recurring types of mistakes. For example, are you struggling more with passage comprehension, grammar rules, or time management?

Use Mistakes as Learning Opportunities

Remember, mistZakes are a normal part of the learning process. Treat them as opportunities to refine your skills and deepen your understanding of the test.

6. Track Your Progress

Preparation for the GRE is a journey, and tracking your progress helps you stay motivated and focused. Use this book as a tool to monitor your improvement over time.

Why Track Progress?

- It allows you to see tangible improvements in your scores.
- It helps you adjust your study plan based on your evolving needs.
- It builds confidence as you approach your target score.

How to Track Progress?

- **Analyze trends:** Look for consistent improvements or recurring issues.
- **Set goals:** Break down your target score into smaller, achievable milestones.

Remember, progress may not always be linear. Some tests may feel harder than others, but consistency in practice is key.

7. Use Effective Test-Taking Strategies

Success on the GRE isn't just about knowing the content; it's also about applying the right strategies.

- **Time management:** Learn how to pace yourself to complete each section without rushing.
- **Eliminate wrong answers:** Narrow down your choices, especially on multiple-choice questions.
- **Guess wisely:** There's no penalty for guessing on the GRE, so make sure to answer every question.
- **Focus on high-value questions:** Prioritize questions you're more confident about before tackling harder ones.

By practicing these strategies during your preparation, you'll feel more prepared and less anxious on test day.

8. Prepare for the Real Exam

As your test date approaches, use the *Practice Tests for the GRE®* for a full-length simulation. This will help you fine-tune your readiness and reduce any last-minute nerves.

Tips for Final Preparation

- **Review key concepts:** Enhance your vocabulary by revisiting 75 high-frequency GRE words, accessible at no cost through the book's exclusive online resources.
- **Practice pacing:** Take at least one full test under strict timed conditions.
- **Build confidence:** Use your previous successes to boost your morale. Remind yourself of how much you've improved.
- **Consistency is key:** GRE preparation is most effective when done consistently over time. Avoid cramming in the weeks leading up to the test. Instead, set aside regular study sessions and stick to a schedule.

The final days before the test should focus on reviewing rather than learning new material. This will help you feel calm and prepared.

For more practice, visit www.vibrantpublishers.com

A Final Word

This book is more than just a collection of practice questions—it's a comprehensive tool to help you achieve your best GRE score. By solving all the questions here, staying consistent in your practice, and reviewing your progress regularly, you'll be well on your way to success. With the right preparation and mindset, you can confidently approach this challenge and open doors to your future aspirations.

Good luck on your GRE journey!

Online Resources

With our test prep books, we also provide Online Resources to help you in your test prep journey! The online resources of this book include:

1. A Stress Management Ebook

The book, titled Conquer the GRE: Stress Management and a Perfect Study Plan, is designed for test takers to manage the commonly experienced stress during GRE prep. It includes:

- Stress Management Techniques
- A 6-month Deep Study Plan
- An 8-week Sprint Plan
- Practical Tips to Get a Good Score on the GRE
- GRE Score Scale Parameters

2. Vocabulary List of Essential Words

Mastering vocabulary is key to scoring well on the GRE verbal section. This exclusive list features 75 high-frequency GRE words. It includes:

- **Part of Speech** – States if the word is a noun, verb, adjective, or more.
- **Meaning** – Defines the word clearly and concisely.
- **Usage** – Demonstrates how the word appears in real use.

How to Access the Online Resources

Step 1: Scan the QR code

Step 2: Fill in your details and submit to request the online resources

Step 3: Check your email inbox to download the resources

Have fun learning!

bit.ly/GRE-VPQ

Focused Book Plan

> **Which Plan Is Right For You?**
>
> Want to study both Verbal and Quant quickly?
> ✓ **8-Week Sprint Plan (Online)**
>
> Prefer a slower pace with deeper study?
> ✓ **6-Month Deep Study Plan (Online)**
>
> Only interested in Verbal Reasoning?
> ✓ **6-Week Focused Book Plan**

If you're aiming to master the Verbal Reasoning section and prefer a dedicated, streamlined approach, this focused 6-week plan is for you. Whether you're starting from scratch or need to sharpen specific skills, this plan helps you build a strong foundation, boost your vocabulary, and develop the strategies needed to tackle every Verbal question type with confidence.

Week 1: Foundation Review

Day 1-3: Begin by reviewing the structure of the GRE Verbal section. Understand the three key question types: Reading Comprehension (RC), Text Completion (TC), and Sentence Equivalence (SE). Focus on the format, scoring, and general strategies for approaching each.

Day 4: Take a GRE Verbal test under timed conditions to establish your baseline performance.

Day 5-7: Analyze your test results thoroughly. Identify your weakest question types and content areas, and set specific improvement goals to guide the next five weeks.

Week 2: Content Review

Day 1-3: Dive into Reading Comprehension. Practice passages from a range of topics—sciences, humanities, business, and social sciences—while focusing on main ideas, inferences, and tone.

Day 4: Review key strategies for tackling Text Completion questions. Learn to use contextual and structural clues to eliminate wrong answers and select the most logical fit. Complete 10–15 practice TC questions.

Day 5-7: Work on Sentence Equivalence questions by focusing on synonym recognition and eliminating misleading options. Begin learning the first 25 vocabulary words from the *Online Resources*.

Week 3: Reading Comprehension Focus

Day 1-3: Complete all remaining RC practice questions in the book, maintaining a timed pace and reviewing explanations for every answer—especially the incorrect ones.

Day 4: Try different reading strategies: skim the passage first or read the questions first, and observe which method improves your comprehension and timing.

Day 5-7: Reflect on your RC performance to find patterns in errors. Target those weaknesses with additional RC drills. Begin studying the next set of 25 vocabulary words.

Week 4: Text Completion Mastery & Strategy Development

Day 1-3: Complete 20–25 Text Completion questions under timed conditions. Focus on improving both speed and accuracy.

Day 4: Deepen your understanding of test-taking strategies, including predicting answers before reading the choices, eliminating extreme or illogical options, and identifying transition words and structure clues.

Day 5-7: Apply these strategies consistently while completing the remaining TC questions. Track your performance and make a note of which techniques are most effective for you.

Week 5: Sentence Equivalence Mastery & Strategy Refinement

Day 1-3: Complete 20–25 Sentence Equivalence questions, aiming for speed and precision. Focus on recognizing pairs of synonyms and understanding sentence structure.

Day 4: Refine your test-taking strategies further by reviewing what has worked best for each question type. Adjust your pacing and approach based on previous results.

Day 5-7: Continue with focused SE practice. Begin reviewing the final 25 vocabulary words from the list.

Week 6: Simulated Testing & Final Review

Day 1-3: Take the next GRE Verbal test. Make sure to simulate real test conditions.

Day 4: Thoroughly review your performance. Identify recurring mistakes, time management issues, and any final content gaps that need attention.

Day 5-7: Review all 75 vocabulary words and skim your notes to reinforce strategies and key concepts.

Adjust the study plan according to your individual needs and schedule, ensuring a balance between content review, practice, and relaxation. Stay committed, stay focused, and trust in your preparation as you approach the GRE.

Icons in this Book and Their Meanings:

 — Key points to remember

 — Quick glance

 — Solved examples

 — Expert tips to help you excel

Chapter 1
Overview of the GRE® General Test

The **Graduate Record Examinations (GRE) General Test** has traditionally been a key component in graduate admissions. While its role is now part of a broader evaluation process, a strong GRE score remains a valuable asset—it can serve as evidence of a strong scholarship on an application. This book is designed to prepare you thoroughly for the GRE General Test, formerly known as the GRE revised General Test (renamed in 2016). While the name has changed, the test's structure and scoring have remained consistent.

It's important to note that some graduate programs may also require GRE Subject Tests. These are designed to assess knowledge in specific academic disciplines and are not covered in this book. Before beginning your GRE preparation, review the admissions criteria of your target programs to determine whether a Subject Test is also required. For more information, visit the Subject Tests section on ets.org.

What the GRE Measures

The GRE General Test is not designed to measure your knowledge of specific fields. It does not measure your ability to be successful in your career or even in school. It does, however, give a reasonably accurate indication of your capabilities in certain key areas such as:

- Comprehending and analyzing complex written material
- Understanding basic mathematical concepts
- Interpreting and evaluating data
- Applying logical reasoning and critical thinking

By preparing for the GRE using this book, you'll not only enhance your test performance but also strengthen foundational skills that are crucial for success in graduate studies.

Format of the GRE General Test

The GRE General Test is offered as a computer-delivered test throughout the year. Post-COVID, ETS provides test-takers with the option to take the test from home. Whether you are taking the GRE General Test at the testing center or at home, the format of the test will essentially be the same. The total time for the test will be about **1 hour and 58 minutes**. The test consists of three main components:

- Analytical Writing
- Verbal Reasoning
- Quantitative Reasoning

Note: The unscored section has also been removed for the shorter GRE General Test, along with the 10-minute scheduled break, which was granted to the students after the 2-hour mark of the 3-hour 45-minute test.

Inside the GRE: What's Tested

The Verbal Reasoning and Quantitative Reasoning sections of the GRE General Test are **section-level adaptive**. This means that the computer will adapt the test to your performance. Since there are two sections, each for Verbal Reasoning and Quantitative Reasoning, the difficulty of the second section will depend on how well you did in the first section. The overall format of the GRE General Test will be as follows:

Measure	Number of Questions	Time Allowed
Analytical Writing (1 section)	1 Analyze an Issue	30 minutes
Verbal Reasoning (2 sections)	12 questions (first section) 15 questions (second section)	18 minutes (first section) 23 minutes (second section)
Quantitative Reasoning (2 sections)	12 questions (first section) 15 questions (second section)	21 minutes (first section) 26 minutes (second section)
		Total Time: 1 hour 58 minutes

1. Analytical Writing Measure

The first section of the GRE General Test is the Analytical Writing measure. This section of the GRE is designed to test your ability to use basic logic and critical reasoning to make and assess arguments. The Analytical Writing measure comprises a singular assignment, which must be completed within 30 minutes. You will be given an issue and a prompt with some specific instructions on how to approach the assigned issue. You will be expected to take a position on the issue and then write a clear, persuasive, and logically sound essay defending your position in correct English.

The tasks in the Analytical Writing measure are designed to reflect a wide range of subject areas—from the arts and humanities to the social and physical sciences—but they do **not require specialized content knowledge.**

To support your preparation, the GRE Program has published the complete pool of **Issue topics** from which the prompts are drawn—you can access this resource as a downloadable PDF from the official ETS website.

 Quick Glance at the Analytical Writing Measure

- **Duration:** The task must be completed within 30 minutes.

- **Task format:** A short essay must be written in response to an issue of general interest. The prompt should be addressed clearly and thoughtfully.

- **Skills measured:** This task assesses the ability to develop complex ideas coherently, structure writing in a focused and organized way, support claims with relevant evidence, and demonstrate a strong command of standard written English.

- **Subject knowledge:** The task is designed to measure reasoning, writing, and analytical skills, not familiarity with specific academic topics.

- **Evaluation criteria:** Responses are evaluated based on clarity of argument, depth of reasoning, use of evidence, organization, and language proficiency.

2. Verbal Reasoning Measure

The Verbal Reasoning measure of the GRE assesses your reading comprehension, ability to draw inferences, and vocabulary skills. You will encounter two Verbal Reasoning sections containing 12 and 15 questions, with time limits of 18 and 23 minutes, respectively.

Most questions are multiple-choice and fall into three main types:

- **Reading Comprehension (RC):** You will read a short passage (1 to 3 paragraphs) and answer questions that test your understanding of the content.

- **Text Completion (TC):** These questions present a brief passage with one to three blanks. You will select the best choices from multiple options to fill in the blanks appropriately.

- **Sentence Equivalence (SE):** You will complete a sentence by selecting two words that both fit the blank and produce sentences with similar meanings.

Together, these question types assess how well you understand and analyze written material, as well as your command of vocabulary in context.

 Quick Glance at the Verbal Reasoning Measure

- **Duration:** The section is split into 12 questions with a 18-minute time limit and 15 questions with a 23-minute limit.

- **Question types:** This section includes Reading Comprehension, Text Completion, and Sentence Equivalence questions.

- **Choices:** RC questions may require selecting one or more correct answers or highlighting a relevant portion of the text. TC questions involve choosing the correct words to fill one or more blanks in a passage. SE questions ask for two answer choices that produce sentences with similar meanings.

- **Skills measured:** The section tests the ability to understand complex texts, apply vocabulary in context, and make logical inferences based on written material.

3. Quantitative Reasoning Measure

The Quantitative Reasoning section of the GRE tests your ability to apply basic math skills, interpret data, and reason with numbers. You'll face two sections: one with 12 questions in 21 minutes, and another with 15 questions in 26 minutes.

Questions may be set in real-world or purely mathematical contexts, with many presented as word problems that require mathematical modeling. The section covers **four** content areas: Arithmetic, Algebra, Geometry, and Data Analysis.

You'll encounter four types of questions:

- **Quantitative Comparison**
- **Multiple Choice — Select One Answer**
- **Multiple Choice — Select One or More Answers**
- **Numeric Entry**

Quick Glance at the Quantitative Reasoning Measure

- **Time Allotted:** The section is split into 12 questions with a 21-minute time limit and 15 questions with a 26-minute limit.

- **Question Types:** This section includes Multiple Choice, Numeric Entry, Quantitative Comparison, and Data Interpretation questions.

- **Skills Measured:** This section tests the ability to use Arithmetic, Algebra, Geometry, and Statistics, interpret and analyze quantitative data, and apply mathematical reasoning to real-world problems..

Features of the Computer-delivered Test

1. **Review and Preview Questions**
   Test takers can review and preview questions within a section, which allows them to manage their time effectively and focus on the most challenging questions first.

2. **Mark and Return to Questions**
   Questions can be marked within a section and revisited later. This enables moving past difficult questions and returning to them, as long as the time limit for the section is respected.

3. **Change or Edit Answers**
   Answers can be changed or edited within a section. If a mistake is noticed, test takers can correct their responses before the section time expires.

4. **On-Screen Calculator**
   An on-screen calculator is provided during the Quantitative Reasoning measure, facilitating quick and accurate calculations. However, you should only use the calculator for complex equations that will take a longer time to do manually, such as square roots, addition, subtraction, and multiplication of numbers with several digits.

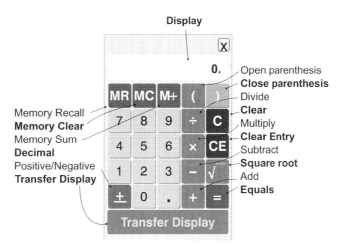

Guidelines for using the on-screen calculator

- The on-screen calculator follows the order of operations (PEMDAS). This means that it computes equations in the following order - parentheses, exponentiation (including square roots), multiplication and division (left to right), addition and subtraction (left to right). So, for an equation like 2 + 3 * 6, the on-screen calculator will give the answer 20 but some calculators will give the answer 30 as they first add 2 and 3 and get 5 which is multiplied by 6 to get the final answer 30.

- The Transfer Display button will be useful for Numeric Entry questions. The button will transfer the number on your calculator display to the numeric entry answer box. But remember to check the transferred answer as sometimes you may be required to round up your answer; adjust it accordingly.

- The Memory Recall (MR), Memory Clear (MC), and Memory Sum (M+) buttons work as per normal calculators.

Registering for the GRE

Before you register to take the GRE, be sure to consider your schedule and any special accommodations that you may need. Be aware that the availability of testing dates may vary according to your location. Be sure to give yourself plenty of time to prepare for the GRE and be sure that you know the deadlines for score reporting and application deadlines for all the schools you are applying to. For general information about deadlines and the GRE, visit the GRE section at ets.org. For more information on how to register for the GRE, visit the Registration section at ets.org. For information on special accommodations for disabled students, visit the Disability Accommodations section on ets.org.

If you are taking the GRE General Test at home, there are certain equipment, environment, and testing space requirements that you need to fulfill before you can start the registration process. For more information on these requirements, read the At Home Testing section on ets.org.

How the GRE General Test is Scored

Scoring for the Analytical Writing Section

In the Analytical Writing section, you will be scored on a scale of 0-6 in increments of 0.5. The Analytical Writing measure emphasizes your ability to engage in reasoning and critical thinking over your facility with the finer points of grammar. The highest scores of 5.5-6.0 are given to work that is generally superior in every respect - sustained analysis of complex issues, coherent argumentation, and excellent command of the English language. The lowest scores of 0.0-0.5 are given to work that is completely off-topic or so poorly composed as to be incoherent.

Scoring for the Verbal and Quantitative Reasoning Sections

The Verbal and Quantitative Reasoning sections are now scored on a scale of 130-170 in 1-point increments.

Preparing for Test Day

How you prepare for the test is completely up to you and will depend on your own test-taking preferences and the amount of time you can devote to studying for the test. At the very least, before you take the test, you should know the basics of what is covered on the test along with the general guidelines for taking the GRE. This book is designed to provide you with the basic information you need and give you the opportunity to prepare thoroughly for the GRE General Test.

Remember, you don't need to spend an equal amount of time on each of these areas to do well on the GRE - allot your study time to your own needs and preferences. Following are some suggestions to help you make the final preparations for your test, and help you through the test itself.

- In the time leading up to your test, practice, then practice some more. Practice until you are confident with the material.

- Know when your test is, and when you need to be at the testing center or in front of your computer at home.

- Make a "practice run" to your testing center, so that you can anticipate how much time you will need to allow to get there. For the at home test, make sure to sign in at least 15 minutes before the test.

- Understand the timing and guidelines for the test and plan accordingly. Remember that you are not allowed to eat or drink while taking the GRE, although you will be allowed to snack or drink during some of the short breaks during testing. Plan accordingly.

- Know exactly what documentation you will need to bring with you to the testing center. If you are testing at home, you will have to provide a valid government-issued identification document as well.

- Relax, especially on the day or night before your test. If you have studied and practiced wisely, you will be well prepared for the test. You may want to briefly glance over some test preparation materials but cramming the night before will not be productive.

- Eat well and get a good night's sleep. You will want to be well-rested for the test.

The Test Day

- Wake up early to give yourself plenty of time to eat a healthy breakfast, gather the necessary documentation, pack a snack and a water bottle, and make it to the testing center well before your test is scheduled to start.

- Have confidence; you've prepared well for the test, and there won't be any big surprises. You may not know the answers to some questions, but the format will be exactly like what you've been practicing.

- While you are taking the test, don't panic. The test is timed, and students often worry that they will run out of time and miss too many questions. The sections of the test are designed so that many students will not finish them, so don't worry if you don't think you can finish a section on time. Just try to answer as many questions as you can, as accurately as possible.

- If there's a question you're not sure of, don't panic—the GRE test allows you to skip and return to questions when you are ready, so take advantage of that. Remember, the value of each easy question is the same as the hard questions!
- Remember the strategies and techniques that you learn from this book and apply them wherever possible.

General Strategies for Taking the GRE

The following is a list of strategies that will help to improve your chances of performing well on the GRE:

- Learn the basics about the test - what is being tested, the format, and how the test is administered.
- Familiarize yourself with the specific types of questions that you will see on the GRE General Test.
- Review basic concepts in math, logic, and writing.
- Work through the test-taking strategies offered in this book.
- Work through mock GRE tests until you feel thoroughly comfortable with the types of questions you will see.
- As you are studying for the GRE, focus your energy on the types of questions that give you the most difficulty.
- Learn to guess wisely. For many of the questions in the Verbal and Quantitative Reasoning Sections, the correct answer is in front of you - you only need to correctly identify it. Especially for questions that you find difficult, you should hone your ability to dismiss the options that are clearly wrong and make an educated guess about which one is right.
- Answer every question. You won't lose any points for choosing the wrong answer, so even a wild guess that might or might not be right is better than no answer at all.

Frequently Asked Questions

General Questions

1. **What changes have been made to the GRE General Test after the announcement on May 31, 2023?**

    The main changes to the test are a reduction in the time (from 3 hours 45 minutes to 1 hour 58 minutes), and the removal of the "Analyze an Argument" essay task (which was a part of the Analytical Writing section) and the unscored section. The time has been curtailed by decreasing the number of questions in each section, reducing the total number of questions from 40 to 27. Furthermore, the removal of the "Analyze an Argument" task and the unscored section also aided in shortening the total duration. The official scores will also be delivered more promptly and will now take 8-10 calendar days, facilitating faster applications to their desired institutes by the students. For more information on the changes, visit the GRE section at ets.org.

2. **Can I take the GRE test at home?**

   Yes. ETS now provides students with the option to take the test from home. If your local test centers are closed or you prefer a familiar testing environment, you can take the GRE from home. You will have to check the equipment, environment, and testing space requirements for the at home test and whether it's an option for you. For detailed information on the requirements for the home test, check the At Home Testing section at ets.org.

3. **How do I get ready to take the GRE General Test?**

   To take the GRE General Test, there are several steps you'll need to take:

   - Find out what prospective graduate/professional programs require: Does the program you're interested in require additional testing beyond the GRE General Test? What is the deadline for receipt of scores?

   - Sign up for a test date. You need to sign up for any GRE testing. Act in a timely manner so that you have plenty of time to prepare and are guaranteed that your scores will be sent and received on time. For the in-center test, testing dates are much more restricted, so if you know that you will need to take the GRE General Test at the center, make arrangements well in advance of the application deadline for your program. There are additional requirements if you're taking the test at home, so make sure to check the requirements well in advance.

   - Use resources provided by ETS and Vibrant Publishers to familiarize yourself with the format of the GRE and the types of questions you will face. Even if you are confident about taking the test, it is essential to prepare for the test.

4. **Does the GRE General Test measure my proficiency in specific subject areas?**

   No. The GRE General Test is designed to measure general proficiency in reading, critical reasoning, and working with data, all abilities that are critical to graduate work. However, you won't be tested on your knowledge of any specific field.

5. **Where can I get additional information on the GRE General Test?**

   Educational Testing Service (ETS), the organization that administers the GRE, has an informative website entirely devoted to information about the test in the GRE section at ets.org. There, you can find links that further explain how to sign up for testing, fees, score reporting, and much more.

Preparing for the Test

1. **How should I start to prepare for the test?**

   The first thing you should do is thoroughly familiarize yourself with the format of the GRE General Test. Read about each section of the test, how many questions are there per section, and the required format for answers. You can find general information about the structure of the test earlier in this chapter.

2. **How do I prepare for the questions I will be asked on the GRE General Test?**

   There are plenty of resources by Vibrant Publishers, including this book to help you prepare for the questions you will face on the GRE General Test. A list of books is provided at the beginning of this book. For the most updated list, you may visit the Test Prep Series section on www.vibrantpublishers.com.

3. How much should I study/practice for the GRE?

Study and practice until you feel comfortable with the test. Practice, practice, and practice some more until you feel confident about test day!

4. Are there additional materials I can use to get even more practice?

Yes. ETS offers a free full-length practice test that can be downloaded from the GRE section at ets.org. Also, after you have signed up for testing through ETS, you are eligible for some further test preparation materials free of additional charge.

Test Content

1. What skills does the GRE test?

In general, the GRE is designed to test your proficiency in certain key skills that you will need for graduate-level study. More specifically:

- **The Analytical Writing section** tests your ability to write about complex ideas in a coherent, focused fashion as well as your ability to command the conventions of standard written English, provide and evaluate relevant evidence, and critique other points of view.

- **The Verbal Reasoning section** is an assessment of your ability to understand, interpret and analyze complex passages, use reasoning to draw inferences about written material, and use sophisticated vocabulary in context.

- **The Quantitative Reasoning section** is an assessment of basic, high school-level mathematical skills and knowledge, as well as your ability to analyze and interpret data.

2. What level of math is required for the Quantitative Reasoning section?

You will be expected to know high school-level math: arithmetic, and basic concepts in algebra and geometry. You will also be expected to be able to analyze and interpret data presented in tables and graphs.

Scoring and Score Reporting

1. How are the sections of the GRE General Test scored?

The GRE General Test is scored as follows:

- **The scores of the Verbal Reasoning section** are done in 1-point increments on a scale of 130-170.

- **The scores of the Quantitative Reasoning section** are done in 1-point increments on a scale of 130-170.

- **The scores of the Analytical Writing section** are done in increments of 0.5 on a scale of 0-6.

2. When will my score be reported?

It depends on when you decide to take the GRE General Test. In general, scores for the test are reported in 8-10 days. You can find your scores in your official ETS account. An email notification from ETS is sent when the test scores are made available. ETS will also send an official Institution Score Report to the institutions you've chosen to send the test scores to. Check the GRE section at ets.org for updates on score reporting and deadlines.

3. **How long will my scores be valid?**

   Your score for the GRE General Test will remain valid for five years.

Other Questions

1. **Do business schools accept the GRE instead of the GMAT?**

   An increasing number of business schools accept the GRE as a substitute for the more standard test for admission to an MBA program, the GMAT. Before you decide to take the GRE instead of the GMAT, make sure that the programs you are interested in applying to will accept the GRE. You can find a list of business schools that currently accept the GRE in the GRE section at ets.org.

2. **How is the GRE administered?**

   The GRE is administered continuously year-round at designated testing centers, where you can take the test free from distractions in a secure environment that discourages cheating. The GRE Test at home is also available for those who are more comfortable in a familiar environment. For information on testing centers in your area and important dates, visit the GRE section at ets.org.

3. **I have a disability that requires me to ask for special accommodation while taking the test - what sort of accommodation is offered?**

   ETS does accommodate test-takers with disabilities. For information on procedures, visit the GRE Disability Accomodations section at ets.org.

4. **Will there be breaks during testing?**

   No. There are no breaks. If you take an unscheduled break, testing time will not stop.

5. **Will I be given scratch paper?**

   Yes. The test administrator will provide you with scratch paper to use during the test, which has to be returned to the testing center staff without any pages missing.

   For the at home test, you cannot use regular notepaper. You may use either of the following materials:

   - One small desktop whiteboard with an erasable marker.
   - A sheet of paper placed inside a transparent sheet protector. You can write on this with an erasable marker.

   At the end of the test, you will need to show the proctor that all the notes you took during the test have been erased.

6. **Should I bring a calculator to the test?**

   No. There will be an on-screen calculator for you to use.

This page is intentionally left blank

Chapter 2
Introduction to Verbal Reasoning

The Verbal Reasoning measure of the GRE is designed to evaluate your skill at reading, interpreting, and analyzing sentences and passages written in standard English. The GRE General Test will have two Verbal Reasoning sections of 12 and 15 questions each. You will have 18 and 23 minutes to complete the sections. Each section will consist of three distinct types of questions: Reading Comprehension, Text Completion, and Sentence Equivalence. This chapter will provide an overview of the types of questions you will face on the Verbal Reasoning measure of the GRE and list some general techniques and strategies for approaching Verbal Reasoning questions. In addition, it gives a more detailed look at each type of question, providing worked examples with in-depth explanations and strategies.

- The Verbal Reasoning measure of the GRE features three distinct question types: Reading Comprehension, Text Completion, and Sentence Equivalence.

- Text Completion and Sentence Equivalence will be in multiple-choice format; Reading Comprehension will consist of some multiple-choice and some questions where you will be asked to highlight a section of text.

- There will be two Verbal Reasoning sections, and you will be given 18 and 23 minutes for finishing the sections.

Reading Comprehension Questions

For Reading Comprehension questions, you will be asked to read a passage and answer several questions on the passage. Passages may cover topics from physical, biological, or social sciences; the arts; the humanities; business; or everyday life. Passages will be between one to five paragraphs in length. After reading the passage, you will be asked to answer several questions about the passage. In some cases, the questions will require you to identify key aspects of the passage or draw inferences about the meaning or the author's intent. In others, you will be asked to highlight the section of the passage that addresses a particular consideration or identify components of the passage that point to a given conclusion.

Reading Comprehension questions will have three formats: multiple-choice in which you choose the single solution that best answers the question, multiple-choice in which you choose one or more solutions that best answer the question, and passage highlighting, in which you highlight the portion of the passage that best addresses a given question. To do well on the Reading Comprehension questions in the Verbal Reasoning measure, you will need to be able to quickly read a passage and identify key points and the central themes of the passage.

> **Reading Comprehension questions test your ability to understand and interpret complex passages and quickly determine key points and details.**

Text Completion Questions

Text Completion questions consist of a short passage one to five sentences long with one or more blanks. The passages will cover topics from the physical, biological, or social sciences, the arts, the humanities, business, or everyday life. You will be asked to choose the best option to fill in the blank (or blanks) and complete the passage. Text Completion questions have been designed with the aim of testing your vocabulary and your ability to draw plausible inferences about the intended meaning of passages written in standard English.

All Text Completion questions are multiple-choice: the number of options you are given will vary from three (usually for passages with two or more blanks) to five (usually for passages with a single blank). To do well on Text Completion questions, you will need to review the given vocabulary, be able to draw quick inferences about the intent of a passage, and be able to choose the word that completes the passage best given the context.

> **Text Completion questions test your ability to apply sophisticated vocabulary in context and to draw inferences about the meaning of passages based on incomplete information.**

Sentence Equivalence Questions

Sentence Equivalence questions consist of short sentences with a single blank. The sentence will be on a topic from the physical, biological, or social sciences; the arts; the humanities; business; or everyday life. You will be given six possible answer options to fill in the blank. You must choose the two options that (a) complete the sentence grammatically and (b) produce two completed sentences with the most similar meanings.

All Sentence Equivalence questions are multiple-choice and will ask you to choose the best two options from a total of six. To do well on Sentence Equivalence questions, you will need to review the given vocabulary and be able to identify words with similar meanings, and you will also need to review the basic rules of English grammar.

> **Sentence Equivalence questions test your knowledge of basic rules of grammar, draw correct inferences about the meaning of a passage based on incomplete information, and identify words with similar meanings.**

Tips for Verbal Reasoning Measure

The Verbal Reasoning Measure of the GRE tests your command of certain key areas of written English. Doing everything you can to solidify your vocabulary, your grammar, and your ability to understand complex passages will help you prepare for the Verbal Reasoning Measure of the GRE. Below is a list of general strategies that will help you with the verbal portion of the test:

- Familiarize yourself with the types of questions that will be asked. There are a limited number of possible types of questions; once you know the format, you won't face anything unfamiliar.

- Read any instructions on the test carefully - always be sure that you are answering the question that you've been asked.

- Brush up on your vocabulary. You can find a list of common GRE words in the *Online Resources*. Also, using the examples provided in this book, you can get a good sense of the kind of words you will encounter on the GRE. Be sure that you know what they mean.

- Work on your critical reading skills. For anything you read while preparing for the GRE, try to ask yourself: What are the key points? What is the author trying to say? What information supports the author's claims?

- Use basic logic and common sense to draw inferences about the passage you are working with.

- If you are unsure of how to answer a multiple-choice question, you can often use the process of elimination. Often by getting rid of answers that are obviously wrong, you can get the right answer, even if you're not sure about some of the options.

Pro Tip

Work on identifying keywords—words like "although", "moreover", and "therefore"—that signal important information or shifts in perspective. Doing this will help you quickly grasp the sense of a passage even if some information is missing.

Chapter 3
Reading Comprehension

Chapter 3: Reading Comprehension

Reading Comprehension questions are designed to test your ability to understand, interpret and analyze what you read. You will be asked to read a short passage between one or more paragraphs long and then answer several questions about the passage. To answer them you will need to recognize what the passage explicitly states and be able to draw inferences about the implications of the passage.

The passages used for Reading Comprehension questions will be drawn from a variety of topics, including the physical, biological, and social sciences; the arts and the humanities; business; and everyday life. To answer the questions on these passages, you do not need to be an expert on the topic covered; you only need to read the passage attentively enough to answer basic questions about it. You will not be asked to evaluate the passage for truth or falsity; you will only need to understand what the author said, and what implications can be drawn from what the author said.

The questions will appear in three formats: two types of multiple choice and highlighting a section of the passage. The first type of multiple-choice will ask you to choose the single best answer from several options. The second type of multiple-choice will ask you to choose one or more answers from several options. For select-in passage, you will be asked to highlight the section of text that best addresses the question.

What Skills do Reading Comprehension Questions Test?

Reading Comprehension questions test your ability to understand, interpret and analyze complex passages of the kind you will encounter in graduate school. Some key skills that are tested include your ability to:

- understand a text holistically and be able to determine the meaning of individual components
- distinguish major and minor points
- succinctly summarize the meaning of an entire passage
- use inference to draw conclusions about implied meaning and intent
- understand how individual parts of a text support the key points
- identify an author's assumptions, biases and perspective
- determine the potential strengths and weaknesses of the author's position

Types of Questions

There are several types of Reading Comprehension questions that you can expect to find. Reviewing the kinds of questions you can expect to be asked, and looking at strategies for answering them, will help you prepare for the test. The following is a list of typical questions:

- What is the main idea?
- What is the purpose?
- Identify specific details
- Identify the purpose of specific details
- Infer a conclusion based on the evidence presented in the passage
- Identify assumptions made by the author

- Identify additional evidence that might undermine/bolster the author's argument
- Highlight a specific section of text that addresses a question
- Other

1. Main Idea

Some questions will be quite straightforward—you will be asked to answer a "big picture" question about the passage, such as questions about the main topic, intended audience, and scope.

Assuming that you have skimmed the passage well and answered the questions listed above in the section on determining what the passage is about, answering this type of question should be quite easy. Practice reading passages to quickly grasp the key points, and then have confidence in your ability to apply this skill on test day.

2. Purpose

Some questions will ask you to say something about the purpose of the passage. Here you are being asked to make an educated guess as to why the author bothered to write the passage—did they intend to educate? To entertain? To undermine a commonly held belief? To develop an argument as to why their perspective is better than another?

When answering questions about the purpose of a passage, look for clues in structure and wording. Does the author develop and then dismiss a certain view? What is the tone—is it adversarial or merely stating facts? Does the passage present a course of action, or does it simply present information? Answering questions such as these will help you determine some basic points about the passage, such as whether the author is advocating something or just trying to educate. You can then look over some of the details of the passage to gain a sense of exactly what position the author is advocating, or who the intended audience might be for the information given.

3. Details

Some questions will ask you to identify specific points within the passage. Here you are being asked to find the place in the passage where the author discusses some particular aspect of the main topic or detail that supports something that they have said.

To answer these questions, you will need to have good skimming skills. As you skim, learn to mentally bookmark the passage so that you know where to find certain information whether or not you have read it carefully or understood it perfectly. Doing this will allow you to quickly refer back to the right section of the passage to find the specific point you are being asked about.

4. Purpose of Detail

Some questions will ask you to identify why the author chose to use certain details in their discussion. If the author is making an argument, you will need to think why they chose to include a certain point to support it; if they are attempting to educate, you will need to decide why they thought a given detail would help make the discussion more informative.

To do well with these types of questions, you will need to have a good grasp on the topic and purpose of the passage, and you will need to know where to find the relevant detail to see where and how it fits into the whole discussion. As you read through the passage, try to read actively rather than passively—ask yourself why the author has chosen to include particular information, and how it fits into the piece as a whole. If you can get a good sense of how and why things hang together in the passage as you skim through it, you will be able to answer this type of question much more rapidly.

5. Additional Conclusions

Sometimes you will be asked to put together the evidence provided in a passage to draw a conclusion. In some cases, the author will have stated a clear conclusion and you will be asked to use the evidence presented to find other implied conclusions. In others, the author will have left their conclusions implied, and you will be asked to say something about them given the evidence.

To answer questions about implied conclusions, you need to grasp the main idea of the passage. There is no way to answer questions about what conclusion you might draw from the passage without knowing the 'big picture' information about the passage. Once you have that, you can use clues from the author's tone and the details they provide to determine what conclusions can be inferred

6. Assumptions

Some questions may ask you what assumptions are implied in the passage. Here, you will need to consider what the author is assuming to develop their position—what do they consider so completely uncontroversial that they rely on it without even mentioning it?

To answer questions about assumptions, you will need to have a solid grasp of what the author is trying to say and why, and how they have structured the passage. You need to focus on ideas or points that are essential to what the author is trying to say but have been left unstated.

7. Bolster/Undermine

Sometimes you will be asked to identify another point that would either strengthen or weaken the author's case in the passage. Here you are looking for any additional evidence that can be brought to bear on the passage.

To answer this type of question, you need to have a clear grasp of the main idea, purpose, and structure of the passage. Focus on only those potential answers that have a direct bearing on the topic, and weigh how the additional information would affect the development of the passage.

8. Highlight

Sometimes you will be asked to find a specific point in the passage and highlight it. For these questions, rather than being given possible answers, you will need to find the answer in the text and highlight it.

If you have skimmed the passage well and know where to find different points, these questions will be quite similar to multiple-choice questions that ask for specific details. Focus your attention only on those parts of the passage that deal specifically with the question asked, and answer the question based on that.

9. Other

You may be asked other types of questions about passages, although any additional type of question will test the same skills that the types listed test. To answer other question types, apply the techniques discussed above in the appropriate combination.

Introduction to Reading Comprehension

 ## What Does a Reading Comprehension Question Look Like?

Reading Comprehension questions will always be based on a short passage of one or more paragraphs. You will be asked to read the passage and then answer 1-3 questions about it.

Below is an example of what a Reading Comprehension question will look like on the GRE General Test:

Questions 1 to 3 are based on the following passage.

Sometimes hype can create impossible expectations. Nowhere is this phenomenon more pronounced than in the world of popular music. Two bands that came to prominence in the first years of the 2000s exemplify this. New York's 'The Strokes' and England's 'Arctic Monkeys' were both hailed by critics as the leaders of a garage rock revival and more grandiosely, as saviors of rock music. Despite successes and considerable popularity, neither band has entirely lived up to these overblown expectations. Although both bands helped to bring greater awareness to the burgeoning indie music scene, rock music still struggles to compete with other genres of popular music. And although both bands have gained considerable popularity, they still don't have the ability to fill stadiums and arenas the way that some of their older and less heralded peers do.

Select only one answer choice.

1. Which of the following statements best characterizes the main idea of the passage?

    - Ⓐ Popular music is more diverse than many people realize
    - Ⓑ The Strokes and Arctic Monkeys are both highly successful bands
    - Ⓒ A single band can revolutionize popular music
    - Ⓓ Critics of popular music sometimes create exaggerated expectations for bands
    - Ⓔ Older bands draw bigger crowds than newer bands

Consider each of the three choices separately and select all that apply.

2. The author most likely uses the phrase "saviors of rock music" to:

    - A characterize the strokes
    - B make a plea for the future of the genre
    - C indicate the hyperbolic expectations created by music critics

3. Select the sentence that suggests rock music's struggles in competing with other types of popular music.

Answer Key

The correct answers to the questions are:

1. **Choice D:** Critics of popular music sometimes create exaggerated expectations for bands
2. **Choice C:** indicate the hyperbolic expectations created by music critics
3. Although both bands helped to bring greater awareness to the burgeoning indie music scene, rock music still struggles to compete with other genres of popular music.

For more practice, visit www.vibrantpublishers.com

Chapter 3: Reading Comprehension

> ## Quick Glance at the Reading Comprehension Questions
>
> - Questions will be based on short passages of one or more paragraphs
> - You will be required to answer 1-3 questions per passage
> - Passages will be on a variety of topics including the physical, biological and social sciences, the arts and the humanities, business and everyday life
> - Questions will be answerable based on the passage alone—you will not need any prior knowledge of the subject matter being discussed
> - Questions will ask you to select one or more correct answers from several, or highlight a relevant portion of the passage

Strategies for Reading Comprehension Questions

You will have 18 and 23 minutes to complete the Verbal Reasoning sections. To complete a section successfully, you will need to budget your time well, and this is especially important with Reading Comprehension questions. It is essential that you do not lose too much time reading passages too carefully. Remember, to do well on Reading Comprehension questions, you do not need to have a mastery of the material covered in a given passage; you just need to be able to answer a few highly directed questions about the passage. If you are able to read the passage both thoroughly and quickly, so much the better. However, if you find yourself taking too much time over a passage, it is better to gather key information quickly than to grasp everything and lose too much time. As you read passages for Reading Comprehension questions, your reading should be goal-oriented: read quickly and "loosely" and focus only on information that is important. Remember, you won't need to remember anything about the passage after the test, and you only need to grasp the key points while taking the test.

Another key consideration is how to approach passages that cover unfamiliar material. Remember, passages can be drawn from many different fields, and chances are you will come across a passage that deals with something you are unfamiliar with. However, the questions about the passage will not demand any prior knowledge of the subject matter. Don't panic if you are asked to read about something that you know nothing about, since the questions will not ask you to evaluate the truth of the claims made in the passage. By the same token, don't let any expertise that you may possess lead you to make unnecessary judgments about the passage. Focus your attention on answering the questions and always keep in mind that your knowledge or lack of knowledge about the subject matter will have no bearing on how well you are able to answer those questions.

Finally, keep in mind that the key skills for Reading Comprehension are skimming and paraphrasing. To skim effectively, you will need to read quickly and gather key information. To paraphrase, you will need to be able to summarily restate the key points of the passage in other words. Skimming will help you quickly understand what the passage is about while paraphrasing will allow you to recognize which possible answers are the best.

Introduction to Reading Comprehension

> **Key Points to Remember**
>
> - Don't lose too much time on reading a passage carefully; read quickly, and read with the goal of answering the questions.
>
> - Don't worry too much about understanding everything—remember, you don't need to learn the material covered in the passage thoroughly, you simply need to answer a few highly directed questions.
>
> - Don't let your knowledge or lack of knowledge of the subject matter distract you—every question you are asked will be answerable solely on the basis of the information in the passage.
>
> - Use your abilities to skim and paraphrase to your advantage; gather relevant information rapidly, and be able to reformulate it to determine what answer choice best answers the question.

What follows are some more specific strategies for answering Reading Comprehension questions. Later in this section, you'll have a chance to put your skills to the test and learn how to hone them in several in-depth worked examples.

1. Determine What the Passage is About

Your first task as you read a passage should be to find out what is being discussed. You should immediately look for clues as to what the main idea of the passage is—doing so will help you address any broad questions about the big picture that the passage is trying to convey. The following three questions will help you find the main idea of the passage:

- **What is the passage about?** This question should be the easiest of the three to answer, and could be fairly broad (e.g. "European history")

- **What is the scope of the passage?** This question asks how narrowly/broadly the passage addresses its subject matter

- **What is the purpose of the passage?** Here you are asking why the author wrote the passage to begin with—is it to educate? To persuade? Who is the intended audience, and what reaction is the author trying to get?

2. Skim the Passage

You need to gather key information quickly to do well and one of the best ways to do that is to skim. As you skim the passage, keep several key points in mind. First of all, skim to determine what the passage is about. You shouldn't need to read every word carefully to be able to address the questions listed in the section above. Also, as you skim the passage, try to keep in mind how the passage is organized—try to have a general idea of what information can be found where. Some questions will ask you to refer to very specific sections of the text—by skimming effectively, you can form an idea of where you need to look to address specific questions. Finally, don't be afraid to skip over sentences or phrases that you don't understand. In many cases, you will be able to learn all you need from a passage without understanding every word. In those rare cases when a question directly addresses something that you didn't understand on the first read-through, you can always read the section again more carefully when you are trying to answer the question.

As you are reading the passage, try to get a quick feel for the structure of the text. If there is more than one paragraph, how are the paragraphs organized? What is the topic and purpose of each paragraph? How are evidence and supporting material presented?

3. Understanding the Questions

After skimming the passage as described above, you will need to be prepared to answer questions about it. You can use the following strategies to help you answer the questions well:

- Read the question carefully. While you usually don't need to read more than a small part of the passage carefully, it's important that you read the question and the possible solutions with care—you need to have a clear sense of what you are being asked in order to find the right answer.

- If the question is in multiple-choice format, read every possible answer choice. Even if you think you can identify the right answer immediately, make sure you read all of the options.

- If the question is general and asks you to describe what the passage is about, or what the purpose is, you should already have a pretty good idea of what the answer is from skimming and determining what the main idea of the passage is.

- If the question is specific, you may need to find a particular section of the passage and read over it more carefully. Make "mental bookmarks" as you skim the passage to give you some idea of where to find which idea so that when you're asked to answer a question on something very specific, you'll know where to find it.

- Be prepared to use the information in the passage to draw an inference to a conclusion that was not explicitly stated. Sometimes you'll be asked to determine the next step in a passage—given what's said in the passage, what sort of conclusions can be drawn?

- Paraphrase. Sometimes you will find that you just can't understand the way that a particular question applies to the passage. By trying to reformulate the question, the relevant section of the passage, or both, in your own words, you can often grasp the key idea that you need to address.

4. Answering the Questions

Once you have read and understood the questions, you'll need to select the best answer (or in some cases, answers).

- Be sure you know what kind of answer you need to find. Some questions will be straight multiple-choice, where you pick only one answer; others will allow you to choose more than one answer, and still, others will ask you to highlight a portion of the text. Be aware of what you're expected to provide in your answer.

- Be sure you are answering the question that was asked. Just because an answer choice is true, doesn't necessarily mean that it is right. Sometimes you will have more than one option that correctly addresses a point made by the passage—be sure that you choose the option that answers the question asked.

- Don't allow any personal opinion or prior knowledge of a topic distract you—again, you should only answer the question as it bears on the passage. You are not being asked to express your opinions about a passage or critique the content.

- Use logic. To correctly answer some questions, you will need to use basic logic. Learn to recognize implicit assumptions made by the author, and draw inferences to see what unstated conclusions might follow from a passage.

Introduction to Reading Comprehension

- Apply the process of elimination. For multiple-choice questions, you will often be given several potential answers that are more obviously wrong than others. Be sure to dismiss these answers first of all, since even if you don't know which of the remaining options is the right answer, you'll increase your odds of choosing it by dismissing those that are clearly wrong.

⫸ Key Strategy # 1

Always use the process of elimination. Many multiple-choice questions of any type will have some options that are more obviously wrong than some others—perhaps they fall beyond the scope of the question, or perhaps they produce an absurd result. If you are not immediately certain of the correct answer, dismiss those answers that are obviously wrong and work with what remains. Even if you end up having to guess the right answer, you'll increase your odds of guessing right by eliminating answers that are obviously incorrect.

⫸ Key Strategy # 2

Some questions on the test are designed to make you waste time if you haven't read effectively. If you did not do a good job of skimming the passage, you could easily waste minutes searching through the passage trying to determine which answers are right and which aren't. Don't let this happen. Hone your skimming skills so that you already have an idea of which information is right and which isn't before you look back over the passage for any final confirmation.

⫸ Key Strategy # 3

As you work on Reading Comprehension questions, remember to use elementary logic to your advantage. One very basic rule of logic is the following: for two propositions p and q, if p then q and not q entails not p. In other words, if you know that it is true that proposition p implies proposition q, and you know that proposition q is not true, then you know that proposition p is also not true. Use this and other strategies from basic logic to answer Reading Comprehension questions that require reasoning.

Tips for Answering Reading Comprehension Questions

- Be sure that you read the instructions for the question carefully. Remember that Reading Comprehension questions can appear in three distinct formats, and to correctly answer a given question, you'll need to understand the format.

- For all types of multiple-choice questions, always review every potential answer before you choose the correct answer or answers.

- For multiple-choice questions that ask for the single best answer, select only the option that best addresses the question.

- For multiple-choice questions that ask you to select one or more answers, don't be alarmed if more than one of the options looks correct. For this type of question, you can select all of the options that accurately answer the question.

- Don't be deceived by answers that are only partially true, or do not completely address the question—make sure that you select only those answers that fully and appropriately answer the question you were asked, especially for those questions that ask you to select a single option out of several or a passage.

Chapter 3: **Reading Comprehension**

This chapter is devoted to helping you develop your skill with Reading Comprehension questions using practice questions. You will find sets of passages related to subjects namely *Arts and Humanities, Biological Sciences, Business, Everyday Topics, Physical Sciences and Social Sciences,* that are similar to the sort of passages you will encounter on an actual GRE test. Each passage has a set of questions and a detailed explanation of the solution to each question. The questions and their solutions will be presented as follows:

In Each Set:

- A passage related to a particular subject similar to what you can expect on an actual GRE test

- Several questions about the passage similar to those you will encounter on an actual GRE test

In Answers & Explanations for Each Set:

- In most sets, a quick summary that paraphrases the main issues of the passage and points out important words or phrases that indicate the meaning or intent of the passage. Being able to answer a few basic questions about Reading Comprehension passages before you even see any of the questions is a key skill that will help you answer questions more quickly and more accurately. The summaries provided here will give you some sense of how to approach summarizing when looking at actual questions.

- Detailed solutions that explain what the correct answer is, and what strategy or strategies you could use to determine the correct answer are included. Explanatory answers will usually refer back to the summary.

Practice Set 1: Arts and Humanities

PASSAGE 1
Question 1 is based on the following passage.

It is little realized how slowly, how painfully, we approach the expression of truth. We are so variable, so anxious to be polite, and alternately swayed by caution or anger. Our mind oscillates like a pendulum: it takes some time for it to come to rest. And then, the proper allowance and correction has to be made for our individual vibrations that prevent accuracy. Even the compass needle doesn't point the true north, but only the magnetic north. Similarly, our minds can at best only indicate magnetic truth, yet they are distorted by many things that act upon them as iron filings do on a compass. The necessity of holding one's job—what an iron filing that is on the compass card of a man's brain!

1. Which of the following sentences supports the conclusion about "truth"?

    (A) Desperation causes people to do things they wouldn't normally do.
    (B) Compasses sometimes lack accuracy, just like people.
    (C) Truth is not "black or white", it only exists in shades of grey.
    (D) Past experiences have a significant effect on a person's behavior.
    (E) People are often very dishonest and seldom can be trusted 100%.

PASSAGE 2
Questions 2 and 3 are based on the following passage.

Out we drove at last. It was December, but by luck we found a halcyon morning which had got lost in the year's procession. It was a Sunday morning, and it had not been ashore. It was still virgin, bearing a vestal light. It had not been soiled yet by any suspicion of this trampled planet, this muddy star, which its innocent and tenuous rays had discovered in the region of night. I thought it still was regarding us as a lucky find there. Its light was tremulous, as if with joy and eagerness. I met this discovering morning as your ambassador while you still slept, and betrayed not, I hope, any greyness and bleared satiety of ours to its pure, frail, and lucid regard. That was the last good service I did before leaving you quiet. I was glad to see how well our old earth did meet such a light, as though it had no difficulty in looking day in the face. The world was miraculously renewed.

2. In the context of this passage, which of the following is the best definition for "lucid"?

    (A) Easily understood
    (B) Shining or bright
    (C) Rational or sane
    (D) Clear, transparent
    (E) Evident

For the following question, consider each of the choices separately and select all that apply.

3. Select the statement that can replace the second sentence of the passage without altering the overall meaning of the author's words.

    [A] Although it was December, we were fortunate to discover tranquil weather that seemed a better fit for a warmer month.
    [B] It was December, and we discovered a holiday celebration that we had neglected to observe earlier in the year.
    [C] Because it was December, we felt as carefree on that morning as we had in the summer month.

PASSAGE 3

Questions 4 to 6 are based on the following passage.

There seem to be two literary factions pitted against each other. Those of one class employ their best effort in dissuading young writers from writing; those of another set forth an author's life in glowing colors. **One faction will tell you that half the manuscripts sent to editors are not even accorded the courtesy of an examination unless signed by a well-known name.** Another says that editors are keenly on the outlook for original matter, seizing with avidity anything that promises to make a new element in current literature.

A noted author writes to a young aspirant: "Sweet and natural though your utterance seems to be, let me ask you in the friendliest spirit not to write at all. The toil is great, the pursuit incessant, the reward not outward." To the same young woman writes another equally well-known writer: "Your work is excellent; you can and will succeed."

4. This passage primarily sets out to prove which of the following ideas?

  (A) Accomplished writers view work with a critical eye and have differing opinions on the rhythm and cadence in a writer's work.

  (B) Authors are opinionated and base their criticism of aspiring writers' works on their own experiences.

  (C) The profession of writing is difficult and toilsome, yet can also be rewarding.

  (D) The opinions of established writers differ greatly and can be distinguished by their outlook on the perceived difficulty of writing as a profession.

  (E) In order to earn money, aspiring authors must make their own decisions regarding how to submit their work to editors so that pessimistic people will not dissuade them from reaching their goals.

5. What is the primary effect of the sentence in **boldface** on the passage's overall message?

  (A) To indicate the severity with which editors express their opinion of work that does not meet the high standards of publishing companies.

  (B) This sentence demonstrates the clout that well-known authors have in the publishing world; without a good reputation, it is very difficult to solicit an editor for advice on completed works.

  (C) It indicates the fragility of amateur writers' careers and the detrimental effects that harsh criticism can have on their aspirations.

  (D) To explain that editors rudely ignore at least fifty percent of submitted manuscripts without so much as a cursory glance unless the work comes highly recommended by one of their colleagues.

  (E) It establishes the opinion of one group of people in the writing business who warn about the regimented approach that editors often take to critiquing unpublished manuscripts.

6. Select a sentence from the passage that provides support for the author's viewpoint that writing is too subjective for one person to determine the fate of an aspiring writer's career.

PASSAGE 4

Question 7 is based on the following passage.

Is human nature intrinsically good or inherently evil? One of the most prominent and influential arguments for the latter was put forward by the British political philosopher Thomas Hobbes. In his seminal work, *Leviathan*, Hobbes established his theory of the social contract, in which he claimed that humans without government exist in a state of nature where each individual has a right to everything, engendering a "war against all". This environment creates a constant fear of death and prevents humans from both obtaining and hoping for the necessities needed to survive. It is only through the establishment of a civil society by way of a social contract that individuals are able to unite and thrive collectively. For Hobbes, society is what tames and controls the ultimately selfish and corrupt natural state of the human being.

7. Select the sentence that best illustrates Hobbes' view on human nature.

PASSAGE 5

Questions 8 and 9 are based on the following passage.

Friends—This lecture has been delivered under these circumstances: I visit a town or city, and try to arrive there early enough to see the postmaster, the barber, the keeper of the hotel, the principal of the schools, and the ministers of some of the churches, and then go into some of the factories and stores, and talk with the people, and get into sympathy with the local conditions of that town or city and see what has been their history, what opportunities they had, and what they had failed to do—and every town fails to do something—and then go to the lecture and talk to those people about the subjects which applied to their locality. "Acres of Diamonds"—the idea—has continuously been precisely the same. The idea is that in this country of ours every man has the opportunity to make more of himself than he does in his own environment, with his own skill, with his own energy, and with his own friends.

8   Based on the information in this passage, select the word that best describes his purpose in delivering his presentation, "Acres of Diamonds".

   (A) Information
   (B) Confirmation
   (C) Innovation
   (D) Motivation
   (E) Intimidation

9   What is the relationship of the last two sentences to the preceding portion of the passage?

   (A) They invalidate the process of the writer's visiting local officials and work places.
   (B) They contrast the universality of the idea with the specificity of the points for each town or city.
   (C) They cast aspersions on the officials and townsfolk that he has visited.
   (D) They summarize the information that he has discovered from his visits to officials and work places.
   (E) They support the assumption of failure on the parts of the town's inhabitants.

PASSAGE 6

Questions 10 to 12 are based on the following passage.

By the mid-nineteenth century, numerous expeditions funded by a few countries had reached the North Pole for exploratory purposes. However, Charles Francis Hall was delegated to be the only Arctic explorer under the patronage of the United States. Born in 1821, Charles Francis Hall established a lifestyle of transformation and change. He moved from employment as a blacksmith to a journalist to a stationer and then to an engraver before getting his hands on travel books, setting his sights on the Arctic environment as an explorer.

The lost explorer, John Franklin, fascinated Hall, and Hall's belief that Franklin's crew might still be alive prompted him to visit King William Land, the final whereabouts of Franklin's expedition. Seeking assistance, Hall distributed circulars calling for public aid and requested personal tales from other explorers and whalers.

10   Which of the following best describes the main idea of the passage?

   (A) Franklin's potential demise resulted in Hall's intention of becoming the first American explorer of the Arctic Circle.
   (B) At first, Hall could not pinpoint his exact employment interest until learning about the Arctic and Franklin's expedition.
   (C) Hall's captivation with exploration and the Arctic areas led to his desire to learn about the ecosystem of King William Land.
   (D) Hall would stop at nothing, even without the necessary financial resources, to locate Franklin's crew.
   (E) Hall realized the need to connect with other explorers, like Franklin, to further his likelihood of reaching the Arctic Circle.

For Questions 11 and 12, consider each of the choices separately and select all that apply.

11   Which of the following most strongly supports the claim that Hall's observations directly affected and led to his interest in John Franklin's expedition?

   [A] His reading of travel books, particularly about the Arctic.
   [B] The belief that the crew members of the Franklin expedition might have survived.
   [C] Hearing the personal tales from whalers and explorers of King William Land.

12. From the passage, it could be inferred that the author would agree with which of the following statements?

   A. Charles Francis Hall's expedition, under the patronage of the United States, would be to King William Land in search of Franklin's crew.
   B. The journey and exploration of the Arctic Circle included an element of danger and risk.
   C. John Franklin's expedition originated within the past year of Hall becoming interested in it.

PASSAGE 7

Question 13 is based on the following passage.

Together with the Mayans, the Andean peoples weave their stories and myths into their clothing. They attire themselves in their myths, legends, and folk stories which, at times, are displayed in their clothing. Histories merge with these tales, augmenting a powerful tradition. The visual metaphors that evolve link these indigenous peoples through their ancestors and varied cultures to the beginnings of time forging an identity and creating a sense of security and order. The daily dress cultivates this harmony. Thus, it can be said that weavers are bearers of tradition and are representatives of the Archetypal Feminine.

13. Select the sentence that suggests the ways in which the traditional attire promotes a sense of emotional well-being.

PASSAGE 8

Questions 14 and 15 are based on the following passage.

Nowhere is there anything just like them. In his best work—and his tales of the great metropolis are his best—he is unique. The soul of his art is unexpectedness. Humor at every turn there is, and sentiment and philosophy and surprise. One never may be sure of himself. The end is always a sensation. No foresight may predict it, and the sensation is always genuine. Whatever else O. Henry was, he was an artist, a master of plot and diction, a genuine humorist, and a philosopher. His weakness lay in the very nature of his art. He was an entertainer bent only on amusing and surprising his reader. Everywhere brilliancy, but too often it is joined to cheapness; art, yet art merging swiftly into caricature. Like Harte, he cannot be trusted. Both writers on the whole may be said to have lowered the standards of American literature, since both worked in the surface of life with theatric intent and always without moral background, O. Henry moves, but he never lifts.

14. Consider the words of this critic and select the word or phrase that best identifies what is missing from O. Henry's writing.

   A. Tension
   B. Style
   C. Subtlety
   D. Plot
   E. Conflict resolution

For the following question, consider each of the three choices separately and select all that apply.

15. Which of the following statements, if true, would have altered this critic's opinion of both O. Henry's and Harte's literary endeavors?

   A. The readers of the stories crafted by Harte and O. Henry are left with a sense of satisfaction.
   B. Harte's and O. Henry's stories continue to appear in secondary school anthologies.
   C. The themes in the works of both writers provide significant insight into the motivations of human behavior.

PASSAGE 9

Questions 16 to 18 are based on the following passage.

For thousands of years, until relatively recently, making money from creating music was almost unheard of. While music is much older than most people realize, humans have always made and continue to make music for many reasons beyond just financial gain. Making, hearing, and talking about music are fundamental parts of the human experience. Given that the creation of music is such an integral, almost compulsory, component of humanity, AI probably will not destroy music, but it can radically affect who makes the music that we hear and why we even make it to begin with.

In modern times, there are millions of people who depend on music for their survival, and machines that make music pose a threat to these individuals' livelihoods. A commercial that employs an AI-created jingle might not seem like that big of a deal, but that 30-second ditty represents a paycheck for a human being. Small jobs like these allow artists to do what they do best so that they can survive and develop their talents on their way to becoming the next Elton John or Taylor Swift. That jingle might sell a lot of cereal, but it will probably not make a classic record or sell out a stadium while also enriching the lives of millions of people.

16. Which of the following options best expresses the main idea of the passage?

    Ⓐ Human beings have been making music for thousands of years, and they continue to do so for a variety of reasons.

    Ⓑ The music industry is being taken over by AI, and it is impossible for musicians to make a living.

    Ⓒ By resorting to the use of AI to generate music, entities run the risk of contributing to a landscape of lackluster music that won't really mean much to anybody.

    Ⓓ There are millions of people in the world who make their living composing and selling music.

    Ⓔ Artists such as Elton John and Taylor Swift are in danger of being replaced by AI.

For Questions 17 and 18, consider each of the choices separately and select all that apply.

17. Which of the following statements, if true, would undermine the author's central argument?

    Ⓐ AI is constantly developing in many areas of human activity, and its uses have yet to be fully realized.

    Ⓑ Music created by AI delivers value to companies looking to use music to advertise products and services.

    Ⓒ Making music is cost-prohibitive, but AI makes creating music more affordable to new artists.

18. The author would probably agree with which of the following statements?

    Ⓐ Elton John and Taylor Swift would never use AI because it would threaten their business models.

    Ⓑ Ancient humans did not care about being compensated financially for making music.

    Ⓒ The use of AI in the creative arts undermines humans' ability to express themselves artistically.

PASSAGE 10

Question 19 is based on the following passage.

For Africans, movement is a great way of communicating with others. Because of this, the dances often utilize symbolic mime, gestures, masks, props, visual devices, and body painting. Most of the basic movements of African dances emphasize the use of torso, upper body, and feet. There are also complex dances that use intricate action and various body parts. Team dances are common but there are also times when the dance involves 2-4 individuals taking turns on the dancing ring.

There are also different formations used by the dancers like columns, serpentine, circular, and linear linear patterns. These formations are not only visually striking but also carry cultural and symbolic significance, often representing unity, continuity, and connection to the community or the spiritual world.

19. Select the sentence that suggests that some dancing exhibitions may be competitive in nature.

PASSAGE 11

Questions 20 and 21 are based on the following passage.

The Pop Art movement is generally seen as the aesthetic expression of capitalism, its motifs and imagery centering on mass production and consumer culture. The hallmark of Pop Art is its ability to make the viewer feel that it is pretend and not worthy of serious critique. A good example of such a work is pop artist Andy Warhol's images of Campbell's Soup cans. While Pop Art seems superfluous at the surface level, it is actually produced with marked intentionality and has a message that splinters in two directions. In Britain, Pop Artists use the capitalist aesthetic to mock and critique the vapidity of American consumer society while American Pop Artists tend to use their work as a celebration of reality and a slight re-imagining of familiar surroundings.

20. How does British Pop Art differ from American Pop Art?

    Ⓐ There is no difference.

    Ⓑ British Pop Art lampoons American consumer culture while American Pop Art focuses on recreating reality.

    Ⓒ British Pop Art is not worthy of serious critique while American Pop Art is highly valued as a legitimate form of aesthetic expression.

    Ⓓ British Pop artists are more famous than American Pop artists.

    Ⓔ British Pop artists avoid exploring capitalism in their work while American Pop artists use their work to address issues related to capitalism.

For the following question, consider each of the three choices separately and select all that apply.

21. What traits of capitalistic culture does Pop Art seek to explore?

    Ⓐ Consumerism

    Ⓑ Mass production

    Ⓒ Free markets

PASSAGE 12

Questions 22 to 24 are based on the following passage.

The first step in preparing a manuscript for printing is to gather essential details such as the total word count, the chosen typeface, the desired "leading" or spacing between the lines, and the size of the page. Thoughtful consideration of these factors is crucial. If the manuscript is a short story by a well-known author, it may be printed with wide margins and wide leading in order to make a book of fair size. In contrast, if it is a lengthy manuscript that will be likely to sell at a moderate but not a high price, it is best to use only as much leading as is necessary to make the line palpable and to print with a margin not so wide as to increase the expense of the book.

22. According to the passage, which of the following is true about the margin size?

    (A) A shorter margin takes less time to print.
    (B) No margins should be considered when printing a fair-sized book.
    (C) Use as many margins as possible to get the best result.
    (D) A wider margin results in a more expensive book.
    (E) The size of the margins should be determined by the popularity of the author.

23. Select the sentence that identifies the structure of the passage.

24. In the context of the passage, the word "palpable" refers to

    (A) detectable
    (B) thick and dark
    (C) ambiguous
    (D) reproducible
    (E) asynchronous

PASSAGE 13

Question 25 is based on the following passage.

The aim of this little work is, therefore, limited to the gathering of such facts and phenomena as may serve to throw light upon the nature of the magic powers with which man is undoubtedly endowed. Its end will be attained if it succeeds in showing that he actually does possess powers which are not subject to the general laws of nature, but more or less independent of space and time, and which yet make themselves known partly by appeals to the ordinary senses and partly by peculiar phenomena, the result of their activity. These higher powers, operating exclusively through the spirit of man, are part of his nature, which has much in common with that of the Deity, since he was created by God "in His own image," and the Lord "breathed into his nostrils the breath of life and man became a living soul."

25. Based on the information in this passage, what makes it likely that the author will find it difficult to conduct an objective investigation?

    (A) His belief in God
    (B) His preconceived idea that man has magical powers
    (C) The lack of previous research on the subject
    (D) The refusal of the church to cooperate in his endeavor
    (E) The likelihood that the public will scoff at his ideas

PASSAGE 14

Questions 26 and 27 are based on the following passage.

Jacques Derrida famously proclaimed, "There is nothing outside the text." By this he meant that analyzing a work of literature could only be done by way of investigating its labyrinthine relationships to other contexts. As a literary critic and founder of deconstructionist theory, Derrida advocated the position that there is no true or objective reference that can serve as a hermeneutical springboard; narratives can only be understood by deconstructing the various frameworks that inform the interpretive process.

26. It can be inferred that Derrida prefers a subjective approach to literary analysis because

    (A) textual analysis is dependent on deconstructing complex narratives
    (B) all texts are context sensitive and thus subjectivity is a more illuminating approach to finding meaning than objectivity
    (C) subjectivity accounts for the different ways readers experience and interpret a text
    (D) deconstructionist theory is predicated on the inner experience of each reader
    (E) subjectivity allows for a wider array of interesting interpretations of a given text

For the following question, consider each of the three choices separately and select all that apply.

27 Derrida's claim "There is nothing outside the text" can be taken to mean that

  A texts are connected to the myriad of contexts that contribute to their overall meaning
  B texts cannot be studied as independent entities
  C there is no reality outside of the text

PASSAGE 15

Questions 28 to 30 are based on the following passage.

Mozambique was partitioned into "holdings" where each holding's rental amount was determined by the number of huts located within each holding. Each holding was let out to anyone of Portuguese descent who guaranteed to pay the total levies of all residences. The tax per residence was one pound annually. The landlord also is required to build new roads, conduct maintenance on the other roads, and hire an appropriate police force for law enforcement and order. Numerous scandals have been initiated by the holdings' lessees. Most of the time, the lessee exudes tyrant behavior over his district by taxing its citizens up to ten times the amount these people were at one time required to pay, but he has escaped all authority and consequences from anyone whatsoever.

28 The passage's structure can best be defined as

  A a description of the hierarchy associated with this Mozambique town
  B a resolution of challenges faced by tenants
  C a causal relationship of letting a holding
  D a spatial explanation of the layout of a town with native huts
  E a sequential list of situations and examples that might occur with a holding

For the following question, consider each of the choices separately and select all that apply.

29 The passage suggests that the author's perspective of the lessee is

  A an avaricious and reluctant tyrant towards their tenants
  B an inhumane and apathetic entrepreneur
  C a leader with violent tendencies to their subordinates

30 The passage suggests that another explanation for the lessee's actions could be that

  A the lessee did not understand how to treat the natives
  B the natives misused the money and hut that was given to them
  C the lessee needed the money to perform all duties required of him
  D the natives were living in the wrong holding
  E the rent on each holding was less than what was first believed

PASSAGE 16

Question 31 is based on the following passage.

I must confess, though, that I am a bibliophile with War books. Any book about the Great War is good enough for me. I am to that class of literature what little boys are to stamps. Yes; I know well the dreaded implication. I am aware of the worm in the mind; that I probe a wound; that I surrender to an impulse to peer into the darkness of the pit; that I encourage a thought which steals in with the quiet of midnight, and that it keeps me awake while the household sleeps. I know I consort with ghosts in a region of evil. I get the horrors, and I do not repel them. For some reason I like those ghosts. Most of them have no names for me, but I count them as old friends of mine; and where should I meet them again, at night, but amid the scenes we knew.

31 Select the sentence that suggests that the writer may be performing a cathartic act in this passage.

PASSAGE 17

Questions 32 and 33 are based on the following passage.

Giving credence to the proverb "one man's trash is another man's treasure," Bulgarian archaeologists found a well-preserved marble statue while excavating an ancient Roman sewer system. It is hoped that the statue, believed to depict the god Hermes, will help to shed light on how worshippers in the area maintained their religion in the face of prevailing Christianity. Pagans may have used the sewer as a hiding place to protect their canonical icons from Christian extremists who occasionally destroyed the heads of such pagan idols. Judging from the statue's condition, the pagan ploy succeeded, as the face and head of the statue showed no signs of damage.

32. In the context of the passage, what does the term "one man's trash is another man's treasure" refer to?

    (A) The ancient Romans threw out most of their objects of worship fearing that Christian zealots would discover them.
    (B) The ancient Romans buried treasures in their sewer systems.
    (C) The pagans thought of their statues as valuable, whereas the Christians thought of the statues as worthless.
    (D) It is ironic valuable items ended up in a sewer system.
    (E) People should be careful about what they throw out.

33. Select the sentence that indicates that this statute will be used for further research.

PASSAGE 18

Questions 34 to 36 are based on the following passage.

After protracted discussions, Royal Exchange Theatre, a prominent venue in Manchester, decided to cancel the running of a modern adaptation of Shakespeare's *A Midsummer Night's Dream*. In response to the lack of transparency in the cancellation, the production alleges that the revocation stems from a growing climate of censorship that undermines artistic integrity. With controversy surrounding social issues and military conflicts around the world, artists decried the decision as a blatant stifling of expression and voice. Two major points of contention were a reference to war in the Middle East and the rights of people who identify as transgender. According to the artists, it behooves a society that is demonstrably pluralistic to engage in debate on such pertinent issues both on and off the stage.

The theater, which had expressed interest in working with artists who "address complex issues," however, claimed there were certain technical setbacks and last-minute changes that proved insurmountable. And while denounced by union officials and associates as a frustrating attack on the artistic principle, exact reasons for the cancellation were not cited. Such a lack of clarity raises doubt about whether this Midsummer's Night Dream will ever see the light of day.

34. In the context in which it appears, the word "decried" most nearly means

    (A) showed the decision to lack merit
    (B) discarded as unreasonable
    (C) offered alternatives
    (D) denounced as unfair
    (E) considered confusing

35. Which of the following statements expresses the perspective of the author?

    (A) The theater has adequately explained the motives behind the cancellation.
    (B) It remains uncertain whether the production will have a theatrical premiere.
    (C) The cancellation came suddenly without any previous warning.
    (D) The theater failed to mediate between the production crew and critical audience members.
    (E) Claims that certain controversial topics were being censored have been substantiated by theater staff.

36. Select a sentence that contextualizes the cancellation within what is perceived as an increasing trend that is examined later in the passage.

PASSAGE 19

Question 37 is based on the following passage.

One of the defining features of the Art Nouveau movement was its desire to distance itself aesthetically from previous methods of artistic expression. Art Nouveau arose at the turn of the 20th century as a reaction to the Neoclassicist movement's propensity to simply mimic the style of the Greeks and Romans. Art Nouveau artists sought to create a truly new and distinct way of representing the world and this is best exemplified in their architectural approach. They used asymmetry and curvy lines and forms in conjunction with leaves, vines, and other unusual patterns to construct and decorate their buildings in a way that had never before been seen.

37 Select the sentence that best describes why Art Nouveau artists were looking to radically alter artistic expression.

PASSAGE 20

Questions 38 and 39 are based on the following passage.

Sun Tzu's The Art of War is one of the earliest and most celebrated books on military strategy in the world. The Art of War covers a variety of topics related to success on the battlefield and, astoundingly, people at nearly all levels of Chinese society in both the past and present are familiar with the text. One of the most influential themes in the book is its emphasis on the ability to evolve and change plans in the present moment instead of focusing solely on developing rigidly thought-out, long-term strategies. This efficacious strategy defined success as the ability to evolve and utilize a quick wit when the situation calls for such action.

38 The author's personal opinion on The Art of War can be best described as

   Ⓐ light-hearted
   Ⓑ aloof
   Ⓒ unaligned
   Ⓓ inert
   Ⓔ phlegmatic

39 The author intends the term "efficacious" in the passage to be analogous to

   Ⓐ ambitious
   Ⓑ useful
   Ⓒ potent
   Ⓓ adequate
   Ⓔ unorganized

PASSAGE 21

Questions 40 to 42 are based on the following passage

The remnants of colonialist societal hierarchy, as they continue to reverberate through contemporary racial dynamics, are explored in Chimamanda Ngozi Adichie's novel, Americanah. Subalternity, the condition of being disenfranchised from the dominant social group and deemed inferior in mainstream narratives, pervades the path of two lovers in their immigration to the United States and the United Kingdom from their homeland, Nigeria. Through the characters' distinct responses to the marginalization they both encounter, Adichie explores the postcolonial challenges faced by subaltern communities who aim to ´fit in´ a world that retains a colonialist mindset.

Assimilation is examined through the lens of its assault on personal identity. One can either resist the demands of mainstream culture through insubordination or, on the other hand, adapt through a form of mimicry of expected behaviors at the expense of one's personality. Both paths entail a certain sacrifice in one's degree of engagement within a society that precludes any genuine integration. Delving into the nature of such sacrifices, Americanah shows them to stem from the psychological tension of being compelled to respond to the dominant culture's implicit or explicit resistance to those from the so-called social "periphery."

40 According to the passage, which of the following summarizes the main idea of the novel?

   Ⓐ Every immigrant has a different experience in terms of integrating into mainstream society depending on the status of their home country during colonial times.
   Ⓑ Relationships endure great hardships during immigration as some individuals find it more difficult to adapt than others.
   Ⓒ Even in the postcolonial era, certain colonialist attitudes remain, resulting in a social climate that excludes outsiders.
   Ⓓ Immigrants from marginalized communities assimilate more smoothly into mainstream culture when they mimic behaviors.
   Ⓔ Unresolved grievances from colonial times result in challenges to integrate into postcolonial societies.

For Questions 41 and 42, consider each of the choices separately and select all that apply.

41 Which of the following statements corresponds with a minor point in the passage?

   ☐ A Postcolonial racial dynamics result in subaltern communities failing to integrate fully whether they comply or not.
   ☐ B The act of behaving in a way that is expected rather than according to one's personality creates a barrier to integration as it entails denying one's personality.
   ☐ C Despite political changes, certain colonialist barriers persist in formerly colonialist societies in the form of psychological tensions.

42. Which of the following conclusions can be made from the passage?

   A. The novel Americanah deals with the persistence of racist attitudes in postcolonial societies.

   B. The author rejects the possibility of integration of people of one culture into another.

   C. A colonialist mindset presumes that one's culture is inherently superior to others and offers little flexibility to outsiders from previously colonized societies.

PASSAGE 22

Question 43 is based on the following passage.

Modernist literature bloomed at the beginning of the 20th century and was characterized by concise language and precise imagery. Modernist writers such as Ezra Pound and T.S. Eliot used their poetry and prose to express sentiments of radical individualism and methodical order. However, this conviction quickly deteriorated from praise of autonomy to a more introspective, darker look at humanity and the role of the individual as the exactitude of form that modernists so cherished in their writing came to represent the meticulousness with which the industrialized world could extinguish human life during World War I and World War II.

43. Given the information in the passage, all of the following are true relative to modernist writing except

   A. Modernist writing evolved to mirror cultural changes

   B. Modernist writing lauds the primacy of coherent form

   C. Modernist writing is at its crux deeply reflective.

   D. Modernist writing eschews florid prose

   E. Modernist writing is mechanical in nature

PASSAGE 23

Questions 44 to 45 are based on the following passage.

Wood has been used throughout centuries for countless practical purposes such as building homes, boats, and weapons. Since the start of recorded history, wood has also been used for aesthetic enjoyment. Wood welcomes a variety of artistic tools such as many types of paint or a carving scalpel. However, one of the most traditional manipulations of wood for creative purposes is through the use of heat.

Pyrography is a style of art that involves using a heated tool to burn markings onto a piece of wood. When traced to its Greek roots, the word, "pyrography," means "writing with fire." While literal fire is not often used in modern pyrography, metal pens known as "pokers" can seamlessly beget detailed works of art.

44. In the second paragraph, what does the word, "beget" most likely mean?

   A. emend
   B. generate
   C. amplify
   D. efface
   E. approximate

45. Select a sentence from the passage that introduces the concept of wood acting as an artistic medium.

PASSAGE 24

Questions 46 to 48 are based on the following passage.

Purportedly a platform to commemorate authors on the merit of their corpus, the Nobel Prize for Literature has become the quintessential recognition of literary achievement. Nonetheless, does the nominating process, and consequently, the selection, suffer from circumscribed perceptions that reduce its purview? Modern interdisciplinary literary studies question the process by which literary achievement is gauged, uncovering certain biases that, perhaps inadvertently, narrow the selection to authors of certain national identities, whose social and cultural milieu render their voice more resonant with the pervading ethos of international readers. Other factors, ranging from linguistic status to translation challenges have been found to play a restrictive role in selection. Moreover, subject matter that touches upon global and national events of wider appeal typically garners more support through previously developed sympathy for the topic than those farther removed from the eye of international attention.

Beyond a prestigious accolade, the Nobel Prize serves to catapult events, trends, and perspectives into a wider social discussion. By amplifying attention on certain human stories over others, any predispositions deserve careful and transparent examination. Critical scrutiny would ensure the prize is reflective of a more thorough selection process, benefiting readers with access to all authors of unique creativity and vision, as well as universal caliber.

46 Based on the passage, the word "restrictive" most nearly means

   A penitent
   B partial
   C facilitative
   D limiting
   E forbidden

47 Based on the information in the passage, which of the following can be inferred about Nobel Prize laureates?

   A They have received a nomination from someone in their families or places of work.
   B They rarely come from countries or languages that differ from that of the selecting committee.
   C Their works have enjoyed international success prior to winning the Nobel Prize.
   D Their writing touches upon themes that are obscure and underrepresented in the international media.
   E They don't come from national backgrounds where the Nobel Prize is not considered prestigious.

48 According to the author's perspective, which of the following conclusions can be drawn about the Nobel Prize?

   A It falls short of its potential in honoring literary achievement, as its scope is not entirely inclusive.
   B It is an instrument for projecting lesser-known authors onto the international stage.
   C It is a prestigious award but only ftor authors from its base country.
   D It should not be bestowed to works that had to be translated from their original language.
   E It is unable to assess literary works that deal with issues not typically presented in mainstream media.

PASSAGE 25

Question 49 is based on the following passage.

The latter half of the 20th century witnessed the rise of a new epistemological approach in the humanities: postcolonial theory. Postcolonial theory was a reaction to the Western meta-narratives of European Imperialism that had been deeply entrenched in global society. It sought to give the colonized and their experience a voice in literature, cultural studies, politics, and philosophy in order to illuminate the fact that global reality had been constructed by European cultural power and that cultural space is really a fluid interaction of a "multiplicity of positionalities."

49 According to the passage, what was the primary consequence of European Imperialism?

   A European imperialism created norms that dictated the structure of global society
   B European Imperialism made it difficult for diversity to thrive
   C The colonized were unable to participate in the political systems erected by colonial societies
   D European Imperialism had little effect on global society
   E European Imperialism promoted a cultural space comprised by a variety of cultural perspectives

PASSAGE 26

Question 50 is based on the following passage.

Certain things are true of all news stories; whether the story be the baldest recital of facts or the most sensational featuring of an imaginary thrill in a commonplace happening, certain characteristics are always present. And these characteristics can always be traced to one cause—the effort to catch and hold the reader's interest. When a busy American glances over his newspaper while he sips his breakfast coffee or while he clings to a strap on the way to his office, he reads only the stories that catch his interest—and he reads down the column in any one story only so long as his interest is maintained. Hence the ideal news story is one which will catch the reader's attention by its beginning and hold his interest to the very end. This is the principle of all newspaper writing.

50 Which statement below casts the most doubt upon a main assumption in the passage?

   A The reader's past experiences will heavily affect his reaction to news articles.
   B Only carefully written articles will interest the reader for its entirety.
   C Many Americans only read the front page of the newspaper.
   D The beginning and ending are the best remembered portions of any news article.
   E There are many distractions competing for one's time, that could be spent reading the newspaper

Answer Key

Q. No.	Correct Answer	Your Answer	Q. No.	Correct Answer	Your Answer
1	C		27	A, B	
2	D		28	C	
3	A		29	A, B	
4	D		30	C	
5	E		31	I must confess... War books.	
6	To the same... succeed.		32	D	
7	For Hobbes,...being.		33	It is hoped... Christianity.	
8	D		34	D	
9	B		35	B	
10	B		36	In response... integrity.	
11	A, B		37	Art Nouveau... Romans.	
12	B, C		38	C	
13	The visual...order.		39	C	
14	C		40	C	
15	C		41	B	
16	C		42	A, C	
17	C		43	C	
18	B		44	B	
19	Team dances...ring.		45	Since the start... enjoyment	
20	B		46	D	
21	A, B		47	B	
22	D		48	A	
23	The first...page.		49	A	
24	A		50	A	
25	B				
26	B				

Practice Set 1: Answers & Explanations

PASSAGE 1

1 **Choice C is correct** because this comment indicates that truth does not exist on a 100% basis. Truth varies according to experiences and needs. What is considered "true" may have tinges of dishonesty in it, changing the "color" from white to grey.

Choice A is incorrect because this passage refers to people's behavior most of the time. Just as a compass doesn't point true north, neither are people entirely honest. The sentence just describes the unusual times. **Choice B is incorrect** because the passage just speaks of usual behavior of people and of compasses. This sentence describes an unusual situation. **Choice D is incorrect** because while past experience does affect a person, it is only a small portion of what this article addresses. Therefore, this is not the best answer. **Choice E is incorrect** because this statement is too extreme for the passage. The passage didn't focus on extreme dishonesty and lack of trustworthiness. The passage just suggested that people have trouble being 100% honest, on account of other situations influencing them.

PASSAGE 2: SUMMARY/PARAPHRASE

The passage is about morning as a metaphor for renewal. The main idea is that, although the author is apparently rather world weary, the beauty of the morning renews some sense of hope in the world. The major points contrast (a) the freshness and innocence of the morning to (b) the sense of the world as "trampled" and the characters as 'grey' and 'sated'. The purpose of the passage is to contrast the author's general state of mind with the symbolic purity of the morning.

2 **Choice D is correct** because in the context of the passage, "lucid" is used to describe the morning's light as "pure, frail, and lucid," emphasizing its clarity and transparency. The description evokes an image of a clear, natural light shining gently on the world, aligning best with the meaning "clear, transparent."

Choice A is incorrect because although "lucid" can mean "easily understood," it applies to ideas or explanations, not to light or physical descriptions, which is the case in this passage. **Choice B is incorrect** because while "lucid" can imply brightness, the word "shining" would more directly convey that meaning. Here, the passage already describes the light as "frail" and "pure," suggesting delicacy and clarity more than brilliance. **Choice C is incorrect** because the meaning "rational or sane" applies to people or states of mind, not to the morning light being described in this poetic and atmospheric passage. **Choice E is incorrect** because although "lucid" can be used to mean "evident," the passage's focus is more on the visual and emotional clarity of the morning light, making "clear, transparent" a better fit.

3 **Choice A is correct** because the author describes the morning as unusually calm and tranquil for December, suggesting it felt out of place in the "year's procession." The word halcyon, when used to describe weather, refers to a peaceful or serene state. Choice A is the only option that captures both the calmness and the sense of an unexpectedly pleasant day.

Choice B is incorrect because although the morning is described as special, there is no indication of a holiday or any form of celebration. The passage focuses solely on the natural qualities of the day. **Choice C is incorrect** because the author does not describe the emotions or attitudes of the people ("we") in the passage. His focus is entirely on the morning itself—its purity, light, and tranquil beauty—not on human sentiment.

PASSAGE 3

4 **Choice D is correct** because the question asks for the main idea of the passage, which is that people have different opinions on the trials that aspiring writers will face in their attempt to make a career of writing.

Choice A is incorrect because it focuses too closely on the details of written work; the passage makes no mention of specific details regarding what makes a writer good or bad. **Choice B is incorrect** because though it may be true, the idea of the passage as a whole does not focus on how established authors and editors form their opinions. It simply states that people have differing opinions but does not attempt to state why that is so. **Choice C is incorrect** because while the passage mentions, in one author's opinion, the toilsome nature of the writing business, it does not discuss ways in which success can be rewarding. The writers who offer encouraging advice simply focus on expressing the possibility for success rather than the benefits that will come with it. **Choice E is incorrect** because the passage does not supply advice to writers on how to make money from writing. While differing opinions are set forth, the author does not outline any explicit advice to young writers.

5 **Choice E is correct** because this sentence outlines the opinion of the more pessimistic people who focus on the harsh reality of the writing business.

Choice A is incorrect because it expresses a stronger opinion than what the passage supplies; while the author indicates that there are people who understand that editors do not read all submitted manuscripts, the passage does not intend to make such a claim. **Choice B is incorrect** because although the sentence mentions that manuscripts without a recommendation may not be read by an editor, it focuses too closely on the benefits of being well-established. The sentence serves to outline reasons why a manuscript may not be read, not to explain the benefits of having connections in the business. **Choice C is incorrect** because it goes beyond what is stated in the passage; though perhaps implied, the text does not support any claims that describe the effects that lack of attention from an editor would have on aspiring writers. **Choice D** is incorrect because though true, it goes too far in bringing emotion into the actions of editors who do not read certain works, calling them "rude." While the sentence does indicate a lack of courtesy in this process, the purpose of the sentence is not to judge the editors but to highlight that some people view this as evidence of the difficulty in breaking into the writing industry.

6 "**To the same young woman writes another equally well-known writer: "Your work is excellent; you can and will succeed."**" This sentence indicates the unreliability of judging a writer's potential on only one opinion. By indicating that the work being judged was written by the 'same' girl, the author establishes a controlled variable. Also, by pointing out that the differing opinion of this same work was that of an 'equally well-known writer', the author of this passage upholds the credibility of both judgments, thus demonstrating the subjective nature of writing and the unreliability of a single opinion.

PASSAGE 4: SUMMARY/PARAPHRASE

The passage is about the political philosophy of Thomas Hobbes. The main idea is that Hobbes developed a theory in which humans are seen as naturally inclined to do evil and require a government to reign in their naturally evil tendencies. The main points are: (a) that Hobbes believes that in a state of nature, humans are engulfed in perpetual state of conflict (b) that Hobbes believes that only in civil society governed by a social contract are humans able to escape the evils of their "natural" condition. A minor point, the mention of the age-old debate between whether human nature is inherently good or bad, is used to introduce the discussion of Hobbes' ideas. The purpose of the passage is to briefly summarize Hobbes' political thought: although the passage presents a potentially controversial matter, the author avoids any indication of bias and merely presents the content.

7 "**For Hobbes, society is what tames and controls the ultimately selfish and corrupt natural state of the human being.**" Hobbes' view on human nature is clearly stated: it is corrupt and selfish.

PASSAGE 5: SUMMARY/PARAPHRASE

The passage is about the author's strategy for speaking to local populations. The main idea is that the author always attempts to learn some particulars about the place where he is going to speak before overlaying the particulars with a more general theme. The major points are (a) that the author speaks to various townsfolk to find out about their town, what they are proud of, and where they see failures and (b) that the author then modifies his speech with its general themes of civic pride with certain specific features. The purpose of the passage is to reveal the author's way of addressing each town. The rhetoric suggests that the author may be somewhat cynical about his vocation.

8 **Choice D is correct** because the purpose of his presentation is to help the residents realize their potential for improvement. He aims to motivate them, making Choice D the best answer. The writer gathers information in order to confirm what he believes about the inhabitants of towns everywhere. He hopes that their behavior will become new or innovative. There is nothing in this passage that suggests he attempts to intimidate them or cause fear. He desires to use what he knows to motivate them to realize their full potential.

Choice A is incorrect because there is no indication that the author seeks to criticize the residents or their past behavior. His goal is motivational, not judgmental. **Choice B** is incorrect because the passage does not suggest that he is attempting to entertain. His tone and purpose are serious and focused on inspiring change. **Choice C** is incorrect because while he may use examples and observations, the main purpose is not to inform in a neutral way but to inspire improvement. **Choice E** is incorrect because the author does not try to instill fear or threaten the audience. His approach is constructive and optimistic, aimed at encouragement rather than intimidation.

9 **Choice B is correct** because the writer's basic assumption is that, although each town has its unique characteristics, they all fail in the same way. The last two sentences provide the general idea that he uses to illuminate the specific failure of the town he is visiting.

Choice A is incorrect because he uses those visits to tailor his presentation, not to make generalizations about the towns themselves. **Choice C** is incorrect because there is no indication that he looks down on the people in positions of power in the town. **Choice D** is incorrect because this passage is an overview of his process and reveals nothing specific about any town. **Choice E** is incorrect because the lecture focuses on possibilities, not failures

PASSAGE 6

10 **Choice B is correct** because the passage describes how Charles Francis Hall became interested in the Arctic Circle after working several diverse jobs before finding a topic that piqued his interest. The passage states that his jobs changed from "a blacksmith to a journalist to a stationer and then to an engraver" and then he became fascinated with the Arctic Circle through reading books which led to him learning about Franklin's expedition.

Choice A is incorrect because there is no connection between Franklin's demise and Hall's intentions of becoming an explorer. Hall became interested in becoming an explorer of the Arctic Circle before learning about Franklin's demise. **Choice C** is incorrect because Hall was captivated by the exploration of the Arctic areas, but he didn't want to travel to King William Land to learn about its ecosystem. Instead, he wanted to see if Franklin's crew was still alive .**Choice D** is incorrect because Hall needed resources to travel on that journey which is why he was "calling for public aid." **Choice E** is incorrect because there is no evidence that Hall and Franklin interacted or communicated with each other.

11 **Choice A is correct** because when Hall read travel books, some of which must have been about the Arctic, he set "his sights on the Arctic environment as an explorer." After this, he learned about John Franklin's expedition and then became interested in it. It can be concluded that Hall may have read about John Franklin's expedition in a book or newspaper. He would have been drawn to this story since he was eager to learn more about the Arctic. **Choice B is correct** because Hall wanted to find Franklin's crew to see if they had survived the expedition. He wanted "to visit King William Land, the final whereabouts of Franklin's expedition" to find evidence of the crew of Franklin. His journey would be to travel to the Arctic Circle in search of possible survivors.

Choice C is incorrect because the personal tales being told from whalers and explorers would only be told after Hall learned about Franklin's expedition. He wanted to hear those tales in order to understand more about King William Land.

12 **Choice B is correct** because the journey and expedition to the Arctic Circle would be dangerous due to Hall traveling to the site of the "lost explorer, John Franklin." Since Franklin had died and his crew may have encountered the same fate as Franklin, Charles Hall might also have experienced the same dangers and threats that took the life of John Franklin. Also, survival would be difficult in the Arctic Circle due to the scarcity of people and vegetation. Any journey to the Arctic Circle would be risky for the captain and the crew. **Choice C is correct** because John Franklin's crew "might still be alive" So they most likely could not or would not be alive if this expedition took place many years ago. It would be unlikely that a crew of people could survive for a long time in the Arctic Circle without enough resources to live off of, especially with their leader deceased.

Choice A is incorrect because Hall's expedition would have been funded by an agency or organization of the United States instead of him having to request aid from the general public.

PASSAGE 7

13 "The visual metaphors that evolve link these indigenous peoples through their ancestors and varied cultures to the beginnings of time forging identity and creating a sense of security and order." The last part of this sentence informs the reader that the clothing helps to forge an identity and create a sense of security and order, all of which lead individuals to feel better about their place in society.

PASSAGE 8: SUMMARY/PARAPHRASE

The passage is about O. Henry. The main idea is that although O. Henry was a superb literary craftsman, his work is gimmicky and lacking in depth. The major points are (a) O. Henry was a unique and skillful writer (b) that his work favors sensation and surprise over genuine substance and (c) that he can be accused of lowering the overall standards of American literature. The main purpose of the passage is to severely critique O. Henry's works while giving some credit for certain topical skill.

14 **Choice C is correct** because the writer's use of words like "caricature" and "cheapness" describe the overall effect of O. Henry's writing, and they point to a lack of subtlety, making Choice C the correct answer.

Choice A is incorrect because the critic states that the reader can never be sure of himself, indicating that the stories do create "tension." **Choice B** is incorrect because the writer of this passage deals with O. Henry's style extensively, so it is not accurate to say that style is missing. **Choice D** is incorrect because the writer provides information about plot elements, so it would be incorrect to assume that plot is a weakness. **Choice E** is incorrect because there is too little information provided to select conflict resolution as a weakness.

Chapter 3: Reading Comprehension

15 **Choice C is correct** because if the themes in the works of both writers provided significant insight into human motivation, it would directly challenge the critic's claim that their writing only skimmed the surface of life and lacked a moral background. This deeper layer of meaning could elevate their work in the critic's eyes and potentially revise his view of their contributions to American literature.

Choice A is incorrect because the critic already acknowledges that O. Henry was an entertainer who amused and surprised his readers. Reader satisfaction aligns with this view but would not alter the critic's core concern—namely, the lack of depth and moral grounding. **Choice B** is incorrect because the presence of Harte's and O. Henry's stories in school anthologies does not, by itself, speak to the literary merit or depth the critic finds lacking. The critic would need to know why their work is included to reconsider his stance.

PASSAGE 9

16 **Choice C is correct** because the thrust of the passage is that using AI to compose music poses a threat to the livelihoods of musicians, and this may result in, not only musicians' ability to earn a living but also to the overall quality of new music.

Choice A is incorrect because it is too narrow in scope. While it does mention that human beings have made and continue to make music, it is not the main point of the passage. It only sets up a historical context in order to make a main point about AI and music. **Choice B** is incorrect because it takes a presented fact and overstates causality. The passage suggests that, although musicians getting paid to make music might be in jeopardy, it does not go so far as to say it is inevitable that they will never be able to be compensated. **Choice D** is incorrect because it is just a fact presented in the passage and not the main topic. **Choice E** is incorrect because it misrepresents a statement made in the passage. The passage suggests that developing artists looking to gain recognition might not be able to do so because of AI. Elton John and Taylor Swift are used as examples of a level of recognition unattainable by new artists. They themselves are not under consideration per se.

17 **Choice C is correct** because this answer provides a benefit to musicians who use AI and goes against the author's intention of arguing why AI is bad for music.

Choice A is incorrect because it is beyond the scope of the passage. While perhaps true, it is off-topic. **Choice B** is incorrect because it is a direct statement of an implication in the passage.

18 **Choice B is correct** because the author states that humans had been making music before money was invented, so it would be unlikely for them to care about something that they did not know.

Choice A is incorrect because the author uses Elton John and Taylor Swift as examples of what professional musicians aspire to be, and whether or not they would use AI is not within the scope of the argument. **Choice C** is incorrect because the passage addresses financial compensation to musicians and not artistic expression per se.

PASSAGE 10

19 "Team dances are common but there are also times when the dance involves 2-4 individuals taking turns on the dancing ring." The other sentences in the passage describe the types of movement and props that the dancers incorporate. The statement "individuals taking turns on the dancing ring", suggests that some competition may have existed. The remaining sentences in the passage fail to mention individual dances. The previous sentence suggests that various body parts (e.g., legs, arms, and head) performed intricate motions but not necessarily by individuals in a competitive manner.

PASSAGE 11

20 **Choice B is correct** because the passage states that British Pop artists mocked (lampooned) America's consumer culture, while American Pop artists were more interested in representations of reality.

Choice A is incorrect because the passage clearly states that there is a difference between British and American Pop Art. **Choice C** is incorrect because both American and British Pop Art are presented as worthy of critique according to the passage. **Choice D** is incorrect because the passage does not discuss whether British or American Pop artists are more famous. **Choice E** is incorrect because the passage clearly states that British Pop artists explored capitalism in their work since they were highly critical of American consumer culture.

21 **Choice A is correct** because the passage lists consumerism as one of Pop Art's themes relative to its exploration of capitalism. **Choice B is correct** because the passage lists mass production as one of Pop Art's themes relative to its exploration of capitalism.

Choice C is incorrect because the passage does not indicate that Pop Artists used free markets as a part of their artistic expression relative to capitalism.

PASSAGE 12

22 **Choice D is correct** because it states in the passage that "to print with a margin not so wide as to increase the expense of the book" which implies that a wider margin would make the book longer and bigger, so it might make it more expensive.

Choice A is incorrect because a shorter margin does not necessarily mean it will take less time to print, and there is no evidence in the passage to support this statement. **Choice B** is incorrect because there is no mention in the passage that there should be no margins. The option instead contradicts the passage. **Choice C** is incorrect because the passage does not advocate for using numerous margins. Instead, it discusses the balance of margin size based on the manuscript length and the author's popularity, suggesting that excessive margins can lead to higher costs. **Choice E** is incorrect because the popularity of the author is mentioned in the passage, but it doesn't state that margin size should solely be determined by the author's popularity. It implies consideration of cost and the type of manuscript as well.

23 The sentence, "**The first step in preparing a manuscript for printing is to gather essential details such as the total word count, the chosen typeface, the desired "leading" or spacing between the lines, and the size of the page.**" is correct because this sentence states the characteristics included in the rest of the passage. For example, the rest of the paragraph goes on to discuss the length of margins based on the size of the book and how expensive the book will be.

24 **Choice A is correct** because "palpable" often refers to something that is clear or obvious enough to be perceived or recognized. In the context of the manuscript formatting, using "as much leading as is necessary to make the line palpable" implies that the leading should be sufficient to make the text easy to read, or detectable to the reader's eye.

Choice B is incorrect because this option suggests a visual quality (thickness and darkness) rather than clarity or perceptibility. "Palpable" does not specifically describe the physical characteristics of the text in this way. **Choice C** is incorrect because the line would be the opposite of ambiguous since ambiguous means unclear and a lengthy margin would make the line stand out instead of being unclear. **Choice D** is incorrect because there is nothing that provides evidence that this line could be reproducible. This relates to the ability to be copied or duplicated, which is not applicable to the readability or clarity of text in this context. **Choice E** is incorrect because asynchronous refers to events occurring at different times or without uniform timing, which is unrelated to text clarity or spacing. "Palpable" does not convey any notion of timing.

PASSAGE 13: SUMMARY/PARAPHRASE

The passage is about supernatural powers for humans. The main idea is that, since man is created in God's image, man too must possess supernatural abilities. The major point is that the work from which the passage is excerpted hopes to demonstrate that humans possess powers "not subject to the general laws of nature"; in other words, that humans have supernatural powers. The purpose of the passage is to serve as a primer for demonstrating that humans are capable of possessing magical abilities.

25 **Choice B is correct** because the author states his conviction that man is undoubtedly endowed with magic powers. This belief may lead him to make the facts fit his theory, which is contrary to objective, scientific research.

Choice A is incorrect because his belief in God should not be an impediment, as many who conduct scientific research also believe in God. **Choice C** is incorrect because the reader cannot tell from the information presented here if there is little or no research on this topic. **Choice D** is incorrect because the reader cannot assume that the church will not cooperate. **Choice E** is incorrect because the reader cannot assume that the public will scoff at his ideas.

PASSAGE 14: SUMMARY/PARAPHRASE

The passage is about Jacques Derrida's critical theory. The main idea is that Derrida believed that the critical analysis of a literary work could only be done by thoroughly investigating its context. The major points are that (a) Derrida believed that there was no objective starting point to begin the analysis of a work and (b) analysis of narrative could only begin by deconstructing the assumptions underlying the interpretive process. The main purpose of the passage is to introduce the reader to Derrida's idea about critical theory.

26 **Choice B is correct** because the passage shows that Derrida insisted that textual analysis was ultimately dependent on understanding and interpreting the various contexts that inform the text, an act that is an exercise in subjectivity since subjectivity is concerned with engaging a diversity of perspectives.

Choice A is incorrect because while this statement is true according to the passage, it does not explicate why subjectivity is needed to deconstruct complex narratives. **Choice C** is incorrect because the passage does not give enough information about how readers read in order to make a judgment as to whether or not subjectivity accounts for the interpretive process of readers. **Choice D** is incorrect because the passage does not give enough specific information about readers to make the inference that the inner experience of the reader is what characterizes deconstructionist theory. **Choice E** is incorrect because the problem word here is interesting. While it may be true that subjectivity may allow for a wider array of textual interpretations, this does not necessarily mean that they would be more interesting than objective interpretations, or at least there is not enough information given in the passage for the reader to make such an inference.

27 **Choice A is correct** because the passage states that Derrida believed that the contexts informing a given text's content are not outside of but in relationship with the text. **Choice B is correct** because texts cannot be independent of contexts; they can never exist completely alone.

Choice C is incorrect because the passage does not indicate that Derrida believed that the text was the only form of reality—reality can still exist without a text.

PASSAGE 15

28 **Choice C is correct** because the passage begins describing a situation in Mozambique and then this causes another set of events to occur, like raising taxes on the lessees.

Choice A is incorrect because the hierarchy of the town is not provided. The only information that is provided would be the tenants and the lessee. **Choice B** is incorrect because a resolution about the taxes to the natives was not provided, only explained. **Choice D** is incorrect because an explanation of the layout where all the huts and tyrants are located is not provided. **Choice E** is incorrect because situations and examples are given, but they are described in a cause/effect way.

29 **Choice A is correct** because the Portuguese who oversaw the holding is described as a "tyrant" and "taskmaster" who overcharges his tenants with taxes. **Choice B is correct** because the Portuguese man is acting inhumanely in the way he operates his business.

Choice C is incorrect because there is no mention or proof in this passage that the Portuguese man is violent towards his tenants.

30 **Choice C is correct** because the passage describes several duties the lessee must do after acquiring this holding, including building new roads and providing police officers.

Choice A is incorrect because the lessee would not have been told how to treat people. He would have done this the way he deemed appropriate to himself. **Choice B** is incorrect because there is no evidence to show that the natives misused the money. **Choice D** is incorrect because there would be no wrong holding to live in. The natives would be provided with a hut if they lived in that area. **Choice E** is incorrect because the rent would have increased with the increase of taxes and not lessened.

PASSAGE 16: SUMMARY/PARAPRASE

The passage is about the author's fascination with books about wars. The main idea is that although the author is aware that his fascination may seem horrific, he is nonetheless unable to resist it. The major point is that the author feels comfortable in the setting and characters of the war, however appalling the war itself may have been. The purpose of the passage is confessional: the author is admitting the oddities of his fascination while justifying and affirming it.

31 The sentence, "**I must confess, though, that I am a bibliophile with War books.**" is the correct answer. Confession is generally a form of catharsis. One may confess to a priest or someone he/she has harmed in the past. In this case, the author thinks that others may find his love of war books strange as the author; himself was most likely a witness to the horrors about which he reads. By revealing his love of these books, he has eliminated the necessity to keep it a secret and probably feels relieved.

PASSAGE 17

32 **Choice D is correct** because it is ironic that valuable items, such as the statue, would end up in a place designated for waste.

Choice A is incorrect because the Romans were hiding the statues. They did not throw them out. This answer may be based on a misinterpretation of the text. **Choice B** is incorrect and may be based on a misinterpretation of the text. Although the pagans may have buried sacred objects, it cannot be concluded that they engaged in the habit of burying treasures in their sewer systems. **Choice C** is incorrect because it does not capture the meaning of the proverb. The reference to trash does not apply to the Christian's opinions of the statue, but rather their unusual location. **Choice E** is incorrect because the pagans deliberately buried their statues in the sewer. They did not deliberately discard their religious icons.

33 The sentence "**It is hoped that the statue, believed to depict the god, Hermes, will help to shed light on how worshippers in the area maintained their religion in the face of prevailing Christianity.**" is correct because it states that the archaeologists are going to use the statue to find out more about how pagans worshipped secretly.

PASSAGE 18

34 **Choice D is correct** because the passage states that artists believed the decision was a "blatant stifling of expression and voice," which is something that they publicly declared as wrong. Further on, the passage suggests that they believe it is important to "engage in debate on such pertinent issues both on and off the stage," therefore, the "stifling" of such voices would be denounced as unfair. Given that the theater supported the idea of tackling "complex issues," the artists of this production likely felt targeted for the particular positions they expressed.

Choice A is incorrect because although the artists disagreed with the decision, "decried" carries a more intense connotation of criticism and strong disapproval. **Choice B is incorrect** because the term has more to do with the nature of the decision being considered morally contemptible, whereas "discarded" has more to do with a rejection of a certain option. **Choice C** because the passage does not state any alternatives provided, but rather a criticism of the decision made to cancel the production. **Choice E is incorrect** because the sentence does not indicate any confusion over the decision, instead it indicates that it "stifled expression." Later in the passage, it becomes clear that the exact reasons for the cancellation were "not cited," but that lack of transparency is not reflected in the sentence where it is said the artists "decried" the decision.

35 **Choice B is correct** because the passage ends on the dubious note that it wasn't clear whether the play would "see the light of day." In other words, whether it would ever have a theatrical release or premiere.

Choice A is incorrect because the passage states there was a "lack of transparency" and that "exact reasons for the cancellation were not cited." Therefore, although it was said that the cancellation was due to "certain technical setbacks and last-minute changes," the ambiguity of these reasons means an adequate explanation for the cancellation was not given. **Choice C is incorrect** because the passage states that there were "protracted discussions," which indicates that there was a process that took place prior to the making of the decision. Therefore, it did not come about suddenly. **Choice D is incorrect** because there were no audience members, given that the cancellation occurred prior to the opening day. Furthermore, theater management was the party that was critical and it was not clear to what extent mediation had occurred, if any. However, discussions were said to have been "protracted." **Choice E is incorrect** because there were no references to theater staff corroborating the claim, but rather shared indignation at the decision within a "growing culture" of censorship.

36 This sentence, "**In response to the lack of transparency in the cancellation, the production alleges that the revocation stems from a growing climate of censorship that undermines artistic integrity,**" makes reference to the "growing climate of censorship," which conveys that this cancellation is not considered to be an isolated incident, but rather another event in a series of related cases of suppressing artistic voices. Later in the first paragraph, the controversies "surrounding social issues and military conflicts…" are mentioned. The paragraph ends by presenting the artists' idea of debating such topics "on and off stage" as a more beneficial approach.

PASSAGE 19: SUMMARY/PARAPHRASE

The passage is about the Art Nouveau movement. The main idea is that Art Nouveau developed art in directions that had never before been seen. There is a major point that Art Nouveau represents a conscious break from Neoclassicist attempts to mimic Greco-Roman aesthetics. A minor point develops the ways in which Art Nouveau differs from art based in classical aesthetics by discussing the use of asymmetry and unusual patterns. The purpose of the passage is to inform, which is reflected in the descriptive tone.

37 The sentence, "**Art Nouveau arose at the turn of the 20th century as a reaction against the Neoclassicist movement's propensity to simply mimic the style of the Greeks and Romans.**" is correct because Art Nouveau artists wanted to find new ways of creating art because they were tired of forms that were constantly mimicking the past.

PASSAGE 20: SUMMARY/PARAPHRASE

The passage is about Sun Tzu's The Art of War. The main idea is that The Art of War is a seminal text on military strategy that is familiar to a broad swath of people. The major point is that The Art of War emphasizes the ability to be flexible and alter strategies as required by circumstances. The main purpose of the passage is to inform: the tone of the passage emphasizes summary facts about the work.

38 **Choice C is correct** because unaligned is a synonym for dispassionate and detached, which are the characteristics of the author's personal opinion of The Art of War. Unaligned also lacks overly positive or negative connotations, making it a good term to convey neutrality.

Choice A is incorrect because while the author clearly delineates that The Art of War is a seminal work on military strategy, the tone does not betray a sense of buoyancy, positivity, or liveliness; the author is quite neutral toward Sun Tzu's work. **Choice B** is incorrect because while the author's personal opinion can be best described as dispassionate toward The Art of War, the tone is not cold. Aloof implies a kind of uppity or icy detachment, which is not accurate here. **Choice D** is incorrect because the author's opinion is neutral due to a lack of direct expression, but inert is too strong a word. To be inert implies apathy, immobility, or laziness, which goes beyond simple neutrality. **Choice E** is incorrect because although phlegmatic can describe someone calm and collected, it does not necessarily convey neutrality. It's not the best term to describe the author's personal opinion toward The Art of War.

39 **Choice C is correct** because efficacious means the power to produce a desired effect, and thus potent can be substituted here since potent also means the same. The author intends to show that Sun Tzu's military strategy is powerful and effective.

Choice A is incorrect because ambitious is not a synonym for efficacious, as ambitious means having the determination to succeed, whereas efficacious means having the power to produce a desired effect. **Choice B** is incorrect because while useful can be a synonym for efficacious, the author is making the point that Sun Tzu's strategy is more than just useful—it leads to military success, which demands a stronger adjective. **Choice D** is incorrect because adequate can also be a synonym for efficacious, but it does not properly convey, from the author's viewpoint, the strength and effectiveness of Sun Tzu's military strategy. **Choice E** is incorrect because unorganized is not a synonym for efficacious, as it means not organized or incoherent.

PASSAGE 21

40 **Choice C is correct** because the novel is said to discuss the challenges of integrating into a postcolonialist society, particularly for "subaltern communities who aim to ´fit in´ a world that retains a colonialist mindset." In other words, certain colonialist attitudes prevail that exclude outsiders due to such attitudes that preclude "genuine integration."

Choice A is incorrect because the two main characters of the novel had "distinct responses" to the challenges they encountered even though they both came from Nigeria. Therefore, the experience of individuals from different cultures has not been explored. **Choice B** is incorrect because the focus of the novel, according to this passage, is not on the relationship itself. Furthermore, although the two characters responded differently, both are said to have suffered from the "psychological tension" of not fitting in society. **Choice D** is incorrect because both responses to the marginalization, insubordination, and mimicry, were said to lead to sacrifices, and neither resulted in a "genuine integration." **Choice E** is incorrect because the passage does not discuss historical grievances or what addressing them might entail. Instead, it explores the fact that a colonialist mindset leads to certain cultures being "deemed inferior in the mainstream narrative."

41 **Choice B is correct** because the point about mimicking social behavior instead of rejecting it, and the impact this has psychologically, is secondary to the main point about postcolonialist challenges that deter subaltern communities from truly being able to fit it.

Choice A is incorrect because the passage explores this as a major theme in the novel, referring to the path of the two characters who respond to the marginalization they encounter in postcolonialist societies by complying or resisting, and the psychological tension that results in either case, precluding "genuine integration." **Choice C** is incorrect because this is essentially a rewording of the main theme, which is that colonialist barriers remain a facet of postcolonialist society, particularly in the arena of psychological impact.

42 **Choice A is correct** because the passage discusses the novel's main theme as having to do with "postcolonialist racial dynamics," particularly certain cultures being deemed "inferior." Therefore, the theme explores racism and its prevalence in modern social interactions. **Choice C is correct** because the passage refers to the "remnants" of a colonialist mindset remaining present in modern postcolonialist societies. It further discusses the challenges faced by marginalized communities and particularly the difficulty of "fitting in" due to being considered from the "periphery." This all points to the superiority that mainstream cultures continue to believe they possess. Also, this phenomenon is discussed as an inflexibility by referring to the dominant culture's "implicit or explicit resistance" to those who have immigrated, in other words, outsiders.

Choice B is incorrect because the passage does not discuss the author's position on whether integration is possible or not in general. The focus is on individuals from cultures that had been colonized assimilating into mainstream cultures within colonizing nations. This cannot be extrapolated to reflect the processes of any culture potentially integrating into any other.

PASSAGE 22

43 **Choice C is correct** because while the passage states that modernist writing evolved to become more introspective in nature, introspection is not a hallmark feature of modernist writing—autonomy and the exactitude of form lie at the heart of modernist writing.

Choice A is incorrect because the passage states that modernist writing shifted toward a more cynical, introspective tone to reflect the realities surrounding the World Wars, thus it evolved to mirror cultural changes. **Choice B** is incorrect because the passage makes it clear that modernist writing is characterized by concise language and structure, so the coherency of form is a highly esteemed feature of modernist writing. **Choice D** is incorrect because precise language is a hallmark feature of modernist writing; therefore, modernist writers avoid florid or elaborate prose. **Choice E** is incorrect because modernist writing has a very mechanistic quality, as it is chiefly concerned with form, structure, and precision.

PASSAGE 23

44 **Choice B is correct** because "generate" means something is being created and "beget" means to bring into existence. "Creating" and "bringing something into existence" are equivalent. The passage also suggests that pokers create, or bring about, new works of art.

Choice A is incorrect because "emend" means to correct or revise something. A poker is not necessarily correcting an existing work of art but is instead creating something entirely new. **Choice C** is incorrect because "amplify" means to add on or enhance something. A poker is not necessarily adding to an already-created work of art, but is birthing its own. **Choice D** is incorrect because "efface" means to erase. A poker does not remove a work of art but creates one. **Choice E** is incorrect because "approximate" means to create a near copy. The passage does not mention anything related to recreating unoriginal works of art.

45 The sentence **"Since the start of recorded history, wood has also been used for aesthetic enjoyment"** is correct. Prior to this sentence the passage only discusses other uses of wood. This sentence first mentions the use of wood in art or, "aesthetic enjoyment." After this sentence, more details about how people create art with wood are discussed.

PASSAGE 24

46 **Choice D is correct** because the passage discusses the committee´s "circumscribed perspectives," which means they are limited. "Language status and translation challenges" are cited as examples of what leads to this narrow view, in other words, how they "limit" the selection.

Choice A is incorrect because "penitent" refers to feeling humbled or regretful, which does not apply to the role these factors play in the selection process. **Choice B** is incorrect because, although there are several factors playing a role, "partial" does not capture the meaning of the impact of these factors, which is a narrowing of options. **Choice C** is incorrect because "facilitative" means allowing something to happen, which is contrary to the intended meaning. **Choice E** is incorrect because, while the narrow selection prevents certain authors from winning the prize, the list of factors involved suggests it is more a matter of a reduced "purview," rather than a formal exclusion.

47 **Choice B is correct** because the passage explains that the selection for the Nobel Prize has been shown to involve "certain biases that, perhaps inadvertently, narrow the selection to authors of certain national identities…" Therefore, it is safe to assume that the authors rarely come from backgrounds that differ greatly from those of the selection committee.

Choice A is incorrect because, based on the information in the passage, the nomination of the author does not necessarily have to come from their close community. The limitations are rather those related to language and national identity in general and not a lack of contacts. **Choice C** is incorrect because the passage mentions that one of the roles of the Nobel Prize is to "catapult events, trends, and perspectives into a wider social discussion." In other words, to expand readership. This wouldn't be the case if all laureates already enjoyed international success with their literary works. **Choice D** is incorrect because it contradicts the passage. The passage suggests authors whose themes are already in international discussion get more recognition, not obscure or underrepresented topics. **Choice E** is incorrect because nowhere in the passage does it discuss how the prize is perceived or what correlation that perception may have on whether or not a writer is considered.

48 **Choice A is correct** because the passage discusses the factors that "reduce the purview" of the selection process. It further suggests that scrutiny of this process would ensure a "more thorough selection process," recognizing the "prestigious accolade" as one that "catapults" certain "events, trends, and perspectives" onto the global stage.

Choice B is incorrect because the passage states that the prize "amplifies attention on certain human stories," rather than pulls unknown authors out of obscurity. Given the limitations outlined in the passage to incorporate lesser-known authors, it would seem more likely that the authors who receive the award are already well-known. **Choice C** is incorrect because there is no discussion in the passage of a "base country" for the prize, and it is more likely the committee is composed of members from different countries. However, it may be the case that winning authors tend to come from the countries represented in the committee. **Choice D** is incorrect because one cannot conclude that all languages face the same challenges in translation. Therefore, it would not be necessarily true for the prize to be bestowed only on works the committee can read in its original language. **Choice E** is incorrect because, although the passage discusses the fact that "subject matter that touches upon global and national events of wider appeal typically garner more support," it does not mean that the committee is unable to "assess" literary works that deal with lesser-known occurrences, even if these are less likely to be selected.

PASSAGE 25: SUMMARY/PARAPHRASE

The passage is about a recent theoretical development in the humanities called postcolonial theory. The main idea is that later 20th century academics reacted to the dominant sociocentric paradigm with a more pluralistic theory. The main points are (a) that postcolonial theory attempts to give colonized peoples more of a voice in the humanities and (b) that postcolonial theory looks at the "cultural space" as a complex interaction of European and other cultures. The main purpose of the passage is to give a brief primer on what postcolonial theory is.

49 **Choice A is correct** because the passage states that the main consequence of European Imperialism was that it shaped global society by exercising cultural dominance.

Choice B is incorrect because although it is true that diversity could not thrive under European Imperialism, this is more of a byproduct of the fact that European cultural norms were dominant. **Choice C** is incorrect because the passage does not discuss whether or not the colonized participated in the colonial political process. **Choice D** is incorrect because the passage clearly states that global society was heavily influenced by colonialism. **Choice E** is incorrect because the passage clearly shows the culturally hegemonic nature of European Imperialism.

PASSAGE 26

50 **Choice A is correct** because this response describes influences external to the newspaper itself that have much bearing on the amount of interest a person has in reading an article. The writer is attributing the ability to influence strictly to the responsibility of the writer of the article, not on the side of the reader. Therefore, a shift to the reader's responsibility will negate the writer's assumption.

Choice B is incorrect because special techniques used in writing do influence interest. This question instructs one to find the negation of the assumption, therefore this response is incorrect. This response is in support of the assumption. **Choice C** is incorrect because this comment is supportive of the assumption rather than a negation of the assumption. The fact that Americans read the front page only goes along with the interest factor the writer was describing. **Choice D** is incorrect because this tendency applies to many situations. However, it more closely relates to the assumption—the interest factor—than the negation of the assumption. **Choice E** is incorrect because this comment may explain the reason why Americans are in such a hurry when they read, thus limiting what they read. However, this does not illustrate the main point of the article or negate it either.

Practice Set 2: Biological Sciences

PASSAGE 27

Question 51 is based on the following passage.

When we examine a simple cell, we find we can distinguish morphological parts. In the first place, we find in the cell a round or oval body known as the nucleus. Occasionally the nucleus is stallate or angular; but as a rule, so long as cells have vital power, the nucleus maintains a nearly constant round or oval shape. The nucleus in its turn, in completely developed cells, very constantly encloses another structure within itself—the so-called nucleolus. With regard to the question of vital form, it cannot be said of the nucleolus that it appears to be an absolute essential, and in a considerable number of young cells it has as yet escaped detection. On the other hand, we regularly meet with it in fully-developed, older forms, and it therefore seems to mark a higher degree of development in the cell.

51. All of the following would help to clarify the author's point and to improve the passage EXCEPT:

    (A) A diagram specifying cell parts and their locations
    (B) A brief glossary of infrequently used phrases that the reader is unfamiliar with
    (C) Further explanation of or informed speculation about the function of the nucleolus
    (D) Differences between old and young cells in an organism
    (E) Scaling back the explanation of the nucleus and its functions

PASSAGE 28

Questions 52 and 53 are based on the following passage.

When Donato di Niccolo di Betto Bardi, called Donatello because men loved his sweet and cheerful temper, died in 1466 at the age of eighty, the brightest light of Italian sculpture in its most promising period was extinguished. Donatello's influence, felt far and wide through Italy, was of inestimable value in correcting the false direction toward pictorial sculpture which Ghiberti, had he flourished alone at Florence, might have given to the art. His style was always eminently masculine. However tastes may differ about the positive merits of his several works, there can be no doubt that the principles of sincerity, truth to nature, and technical accuracy they illustrate, were all–important in an age that lent itself too readily to the caprices of the fancy and the puerilities of florid taste. To regret that Donatello lacked Ghiberti's exquisite sense of beauty, is tantamount to wishing that two of the greatest artists of the world had made one man between them.

52. Which of the following best summarizes this passage?

    (A) The author presents several arguments supporting his assertion that Donatello and Ghiberti were the greatest sculptors of their era.
    (B) The author describes the positive influence that Donatello's work had upon Ghiberti's style.
    (C) The author describes the negative influence that Ghiberti's work had upon Donatello's style.
    (D) The author argues that Donatello's style had a favorable influence upon the art of sculpture.
    (E) The author argues that the styles of Donatello and Ghiberti actually complemented one another.

53. Which of the following best describes the author's assessment of Ghiberti?

    (A) Ghiberti's work tended toward the masculine while Donatello's had a more graceful form.
    (B) Ghiberti's work, while often beautiful, tended to be too fanciful and overwrought.
    (C) Ghiberti's work heavily influenced Florentine sculpture until Donatello came along.
    (D) Ghiberti's work is significantly overrated.
    (E) Ghiberti's work is significantly underrated.

Chapter 3: Reading Comprehension

PASSAGE 29

Questions 54 to 56 are based on the following passage.

We have already given a description of the mammalian skull, and we have stated where the origin of the several bones was in membrane, and where in cartilage; but a more complete comprehension of the mammalian skull becomes possible with the handling of a lower type. We propose now, first to give some short account of the development and structure of the skull of the frog, and then to show briefly how its development and adult arrangement demonstrate the mammalian skull to be a fundamentally similar structure, complicated and disguised by further development and re-adjustment.

54. Which of the following is the most appropriate audience for the information in this passage?

   A. Herpetologists
   B. Zoologists
   C. Endocrinologists
   D. Thoracic surgeons
   E. Craniologists

55. Select from the following list the definition of "fundamentally" that most closely matches the use of the word in this context.

   A. Primarily
   B. Basically; underlying
   C. Of or affecting the foundation or basis
   D. Originally
   E. Indispensably

For the following question, consider each answer choice separately and select all that apply.

56. Based on the information in this passage, which of the following is likely to be true about the study of human anatomy?

   A. Every aspect of human anatomy has a corresponding structure in a lower life form
   B. Examining amphibian anatomy leads to a better understanding of human anatomy
   C. Examining anatomical structures of other life forms may lead to a better understanding of human anatomy

PASSAGE 30

Question 57 is based on the following passage.

We may note here the meaning of certain terms we shall be constantly employing. The head end of the rabbit is anterior, the tail end posterior, the backbone side of the body—the upper side in life—is dorsal, the breast and belly side, the lower side of the animal, is ventral. If we imagine the rabbit as if sawn asunder by a plane passing through the head and tail, that plane would be the median plane. Parts on either side of it are lateral, and designated left or right according to whether they lie on the animal's left or right side. In a limb, or in the internal organs, the part nearest the central organ, or axis, is proximal, the more remote or terminal parts are distal. For instance, the mouth is anteriorly placed, the tongue on its ventral wall; the tongue is median, the eyes are lateral, and the fingers are distal to the elbow. The student must accustom himself to these words, and avoid, in his descriptions, the use of such terms as "above," "below," "outside," which vary with the position in which we conceive the animal placed.

For the following question, consider the answer choices separately and select all that apply.

57. Select the scenario below that best reflects the writer's purpose in this passage.

   A. Sailing a yacht in the America's Cup race
   B. Performing brain surgery
   C. Repairing a truck engine

PASSAGE 31

Questions 58 and 59 are based on the following passage.

Based on a beekeeper's own sequential observations, the Queen or Mother Bee of a hive unquestionably reigns supreme over her common and working bees as well as the male drones. Inside this community, the Queen's office is where she lays her eggs. The birth from these eggs can produce more workers, drones, or even future queens.

Armed with a stinger that is rarely used, the Queen determines the survival of the hive. If she becomes separated or isolated from the rest of her family, the labor inside the hive would be halted resulting in a dispersion of the community members. She never acknowledges nor identifies anyone as being her enemy or her equal.

58 In the context of the passage, what does "community members" refer to?

- (A) Male drones
- (B) Common working bees
- (C) All the queen bees in all the surrounding hives
- (D) The bees in the hive related to the Queen
- (E) All bees in the entire hive, except the Queen

59 Select a sentence that best describes the organization of the passage.

PASSAGE 32

Questions 60 to 62 are based on the following passage.

Many attempts have been made and are still being made to increase the length of the staple of the upland types. The methods used are as follows: selection of seed having a long fiber; special cultivation and fertilization; crossing the short-stapled cotton on the long-stapled cotton. This last process, as already explained, is called hybridizing. Many of these attempts have succeeded, and there are now a large number of varieties which excel the older varieties in profitable yield. The new varieties are each year being more widely grown. Every farmer should study the new types and select the one that will best suit his land. The new types have been developed under the best tillage. Therefore, if a farmer would keep the new type as good as it was when he began to grow it, he must give it the same good tillage, and practice seed-selection.

60 Select the sentence in the passage that justifies the writer's purpose in this piece.

61 Which of the following is a reasonable conclusion based on the content of the passage?

- (A) Hybridization is a long and costly endeavor.
- (B) The benefit of a hybrid is that it can adapt to any condition.
- (C) Fertilization produces the best results with hybrid plants.
- (D) Overlooking one of the cultivation criteria will reduce the success of a hybrid seed.
- (E) Farmers should select the hybrid that demands the highest price after harvesting.

62 The use of the word "tillage" in this context implies that which of the following is most important to insure crop success?

- (A) Good soil preparation
- (B) Correct nutrient application
- (C) Sufficient use of pesticides
- (D) Adequate irrigation
- (E) Widespread application of mulch

PASSAGE 33

Question 63 is based on the following passage.

From this you can see that it is especially important to know all you can about the life of injurious insects, since it is often easier to kill these pests at one stage of their life than at another. Often it is better to aim at destroying the seemingly harmless beetle or butterfly than to try to destroy the larvae that hatch from its eggs, although, as you must remember, it is generally the larvae that do the most harm. Larvae grow very rapidly; therefore, the food supply must be great to meet the needs of the insect.

63 Consider the information in this passage and select what relationship it likely has to the text that precedes it.

- (A) It functions as the conclusion
- (B) It functions as an explanation of an idea from the preceding paragraph
- (C) It functions as a warning about a situation mentioned in the previous paragraph
- (D) It serves as a transition between the previous paragraph and the conclusion
- (E) It reinforces the idea presented in the previous portion of the text

Chapter 3: Reading Comprehension

PASSAGE 34

Questions 64 to 65 are based on the following passage.

Adeno-associated viruses (AAV) show potential as a method of treating a considerable number of long-term metabolic diseases using vivo gene therapy. AAV angles have considerable advantages when transducing dividing and non-dividing cells and bring about sustained episomal transgene articulation. Researchers have identified various AAV serotypes and are using them to treat multiple metabolic diseases in non-human subjects. AAVs possess disparate cell tropism which allows them to be used therapeutically. Various studies on primates have indicated AAV serotypes (AAV8) transduce cells in a variety of tissues such as the liver, muscle, and cardiac while progressing transgene expression post-delivery in excess of five years. However, human applications involving AAV8 remain unattainable due to the triggering of dangerous immune responses.

64. What is the meaning of the passage based on the context?

   A) Long-term, episomal transgene expression is the goal of the study.
   B) Primates can be treated with AAV8 serotypes.
   C) Adeno-associated viruses (AAV) for gene transfers can help treat many metabolic diseases.
   D) The ultimate goal of the study is to apply adeno-associated viruses (AAV) for the treatment of genetic disorders in humans.
   E) Adeno-Associated viruses are not a viable avenue for the treatment of genetic metabolic disorders.

65. Select the sentence that best describes the structure of the passage.

PASSAGE 35

Questions 66 to 68 are based on the following

It may seem somewhat superfluous to say that fish cannot live in any water unless that water contains the food supply necessary for them to thrive upon, and yet this is the point most often overlooked in stocking waters with fish. Small attempts at stocking with creatures suitable for food, particularly after the fish have been already introduced, are not at all likely to succeed. Such an important matter when treated as a small afterthought is almost sure to end in failure of the whole business of stocking.

66. Select the sentence that most closely exemplifies the adage, "An ounce of prevention is worth a pound of cure".

67. What assumption about fish is the reader apt to make after reading this passage?

   A) Fish have specific diets
   B) Fish in a pond with no food source will be easier to catch
   C) Fish are slow to adapt to a new food source
   D) Fish become cannibalistic when deprived of a natural food source
   E) Fish will migrate to a source of food

68. In a presentation on stocking a pond with fish, where, in the sequence, is the best place for the information in this passage?

   A) The introduction
   B) The conclusion
   C) Immediately following a discussion of the types of food necessary for fish to thrive in a pond
   D) Immediately prior to a discussion of the types of food necessary for fish to thrive in a pond
   E) Immediately prior to a discussion of the vegetation needed in the pond

PASSAGE 36

Question 69 is based on the following passage.

The reason for mixing clover and grass is at once seen. The true grasses, so far as science now shows, get all their nitrogen from the soil; hence they more or less exhaust the soil. But, as several times explained in this book, clovers are legumes, and all legumes are able by means of the bacteria that live on their roots to use the free nitrogen of the air. Hence, without cost to the farmer these clovers help the soil to feed their neighbors, the true grasses. For this reason, some light perennial legume should always be added to grass seed.

69. Select the sentence in this passage that demonstrates that growing clover is preferable to adding nitrogen-rich fertilizer to the soil.

PASSAGE 37

Questions 70 and 71 are based on the following passage.

Haplotypes, sets of unique genetic markers, help ascertain the extent to which certain lineages have spread. The Y chromosome carries few alleles with phenotypes expressed in typical traits, such as appearance or body build, that would account for favorability in reproductive selection. Consequently, the presence of Y-chromosome haplotypes dispersed across a region points to a certain line of male dominance, which, over the ages, has been preferred among—or imposed on—women in their reproductive years. To wit, this occurrence is typically associated with warrior dynasties of significant duration.

Recent studies of a particular eastern Asian haplotype revealed that 1 out of every 200 men were direct descendants of the Mongolian warlord Ghengis Khan. Similar findings may be discovered for other bellicose emperors, although data is yet lacking.

70 In the context of the passage, what does "favorability" most likely refer to in terms of reproductive success?

Ⓐ Males carrying these haplotypes exhibited qualities that more likely resulted in their being chosen for reproduction.

Ⓑ Males carrying this Y chromosome were more likely to pass on their genes than those who were not.

Ⓒ The haplotypes resulted in pregnancies with a higher likelihood of coming full term.

Ⓓ Males carrying this Y chromosome were more fit in their reproductive health than those who were not.

Ⓔ The offspring of males carrying this haplotype were more likely to exhibit similar features.

For the following question, consider each of the choices separately and select all that apply.

71 Which of the following conclusions can be made from the information in the passage?

[A] Given the reproductive favorability of certain historical lineages, most human males can be traced back to a certain dynasty of the past.

[B] Genetic research analyzing reproductive variance can lead to insight into historical social tendencies.

[C] Certain widespread lineages can be traced back to dominant male figures through the inheritance of haplotypes on the Y chromosome.

PASSAGE 38

Questions 72 to 74 are based on the following passage.

Whether, therefore, a tree might possibly continue living and growing forever is a question of less entertainment than the question of its possible duration in the common state of nature and under the irreversible conditions of climate, soil, and the elements. What age may we ascribe to some of our largest specimens, either still existing or recorded in trustworthy history? Is the period of one thousand years, the favorite figure of tradition, a common or probable period of arboreal longevity, or have our proudest forest giants attained their present size in half the time that is commonly claimed for them?

In the discussion of this question we have but little known data to guide us, since statistics of the rate of growth, as afforded by careful measurement, date only from about the beginning of the eighteenth century. Of such statistics we may dismiss at once measurement of height or of the spread of a tree's boughs, the measurement of girth being far easier and more conclusive.

72 Select the sentence that implies that the ages of apparently old trees were arbitrarily determined.

73 Select the most accurate definition of entertainment as it appears in the first sentence of this passage.

Ⓐ Amusement

Ⓑ Something affording pleasure

Ⓒ A performance

Ⓓ An agreeable occupation of the mind

Ⓔ Consideration

74 Use the progression of ideas in this passage to select which of the following is the most probable topic of the writer's next paragraph.

Ⓐ Other means of determining the age of trees

Ⓑ How soil and climate conditions contribute to arboreal longevity

Ⓒ The progress made in ageing trees between the end of the eighteenth century and the end of the nineteenth century

Ⓓ An argument for replacing the one-thousand-year measurement for very old trees with a more moderate five-hundred-year measurement

Ⓔ The part of the world that is home to the oldest trees

Chapter 3: Reading Comprehension

PASSAGE 39

Question 75 is based on the following passage.

Research on barn swallows gives us insight into the ways in which hormones affect the behavior of various species, including our own. Male barn swallows with the most vibrantly colored feathers are most attractive to females and thus mate much more frequently than their dull-feathered male counterparts. Scientists, however, have discovered that simply darkening the feathers of the lusterless males with a marker can change their hormone levels, turning beta males into alpha males since their mating rates increase dramatically. This is due not only to an increase in attractiveness to females but also an increase in the confidence of the males, consequently engendering higher levels of testosterone.

75. Given the information in the passage, what is the relationship between confidence and hormones in male barn swallows?

   (A) Confidence plays a minor role in the increase of certain hormones in male barn swallows.
   (B) Physically attractive male barn swallows are more confident and thus experience higher levels of testosterone.
   (C) Only inherently attractive alpha male barn swallows have confidence due to high testosterone levels.
   (D) Confidence is the sole factor in raising the testosterone levels of male barn swallows.
   (E) Confidence plays no role in the hormonal patterns of male barn swallows; mating is the key factor in fluctuating hormone levels.

PASSAGE 40

Questions 76 and 77 are based on the following passage.

Far from being solitary figures, trees within forest communities are thought to participate in a synergistic web of underground resource-sharing through a web of opportunistic mycelium, the fungal body responsible for the fruition of mushrooms. International research has recently explored the extent to which this highly intricate network engages in nutrition distribution, and subsequently, the role that it plays in tree resiliency and health.

These subterranean meshes, called mycorrhizal networks, extend from minuscule tendrils coiled around and integrated into tree roots and are the site of massive nutrient exchange. Nonetheless, theories on the nature of their operation abound. There is some evidence that older, more seasoned trees, known as "mother" or "hub" trees, direct more nutrients towards seedlings and more vulnerable members, however, a definitive theory remains tenuous.

76. Which of the following best summarizes the main point of the passage?

   (A) The presence of subterranean mycorrhizal networks may indicate a natural altruism among trees, in which older trees direct nutrients towards fellow trees in distress.
   (B) There is a direct correlation between the presence of mycorrhizal networks and the resilience of trees in the face of disturbance.
   (C) While it is known that trees are connected through underground networks of mycelium, it remains unclear what role these play in resource distribution.
   (D) Underground networks of mycelium point to a greater level of interdependence among trees than previously considered.
   (E) While trees have been shown to be connected through mycelium webs, there is no evidence to suggest these play a role in resource acquisition, trading, or sharing.

77. Select a sentence in the passage that suggests that mycelium webs retain a portion of the nutrients they acquire from tree roots.

PASSAGE 41

Questions 78 to 80 are based on the following passage.

According to anthropologists, observing primates in Senegal is like opening a window to the world of understanding the behavior of early humans, particularly related to sharing. They have found that the chimpanzees display an intentional willingness to share food and rudimentary hunting tools with each other, an important detection since it was previously thought that chimpanzees usually only shared meat. However, this sharing is not altruistically motivated. Since it is an exchange that primarily takes place from males to females, anthropologists have postulated a "food for sex" theory. This claim is further backed up by the fact that sexually receptive females in their reproductive years were most likely to receive food and supplies from males.

78. What is inferred by the "food for sex" theory in primates?

   (A) Attractive females have the best chances for survival
   (B) Sexual gratification is the primary motivation of male primates
   (C) Male primates are ultimately exploitative
   (D) Primates display a high level of magnanimity
   (E) Male primates are lazy

79. According to the passage, understanding group behavior in primates is important because

   (A) Primates are closely related to humans and thus can help us better understand our own species
   (B) Group behavior in primates can help us understand specifically the way males and females share
   (C) Primates can help humans see why it is important to learn to be altruistic
   (D) Group behavior in primates is the key to understanding behavior patterns in all species
   (E) The sexual habits of primates can enlighten humans as to their own motivations for sex

80. Select the sentence that makes use of the rhetorical device of the trope.

PASSAGE 42

Question 81 is based on the following passage.

Starvation-induced antibiotic resistance is one of the primary reasons many bacteria are elusive when it comes to treatment and as a result some infections are actually impossible to cure. This situation proves paradoxical to scientists, as many of the bacteria that are antibiotic-sensitive still exhibit remarkable survival skills. As soon as bacteria, which typically gather in clusters, sense that their supply of nutrients is waning, they issue a chemical warning that causes them to modify their metabolic rates as a means of defending against starvation, which in turn halts their growth. Many forms of antibiotic treatment, which target active bacteria, are then rendered ineffective since starving bacteria stall cellular growth and lie dormant.

For the following question, consider each of the three choices separately and select all that apply.

81. According to the passage, starvation protects bacteria from medications by

   (A) Modifying its growth patterns
   (B) Making it impervious to antibiotic attack
   (C) Changing its chemical composition

PASSAGE 43

Questions 82 and 83 are based on the following passage.

Self-organization takes place through a number of undirected behaviors that are neither pre-planned nor centrally controlled. It is a feature found in a variety of realms, from cells to plants, from insects to animal groups. One of the ways by which these processes come about is called stigmergy, which entails leaving a sign of a "work in progress" that is then perceived and built upon by others.

Some termite architecture is a preeminent illustration of self-organization. As termites randomly walk about, they inadvertently leave behind sand grains imbued with their pheromone scent. This increases the likelihood of another termite walking over the same spot and leaving sand. Such random behavior results in a distribution pattern, gradually forming pillars that become the basis of termite nest formation.

82. According to the passage, what assumption is being made about termite behavior?

   (A) Termite nest formation is directed by a guiding agent that does not participate in the construction of the nest.
   (B) Pheromones can be perceived by proximal termites passing through the area.
   (C) Self-organization takes place predominantly in the formation of nests and related structures for residence.
   (D) Stigmergy requires a blueprint for members to be able to build upon previous work completed.
   (E) Termites move around without a preconceived plan and without the intention of participating in nest formation.

83. Based on the information provided in the passage, which of the following conclusions can be drawn about termite nest formation?

   (A) Nest formation begins with a signal from certain termites to the rest of the colony that a nest is to be built at that location.
   (B) The final structures of termite nests are all identical since they follow the same steps in construction.
   (C) Sand grains are discarded by termites working on a nest as a way to engage more termites in the construction process.
   (D) Nest formation is accelerated in colonies with a higher number of termites and with ample access to sand, or a similar building material.
   (E) Termites are self-organized insects, therefore, their entire nests are completed through self-organized efforts.

PASSAGE 44

Questions 84 to 86 are based on the following passage.

Ocean acidification due to the absorption of atmospheric carbon dioxide is a major threat to coral reef ecosystems worldwide and scientists are looking for ways to both understand and combat this phenomenon. This is an especially vital area of exploration since coral reefs are home to 25% of all marine species. Studies pertaining to ocean acidity and the coral reef have been conducted at the submarine springs near the Yucatan Peninsula in Mexico, a perfect environment due to the naturally occurring high acidity (low pH). They have found that the type of coral that serves as the foundation of the reef is unable to calcify and grow in high acidity, which means that the continued absorption of carbon from the atmosphere could halt or dramatically change the growth of the ocean's coral reefs—a terrible catastrophe for the delicate balance of life undersea.

84. From the information given in the passage, what are the implications of the continued occurrence of low pH levels in the world's oceans?

   (A) The atmosphere will continue to absorb carbon from the high acidity ocean
   (B) At least 25% of all marine species will die
   (C) The low acidity will negatively impact the growth of the foundation of the coral reefs
   (D) Since many types of coral can grow in high acidity, coral reefs are not in any dramatic danger
   (E) Continued acidification will make it difficult for coral reefs to grow and support marine life

85. The rhetorical goal of this passage is

   (A) To delineate the danger atmospheric carbon dioxide poses to the world's oceans
   (B) To invoke an emotional response in the reader relative to ocean acidification
   (C) To persuade the reader that ocean acidification is harmful
   (D) To delve deeper into the specifics of how pH levels affect coral reefs
   (E) To persuade the reader that the coral reefs are in grave danger

86. Select the sentence that best describes the importance of coral reefs in the ocean ecosystem.

PASSAGE 45

Question 87 is based on the following passage.

Malaria is a mosquito-borne disease that attacks its victims by way of parasites within the red blood cells that cause serious illness that can result in coma and death. Researchers have recently gained a crucial understanding of the disease after discovering why people who have sickle-cell anemia, a prominent hereditary mutation of the red blood pigment hemoglobin, are immune to malaria. The successful transmission of malaria requires that the red blood cells infected by the parasite establish a trafficking system that allows the parasite to access the exterior of the blood cells via its adhesive proteins known as adhesins. However, the mutated hemoglobin present in sickle cell anemics causes these adhesions to occur rarely and often not at all. Thus, mutated hemoglobin (which does not only occur in sickle cell anemia) protects the human body from the malaria parasite.

For the following question, consider each of the three choices separately and select all that apply.

87. Which of the following, if true, would weaken the author's contention?

   [A] Hemoglobin mutations facilitate the bonding of adhesins

   [B] Adhesins have the ability to attach to blood cells

   [C] Malaria is able to infect the blood cells of sickle cell anemics

PASSAGE 46

Questions 88 and 89 are based on the following passage.

Curiously enviable, the "immortal jellyfish" was given its moniker for its coveted capacity of outwitting death by reverting to an earlier developmental stage in response to injury. Having matured to adulthood, the Turritopsis dohrnii is able to convert itself back to the stage of a budding polyp, thereby availing itself of yet undifferentiated cells that can then develop and spawn into several genetically identical and healthy adults.

Behind this remarkable feat of cellular recycling is a mechanism called transdifferentiation. Essentially, it accomplishes the idea behind stem cell research, which is to provide cells capable of developing into and substituting any kind of damaged tissue. Cells that specialized for one tissue could theoretically be "rebooted" to replace cells in other tissues damaged by disease.

88. In the context of the passage, what is the closest meaning of the word "undifferentiated"?

   (A) Underdeveloped, as in, a cell that has not matured into an adult cell.

   (B) Non-specific, as in, a cell that has not yet turned into a specific tissue cell.

   (C) Indeterminate, as in, a cell whose species cannot be identified.

   (D) Indiscriminate, as in, a cell that can complete the functions of any tissue cell.

   (E) Inapplicable, as in, a cell that serves no purpose in the development of the organism.

89. Select a sentence in the passage that implies efforts have been made to replicate the transdifferentiation mechanism for potential medical applications.

PASSAGE 47

Questions 90 to 92 are based on the following passage.

Oxytocin, also known as the love hormone, bonds mothers to their children and promotes intimacy and relationships in various species including humans. Researchers have recently discovered that administering oxytocin nasally enhances prosocial choices among macaque monkeys. Exposure to the oxytocin caused the monkeys to more frequently share their juice without the expectation of receiving something in return. Scientists believe that it is important to understand how the hormone can impact behavior in a positive way and monkeys provide valuable information in this regard since they are so closely related to humans.

90. Based on the information given in the passage, what can be inferred about the scientific motivation to study oxytocin relative to humans?

   (A) Humans are closely related to macaques and thus will behave in the same way as them under the influence of oxytocin

   (B) Understanding the behavior of macaque monkeys under the influence of oxytocin can help scientists discern how oxytocin can potentially affect behavior in humans

   (C) Scientists can find ways of treating antisocial behavior in humans with oxytocin

   (D) Scientists can learn how to reproduce oxytocin synthetically as a treatment for depression

   (E) Humans are not the focal point of scientific motivation for studying oxytocin

91. What is meant by "prosocial choices" in the second sentence?

   (A) Choices that promote the well-being of others

   (B) Choices that are made as a result of higher levels of altruism

   (C) Choices that create a hierarchy in the community

   (D) Choices that influence hormonal patterns

   (E) Choices that cannot be made without the influence of oxytocin

92. Select the sentence that best describes why oxytocin is a crucial component of social attachment.

Chapter 3: Reading Comprehension

PASSAGE 48

Question 93 is based on the following passage.

Scientists have taken another step in the direction of better understanding the biological underpinnings of various psychiatric disorders. They have homed in on the gene named RNF123 because of its effect on the hippocampus, the area of the brain that is altered in people with major depression. They hope to be able to then ascertain more information about the relationship between the gene, the hippocampus, and the subjective experiences of the patient in order to establish a more holistic approach to understanding the delicate amalgamation of nature vs. nurture in psychiatry and mental health treatment.

93. Select the sentence that best indicates scientists' initial interest in the role of genetics in depression.

PASSAGE 49

Questions 94 and 95 are based on the following passage.

Gut microbiota has been implicated in a plethora of local and systemic health benefits, with commensal bacteria playing a particularly indispensable role in the robustness of immune response against disease. This is evidenced, for instance, by the fact that germ-free animals, those reared in sterile conditions without exposure to foreign bacteria, have been shown to develop diseases at higher rates than their bacteria-containing counterparts.

Recent studies have uncovered yet another way microbiota performs a pivotal function in immune health: by maintaining the homeostasis needed to prevent autoimmunity. Self-tolerance, the immune system's ability to recognize host cells and tissue, thereby refraining from attack, is the cornerstone of autoimmune prevention. It is now apparent that gut microbiota is an invaluable actor in self-tolerance by influencing the development and function of immune cells.

94. Based on the information presented in the passage, which of the following conclusions can be drawn?

   (A) Autoimmunity can be caused by the activation of certain colonies of gut microbiota.
   (B) Gut microbiota, being commensal, is perceived by the host as non-foreign cells and thereby does not trigger an immune response.
   (C) Self-tolerance can be undermined in viral infections, possibly leading to autoimmune diseases.
   (D) Autoimmunity comes about from a battle between the immune system and gut microbiota.
   (E) Gut microbiota develops on its own within the organism, without exposure to outside germs.

For the following question, consider each of the choices separately and select all that apply.

95. Based on the information provided, which of the following statements can be classified as a major point of the passage?

   [A] The diverse roles that gut microbiota is known to play in the immune system have been expanded to include its vital contribution to an organism's self-tolerance.
   [B] Organisms grown in sterile conditions fail to develop certain facets of the immune system necessary for a healthy response against disease.
   [C] Autoimmune diseases come about from a disturbance to homeostasis and a breakdown of the host's self-tolerance.

PASSAGE 50

Questions 96 to 98 are based on the following passage.

Stem cells are found in all multicellular organisms and their value in research is their ability to differentiate into specialized types of diverse cells as a result of mitosis (cell division). Medical researchers are convinced that human embryonic stem cell therapy has the potential to treat or cure various diseases and physical ailments from cancer to muscle damage; many even go as far as to claim it is a miracle treatment. However, many people stand in opposition to embryonic stem cell therapy, as they believe it is interfering with and exploiting natural life. Furthermore, some scientists believe that stem cell therapy could potentially aggrandize medical conditions rather than cure them. Thus, human embryonic stem cell research remains a highly controversial method of medical treatment.

96. Mitosis is a specifically important factor in stem cell research because

   A. Mitosis allows scientists to use large quantities of stem cells since they reproduce so quickly
   B. Stem cells after mitosis are stronger and easier for scientists to study
   C. Mitosis generates cells that can be manipulated for a variety of medical purposes
   D. Mitosis is not really an important factor in stem cell research
   E. Stem cells undergo mitosis and become diversified as a result

97. The author would agree with all of the following except.

   A. Stem cell therapy is a sensitive issue
   B. Medical benefits sometimes come at a cost
   C. The outcomes of scientific research do not always align themselves with social mores
   D. The exploitation of natural life is the white elephant in the room of stem cell therapy debate
   E. Stem cells are a testament to the regenerative nature of the human body

For the following question, consider each of the three choices separately and select all that apply.

98. According to the passage, stem cell therapy is an ethical conundrum because

   A. Some believe that, despite its efficacy, it is the immoral treatment of natural life
   B. Many maintain that it promotes a culture of death, despite the fact that it is an extremely useful form of medical treatment
   C. Despite its flexibility as a treatment, stem cell therapy can also have adverse effects

PASSAGE 51

Question 99 is based on the following passage.

Mankind are always happier for having been happy; so that if you make them happy now, you make them happy twenty years hence, by the memory of it. A childhood passed with a due mixture of rational indulgence, under fond and wise parents, diffuses over the whole of life a feeling of calm pleasure; and, in extreme old age, is the very last remembrance which time can erase from the mind of man. No enjoyment, however inconsiderable, is confined to the present moment. A man is the happier for life, from having made once an agreeable tour, or lived for any length of time with pleasant people, or enjoyed any considerable interval of innocent pleasure: and it is most probably the recollection of their past pleasures, which contributes to render old men so inattentive to the scenes before them; and carries them back to a world that is past, and to scenes never to be renewed again

99. Which one of the following statements most directly contrasts with the concept proclaimed in the passage above?

   A. My grandparents enjoy a "walk down memory lane" as we share stories at family reunions.
   B. Kevin did not have a happy childhood, this accounts for his sour disposition today.
   C. Julie is much happier now that she has a new house with new furniture.
   D. The saddest people on earth are those with too many material possessions, to which they are held in bondage.
   E. A trip to Disneyland for my family would be a waste of money, it is very expensive and there is little to show for it afterward

PASSAGE 52

Question 100 is based on the following passage.

Taming captive young animals is no simpler than taming the animals that were removed from their own natural habitats. If the animals remain in their natural habitat and are maternally raised, the young animals frequently become more reserved and intolerably connected to adult men, surpassing even their mothers. There is no such thing as tameness or obedience that is genetic. A broad review of the evidence supports the theory that taming is nothing more than the conveyance of a young animal's innate assurance and fondness for humans.

100. The passage suggests that an animal trainer's strength in taming animals relies on

   A. if the young animal is shy or energetic
   B. whether the young animal was born in captivity or in the wild
   C. the process he has set for taming the young animal
   D. the young animal's viewed connection between the trainer and its mother
   E. the expertise of the trainer in regard to the type of animal

Answer Key

Q. No.	Correct Answer	Your Answer
51	E	
52	D	
53	B	
54	E	
55	B	
56	C	
57	A, B, C	
58	E	
59	Based on… male drones.	
60	Many of… profitable yield.	
61	D	
62	A	
63	E	
64	D	
65	However,… immune responses.	
66	Small…to succeed.	
67	A	
68	D	
69	Hence,…true grasses.	
70	B	
71	B, C	
72	Is the…for them?	
73	E	
74	A	
75	B	

Q. No.	Correct Answer	Your Answer
76	C	
77	Far from… mushrooms.	
78	A	
79	B	
80	According to… sharing.	
81	A, B	
82	E	
83	D	
84	E	
85	E	
86	This is… species.	
87	A, C	
88	B	
89	Essentially,…tissue.	
90	B	
91	A	
92	Oxytocin,…humans.	
93	Scientists…disorders.	
94	B	
95	A	
96	C	
97	D	
98	A, C	
99	E	
100	D	

Practice Set 2: Answers & Explanations

PASSAGE 27

51 **Choice E is correct** because scaling back the explanation of the nucleus and its functions would reduce clarity. The passage centers on identifying and distinguishing cell structures, starting with the nucleus. Reducing this detail would undercut the author's goal of explaining the cell's morphological parts.

Choice A is incorrect because a diagram would visually clarify the structural parts of a cell, supporting the author's descriptive points. **Choice B is correct** because a glossary of technical or uncommon terms (e.g., "stallate" or "nucleolus") would aid reader understanding. **Choice C is correct** because further explanation or speculation about the nucleolus's function would enhance the passage, which currently notes that its role is not essential but offers no functional detail. **Choice D is correct** because information on differences between young and old cells would clarify how the nucleolus's presence signifies development, directly relating to a key point in the passage.

PASSAGE 28

52 **Choice D is correct** because besides lauding Donatello as "the brightest light," the passage specifically states that his style acted as a corrective to Ghiberti's influence and that Donatello's proclivity for natural realism and accurate detail helped steer sculptural trends away from more fanciful and less tasteful styles.

Choice A is incorrect because the author clearly states that Donatello was the greatest of his time and admits that Ghiberti was a great artist of the world, but does not clearly place Ghiberti on the same level aesthetically, to the exclusion of other artists. **Choice B is incorrect** because the passage describes Donatello's positive effect on Renaissance sculpture in general, not on Ghiberti. **Choice C is incorrect** because the negative influence discussed applies to the art world in general, not Donatello. **Choice E is incorrect** because the author admits that Ghiberti was a great artist and superior to Donatello in one specific aspect, but does not suggest that their styles complemented one another.

53 **Choice B is correct** because the author characterizes Ghiberti's work as exemplary of the overly "florid" style criticized in the passage. He does admit, however, that the artist was great and had an exquisite sense of beauty.

Choice A is incorrect because the "masculine" work referred to is Donatello's. **Choice C is incorrect** because the author only states that Ghiberti "might" have been influential had Donatello not been there. **Choice D is incorrect** because the author does not imply that the artist's work is underrated. **Choice E is incorrect** because the author does not imply that the artist's work is overrated. He both criticizes and compliments the artist, but does not suggest that popular opinion has placed Ghiberti higher or lower than where he ought to be.

PASSAGE 29

54 **Choice E is correct** because craniologists study the cranium, another word for skull, which is the apparent focus of the writer.

Choice A is incorrect because herpetologists study snakes and amphibians; even though the frog is an amphibian, it is not the focus of the information in this passage. **Choice B is incorrect** because zoologists study animals, but the focus of the passage is specifically the human skull. **Choice C is incorrect** because endocrinologists study and treat malfunctions and disorders of the endocrine system, which is unrelated to the content of the passage. **Choice D is incorrect** because thoracic surgeons operate in the area of the chest, not the skull, eliminating it as a correct answer choice.

55 **Choice B is correct** because the word "fundamentally" in the passage refers to a basic or underlying similarity in the structure of the mammalian and frog skulls. The passage is explaining that although the skulls differ in complexity, their basic structure is similar.

Choice A is incorrect because "primarily" refers to the main or chief focus, which is not the context in this sentence. The sentence is not focusing on the main purpose of the skull, but on its underlying structure. **Choice C is incorrect** because this definition is more formal and structural, implying a literal foundational effect. The passage is discussing the conceptual similarity of the skulls, not a literal physical foundation, making this option too literal. **Choice D is incorrect** because "originally" refers to something that existed from the beginning, indicating a temporal origin. The passage is not talking about the temporal origin of the skulls' similarity, but about their basic structural similarity. **Choice E is incorrect** because "indispensably" means absolutely necessary or essential. The passage does not state that the similarity of the skulls is essential; it is simply explaining that they share a basic similarity in structure, making this option irrelevant to the context.

56 **Choice C is correct** because studying anatomical structures of other life forms, like the frog's skull, can help lead to a better understanding of human anatomy in various parts, which is supported by the context of the passage.

Choice A is incorrect because the passage only mentions the human skull, so it would be incorrect to assume that other anatomical structures in lower life forms correspond to human anatomical structures. **Choice B** is incorrect because there is no indication in the passage that all amphibian anatomy corresponds to human anatomy.

PASSAGE 30: SUMMARY/PARAPHRASE

The passage is about basic locational terminology in anatomy. The main idea is that students of anatomy need to master a specialized lexicon of locational terms. The major point is the discussion of key locational terms used in anatomy. The major point is supported by (a) several examples of how to use the terms when discussing the anatomy of a rabbit and (b) a brief justification for why anatomists prefer a specialized locational terminology to more general terms. The purpose of the passage is to introduce the reader to anatomical terminology.

57 **Choices A, B and C are correct** because the passage emphasizes the importance of using correct and uniform terminology depending on the task or occupation. When sailing, for example, it is crucial to know the parts of a ship in relation to the bow. If one were to use the word left instead of port, the listener might think that the speaker is referring to his own left rather than the left side of the boat. When performing brain surgery, the terms front, back, top, or bottom can change depending on the patient's position. Medical terminology for the parts of the brain and their relative position in the cranium remain constant enabling everyone involved in the procedure to understand what is happening. In the same way, a mechanic must know and use the correct names for parts of an engine, especially if he is working with another mechanic or ordering parts.

PASSAGE 31

58 **Choice E is correct** because the community refers to all of the bees in the entire hive, excluding the Queen. The community members would refer to the common and working bees as well as the male drones. This analogy refers to the community being those that work and then there would be a leader, like a mayor in a community. When the Queen leaves or is separated, this would result "in a dispersion of the community members" which refers to the rest of the bees.

Choice A is incorrect because "community members" would not only include the male drones but would also include the common working bees because they would all be a part of this community inside the hive. **Choice B** is incorrect because "community members" would not only include the common working bees but also the male drones. **Choice C** is incorrect because "community members" does not refer to all the queens in all surrounding hives because the term "community" typically means one particular hive only. **Choice D** is incorrect because the term "family" might refer to the bees in the hive that are related to the Queen, but the "community members" would refer to the workers in the hive.

59 The sentence **"Based on a beekeeper's own sequential observations, the Queen or Mother Bee of a hive unquestionably reigns supreme over her common and working bees as well as the male drones"** is correct because the beginning of this first sentence, "based on a beekeeper's own sequential observations," means that a beekeeper possibly kept a journal detailing what they observed with the hive. These observations were listed sequentially; each event noted in the journal was listed in the order in which these events took place.

PASSAGE 32: SUMMARY/PARAPHRASE

The passage is about strategies for cotton growing. The main idea is that through a variety of methods, farmers have succeeded in generating cotton crops with higher yields than were possible historically. The major points are: (a) that using seed selection, special cultivation, and hybridization, cotton farmers have created new varieties of cotton that produce unprecedented yields and (b) that farmers need to carefully consider numerous factors in order to optimize their results when using one of these new varieties. The purpose of the passage is to inform the reader about how cotton varietals affect yields and advise on how to optimize them.

60 The correct answer is **"Many of these attempts have succeeded, and there are now a large number of varieties which excel the older varieties in profitable yield."** The writer is advising farmers to select and plant hybrid cotton. His justification for this recommendation is the success that others have had doing so. The increasing popularity of the hybrids is evidence of their effectiveness.

61 **Choice D is correct** because the writer states that hybrids are developed under ideal conditions, so for farmers to achieve optimal yields, they should mimic those same conditions.

Choice A is incorrect because although hybridization can be long and costly, the passage does not provide evidence to support this as a reasonable conclusion. **Choice B** is incorrect because hybrids are developed for specific soil and climate conditions, making the idea that they are broadly adaptable inaccurate. **Choice C** is incorrect because while fertilizers may help increase yield, it is not the only factor contributing to a plant's success, so it cannot be the sole conclusion. **Choice E** is incorrect because the passage does not support the idea that a hybrid's price determines the value of the harvested crop, as market demand can also influence pricing.

62 **Choice A is correct** because the word tillage refers to the preparation of soil for growing crops, including plowing, turning, and conditioning the soil. The passage emphasizes that the new cotton varieties were developed under "the best tillage," implying that proper soil preparation is crucial for maintaining the success of these varieties.

Choice B is incorrect because while fertilization is mentioned earlier in the passage as one of several methods used, it is not directly tied to the term tillage nor emphasized as the primary requirement for maintaining crop quality. **Choice C** is incorrect because the passage makes no mention of pesticide use at all, so it cannot be inferred that pesticide use is relevant to the meaning or importance of tillage in this context. **Choice D** is incorrect because although irrigation is often important in agriculture, it is not discussed or implied in the passage, nor is it associated with the term tillage. **Choice E** is incorrect because mulch application is not mentioned in the passage and is unrelated to the concept of tillage, which focuses more on soil manipulation than on covering the soil surface.

PASSAGE 33: SUMMARY/PARAPHRASE

The passage is about strategies for dealing with insect pests. The main idea is that while an insect may do the most harm during one point in its lifecycle, it may be easier to destroy at another point in its cycle. The major point is that it may be easier to destroy a mature insect than its larvae even though the larvae may be more harmful. There is a minor point that underscores the potential harmfulness of larvae by explaining that larvae require a large food supply to furnish their tremendous growth rate. The purpose of the passage is to provide information on pest control. Although the passage features normative language such as "it is better to", it is mainly factual; the reader is not being told that they ought to kill pests, merely the most strategic approach to dealing with them should they desire pest control.

63 **Choice E is correct** because the phrase "from this" indicates the author is reinforcing a previous point, suggesting that the current text supports or restates an earlier explanation or example.

Choice A is incorrect because there is too little information to conclude that this is a final statement or conclusion; the author may continue developing the topic. **Choice B** is incorrect because the writer is not offering a new example but rather reiterating or reinforcing a previous statement. **Choice C** is incorrect because the passage presents alternatives, not a cautionary message, so it does not function as a warning. **Choice D** is incorrect because there is no clear indication that the author intends to further develop a new idea introduced in this excerpt.

PASSAGE 34

64 **Choice D is correct** because the passage concludes by implying that non-human trials are being conducted with the purpose of applying the therapy to human metabolic diseases.

Choice A is incorrect because, although it mentions a finding of the study, it does not speak of the study's ultimate goal. **Choice B** is incorrect because it only addresses a narrow finding in one experiment. **Choice C** is incorrect because it is true in general, but it does not address the ultimate goal. **Choice E** is incorrect because it undermines the entire point of the passage and states the exact opposite in terms of meaning.

65 The sentence **"However, human applications involving AAV8 remain unattainable due to the triggering of dangerous immune responses"** is correct because it articulates the logical progression of facts and examples as they have been organized in the passage.

Chapter 3: **Reading Comprehension**

PASSAGE 35: SUMMARY/PARAPHRASE

The passage is about stocking water with fish. The main idea is that, although it may seem obvious that fish being stocked need to be fed, the issue of feeding is often overlooked. There is a major point that stocking feed after the fish have been introduced is often a failure. The main purpose of the passage is to inform. The author leaves unstated the explanation of why introducing feed after the fish does not work.

66 **"Small attempts at stocking with creatures suitable for food, particularly after the fish have been already introduced, are not at all likely to succeed"** is the correct answer. Attempting to treat an illness is more time-consuming and expensive than taking steps to prevent the illness in the first place. One may succeed in curing the patient, but success is not guaranteed. In much the same way, stocking the body of water with food before introducing the fish is more likely to have a successful result than stocking the water with fish and, then, introducing the food. Many or all of the fish will have already died.

67 **Choice A is correct** because failing to provide food that the fish will eat ensures their death, and this is directly supported by the passage.

Choice B is incorrect because although one may stock a pond to catch fish, the passage makes no mention of this purpose. **Choice C** is incorrect because the writer states that an appropriate food source is necessary but does not indicate that fish will adapt to a new type of food. **Choice D** is incorrect because there is no evidence in the passage suggesting that the fish would engage in cannibalism. **Choice E** is incorrect because there is no indication in the passage that the fish will migrate, and a pond may not even have an outlet for such movement.

68 **Choice D is correct** because the passage emphasizes the often-overlooked importance of ensuring a food supply before stocking fish. Presenting this information just before discussing the specific food types sets the stage by stressing the need for such a discussion, making the following information more relevant and impactful.

Choice A is incorrect because introducing the presentation with this point might be too specific and negative. Introductions should provide a general overview or hook, not jump directly into a cautionary detail. **Choice B** is incorrect because placing it at the conclusion would reduce its preventive value. The warning is meant to influence decisions early in the stocking process—not after all other points have been made. **Choice C** is incorrect because placing it after the discussion of food types misses the opportunity to highlight why food is important before exploring what food is needed. **Choice E** is incorrect because while vegetation can contribute to the food supply, the passage does not specifically focus on vegetation but rather on the concept of food availability in general. Therefore, this positioning would be too narrow.

PASSAGE 36: SUMMARY/PARAPHRASE

The passage is about effective planting. The main idea is that true grasses thrive best with the addition of another type of plant, legumes. The major points are: (a) that true grasses will exhaust the nitrogen supply in soil because they can only get nitrogen from the soil (b) that legumes such as clover are able to extract free nitrogen from the air as well as from the soil and (c) that in order to optimize planting, farmers should add legume to grass seed in order to keep the grass from exhausting all the nitrogen in the soil. The main purpose of the passage is to inform and persuade by explaining to the reader why it is optimal to add in legume.

69 The correct answer is **"Hence without cost to the farmer these clovers help the soil to feed their neighbors, the true grasses."** Adding fertilizer with the correct proportion of nitrogen is probably as effective as growing clover in tandem with the true grasses. The downside is the cost. Since the clover is perennial, it will grow every year without replanting, whereas chemical fertilizers must be added to the soil every year at great cost to the farmer.

PASSAGE 37

70 **Choice B is correct** because the passage states that haplotypes help ascertain the spread of certain lineages. It also says it has to do with a lineage that was preferred or imposed, thereby leading to the fact that males with this Y chromosome were more likely to pass on their genes, by virtue of their lineage, than males from other lineages.

Choice A is incorrect because the passage states that the Y chromosome carries few alleles for phenotypes that would be visually distinguishable. That is to say, the males carrying this Y chromosome did not stand out for any visible characteristic, but rather solely for being direct descendants of a certain prominent lineage. **Choice C** is incorrect because there was no connection made between a fetus carrying this chromosome and pregnancy outcomes. Therefore, one cannot conclude that these haplotypes had any impact on the rate of pregnancies coming to term. **Choice D** is incorrect because the passage states that the haplotypes do not result in significant phenotype expression, and it does not indicate or suggest they have any bearing on reproductive health either. Therefore, one cannot conclude there was a link between the haplotypes and reproductive health. **Choice E** is incorrect because the passage points to a social tendency at a time when males of a certain lineage were more likely to procreate, passing on their genes, than others. This occurred by virtue of merely being of a certain lineage, rather than expressing any qualities or features. While these men were related through their paternal bloodline, the broad distribution of the lineage suggests they did not necessarily share any common characteristics beyond claim to this lineage, as supported by the passing on of haplotypes that yield few recognizable phenotypes.

71 **Choice B is correct** because the passage states that the analysis of genetic markers, haplotypes, "helps ascertain the extent to which certain lineages have spread." This establishes a link between the research of such markers and gleaning insight as to the way certain male lines dominated in a certain period, as reflected in the spreading of the lineages. **Choice C is correct** because it states that one such haplotype revealed the predominance of the line descended from Ghengis Khan. It further suggests that similar findings may be discovered for other emperors.

Choice A is incorrect because the passage does not suggest the presence of one single line of male dominance from a certain dynasty, but rather several. It concludes by suggesting that other emperors may also have spread a line of genetic dominance. The passage also does not suggest that most males descended from some dynasty, only that certain lineages present today can be traced back to dynasties in the past.

PASSAGE 38: SUMMARY/PARAPHRASE

The passage is about determining the age of trees. The main idea is that many methods of determining a tree's age are unreliable. The major points are that (a) scientifically rigorous measurement of growth rates has only existed since the eighteenth century and (b) that only the measurement of a tree's girth is reliable for telling its age. The main idea of the passage is primed by an extensive preamble that ponders questions of our knowledge of a tree's age. The purpose of the passage is to briefly discuss the longevity of trees and several methods for determining it.

72 The correct answer is **"Is the period of one thousand years, the favorite figure of tradition, a common or probable period of arboreal longevity, or have our proudest forest giants attained their present size in half the time that is commonly claimed for them?"** The phrase "favorite figure of tradition" suggests that scientific methods were not used to determine the ages of old trees. It may be that the only way people could judge the age of an apparently antique specimen was through a family or village oral history.

73 **Choice E is correct** because to entertain an idea is to consider it; one may also do this with a question, making it the most appropriate interpretation in context.

Choice A is incorrect because the writer is not referring to something that amuses. **Choice B** is incorrect because pleasure and amusement have similar connotations, and the context does not support this interpretation. **Choice C** is incorrect because the author is clearly not describing a performance of any kind. **Choice D** is incorrect because this implies leisurely mental engagement. The passage is focused on serious inquiry.

74 **Choice A is correct** because by the end of this passage, the writer has discussed how scientists have measured the ages of trees, so it is logical to assume he will continue discussing methods or findings related to that theme.

Choice B is incorrect because although the writer briefly mentions that tree location affects longevity, he does not elaborate and shifts to other topics, making it unlikely to be the focus. **Choice C** is incorrect because the passage is informational, not persuasive, so it is not logical to assume the writer is about to make an argument. **Choice D** is incorrect because there is no indication in the passage that the writer intends to address specific geography next. **Choice E** is incorrect because the passage has not yet focused on geographical details, so it is unlikely that will be the immediate topic.

PASSAGE 39: SUMMARY/PARAPHRASE

The passage is about the effects that hormones have on behavior. The main idea is that hormone levels have a more significant effect on mating potential than other indicators such as attractiveness. There are two major points: (a) that the behavior observed in swallows correlates to other animal species, including humans and (b) that the increased confidence and higher testosterone levels affected mating outcomes as much as the changes to the vibrancy of the birds' coloring. The purpose of the passage is to inform the reader of the important role that hormones play in animal behavior

75 **Choice B is correct** because the passage claims that confidence is caused by an attractive physical appearance.

Choice A is incorrect because the passage lists confidence as one of two main factors involved in increasing male barn swallows' testosterone levels. **Choice C** is incorrect because the passage states beta males can turn into alpha males and thus have increased levels of testosterone, ruling out the idea that high levels of testosterone are inherent or unchangeable. **Choice D** is incorrect because the passage lists confidence as one of two main factors involved in increasing male barn swallows' testosterone levels. **Choice E** is incorrect because the passage does not attribute fluctuating levels solely to mating.

PASSAGE 40

76 **Choice C is correct** because it states that mycelium has a role to play in tree health, but it also states that theories on the specific role "abound" and that the idea of resource-sharing is a theory that remains "tenuous," which means still lacking in rigorous evidence.

Choice A is incorrect because, although the theory of "hub" trees acting altruistically is presented as a possibility, it has yet to be verified and is not the primary focus of the passage. **Choice B** is incorrect because, although research has explored the role these networks play in resiliency, a direct correlation has not been established, making this a supportive point, rather than the primary one. **Choice D** is incorrect as there is no emphasis on new findings supplanting the theories of previous studies. The passage states that they "have been thought to participate" in some form of synergistic interaction, which indicates that the idea of interdependency has been previously considered. **Choice E** is incorrect because international studies are exploring "the extent to which" there is distribution-sharing, which means its specific function is unclear. Also, it states that "some evidence" points to hub trees sharing resources with vulnerable members. Therefore, it cannot be said that no evidence exists to support such theories.

77 "Far from being solitary figures, trees within forest communities have been thought to participate in a synergistic web of underground resource-sharing through a web of opportunistic mycelium, the fungal body responsible for the fruition of mushrooms." This sentence is correct because it states that trees may participate in "a synergistic web of underground resource-sharing," which implies that the distribution of nutrients is not one-sided. In addition, the term "opportunistic" used in reference to the mycelium indicates that the fungal networks also benefit from the relationship with the trees, suggesting that they too obtain nutrients in the process.

PASSAGE 41: SUMMARY/PARAPHRASE

The passage is about primate behavior. The main idea is that sharing among primates is often not strictly altruistic. The main points of the passage are (a) that anthropologists believe that chimpanzee behavior is analogous to the behavior of early humans and (b) that chimpanzees are mainly motivated to share food and tools in exchange for sex. Major point (b) is backed up by additional facts that male chimpanzees are most likely to share food and supplies with sexually receptive females. The purpose of the passage is to inform and to draw a comparison between human behavior and that of other primates.

78 **Choice A is correct** because sexually receptive females in their reproductive years have a higher chance of receiving food and supplies, giving them the highest chance for survival.

Choice B is incorrect because the passage actually infers that male primates' motivation is to perpetuate the species, as they are most likely to exchange food for sex with females in their reproductive years. **Choice C** is incorrect because male primates trade food for sex as a means of survival, not exploitation. Their ultimate goal is to perpetuate the species. **Choice D** is incorrect because the passage states that the food-for-sex process is not altruistically motivated; therefore, primates cannot possess a high level of magnanimity or selflessness. **Choice E** is incorrect because the passage does not infer that male primates are in any way lazy. In fact, it infers the opposite: that male primates work to gather supplies to exchange.

79 **Choice B is correct** because the passage explores gender relationships among primates and focuses on sharing as the central reason anthropologists want to study their behavior.

Choice A is incorrect because the passage states that primate behavior likely mirrors that of early humans, but then makes it clear that sharing is the primary reason anthropologists are interested in understanding group behavior in primates. **Choice C** is incorrect because the author makes it clear that the sharing among primates is not altruistically motivated; therefore, group behavior in primates cannot teach humans about the importance of altruism. **Choice D** is incorrect because the passage indicates that group behavior in primates can only be related to humans. **Choice E** is incorrect because the sexual behavior of primates (or humans for that matter) is not the primary focus of the passage; sex is mentioned as a byproduct of the main goal of anthropological studies on group behavior in primates: sharing.

80 "According to anthropologists, observing primates in Senegal is like opening a window to the world of understanding the behavior of early humans, particularly related to sharing." One type of trope is a metaphor employed for rhetorical purposes - to either clarify or enhance a reader or listener's understanding of something. The first sentence uses a metaphor comparing anthropological research to a window that opens to knowledge and thus makes use of the trope rhetorical device.

PASSAGE 42: SUMMARY/PARAPHRASE

The passage is about bacterial resistance to antibiotics. The main idea is that even bacteria that are affected by antibiotics are capable of surviving an antibiotic onslaught. The main points are that (a) many antibiotic treatments work by targeting active bacteria, with the implication that they do so by cutting nutrients and (b) some bacteria are able to slow their growth rate into dormancy when their source of nutrients is threatened, thus rendering them immune to the antibiotic. The purpose of the passage is to explain how some bacteria resist antibiotics.

81 **Choice A is correct** because the passage states that starvation causes the bacteria to stop growing and lie dormant. **Choice B is correct** because the passage states that starving bacteria are immune to medications because they are dormant; most antibiotics are only effective against active bacteria.

Choice C is incorrect because starvation does not change the bacteria's chemical composition according to the passage.

PASSAGE 43

82 **Choice E is correct** because the passage discusses termite behavior as an example of self-organization, which is defined as "undirected" behavior that is not "preplanned." Therefore, the analysis of the termites engaging in self-organization is predicated on their "random" movements, in other words, without a preconceived plan.

Choice A is incorrect because, as an example of self-organization, the process of nest-building can't be "centrally controlled." Therefore, there cannot be a guiding agent orchestrating the process, at least not for the base of the nest used as an example. **Choice B** is incorrect because this is not an assumption in the text but rather the definition of pheromones. These are scents left behind that serve as chemical signals to other members of the group or other elements of the organism. The fact that they would be perceived by other termites once in proximity is in the very nature and function of pheromones. **Choice C** is incorrect because it is stated in the first paragraph that self-organization is a process that takes place in a variety of realms, including plants and cells. Therefore, it cannot be limited to only nest formation. **Choice D** is incorrect because the use of a blueprint would require some pre-planning or some kind of envisioning of the final structure before beginning the work. However, one of the conditions presented for behavior to be self-organized is that it comes about on its own and it is not pre-planned or directed in any way.

83 **Choice D is correct** because the passage explains that the base of a nest is built by termites walking about "randomly" and inadvertently dropping sand grains with a certain scent. It stands to reason that higher traffic of termites in close vicinity to building material, such as sand, would result in more frequent intercrossing of termite paths and an accelerated piling up of sand grains.

Choice A is incorrect because the passage states that the base of a nest is built through self-organized activity, which is "undirected" and inadvertent. Therefore, it cannot be the result of a signal that would intentionally direct worker termites to start constructing a nest. **Choice B** is incorrect because the process of nest building begins with "random" paths that lead to sand grains collecting in certain spots where termites had passed. So, although there may be steps the termites appear to be following, they are internally "undirected." Therefore, a series of randomly piled grains of sand may resemble each other, but one cannot infer they are identical. In fact, given the random nature of the early composition process, one can presume each is unique. **Choice C** is incorrect because if termites were intentionally leaving grains of sand in their path, they would be consequently directing work to proceed on nest formation. However, that would contradict the self-organized nature of the phenomenon, which is, by definition, "undirected," which is to say, it takes places of its own accord and without being intentionally prompted. **Choice E is incorrect** because the passage states that "some" termite architecture is an example of self-organization, not that all activities in termite colonies are self-organized. So, one cannot infer that the entire nest is constructed in a self-organized way, but only its base.

PASSAGE 44: SUMMARY/PARAPHRASE

The passage is about the phenomenon of ocean acidification. The main idea is that increasing acid levels in ocean waters are disrupting the growth of coral reefs that are vital to maintaining the diverse ecosystem of the ocean. There are several major points: (a) that increased levels of carbon dioxide in the atmosphere are leading to the acidification of the oceans due to the way the ocean absorbs atmospheric carbon dioxide (b) that increased acidification of ocean water prevents the proper growth of coral reefs and (c) the alteration of coral reefs could be disastrous for oceanic life, since coral reefs support a notable percentage of marine species. The main purpose of the passage is to explain and call to action; the process by which carbon dioxide affects the oceans is concisely explained and loaded rhetoric such as the use of terms like "threat" and "terrible catastrophe" indicates that there is an implied intention we take action on atmospheric carbon dioxide levels.

84 **Choice E is correct** because the information in the passage implies that since the base of the coral reefs cannot calcify in low pH environments, the reefs as an aggregate will struggle to grow and this will harm the marine life they support.

Choice A is incorrect because the ocean absorbs carbon from the atmosphere. **Choice B is incorrect** because while it is true that 25% of marine species depend on the coral reef ecosystem, low pH in the ocean does not mean they will all go extinct. **Choice C is incorrect** because the statement is correct except that low pH means high acidity and not low acidity, and thus the answer is ultimately incorrect. **Choice D is incorrect** because while it is true that many types of coral reefs can grow in low pH environments, the passage nonetheless leads us to believe that the coral reef ecosystems are still in danger from acidification.

85 **Choice E is correct** because the rhetorical goal of the passage is to convince the reader that ocean acidification is harmful specifically because of the damage it does to coral reefs.

Choice A is incorrect because while it is true that the passage delineates the dangers of carbon dioxide in the world's oceans, description is not a rhetorical strategy; the goal of rhetoric is always to persuade and not describe. **Choice B** is incorrect because while the information in the passage may stimulate an emotional response in the reader, the actual rhetorical goal of the passage is to persuade the reader of the harms of ocean acidification. **Choice C** is incorrect because persuasion is always the goal of rhetoric and this passage seeks to persuade the reader that ocean acidification is harmful, but the answer needs to be more specific—the author ultimately wants to convey the danger that coral reefs are in as a result of ocean acidification. **Choice D** is incorrect because again, a rhetorical goal must always be persuasive and not merely descriptive; therefore, explaining the specifics of pH levels' effect on coral reefs is not a rhetorical goal.

86 "This is an especially vital area of exploration since coral reefs are home to 25% of all marine species." While the passage later goes on to describe how ocean acidification damages coral reefs, the primary importance of the coral reefs, from an ecological standpoint, is that they house 25% of the world's marine species.

PASSAGE 45: SUMMARY/PARAPHRASE

The passage is about the parasitic disease malaria. The main idea is that the pathology of malaria makes those affected by sickle-cell anemia immune. The main points are that (a) malaria requires access to the exterior of blood cells by using certain adhesive proteins and (b) that mutations to the hemoglobin of those affected by sickle cell anemia mean that they rarely, if ever, possess the adhesive proteins needed for the malaria parasite to establish itself. The purpose of the passage is to inform - the tone is mostly dry and factual.

87 **Choice A is correct** because sickle cell anemics are protected from malaria because of a hemoglobin mutation, but this mutation does not facilitate adhesion bonding, it impedes it. The author's contention is that sickle cell anemics are protected from malaria as a result of a hemoglobin mutation that impedes adhesin bonding, and thus the author's contention would be incorrect if sickle cell anemia hemoglobin mutations facilitated adhesion bonding. **Choice C is correct** because according to the information given in the passage, the malaria parasite is not able to infect the blood of sickle cell anemics; sickle cell anemics are immune to malaria and hence this statement would weaken the author's contention if true.

Choice B is incorrect because adhesins can sometimes attach to the blood cells of sickle cell anemics and therefore this statement merely reinforces the author's claim that adhesin adhesions occasionally occur in sickle cell anemics, but still not frequently enough to successfully transmit the malaria virus.

PASSAGE 46

88 **Choice B is correct** because the passage states that these cells have undergone "transdifferentiation" which reverts them to cells "capable of developing into and substituting any kind of damaged tissue." Therefore, as they are cells that have not yet developed into a specific tissue cell, they remain "non-specific."

Choice A is incorrect because the state of being undifferentiated means the cell has not developed into a specific tissue cell, but it does not mean that as a specialized tissue cell, it has not matured as an adult. It is a question of its genetic identity rather than its stage of development as a specialized, or differentiated, cell. **Choice C** is incorrect because the passage does not mention anything about identifying cells according to their species. Undifferentiated cells are variable in their ultimate function, but this is not necessarily a result of lacking markers particular to the species. **Choice D** is incorrect because although an undifferentiated cell can develop into any tissue cell, while still undifferentiated, it cannot complete the functions of different kinds of cells. It has to differentiate before it can be applied "to replace cells in other tissues." **Choice E** is incorrect because the cells develop into "healthy adults," thereby allowing the organism to recover from injury. As the passage states originally, by virtue of reverting to undifferentiated cells, the jellyfish is able to "outwit death," which serves the purpose of ensuring the organism's survival.

89 **"Essentially, it accomplishes the idea behind stem cell research, which is to provide cells capable of developing into and substituting any kind of damaged tissue."** This sentence refers to "stem cell research," which is a field of medical research that aims to "provide cells capable of … substituting any kind of damaged tissue." This would have vast applications in the reparation of tissue "damaged by disease." The transdifferentiation that the Turritopsis dohrnii is capable of aligns with the objectives of this research.

PASSAGE 47: SUMMARY/PARAPHRASE

The passage is about how hormones influence primate behavior. The main idea is that exposure to oxytocin, known as the "love hormone", has been shown to increase altruistic behavior in monkeys. The main point is that since the monkeys are closely related to humans, study of the hormone's effects in the monkeys can help us better understand how it affects human behavior. There are minor points that underscore the effect of the hormone: (a) its effects on developing intimate relationships such as that between mother and child and (b) a specific instance of the prosocial behavior it helped to promote in the affected monkeys. The purpose of the passage is to explain and inform.

90 **Choice B is correct** because the information in the passage implies that studying oxytocin's effects on monkeys can be used to have deeper insight into human behavior related to the hormone.

Choice A is incorrect because humans may be closely related to the macaque, but the passage does not indicate that oxytocin will affect humans in the exact same manner as the monkeys. **Choice C** is incorrect because while oxytocin could theoretically be used for this purpose, the passage does not indicate that the information garnered from the study on the macaques will be used to create medication to treat antisocial behavior in humans. **Choice D** is incorrect because the passage actually infers that scientists have already produced oxytocin synthetically for research purposes. **Choice E** is incorrect because the passage makes it clear that studying macaques could have long-term benefits on understanding humans relative to oxytocin.

91 **Choice A is correct** because the passage indicates that prosocial choices are about sharing, which clearly benefits the well-being of two parties, in this case the two macaques.

Choice B is incorrect because the passage states prosocial choices, not antisocial ones. **Choice C** is incorrect because the passage does not indicate that prosocial choices play a role in the creation of social hierarchies. **Choice D** is incorrect because according to the passage, prosocial choices are the result of changes in hormonal patterns and thus do not influence them. **Choice E** is incorrect because the passage states that prosocial choices are often made under the influence of oxytocin, not in its absence.

92 **"Oxytocin, also known as the love hormone, bonds mothers to their children and promotes intimacy and relationships in various species including humans."** This sentence explicates why oxytocin is vital to the forging of social connections among species.

PASSAGE 48: SUMMARY/PARAPHRASE

The passage is about the biological causes of psychiatric disorders. The main idea is that scientists hope to be able to combine their findings about the RNF123 gene with a holistic understanding of mental health. The main points are (a) that the RNF123 gene affects the hippocampus and (b) that the hippocampus is altered in people with depression and (c) that scientists are looking at this information along with the experiences of patients to form a fuller understanding of the issues affecting mental health. The purpose of the passage is to present an objective account of a current trend in the life sciences.

93 "**Scientists have taken another step in the direction of better understanding the biological underpinnings of various psychiatric disorders.**" While the passage ultimately indicates that scientists are interested in both genes and environment, at first their main interest is discerning the biological factors underlying mental health issues.

PASSAGE 49

94 **Choice B is correct** because the passage discusses the role that gut microbiota plays in the immune system's response to "disease." It states it is "commensal," which means it does not harm the host. It further states that it is an "invaluable actor" in the organism's development of "self-tolerance," by which it "refrains from attack," a task that would not be possible were the microbiota considered foreign and subsequently targeted and attacked.

Choice A is incorrect because the passage states that gut microbiota prevents the development of autoimmunity by playing a role in the immune system's self-tolerance. This would be contradicted if somehow activated gut microbiota led to autoimmunity. **Choice C** is incorrect because, whether or not this is true, there is no discussion of viral infections in the passage or how certain diseases may lead to autoimmunity. Therefore, based on the information presented, one cannot make any conclusions on the effects viral infections might have on suppressing self-tolerance or the immune response in relation to gut microbiota. **Choice D** is incorrect because the passage discusses gut microbiota playing a facilitative role, "influencing the development and function of immune cells." There is no indication that gut microbiota enters into battle with the immune system, but rather that the two work together. This fact is further supported by the use of the word "commensal," indicating that microbiota inhabits without doing any harm to the host. **Choice E** is incorrect because, in the first paragraph, organisms with gut microbiota are contrasted with those that are "germ-free," described as "those reared in sterile conditions without exposure to foreign bacteria." Therefore, it suggests that organisms require some exposure to germs to develop gut microbiota, contradicting the statement that gut microbiota can develop on its own.

95 **Choice A is correct** because the passage opens up by stating there is a "plethora of local and systemic health benefits" that gut microbiota offers, particularly in relation to the immune system. In the second paragraph, it goes on to indicate that new studies have determined "yet another" way in which microbiota "performs a pivotal function," namely, its role in self-tolerance and preventing autoimmunity. This makes it a major point of the passage, focusing on the wide range of functions performed by microbiota and adding to that list another invaluable contribution recently discovered.

Choice B is incorrect because the case of "germ-free" organisms was mentioned as evidence of the claim that gut microbiota plays an important role in the functioning of the immune system. This does not make it a major point, but rather a supportive point to the main idea. **Choice C** is incorrect because the importance of self-tolerance in the prevention of autoimmunity is a point made in support of the idea that gut microbiota is shown to play a role in facilitating self-tolerance. The passage states that it helps maintain homeostasis and influences "the development and function of immune cells," which in turn contributes to self-tolerance. Therefore, the definition of self-tolerance on its own is not a major point, but rather it is the link that has been made between self-tolerance and gut microbiota.

PASSAGE 50: SUMMARY/PARAPHRASE

The passage is about stem cell research. The main idea is that while some scientists have promoted stem cells as having "miracle cure" potential, there is considerable trepidation about using stem cells in both the scientific community and among laymen. The main points are (a) that stem cells have been posited as a potential treatment for a wide variety of diseases and conditions (b) that there is opposition to stem cell research from those who see it as a disruption of the natural order of life and (c) there is caution from some scientists who worry that stem cell research may not be as effective as some claim. The main purpose of the passage is to briefly summarize the chief arguments for and against the use of stem cell research.

96 **Choice C is correct** because diverse cells, the byproducts of mitosis, can be controlled by scientists and manipulated toward diverse medical outcomes, thus rendering mitosis a key factor in stem cell research.

Choice A is incorrect because the passage does not claim that mitosis is specifically useful because it allows scientists to use stem cells in abundance. **Choice B** is incorrect because the passage does not claim that stem cells are stronger after mitosis. **Choice D** is incorrect because the passage makes it clear that mitosis is important to stem cell research because it engenders a diversity of cells, not simply because the process occurs. **Choice E** is incorrect because this answer is true, but more information should be given to explain exactly why diversified cells are useful in stem cell research; the reason why—not just the fact that—diverse cells are useful to stem cell therapy specifies the importance of mitosis.

97 **Choice D is correct** because for the author to believe that the exploitation of natural life was the elephant in the room of the stem cell therapy debate, he or she would have to be anti–stem cell therapy. "The white elephant in the room" is a metaphor in the English language that serves as a rhetorical strategy to underline a glaring truth that is being ignored. Since the author's tone is objective regarding stem cell therapy as a whole in the passage, the author would not agree with the elephant-in-the-room idiom for stem cell therapy, because that would mean the author also believes that stem cell therapy is the exploitation of life.

Choice A is incorrect because the author agrees that stem cell therapy is a highly sensitive issue, given that he or she highlights the fact that many people believe stem cell therapy exploits human life. **Choice B** is incorrect because the author states that many medical doctors believe stem cell therapy can have adverse effects despite being an extremely useful treatment method. Thus, the benefits of stem cell therapy are sometimes overshadowed by its pitfalls. **Choice C** is incorrect because the author would agree that the outcomes of scientific research do not always align with social mores, since stem cell therapy is a successful treatment method that also causes social controversy. **Choice E** is incorrect because the entire passage is about how stem cells regenerate and can be used to treat a diverse variety of medical conditions, and thus the author would agree that stem cells underscore the regenerative nature of the human body.

98 **Choice A is correct** because the passage states that some people believe that stem cell therapy exploits and interferes with natural life, even though it is a very effective method of medical treatment. **Choice C is correct** because the passage states that scientists worry about the potential for stem cell therapy to worsen various medical conditions, despite its ability to treat a wide array of medical issues.

Choice B is incorrect because the passage does not explicitly state that those opposed to stem cell therapy believe it promotes a culture of death.

PASSAGE 51: SUMMARY/PARAPHRASE

Mankind are always happier for having been happy; so that if you make them happy now, you make them happy twenty years hence, by the memory of it. A childhood passed with a due mixture of rational indulgence, under fond and wise parents, diffuses over the whole of life a feeling of calm pleasure; and, in extreme old age, is the very last remembrance which time can erase from the mind of man. No enjoyment, however inconsiderable, is confined to the present moment. A man is the happier for life, from having made once an agreeable tour, or lived for any length of time with pleasant people, or enjoyed any considerable interval of innocent pleasure: and it is most probably the recollection of their past pleasures, which contributes to render old men so inattentive to the scenes before them; and carries them back to a world that is past, and to scenes never to be renewed again

99 **Choice E is correct** because a trip to Disneyland would provide a lot of happy memories to generate pleasant feelings at a later date. The idea of happiness in the future as a result of special happy moments in the past is what this passage is all about. By calling the trip a "waste of money," that directly contrasts with the main concept of the passage.

Choice A is incorrect because the question asks for a contrast to the concept, rather than one consistent with it. This statement is consistent rather than contrasting. **Choice B** is incorrect because it is also consistent with the concept of the passage. A lack of happiness as a child has led to unhappiness now. **Choice C** is incorrect because this statement describes happiness in relation to material possessions rather than memories. That is slightly inconsistent, but mostly irrelevant to the main topic. **Choice D** is incorrect because being sad contrasts with happiness, but again, the discussion is not about materialism; it is about experiences and memories.

PASSAGE 52

100 **Choice D is correct** because the passage states that "There is no such thing as tameness or obedience that is genetic" and "taming is nothing more than the conveyance of a young animal's innate assurance and fondness for humans." So, it would need to associate the trainer with its mother.

Choice A is incorrect because While the passage doesn't explicitly discuss the temperament of the animal in terms of "shy" or "energetic," it does suggest that the behavior of the animal can vary, especially regarding the connection with the trainer and its mother. However, the passage does not focus on these two traits specifically, so this is not the best answer. **Choice B** is incorrect because the option seems promising at first, as the passage discusses the challenges of taming animals raised in different environments. However, the passage doesn't directly emphasize the difference between captivity and wild birth, making this choice not quite precise. **Choice C** is incorrect because the passage implies that taming is a process that involves how the animal's inherent traits (such as its "innate assurance and fondness for humans") are nurtured. The idea of a specific "process" is close to what the passage suggests, although it doesn't directly outline the trainer's methods. **Choice E** is incorrect because the passage does not delve into the trainer's expertise or experience with different species. The focus is on the animal's inherent traits and the process of taming rather than the trainer's skill in handling specific types of animals.

Practice Set 3: Business

PASSAGE 53

Question 101 is based on the following passage.

The economic crisis that broke through the global floodgates in 2008 has placed the system of capitalism under attack from its opponents. Capitalism, however, has been under scrutiny since its inception, and thus this is not a new phenomenon. However, as society has evolved so have the criticisms launched against capitalism; imperialist oppression, market failure and the wasteful and inefficient use of resources are all common gripes that constitute the anti-capitalism jeremiad. One of the prominent denunciations vaulted against capitalism over the course of the last fifteen years is its opposition to sustainability. Critics claim that capitalism promotes a milieu of exploitation because of its unbridled focus on consumption. Consequently, capitalism is a danger to a world that is increasingly strapped for natural resources, the foundation stones of capitalist enterprise.

101. According to the information given in the passage, why is consumption seen as a negative attribute of capitalism?

   (A) Consumption led to the financial crisis in the late 2000s
   (B) Consumption results in the overuse of natural resources that are currently in high demand globally
   (C) Consumption contributes to the destabilization of the market in a capitalist economic system
   (D) Consumption is the way in which proponents of capitalism distract people from the system's penchant for imperialistic oppression
   (E) Consumption leads to an increase in wasteful consumer choices

PASSAGE 54

Questions 102 and 103 are based on the following passage.

Time is an asset that is critically important to the health of a business, particularly in the upper management domain; wasted time can be especially noxious to an organization's overall success. Despite the prevalence of the platitudes "time is money" and "time is of the essence", many people working in the higher echelons of a company are unaware of how they distribute their time relative to the tasks that they need to accomplish. Such oversight of fundamental management principles can cause a business to stagnate because it shows a lack of self-reflexivity that leads to disorganization, wasted resources, and a lack of solid leadership.

102. Based on the information in the passage, the reader can infer all of the following except

   (A) Upper management in an organization is often characterized by disorganization
   (B) The principles of business theory are not often practiced
   (C) Time management skills correspond to money management skills
   (D) A lack of organizational leadership is a harbinger of poor time management
   (E) Successful organizations have the ability to critically evaluate themselves

For the following question, consider each of the three choices separately and select all that apply.

103. Poor time management is paradoxical in businesses because:

   [A] Upper management is the guilty party
   [B] Businesses know that time is a valuable asset
   [C] It leads to poor business decisions

PASSAGE 55

Questions 104 to 106 are based on the following passage.

Men should be systematic in their business. A person who does business by rule, having a time and place for everything, doing his work promptly, will accomplish twice as much and with half the trouble of those who do it carelessly and **slipshod**. By introducing system into all your transactions, doing one thing at a time, always meeting appointments with punctuality, you find leisure for pastime and recreation; whereas the man who only half does one thing, and then turns to something else, and half does that, will have his business at loose ends, and will never know when his day's work is done, for it never will be done. Of course, there is a limit to all these rules. We must try to preserve the happy medium, for there is such a thing as being too systematic.

104. Which of the following best summarizes the passage?

   (A) One must be systematic, as this ensures that one will have excellent management strategies.
   (B) To be an excellent businessman, one should be rigidly systematic in one's work.
   (C) A man should be systematic but maintain temperance.
   (D) The benefits of organization can be felt in varied areas of life.
   (E) Systematic men will be respected in business for their organization.

105. The underlined and bolded word "slipshod" means more nearly in the context of the passage:

   (A) Bedraggled
   (B) Slovenly
   (C) incorrectly shod
   (D) Absent-mindedly
   (E) Painstakingly

106. Which of the following must be true in order for the author's claim to be valid?

   (A) Systematic methods always improve one's working ability
   (B) One can excel by performing one task at a time, or by taking short breaks between tasks
   (C) The most successful businessmen developed organizational strategies early in life
   (D) It is more important to follow a routine than an organization strategy
   (E) To be systematic, businessmen should utilize employees beneath them

PASSAGE 56

Question 107 is based on the following passage.

Price is generally impacted when wages increase due to changes in the value of money. Because of this, there is no discernible impact on profitability. Conversely, a rise in wages resulting from a more generous reward system for workers or from the challenge of obtaining the necessities for paying wages does not have the effect of driving up prices. It does, nonetheless, significantly reduce profitability.

107. According to the passage, what advantage is mentioned regarding the increase in labor wages?

   (A) A laborer will be rewarded for a difficult production of goods.
   (B) There will be no increase in what the consumer pays for goods.
   (C) The price of goods will be affected if wages are raised.
   (D) When wages increase, there is a direct correlation to the product's value.
   (E) An increase in wages results in a decrease in profits.

PASSAGE 57

Questions 108 and 109 are based on the following passage.

However, there are also important implications for capitalism itself; not only is the value of labor decreased, the value of capital is also diminished. In the classical model, investments in human capital and financial capital are important predictors of the performance of a new venture. However, as demonstrated by Mark Zuckerberg and Facebook, it now seems possible for a group of relatively inexperienced people with limited capital to succeed on a large scale

108. Based on the information in the passage, which of the following statements best defines the word "capital" in this context?

    (A) material wealth owned by an individual or business enterprise and wealth available for or capable of use in the production of further wealth

    (B) any assets or resources, especially when used to gain profit or advantage and the nominal value of the authorized or issued shares

    (C) the ownership interests of a business as represented by the excess of assets over liabilities and material wealth owned by an individual or business enterprise

    (D) the nominal value of the authorized or issued shares and the abilities and skills of any individual

    (E) wealth available for or capable of use in the production of further wealth and the abilities and skills of any individual

109. Including the example of Mark Zuckerberg and Facebook at the end of the passage achieves which of the following purposes?

    (A) It supports the claim that industry is becoming more information – intensive.

    (B) It illustrates the rapid growth of social media as an important component of modern industry.

    (C) It contrasts with the idea that the amount of human and capital investment in a company is proportional to the success of the company.

    (D) It suggests that a company doesn't have to be especially productive to be successful.

    (E) It supports the idea of getting more work from employees while providing lower salaries

PASSAGE 58

Questions 110 to 112 are based on the following passage.

Social entrepreneurship has become a vitally important concept in the business world. Global attitudes increasingly desire the promotion of the unselfish concern for the common good. Social entrepreneurs believe that business emphasis should be placed on the creation of social capital and not the traditional goals and objectives of industry that revolve around profit and return. Social capital is the value of social relations. It is engendered when entrepreneurs identify a pressing social problem and then use the principles of business and management to erect ventures that address these issues by way of social dialogue and collaboration. Thus, cooperation and social relationships facilitate economic results.

110. Based on the information given in the passage, what main difference can be inferred between social entrepreneurs and conventional entrepreneurs?

    (A) Social entrepreneurs build better relationships with clients than traditional entrepreneurs

    (B) Social entrepreneurs don't rely on the axioms of business while traditional entrepreneurs do

    (C) Social entrepreneurs are concerned with quality of life and traditional entrepreneurs are concerned with fiscal gain

    (D) Social entrepreneurs are more concerned with climate change than traditional entrepreneurs

    (E) Social entrepreneurs and traditional entrepreneurs are essentially the same

111. The author would agree with all of the following statements regarding social capital EXCEPT

    (A) Social capital is the product of collaborative problem solving

    (B) Social capital is the salient feature of social entrepreneurship

    (C) Social capital is a tangible feature of social entrepreneurship

    (D) Business management principles support social capital

    (E) Social capital has monetary value

112. According to the information given in the passage, what is meant by the term social capital?

  (A) The author does not give enough information to define social capital.
  (B) Social capital means building community.
  (C) Social capital means building relationships.
  (D) Social capital is synonymous with social problems.
  (E) Social capital is money created by people sharing in a concerted effort towards a common goal.

PASSAGE 59
Question 113 is based on the following passage.

In 1980, the federal government began encouraging academic-industry relationships by creating a uniform federal patent policy, allowing federal grantees to collaborate with commercial interests to promote inventions, and permitting universities to retain the title on inventions developed through government funding.

As a result, as many as 90 percent of life-science companies now have a financial relationship with academia. Corporate licensing of academic inventions accounts for more than $20 billion of the universities' annual revenue. In most cases, the researchers making the discoveries get some portion of the money.

Another recent byproduct of the increased privatization of research has been the right of companies under patent law to refuse to allow foreign competitors to create generic—and often significantly cheaper—treatments for life-threatening diseases. Poorer countries in Africa, particularly, say they need the less-expensive generic drugs to fight AIDS, leaving the federal government in the awkward position of equivocating between protection of U.S. corporate interests and global humanitarian interests.

113. Select a word from the following list that would be a better choice than "equivocate" in the final sentence of the passage.

  (A) Hesitate
  (B) Prevaricate
  (C) Pontificate
  (D) Vacillate
  (E) Abrogate

PASSAGE 60
Questions 114 and 115 are based on the following passage.

In the last twenty years trading on the stock market has gone from the stock room floors to computer screens. This has resulted in the rapid rise of high frequency trading, which researchers now believe leads to increased volatility in the stock market. High frequency trading makes it possible for large volumes of stocks to be traded in milliseconds, much faster than they can be tracked with the human eye. Multitudinous problems arise from high frequency trading, one of the most potent being the potential to disrupt the global economic balance more frequently and with little warning.

114. Based on the information given in the passage, how does the author intend to define high frequency trading?

  (A) High frequency trading is when stocks are traded continuously
  (B) High frequency trading is computer-generated stock trading on a grandiose scale
  (C) High frequency trading is computer generated stock trading
  (D) High frequency trading is stock trading that is done at a rapid pace
  (E) High frequency trading is when large volumes of stock are traded on the stock room floor

115. Based on the information given in the passage, what can be inferred about the global economic balance?

  (A) The global economic balance cannot be sustained if high frequency trading is continued
  (B) High frequency trading keeps the global economic balance at a healthy equilibrium
  (C) High frequency trading makes rapid and unforeseen fluctuations in the global market more possible
  (D) Nothing can be inferred about the global economic market based on the information given in the passage
  (E) The global economic balance was more stable before the introduction of high frequency trading

PASSAGE 61

Questions 116 to 118 are based on the following passage.

Countering the movement to shorten the workweek, an approach that has been gaining support in Europe, North America, and Japan, the government of Greece recently adopted legislation that allows people to work up to 48 hours per week. Greece based its decision to raise the maximum weekly hours limit on concerns about persistent low productivity and labor shortages, but labor rights advocates argue the new law is misguided. According to research, increases in working hours lead to declines in worker well-being, including evidence of more workplace errors, higher levels of illness and anxiety, and, paradoxically, lower overall productivity. The Greek government is not, however, insensitive to the plight of workers. Their reform also seeks to address pressing labor issues, such as unpaid overtime and undeclared work, that they believe harm workers financially; the scale of the informal economy that facilitates worker exploitation may present Greece with challenges that are no longer critical in the world's major economies.

116. The passage is primarily concerned with

  (A) questioning emerging research on a workplace trend
  (B) examining considerations underlying a legal reform
  (C) contrasting the methodologies of two academic disciplines
  (D) critiquing the Greek government's unconventional decision
  (E) advocating for greater awareness of worker wellbeing

For Questions 117 and 118, consider each of the choices separately and select all that apply.

117. The author does which of the following to dispute the perception that Greek lawmakers are indifferent to research on worker wellbeing?

  [A] She asserts the presence of factors that may affect aspects of well-being not addressed in the research.
  [B] She cites existing dangers to Greek workers that may be linked to dynamics not present in other countries.
  [C] She mentions an example to suggest that longer worker hours might not be correlated with burnout.

118. The passage implies that a shorter workweek creates which of the following possibilities:

  [A] Employers would enjoy lower costs associated with absenteeism.
  [B] Workers would spend more time cultivating healthy behaviors.
  [C] Companies would hire more workers to maintain productivity.

PASSAGE 62

Question 119 is based on the following passage.

According to a recent study conducted at the University of Minnesota, men spend more money when there is a dearth of women in their locale. Researchers were able to determine that U.S. cities with a higher male to female ratio had correspondingly higher levels of male debt. Consequently, men are much more willing to take financial risks and engage their consumer habits in the aforementioned areas than men in regions with gender equilibrium.

119. The author intends "a dearth of women" to be analogous to

  (A) An abundance of women
  (B) The rarity of women
  (C) A surplus of men
  (D) A total lack of women
  (E) A paucity of women

PASSAGE 63

Questions 120 and 121 are based on the following passage.

The tourist industry on the Mediterranean coasts of Spain has been under considerable criticism by local residents this summer. As the population on the Iberian peninsula triples with the influx of over 100 million tourists, transport and public spaces fill to the brim. However, it is local housing that is most impacted with tourist-accommodating condos gentrifying formerly affordable neighborhoods.

Residents have taken to the streets in hot-spot cities like Malaga and Barcelona in protest against the skyrocketing prices of rent that force many to move from their ancestral homes. Small businesses similarly cannot compete with multinational chains as rising property values push them out from central locations. Solutions are demanded for a more considerate and less disruptive tourist presence.

120. Based on the passage, "gentrifying" most nearly means

   A. renovating
   B. improving
   C. restoring
   D. modernizing
   E. exclusivizing

121. Select the sentence that states both the impact of massive tourism and the reaction of locals.

PASSAGE 64

Questions 122 to 124 are based on the following passage.

When creating a business plan for a nonprofit organization, one must make unique considerations. The purpose of creating a business plan is to outline how the business will operate and prepare for future adversities. For nonprofit organizations in particular, business plans should be easy to understand and present to those who are not intimate with the day-to-day operations. The nonprofit's mission and values should be at the forefront of the business plan, but it should also examine practical matters such as present sources of income, future sources of income, diversity in revenue streams, and plans for economic impacts. When formulating a business plan for a nonprofit, leaders should consider how much money they plan to receive from government grants and how much money will be brought in from alternative sources. Additionally, nonprofits must carefully consider their current and future expenditures. Sometimes, a "competitive analysis" is completed in order to describe other entities that deliver similar services as well.

122. Based on the passage, which of the following audiences is the author most likely writing to?

   A. A group of business owners who run a nonprofit organization
   B. A group of business individuals who approve grants for nonprofits based on business plans
   C. A group of aspiring business owners who are looking to start a nonprofit
   D. A finance executive of a nonprofit organization
   E. A group of aspiring finance executives

123. Based on the context of the passage, what is a "competitive analysis"?

   A. A required part of the business plan that analyzes other business that offer the same products
   B. A part of the business planning process that focuses on understanding weaknesses in competing companies
   C. A part of the business planning process that focuses on ways of acquiring customers that are currently working with competing companies
   D. A portion of a business plan that discusses other businesses in the area that offer the same products
   E. A required part of the business planning process that focuses on ways of acquiring customers that are currently working with competing companies

124. Which of the following is a major point being made by the author?

   A. Nonprofit business planning is different because it requires focusing on values while still analyzing practical operations.
   B. Composing a strong business plan can have significant impacts on a company's ability to handle adversity and overcome obstacles.
   C. It is crucial that nonprofit organizations obtain at least three diverse sources of revenue, rather than relying on one stream.
   D. A competitive analysis should always be completed for nonprofit business plans, but is not needed for other types of businesses.
   E. Creating a business plan for a nonprofit is much more difficult than creating a business plan for another type of business.

PASSAGE 65
Question 125 is based on the following passage.

Although professional women make up over 40% of the employees at organizations in the United States, they are still woefully underrepresented in the corporate upper echelons; only 21% of women serve among the ranks of business executives. However, in the post-feminism world this is not due to outright discrimination but rather covert bias. There is a strong pipeline of female talent that is fed into the corporate sphere, but women rarely make the executive suite due to high levels of attrition that typically occur after they have reached the management level. Many researchers claim that this is due to the fact that U.S. businesses make it extremely difficult for women to advance up the chain of command when they decide to have a family—U.S. businesses do not focus on maternity leave options for women that allow them to easily re-access the upper levels of the company.

125 According to the passage, in what clandestine way are U.S. businesses anti-female?

(A) U.S. businesses do not provide women with the professional development needed for career advancement

(B) U.S. businesses do not afford women the opportunity to the management level

(C) U.S. businesses do not provide women with maternity leave

(D) U.S. businesses do not equip themselves to deal with issues important to women in the workplace

(E) U.S. businesses do not place emphasis on family friendly policies

PASSAGE 66
Questions 126 and 127 are based on the following passage.

A paramount principle in being a good collector of debts is to never lose the goodwill of patrons. So long as one is on friendly terms with a man, one can approach him and talk over the matter. When a debt collector keeps in contact with their patron, this will make it easy to know when he is expecting to receive money. The time will come when he can pay at least a part or secure the claim. It is best to not lose sight of the fact that in this country, poor men sometimes become rich, and rich men sometimes become poor. Collectors should deal with them accordingly. It is poor business policy to permit well-to-do clients to run up big bills and at the same time hound the poor patrons.

126 The passage uses the word "paramount" to describe the principle as being

(A) problematic

(B) initial

(C) similar

(D) essential

(E) distinguished

127 All the following statements are true about the qualities that a good debt collector should possess EXCEPT

(A) Aggressive behavior and planning

(B) Preparation and courtesy of its patrons

(C) An advanced business degree

(D) Extreme generosity to patrons

(E) A complete understanding of the business

PASSAGE 67

Questions 128 to 130 are based on the following passage.

In today's world, selling a product can be incredibly complex. Unlike simple newspaper advertisements, modern commercials must break through the noise and captivate the target audience in just a few short seconds. There are many vital aspects of every advertising campaign, no matter what the product or service relates to. Most importantly, the objective of the campaign must be clear to the creators and the consumers. The business putting forth the campaign should know what they are trying to accomplish, and the customer should understand what the item being advertised entails. Next, the campaign must display a compelling message that speaks directly to the targeted buyer. The demographics and behaviors of those being reached should be well understood by the designers. Furthermore, a call to action must be included at the end of the advertisement. Provided that the audience has been adequately persuaded, they should know how to proceed.

128. Based on the passage, which of the following conclusions can be drawn about modern advertising?

   A. The most crucial aspects of the advertising campaign depend on the type of product or service being sold.
   B. More time and effort must be put into modern advertisements than has been needed historically.
   C. Reaching a massive audience is more important than pinpointing particular customers.
   D. Strong advertisements include contact information of the company at the end so that the customers can proceed.
   E. A clear objective, a compelling message, and a call to action are three equally important aspects of creating a strong advertisement.

129. Which of the following statements best summarizes the passage?

   A. The audience must know what to do after they've been successfully persuaded by the advertisement.
   B. The job of modern advertisers is simply to create a message that will be easily received by customers.
   C. Regardless of the product being sold, there are three specific and necessary aspects of an advertisement.
   D. Today's advertisements require less effort due to the capabilities of technology.
   E. Modern advertisements should consider clear objectives, the ideal audience, and how that audience should respond in order to be successful.

130. Which sentence from the passage best supports the idea that details about the target audience should be understood when creating a campaign?

PASSAGE 68

Question 131 is based on the following passage.

The newspaper is a private enterprise. Its object is to make money for its owner. Whatever motive may be given out for starting a newspaper, expectation of profit by it is the real one, whether the newspaper is religious, political, scientific, or literary. The exceptional cases of newspapers devoted to ideas or "causes" without regard to profit are so few as not to affect the rule. Commonly, the cause, the sect, the party, the trade, the delusion, the idea, gets its newspaper, its organ, its advocate, only when some individual thinks he can see a pecuniary return in establishing it.

131. Which statement, if true, provides the most strength for the validity of the conclusion?

   A. Many religious groups publish newspapers to tell about missionary support.
   B. Newspapers are designed to be attractive and interesting for the reader.
   C. Newspaper printing is one of the most dependable sources of income because there is always news happening somewhere.
   D. The price of newspaper subscriptions has risen 25% in the past 10 years.
   E. The new owners of the local newspaper are seeking the most relevant issues facing the community because they hope to increase the number of subscribers.

PASSAGE 69

Questions 132 and 133 are based on the following passage.

An audit is an examination and evaluation of financial documents belonging to a company or individual that is completed by a third party. There are three main types of audits. First, internal audits are done by company employees and used for managerial reasons. Second, external audits are done by someone outside of a company who can provide an unbiased opinion for stakeholders and decision makers. Third, governmental audits are performed to verify the amount of taxable income. The governmental entity known as the Internal Revenue Service, or the IRS, regularly takes part in governmental financial audits. Though often thought of as an unpleasant ordeal, one of the primary purposes of an audit is to ensure financial information is represented accurately, ethically, and according to the necessary standards.

132. Based on the context, which of the following words could best replace, "ordeal"?

    (A) Capital
    (B) Coincidence
    (C) Predicament
    (D) Amusement
    (E) Leisure

133. Which of the following assumptions can be drawn from information provided in the passage?

    (A) Decisions cannot be made based on internal audits.
    (B) It is expensive for companies to have an external audit completed.
    (C) The IRS is not involved in all audits.
    (D) Financial information is not the primary focus of most audits.
    (E) Multiple governmental agencies can take part in audits of certain companies.

PASSAGE 70

Questions 134 to 136 are based on the following passage.

When starting a new business entrepreneurs may decide to legally organize their company as a limited liability company (LLC) or a sole proprietorship. While sole proprietorships are appealing due to their simplicity, there are many advantages to conducting business as an LLC.

Perhaps the most compelling reason for forming an LLC over a sole proprietorship is the financial protection. In a sole proprietorship, the owner of the business is fully responsible for business expenses and obligations. So, in the event of a lawsuit or debt, personal resources are at risk. Contrarily, in an LLC personal assets are considered separate. Another reason for forming an LLC instead of a sole proprietorship is the credibility that the title holds. Because LLCs require more documentation and stricter procedures, consumers tend to trust LLCs more than sole proprietorships. Moreover, LLCs allow for greater options when raising financial capital than sole proprietorships do. Investors are more confident when funding LLCs, so sole proprietors are often challenged with larger business expenses.

For Questions 134 and 135, consider each of the choices separately and select all that apply.

134. Based on the passage, which of the following could be listed as potential benefits of forming a sole proprietorship instead of an LLC?

    [A] A sole proprietorship is easier to manage since all personal and professional accounts are under the owner's name.
    [B] It requires less documentation so more time and effort can be put into other aspects of the business.
    [C] Business owners are less likely to be in debt because there are fewer ways to raise capital.

135. Which of the following are minor points presented by the author that support the idea that LLCs are superior to sole proprietorships?

    [A] Consumers tend to believe LLCs are more reliable than sole proprietorships.
    [B] Overall, there are more advantages to forming an LLC than a sole proprietorship.
    [C] In the event of a lawsuit or debt, an LLC provides protection over personal assets

136. Which of the following is the greatest strength of the author's argument in favor of LLCs?

- (A) The author explains the opposing arguments and makes counterpoints to each.
- (B) The author provides multiple reasons to support the argument that LLCs are superior to sole proprietorships.
- (C) The author provides both the pros of LLCs and cons of sole proprietorships when making each minor point.
- (D) The author provides examples to illustrate each minor point.
- (E) The author uses highly technical business terms to convince the reader of subject matter expertise.

PASSAGE 71

Question 137 is based on the following passage.

Traditionally, the hierarchy of positions and titles within companies has been laid out using organizational charts. However, with modern businesses no longer following a classic pyramidal structure, organigraphs have been developed to meet the needs of more complex networks of employees. Organigraphs display how parts of a company connect with one another beyond who reports to whom.

Organigraphs differ from organizational charts because they use webs and hubs rather than simple, labeled boxes. This format better represents the possible routes that leaders of the company can take in order to get something done. Like using a map, managers can develop strategic options without the constraints of organizational boundaries getting in the way.

137. How do the first and second paragraphs relate to one another?

- (A) The first paragraph explains the need for organigraphs before the second paragraph outlines the differences between organigraphs and organizational charts.
- (B) The first paragraph explains the functions of organigraphs before the second paragraph explains the need for organigraphs.
- (C) The first paragraph describes how to use an organizational chart before the second paragraph explains why they are no longer needed.
- (D) The first paragraph explains the need for organigraphs before the second paragraph explains the functions of organigraphs.
- (E) The first paragraph describes how to use an organizational chart before the second paragraph outlines differences between organigraphs and organizational charts.

PASSAGE 72

Questions 138 and 139 are based on the following passage.

Many people aspire to open their own businesses, but pursuing a degree in business first can make an impactful difference in long term success. Business school may not be for everyone, but for serious entrepreneurs who desire a strong professional stance it is an important step. Having a degree in business can increase overall career flexibility. For those that aren't entirely certain what their future business will look like, obtaining a multitude of skills and credibility in numerous areas of business will be helpful. Additionally, attending business school can embed individuals in a powerful group of like-minded peers and mentors. Interactions with other aspiring professionals can increase preparedness for business interactions after graduation. Relatedly, one can gain experience leading groups in a safe and supported environment.

138 Based on the passage, which of the following conclusions can be drawn about attending business school?

(A) There are some benefits to attending business school, but it is not a necessary prerequisite for entrepreneurs.

(B) Those who obtain a degree in business are locked into a more specific route than those without a degree.

(C) Peers attending business school often have trouble working together due to the competitive nature of the discipline.

(D) There will likely be few opportunities to lead groups until after earning a degree.

(E) Obtaining a degree in business is a requirement before becoming an entrepreneur.

For the following question, consider each of the three choices separately and select all that apply.

139 Which of the following are minor points presented by the author in favor of attending business school?

A Business students can gain experience leading groups.

B Business students will learn an array of skills across the discipline.

C After graduation, business students are more prepared for real professional interactions.

PASSAGE 73

Questions 140 to 142 are based on the following passage.

Search engine optimization, or SEO, is the process of creating and enhancing content in a way that helps consumers find what they are looking for. The purpose of utilizing SEO is to increase the amount of relevant content being displayed on a website. Internet output is no longer a one-size-fits-all model. Rather, it has become a systematic and individualized machine delivering specific information to specific people.

Search engine crawlers, known as bots, dissect all of the content found on the internet by following internal links within and across websites. Then, the bots analyze the content on each page and develop an index. The index is then used to construct search engine results pages, or SERPs. These SERPs are organized using a ranking scheme that considers keywords, page loading speed, social media signals, and other metrics.

140 Which of the following best summarizes the first paragraph?

(A) Search engine optimization is used to individualize the content being delivered on websites.

(B) SEO works by utilizing bots to analyze content and build ranked indexes.

(C) Search engine optimization is done by using bots that can analyze and rank content in order to deliver more relevant information to people.

(D) SEO is the process of generating and delivering content that consumers desire.

(E) Search engine optimization allows for greater masses of people to be reached with one, consistent message.

141 Based on the first paragraph, which of the following can be inferred about the internet?

(A) SEO helps consumers find the content they are looking for.

(B) Prior to the development of SEO, the content available on the internet was blanket for all users.

(C) Bots are programmed by humans before operating independently.

(D) The utilization of SEO practices can occur outside of websites on the internet.

(E) Before the utilization of SEO, only irrelevant content was displayed on websites.

For the following question, consider each of the three choices separately and select all that apply.

142 Which of the following purposes are served by the first sentence of the passage?

A To outline the author's argument that will be proven throughout the rest of the passage

B To define the key term being discussed throughout the rest of the passage

C To act as a hook that grabs the reader's interest

PASSAGE 74

Question 143 is based on the following passage.

It can be challenging for new business owners to justify hiring a personal accountant when most accounting tasks can be completed by amateurs. However, accountancy is a demanding task with many opportunities to make mistakes, as well as multiple tricks to save money that may not be known to laypersons.

A Certified Public Accountant, or CPA, is an accountant who has completed required coursework and passed a certification exam. Hiring a CPA ensures a higher likelihood that bookkeeping and financial management will be completed at a certain standard. Trained accountants hold skills and experience to maximize financial benefits and find possible tax breaks. Plus, some accountants can help with marketing, technology, and legal matters as well.

143. Which sentence from the passage best illuminates the possible opposing arguments to the author's position?

PASSAGE 75

Questions 144 and 145 are based on the following passage.

The study of the economy is broken into two realms: macroeconomics and microeconomics. Macroeconomics analyzes how the broader economy operates including inflation, employment rates, and international products. This is often a primary concern of federal government officials. On the other hand, microeconomics examines smaller, individual markets and behaviors of single consumers. For instance, microeconomists may study changes in price for oil or automobiles.

Economics have not always been separated in this manner. The occurrence of the Great Depression propelled a desire to better understand how various factors influence the health of the economy. While early economists focused on maintaining equilibrium, economists now understand the need to understand the flow of goods, labor, and financial capital as well.

144. Which of the following conclusions can be drawn from the second paragraph?

    (A) The Great Depression led to setbacks in the field of economics.
    (B) Modern economists no longer think about how to maintain equilibrium.
    (C) The federal government is typically less concerned with the study of microeconomics.
    (D) The study of the economy has always been separated into two realms.
    (E) Studying equilibrium in the economy was not sufficient to prevent an enormous economic collapse like the Great Depression.

145. Based on the information provided in the passage, which of the following topics would not fall under the category of macroeconomics?

    (A) International trade
    (B) Social security
    (C) Recessions
    (D) National energy usage
    (E) Competition between two businesses

PASSAGE 76

Questions 146 to 148 are based on the following passage.

Business ethics are important for every company to uphold. Behaving in an ethical manner means doing what is right in order to keep workers safe, maintain integral intercompany relationships, and provide good service to customers. There are basic standards of ethical guidelines that exist in the business world. For instance, putting too many workers on one floor can create a crowded space that is uncomfortable and dangerous in emergency situations. Therefore, this would be considered an unethical practice.

Many unethical business practices are somewhat conspicuous and easy to avoid. However, others can be much more complex and difficult to navigate. Each individual organization should make a point to explicitly outline acceptable and unacceptable behaviors. It should be clear to management and employees what is permitted and what is considered unethical.

146. Which of the following words would most drastically change the meaning of the text if it replaced, "conspicuous," in the second paragraph?

   (A) Obvious
   (B) Imperceptible
   (C) Evident
   (D) Uncomplicated
   (E) Elementary

For the following question, consider each of the three choices separately and select all that apply.

147. Which of the following are purposes served by the example of putting too many workers on one floor in the first paragraph?

   [A] It helps the reader understand what a basic ethical practice looks like.
   [B] It illustrates some of the issues with making unethical decisions.
   [C] It provides a segue into a further conversation in the following paragraph about employee relations.

148. Which sentence from the passage best expresses the main idea of why business owners should behave in an ethical way?

PASSAGE 77

Question 149 is based on the following passage.

Leading a business is a strenuous task for even the most seasoned professionals. There are a number of skills that can be helpful when leading a business that operates in any industry. Six of the most crucial leadership skills are the abilities to anticipate, challenge, interpret, decide, align, and learn. All of these skills have been examined in leadership literature. Ultimately, an adaptive strategic leader is one who can apply all six of these essential skills at once.

149. If this passage were to continue, what would the remainder of the essay most likely be about?

   (A) Reasons that leading a business is so strenuous
   (B) Ways to learn important leadership skills
   (C) Other skills that are important to leadership beyond the six described
   (D) A breakdown of the six crucial leadership skills
   (E) Common complaints of seasoned business owners

PASSAGE 78

Question 150 is based on the following passage.

Many businesses recognize the importance of creating a positive brand identity including a strong social media presence. However, some companies do not fully realize how easily this can be done by using brand ambassadors. Brand ambassadors require little investment but play a major role in promoting product awareness and increasing revenue.

Brand ambassadors may be specifically hired, or current employees can be appointed for the role. Current employees may already have genuine enthusiasm over the company and find it easy to promote products among friends and family. Brand ambassadors are often confused as social media influencers. However, advertisement through brand ambassadors can be done online, but it may also be done in offline networks.

For the following question, consider each of the three choices separately and select all that apply.

150. Based on the passage, which of the following are points that support the author's argument for the use of brand ambassadors?

   [A] Brand ambassadors are not costly to hire.
   [B] Brand ambassadors require minimal training.
   [C] Brand ambassadors increase a desire for employment at the company.

Answer Key

Q. No.	Correct Answer	Your Answer
101	B	
102	C	
103	A, B	
104	C	
105	D	
106	A	
107	B	
108	E	
109	C	
110	C	
111	C	
112	E	
113	D	
114	B	
115	C	
116	B	
117	A	
118	A	
119	C	
120	E	
121	Residents...homes.	
122	C	
123	D	
124	A	
125	E	

Q. No.	Correct Answer	Your Answer
126	D	
127	B	
128	B	
129	E	
130	The demographics... designers.	
131	E	
132	C	
133	C	
134	A, B	
135	A, C	
136	C	
137	A	
138	A	
139	A, B, C	
140	A	
141	B	
142	B, C	
143	It can...amateurs.	
144	E	
145	E	
146	B	
147	A, B	
148	Behaving...customers.	
149	D	
150	A	

Practice Set 3: Answers & Explanations

PASSAGE 53: SUMMARY/PARAPHRASE

The passage is about the evolution of criticisms leveled against capitalism. The main idea is that critiques of capitalism tend to evolve to match the concerns of the day. The major points are (a) that critics of capitalism carry over many older complaints and (b) in light of current concerns about the environment and resource depletion, current critiques of capitalism claim that it is a danger to the world itself as well as its social structures. The main purpose of the passage is to inform the reader about the history of the ways in which capitalism has been attacked. The tone of the passage suggests that the author may be trying to undermine current critiques of capitalism by lumping them with earlier critiques - the phrase "this is not a new phenomenon" seems dismissive in the context.

101 **Choice B is correct** because the passage states that consumption leads to the exploitation of natural resources that are in high demand. Since the passage also states that consumption is a main focus of capitalism, it is thus a negative attribute of capitalism.

Choice A is incorrect because the passage does not in any way discuss consumption leading to the financial crisis of the late 2000s. **Choice C is incorrect** because while the passage mentions that market failure (a result of destabilized markets) is often seen as a negative attribute of capitalism, it does not directly link consumption with this specific issue. **Choice D is incorrect** because the passage makes no claims directly linking imperialistic oppression and consumption within the paradigm of capitalism. **Choice E is incorrect** because while it is true that consumption leads to the overuse (and waste) of natural resources, the passage does not explicitly state that consumption leads directly to wasteful consumer choices, even if the reader can infer this from the information given in the text.

PASSAGE 54: SUMMARY/PARAPHRASE

The passage is about the importance of time management in business. The main idea is that inefficient time management among higher management may lead a business to stagnate. The major point is that in spite of many platitudes about the importance of effective time management, many business leaders actually use their time poorly. A minor point reinforces this notion by explaining how poor time management affects a business. The purpose of the passage is to raise awareness of the harmful effects of poor time management.

102 **Choice C is correct** because while the author draws attention to the fact that sayings like "time is money" highlight a link between time management and money, there is not enough information given to conclude that time management skills are analogous to money management skills.

Choice A is incorrect because the passage pinpoints upper management as an area of a business where time is most often poorly managed, so the reader can infer that upper management is generally disorganized, since the ability to distribute time correctly is a feature of the ability to organize. **Choice B is incorrect** because the passage indicates that time management is a principle of business, and thus it can be inferred that businesses struggle to implement their theoretical maxims in practice. **Choice D is incorrect** because the passage claims that businesses lacking in time management skills also lack the ability to be self-evaluative, which often leads to poor leadership. Therefore, poor leadership is a major indicator that an organization is also deficient in time management. **Choice E is incorrect** because the passage points out that businesses stagnate when they lack organizational self-reflexivity, so the reader can infer that businesses do better when they are able to critically evaluate their own methods and practices.

103 **Choice A is correct** because people in upper management should be the most responsible and time-conscious given their position of power, but according to the passage, they are the party that lacks critical time management skills and hence the understanding of the principles of business management—a clear incongruence. **Choice B is correct** because despite the fact that people know how valuable time is, as evidenced by the aphorisms "time is money" and "time is of the essence," businesses still commit the crime of wasting time.

Choice C is incorrect because while wasting time may indeed lead to making poor business decisions, this is not a paradox; poor time management would logically lead to poor decision-making. A paradox would require that the result be in logical conflict with the original statement.

PASSAGE 55

104 **Choice C is correct** because the passage mentions that people should be systematic, but also says that they must retain balance in their lives.

Choice A is incorrect because the passage never mentions developing management strategies. Choice B is incorrect because the passage says that men should be systematic, but retain balance. Choice D is incorrect because this is true, but it is not the point of the passage. Choice E is incorrect because the passage does not mention respect for others; it suggests that organized businessmen will be respected, but this is not the main point of the passage.

105 Choice D is correct because it is the closest in meaning to slipshod.

Choice A is incorrect because bedraggled is not a synonym for slipshod. Choice B is incorrect because slovenly is a synonym of slipshod, but it does not fit the meaning of the sentence. Choice C is incorrect because it is not a synonym for slipshod. Choice E is incorrect because painstakingly is an antonym of slipshod.

106 Choice A is correct because the passage assumes that being systematic will always help people work better.

Choice B is incorrect because the author suggests that working on one task at a time is most efficient. The author does not say that taking breaks will help efficiency, so the validity of breaks increasing efficiency does not matter for this claim. Choice C is incorrect because the passage does not depend on people learning to be organized early in life. Choice D is incorrect because the author suggests that a routine and a way of organizing are both important. Choice E is incorrect because while this might be true, the passage discusses being systematic as an individual, so working with others is not relevant to the author's point.

PASSAGE 56

107 Choice B is correct because the passage states that an increase in wages due to changes in the value of money doesn't "drive up prices."

Choice A is incorrect because the passage doesn't directly mention rewarding laborers for the difficulty of production. Instead, it focuses on the effects of wage increases on prices and profitability, so this option is not accurate. Choice C is incorrect because the passage mentions that an increase in wages may affect prices depending on the situation. However, the passage does not suggest that this is an "advantage," as the impact on prices can vary. This option doesn't match the intended meaning. Choice D is incorrect because the passage does not establish a direct correlation between wage increases and the product's value, so this option is not accurate. Choice E is incorrect because an increase in wages and a decrease in profits would not be considered a strength.

PASSAGE 57

108 Choice E is correct because wealth available for use in the production of further wealth implies investing it, and the abilities and skills of any individual define human capital.

Choice A is incorrect because the second definition could be correct, but the first part is not correct. Choice B is incorrect because the first definition could be correct in a broad sense if one considered humans as an asset to a business, but the second part, referring to shares in a business, is not correct. Choice C is incorrect because the first part defines capital as the money that is left after the bills have been paid, not as something to invest, eliminating this as the correct answer. Choice D is incorrect because it defines an investment that already exists.

109 Choice C is correct because the phrase relatively inexperienced people with limited capital supports the idea that success can come from those with limited resources and experience, aligning with the model described.

Choice A is incorrect because although Facebook is likely information-intensive, this idea does not address the model of limited capital and inexperience leading to success. Choice B is incorrect because while Facebook is a form of social media, that fact is irrelevant to the point about how success was achieved under the conditions described. Choice D is incorrect because the reader is not given enough information to determine that Facebook is not productive. Choice E is incorrect because value and salary are not synonymous; lower value of labor does not mean that the laborers are being paid low salaries.

PASSAGE 58: SUMMARY/PARAPHRASE

The passage is about social entrepreneurship. The main idea is that social entrepreneurship is a form of doing business that places a higher value on serving the common good than traditional business practices. The main points are that (a) attitudes have shifted so that people now demand businesses to conduct themselves in a more socially conscious fashion and (b) social entrepreneurship is a corollary of these shifts. There is a minor point that socially responsible business can have positive economic outcomes, although it is not developed. The purpose of the passage is to inform.

110 Choice C is correct because it can be inferred from the passage that social entrepreneurs are more concerned with quality of life than their traditional entrepreneur counterparts, as their main objective is to use business as a method of addressing social problems.

Choice A is incorrect because the passage does not suggest that social entrepreneurs build better client relationships than traditional entrepreneurs. While it is true that social entrepreneurs must be adept at building relationships to promote social capital, traditional entrepreneurs can be just as skilled at creating client relationships for profit. **Choice B** is incorrect because the passage clearly states that social entrepreneurs rely on the traditional principles of business, and in this context, axiom is analogous to principle. **Choice D** is incorrect because the passage does not suggest that social entrepreneurs are more concerned with climate change. **Choice E** is incorrect because the passage delineates clear differences between the two categories, particularly in their conceptions of capital.

111 **Choice C is correct** because while it is true that social capital is a feature of entrepreneurship, the author would not agree that social capital is concrete or tangible; he or she describes it as the value of social relations, which in and of itself cannot be materially embodied.

Choice A is incorrect because the author states that social capital is engendered by social dialogue and collaboration, and thus the author would agree that it is a product of collaborative problem solving. **Choice B** is incorrect because the author states that social capital is the prominent feature that distinguishes social entrepreneurship from other business ventures and entrepreneurs, and would thus agree that social capital is the salient feature of social entrepreneurship. **Choice D** is incorrect because the passage states that the principles of business management are used to create social relations and social capital. **Choice E** is incorrect because since the passage states that social capital facilitates economic results, the author would clearly agree that it has monetary value.

112 **Choice E is correct** because the passage indicates that social capital is the monetary result of people cooperating and building relationships in order to reach a goal.

Choice A is incorrect because the author clearly gives enough information to define social capital, stating that cooperation and social relationships facilitate economic growth. **Choice B** is incorrect because the author intends social capital as capital in the traditional sense, referring to financial assets, and thus it does not mean community building. **Choice C** is incorrect because the author intends social capital as capital in the traditional sense that refers to financial assets, and thus it does not mean relationship building. **Choice D** is incorrect because the author intends social capital as capital in the traditional sense that refers to financial assets, and thus it does not mean social problems.

Practice Set 3: Answers & Explanations

PASSAGE 59: SUMMARY/PARAPHRASE

The passage is about changes to patent law. The main idea is that while the privatization of research was designed to promote innovation, it has had some adverse effects as well. The major points are: (a) the government allowed commercial interests and public institutions to collaborate and share revenues in order to foster innovation (b) firms now have the right to deny foreign competitors the right to produce generic versions of products for which they hold the patent (c) the exclusivity of the licensing process makes it difficult for poorer countries to produce generic drugs to combat diseases such as AIDS. The purpose of the passage is to raise awareness of a flaw in the way the patent process works.

113 **Choice D is correct** because "vacillate" means to waver between different opinions or actions, especially when faced with a difficult decision. This precisely captures the federal government's dilemma between protecting U.S. corporate interests and supporting humanitarian needs abroad. It conveys the intended meaning without the misleading connotation of dishonesty.

Choice A is incorrect because "hesitate" implies a momentary pause or delay in action, but does not fully convey the idea of ongoing uncertainty or indecision between two positions. **Choice B** is incorrect because "prevaricate" means to speak or act in an evasive or misleading way, often with the intent to deceive. This implies dishonesty, which is not necessarily suggested in the passage. **Choice C** is incorrect because "pontificate" means to speak pompously or dogmatically, which does not fit the context of internal conflict or indecision. **Choice E** is incorrect because "abrogate" means to repeal or do away with a law or formal agreement, which does not relate to the act of wavering or struggling between two courses of action.

PASSAGE 60: SUMMARY/PARAPHRASE

The passage is about changes in the way stock market trading is conducted. The main idea is that increased computerization in stock market trading has led to greater volatility in the global economy. The main points are (a) computerization has facilitated high frequency trades and (b) high frequency trading can disrupt global economic equilibrium without warning. The purpose of the passage is to inform and explain; the passage summarily informs the reader about the volatility caused by high frequency trading while explaining why this is the case.

114 **Choice B is correct** because high frequency trading occurs rapidly and on a massive scale with the assistance of a computer program.

Choice A is incorrect because stocks being traded continuously does not account for the fact that a high volume of stocks are being traded digitally, as is the case with high frequency trading per the information relayed by the author in the passage. **Choice C is incorrect** because while high frequency trading is computer-generated, this answer does not account for the fact that the author makes it explicitly clear that high frequency trading entails the rapid transference of huge quantities of stocks. **Choice D is incorrect** because it is true that high frequency trading means that stocks are being traded rapidly, but this does not account for the fact that stocks are also being traded digitally, as is the case per the information relayed by the author in the passage. **Choice E is incorrect** because the passage makes it clear that high frequency trading is done by computers and not on the stock room floor.

115 **Choice C is correct** because the information in the passage indicates that the global economic balance can be affected quickly and in an unforeseen manner by high frequency trading; thus, it can be inferred that this will lead to trends of irregularity.

Choice A is incorrect because the author does not indicate that the global market cannot be sustained if high frequency trading continues—only that high frequency trading is potentially dangerous to the global economic balance. **Choice B is incorrect** because the author makes it explicitly clear that high frequency trading has a negative impact on the global economic balance and thus does not facilitate equilibrium, making this inference inaccurate. **Choice D is incorrect** because the author provides sufficient information for the reader to make inferences regarding the global economic balance. **Choice E is incorrect** because the passage does not offer any indication about the state of the global economic balance before high frequency trading was introduced as a method on the stock market.

PASSAGE 61

116 **Choice B is correct** because it identifies the main purpose of the passage, which is to explore some of the factors that led the Greek government to adopt new legislation lengthening the workweek.

Choice A is incorrect because the passage does not focus on analyzing the validity of the research. It mentions research on the shorter workweek as an example of a consideration the Greek government might have disregarded in its decision. **Choice C is incorrect** because the passage does not explicitly mention academic disciplines or methodologies. The reference to research is generic, and the passage does not discuss any contrasting academic approach. **Choice D is incorrect** because the passage presents a balanced view of the Greek government's decision. It discusses views that question the wisdom of the decision as well as counter-vailing concerns that may justify the increasingly unpopular approach. **Choice E is incorrect** because the passage does not take an explicit position on the importance of worker wellbeing. It presents well-being as one concern underlying discussions about the length of the workweek.

117 **Choice A is correct** because the author introduces financial harm as an example to dispute the idea that the Greeks are "insensitive to the plight of workers." As described in the passage, the research cited links well-being only to workplace performance (errors, productivity) and physical and emotional health. **Choice B is correct** because the author suggests that financial exploitation of workers may be more prevalent in Greece than in "the world's major economies." This phrase refers back to Europe, North America, and Japan, countries where a shorter workweek is gaining support.

Choice C is incorrect because the author does not seek to disprove the research indicating a link between longer hours and higher rates of illness and anxiety. Instead, the passage shifts the focus to different factors, specifically those related to financial exploitation.

118 **Choice A is correct** because the passage indicates that, with shorter workweeks, employees experience less illness and anxiety. One could reasonably infer that employees would, therefore, take less sick leave. Put another way, they would have fewer absences.

Choice B is incorrect because the passage does not provide any basis for inferring how employees would spend their non-working time. The lower rates of illness and anxiety may result simply from less time in the workplace, regardless of how employees spend their additional non-working time. **Choice C is incorrect** because the passage does not provide any basis to infer how the length of the workweek affects employer hiring choices, only employee behaviors. The discussion of research suggests that shorter workweeks improve productivity, implying the same number of employees can produce more. Additionally, the reference to longer legal workweeks as a solution for labor shortages implies that some workers may not find short workweeks attractive, making it difficult for employers to hire.

PASSAGE 62: SUMMARY/PARAPHRASE

The passage is about the spending habits of men. The main idea is that men tend to spend more liberally if they live in a region with a disproportionately high male population than if they live in a region with relative gender equilibrium. The main idea is supported by the mention of a relevant study. The purpose of the passage is to inform, as indicated by the dispassionate rhetoric and clear summary of research findings.

119 **Choice C is correct** because the author uses this passage to discuss the implications of higher ratios of men than women on debt, and thus a dearth of women can be understood as a synonym for a surplus of men.

Choice A is incorrect because the word dearth is not synonymous with abundance under any circumstances, regardless of the author's intent. **Choice B is incorrect** because while rarity can be a synonym for dearth, in this context dearth is more indicative of a higher rate of men than women, and not simply that women are rare. **Choice D is incorrect** because a total lack of women would imply there are no women at all, while the author clearly states that there are women—just fewer women than men. **Choice E is incorrect** because paucity is synonymous with scarcity and thus does not adequately convey the author's intention that the dearth of women implies a surplus of men.

PASSAGE 63

120 **Choice E is correct** because the passage mentions a higher cost of living that "forces many to move from their ancestral homes," making the neighborhoods available exclusively to high-income residents or tourists.

Choice A is incorrect because "renovating" suggests making design reforms or improvements to infrastructure, which is not referenced in the passage. **Choice B is incorrect** because "improving" has a positive connotation that is not in line with the critical tone of the passage, particularly with the residents demanding more "considerate" treatment. **Choice C is incorrect** because "restoring" means returning to a previous state, as in an earlier time period in architecture or design, whereas the passage speaks about an economic impact leading to unprecedented and "disruptive" change that is a result of massive tourism.**Choice D is incorrect** because "modernizing" refers to cultural, systemic, or architectural modifications that typically include changes such as amenities and new features not previously available, none of which were mentioned in the passage.

121 "Residents have taken to the streets in hot-spot cities like Malaga and Barcelona in protest against the skyrocketing prices of rent that force many to move from their ancestral homes." In this sentence, the impact of over-tourism is a rise in housing costs due to the increase in higher-income accommodations and tourist-oriented apartments. This results in rent spikes for local residents and an untenable situation for small businesses. The reaction to this trend is a series of demonstrations in the streets of impacted cities, in which locals voice their complaints and demand equitable solutions.

PASSAGE 64

122 **Choice C is correct** because the passage discusses how to create a business plan, suggesting that a business plan has not yet been created and the audience is only aspiring to become involved in business. Also, the passage focuses on writing business plans for nonprofit organizations in particular. So, it is likely that the aspiring business owners in the audience are hoping to start a nonprofit.

Choice A is incorrect because if the audience were people who already owned business, they would likely not need to learn about writing a business plan. **Choice B is incorrect** because the passage focuses on writing a business plan, not analyzing a business plan that someone has already written. **Choice D is incorrect** because if someone was already employed as a finance executive at a nonprofit organization, then a business plan would have likely already been written because the business is already operating. **Choice E is incorrect** because, if the audience were only aspiring to become finance executives, they would not need to learn so much about writing business plans in particular.

123 **Choice D is correct** because the passage states that sometimes a competitive analysis is done, suggesting it is not a requirement. It also says that a competitive analysis, "describes other entities that deliver similar services." So, it simply talks about other businesses in the area that sell related items.

Choice A is incorrect because the passage states that sometimes a competitive analysis is done, suggesting it is not a requirement. **Choice B is incorrect** because the passage explains that a competitive analysis "describes other entities that deliver similar services," but does not make any mention of focusing on weaknesses of those companies. The focus of the competitive analysis cannot be assumed based on the information provided. **Choice C is incorrect** because the passage explains that a competitive analysis "describes other entities that deliver similar services," but does not make any mention of focusing on ways of acquiring customers who are currently with other companies. The focus of the competitive analysis cannot be assumed based on the information provided. **Choice E is incorrect** because the passage states that sometimes a competitive analysis is done, suggesting it is not a requirement. Also, the passage explains that a competitive analysis "describes other entities that deliver similar services," but does not make any mention of focusing on ways of acquiring customers who are currently with other companies. The focus of the competitive analysis cannot be assumed based on the information provided.

124 **Choice A is correct** because the thesis statement presented by the author is, "The nonprofit's mission and values should be at the forefront of the business plan, but it should also examine practical matters such as present sources of income, future sources of income, diversity in revenue streams, and plans for economic impacts." In this sentence, the author states the main idea while also outlining several of the points that will be addressed throughout. The remainder of the sentences in this passage touch on various minor points.

Choice B is incorrect because, although the author does mention that creating a business plan helps to "prepare for future adversities," this is included in a list with another purpose for writing a business plan. Therefore, it is not a major point. In addition, there are no other sentences that discuss overcoming obstacles or how a business plan results in getting through adversities. **Choice C** is incorrect because the author does discuss outlining diverse sources of income but does not mention having at least three sources. Also, this is a minor point that fits into the major point being made, which is outlined in choice A. **Choice D** is incorrect because the author explains that a competitive analysis is sometimes done, but does not specify which business should complete them or why. Also, this is discussed in one sentence at the bottom of the passage, suggesting it is not a major point. **Choice E** is incorrect because the author does not attempt to compare the difficulty of creating business plans based on business types. The author only mentions that nonprofit business plans come with unique considerations.

PASSAGE 65: SUMMARY/PARAPHRASE

The passage is about gender disparity in upper management. The main idea is that while women play an increasing role in the corporate world, they are far less likely to be represented in higher management. There are two major points: (a) that the gender disparity is not the result of explicit discrimination and (b) that the relative lack of women in high management positions can be attributed to a "covert bias" that can discourage women from advancing. There is a minor point that specifies an example of "covert bias": corporate policies on maternity leave that force women to choose between their career and having a family. The purpose of the passage is to explain - the passage tackles a known phenomenon and offers an explanation of why it is the case.

125 **Choice E is correct** because the passage states that U.S. businesses do not provide adequate maternity leave that allows for the successful re-entry of women into the company after their time off. This makes it difficult for women with children to balance family and work obligations, impeding their ability to rise to the upper echelons of business organizations.

Choice A is incorrect because the passage does not discuss professional development and in fact infers that women have adequate professional development based on their ability to rise to the management level. **Choice B** is incorrect because the passage states that the attrition of female employees occurs after they have reached the management level. Thus, women can reach management but are typically unable to rise beyond it. **Choice C** is incorrect because the passage does not state that U.S. businesses do not provide maternity leave; it only states that the maternity leave options do not allow women to easily reintegrate into the company. **Choice D** is incorrect because the passage does not mention anything about women's issues specifically; it focuses on maternity leave and its impact on women's advancement in the workplace.

PASSAGE 66

126 **Choice D is correct** because "paramount" means essential as the term signifies something crucial and fundamental, which aligns with the passage's emphasis on the importance of maintaining good relations with patrons.

Choice A is incorrect because, according to the passage, if someone wants to be a good debt collector, the principle they would follow shouldn't be problematic. **Choice B** is incorrect because the word 'initial' refers to something that occurs first in time or order. The passage discusses an ongoing principle in debt collection, rather than something that is merely initial or introductory. **Choice C** is incorrect because the passage does not discuss similarities; instead, it focuses on the importance of maintaining goodwill in debt collection, making this option irrelevant. **Choice E** is incorrect because there is no reference that this principle is distinguished, but it is important.

127 **Choice B is correct** because the last sentence specifies that good debt collectors should not "hound the poor patrons" and show goodwill towards the patrons. Also, they should prepare so that the rich will not run up bills.

Choice A is incorrect because the passage states that good debt collectors should do the opposite of being aggressive and show goodwill towards the patrons. **Choice C** is incorrect because there is no mention of needing a certain level of education to be a good debt collector. **Choice D** is incorrect because even though the passage states for good collectors to show goodwill, that does not mean they need to be extremely generous. **Choice E** is incorrect because the main principle explained is that good debt collectors should show goodwill and plan instead of knowing the business.

PASSAGE 67

128 **Choice B is correct** because the passage states, "Unlike simple newspaper advertisements, modern commercials must break through the noise and captivate the target audience in just a few short seconds." The passage also expresses that modern advertising is complex. In other words, commercials require more from the creators than in previous eras.

Choice A is incorrect because the passage states, "There are many vital aspects of every advertising campaign, no matter what the product or service relates to." Therefore, the crucial aspects of the campaign are unchanged based on the product. **Choice C** is incorrect because the passage discusses knowing the audience and speaking directly to a targeted buyer, not reaching a massive amount of people. **Choice D** is incorrect because a call to action should come at the end of the advertisement so that customers know how to proceed. However, the passage does not state that this should include contact information of any kind. **Choice E** is incorrect because the passage starts discussing clear objectives with the transitional phrase, "Most importantly." Therefore, the author feels that having clear objectives is the most important aspect of the three topics discussed.

129 **Choice E is correct** because it includes the three main points in the passage, which are clear objectives, target audiences, and a call to action. It also provides the main idea, which is creating modern advertisements successfully.

Choice A is incorrect because it does not summarize the passage overall, but only restates one point from the text. This statement only discusses one aspect of a call to action. **Choice B** is incorrect because the passage focuses on the creation of advertisements but does not discuss the specific job of the advertiser. Additionally, it is not a "simple" task based on the sentence, "In today's world, selling a product can be incredibly complex." This is emphasized in the following sentence as it contrasts simple newspaper advertisements with modern advertising. Furthermore, the remainder of the passage addresses the many considerations in an advertisement, not just creating a message that will be easily received. **Choice C** is incorrect because the passage states, "There are many vital aspects of every advertising campaign." Therefore, there are more than only the three aspects discussed in this passage. So, choice E is the better option. **Choice D** is incorrect because the passage expresses that today's advertisements are complex and require many components, not that they require less effort. Also, modern technology and its role in advertising is not discussed in the passage.

130 "The demographics and behaviors of those being reached should be well understood by the designers." There are only two sentences relating to the idea of understanding the target audience. The sentence prior to this is incorrect because it simply introduces the idea of speaking to a specific consumer. This sentence is correct because it supports the idea of understanding details of the audience by talking about demographics and behaviors.

PASSAGE 68

131 **Choice E is correct** because it addresses the conclusion that all people owning newspapers are more interested in the money than the cause. The fact that the new owners are hoping to increase subscribers (and therefore funds) is the most significant comment. The method of accomplishing an increase in business is based upon relevancy of the content of the paper.

Choice A is incorrect because it just illustrates an example of one reason to print a newspaper. **Choice B** is incorrect because it only offers a detail. It does not address the concern of the profits of the owner. **Choice C** is incorrect because, while it addresses some income benefits of printing a newspaper, it does not specifically compare profit with the cause for publishing newspapers. **Choice D** is incorrect because the increased price of subscriptions could help the newspaper owner earn more income. However, the response does not address the income of the owner. It merely states a fact that the price has increased, only showing weak support for the conclusion.

PASSAGE 69

132 **Choice C is correct** because, "ordeal," means a painful or horrific experience. So, audits are often thought of as unpleasant, painful, or horrific experiences. Similarly, "predicament," means a difficult or unpleasant situation. These definitions mirror one another. Therefore, "predicament" could replace "ordeal" without changing the meaning of the sentence.

Choice A is incorrect because, "capital," means financial and monetary assets. Although this passage relates to the concept of financial management, this word would not make sense in the context of the sentence because it has a very different meaning from the word, "ordeal," which means a painful or horrific experience. **Choice B** is incorrect because, "coincidence," means a remarkable concurrence of events without apparent connection. There is nothing concurring with an audit in this passage, so the word, "coincidence," would not make sense. It does not mean the same thing as, "ordeal," which is a painful or horrific experience. **Choice D** is incorrect because,

Chapter 3: Reading Comprehension

"amusement," means a funny or enjoyable experience. However, the sentence describes audits as unpleasant. Therefore, the word, "amusement," would not fit in the context of the sentence. **Choice E** is incorrect because, "leisure," means free time used for enjoyment. However, the sentence describes audits as unpleasant. Therefore, the word, "leisure," would not fit in the context of the sentence.

133 **Choice C is correct** because the passage explains three types of audits: internal, external, and governmental. The passage states that internal audits can be done by company employees and external audits can be done by third parties. Therefore, the IRS is not involved in all types of audits.

Choice A is incorrect because the passage states that internal audits are done for managerial reasons. Managerial tasks can include a variety of things including decision making. **Choice B** is incorrect because the passage does not indicate anywhere that audits are costly. It only states that external audits are completed by third parties outside of the company to share objective opinions. **Choice D** is incorrect because the passage expresses multiple times that financial information is the focus of audits. It states that financial documents are examined and evaluated, as well as the fact that the focus of an audit is to ensure that financial information is accurate. **Choice E** is incorrect because the text explains, "The governmental entity known as the Internal Revenue Service, or the IRS, regularly takes part in governmental financial audits." The text makes no other mention of additional governmental agencies.

PASSAGE 70

134 **Choice A is correct** because the text explains that in an LLC personal and business obligations are separate, but in a sole proprietorship the owner of the business is fully responsible for both. Plus, it is mentioned that sole proprietorships are simpler. Therefore, one benefit of a sole proprietorship could be the ease of management without having to worry about two separate entities. **Choice B is correct** because the text states that LLCs require more documentation than sole proprietorships. Therefore, it can be assumed time would be saved if an owner opted for an LLC and more effort could be put into other aspects of the business.

Choice C is incorrect because, although the text does state that sole proprietorships have fewer options for raising financial capital, it cannot be assumed that this would lead to the accrual of less debt. Having fewer options for revenue sources would not serve as an advantage.

135 **Choice A is correct** because the author expresses that the title of LLC holds more credibility and states, "consumers tend to trust LLCs more than sole proprietorships." Therefore, consumers find LLCs more reliable. This is a minor point because it is a part of a list of several other points that prove LLCs are superior. **Choice C is correct** because the passage states, "in the event of a lawsuit or debt, personal resources are at risk" in a sole proprietorship, while an LLC offers financial protection. This is a minor point because it is a part of a list of several other points that prove LLCs are superior.

Choice B is incorrect because this is the main idea of the text, not one of the minor points presented.

136 **Choice C is correct** because the author does provide pros of LLCs and cons of sole proprietorships when discussing liability, credibility, and raising capital. Of all options given, this is the greatest strength of the argument.

Choice A is incorrect because the author does not explain any opposing arguments, which would be reasons that sole proprietorships are said to be superior to LLCs. Thus, no counterpoints are given either.**Choice B** is incorrect because, although the author does provide multiple reasons to support the argument, that is not the greatest strength of the argument. Providing multiple reasons in order to make a point is a minimal requirement. Therefore, choice C is the better option. **Choice D** is incorrect because the author does not provide examples to illustrate the points. Examples would include stories of specific businesses, and no specific businesses are mentioned in the passage. **Choice E** is incorrect because the author does not use highly technical business terms but writes in a way that can be easily understood by most adult audiences. The only two terms that may be considered highly technical are, "LLC," and "sole proprietorship," both of which are explained in detail.

PASSAGE 71

137 **Choice A is correct** because the passage explains why entrepreneurs may want to earn a degree, but also expresses that it may not be for everyone and it, "can," make a long term difference. This suggests that it is not guaranteed to make a difference and is not completely necessary.

Choice B is incorrect because the author explains that obtaining a degree in business increases career flexibility, which is the opposite of locking into a specific route. **Choice C** is incorrect because the author expresses that students can become embedded in a powerful group of like-minded peers. This suggests that students work together and support one another rather than letting competition interfere negatively. **Choice D** is incorrect because the text states, "one can gain experience leading

Practice Set 3: Answers & Explanations

groups in a safe and supported environment." This indicates that there are opportunities during school to practice leading groups before graduation. **Choice E** is incorrect because the author expresses that business school may not be for everyone and it, "can," make a long term difference. This suggests that it is not guaranteed to make a difference and is not completely necessary.

PASSAGE 72

138 **Choice A is correct** because the passage explains why entrepreneurs may want to earn a degree, but also expresses that it may not be for everyone and it, "can," make a long term difference. This suggests that it is not guaranteed to make a difference and is not completely necessary.

Choice B is incorrect because the author explains that obtaining a degree in business increases career flexibility, which is the opposite of locking into a specific route. **Choice C** is incorrect because the author expresses that students can become embedded in a powerful group of like-minded peers. This suggests that students work together and support one another rather than letting competition interfere negatively. **Choice D** is incorrect because the text states, "one can gain experience leading groups in a safe and supported environment." This indicates that there are opportunities during school to practice leading groups before graduation. **Choice E** is incorrect because the author expresses that business school may not be for everyone and it, "can," make a long term difference. This suggests that it is not guaranteed to make a difference and is not completely necessary.

139 **Choice A is correct** because the text states, "one can gain experience leading groups in a safe and supported environment." This concept is not mentioned in any other place throughout the paragraph, making it a minor point in support of attending business school. **Choice B is correct** because the text states, "obtaining a multitude of skills and credibility in numerous areas of business will be helpful." This concept is not mentioned in any other place throughout the paragraph, making it a minor point in support of attending business school. **Choice C is correct** because the text states, "Interactions with other aspiring professionals can increase preparedness for business interactions after graduation." This concept is not mentioned in any other place throughout the paragraph, making it a minor point in support of attending business school.

PASSAGE 73

140 **Choice A is correct** because this sentence is concise but still includes the most important aspects of the first paragraph, which are the term, "search engine optimization," the idea that it is used to individualize content, and the fact that this content is delivered on websites.

Choice B is incorrect because it summarizes the second paragraph, not the first paragraph. **Choice C** is incorrect because it accurately summarizes the entire passage, not the first paragraph. The information relating to bots, analysis, and ranking should not be included. **Choice D** is incorrect because this sentence simply restates the first sentence of the paragraph rather than summarizing the entire paragraph. Therefore, choice A is the better option. **Choice E** is incorrect because it states the opposite of the information provided in the first paragraph. SEO does not aim to reach masses with one consistent message, but strives to deliver individualized information to specific people.

141 **Choice B is correct** because the passage explains, "Internet output is no longer a one-size-fits-all model," and that after the creation of SEO, content became individualized. Therefore, prior to the utilization of SEO, the content that was displayed was the same across the board.

Choice A is incorrect because it does not make an inference, but simply restates the first sentence using the information that was directly provided. **Choice C** is incorrect because it makes a correct inference regarding the information in the second paragraph, not the first. **Choice D** is incorrect because the passage does not indicate in any way that SEO practices could be used in other ways besides optimizing internet and website use. This is not an accurate inference. **Choice E** is incorrect because, although the text states, "The purpose of utilizing SEO is to increase the amount of relevant content being displayed on a website," this does not necessarily mean that previous content was irrelevant. Rather, it suggests that the content being displayed is merely becoming more relevant than it was previously.

142 **Choice B is correct** because the term, "search engine optimization," is clearly defined in the sentence by saying it, "is the process of creating and enhancing content in a way that helps consumers find what they are looking for." This term is then discussed throughout the rest of the passage. **Choice C is correct** because it is a strong sentence that captivates the reader before the rest of the paragraph provides additional background information.

Choice A is incorrect because this is an informative passage with no argument being made. The author uses no persuasive techniques throughout the passage. This sentence only serves to educate and interest the reader.

PASSAGE 74

143 **"It can be challenging for new business owners to justify hiring a personal accountant when most accounting tasks can be completed by amateurs."** This sentence is correct because the author's argument is that hiring a professional CPA is a better idea for a business owner than attempting to complete accounting tasks independently. This sentence illuminates the opposing argument because it is the only sentence from the text that does not support hiring a CPA. Instead, it explains that business owners can do their own accounting because most accounting tasks can be completed by untrained people.

PASSAGE 75

144 **Choice E is correct** because the paragraph explains that prior to the Great Depression economists only focused on maintaining equilibrium. This changed after the Great Depression. Therefore, they now understood the need to go beyond the study of equilibrium because it had been insufficient.

Choice A is incorrect because the passage explains that the study of economics developed after the Great Depression because it, "propelled a desire to better understand how various factors influence the health of the economy." This is the opposite of undergoing setbacks. **Choice B is incorrect** because the last sentence states, "While early economists focused on maintaining equilibrium, economists now understand the need to understand the flow of goods, labor, and financial capital as well." The phrase, "as well," suggests economists still focus on maintaining equilibrium in addition to the newer topics. **Choice C is incorrect** because it provides an accurate conclusion that can be drawn from the first paragraph, not the second paragraph. **Choice D is incorrect** because the text states, "Economics have not always been separated in this manner." Thus, there have not always been two realms of economics.

145 **Choice E is correct** because competition between two businesses would be a smaller scale topic that would fall under microeconomics. The text explains that macroeconomics examines the broader economy and, "microeconomics examines smaller, individual markets."

Choice A is incorrect because international trade would fall under macroeconomics due to its broad economic impacts across multiple countries. **Choice B is incorrect** because social security is used by millions of older citizens across the country. Thus, it would fall under macroeconomics due to its broad economic impacts across an entire nation. **Choice C is incorrect** because recessions, such as the Great Depression, would fall under macroeconomics due to its broad economic impacts across an entire nation and a multitude of entities. **Choice D is incorrect** because national energy usage would fall under macroeconomics due to its broad economic impacts across an entire nation.

PASSAGE 76

146 **Choice B is correct** because, "conspicuous," means something is clearly visible. So, the sentence is saying that many unethical practices are very easy to spot. On the other hand, "imperceptible," means impossible to perceive. So, if this word was the replacement the sentence would be saying that many unethical practices are hard to spot. This would make the meaning of the sentence opposite of the original.

Choice A is incorrect because, "obvious," means easily perceived or apparent. This is very similar to the definition of, "conspicuous," which is something that is clearly visible. So, if the word, "obvious," replaced "conspicuous," the sentence would still be saying that unethical practices are very easy to spot. **Choice C is incorrect** because, "evident," means plain or obvious. This is very similar to the definition of, "conspicuous," which is something that is clearly visible. So, if the word, "evident," replaced "conspicuous," the sentence would still be saying that unethical practices are very easy to spot. **Choice D is incorrect** because, "uncomplicated," means something is simple. Although this is not synonymous with the definition of, "conspicuous," it would still align with the point of the sentence, which is the fact that some unethical practices are easy to spot. Therefore, choice B is the better option. **Choice E is incorrect** because, "elementary," means something is basic and straightforward. Although this is not synonymous with the definition of, "conspicuous," it would still align with the point of the sentence, which is the fact that some unethical practices are easy to spot. Therefore, choice B is the better option.

147 **Choice A is correct** because the example follows the statement, "There are basic standards of ethical guidelines that exist in the business world." So, the purpose of this example is to illustrate some basic ethical guidelines. **Choice B is correct** because the example states that the ethical violation can be uncomfortable for employees and dangerous in emergency situations. Thus, these are some of the issues that result from the unethical decision of putting too many workers on one floor.

Choice C is incorrect because it ends the paragraph and does not provide a segue to the next paragraph in any way. The next paragraph does not discuss employee relations, but transitions to the topic of how companies can navigate ambiguous ethical boundaries.

148 **"Behaving in an ethical manner means doing what is right in order to keep workers safe, maintain integral intercompany relationships, and provide good service to customers."** This sentence is correct because it provides three reasons for behaving in an ethical manner. The other sentences do not explain overall why behaving ethically is important. Instead, they either state that behaving ethically is important (without explanation) or provide minor details supporting the claim.

PASSAGE 77

149 **Choice D is correct** because the focus of this passage is to introduce the six crucial skills and state that they are essential for strong leadership. It would make sense for the remainder of the essay to continue that message and break down each of the six skills in detail.

Choice A is incorrect because the passage starts with the sentence, "Leading a business is a strenuous task for even the most seasoned professionals." However, this is only the hook that leads into a discussion about leadership skills. Leadership being strenuous is not a concept that is mentioned anywhere else in the paragraph, so it is unlikely that the passage would go on to discuss it. **Choice B** is incorrect because the focus of this passage is to introduce the six crucial skills and state they are essential for strong leadership. The passage does not mention anything about learning these skills, business school, or new leaders. Therefore, it would make sense for the remainder of the essay to break down each of the six skills, making choice D the better option. **Choice C** is incorrect because the passage states, "There are a number of skills that can be helpful when leading a business," only to lead into the introduction of the crucial six. The remainder of the paragraph continues discussing the six skills. Therefore, it would be unlikely that the following paragraphs would transition to talking about other skills beyond the six. **Choice E** is incorrect because the passage does not relate to common complaints of business owners. It does mention, "Leading a business is a strenuous task for even the most seasoned professionals." However, this is only to segue into the discussion of important leadership skills.

PASSAGE 78

150 **Choice A is correct** because the passage states, "Brand ambassadors require little investment," suggesting that they are not costly to hire.

Choice B is incorrect because the passage does not discuss training of brand ambassadors. Therefore, this is not a point that is used in the text to support the author's argument. **Choice C** is incorrect because the passage does not discuss how brand ambassadors change a desire to work at the company. Therefore, this is not a point that is used in the text to support the author's argument.

Practice Set 4: Everyday Topic

PASSAGE 79

Question 151 is based on the following passage.

Lenny's Lemonade provides concession stands for large agricultural fairs throughout New England between the months of May and October each year. Lenny's Lemonade squeezes fresh organic lemons into filtered water and adds just the correct amount of organic cane sugar while the customer waits. Over the years, Lenny has developed a loyal following, and his lemonade is in great demand. In fact, last year, Lenny's sales increased twenty percent over the previous year. Lenny predicts that sales will continue to climb and has placed an order for twenty-five percent more lemons for the coming season.

151. Which of the following, if true, undermines Lenny's prediction?

   (A) The price of organic lemons has increased by twenty percent.
   (B) Last summer, almost all of New England experienced record high temperatures.
   (C) Sales of organic products have increased in stores across New England.
   (D) Fair organizers have announced a decrease in the entrance fee for attendees.
   (E) Fair organizers have increased the percentage of sales that concessionaires must pay to reserve their spaces

PASSAGE 80

Questions 152 and 153 are based on the following passage.

The number of homeless female military veterans in the United States has intensified, with rates nearly doubling between 2006 and 2010 according to the most recent government surveys. While it is true that this increase can be attributed to an overall increase in female representation in the U.S. military, the trend is nonetheless deeply disturbing. Women are particularly vulnerable since many have to care for young children and a lack of access to veteran shelters that also provide family services only compounds the problem—more women and children have nowhere to go while many male veterans can still rely on traditional veteran shelters.

152. Rhetorically speaking, the author is appealing to the reader's:

   (A) Logos
   (B) Pathos
   (C) Metaphysical sensibilities
   (D) Ethos
   (E) Political sensibilities

153. The reader can most reasonably infer that:

   (A) The United States military does not take care of its veterans
   (B) United States veterans are usually homeless
   (C) Gender inequality is a problem among military veterans
   (D) Women should not serve in the U.S. military
   (E) Female veterans of the U.S. military have more children than male veterans

PASSAGE 81

Questions 154 to 156 are based on the following passage.

It is an even thing: New York society has not taken to our literature. New York publishes it, criticizes it, and circulates it, but I doubt if New York society much reads it or cares for it, and New York is therefore by no means the literary center that Boston once was, though a large number of our literary men live in or about New York. Boston, in my time at least, had distinctly a literary atmosphere, which more or less pervaded society; but New York has distinctly nothing of the kind, in any pervasive sense. It is a vast mart, and literature is one of the things marketed here; but our good society cares no more for it than for some other products bought and sold here; it does not care nearly so much for books as for horses or for stocks, and I suppose it is not unlike the good society of any other metropolis in this. To the general, here, journalism is a far more appreciable thing than literature, and has greater recognition, for some very good reasons; but in Boston literature had vastly more honor, and even more popular recognition, than journalism.

154. The author uses which of the following formats to achieve his purpose in this passage?

   (A) Persuasive writing
   (B) Logical appeal
   (C) Narrative
   (D) Symbolism
   (E) Compare/contrast

155. According to this writer, in what way is New York similar to any other large city?

   (A) It is home to many writers
   (B) It treats literary work as a commodity
   (C) It is a center of commerce
   (D) It has great journalists
   (E) It has a stock exchange

156. Consider the content of this passage as you select the pair of descriptors that contrast New York City and Boston

   (A) Pragmatic versus aesthetic
   (B) Industrial versus agrarian
   (C) Competitive versus complacent
   (D) Stereotypical versus unique
   (E) Progressive versus stagnant

PASSAGE 82

Question 157 is based on the following passage.

Realtors in Commonville have noticed a marked increase in home sales in the neighboring town of Placeton. Additionally, those houses are selling for 5 to 10 percent over the asking price, which, in turn, increases the realtors' commissions. Last year, a home staging company opened in Placeton, and several homeowners have used their services when putting their houses on the market. The realtors in Commonville have recommended that their clients use the staging company and predict that not only will their homes sell more quickly but for higher prices.

157. Which of the following conditions weakens the prediction made by the Commonville realtors?

   (A) Realtors in Commonville use a variety of media to market the houses they are selling.
   (B) Homes in Placeton have consistently been priced below market value.
   (C) A large employer in Commonville recently reduced its workforce by half.
   (D) A majority of the homes in Placeton are ranch style, while a majority of the homes in Commonville are Victorian style.
   (E) Thirty percent of Commonville homeowners are single parents.

PASSAGE 83

Questions 158 and 159 are based on the following passage.

A fourth approach advocates using the power of the free market to improve public education. Supporters assert that public schools don't improve because they have no real competition. By giving parents vouchers that could be used for students to attend either public or private schools, parents could choose the best school for their child, and public schools would be forced to improve to compete. "School choice" programs for public schools are now officially part of the No Child Left Behind Act, which permits parents in failing schools to transfer their children to another public school. Only a few communities, like Milwaukee, Cleveland, Dayton, Fla., and Washington D.C., have attempted to include private and religious schools in their voucher plans. That raises concerns about the separation of church and state, but the U.S. Supreme Court has upheld Cleveland's plan.

158. Which of the following attitudes is a likely result of the lack of competition to enroll students in public schools?

   (A) Optimism
   (B) Pessimism
   (C) Complacency
   (D) Defeatism
   (E) Lethargy

159. In addition to concerns about separation of church and state, what other weakness lies in choosing a private or religious school in an effort to improve public education?

   (A) Students may have to purchase their own books and uniforms
   (B) Private schools do not have to comply with the No Child Left Behind act
   (C) Private schools may not offer extracurricular activities
   (D) Religion classes may be part of the curriculum
   (E) Private schools might not offer transportation to school

PASSAGE 84

Questions 160 to 162 are based on the following passage.

Debt is a hot topic and a major concern at all levels of American society and yet there is one group of Americans who are less troubled by the financial albatross that they bear than the rest: college students. Despite the high average student loan debt of $23,000 for graduating seniors, many students are not stressed about the money they owe—they in fact feel confident and empowered. Researchers attribute this response to student loan debt as atypical and evidence that college students see their education as an investment and feel that their level of debt indicates their commitment to opportunities for greater growth and later career advancement.

160. What can be inferred about American college students based on the information given in the passage?

   (A) American college students have high levels of student debt
   (B) American college students resent taking out student loans
   (C) American college students are not as heavily affected by debt as their older adult counterparts
   (D) American college students choose to view debt through a positive lens
   (E) American college students feel that debt is not an important issue

161. College students' attitude to student loan debt is best described as:

   (A) Naive
   (B) Predictable
   (C) Preternatural
   (D) Banal
   (E) Unexceptional

162. The author intends the term "albatross" in the passage to be analogous to:

   (A) The level of debt
   (B) The burden of debt
   (C) The stresses in American society
   (D) A bank account
   (E) Credit card debt

PASSAGE 85

Question 163 is based on the following passage.

Over the past few years, the deer population in northern Maine has declined significantly. Three years ago, a large landowner began clear cutting woodlands in areas of northern Maine, destroying underbrush that the deer feed on. Stopping the clear cutting will reestablish a healthy deer population.

163. Which of the following, if true, weakens the argument?

   (A) The large landowner has placed salt licks near the deer yards.
   (B) Five years ago, the state issued a large number of doe permits to hunters in northern Maine.
   (C) The landowner has plans to plant seedlings where it has clear cut.
   (D) The clear cutting has led to erosion which has caused soil to wash into a nearby river.
   (E) The state has employed more game wardens to curtail the illegal hunting of deer.

PASSAGE 86

Questions 164 and 165 are based on the following passage.

The year 1919 awarded coffee one of its brightest honors. An American general said that coffee shared with bread and bacon the distinction of being one of the three nutritive essentials that helped win the World War for the Allies. So, this symbol of human brotherhood has played a not inconspicuous part in "making the world safe for democracy." The new age, ushered in by the Peace of Versailles and the Washington Conference, has for its hand-maidens temperance and self-control. It is to be a world democracy of right-living and clear thinking; and among its most precious adjuncts are coffee, tea, and cocoa—because these beverages must always be associated with rational living, with greater comfort, and with better cheer.

164. If this paragraph were an introduction to a longer piece of writing, which of the following topics would logically be the focus of the next paragraph?

   (A) How the properties of bacon sustained the soldiers during the war
   (B) How bread served as the most important food item for the troops during the war
   (C) How important right living and clear thinking are to democracy
   (D) How coffee, tea, and cocoa are associated with rational living, greater comfort, and better cheer
   (E) How coffee, tea, and cocoa might have deleterious effects on humans

For the following question, consider each of the three choices separately and select all that apply.

165. Which of the following is a possible topic for the longer piece of writing that contains this passage?

   [A] Coffee has accumulated a number of honors throughout history
   [B] Throughout history, a number of relatively commonplace commodities have helped to make the world safe for democracy
   [C] Coffee, tea, and cocoa are essential to a world democracy of right living and clear thinking

PASSAGE 87

Questions 166 to 168 are based on the following passage.

Coffee is a brewed beverage prepared from the roasted seeds of several species of an evergreen shrub of the genus Coffea. Coffee is one of the most consumed drinks in the world. The earliest evidence of coffee drinking appears in the middle of the fifteenth century in the Sufi monasteries in Yemen. From the Middle East coffee spread to different places around the world and gained popularity as a drink.

The primary psychoactive chemical in coffee is caffeine, an adenosine antagonist that is known for its stimulant effects. Coffee also contains the monoamine oxidase inhibitors β-carboline and harmane, which may contribute to its psychoactivity. Although recent research suggests that moderate coffee consumption is benign or mildly beneficial, coffee can worsen the symptoms of conditions like anxiety due to the caffeine and diterpenes it contains.

Polymorphisms in the CYP1A2 gene may lead to a slower metabolism of caffeine and in patients with a slow version of this enzyme the risk for myocardial infarction is increased by a third to two thirds, depending on the amount of coffee consumed (2–3 cups and >4 cups respectively). Interestingly, paper coffee filters bind to lipid-like compounds, removing most of the cafestol and kahweol found in coffee, and might present health benefits compared to boiled coffee or espresso.

166. The passage addresses which of the following issues revolving around caffeine use and coffee drinking?

   (A) The higher risk to geriatric patients leading from coffee consumption
   (B) The long-term risks of psychoactive chemicals
   (C) The side effects of psychoactive chemicals
   (D) The reasoning doctors have for suggesting a limited caffeine intake
   (E) The knowledge needed for patients to choose to abstain from caffeine

167. The passage explains or implies the potential physiological effects of ingesting all of the following EXCEPT

   (A) harmane
   (B) caffeine
   (C) cafestol
   (D) diterpenes
   (E) monoamine oxidase inhibitors

Chapter 3: Reading Comprehension

For the following question, consider each of the three choices separately and select all that apply.

168. The author would most likely agree with which of the following?

    |A| Caffeine's stimulatory effect is somewhat mitigated by potential side effects.
    |B| Caffeine has made itself indispensable to humans.
    |C| People should drink no more than 4 cups of coffee per day.

PASSAGE 88

Question 169 is based on the following passage.

The rise in popularity of Oxycontin, an addictive prescription pain reliever, illustrates the challenge facing authorities trying to prevent drug use. The drug was first released in 1995, and its use has particularly spiked in the Appalachian states, which are more isolated from traditional illegal drug routes. Oxycontin is obtained through fake prescriptions, other people's legal prescriptions, theft, diversion from pharmacies and the practice of "doctor-shopping," in which people go from one doctor to another seeking multiple prescriptions. The problem for officials is how to separate legitimate users and legitimate prescription-writing doctors from addicts and dealers.

169. Which of the following, if true, might weaken the position that isolation from traditional illegal drug routes is the reason for increased use of OxyContin in Appalachian states?

    (A) Residents of the Appalachian states, where coal mining is a common occupation, more commonly suffer from painful injuries
    (B) There are fewer pharmacies per capita in the Appalachian states
    (C) There are fewer doctors per capita in the Appalachian states
    (D) The population density in the Appalachian states is lower than in other areas of the country
    (E) OxyContin is more expensive than other prescription painkillers

PASSAGE 89

Questions 170 and 171 are based on the following passage.

The debate surrounding the Second Amendment to the United States Constitution has the ability to bring out the pugnacious nature of American politicians and civilians alike. Gun control discussions often raise pulses, but more importantly, they underscore the myopic nature of the American civic milieu. For example, the Virginia Tech University Massacre in 2007 engendered public and political outrage and gun control issues took center stage in American public discourse. At the time, many Americans believed that gun control laws were too lax and that stricter regulations needed to be put in place to protect the public from firearms. However, in just five short years the gun control tides have turned. Americans have relaxed their opposition to and de-centered their focus from firearms control, likely resulting in the new laws that allow the carrying of concealed weapons in states like Wisconsin and even on university campuses, such as the University of Texas.

170. What overall message does the author intend to convey to the reader about American society?

    (A) America needs stricter gun control laws
    (B) Issues related to the Second Amendment typically do not concern Americans
    (C) American society is characterized by emotionally driven rhetoric
    (D) American public discourse is often short-sighted relative to civic issues
    (E) The Second Amendment is the cornerstone of American society

171. The author mentions "the pugnacious nature of American politicians and civilians alike" as

    (A) A way to show how confused Americans are when it comes to the rules governing civil society
    (B) A method of underscoring the belligerence of the American national character
    (C) A means of capturing the reader's attention
    (D) An argumentative strategy to convince the reader that Americans are aggressive by nature
    (E) A narrative rhetorical strategy to convince the reader that Americans are short-sighted relative to civil issues

PASSAGE 90

Questions 172 to 174 are based on the following passage.

Since the advent of robotics, an ethical quagmire has emerged regarding the ramifications of developing potentially dangerous metallic creatures. Concerns range from their intentional misuse for destructive purposes to their capacity to outwit their creators and take charge to destructive ends. Many allude to the laws of Isaac Asimov, a famous writer of science fiction and popular science, who saw AI as a looming threat to humanity, should it be possible for robots to one day emancipate themselves from their programmers and roam of their own accord. In anticipation of the mayhem that might ensue, Asimov wrote the "Three Laws for Robotics" in one of his novels, aimed to prevent any destruction such aberrations could cause.

These laws revolve around the idea that robots must never take action to injure humans, nor allow injury to occur. They must also obey orders and protect themselves to the degree that no harm is caused. However, while these laws theoretically ensure the human race safety from their electronic offspring, in many cases, they contradict the very raison d'être for which robots are constructed today: military engagement. Apart from the challenge of coding ethical considerations into machinery with a limited cognitive architecture, the real conundrum is: What is guiding the ethics of robotic engineers?

172 Which of the following statements expresses the perspective of the author?

(A) Although some may consider there to be ethical ambiguity about the development of robotics, such misgivings are generally misinformed.

(B) The ethics of robotic engineering have been addressed through the application of Asimov's Laws.

(C) Ethical concerns over the dangers of robotics are complex and difficult to address, given their application is intentionally harmful.

(D) Robotics are inherently ethically unjustifiable and pose an immediate threat to humanity.

(E) Ethical considerations impede the development of robotics, putting the engineering industry at risk.

173 In the first paragraph, the word "aberrations" most nearly means:

(A) physical assaults on human beings.

(B) deviations from expected behavior.

(C) a failure to function.

(D) actions programmed to cause destruction.

(E) activities under the control of malevolent engineers.

174 Which of the following is a major point in the passage?

(A) Science fiction authors, such as Isaac Asimov, have been visionaries in foreseeing the rise of robotics and predicting dilemmas.

(B) Ethical concerns over the dangers of robotics are further complicated by the fact that they are often created for the purpose of doing harm.

(C) An ethical framework should be programmed into robotic behavior to prevent potential injury to human beings.

(D) Robotic engineers need to be held accountable for any ethics violations in the field of combat when robotics are involved.

(E) There is an alarming lack of control over the development of robotics in the military industry that deserves closer ethical scrutiny.

PASSAGE 91

Question 175 is based on the following passage.

Studies recently conducted in Japan reveal that natural scenery, be it a forested area or even flowers in a vase, has anodyne effects on the psyche, reducing stress, and boosting resilience against disease. Scenes of nature have also been shown to result in higher levels of productivity and creativity in EEGs. Similarly, the wafting of natural fragrances, such as that of roses, has been linked to more relaxed states of driving when present in vehicles.

Psychologists posit that these positive effects are atavistic remnants from earlier times when human beings inhabited savannah-type settings scattered with greenery, which attracted their attention as places of refuge. By enticingly drawing the eye and pleasantly stimulating the olfactory sense, nature provides therapeutic benefits simply by being present.

175. Based on the passage, what conclusion can be drawn about exposure to nature?

    (A) Nature has a therapeutic effect only when experienced in the outdoors, as in the savannah or the woodlands.
    (B) Human beings, nowadays, have a deeper appreciation for nature than in previous eras.
    (C) Workers in offices with plants and flowers are more frequently distracted than those without.
    (D) Some patients in hospital settings with views of greenery recover faster than those without.
    (E) Strong smells emitted from air fresheners in vehicles lead to safer driving.

PASSAGE 92

Questions 176 and 177 are based on the following passage.

The number of homeless female military veterans in the United States has intensified, with rates nearly doubling between 2006 and 2010 according to the most recent government surveys. While it is true that this increase can be attributed to an overall increase in female representation in the U.S. military, the trend is nonetheless deeply disturbing. Women are particularly vulnerable since many have or care for young children and a lack of access to veteran shelters that also provide family services only compounds the problem—more women and children have nowhere to go while many male veterans can still rely on traditional veteran shelters.

176. Rhetorically speaking, the author is appealing to the reader's

    (A) Logos
    (B) Pathos
    (C) Metaphysical sensibilities
    (D) Ethos
    (E) Political sensibilities

177. The reader can most reasonably infer that

    (A) The United States military does not take care of its veterans
    (B) United States veterans are usually homeless
    (C) Gender inequality is a problem among military veterans
    (D) Women should not serve in the U.S. military
    (E) Female veterans of the U.S. military have more children than male veterans

PASSAGE 93

Questions 178 to180 are based on the following passage.

The ubiquity of microplastics continues to astound researchers as new sources of contamination seem to be discovered at an exponential rate. Most recently, the laundry machine has been implicated in the draining of millions of microplastics shed from microfibers during the friction of the wash, as well as from the centrifugal force of the dryer. These microplastics are often imbued with toxic chemicals, such as phthalates and bisphenol A, as well as flame retardants and other pollutants. All of these deposit into the sewage system, which, upon treatment, becomes part of the "sludge sewage" that is often applied to soil as fertilizer. Once contaminants enter the earth, they are easily absorbed by crops, becoming the covert ingredients of our meals. Additionally, even natural fabrics, made from cotton or wool, were also found to shed pollutants ensconced among the fibers, having collected them from the environment.

Even those who strive to be the paragon of sustainable practices—painstakingly opting for green products, used over new purchases, and low-footprint modes of transport—find themselves hard-pressed to countervail the cycle of contaminants produced in quotidian activities. However, a few remedies are advised to curb the shedding, at least come laundry time. Researchers recommend washing in cold water, less frequently, and avoiding the dryer altogether in favor of the clothes line.

178. Which of the following statements summarizes the passage?

    Ⓐ The shedding of microplastics from clothes items can be prevented by changing one's purchasing choices.

    Ⓑ Added to the myriad sources of microplastic pollution is the laundry machine, whose adverse impact cannot be avoided, only mitigated.

    Ⓒ Avoiding the microplastics pollution caused by doing the laundry requires a series of conscientious changes to behavior.

    Ⓓ Microplastic contamination in soil, and its subsequent entry into the food cycle, has been traced to a few house chores that were found to be predominantly the source.

    Ⓔ Those who pursue an eco-friendly lifestyle are responsible for fewer contaminants entering the environment that those who do not.

179. Select a sentence in the text that explains the final link in the "cyle of contamination" mentioned in the second paragraph.

180. Which of the following points would strengthen the position expressed in the passage?

    Ⓐ The use of "sewage sludge" additionally introduces other contaminants, such as medical byproducts and chemical additives, which seep into the soil of farmlands.

    Ⓑ Organic farming avoids the use of harmful pesticides, which reduces the content of crop contamination.

    Ⓒ Cities with improved air quality are shown to experience fewer pollutants collected on the natural fibers of clothing.

    Ⓓ Microplastic introduced into the ocean are often consumed by fish, thereby entering the marine, and ultimately human, food chain,

    Ⓔ Treatment procedures are able to clear some of the microplastics, however, with millions of particles introduced per wash, it is a staggering challenge.

PASSAGE 94

Question 181 is based on the following passage.

The term domestic violence generally conjures images of defenseless women being attacked by abusive and domineering men. However, statistics show that males account for 2 out of 5 cases of domestic violence; thus, men are frequently at the receiving end of abuse. Researchers also believe that these numbers could be misleading; in many Western societies, there is still a strong social stigma surrounding men being victims of abuse. Many men feel that it is socially unacceptable for them to display weakness or seek help in abusive situations. This may very well cause many cases of female on male domestic violence to go unreported.

181. The statistics relative to the domestic abuse of males are inaccurate because:

    Ⓐ Women in Western society stigmatize abused men

    Ⓑ Researchers demonstrate a bias that supports the feminist agenda

    Ⓒ Men worry that reporting abuse will negatively impact their relationships with women

    Ⓓ Statistics in general can never be 100% accurate

    Ⓔ Men worry that reporting abuse will tarnish their image

Chapter 3: Reading Comprehension

PASSAGE 95

Questions 182 and 183 are based on the following passage.

One of the major roadblocks impeding equal opportunities for success in the United States is low literacy rates. While many people often lump low literacy and children together as one problem set, experts estimate that nearly 30 million American adults have literacy skills that are "below basic." This phenomenon is particularly harmful because low literacy among adults engenders a cycle of literacy problems; the children of adults with low literacy are more likely to struggle with school, drop out of school, and live in poverty. **This is why literacy initiatives are such an important part of the fabric of American society: they help keep opportunities for success open to all individuals by fostering the development of critical language skills.**

182. The two parts in **boldface** demonstrate how the author

    Ⓐ Delineates the problems associated with low literacy

    Ⓑ Appeals to the reader's emotional sensibilities relative to low literacy

    Ⓒ Reinforces his or her beliefs as well as opposing beliefs relative to low literacy

    Ⓓ Reaches a solution to the problem posed in his or her original claim

    Ⓔ Makes use of paradox relative to low literacy

For the following question, consider each of the three choices separately and select all that apply.

183. The author would agree with which of the following statements?

    ☐A Low literacy is especially problematic in children

    ☐B Low literacy stonewalls equal opportunities

    ☐C Low literacy leads to higher crime rates

PASSAGE 96

Questions 184 to 186 are based on the following passage.

Proponents of education reform in the United States point to its abysmal performance in mathematics and science as compared to other countries, as well as its high dropout rate. There is a growing consensus among educators and parents alike that modifications to the current approach are in order. However, models employed by leading school systems, such as the one in Finland, present a different paradigm of learning altogether. One glaring difference is that while the US system relies almost exclusively on standardized testing, Finland offers a student-centered approach that bases evaluations on in-depth feedback from teachers, most of whom are highly qualified, holding a Master's in education. Teachers also remain consistently with each student year after year, permitting a stronger bond to form over time. In addition, school hours begin later in the morning, allowing adolescents to get a better night's rest, with ample time to rest and reflect throughout the school day.

Admittedly, mirroring such features in the US would require nothing short of an overhaul of its current structure, as well as mitigating related challenges. But while many find the prospect of upending the US model rather bleak, more sanguine supporters believe that gradual changes can be introduced to shift the culture of learning towards a more positive experience with superior results.

184. Based on the passage, what conclusion can be drawn about the Finnish education system?

    Ⓐ It is a facet of a unique cultural framework in Finland, which would make it difficult to implement in other countries.

    Ⓑ Lacking a standardized system, it prevents students from integrating into international universities for lack of a transcript equivalent.

    Ⓒ It is prone to teacher's bias, which leads to inequitable evaluations that reflect on academic results.

    Ⓓ It has based its model on exam-centered learning, which has resulted in superior scores.

    Ⓔ Despite being different to other education models, its students outcompete in academic performance.

For Questions 185 and 186, consider each of the choices separately and select all that apply.

185 Based on the information in the passage, what could be an alternative theory to high academic performance in Finland and other leading nations?

- [A] Students in other nations may not have some of the impediments to academic performance faced by students in the US, such as gun violence and food insecurity.
- [B] Students in other nations may be taught certain subjects that do not correlate with the US academic curriculum.
- [C] Students in other nations may have other cultural support, such as stronger family involvement, which translates into higher performance academically.

186 According to the passage, which is a minor point regarding differences in education systems?

- [A] In lieu of an entire makeover, piecemeal changes might help steer the US system in the right direction.
- [B] Although changes need to be made in the US education system, they may be more complex than anticipated.
- [C] Addressing academic performance and dropout rates may require the challenge of shifting the entire approach to education.

PASSAGE 97

Question 187 is based on the following passage.

By the 1890s Social Darwinist ideas were popular and were making themselves felt, influencing social policies in the United States and elsewhere. Social Darwinism saw human society as based on a struggle for survival, in which the superior, the fittest, would triumph and the inferior would be swept to the wayside. It was more or less the ancient "predator ethic"—the idea that might makes right, that the strong are entitled to oppress the weak—dressed up in pseudoscientific clothes. If the struggle for survival was the way of the world, then it was only natural that human society should operate in the same way. Social Darwinism also dovetailed with racist thinking: American segregationists used the idea to promote the second-class status of black folk as a positive good. In Germany, Ernst Haeckel took the idea even farther, using it as a framework to propose Aryan race-supremacy notions and German.

For the following question, consider each of the three choices separately and select all that apply

187 According to the passage, which of the following are examples of "predator ethic"?

- [A] Cyber- bullying
- [B] Involuntary commitment to a mental institution
- [C] Incarcerating people based on their race

PASSAGE 98

Questions 188 and 189 are based on the following passage.

Although guidebooks have directed tourists toward recommended destinations since the illustrated travelogues of the 1800s, today's travel influencers, aided by the surge in image-based social media and affordable airfare, have generated dangerous over-tourism. The impact of social media influencers as instigators of unsustainable travel patterns is evident in Japanese tourism trends. Influencers provide visual checklists of sites in well-known locations, spurring throngs of travelers seeking their own picturesque images to crowd into narrow Kyoto districts or Mount Fuji hiking trails. In contrast, influencers very rarely steer their followers to obscure destinations, where travelers could enjoy authentic experiences without the hordes. Additionally, influencer tactics—such as organizing early morning shoots with professional photographers—fool audiences about the ease of capturing pristine scenery unspoiled by masses of other visitors.

188 In the context in which it appears in the passage, "obscure" most nearly means:

- (A) remote
- (B) unseen
- (C) mysterious
- (D) little-known
- (E) strange

189 Select the sentence that describes a desirable effect that influencers could have that does not occur.

Chapter 3: Reading Comprehension

PASSAGE 99

Questions 190 to 192 are based on the following passage.

Studies recently published in European Health Journal refute the long-held notion that only prolonged exercise routines benefit cardiovascular health. Even as few as 15-20 minutes a week were shown to ameliorate chances of developing heart conditions, lowering the risk of heart attack and early death. To track activity regimes and gauge impact, healthy, low-risk participants donned wrist activity trackers that monitored instances of increased heart rates over the course of a long-term study. Subjects were examined periodically to check for the development of heart disease as they aged, and these findings were then correlated to their activity habits. A sedentary lifestyle and inadequate physical activity were shown to be effective indicators of disease development.

Also germane to the research was the way in which activity was carried out. Bursts of vigorous activity (defined as at a level that prevented speaking in complete sentences) as short as 2 minutes each contributed to improved outcomes, which researchers say, included everyday walks, house chores, and yard work. Such activity over time correlated with reduced mortality and heart disease. In addition to cardiovascular benefits, there was an evident decrease in the overall risk of cancer as well.

190. Which of the following statements would strengthen the arguments made in the passage?

    (A) The wrist activity trackers allow for long-term tracking, providing reliable, observational data for longitudinal studies.
    (B) It's been shown that the risk in heart disease, cancer, and death is inversely correlated to the time spent exercising per week.
    (C) Study participants were free of cardiovascular disease and cancer at the time of the study and were tested periodically.
    (D) The average age of participants was 62, and over 70,000 adults took part in the study.
    (E) The wrist trackers only measured vigorous activity that lasted for at least 2 minutes.

191. Which of the following is the best description of how the first paragraph relates to the second?

    (A) The first paragraph introduces the main idea about exercise benefits, while the second discusses some contrary findings.
    (B) The first paragraph discusses the importance of exercise, whereas the second explores other factors of a healthy lifestyle.
    (C) The first paragraph discusses recent findings on beneficial exercise time, while the second specifies the kind of exercise that is most effective.
    (D) The first paragraph explores some of the diseases caused by a sedentary lifestyle, while the second makes recommendations for healthier living.
    (E) The first paragraph presents the current recommendations for weekly exercise routines, while the second refutes them based on research conducted more recently.

192. Which of the following statements expresses an important assumption made by the researchers?

    (A) Wrist activity trackers were worn only when the subject engaged in vigorous activity.
    (B) No other changes were made by the study participants that may have contributed to their reduced risk of certain diseases.
    (C) Absence of heart disease and cancer in participants can be reliably determined prior to the start of the study.
    (D) Study participants were at risk for certain diseases due to their medical history and family background.
    (E) The wrist activity tracker does not contain carcinogenic elements and cannot cause heart problems from its impact on the radial pulse.

PASSAGE 100

Question 193 is based on the following passage.

Several studies on physical and mental health have indicated that the experience and expression of gratitude serves to extenuate feelings of stress, as well as reduce depression, regulate blood pressure, and ameliorate the quality of sleep.

The feeling of gratitude has been correlated with an increase in the release of the neurotransmitters, serotonin and dopamine, as well as the hormone oxytocin, which is instrumental in the forming of human bonds. In fact, actively noting people we are grateful to, as a morning and bedtime ritual, has been shown to promote a deeper sense of well-being. While it used to be considered that "biology is destiny," findings are now indicative of an updated adage that, indeed, "behavior changes biology."

For the following question, consider each of the three choices separately and select all that apply.

193. Which of the following statements is not a major point in the passage?

    A. Gratitude is a feeling that can be invoked at will, resulting in detectable positive changes in several indicators of well-being.

    B. Conscious effort to experience gratitude has been shown to result in numerous health advantages, making it a beneficial habit to form on a daily basis.

    C. Certain paradigms in the field of biology need to be reconsidered in light of new science on the impact of changing mental habits, such as feeling gratitude.

PASSAGE 101

Questions 194 and 195 are based on the following passage.

Current practices for curing meat stem back to ancient times when salts were applied to fresh meat for preservation. Such methods effectively inhibit the growth of microorganisms and delay rancidity. However, modern practices in the meat industry, ranging from the use of additives to preservatives, are repeatedly implicated in the rise of cancer cases within the general population.

In point of fact, studies have indicated that nitrates and nitrites, when used as salts in meat preservation, can both lead to the formation of nitrosamines, which are known carcinogens, thereby classifying "processed meats" as Group 1 products by the International Agency for Research on Cancer (IARC). This category is reserved for food items that evidence sufficiently links with increased cancer rates and are strongly recommended to avoid.

194. Which of the following statements best summarizes the passage?

    A. There is a need to discover healthier ways of processing food, as many preservatives used today involve an increased risk of cancer.

    B. Cured meat has traditionally been a health hazard, as any salt used increases the risk of cancer.

    C. Meat is able to remain fresh for longer times than before by virtue of certain salt compounds used today.

    D. Food processing today poses significant health risks due to the compounds used.

    E. The meat industry is implicated in the rising incidence of cancer patients as a result of the preservatives used in meat processing.

195. Based on the information presented in the passage, which of the following statements can be inferred?

    A. All meat products are categorized by the IARC under Group 1 for their likelihood of leading to cancer.

    B. The meat industry has been associated with more than one cancer-risk augmenting practice.

    C. Salt consumption of any kind is strongly discouraged by the IARC for its implication in cancer development.

    D. Nitrates and nitrites used in the preservation of vegan products do not increase the risk of cancer.

    E. Human ancestors in previous eras who consumed cured meat suffered from a higher incidence of cancer than those who did not.

PASSAGE 102

Questions 196 to 198 are based on the following passage.

Subsequent to organ transplantation becoming a viable medical procedure for replacing diseased or failing organs, questions over candidacy and donor policies have been under debate. Currently, a crisis of organ shortages and an antiquated system of donor-recipient pairing in the United States impede the system with a number of hindrances that lead to an exorbitant number of healthy organs made unavailable to recipients in need. Part of the issue lies in the informed consent required either expressly from the donor or, alternatively, from the next of kin to agree to the operation, typically at a time of duress from having just discovered the death of a loved one.

Presumed consent, on the other hand, a system underway in certain countries, like Spain, makes organ donations a fait accompli. While individuals can opt out of the policy for personal or religious reasons, the tacit understanding is that they participate. Although not a panacea to organ shortages, presumed consent effectively prevents the discarding of usable organs. In turn, these can serve to significantly extend life expectancy in patients with organ disease or failure.

For the following question, consider each of the three choices separately and select all that apply.

196 Which of the following statements accurately describes the relationship between the two paragraphs of the passage?

- [A] The first paragraph discusses an approach, while the second presents an alternative.
- [B] The first paragraph introduces a problem, and the second offers a way to address it.
- [C] The first paragraph introduces an issue, and the second explores the main challenges to resolving it.

197 Select a sentence which reflects the author's perspective that the system of presumed consent would be an improvement, if not a complete solution, to the issue of organ shortages.

198 All of the following are major points in the passage EXCEPT

- (A) An alternative to the US organ donation policy may considerably address the issue of organ shortages.
- (B) A policy of presumed consent allows individuals to opt out of becoming an organ donor.
- (C) Part of the issue with a policy based on informed consent is that donors have to actively opt in or relatives have to decide on their behalf.
- (D) As a result of the need for informed consent, a great number of potentially life-saving organs are unavailable.
- (E) Under presumed consent, fewer organs are discarded, resulting in more viable transplants that lead to improved patient outcomes.

PASSAGE 103

Question 199 is based on the following passage.

Ecological imperatives to consider the environmental impact of transportation choices have led to the development of micromobility units, as exemplified by the electric scooter. Emitting zero greenhouse gasses indubitably favors air quality and reduces contaminants from depositing into the environment.

Nonetheless, manufacturing and recharging burdens play a significant role in overall emissions, as the main sources of material and production energy remain based intensely on fossil fuels or even coal in some areas. Moreover, examining the modal shift, which is the mode of transport that electric scooters tend to replace, one finds an alarming ecological loss. Particularly in cities, it is seen that scooters are typically used in place of more sustainable means of transport, such as walking, biking, or the metro.

199 Which of the following best summarizes the passage?

- (A) Upon closer inspection, the use of electric scooters is not as environmentally friendly as generally considered.
- (B) Electric scooters manufactured in factories that rely on fossil fuels result in considerable carbon emissions.
- (C) In the absence of electric scooters, many riders would make use of a more sustainable form of transport.
- (D) Air pollution is significantly improved by virtue of micromobility vehicles.
- (E) Consumers considering the purchase of an electric scooter are advised to research its manufacturing plant and its pollution levels.

PASSAGE 104

Question 200 is based on the following passage.

Many ambitious souls have entertained hopes about immortality, a concept buttressed by the ever-increasing ages reached by supercentenarians. Mounting empirical evidence challenges the hypothesis that human longevity has no maximum value. Findings suggest that biology poses certain limits to aging that cannot be breached.

In fact, in studies of historical birth cohorts, mortality trajectories have shown a deceleration at advanced ages. While research on the topic is not yet conclusive, conservative estimates point to a "mortality plateau" at around 120 years.

200. Based on the information presented in the passage, which of the following conclusions can be made?

- (A) Current estimates for mortality limits do not take into account biological thresholds.
- (B) Mortality trajectories differ greatly in relation to location, lifestyle, and time period.
- (C) Analysis of historical birth cohorts are an unreliable method for extrapolating mortality limits.
- (D) It is possible that after more exhaustive research, the "mortality plateau" will be higher.
- (E) Prospects of limitless aging are corroborated by an ever increasing number of supercentenarians.

Answer Key

Q. No.	Correct Answer	Your Answer
151	B	
152	B	
153	C	
154	E	
155	B	
156	A	
157	C	
158	C	
159	B	
160	D	
161	C	
162	B	
163	B	
164	D	
165	A, B, C	
166	C	
167	C	
168	A	
169	A	
170	D	
171	B	
172	C	
173	B	
174	B	
175	D	

Q. No.	Correct Answer	Your Answer
176	B	
177	C	
178	B	
179	Once...our meals.	
180	E	
181	E	
182	D	
183	B	
184	E	
185	A, C	
186	A	
187	C	
188	D	
189	In contrast...hordes.	
190	B	
191	C	
192	B	
193	C	
194	D	
195	B	
196	A, B	
197	Although not...organs.	
198	B	
199	A	
200	D	

Practice Set 4: Answers & Explanations

PASSAGE 79

151 **Choice B is correct** because higher temperatures can explain the increase in lemonade sales. Record high temperatures occur infrequently, and expecting to sustain high sales numbers during an average summer may be too optimistic.

Choice A is incorrect because it is outside of the scope of the argument. It is impossible to say if this factor would have any impact on sales. **Choice C** is incorrect because the general increase in the sale of all organic products does not necessarily affect lemonade sales at seasonal events. In fact, it could make Lenny's lemonade more attractive to a number of fair attendees. **Choice D** is incorrect because it may encourage higher attendance numbers at the fairs. Visitors will have more money to spend on food and entertainment, so Lenny might sell more lemonade as a result. **Choice E** is incorrect because it has no predictive value concerning lemonade sales. Increased rent may force Lenny to raise his lemonade price, but the argument does not indicate that customers either choose or ignore Lenny's product because of price.

PASSAGE 80: SUMMARY/PARAPHRASE

The passage is about homelessness among female veterans in the United States. The main idea is that homelessness among female veterans can be attributed to a combination of increased female participation in the military and a lack of veterans' services targeted specifically at women. The major point of the passage is the problematic increase in homelessness among female veterans. There are two minor points: (a) that the increase in homelessness is partly attributable to an increase in female enlistment and (b) that traditional veterans' shelters do not provide enough appropriate services for female veterans. The purpose of the passage is to inform the reader of a problem. The tone of the passage suggests that the problem of homelessness among female veterans needs to be addressed. The passage implies that increasing veterans' services targeted specifically at females is a remedy for the problem.

152 **Choice B is correct** because the author uses the example of homeless female veterans not being able to care for their children to underscore the problem of homelessness among female veterans. This is a classic emotional (pathos) appeal that plays on the needs, values, and emotional sensibilities of the reader.

Choice A is incorrect because the passage does not appeal to logos, or logical reasoning, to make the argument regarding the increase of homeless female veterans. Instead, the author appeals to the emotional sensibilities of the reader by illustrating that homelessness prevents these women from caring for their children. **Choice C** is incorrect because the passage in no way addresses metaphysical concerns (i.e., fundamental questions of being in the world according to philosophy), and thus does not appeal to the metaphysical sensibilities of the reader. **Choice D** is incorrect because the reader is not provided with any information about the author's identity. Since ethos is an ethical appeal based on the reputation or credibility of the author, it does not apply here. **Choice E** is incorrect because the political level is not addressed directly in the passage, and therefore the author is not appealing to the reader's political sensibilities.

153 **Choice C is correct** because it can be inferred from the information given in the passage that gender inequality exists among U.S. military veterans. Veteran services are not inclusive of women and their children, thus leaving them more vulnerable.

Choice A is incorrect because the passage does not suggest that the U.S. military offers its veterans no services, only that these services are lacking—particularly in terms of helping female veterans and their children. **Choice B** is incorrect because the passage does not suggest that all U.S. military veterans are homeless. It specifically states that homelessness is increasing among female veterans. **Choice D** is incorrect because the passage in no way indicates that women should not serve in the U.S. military. It merely emphasizes that female veterans require more assistance. **Choice E** is incorrect because based on the information given in the passage, it cannot be inferred that more female veterans have children than male veterans overall. However, it can be inferred that more female veterans are responsible for their children than male veterans.

PASSAGE 81: SUMMARY/PARAPHRASE

The passage is about differences in attitudes toward literature in New York and Boston. The main idea is that although New York is a literary center, Boston society appreciates literature more than New York society. The major points are (a) New York is a center for writers and publishing and (b) New York society values commerce more than literature, while Boston society esteems literature. The purpose of the passage is to compare the attitudes of two major eastern cities toward literature. The author makes a latent assumption that his experience accurately reflects wider attitudes.

154 **Choice E is correct** because the writer is comparing and contrasting the attitudes of New York City's and Boston's regard for literary endeavors. The repetitive use of the word but is a standard tool for this purpose.

Choice A is incorrect because the writer may be making a case for his point of view, but he is not asking the reader to take some action, which is the point of persuasive writing. **Choice B** is incorrect because a logical appeal is a technique used in persuasive writing and not a format in itself. **Choice C** is incorrect because a narrative is simply a story and does not describe the author's purpose here. **Choice D** is incorrect because the writer has not employed symbolism to achieve his purpose.

155 **Choice B is correct** because the author explicitly states that New York treats literature as just another product that is "marketed," and compares society's regard for literature to its regard for "horses or for stocks." This commodification of literature is said to be typical of other metropolises as well, making this the best match for how New York is similar to other large cities.

Choice A is incorrect because although the author notes that many literary men live in or near New York, this detail is not given as a reason New York is similar to other cities. It's presented more as a contrast with its lack of a "literary atmosphere." **Choice C** is incorrect because while New York is described as a "vast mart," the passage does not make a direct comparison between New York and other cities based on being commercial centers. **Choice D** is incorrect because the author acknowledges that journalism receives more recognition in New York, but this is not cited as a point of similarity with other cities. **Choice E** is incorrect because the mention of stocks is used metaphorically to describe society's interests, not as a literal comparison involving a stock exchange, and there is no assertion that all large cities share this trait.

156 **Choice A is correct** because New York City has a more pragmatic or practical attitude toward the literary world; it cares more for the factual reporting of journalism than it does for the aesthetics of great literature. Boston, on the other hand, is more enamored of literature than journalism, preferring its aesthetic sensibilities.

Choice B is incorrect because the reader may conclude that New York is industrial in focus, but there is no evidence that Boston is an agrarian, or agricultural, city. **Choice C** is incorrect because there is no evidence that New York is more competitive than Boston in any sense. **Choice D** is incorrect because although the author reveals contrasts between the two cities, he makes no mention of New York being a stereotypical American city or that Boston is one of a kind. **Choice E** is incorrect because Boston is not described as being less progressive than New York, simply different from New York.

PASSAGE 82

157 **Choice C is correct** because the economy of Commonville has suffered a serious blow. It is not likely that any type of marketing, including home staging, will help homeowners sell their homes more quickly and for higher prices.

Choice A is incorrect because using a variety of media makes real estate inventory more visible to the public. If sellers use the staging service, they will want the results to be visible in every medium used by the realtors. **Choice B** is incorrect because it does not address the advantages or disadvantages of home staging and does not relate to results that Commonville residents can expect from staging their homes. **Choice D** is incorrect because the argument does not reveal what style of home the staging company provides its services to. If staging is the difference between a quick sale or having a home sit on the market for several months, the style of home is irrelevant. **Choice E** is incorrect because it doesn't provide enough information. Without knowing the incomes of the single parents or how many children are in their care, the reader cannot discount them as potential buyers.

PASSAGE 83: SUMMARY/PARAPHRASE

The passage is about methods for improving outcomes in primary education. The main idea is that introducing a market system to primary education might be one way to improve outcomes. The main points: (a) that a voucher system will make primary education a free market and (b) that market forces will pressure underperforming public schools to improve their performance vis a vis their better-performing peers in order to compete. There is a minor point that some districts have tried to include private and even parochial schools in their voucher program, raising a potential constitutional issue regarding separation of church and state. The main purpose of the passage is to inform the reader about an approach to improving outcomes in primary education: while the issue is often a charged one, the passage presents relevant information without clearly espousing a position.

158 **Choice C is correct** because when there is no sense of urgency to improve the way a business or school operates, that institution may suffer from complacency. When schools have a captive student body with nowhere else to go, there is a temptation to think, "We're doing all right." It is easy to become complacent, or satisfied with the status quo. Only when a school is striving to improve and is seeing some progress is there a reason to feel optimistic. Conversely, a school that is trying to improve and failing has reason to feel pessimistic or defeated.

Choice A is incorrect because lack of competition does not necessarily lead to the qualities implied by this choice. **Choice B** is incorrect because lack of competition alone does not produce this outcome in the context of school performance. **Choice D** is incorrect because lethargy implies a lack of energy, which may result from complacency, but it is not the most accurate or direct effect. **Choice E** is incorrect because it is not the best choice; complacency more directly fits the described situation.

159 **Choice B is correct** because if the purpose of the voucher system is to ensure that students receive the best educational opportunities, then private schools that attract students under this system should be required to conform to the guidelines set by the No Child Left Behind Act. There is no oversight to ensure that private schools offer a curriculum superior to that of public schools.

Choice A is incorrect because parents are not obligated to select a private school and may choose not to do so due to additional expenses such as books and uniforms. **Choice C** is incorrect because extracurricular activities are not a valid measure of the quality of education provided by a school. **Choice D** is incorrect because parents are typically aware of religion courses offered at religious schools and can choose to enroll their children elsewhere if they disagree with the curriculum. **Choice E** is incorrect because the same reasoning applies—parents have the choice to avoid schools that offer content they do not support.

PASSAGE 84: SUMMARY/PARAPHRASE

The passage is about college students' attitudes toward their student loan debt. The main idea is that college students have an unusual attitude about their debt burden. There are two major points: (a) students are optimistic about their ability to use their education to succeed, and thus inclined to take a positive view of their debt. There is also an implied point (b) that most other Americans who are in debt do not share this positive view of their debt. There is a minor point that student views on empowerment through education are a key influence on their feelings about their debt burden. The main purpose of the passage is to point out an atypical attitude within the broader context of how people respond to being in debt.

160 **Choice D is correct** because the passage states that American college students view student loan debt as a way of advancing their careers and opportunities. This suggests that they are choosing to see debt in a positive light, viewing it as an investment in their future.

Choice A is incorrect because this answer is not an inference about American college students; it is a fact taken directly from the passage. **Choice B** is incorrect because the passage indicates that American college students see debt as a positive thing because it signifies their commitment to the future and provides access to a wider array of opportunities, not as an inherently positive thing in all circumstances. **Choice C** is incorrect because the passage does not provide enough information to compare American college students' debt levels to other adults, and it clearly states that American college students are heavily impacted by their high levels of student loan debt. **Choice E** is incorrect because while the passage shows that American college students do not view student loan debt negatively, it does not indicate that they feel the issue of debt is unimportant—it simply suggests they do not view it as a negative aspect of their experience.

161 **Choice C is correct** because the passage states that researchers view students' reaction to their debt level as atypical or unusual, and since preternatural means unusual, it is a synonym for atypical. This accurately reflects the attitude of college students.

Choice A is incorrect because the term naïve means child-like or inexperienced, which does not align with the passage's description of students' reactions as atypical or unusual. **Choice B** is incorrect because the term predictable means reliable or typical, which contradicts the passage's description of students' reaction as atypical or unusual. **Choice D** is incorrect because the term banal means trite or commonplace, which is the opposite of atypical and does not accurately reflect the attitude of college students. **Choice E** is incorrect because the term unexceptional means typical or usual, which directly contradicts the description in the passage of students' reaction being atypical or unusual.

162 **Choice B is correct** because an albatross is a figure of speech for a burden, and in the passage, it is used to symbolize the burden of debt.

Choice A is incorrect because an albatross cannot represent a specific amount of debt, as it is a metaphor for a burden rather than a numerical value. **Choice C** is incorrect because while an albatross symbolizes a burden, it is not used in the passage to represent the stresses in American society. **Choice D** is incorrect because substituting bank account for albatross would not be logical in the passage. The term albatross represents a burden, while a bank account does not convey the same figurative meaning. **Choice E** is incorrect because while credit card debt is a type of debt and can be seen as a burden, the passage does not specifically mention credit card debt. Therefore, it cannot be substituted for albatross in the passage.

Chapter 3: Reading Comprehension

PASSAGE 85

163 **Choice B is correct** because it logically follows that hunters being given more permits to hunt five years ago would have affected the number of fawns born in the subsequent spring, as it would take a few years to restore the deer population to its prior numbers.

Choice A is incorrect because it is outside the scope of the argument. Salt licks cannot replace the deer's primary food sources, and the passage does not discuss this issue. **Choice C** is incorrect because it does not address the issue of clear-cutting. There is not enough information provided in the passage to suggest that clear-cutting occurred near the deer's food sources. **Choice D** is incorrect because erosion of soil into a nearby river does not directly address the availability of food for the deer. The passage focuses on deer population and hunting permits, not soil erosion. **Choice E** is incorrect because the passage does not discuss illegal hunting nor specify where game wardens will monitor for illegal hunting, making this answer irrelevant to the argument.

PASSAGE 86: SUMMARY/PARAPHRASE

The passage is about public perceptions of coffee. The main idea is that coffee is a symbol of American values. The major points are (a) that an American general remarked that coffee helped the allies win WWI and (b) that coffee is associated with temperance and rationality, qualities needed for the functioning of democracy. The purpose of the passage is to celebrate coffee, and to associate coffee with what the author thinks are essential values of democracy.

164 **Choice D is correct** because it is typical of good writing for the last sentence of a paragraph to preview the content of the next. The sentence in question hints that the next paragraph will provide an explanation or examples of the benefits of coffee, tea, and cocoa, making D the most logical choice.

Choice A is incorrect because bacon is only mentioned briefly in the second sentence of the passage, and there is no reason to believe the writer will return to this topic in the following paragraph. **Choice B** is incorrect because bread, like bacon, is only mentioned briefly earlier in the passage, and the next paragraph is more likely to focus on coffee, tea, and cocoa rather than bread. **Choice C** is incorrect because the passage suggests the writer extols the benefits of coffee, tea, and cocoa, rather than implying these beverages contribute to clear thinking and right living as a result of the other way around. **Choice E** is incorrect because the passage does not focus on the negative effects of coffee, tea, and cocoa, so it is unlikely that the next paragraph will explore harm rather than benefits.

165 **Choice A is correct** because the passage begins by discussing how coffee was honored in 1919 and mentions its significance in the context of the World War. This suggests that a possible larger topic could be the historical honors coffee has received. **Choice B is correct** because the passage implies that coffee, along with tea and cocoa, is important in the context of making the world "safe for democracy," connecting these beverages to the larger theme of commodities helping to foster global peace and democracy. The mention of coffee alongside other beverages could be part of a larger discussion of commodities with historical significance. **Choice C is correct** because the passage emphasizes coffee, tea, and cocoa as being associated with rational living and democracy, suggesting that a longer piece of writing could focus on how these beverages are essential to a world democracy founded on right living and clear thinking.

PASSAGE 87

166 **Choice C is correct** as the passage mentions side effects such as anxiety.

Choice A is incorrect, as the passage does not focus on older patients. **Choice B** is incorrect, as the passage does not mention long-term risks. **Choice D** is incorrect, as the passage does not say anything about doctors' suggestions to drink coffee or not to drink coffee. **Choice E** is incorrect, as the passage does not advocate abstaining from caffeine.

167 **Choice C is correct** the passage implies that there may be some benefit to removing cafestol, but does not suggest or imply the physiological effects of this compound.

Choice A is incorrect, as the passage mentions that harmane may be psychoactive. **Choice B** is incorrect, as the passage suggests caffeine may worsen anxiety. **Choice D** is incorrect, as the passage mentions that diterpenes may worsen anxiety. **Choice E** is incorrect. Monoamine oxidase inhibitors are the general class of potentially psychoactive compounds to which harmane belongs.

168 **Choice A is correct** as the passage describes the general popularity of coffee but then notes some possible undesirable side-effects.

Choice B is incorrect, as while the drink may be the most popular drink worldwide, it is not a necessity. **Choice C** is incorrect, as four or more cups can lead to a risk for only certain people and the author stops short of actually recommending this limit.

PASSAGE 88: SUMMARY/PARAPHRASE

The passage is about prescription drug abuse. The main idea is that the difficulty of determining legitimate drug use from abuse makes the prevention of prescription drug abuse difficult. The major point is that prescription drug abusers can obtain the drug in a variety of ways, many of them difficult to distinguish from proper use. The purpose of the passage is to illustrate the difficulties authorities face in preventing prescription drug abuse.

169 **Choice A is correct** because the lower number of pharmacies and doctors in Appalachian states could lead to reduced access to prescription drugs like OxyContin, thereby decreasing overall drug use in the area.

Choice B is incorrect because a lower number of pharmacies and doctors would not necessarily lead to an increase in the use of prescription drugs. In fact, fewer providers would likely decrease availability and use. **Choice C** is incorrect because population density is not directly related to the rate of drug use. Drug use is typically measured per capita, so it wouldn't matter how densely or sparsely populated an area is. **Choice D** is incorrect because the cost of OxyContin doesn't directly impact its likelihood of abuse. Drugs can be abused regardless of their price, and the passage doesn't provide evidence supporting the idea that the drug's cost is a significant factor in abuse. **Choice E** is incorrect because a spike in the use of OxyContin does not necessarily imply abuse. It may simply mean that people in the region now have access to a more effective painkiller, and the increase in use could be due to legitimate medical reasons.

PASSAGE 89: SUMMARY/PARAPHRASE

The passage is focused on the gun control debate in the United States. The main idea of the passage is that the debate over gun control is a good example of the short-sighted nature of American civic discourse. The major point of the passage is that the reversal of the dominant public opinion on gun control within a 5-year span is a prime example of how short-sighted American public policy debates can be. There is a minor point that Americans are often aggressive in their views on topics such as gun control. The purpose of the passage is to illustrate a point about the nature of civic discourse in the United States. There is an underlying assumption that the legislative initiatives mentioned toward the end of the passage are an accurate reflection of current overall public opinion.

170 **Choice A is correct** because the lower number of pharmacies and doctors in Appalachian states could lead to reduced access to prescription drugs like OxyContin, thereby decreasing overall drug use in the area.

Choice B is incorrect because a lower number of pharmacies and doctors would not necessarily lead to an increase in the use of prescription drugs. In fact, fewer providers would likely decrease availability and use. **Choice C** is incorrect because population density is not directly related to the rate of drug use. Drug use is typically measured per capita, so it wouldn't matter how densely or sparsely populated an area is. **Choice D** is incorrect because the cost of OxyContin doesn't directly impact its likelihood of abuse. Drugs can be abused regardless of their price, and the passage doesn't provide evidence supporting the idea that the drug's cost is a significant factor in abuse. **Choice E** is incorrect because a spike in the use of OxyContin does not necessarily imply abuse. It may simply mean that people in the region now have access to a more effective painkiller, and the increase in use could be due to legitimate medical reasons.

171 **Choice B is correct** because the author uses the phrase to underscore how easily anger and aggression can be provoked in American civic debate, particularly around gun control. This supports the broader point about the short-sighted and reactionary nature of American civil discourse.

Choice A is incorrect because the passage does not suggest Americans are confused about the rules of civil society. Their familiarity with the Second Amendment demonstrates a level of legal awareness, not confusion. **Choice C** is incorrect because while the phrase might indeed grab attention, its function in the passage is deeper—it emphasizes both the aggressive tone and the short-sightedness of civic debate, not just its emotional appeal. **Choice D** is incorrect because the phrase itself is not used as an argumentative strategy. Although the author builds a case using reasoning, this specific phrase is illustrative rather than logical evidence meant to persuade the reader of American aggression. **Choice E** is incorrect because the phrase does not reflect a narrative rhetorical strategy. There is no storytelling or recounting of events; instead, the phrase is a vivid example that supports the author's analytical point.

PASSAGE 90

172 **Choice C is correct** because in the passage, the ethical considerations are called a "quagmire" and later a "conundrum," which both mean a confusing and difficult situation. The crux of this challenge is expressed by the fact that robotics are demonstrably made for destruction, which renders senseless any attempts to maintain them as safe and unthreatening creatures.

Choice A is incorrect because the passage states that there is an "ethical quagmire" over the development of robotics, which is later explained as the concern over the "potentially dangerous" creatures and the "threat" they pose. These concerns are not discarded, instead they are compounded with the consideration of the "ethics guiding the engineers." **Choice B is incorrect** because the three laws developed by Asimov were "contradicted" by the fact that robots these days are made for the purpose of destruction. Therefore, a law preventing them from committing harm would be nonsensical. **Choice D is incorrect** because the passage does not suggest robots pose a threat unless one day they "should emancipate themselves from their programmers." Therefore, the threat is not presumed to be immediate outside the destruction they are intended to do. **Choice E is incorrect** because the impact on the engineering industry was not taken into consideration, but rather larger fears concerning their threat on humanity as a whole.

173 **Choice B is correct** because the aberrations stated earlier in the passage were of robots "emancipating themselves from their programmers" and thereby functioning "of their own accord." This would be a deviation from their intended code and the behavior expected of them.

Choice A is incorrect because there is no mention of direct violence, but rather the "mayhem" that might ensue, which could be harmful any number of ways not including assault. **Choice C is incorrect** because there is no indication that the robots would shut down, particularly as they would be "roaming" on their own. **Choice D is incorrect** because the actions would no longer be under the control of programmers, since they would have "emancipated themselves" from such direction. **Choice E is incorrect** because it is said they would have "emancipated themselves," which means they would no longer be under the control of engineers.

174 **Choice B is correct** because the passage refers to the ethical concerns as a "quagmire" and a "conundrum," which both mean they are difficult and complex. Furthermore, it points out the challenges in applying Asimov's protective laws, as well as programming ethics into a "limited cognitive architecture." Finally, it explores the contradiction of questioning the ethics of machinery that is designed specifically for destructive ends within the military.

Choice A is incorrect because the purpose of mentioning Asimov was not to praise him as a visionary, but rather to address his three laws which many refer to as a preventative of robotic mayhem. **Choice C is incorrect** because the passage states as a side the "limited cognitive architecture" that would not permit programming ethical considerations. Therefore, the imperative to do so is not the main idea. **Choice D is incorrect** because although robotic engineers are mentioned in the end as responsible for destructive behavior, how culpability of their code would be defined or pursued was not discussed. **Choice E is incorrect** because the passage states that robotics are made for the purpose of "military engagement," but not that such development is out of control. Although ethical scrutiny is advocated in the final question of the passage, it is not a point developed in the passage.

PASSAGE 91

175 **Choice D is correct** because it states that natural scenery was shown to "boost resilience against disease," which would translate as faster recovery times in certain conditions.

Choice A is incorrect because it states that not only nature experienced outdoors but even "flowers in a vase" could produce therapeutic effects. Therefore, one can be indoors to benefit from natural sceneries. **Choice B is incorrect** because there is no indication that appreciation is different today than it was in previous eras. In fact, it points to the experience of our ancestors being attracted to natural settings as "places of refuge." **Choice C is incorrect** because the passage states that the presence of natural objects resulted in "higher levels of productivity," therefore, one could conclude that workers with views of natural scenes would be less distracted than those without. **Choice E is incorrect** because natural fragrances were shown to result in more relaxed driving, particularly when "wafting" through a vehicle, which implies a gentle intensity. This does not imply that all fragrances, least of all strong ones, would have the same effect.

PASSAGE 92: SUMMARY/PARAPHRASE

The passage is about homelessness among female veterans in the United States. The main idea is that homelessness among female veterans can be attributed to a combination of increased female participation in the military and a lack of veterans' services targeted specifically at women. The major point of the passage is the problematic increase in homelessness among female veterans. There are two minor points: (a) that the increase in homelessness is partly attributable to an increase in female enlistment and (b) that traditional veterans' shelters do not provide enough appropriate services for female veterans. The purpose of the passage is to inform the reader of a problem. The tone of the passage suggests that the problem of homelessness among female veterans needs to be addressed. The passage implies that increasing veterans' services targeted specifically at females is a remedy for the problem.

176 **Choice B is correct** because the author uses the example of homeless female veterans being unable to care for their children to highlight the severity of the problem. This is a classic emotional (pathos) appeal that resonates with the reader's values and emotions.

Choice A is incorrect because the author does not use logical reasoning (logos) to support the argument. Instead, the emphasis is on evoking empathy through emotionally charged examples. **Choice C is incorrect** because the passage does not explore or reference metaphysical issues or philosophical questions of existence, so it cannot be said to appeal to metaphysical sensibilities. **Choice D is incorrect** because ethos involves appealing to the reader through the credibility or reputation of the author. Since the author's identity or credentials are not established, ethos is not used here. **Choice E is incorrect** because the passage does not directly discuss political policies or systems, so it cannot be said to appeal to the reader's political sensibilities.

177 **Choice C is correct** because it can be inferred from the passage that gender inequality exists among U.S. military veterans. The services available do not sufficiently accommodate the needs of female veterans and their children, leaving them particularly vulnerable.

Choice A is incorrect because the passage does not claim that the U.S. military provides no services to its veterans. Rather, it points out that the services are inadequate, especially for women and their children. **Choice B is incorrect** because the passage does not generalize that all veterans are homeless. It focuses specifically on the growing issue of homelessness among female veterans. **Choice D is incorrect** because the passage does not argue that women should not serve in the military. Instead, it emphasizes the need for better support for female veterans after service. **Choice E is incorrect** because the passage does not provide comparative data on the number of male and female veterans with children. It only suggests that more female veterans tend to be responsible for their children.

PASSAGE 93

178 **Choice B is correct** because the passage refers to the "ubiquity of microplastics" and the "exponential rate" of discovering new sources, which means there are myriad sources already known. Moreover, it speaks about "curbing" the shedding of microplastics, which means reducing it rather than eliminating it entirely.

Choice A is incorrect because, according to the passage, even clothing made of natural fibers introduces pollutants into the wash, having been picked up from the environment and "ensconced," or tightly hidden, into the fibers. So, purchasing natural fibers would reduce but not eliminate the shedding of toxins. **Choice C is incorrect** because the passage states that even those who try to be "paragons" of eco-friendly behavior find themselves "hard-pressed," which is to say, those who are the best examples of conscientious decision-making find it difficult to avoid shedding pollutants one way or another. **Choice D is incorrect** because the passage states that the sources are "ubiquitous," which is to say, they are many. There is no discussion of which source or sources are predominant. **Choice E is incorrect** because, while the statement is true, it is not discussed in the passage and does not summarize the main ideas that were raised.

179 **"Once contaminants enter the earth, they are easily absorbed by crops, becoming the covert ingredients of our meals."** This sentence is correct because it explicitly makes the connection between the microplastics shed in the laundry to food that is eaten via soil contamination taken up by crops, thereby establishing the final link of the "cycle" in which we shed toxins from our clothing and later end up consuming them.

180 **Choice E is correct** because this fact introduces a potential solution to the problem of microplastics shed from the laundry and explains why it is insufficient in the face of such massive pollution.

Choice A is incorrect because the focus of the passage is on the issue of microplastics introduced in the wash. Therefore, the release of other contaminants would not strengthen the main point. **Choice B is incorrect** because the ability of organic farming to reduce pesticide contamination does not alleviate the problem of microplastics released in the laundry. **Choice C is incorrect** because even though cleaner air would decrease the number of pollutants picked up on natural fibers, the fact that some cities have better air quality than others does not resolve the main concern of microplastics shed in the laundry, particularly since most of them come from synthetic materials. **Choice D is incorrect** because the passage explains how most of the microplastics enter the human food chain (through the soil). Therefore, their introduction into the food chain through fish consumption would be an additional point that doesn't strengthen the main argument.

Chapter 3: Reading Comprehension

PASSAGE 94: SUMMARY/PARAPHRASE

The passage is about domestic violence. The main idea is that, contrary to popular belief, men are quite often the target of domestic violence. There are two major points: (a) 40% of domestic violence victims are male and (b) due to societal attitudes toward male weakness, domestic violence incidents involving men may be underreported. The main purpose of the passage is to (a) debunk the myth that men are rarely the victims of domestic violence and (b) give one potential reason that domestic violence against men may be underreported.

181 **Choice E is correct** because the passage states that men face social stigma if they admit to being victims of domestic abuse. This stigma, which equates victimhood with male weakness, leads to underreporting of such abuse.

Choice A is incorrect because the passage attributes the stigmatization of abused men to Western society as a whole, not specifically to women. **Choice B** is incorrect because there is no mention of researcher bias—either pro- or anti-female—in the passage. **Choice C** is incorrect because the passage does not claim that reporting abuse damages male victims' relationships with women. **Choice D** is incorrect because while faulty statistics are mentioned, the passage does not blame this on general flaws in statistical methodology but rather on underreporting due to stigma.

PASSAGE 95

The passage is about the difficulty of achieving equal educational opportunities in the United States. The main idea is that while there is a tendency to focus on literacy rates and children, the problem of low literacy has broader implications. There is an explicitly stated major point that low literacy among adults engenders poor educational results in the children of the affected population. In addition, there is an implied major point that literacy is crucial to equal opportunity. The purpose of the passage is to rally support for literacy initiatives by explaining why they are important. Rhetorical cues such as the use of the word 'harmful' and the discussion of adverse outcomes indicate that the passage is a call to action.

182 **Choice D is correct** because the two bold-face parts show how the author presents the claim that low literacy obstructs access to equal opportunities and then offers a solution to that problem: literacy initiatives.

Choice A is incorrect because the non-bold portions of the passage are where the author describes the problems associated with low literacy. The bold-face sections present the author's stance and proposed solution. **Choice B** is incorrect because the emotional appeal to the challenges faced by children with low literacy is made in the non-bold sections, not the bold-face parts. **Choice C** is incorrect because the author's beliefs are consistent throughout the passage. There is no mention of or contrast with an opposing belief. **Choice E** is incorrect because the two bold-face parts are not paradoxical. Instead, they align to support the argument that low literacy limits opportunity and that literacy initiatives can address the issue.

183 **Choice B is correct** because the passage discusses how low literacy rates in American adults impede equal opportunities, emphasizing the broader societal impact and challenges created by adult illiteracy.

Choice A is incorrect because although the author notes that children of low-literacy adults may also struggle, the main focus of the passage is on adult literacy itself, not on children or the perpetuation cycle. **Choice C** is incorrect because the passage does not mention any connection between low literacy and crime rates, so no such inference can be made.

PASSAGE 96

184 **Choice E is correct** because the passage uses the example of Finland as a country that has a "leading school system" and implies that incorporating some of the changes to be more like the Finnish model would lead to "superior results." Therefore, one can conclude that students in Finland outcompete others in academics.

Choice A is incorrect because there is no discussion of cultural influences in the Finnish education model, nor how it would be difficult to incorporate in other countries for that reason. **Choice B** is incorrect because, although standardized tests are not incorporated in the school system, one cannot conclude there are no transcripts reflecting academic achievement. In fact, it states that evaluations are given with "in-depth feedback from teachers." Therefore, it does not necessarily follow that such transcripts preclude international matriculation. **Choice C** is incorrect because, although evaluations are provided by teachers, which runs the risk of introducing bias, the passage does not present this occurrence or discuss it as what would be a drawback to the model. **Choice D** is incorrect because the passage states the learning in Finland is more student-centered, which proposes a different approach to exam-taking in contrast to the USA, which "relies almost exclusively on standardized testing."

185 **Choice A is correct** because the passage explores some of the different approaches that the system in Finland employs but does not look at the root causes of the problems in the US. It stands to reason that students in situations of instability, in low-income households or in situations of violence, would struggle in their academic performance regardless of the education model. **Choice C is correct** because the support students receive at home and the environment they come home to both play a significant role in a child's development and academic performance, regardless of the education model.

Choice B is incorrect because, although this may be the case in certain regions, the passage suggests that other countries are leaders in education, a statement that would not make sense if the curricula were not comparable.

186 **Choice A is correct** because the passage discusses the factors that make Finland stand out as an exemplary model, and they vary so drastically that the US model would need to be "upended," as in, redone with an entire makeover. It makes the minor point at the end, however, that certain "sanguine proponents" believe that some "gradual changes," which could be piecemeal, might steer the system in a better direction. This is not the main idea of the passage, but it is a minor point that offers some hope at the end.

Choice B is incorrect because this is the main point of the passage. It states that there is a "growing consensus" that changes are "in order." Afterwards, the passage explores another education model from a leading country and concludes that it would take "nothing short of an overhaul" to do something similar in the US, which implies that there are considerable challenges to modifying the current system. **Choice C** is incorrect because it is a paraphrasing of the main point also. The passage states that other education models offer a "different paradigm of learning altogether," whose main differences it then proceeds to enumerate in the example of the Finnish system. Therefore, the main idea of the passage is that the change to another leading school system would require a shift in the entire approach.

PASSAGE 97

187 **Choice C is correct** because the new parent in the passage makes a generalization, assuming that all parents respond to their children in the same loving and emotional way that he does. This reflects the main assumption behind the conclusion and reveals the underlying belief that his experience is universal.

Choice A is incorrect because although the statement may be factually accurate, it does not address the core assumption behind the parent's conclusion. It is peripheral to the main idea of the passage. **Choice B** is incorrect because while it touches on an aspect of the assumption (parents watching their children in the crib), it is too narrow and not the central assumption being made. It represents just one expression of the broader generalization. **Choice D** is incorrect because it introduces a possible assumption, but it does not impact the logical validity of the conclusion. It does not directly relate to the universal assumption about parental behavior. **Choice E** is incorrect because although it might be true, it is not the main point the parent is assuming. Like B, it represents a secondary or supporting idea, not the foundational assumption of the passage.

PASSAGE 98

188 **Choice D is the correct** answer because it most logically contrasts with "well-known" used to describe destinations earlier in the passage. As used in this context, "obscure" means little-known suggesting the destinations are unfamiliar to potential travelers to Japan.

Choice A is incorrect because "remote" means isolated. In this context, it does not provide a contrast with all the destinations described in the prior sentence. In particular, the reference to "hiking trails" suggests that Mount Fuji is likely to be remote. **Choice B** is incorrect because "unseen" means hidden or concealed. In this context, it does not provide the best contrast with "well-known." While this response is tempting, it implies some deliberate concealment for which there is no evidence in the passage. **Choice C** is incorrect because "mysterious" means unsolved or puzzling. In this context, it does not provide a contrast with well-known and there is no evidence for this description in the passage. **Choice E** is incorrect because "strange" means odd or peculiar. In this context, it does not provide a contrast with well-known and there is no evidence for this description in the passage. Additionally, it is too similar to Choice C, and both can be eliminated.

189 **"In contrast, influencers very rarely steer their followers to obscure destinations, where travelers could enjoy authentic experiences without the hordes."** The above-cited sentence is the correct answer because it explains that travel influencers could steer their followers to destinations where they would have authentic experiences without crowds. However, influencers only rarely use their power to shift travel away from already crowded destinations.

Chapter 3: Reading Comprehension

PASSAGE 99

190 **Choice B is correct** because the passage states short bouts of vigorous exercises can help improve one's chances against heart disease, cancer, and early death. So, while pointing out that as few as 2 minutes could make a difference, the fact that longer periods of time correlate with an even lower risk helps strengthen the overall message.

Choice A is incorrect because the method used and reliability of the data are not under question in the passage. Therefore, the fact that wrist trackers are effective devices for long-term monitoring does not make an impact on the main idea. **Choice C** is incorrect because the study would not be conducted on participants who were already suffering from heart disease or cancer, as their data would not be indicative of how exercise serves to prevent these diseases. **Choice D** is incorrect because the robustness and scope of the study is not under question. Moreover, it is logical for the study to choose participants at around the age when the diseases in question tend to develop. **Choice E** is incorrect because, in fact, this statement weakens the main argument, as possibly even shorter periods of vigorous activity could lead to certain health benefits and a reduction in the risk for the diseases in question. However, since wrist trackers did not record such activity, this did not enter into the findings.

191 **Choice C is correct** because the passage states that recent findings indicate that even 15-20 minutes of exercise a week reduce the risk of heart disease and other diseases. The second paragraph looks more closely into "the way the exercises were done," specifying the importance of at least 2 minutes of "vigorous activity" a day.

Choice A is incorrect because although the first paragraph presents the main idea, the second paragraph does not discuss any data that might contradict the information presented. **Choice B** is incorrect because the first paragraph suggests that exercise is important for a healthy lifestyle, but the second paragraph reinforces this idea and does not explore other factors that may contribute to it. **Choice D** is incorrect because the diseases in question are referenced but not discussed in and of themselves. Furthermore, suggestions for a healthier lifestyle through activity are made in both paragraphs. **Choice E** is incorrect because current recommendations in the form of "long-held notions" are refuted in the first paragraph, which goes on to present new recommendations of "at least 15-20 minutes a week." These are reinforced and given a specification (including daily "vigorous activity") in the second.

192 **Choice B is correct** because there are many factors that contribute to disease risk reduction and, while the studies focused on physical activity, the underlying assumption must have been that the activity was analyzed ceteris paribus (all other factors remaining the same).

Choice A is incorrect because this was a "long-term study" that "monitored increased heart rates" for as little as 2 minutes. Therefore, it could not rely on subjects putting them on only during anticipated physical activity, as some activity takes place unexpectedly. **Choice C** is incorrect because, although it may be true that not all diseases can be properly cleared during a medical examination, it can be said that "healthy participants" were not suffering from such diseases at any noticeable level. **Choice D** is incorrect because the passage states the study was conducted on "healthy, low-risk" participants in order to test the effects of exercise on preventing certain diseases. **Choice E** is incorrect because, while this is presumed to be true, if the wrist activity trackers had been the cause of disease, they would have affected all participants. Additionally, those with longer exercise times would still be shown to have benefited from the physical activity due to their lower incidence of disease development.

PASSAGE 100

193 **Choice C is correct** because the passage mentions in the end that the old adage, "Biology is destiny" ought to be replaced for the new one, "Behavior changes biology," as a remark on the shifting perceptions on the power that mental habits have in making perceptible physiological changes. However, it is not the main point of the passage, which is centered on the health benefits imparted by the feeling and expression of gratitude.

Choice A is incorrect because the fact that the feeling of gratitude results in detectable physiological changes (e.g., reduced stress, better sleep) is the main idea of the passage, particularly that the feeling can be invoked at will as a "morning and bedtime ritual." **Choice B** is incorrect because this statement is a major point in the passage: the fact that studies show that conscious effort to feeling gratitude has been correlated with health improvement, making it a recommendable mental habit to form.

PASSAGE 101

194 **Choice D is correct** because the passage states that "modern practices" are "repeatedly implicated" in rising cancer cases as a result of the carcinogens ("nitrosamines") that form from the compounds used in curing meat.

Choice A is incorrect because, while this statement would be a suitable conclusion, it is not a proper summary. The passage does not make recommendations to change the compounds used in the practice of curing meat, but rather advises consumers directly to "avoid" purchasing and consuming processed meat. **Choice B** is incorrect because the salts used in traditional methods of curing meats are not the same as those used today. The passage specifies that "modern practices" employ compounds that lead to the formation of "carcinogens," which is not the same as saying any salt would pose an increased cancer risk. **Choice C** is incorrect because, while this statement may be true, it does not summarize the passage, whose main idea is not about comparing preservation time and the effectiveness of different salts. Instead, the main idea is to point out the health risks involved with the use of certain compounds. **Choice E** is incorrect because, while the statement may be true, it is not the focus of the passage and therefore does not justly summarize it. The passage does not explore the legal or ethical implications of incorporating compounds known to lead to carcinogens, which would concern the accountability of the meat industry. Instead, it points out the health risk involved in their consumption.

195 **Choice B is correct** because the passage states that practices in the modern meat industry have been "repeatedly implicated in the rise of cancer cases," which means there are other practices correlated with increasing cancer risk.

Choice A is incorrect because the passage states that "processed meat" falls under this category, particularly for the additives and preservatives applied, which does not imply that all meat naturally does. **Choice C** is incorrect because the passage states that certain salts, particularly nitrates and nitrites, are considered carcinogenic when they lead to the formation of nitrosamines. This does not mean that table salt, which is a different chemical compound, has the same effects. **Choice D** is incorrect because there is no discussion in the passage of nitrates and nitrites outside of the context of meat products. Vegan products are plant-based and do not necessarily induce nitrosamines to form, due to their low level of amines. However, the passage does not provide enough information to infer that processed vegan products pose a cancer risk or not. **Choice E** is incorrect because the passage differentiates between the salt used to preserve meat in previous eras and "modern practices" that employ nitrate salts. Therefore, one cannot infer that the sea salt used in previous times carries an associated cancer risk, as do the nitrate salts used today..

PASSAGE 102

196 **Choice A is correct** because the first paragraph discusses the organ donor policy in the US based on "informed consent." The second paragraph introduces an alternative approach based on "presumed consent." **Choice B is correct** because the first paragraph introduces the problem of organ shortages in the US, whereas the second paragraph offers a way to address it by proposing the system of "presumed consent," which is "able to extend life expectancy" in recipients who would otherwise remain on a waiting list.

Choice C is incorrect because the first paragraph describes the challenges of acquiring "informed consent," which is needed to donate organs. The second paragraph does not further describe complications to this challenge, but rather offers an alternative solution based on the model of "presumed consent."

197 **"Although not a panacea to organ shortages, presumed consent effectively prevents the discarding of usable organs."** This sentence is correct because "a panacea" would be a universal remedy to a difficulty. So, by stating "not a panacea," the author acknowledges that presumed consent would not entirely resolve the issue of shortages, but it would be an improvement.

198 **Choice B is correct** because the main ideas discussed in the passage are in connection to organ shortages in the US, specifically the drawbacks to a policy based on informed consent and the benefits that a policy on presumed consent would offer. The fact that individuals can opt out of presumed consent is an additional point that is secondary to the main idea of increasing organ availability.

Choice A is incorrect because the passage is centered on the main point of exploring presumed consent as an alternative in order to address the "crisis of organ shortages" in the US. **Choice C** is incorrect because it is a major point in the shortcoming of the informed consent system that individuals have to opt in or have relatives opt them in, which is a task often complicated by difficult circumstances. **Choice D** is incorrect because this statement is essentially the crux of the argument against informed consent, the fact that consequently potential organs cannot be transplanted into patients in need, making it a major point in the passage. **Choice E** is incorrect because this is the main benefit of the alternative, presumed consent, the fact that more organs are made available for transplant to help patients in need.

PASSAGE 103

199 **Choice A is correct** because the passage is fundamentally challenging the claim that electric scooters are eco-friendly by exploring a number of factors from manufacturing to modal shift. This contradicts the notion that it is a non-polluting vehicle, thus, it is not as sustainable as generally considered.

Choice B is incorrect because this statement is only one of the points made ("manufacturing....burden"), but it does not summarize the passage as a whole. **Choice C** is incorrect because modal shift is also another point that is made, but it does not summarize the entire passage, which consists of several arguments. **Choice D** is incorrect because while air pollution in the areas the scooter is used may benefit greatly, the air around the factories would not. In either case, this is an argument in support of scooters being environmentally friendly, which later gets refuted in the passage. **Choice E** is incorrect because this is a conclusion in the form of consumer advice that may be gleaned from the passage, but it does not summarize all the points made.

PASSAGE 104

200 **Choice D is correct** because the passage states that research on this topic is "not yet conclusive" and that current estimates are "conservative." Therefore, it is possible that further research may determine a higher bound for the "mortality plateau."

Choice A is incorrect because the passage does not discuss how current limits are calculated, nor that biological thresholds are ignored. It suggests that certain people have "entertained hopes" rather than biology presenting immortality as a possibility. **Choice B** is incorrect because the passage does not discuss factors that are involved in mortality rates, therefore, there may be others more relevant, such as genetic predisposition. **Choice C** is incorrect because the passage refers to the method of studying birth cohorts and does not suggest that it is unreliable for the purpose at hand. **Choice E** is incorrect because the passage states that the ages of supercentenarians are "ever-increasing," not that their number is increasing. However, even if that were true, this statement would not be considered a conclusion to the passage, but rather a minor point made in reference to the central argument of identifying mortality limits.

Practice Set 5: Physical Sciences

PASSAGE 105

Question 201 is based on the following passage.

As pitch depends upon the frequency at which sound waves strike the ear, an object may emit sound waves at a constant frequency yet may produce different pitches in ears differently situated. Such a case is not usual, but an example of it will serve a useful purpose in fixing certain facts as to pitch. Conceive two railroad trains to pass each other, running in opposite directions, the engine bells of both trains ringing. Passengers on each train will hear the bell of the other, first as a *rising* pitch, then as a *falling* one. Passengers on each train will hear the bell of their own train at a *constant* pitch.

201 Which of the following statements best describes the main discrepancy presented by this passage?

- (A) The continuity of sound waves emitted by an object varies in the unreliability of individual perceptions.
- (B) It is unusual for people to hear the same sounds in different ways
- (C) Two trains that are travelling in opposite directions meet at a common point at the moment that they pass each other.
- (D) Though theoretically two trains may emit identical sounds from their bells, the sound emitted is irrelevant to the sound that is heard.
- (E) The rate of change exhibited by a sound is in direct relation to the speed of the train.

PASSAGE 106

Questions 202 and 203 are based on the following passage.

After the first four, no more asteroids were found until 1845, when one was discovered; then, in 1847, three more were added to the list; and after that searchers began to pick them up with such rapidity that by the close of the century hundreds were known, and it had become almost impossible to keep track of them. It was long supposed that Vesta was the largest, because it shines more brightly than any of the others; but finally, in 1895, Barnard, with the Lick telescope, definitely measured their diameters, and proved to everybody's surprise that Ceres is really the chief, and Vesta only the third in rank. They differ greatly in Z.

202 Which of the following statements is the most reasonable explanation for the increased frequency with which asteroids were discovered toward the end of the nineteenth century?

- (A) A shift in the jet stream created larger areas of cloudless skies, making the asteroids more visible
- (B) More colleges and universities offered courses in astronomy
- (C) A period of frequent volcanic activity had finally subsided, reducing the amount of particulate matter in the atmosphere
- (D) Advances in telescope technology made it possible to identify asteroids that had been previously overlooked
- (E) Astronomers had a better understanding of asteroids' identifying characteristics

203 Which of the following predictions about the future of science is likely to be true based on your understanding of this passage?

- (A) New discoveries and accuracy will occur at an increasingly rapid pace
- (B) More asteroids will be discovered and correctly measured
- (C) Astronomers are likely to discover an asteroid larger than Ceres
- (D) Greater investment should be made in astronomical research
- (E) The origins of asteroids will continue to be identified

PASSAGE 107

Questions 204 to 206 are based on the following passage.

The difference between the ways in which snow and rain are formed is very slight. In both cases water evaporates, and its vapor mingles with the warm air. The warm air rises and expands. It cools as it expands, and when it gets cool enough the water vapor begins to condense. But if the air as it expands becomes very cold, so cold that the droplets of water freeze as they form and gather together to make delicate crystals of ice, snow is formed. The ice crystals found in snow are always six-sided or six-pointed, because, probably, the water or ice molecules pull from six directions and therefore gather each other together along the six lines of this pull. At any rate, the tiny crystals of frozen water are formed and come floating down to the ground; and we call them snowflakes. After the snow melts it goes through the same cycle as the rain, most of it finally getting back to the ocean through rivers, and there, in time, being evaporated once more.

204. The use of the phrase, "at any rate" reveals which of the following about the sentence preceding it?

  (A) That the information in that sentence is essential to understanding the passage
  (B) That the information in that sentence cannot be scientifically proven
  (C) That the information in that sentence is an unnecessary digression
  (D) That the process described in that sentence is not true in every case
  (E) That the information in that sentence is not very interesting

205. Consider the context of this passage to decide which of the following most accurately identifies the type of writing exhibited.

  (A) Narrative
  (B) Expository
  (C) Editorial
  (D) Persuasive
  (E) Compare/contrast

206. Based on the information in this passage, decide which of the following meteorological events is a result of the same process described here.

  (A) A rainbow
  (B) Fog
  (C) Wind chill
  (D) Degree days
  (E) Thunder

PASSAGE 108

Question 207 is based on the following passage.

The wear on a well-designed gas valve operating mechanism is practically nil; and even if there was wear, the effect would be to cause the valve to open a trifle later and close sooner than it would otherwise, i.e., it would remain open a shorter time during each charging stroke. This in turn (other conditions remaining the same) would give us a weaker mixture; and although too weak a mixture is preferable to a too rich one, we should have to adopt some means of increasing the richness of the mixture; otherwise the maximum power of the engine would soon be seen to diminish.

207. Choose the option that identifies a topic which, if added to the passage in more detail, would best strengthen the author's argument.

  (A) How to maintain the best overall function of an engine.
  (B) Whether the quality of a gas valve's design will adversely affect engine performance.
  (C) Whether a richer mixture is more detrimental to engine performance than a weaker one.
  (D) The destructive effects of wear on a gas-valve over time.
  (E) The numerous conditions that can affect an engine's maximum performance.

PASSAGE 109

Questions 208 and 209 are based on the following passage.

Evapotranspiration is water transpired from plants and evaporated from the soil. *Rising* air currents take the vapor up into the atmosphere where cooler temperatures cause it to condense into clouds. Air currents move water vapor around the globe; cloud particles collide, grow, and fall out of the sky as precipitation. Some precipitation falls as snow or hail, and can accumulate as ice caps and glaciers, which can store frozen water for thousands of years.

208. Based on the information in the passage, which of the following would be an appropriate visual representation of the text.

   (A) A Venn diagram
   (B) A list
   (C) A flow chart
   (D) A timeline
   (E) A T-chart

209. Based on the sequence of information in this passage, which of the topics listed below might logically be discussed in the paragraph immediately following this one?

   (A) Different cloud formations
   (B) Other forms of precipitation
   (C) Water evaporated from lakes and ponds
   (D) Glaciers and ice caps
   (E) The motion of air currents

PASSAGE 110

Questions 210 to 212 are based on the following passage.

Sound is the sensation peculiar to the ear. This sensation is caused by rapidly-succeeding to-and-fro motions of the air which touches the outside surface of the drum-skin of the ear. These to-and-fro motions may be given to the air by a distant body, like a string of a violin. The string moves to and fro, that is, it vibrates. These vibrations of the string act on the bridge of the violin, which rests on the belly or sounding-board of the instrument. The surface of the sounding-board is thus set trembling, and these tremors, or vibrations, spread through the air in all directions around the instrument, somewhat in the manner that water-waves spread around the place where a stone has been dropped into a quiet pond. These tremors of the air, however, are not sound, but the cause of sound. Sound, as we have said, is a sensation; but, as the cause of this sensation is always vibration, we call those vibrations which give this sensation, sonorous vibrations.

210. What is the correct definition of peculiar as it is used in the first sentence of this passage?

   (A) Odd
   (B) Uncommon
   (C) Distinctive in character or nature from others
   (D) Belonging characteristically
   (E) Belonging exclusively to some person, group, or thing

211. Consider the content of the passage and select the most likely audience for this information.

   (A) Musicians
   (B) Violin manufacturers
   (C) Students
   (D) Sonography technicians
   (E) Acoustics engineers

212. Select the sentence that a seismologist might find useful to describe the effect of an earthquake.

PASSAGE 111

Question 213 is based on the following passage.

The process used to manufacture Biodiesel from pure vegetable oil is called ester interchange. In the process the vegetable oil is combined with a much smaller amount of Methanol. Methanol can be manufactured by the fermentation of starch or sugar and it can also be produced from natural gas. The vegetable oil and methanol are placed in a small quantity of an alkaline catalyst and it is in this process that the chemical makeup of the vegetable oil is altered. The result is a clean burning fuel with a viscosity (flow properties) approximating that of standard diesel fuel. During this process, approximately 90% of what is manufactured is Biodiesel fuel, while the remaining 10% is in the form of the glycerin that was broken down from the vegetable matter. This glycerin can also be used in other applications in the chemical industry, making the manufacture of Biodiesel practically waste-free.

213. Select the sentence that reveals when ester interchange occurs.

Chapter 3: Reading Comprehension

PASSAGE 112

Questions 214 and 215 are based on the following passage.

Star Wars showed us planets with more than one sun and now scientists are doing the same. The Earth only orbits one sun, but astrophysicists now believe in the ubiquity of other planets in the universe that orbit two stars. These so-called circumbinary planets possess rapidly changing flows of energy and wildly varying climates due to the orbital motion around two suns. Scientists believe that since the climate and seasonal change on such planets are in constant flux, the evolution of life in a circumbinary system would be vastly different than on earth. However, scientists can only speculate as to what this difference would entail; they are still unsure of how exactly life could manifest differently on different planets and in different solar systems.

214. The author discusses Star Wars

    A. In order to draw a parallel between science and science fiction
    B. To show how science fiction films often predict scientific truths
    C. As a stylistic device to peak the reader's interest in the text
    D. As a narrative rhetorical strategy to peak the reader's interest in the text
    E. In order to promote the Star Wars films

For the following question, consider each of the three choices separately and select all that apply.

215. Circumbinary planets can help us understand:

    A. How life materializes and evolves on other planets
    B. Climate change on Earth
    C. The role of the sun(s) in climate control

PASSAGE 113

Questions 216 to 218 are based on the following passage.

Scientific progress is often measured in terms of medical progress; chemists, biologists, and even physicists work hard to find ways to keep humans healthy and whole and in doing so advance their respective scientific fields. **Furthermore, many of the medical discoveries engendered by the cooperation of doctors and scientists push the boundaries of our imaginations.** Recent developments within the field of chemistry have led to such a groundbreaking discovery: new "smart" material that could potentially help light be transmuted for medicinal purposes. Chemists report that their new polymer (plastic-like) material could help diagnose diseases and engineer new human tissues; whether or not these claims can be substantiated is another matter.

216. According to the passage, what is so avant-garde about chemists' recent discoveries relative to the new "smart" polymer?

    A. The "smart" polymer will lead to diagnosing more diseases and could even help scientists and doctors engineer new human tissues
    B. The "smart" polymer will give chemistry a competitive edge among the other sciences represented in the medical community
    C. The new polymer could help light be harnessed as a curative property
    D. The "smart" polymer is the cooperative product of chemists, physicists, and biologists
    E. There is nothing avant-garde about the new "smart" polymer

217. The section highlighted in **boldface** is intended to underscore

    A. The fact that scientists and doctors often cooperate
    B. The fact that scientists and doctors are creative
    C. The fact that medicine evolves in unforeseen ways
    D. The fact that medical discoveries could not occur without the cooperation of doctors and scientists
    E. The fact that our imaginations are limited

218. Select the sentence that belies the author's excitement vis-a-vis the new "smart" polymer.

PASSAGE 114

Question 219 is based on the following passage.

Iron differs from the metals so far studied in that it is able to form two series of compounds in which the iron has two different valences. In the one series the iron is divalent and forms compounds which in formulas and many chemical properties are similar to the corresponding zinc compounds. It can also act as a trivalent metal, and in this condition forms salts similar to those of aluminum. Those compounds in which the iron is divalent are known as ferrous compounds, while those in which it is trivalent are known as ferric.

For the following question, consider each answer choice separately and select all that apply.

219. Use the information in the passage to decide which of the following statements is accurate.

   A. Metals referred to as cuprous in a compound have a lower valence number as metals referred to as cupric in a compound

   B. The suffix, - ous, means full of or possessing a certain quality, and the suffix, - ic, means having some characteristics of

   C. Cuprous means possessing the qualities of copper and cupric means having some characteristics of copper

PASSAGE 115

Questions 220 and 221 are based on the following passage.

In particle physics, antimatter is the inverse of matter; antimatter is composed of antiparticles while regular matter is comprised of particles. Antimatter was originally conceptualized in the late 1920s by physicist Paul Dirac as a means of better understanding the behavior of electrons and thus the behavior of our universe. Dirac theorized that nature's predisposition to binary pairs could help him explain the functioning of electrons. He hypothesized that electrons could only exist if there was an antielectron—the opposite of an electron with an opposite electrical charge, but proof of their existence wasn't possible until it could be tested in particle accelerators; a process that could not be undertaken until the 1960's. Today, most antimatter research is centered in Geneva, Switzerland at CERN, the European Organization for Nuclear Research.

220. Dirac's antimatter hypothesis relies on the assumption that

   A. Scientific possibilities are never limited
   B. Electrons are the key to unlocking the structure of the universe
   C. Every extant thing has an inverse
   D. The universe can be fully delineated and understood
   E. Scientific ideas are sometimes ahead of their times in terms of technological capabilities

221. This passage can best be described as:

   A. A narrative
   B. A testimony
   C. A scientific theory
   D. Persuasive prose
   E. Comparative prose

PASSAGE 116

Questions 222 to 224 are based on the following passage.

HVBS Chemists are one mind-blowing step closer than ever to building artificial life forms from scratch. Whether or not this is a good idea is another matter; we are faced here with the "just because we can doesn't mean we should" dilemma. Biochemical researchers have now been able to employ a novel chemical reaction that begets self-assembling cell membranes. Cell membranes are the structural foundation stones for life on Earth and scientists hope that this research breakthrough will allow them to better understand the very origins of life on Earth; one of the great mysteries in science is how non-living matter transmuted to living matter and scientists argue that is important to unlock the secret to the basic chemical and biological principles necessary for the original formation of life. Such research would help us answer the fundamental questions as who we are, where we came from. However, some secrets are meant to stay hidden and the ability to create artificial life could open a Pandora's box with far reaching consequences from exploitation if the technology fell into the wrong hands to annihilation of natural life as we know it.

222. The author makes his or her point primarily by

   A. Offering an objective evaluation of the facts
   B. Dramatically appealing to the reader's fear of the unknown
   C. Providing both a view and counterview
   D. Castigating the mindset of the scientists
   E. Using a specific source of authority to back up his or her claims

223. The author refers to a Pandora's Box in order to:

   Ⓐ Test the reader's intelligence

   Ⓑ Highlight the fact that artificial life could never be controlled

   Ⓒ Show that the creation of artificial life would be evil

   Ⓓ Reinforce his point by way of a trope

   Ⓔ Distract the reader with a red herring

224. In the last sentence the author apparently intends to:

   Ⓐ Explicate how non-living matter transformed into living matter

   Ⓑ Underscore why the scientific research mentioned in the passage is important

   Ⓒ Generalize an argument to make it more appealing to a wider audience

   Ⓓ Give the reader more details related to the information previously discussed in the passage

   Ⓔ Persuade the reader to believe an opinion by way of a rhetorical strategy

PASSAGE 117

Question 225 is based on the following passage.

The reason for this peculiarity of mercury is that the pull between the particles of mercury themselves is stronger than the pull between them and your finger or handkerchief. In scientific language, the cohesion of mercury is stronger than its adhesion to your finger or handkerchief. Although this seems unusual for a liquid, it is what we naturally expect of solid things; you would be amazed if part of the wood of your school seat stuck to you when you got up, for you expect the particles in solid things to cohere—to have cohesion—much more strongly than they adhere to something else. It is because solids have such strong cohesion that they are solids.

225. Select the sentence in the passage which reveals that the writer's audience is most likely comprised of laymen.

PASSAGE 118

Questions 226 and 227 are based on the following passage.

On the retina, each image takes up a specific amount of space. Depending on how close or far away the object is viewed, there is a proportionate amount of space. It may surprise someone to learn how tiny the image appears after staring at the sun. However, this only happens if the person closes their eyes right away after observing it. The individual will always perceive the image as larger in proportion to the distance from the surface it is resting on as long as the individual looks to the edge of the room and examines it in comparison to other items.

For Questions 226 and 227, consider each of the choices separately and select all that apply.

226. The passage suggests that a person's sight of an object can be affected by the location of the viewed object

   Ⓐ In comparison to the proximity of the person

   Ⓑ In comparison to the location of surrounding objects

   Ⓒ And the health of their retinas

227. The passage addresses which issues about the eyesight and retina?

   Ⓐ The actual size of an object can appear incorrectly

   Ⓑ Brightness and darkness affect the appearance of the size of an image

   Ⓒ The retina is responsible for interpreting visual images

PASSAGE 119

Questions 228 to 230 are based on the following passage.

Solar energy is an effective alternative to consider when discussing ways to meet net-carbon-zero goals. Currently, the energy produced by natural gas plants in the United States results in about 1,071 pounds of carbon dioxide emissions for every megawatt-hour (MWh) of electricity produced. By contrast, industrial-scale solar installations result in about 95 pounds per MWh. Such a significant reduction does not only help defray the worst effects of global warming but also leads to better air quality; better air quality in turn reduces the prevalence of respiratory and other diseases.

Of course, solar energy is not a panacea. There are very real drawbacks to building large-scale solar arrays, not the least of which is the amount of land that could be used for other forms of development or agriculture. Placement must be evaluated to mitigate habitat loss and soil erosion. However, if properly installed and maintained, one acre can produce up to about 447 MWh of energy per year.

228. The primary purpose of the passage is to

   (A) discuss a possible implication of the decision to pursue net-carbon-zero goals
   (B) introduce reasons that solar energy is not as wise a solution to meet net-carbon-zero goals as it first appears
   (C) weigh the arguments and counterarguments regarding the use of solar energy
   (D) provide evidence showing how significantly diseases might be reduced by adopting solar energy
   (E) offer recommendations about the most effective use of solar energy in meeting net-carbon-zero goals

229. Which of the following facts is mentioned in the passage as a reason to doubt the assumption that solar energy is a "panacea"?

   (A) Solar installations occupy land that might otherwise be used for agriculture.
   (B) Industrial-scale solar installations can help defray the worst effects of global warming.
   (C) Air quality in many areas will improve if solar energy is a primary energy source.
   (D) Soil erosion is minimized if placement of the solar panels is carefully evaluated.
   (E) Natural gas results in a large amount of carbon dioxide emissions per MWh of energy produced.

230. Based on the passage, it can be inferred that large-scale solar arrays

   (A) reduce the amount of carbon dioxide in the air by about 95 pounds per year
   (B) will produce far fewer than 447 MWh of energy annually if not kept in good repair
   (C) are currently being installed without attention paid to mitigate habitat loss
   (D) are the most efficient solution in the attempt to reach net-carbon-zero goals
   (E) will be more cost-effective to install than building new natural gas plants

PASSAGE 120

Question 231 is based on the following passage.

In the wake of global climate change hysteria, everyone is looking for reasons to explain fluctuating weather patterns, from lay people to meteorologists. Extremely hot summers have everyone convinced global warming is on the rampage and extremely cold winters have everyone convinced a new ice age is coming. Scientists, however, now believe that they have found a way to explain the recent phenomenon of extreme winters: harshly hot summers. Research suggests that hot summers contribute to the melting of ice in the world's Arctic regions, which in turn causes extreme cold and heavy snowfall in the winters of temperate climates. The exact cause of the harshly hot summers is still up for debate, but one thing is certain: Just as extreme behavior begets more extreme behavior in humans, so too does extreme weather beget extreme weather.

For the following question, consider each of the three answer choices separately and select all that apply.

231. The author's attitude towards the public and scientific reaction to climate change can best be described as:

   [A] Petrified
   [B] Incredulous
   [C] Dubious

PASSAGE 121

Questions 232 to 233 are based on the following passage.

The Red Planet is the nearest neighbor to Earth as Venus is on the hither side. It is also in some ways the planet best situated for scientific observations. While the greatest apparent diameter of its disc is considerably less than that of Venus, Mars does not hide close to the Sun's rays like the inferior planets but may be seen all night when in opposition. Not all oppositions, however, are equally favorable. Under the best circumstances, Mars may come as near to the Earth as 35,000,000 miles. When less favorably situated, it may come no nearer than 61,000,000. This very considerable variation in its distance arises from the eccentricity of the planet's orbit, which amounts to nearly one-tenth.

For the following question, consider each of the three answer choices separately and select all that apply.

232. The passage suggests that the best time for scientists to observe Mars is

   A. While Mars is in its last one-tenth orbit
   B. When Earth is positioned between the Sun and Mars
   C. During nighttime hours

233. The main idea of the passage focuses chiefly on

   A. The appearance of Mars and its diameter
   B. The description of Mars' orbit
   C. The location of Mars in comparison to Earth and Venus
   D. The distance of Mars to Earth
   E. The ideal time and place to view Mars

PASSAGE 122

Questions 234 to 236 are based on the following passage.

For the first time ever, researchers have observed quantum entanglement between quarks. This is an elusive quantum state where particles become intertwined, and in doing so lose their distinct identities, which makes it impossible to identify them individually. This breakthrough was made at the Conseil Européen pour la Recherche Nucléaire (CERN), the European particle physics lab in Geneva, Switzerland, and it may pave the way for deeper exploration of quantum information in high-energy particles.

While quantum entanglement has been studied in particles like electrons and photons for many years, it's a fragile phenomenon typically measured in low-energy, stable environments (i.e. ultra-cold conditions in quantum computers). In contrast, particle collisions, like those between protons at CERN's Large Hadron Collider, occur in high-energy and chaotic settings, making it significantly more difficult to detect entanglement in the resulting debris — akin to trying to hear a whisper amidst the noise of a rock concert.

234. In the context of the passage, what does the word "chaotic" mean?

   A. realigned
   B. settled
   C. deleterious
   D. disorganized
   E. unbounded

235. What can be inferred when the author states that observed quantum entanglement between quarks "may pave the way for deeper exploration of quantum information for high energy particles?"

   A. Researchers will now be able to isolate individual quarks in high-energy collisions.
   B. Empirical knowledge of quantum entanglement involving quarks could aid theoretical and practical development in the field of quantum computing
   C. The discovery guarantees that quantum computers will soon function in high-energy environments.
   D. The entanglement of quarks makes it easier to detect other quantum phenomena in low-energy particles.
   E. Future studies will focus exclusively on quarks rather than on electrons or photons.

For the following question, consider each of the three answer choices separately and select all that apply.

236. What statements relate to the primary themes of this passage?

   A. Studies using high-energy particles are more important than those involving low-energy particles
   B. Prior to 2024, quantum entanglement studies involving quarks were insufficiently abundant to inform new quantum computing studies
   C. Advancements in quantum computing cannot be made without the use of quantum entanglement

PASSAGE 123

Question 237 is based on the following passage.

The origin of the universe is a hotly debated topic in the scientific community, but despite the fierce polemics, the Big Bang theory is still the prevailing explanation. Proponents of the Big Bang theory insist that the universe once existed in an incredibly dense and hot state until it exploded out and expanded rapidly, causing cooling and the formation of stars, galaxies, and eventually life. Most scientists estimate this event to have occurred around 14 billion years ago.

For the following question, consider each of the three answer choices separately and select all that apply.

237 Which of the following are analogous to the term "polemic" in the passage?

- [A] Contingency
- [B] Brouhaha
- [C] Argument

PASSAGE 124

Questions 238 and 239 are based on the following passage.

There is a key reason why the Thwaites Glacier in Antarctica has earned the nickname "Doomsday Glacier". If this mass of ice, which is roughly the size of Florida, were to fully melt, global sea levels could rise by 65 centimeters. Additionally, since it acts as a barrier preventing other ice sheets from sliding into the ocean, its collapse could eventually lead to a rise in global sea levels that could exceed 3 feet.

In 2018, a joint U.S. and U.K. initiative launched the International Thwaites Glacier Collaboration (ITGC), a project involving 100 experts, to study the glacier's structure and potential future using field research, submersibles, remote sensing, and computer simulations.

238 From the passage presented, it can be concluded that

- (A) The impact of the Thwaites Glacier is limited to the USA and the UK
- (B) The glacier will only be frozen for a short while longer
- (C) Studies of the glacier are multifaceted and likely ongoing
- (D) The rise in sea level from glacial melting is insufficient to cause a problem
- (E) The next global extinction event will begin in Antarctica

For the following question, consider each of the three answer choices separately and select all that apply.

239 Which of the options best summarizes the passage?

- [A] The condition of the Thwaites Glacier has the potential to be globally impactful
- [B] The Thwaites Glacier presents an immediate threat to humanity
- [C] Studies have been initiated to better understand the current and changing state of the Thwaites Glacier

PASSAGE 125

Questions 240 to 242 are based on the following passage.

Asteroids might seem like nothing more than space rocks of varying sizes, but they are far more intricate. They exhibit remarkable diversity in terms of size, shape, composition, and even how they evolve over time.

If you've previously dismissed asteroids, you're not alone. Until recent decades, astronomers underestimated their significance, once referring to them as "vermin of the sky" because they interfered with observations of stars and galaxies, which were considered more important.

However, as technology and observational methods advanced, asteroids gained recognition. With the advent of spacecraft, we can now study them more closely and fully appreciate their complexity—especially the smaller ones that have tiny moons orbiting them.

240 Select the sentence in the text that highlights flawed perceptions of asteroid importance

241 In the context of the passage, the word "intricate" most closely means

- (A) sophisticated
- (B) showy
- (C) unimportant
- (D) recalcitrant
- (E) underwhelming

242) What is the meaning of the 3rd paragraph within the context of the passage?

- (A) The study of stars and galaxies has eroded in recent years.
- (B) Enhancements to instrumentation and observation better highlight the unique details of asteroids
- (C) Lunar studies are important to the future of human space exploration
- (D) Scientists can now leverage asteroids capabilities for human benefit
- (E) The moons of asteroids are now decreasing as they are more closely observed

PASSAGE 126

Question 243 is based on the following passage.

In physical geography, the earth can be divided into categories of climatic conditions, each with endemic communities of plants, animals, and soil organisms. These groups are known as biomes and it is critically important to understand and protect them because they play a vital role in sustaining the balance of life on the planet. There are four main types of biome: aquatic, forest, desert, and grassland. While each type of biome is different, all are equally important threads woven into the same tapestry: planet earth.

243) Select the sentence that uses metaphor as a rhetorical strategy.

PASSAGE 127

Questions 244 and 245 are based on the following passage.

Volcano science has evolved significantly in recent decades, transforming from a descriptive natural science into a highly advanced, multidisciplinary field within geosciences. Despite this progress, the field still lacks large-scale scientific initiatives comparable to those in other disciplines, like the Large Hadron Collider for particle physics or the Human Genome Project for life sciences. A similar "big science" approach is expected to shape the future of volcanology. Three key developments likely to drive this shift in the 2020s include the Krafla Magma Testbed initiative, the creation of a Global Volcano Simulator, and the increasing importance of big data in volcano research. These efforts will push the boundaries of volcano science and enhance our understanding of volcanic processes.

244) In the context of the passage, the word "initiatives" means

- (A) coordinations
- (B) diminutions
- (C) studies
- (D) declensions
- (E) schemes

245) What events would strengthen the position of this passage if true?

- (A) Public and professional interest in "big science" projects drastically declined after 2022.
- (B) A large hadron collider for volcanology is being developed
- (C) A recent survey demonstrated that public interest in volcanos has grown significantly in recent years
- (D) Innovative scientific research has already been planned based on the Krafla Magma initiative.
- (E) The use of big data has created increased demands on scientists' time.

PASSAGE 128

Questions 246 to 248 are based on the following passage.

Copper remains the only heterogeneous catalyst known to effectively convert electrochemically reduced CO_2 (CO2R) into valuable hydrocarbons and alcohols like ethylene and ethanol. Several factors influence CO2R activity and selectivity, including the catalyst's surface structure, morphology, composition, electrolyte ions, pH, and the design of the electrochemical cell. These factors are often interdependent, making the discovery and optimization of catalysts a complex challenge. A comprehensive, historical approach to examining these aspects and their interactions in CO2R on copper, offering insights, critical evaluations, and recommendations for future research and best practices was taken. First, a discussion regarding the experimental and theoretical methods used to understand the mechanisms of product formation was conducted, followed by an analysis of current reaction networks for CO2R on copper. Next, two key strategies were explored for modifying copper's activity and selectivity: nanostructuring and the use of bimetallic electrodes. Finally, perspectives were provided on future directions in CO2R research.

246. Within the context of the passage, what does the word "heterogeneous" mean?

   (A) uniform
   (B) mixed
   (C) disorganized
   (D) comprehensive
   (E) gelatinous

For Questions 247 and 248, consider each of the choices separately and select all that apply.

247. What can be inferred when the author states "Copper remains the only heterogeneous catalyst known to effectively convert electrochemically reduced CO2 (CO2R) into valuable hydrocarbons and alcohols like ethylene and ethanol."?

   [A] Electrochemical conversion of reduced carbon to hydrocarbons requires very specific circumstances.
   [B] Under the right circumstances, other heterogeneous substances can effectively generate hydrocarbons.
   [C] Nanostructuring and bimetallic electrodes may impact CO2R conversion.

248. What conclusions could likely be drawn about CO2R based on this passage?

   [A] CO2R reacts uniformly with copper under diverse experimental conditions
   [B] Interest in different factors enhancing the activity and selectivity of catalysts for CO2R are a key focus of scientific discussion
   [C] The properties of CO2R can be dictated by a variety of circumstances

PASSAGE 129

Question 249 is based on the following passage.

The use of gravitational lensing serves as a powerful tool for exploring the universe. Instead of using a magnifying glass, the "lens" in this case is the curvature of space itself. According to Albert Einstein's general theory of relativity, spacetime bends in the presence of massive objects, like galaxy clusters. A newly captured image provides strong evidence that Einstein's 1915 theory accurately represents the structure of the universe.

249. Given the content of the passage, what is the most likely conclusion which can be reached about the "newly captured image" referenced?

   (A) it is inferior to those images captured with a "magnifying glass"
   (B) it fails to adhere to the general theory of relativity
   (C) it will be grainy when compared to images from 1915
   (D) it leverages unique cosmetological aspects of the universe to generate an image of galaxy clusters
   (E) it disproves one of Einstein's most important theories

PASSAGE 130

Question 250 is based on the following passage.

Dark matter is still a mysterious phenomenon to astrophysicists. There are large portions of the universe in which mass does not emit or scatter light or any other kind of electromagnetic radiation, so scientists deem these areas to be composed of dark matter. However, there is still no concrete evidence for the existence of dark matter; scientists can only infer that it exists based on the studied gravitational effects of visible matter and the discrepancies in mass that occur in calculations relative to the mass of galaxies and clusters of galaxies. Thus, dark matter provides a good example of how little we really know about the structures that compose our universe.

250. Select the sentence that, according to the author, best describes the current state of astrophysics.

Answer Key

Q. No.	Correct Answer
201	D
202	D
203	B
204	C
205	E
206	B
207	B
208	C
209	D
210	D
211	C
212	The surface... pond.
213	The vegetable...altered.
214	C
215	C
216	C
217	C
218	Chemists...matter.
219	A, B, C
220	C
221	A
222	C
223	D
224	E
225	In scientific... handkerchief.

Q. No.	Correct Answer
226	A, B
227	A, C
228	C
229	A
230	B
231	B, C
232	B, C
233	C
234	D
235	B
236	B
237	B, C
238	C
239	A, C
240	Until... important.
241	A
242	B
243	There...earth.
244	E
245	D
246	B
247	A, C
248	B, C
249	D
250	Thus,... universe.

Practice Set 5: Answers & Explanations

PASSAGE 105

201 **Choice D is correct** because the passage emphasizes that although the sound waves are emitted at a constant frequency, they may be perceived differently depending on the position of the listener. This demonstrates that the sound emitted is not always the same as the sound that is heard, especially when motion is involved (e.g., trains moving in opposite directions). This is a classic example of the Doppler effect.

Choice A is incorrect because the passage does not focus on the unreliability of individual perceptions, but rather on how position and motion affect perception, which is a predictable physical phenomenon. **Choice B** is incorrect because while the scenario described (hearing the same sound differently) is noted as unusual, the main point is not the rarity, but the mechanism (difference in perception due to relative motion). **Choice C** is incorrect because the moment of the trains passing is not the central issue; the changing pitch as perceived due to movement is. The common point of passage is incidental. **Choice E** is incorrect because the passage does not discuss the rate of change of sound in direct relation to the speed of the train in detail. While motion is implied, the focus is on pitch perception, not quantitative rate of change.

PASSAGE 106: SUMMARY/PARAPHRASE

The passage is about asteroids. The main idea is that astronomers originally had little knowledge of asteroids. The main idea is developed by two major points: (a) until the mid-19th century, astronomers had little accurate notion of how many asteroids there were and (b) astronomers mistakenly believed that Vesta was the largest asteroid due to its relative brightness, whereas the largest asteroid is in fact Ceres. A minor point explains that the mistake in determining the relative size of the asteroids stemmed from differences in the reflectivity of Ceres and Vesta. The purpose of the passage is to inform the reader about the history of our knowledge of asteroids.

202 **Choice D is correct** because it is the most logical explanation. The passage suggests that after years with few sightings, asteroids began to be seen with increasing regularity. This implies that something improved the spotters' ability to detect them, such as better instruments or techniques, rather than an actual increase in asteroid numbers.

Choice A is incorrect because the passage does not mention weather conditions as a factor in spotting asteroids, so assuming poor weather had previously obstructed views is speculative and unsupported. **Choice B** is incorrect because while more astronomy courses might educate people, it does not necessarily follow that this would directly result in more astronomers actively spotting asteroids. **Choice C** is incorrect because there is no indication in the passage of volcanic activity or atmospheric ash affecting visibility, making this explanation purely hypothetical. **Choice E** is incorrect because the passage does not state or imply that astronomers were confused about asteroid characteristics, so a shift in definition or classification does not explain the change in sightings.

203 **Choice B is correct** because the passage highlights that after 1845, asteroids began to be discovered with increasing regularity, suggesting that the trend of more discoveries will likely continue. The mention of a large number of asteroids being tracked by the close of the century supports the idea that more asteroids will be discovered and correctly measured in the future.

Choice A is incorrect because although rapid discoveries were made in the past, the passage does not directly predict that discoveries will occur at an even faster pace in the future. The passage simply discusses a historical trend, not a forecast of continuous acceleration. **Choice C** is incorrect because while the passage discusses the discovery of asteroids and their sizes, it does not suggest any likelihood of a larger asteroid than Ceres being discovered. In fact, Ceres was proven to be the largest, which implies a resolution of such doubts rather than future discoveries of larger bodies. **Choice D** is incorrect because the passage does not advocate for increased investment in astronomical research. While research is clearly important, the passage focuses on the progress of discoveries and measurements, not funding. **Choice E** is incorrect because while the origins of asteroids are an interesting topic, the passage does not address the continued identification of their origins. It focuses more on the discovery and measurement of asteroids, not their historical or physical origins.

PASSAGE 107: SUMMARY/PARAPHRASE

The passage is about how snowflakes and raindrops form. The main idea is that snowflakes and raindrops form through a very similar process. The major points are: (a) raindrops form when water vapor reaches cooler temperatures and begins to condense to form droplets and (b) that snowflakes form in almost the exact same conditions except that it is cold enough to freeze the newly condensed water. There is a minor point that speculates on why snowflakes have the crystalline structure they have, and another that mentions that snow and rain are both part of the water cycle. The purpose of the passage is to inform.

204 **Choice C is correct** because the phrase "in any case" signals that the writer is refocusing on the main topic after discussing an unrelated aspect, indicating a return to the original subject of rain and snow formation.

Choice A is incorrect because the information about the effect of cooling air on water vapor is not the focus of the passage at this point. The writer is not addressing this topic in the sentence where "in any case" is used. **Choice B** is incorrect because the phrase "in any case" does not refer to snowflake formation. The sentence is not a return to that subject, but rather to the broader topic of precipitation formation. **Choice D** is incorrect because it does not address the function of the phrase "in any case." The writer is not distancing himself from a discussion of snowflake formation, but returning to the core topic. **Choice E** is incorrect because there is no indication that the writer finds the information uninteresting. The passage does not suggest a shift away due to lack of interest, but rather a change in focus.

205 **Choice E is correct** because the passage explains how rain and snow form through the same process, with differences arising due to temperature. By highlighting both similarities and differences, the author uses a compare-and-contrast structure.

Choice A is incorrect because a narrative tells a story, and this passage does not present a sequence of events or a plot. **Choice B** is incorrect because expository writing typically explains background or context, especially in relation to setting or characters, which is not the focus here. **Choice C** is incorrect because the passage does not present an argument or opinion, which is typical of an editorial. **Choice D** is incorrect because persuasive writing aims to convince the reader of a particular viewpoint, which this passage does not attempt to do.

206 **Choice B is correct** because fog forms when cool air on the surface comes in contact with warm air vapor, leading to the formation of small droplets of water.

Choice A is incorrect because a rainbow forms when light passes through water droplets, not when cool air interacts with warm air vapor. **Choice C** is incorrect because wind chill is a measure of how wind affects the perceived temperature, but it is not a weather event itself. **Choice D** is incorrect because a degree day is a measure used for heating or cooling needs, not a weather event. **Choice E** is incorrect because thunder is the sound produced by lightning, which is not related to the formation of fog.

PASSAGE 108

207 **Choice B is correct** because the passage focuses on how wear affects a gas valve, specifically a well-designed one, and the impact of gas valve design on engine performance. Adding further evidence on how the design influences engine performance would strengthen the author's argument about the importance of quality gas valves.

Choice A is incorrect because the passage does not provide instructions for maintaining engine function in general, but focuses specifically on the gas valve. Adding information about overall engine function would distract from the main focus on the gas valve. **Choice C** is incorrect because while it discusses the quality of performance in a gas valve, it does not address the main argument about why the design of the valve matters for engine performance. It deviates from the author's central point. **Choice D** is incorrect because the passage argues that wear has few destructive effects on a gas valve, particularly one that is well-designed. Adding information about how gas valves deteriorate over time would contradict the author's emphasis on design quality. **Choice E** is incorrect because it introduces irrelevant factors that the passage does not address. By focusing on just one factor—gas valve design—the author avoids complicating the argument with unrelated conditions that could affect overall engine performance.

PASSAGE 109

208 **Choice C is correct** because the passage describes a cycle, which is best represented by a circular diagram. A cycle involves repetitive processes or steps, and a cycle diagram would effectively depict this recurring nature of the information.

Choice A is incorrect because Venn diagrams are used for comparison and contrast, which does not align with the purpose of the passage. **Choice B** is incorrect because a list does not necessarily require any specific organizational pattern and would not be the best method for organizing the information presented in the passage.

Choice D is incorrect because a timeline organizes events chronologically, which would not be suitable for representing a cycle where events do not occur in a strict chronological order but rather repeat over time. **Choice E is incorrect** because T-charts, like Venn diagrams, are used for comparison and contrast and do not match the purpose of the passage.

209 **Choice D is correct** because the passage introduces the process of precipitation and how it leads to the formation of ice caps and glaciers, which logically suggests that the next paragraph will further elaborate on these topics, particularly ice caps and glaciers.

Choice A is incorrect because while clouds and air currents are mentioned, they are not discussed in sufficient detail to be the focus of the next paragraph. The passage emphasizes precipitation and its effects on ice caps and glaciers, rather than on cloud formation. **Choice B is incorrect** because the passage does not cover all forms of precipitation, and the next paragraph would likely focus on ice caps and glaciers, rather than additional forms of precipitation. **Choice C is incorrect** because while lakes and ponds may contribute to the water cycle, the passage does not focus on them or suggest that they will be discussed in the following paragraph. The main focus is on precipitation leading to ice caps and glaciers.

PASSAGE 110: SUMMARY/PARAPHRASE

The passage is about sound. The main idea is that sound is a sensation caused by clearly delineated physical phenomena. The major points are: (a) that sound is a sensation rather than a physical phenomenon (b) that the sensation of sound is caused by a physical phenomenon known as "sonorous vibration" and (c) the sonorous vibrations cause the sensation of sound by reaching the skin of the ear. A minor point that compares sonorous vibrations to ripples in water serves to illustrate the phenomenon. The main purpose of the passage is to clarify and explain the link between a physical phenomenon and a bodily sensation.

210 **Choice D is correct** because the term "peculiar" in this context refers to something characteristic or inherent to the ear, meaning it is natural or typical for the ear to hear sound. This interpretation aligns with the passage's intent.

Choice A is incorrect because sound is not described as odd or uncommon in this context. In fact, the ear is naturally attuned to hearing sound, making this choice inaccurate. **Choice B is incorrect** because this option also implies sound is strange or exceptional, which contradicts the passage's description of sound being a normal and typical experience for the ear. **Choice C is incorrect** because the definition of "peculiar" in this answer refers to something unusual or out of the ordinary, which does not match the intended meaning in the passage where sound is described as a typical experience for the ear. **Choice E is incorrect** because replacing "peculiar" with "belonging characteristically" would alter the meaning. The passage emphasizes the ear's natural ability to hear sound, so "peculiar" correctly conveys this inherent quality rather than suggesting it's simply belonging to the ear.

211 **Choice C is correct** because the passage uses the violin as an example to illustrate how vibrations affect the eardrum, which is suitable for helping students understand the sensation of sound. The explanation is educational rather than technical, making it appropriate for a learning context.

Choice A is incorrect because although the violin is mentioned, the passage is not directed at musicians nor does it provide information specifically tailored to musical performance or technique. **Choice B is incorrect** because the passage does not provide the technical specifications or construction guidelines that would be relevant to violin manufacturers. **Choice D is incorrect** because the passage does not relate to medical imaging or procedures involving sonography technicians, such as conducting or interpreting sonograms. **Choice E is incorrect** because while the passage discusses sound, it does not delve into the design of physical spaces to optimize sound clarity, which would be the focus of acoustics engineers.

212 **"The surface of the sounding-board is thus set trembling, and these tremors, or vibrations, spread through the air in all directions around the instrument, somewhat in the manner that water-waves spread around the place where a stone has been dropped into a quiet pond."** This sentence, in fact, uses some of the same language that is used to report earthquakes such as tremors and trembling. The effects of an earthquake are similar in that the movement of the earth radiates out from the epicenter.

PASSAGE 111

213 **"The vegetable oil and methanol are placed in a small quantity of an alkaline catalyst and it is in this process that the chemical makeup of the vegetable oil is altered."** Prior to the addition of the catalyst, the mixture of vegetable oil and methanol has no ability to be used as fuel. They cannot complete the ester interchange by simply being combined. The information following the highlighted sentence details the byproducts of the ester interchange.

PASSAGE 112: SUMMARY/PARAPHRASE

The passage is about astrophysics. The main idea is that astrophysics now believes that it is not uncommon for planets in other solar systems to orbit more than one star, a notion that was once largely relegated to the realm of science fiction. The major points are (a) that the climate on a planet orbiting two stars would be quite unstable (b) that scientists are unsure of how or if life would come to be on such planets. The main purpose of the passage is to inform the reader about a recent development in astrophysics.

214 **Choice C is correct** because the author uses Star Wars as a stylistic device to pique the reader's interest in a scientific discussion by connecting it to a familiar cultural reference. This makes the scientific content more engaging and accessible without altering the factual focus of the passage.

Choice A is incorrect because while the passage does mention both science fiction and science, the comparison is limited to circumbinary planets, not a broader commentary about science fiction influencing science overall. **Choice B is incorrect** because the author's mention of Star Wars is not intended to imply that science fiction always precedes scientific knowledge; this would be a far-reaching inference beyond what the passage supports. **Choice D is incorrect** because although Star Wars is used to draw the reader in, this is a stylistic rather than a rhetorical strategy. The author is not constructing an argument or trying to persuade the reader of a specific opinion, and no narrative elements are included. **Choice E is incorrect** because the passage does not attempt to promote or advertise Star Wars in any way—it simply references it to help readers connect with the topic.

215 **Choice C is correct** because the passage explains that studying circumbinary planets provides insight into how stellar systems—like dual suns—can affect the climates of planets. This supports a better understanding of how solar forces influence planetary environments, which is the focus of the passage.

Choice A is incorrect because the passage notes that scientists do not yet know how life forms or evolves on such planets. Therefore, circumbinary planets cannot currently help us understand how life develops elsewhere. **Choice B is incorrect** because there is no mention of Earth's climate change in the passage. The connection between circumbinary planets and climate change on Earth is not supported by the information provided. **Choice D is incorrect** because the passage does not suggest that circumbinary planets are common or help us understand how typical such planetary systems are—there is no comparative frequency discussed. **Choice E is incorrect** because while the discovery of circumbinary planets is certainly interesting, the passage does not suggest they challenge or change our fundamental definitions of planets.

PASSAGE 113: SUMMARY/PARAPHRASE

The passage is about the impact of scientific progress on health. The main idea is that developments in all scientific fields can have an impact on medical progress. The main idea is supported by a major point: that chemists have recently discovered new materials that could potentially be used for a variety of medical diagnoses and treatments. The purpose of the passage is to inform the reader about the extent to which medical progress draws on broader scientific progress.

216 **Choice C is correct** because the passage describes the new "smart" polymer as groundbreaking—which aligns with the meaning of "avant-garde." The author emphasizes that this polymer's true innovation lies in its potential to enable light to function as a form of medicine, marking a significant advance in medical science.

Choice A is incorrect because while disease diagnostics and tissue engineering are mentioned as benefits, the passage presents these as secondary applications. The main significance is the polymer's ability to assist in using light as a therapeutic tool. **Choice B is incorrect** because the passage makes no mention of competition among chemists or a competitive advantage in the medical field. There is no information to support this inference. **Choice D is incorrect** because there is no indication in the passage that the polymer resulted from interdisciplinary cooperation. The focus is solely on the polymer's capabilities and potential applications. **Choice E is incorrect** because while it's true the polymer is described as special, this choice repeats information without identifying why the polymer is considered avant-garde, which is the focus of the question.

217 **Choice C is correct** because the section in boldface emphasizes that medical advancements often occur in unexpected ways—beyond what we can currently imagine. This directly supports the idea that the evolution of medicine can be surprising and unpredictable, which is the main point being made.

Choice A is incorrect because although the boldface section shows cooperation between scientists and doctors, its primary purpose is to highlight the unpredictability of medical progress, not the collaboration itself. **Choice B is incorrect** because the focus is not simply that scientists and doctors are creative, but rather that their combined efforts lead to innovations that defy our expectations. **Choice D is incorrect** because the section does not claim that medical advances cannot happen without such cooperation—only that such cooperation can lead to unexpected outcomes. **Choice E** is incorrect because while the boldface section implies that future developments are beyond our current imagination, it does not argue that human imagination is fundamentally limited. The emphasis is on the surprising nature of progress, not on limits of creativity.

218 **"Chemists report that their new polymer (plastic-like) material could help diagnose diseases and engineer new human tissues; whether or not these claims can be substantiated is another matter."** For the majority of the passage the author's tone towards the new "smart" polymer is one of excitement and intrigue. However, the last sentence demonstrates that the author is actually skeptical as to whether or not the new "smart" polymer can live up to the promises of the scientists.

PASSAGE 114: SUMMARY/PARAPHRASE

The passage is about the chemical properties of iron. The main idea is that iron can form two chemically distinct series of compounds. The major points are that: (a) iron can form a series of compounds with chemical similarities to zinc compounds and (b) that iron can also form a series of compounds that are chemically similar to aluminum compounds. The primary purpose of the passage is to inform the reader about the chemical properties of iron compounds.

219 **Choice A is correct** because the passage states that ferrous (lower valence) and ferric (higher valence) compounds follow a naming rule also seen with copper: cuprous (+1) and cupric (+2). **Choice B is correct** because the suffixes –ous and –ic can mean "possessing" and "having characteristics of" in general English, as seen in words like beauteous and heroic. **Choice C is correct** because if B is accepted, then describing cuprous and cupric as relating to copper's qualities or characteristics is reasonable by extension.

PASSAGE 115

The passage is about antimatter. The main idea is that antimatter was posited as a way of understanding the behavior of electrons, but deeper understanding was not possible until the development of particle accelerators. The main points are that (a) antimatter is composed of antiparticles, just as matter is composed of particles (b) Dirac hypothesized the existence of antimatter as a way of better understanding electrons and (c) that the existence of antimatter was only proven by particle accelerators. There is a minor point that most current research on antimatter is at CERN, in Geneva. The main purpose of the passage is to familiarize the reader with some very basic points about antimatter, and give a brief, factual account of how it was initially posited.

220 **Choice C is correct** because Dirac's antimatter hypothesis is founded on the presupposition that everything has an opposite.

Choice A is incorrect because, while this may be the case, the author does not point to this line of thinking as the impetus behind Dirac's investigations into antimatter. **Choice B** is incorrect because the author does not claim that understanding electrons is the key to unlocking the universe, nor does the author show this to be the reasoning behind Dirac's hypothesis. **Choice D** is incorrect because the passage does not indicate that Dirac believed in the idea that the universe could be fully delineated or that he used such thinking to formulate his antimatter hypothesis. **Choice E** is incorrect because the passage discusses that Dirac conceptualized antimatter in the late 1920s but that it couldn't be tested until at least the 1960s, so it can be reasonably inferred that technological capabilities and scientific ideas do not always align.

221 **Choice A is correct** because the author is recounting the conceptualization of the antimatter hypothesis.

Choice B is incorrect because a testimony relays a truth or conviction that something is true; this passage is merely recounting the development of the antimatter hypothesis. **Choice C** is incorrect because the passage itself is not a scientific theory; it is a recounting of the development of a scientific hypothesis. **Choice D** is incorrect because the author is not directly trying to persuade the reader to believe in the antimatter hypothesis. **Choice E** is incorrect because the author does not draw any comparisons relative to the development of the antimatter hypothesis.

PASSAGE 116: SUMMARY/PARAPHRASE

The passage is about advances in biotechnology. The main idea is that while biochemical research is coming ever closer to creating life, actually doing so could have severely adverse consequences. The major points are that (a) biochemists are using a new chemical reaction to create self-assembling cell membranes (b) scientists hope the understanding cell-membranes, which are one of the basic building blocks of life, will lead to insights into how non-living matter becomes life and (c) in the author's view, some questions are best left unanswered, especially in view of the potentially destructive potential of such breakthroughs. The main purpose of the passage is to caution against research that digs too deeply into the origins of life. Rhetorical devices such as the mention of Pandora's Box and the vague danger of total annihilation indicate that the author has a strong bias against the research under discussion.

222 **Choice C is correct** because the author's point that the creation of artificial life is problematic is driven home by the fact that the author also provides a counterview to his point, showing that the author is willing to both understand the other side and yet still maintain his or her own viewpoint.

Choice A is incorrect because the author does provide the facts related to the potential creation of artificial life forms, but the entire passage is infused with the author's bias against this line of scientific inquiry; there is no purely objective evaluation of the facts. **Choice B** is incorrect because, while the last line of the passage is certainly a dramatic way of driving home the author's point about the dangers of the creation of artificial life, the author primarily reinforces his or her claim by providing a counterview to the argument in delineating what scientists think about the matter. **Choice D** is incorrect because the author does not directly and harshly criticize the opinions of the scientists; the author merely disputes them. **Choice E** is incorrect because the author provides no specific authority who agrees with his or her claims; the author's authority in this passage is merely his or her own opinions.

223 **Choice D is correct** because the author is making the point that the creation of artificial life may have far-reaching consequences that can never be undone and uses the trope or metaphor of Pandora's Box as a rhetorical device to reinforce this point.

Choice A is incorrect because, whether or not the reader understands the meaning of the Pandora's box metaphor, the author still clearly delineates what it means in the same sentence by saying that creating artificial life would engender a situation in which scientists could not undo the consequences. The author's strategy is double-layered and provides both the metaphor and its literal meaning simultaneously, showing that the Pandora's box trope is not used to test the reader's intelligence. **Choice B** is incorrect because Pandora's Box is a metaphor for an action with consequences that cannot be undone, and its use does not necessitate that the consequences can never be controlled. **Choice C** is incorrect because Pandora's Box is a metaphor for an action whose consequences can never be undone, but this does not mean that the consequences are evil. Hence, invoking Pandora's Box does not show that the creation of artificial life is evil. **Choice E** is incorrect because Pandora's Box is not a red herring since it is a metaphor that reinforces the author's main claim and not a rhetorical device that distracts the reader from the issue at hand.

224 **Choice E is correct** because the author uses the last sentence to appeal to the reader's sense of values or emotions (pathos).

Choice A is incorrect because the last sentence of the passage is meant to persuade the reader to believe in the author's opinion by way of a rhetorical appeal to the reader's emotions or sense of values (pathos). **Choice B** is incorrect because the author does not believe that the scientific research mentioned in the passage is important; rather, the author views it as dangerous. **Choice C** is incorrect because the author does not generalize a specific argument in the last sentence of the passage, but instead uses the end of the passage to appeal to the sensibilities of the reader as a means of persuading the reader to agree with his or her viewpoint. **Choice D** is incorrect because the last sentence does not lay out more details related to self-assembling membranes; it actually seeks to convince the reader that scientific research regarding self-assembling membranes is dangerous.

PASSAGE 117: SUMMARY/PARAPHRASE

The passage is about the way that particle structure affects how matter interacts with matter. The main idea is that mercury is unusual in that it behaves like a solid even in a liquid state. The major points are: (a) that particles in solids cohere to each other more strongly than they adhere to the particles in other objects (b) that liquid mercury particles also cohere to one another more strongly than they adhere to the particles in other objects. The main purpose of the passage is to inform.

225 **"In scientific language, the cohesion of mercury is stronger than its adhesion to your finger or handkerchief."** The writer's use of the phrase "in scientific language" implies that the text before this is not written in scientific language. The writer also follows this sentence with an example that uses a common object to illustrate the topic of the passage. This indicates that the intended audience is not other scientists.

PASSAGE 118

226 **Choice A is correct** because this option suggests that the distance from the observer to the object affects how the object is perceived, aligning with the passage's mention of space taken up by the image depending on how close or far the object is. **Choice B is correct** because this option emphasizes that perception of an object's size can be influenced by its relationship to the surrounding environment, as noted in the passage about examining the object in comparison to other items in the room.

Choice C is incorrect because the passage does not mention anything about retinal health affecting perception; instead, it focuses on how distance and surrounding items contribute to what a person perceives.

227 **Choice A is correct** because this option is supported by the passage's discussion about how the perceived size of an object changes based on distance and context, implying that the human perception of size can be distorted. **Choice C is correct** because it is implied that the retina plays a crucial role in the way we perceive images based on the light and the images sent to the brain. Thus, it relates to the broader understanding of visual perception.

Choice B is incorrect because the passage does not discuss how brightness or darkness influences size perception; instead, it focuses on distance and surrounding objects.

PASSAGE 119

228 **Choice C is correct** because the passage starts by discussing that solar energy is a possible way to help reach net-carbon-zero goals, and the first paragraph adds statistics to show how much carbon dioxide might be reduced by a switch from natural gas to solar energy. The first paragraph also delves into the benefits of better air quality. However, the second paragraph introduces some counterarguments, such as habitat loss and soil erosion, but concludes that the problems might be "mitigated" or "minimized." The final sentence starts with "however" to show that the production of energy might ultimately outweigh the problems.

Choice A is incorrect because the passage is about solar energy, not the decision to pursue net-carbon-zero goals. There is no discussion of what such goals accomplish, only a discussion of the benefits and drawbacks of solar energy. **Choice B** is incorrect because, while the second paragraph explains that there are some concerns about solar energy, the entire text is not focused on explaining that solar energy is "not wise" or "a bad decision to use." The second paragraph specifically points out that problems can be mitigated. **Choice D** is incorrect because reducing diseases is given as evidence supporting why solar energy should be adopted, not vice versa. The evidence refers to how much carbon dioxide is reduced, there are no facts showing the reductions in disease. There is only a claim that such reductions occur. **Choice E** is incorrect because there are no "recommendations" or "suggestions" other than saying solar energy might help and the allusion that proper installation and maintenance are necessary. However, there is no specific advice about how to implement the installation or placement, or how much should be used.

229 **Choice A is correct** because the question is asking for a fact that shows that solar energy is not a "panacea" or "cure-all." In other words, the answer choice needs to show a problem of solar energy. Choice A is such a problem: solar panels take up land that might be better used for other purposes.

Choices B and C are incorrect because they describe the benefits of solar energy, so they support the claim that solar energy is a panacea rather than "cast doubt on" or "weaken" the idea that it is a panacea. **Choice D** is incorrect because it shows that there is a problem, but that the problem can be minimized. The author is using this fact to show that solar energy can help, not weaken the idea that solar energy can solve all problems. **Choice E** is incorrect because the author uses this fact to establish a baseline for the fact that solar energy is better than the main current energy production technology. Therefore, this fact strengthens the idea that solar energy is a panacea.

230 **Choice B is correct** because the last sentence of the text states that, "if properly installed and maintained, one acre can produce up to about 447 MWh of energy per year." The implication is therefore that "if not properly installed and maintained," the amount of energy produced will be less.

Choice A is incorrect because the text states that solar energy produces about 95 pounds of carbon dioxide per MWh, but that a large-scale installation can produce about 447 MWh of energy per year. If an equivalent amount of gas were used to produce 447 MWh of energy per year, there would be thousands of pounds saved, since each MWh of gas-generated energy emits about 1,071 pounds of carbon dioxide. The savings would be much greater than 95 pounds. **Choice C** is incorrect because, while the text mentions paying attention to mitigate habitat loss, there is no indication that such a process is not occurring now. The statement could be a reminder to continue good practices. **Choice D** is incorrect because the text states that solar energy is "an effective alternative to consider," but does not extend the claim to say that it is the only alternative. There might be better solutions. **Choice E** is incorrect because there is no discussion of expenses in the text, so it is impossible to evaluate this claim based on the information provided.

PASSAGE 120: SUMMARY/PARAPHRASE

The passage is about climate change. The main idea is that although people are prone to jump to conclusions about the climate based on transitory trends in the weather, the real picture is more complex. The major points are (a) that people tend to see extreme temperatures, depending on the nature of the extreme, as either a confirmation or a refutation of global warming and (b) research suggests that factors associated with extreme high temperatures can also be used to explain severe winters. The purpose of the passage is to caution the reader from drawing glib solutions about the phenomenon about climate change by showing at least one way in which doing so has been demonstrated to be wrong.

231 **Choice B is correct** because incredulous means skeptical or suspicious, and since the author seems to be wary of the climate change hysteria permeating public and scientific discourse, incredulous is a good way to characterize the author's attitude. **Choice C is correct** because dubious means to be wary or suspicious of something, and given the author's introductory sentence, it is clear that the author is skeptical of the climate change hysteria permeating public and scientific discourse.

Choice A is incorrect because the author is skeptical of public and scientific reaction to climate change, but there is no indication that he or she is afraid of it.

PASSAGE 121

232 **Choice B is correct** because the passage states that Mars "may be seen" as it is "in opposition". When Mars is in opposition, this means that the Earth is positioned between Mars and the sun. **Choice C is correct** because this opposition, as the passage clearly mentions, would occur "all night."

Choice A is incorrect because Mars can best be viewed when its orbit is in opposition and not during its last orbit.

233 **Choice C is correct** because the passage primarily discusses Mars' location and how it compares to Earth and Venus, which positions Mars favorably for scientific observations despite its distance fluctuations due to its eccentric orbit.

Choice A is incorrect because while the passage briefly mentions the apparent diameter of Mars compared to Venus, it does not focus on the visual aspects or characteristics of Mars itself. The passage is more concerned with Mars' position relative to Earth and its oppositions rather than its visual appearance. **Choice B** is incorrect because the passage only discusses one fact about Mars' orbit. The orbit is mentioned to help explain distances but is not the main subject of the passage. **Choice D** is incorrect because while the passage discusses the distance between Mars and Earth, it is framed within the context of comparing Mars with Venus and discussing the best times for observation, rather than solely focusing on distance metrics alone. **Choice E** is incorrect because while the passage does mention that Mars can be seen at night during opposition, it does not delve deeply into practical observation details or ideal viewing locations. The main focus is on Mars' position relative to Earth and Venus, rather than the specifics of observation times.

PASSAGE 122

234 **Choice D is correct** because it means "in a state of complete confusion or disorder" while disorganized means "not properly planned or controlled". These definitions are closely aligned and could commonly be used to analogize one another.

Choice A is incorrect because realigned refers to "changing or restoring an entity to a different position or state", a definition that cannot be used interchangeably with chaotic in this context. **Choice B** is incorrect because settled is defined as "to sit or come to rest in a comfortable position" which would be the opposite of chaotic in this circumstance. **Choice C** is incorrect because deleterious is defined as "causing harm or damage". While the particles discussed are somewhat spectral with regard to their properties, there is nothing inherently "good" or "bad" about them in the context of the passage. **Choice E** is incorrect because unbounded is defined as something that "lacks or appears to lack limits". While the environment within which these particles are reacting might be difficult to understand, they are, by the nature of the experiment being run, controlled and bounded.

235 **Choice B is correct** because the passage indicates that quantum entanglement involving quarks had never been observed before, and while other reactions related to quantum entanglement had been observed, they involved unstable and dissimilar particles in extreme environments that were significantly dissimilar to the new data.

Choice A is incorrect because the passage stated that particles "lose their distinct identities", implying that these identities (including those of quarks) were characterizable prior to the high energy collisions described **Choice C** is incorrect because there is no explicit guarantee of improvement in functionality, only the possibility of gleaning more knowledge **Choice D** is incorrect because the primary focus of the passage was on high energy, not low energy reactions **Choice E** is incorrect because the passage at no point indicates the exclusion of one form of particle or another, merely the addition of new information to inform those studies.

236 **Choice B is correct** because the passage describes the new possibilities for discovery that now exist by conducting quantum entanglement studies involving quarks. The implication, by proxy, is that information was insufficient to do so prior to this point. **Choice A** is incorrect because the passage never seeks to compare the relative importance of one particle versus another, but merely to highlight the additional information and opportunity gleaned from recent particle studies. **Choice C** is incorrect because it asserts that quantum entanglement knowledge is essential to advancements in quantum computing. While the importance of this knowledge was highlighted, at no point did the passage state or imply that quantum entanglement was essential for all advances in quantum computing

PASSAGE 123: SUMMARY/PARAPHRASE

The passage is about the Big Bang theory. The main idea is that while the origins of the universe are still controversial, the Big Bang theory is the most widely accepted explanation. There are two major points that briefly sketch the basics of the theory: (a) that universe existed in an extremely hot and dense microcosm of itself and then exploded outward and created stars and galaxies in the process and (b) that the Big Bang is estimated to have occurred roughly 14 billion years ago. The main purpose of the passage is to give a brief, factual summary of the current position of science on the origins of the universe without commenting on whether that position is or is not correct.

237 **Choice B is correct** because both brouhaha and polemic are synonyms for dispute, and thus the two terms are analogous. **Choice C is correct** because both argument and polemic are synonyms for dispute, and thus the two terms are analogous.

Choice A is incorrect because contingency means chance or possibility, and polemic means dispute, so the two terms are not analogous

PASSAGE 124

238 **Choice C is correct** because of the passage's reference to the future actions associated with field research, submersibles, remote sensing, and computer simulations.

Choice A is incorrect due to the reference to "global" sea level rise that could exceed 3 feet **Choice B** is incorrect because no reference was made to the glacier's projected melt schedule. **Choice D** is incorrect because of the apocalyptic implications associated with terms like " 'Doomsday Glacier' " and allusions to deleterious cascade effects associated with its potential melting **Choice E** is incorrect because no ordinal references to global catastrophe are present in this passage

239 **Choices A and C are correct** because the global implications of the Thwaites Glacier are explicitly highlighted in the passage as ongoing studies to assess its current and changing condition.

Choice B is incorrect because the immediacy of the glacier's impact is never alluded to within the passage

PASSAGE 125

240 "Until recent decades, astronomers underestimated their significance, once referring to them as "vermin of the sky" because they interfered with observations of stars and galaxies, which were considered more important." This sentence indicates that perceptions, which appropriately consider the menagerie of nuanced characteristics of asteroids at present, were much less considered in past years.

241 **Choice A is correct** because the definition of intricate in this circumstance is "very complicated or detailed" while sophisticated is "a machine, system, or technique developed to a high degree of complexity."

Choice B is incorrect because showy means having a striking appearance or style, which does not align with the definition of intricate in the passage **Choice C** is incorrect because unimportant means lacking in importance or significance which does not align with the definition of intricate in the passage **Choice D** is incorrect because recalcitrant means having an uncooperative attitude towards authority or discipline which does not align with the definition of intricate in the passage **Choice E** is incorrect because underwhelming means failing to impress or have a positive impact on someone which does not align with the definition of intricate in the passage

242 **Choice B is correct** because the passage details the advancements of "technology and observational methods" which enhance the recognition of asteroids and their unique characteristics

Choice A is incorrect because no mention of reduction in study is mentioned within the passage, only that more attention is paid to the distinctive attributes of asteroids **Choice C** is incorrect because the passage addresses lunar studies related to asteroids, but fails to relate those studies to human space exploration. **Choice D** is incorrect because the passage speaks to the observations of asteroids made, rather than any directed applications of those observations **Choice E** is incorrect because there is no direct reference or allusion to lunar bodies of asteroids being perturbed by the observations being made.

PASSAGE 126: SUMMARY/PARAPHRASE

The passage is about the way physical geography divides up the earth by climate zones. The main idea is that climatic zones, known as biomes, are crucial to understanding the balance of life on earth. The major points are (a) that biomes support a rich variety of plant and animal life and (b) the diversity of biomes is vital to sustaining the balance of life. A minor point specifies the major types of biome. The purpose of the passage is to raise awareness of biomes and their importance.

243 "There are four main types of biome: aquatic, forest, desert, and grassland and while all are different, all equally important because they are like threads woven into the same tapestry: planet earth." The last sentence creates a metaphor that likens the earth and its biomes to a tapestry and the author does this to underscore the fact that each part of the biome is unique but all are equally important.

PASSAGE 127

244 **Choice E is correct** because "initiatives" is defined as "acts or strategies intended to resolve a difficulty or improve a situation". Given of the definition of schemes is a "systematic plan or arrangement for obtaining a particular objective" it aligns well with the definition of initiatives.

Choice A is incorrect because coordinations is defined as the organization of different elements of a complex body, which does not align with the definition of initiatives in this context. **Choice B** is incorrect because diminutions means a reduction in the size or importance or something, which does not align with the definition of initiatives in the passage. **Choice C** is incorrect because "studies" describes devoting time or attention to acquiring knowledge, which does not align with the definition of initiatives in this passage. **Choice D** is incorrect because "declensions" are linguistic variations on words to identify grammatical case, gender, and number.

245 **Choice D is correct** because it highlights the utility ensconced within the "big science" initiatives currently underway

Choice A is incorrect because it would indicate that the "big science" projects had failed to achieve their perceived potential of "[pushing] the boundaries of volcano science and [enhancing] our understanding of volcanic processes". **Choice B** is incorrect because the utility of a large hadron collider for volcanology was never established or implied within the passage. **Choice C** is incorrect because it speaks only to public perceptions of volcanoes, which are tethered to the scientific remits at play in the passage. **Choice E** is incorrect because big data is meant to drive scientific evolution of the field of volcanology. The impact on scientist time would be largely immaterial to this goal.

PASSAGE 128: SUMMARY/PARAPHRASE

246 **Choice B is the correct** answer because in the context of the passage "heterogeneous" means diverse in character or content, while "mixed" means consisting of different qualities or elements

Choice A is the incorrect answer because uniform is defined as "unchanging in form or character" which does not align with the definition of heterogeneous. **Choice C** is the incorrect answer because disorganized means not properly planned or controlled, which does not align with the definition of heterogeneous. **Choice D** is the incorrect answer because comprehensive means "complete or containing all aspects of something" which does not aline with the meaning of heterogeneous. **Choice E** is the incorrect answer because gelatinous means "having the consistency of jelly" which does not align with the definition of heterogeneous.

247 **Choices A and C are correct** because heterogeneously copper is highlighted as the singularly identified substance which can facilitate the stated conversion, and studies using nanostructuring and bimetallic electrodes are currently underway which might influence the activity and selectivity of these reactions.

Choice B is incorrect because copper is the only identified heterogeneous substance which can facilitate this conversion.

248 **Choices B and C are correct** because a number of ongoing research efforts and current best practices are alluded to in the passage. Furthermore, a variety of the factors which could impact CO2R reactions with copper are referenced in the text.

Choice A is incorrect because CO2R is stated to be influenced by "several factors" including electrolyte ions and pH

PASSAGE 129

249 **Choice D is correct** because "gravitational lensing" using "curvature of space" which "bends in the presence of massive objects" implies that massive objects like galaxy clusters will be imaged using this technique.

Choice A is incorrect because no discussion of image quality is presented or alluded to in the passage. **Choice B** is incorrect because the passage discusses leveraging Einstein's theory to generate insights, it does not indicate that the theory is not being adhered to. **Choice C** is incorrect because image quality does not come into discussion within the context of the passage. **Choice E** is incorrect because lensing was presented as a result of Einstein's theory, not a tool with which one could prove or disprove the theory

PASSAGE 130: SUMMARY/PARAPHRASE

The passage is about our understanding of the universe. The main idea is that physicists' lack of clear understanding of dark matter is a good example of how little we really understand the universe. The major points are (a) that scientists posit dark matter to explain sizable stretches of the universe that emit no light or electromagnetic radiation and (b) that there is no definite evidence that dark matter exists. The main purpose of the passage is to use dark matter to illustrate a point about the limits of human knowledge.

250 **"Thus, dark matter provides a good example of how little we really know about the structures that compose our universe."** In the last sentence of the passage, the author makes it clear that he or she believes that astrophysics still has a long way to go in fully elucidating the structure and functioning of the universe.

Chapter 3: Reading Comprehension

Practice Set 6: Social Sciences

PASSAGE 131

Question 251 is based on the following passage.

Botel Tobago is an island in the South Seas which has lately been visited by a party of United States naval officers. They were surveying a rock east of the South Cape of Formosa and called at this island. They found a curious race of Malay stock. These aborigines did not know what money was good for. Nor had they ever used tobacco or rum. They gave the officers goats and pigs for tin pots and brass buttons and hung around the vessel all day in their canoes waiting for a chance to dive for something which might be thrown overboard. They wore clouts only, ate taro and yams, and had axes, spears, and knives made of common iron. Their canoes were made without nails and were ornamented with geometrical lines. They wore the beards of goats and small shells as ornaments.

251. Based on the information in this passage, select the list of adjectives that best describes the inhabitants of Botel Tobago.

   (A) Aggressive, amenable, cunning
   (B) Naive, narcissistic, opportunistic
   (C) Vain, opportunistic, overt
   (D) Herbivorous, humble, hardy
   (E) Social, stoic, omnivorous

PASSAGE 132

Questions 252 and 253 are based on the following passage.

The Japanese remained almost entirely ignorant of these preparations. Many of the Japanese military command were suffering from "senshobyo (victory disease)". They had easily won almost every battle they had fought, and they had no reason to believe they would not win just as easily in the future. The defeat at Midway had not been made public and did not disturb this belief. Few senior military officers believed there would be a serious Allied counterstroke against Japan until well into 1943.

There were those among them who were more realistic in their thinking, including Lieutenant Commander Itoo Haruki of the Naval Intelligence Center in Tokyo. In late July, his unit identified two new Allied radio callsigns, both operating on the 4.205 megahertz band and communicating with Pearl Harbor. On 1 August, Japanese radio direction finders pinpointed the location of the stations as Melbourne and Noumea. Itoo correctly guessed these were headquarters for Allied operational forces, massing for an attack on New Guinea or the Solomons. He relayed an urgent warning to Truk, the main Japanese base in the central Pacific, and Rabaul. The warning was ignored.

252. Based on the information in the passage, select the most likely symptom of senshobyo from the following list.

   (A) Optimism
   (B) Courage
   (C) Overconfidence
   (D) Complacency
   (E) Satisfaction

253. What purpose is served by the writer's including the specific details of Lieutenant Commander Haruki's intelligence?

   (A) To show the level of efficiency in the Naval Intelligence Center in Tokyo
   (B) To establish a foundation for Haruki's warning
   (C) To provide information about the location of the Allies in the Pacific
   (D) To justify Haruki's rise to the level of Lieutenant Commander
   (E) To demonstrate the lack of preparedness on the part of the Japanese Navy

PASSAGE 133

Questions 254 to 256 are based on the following passage.

This distinction must be borne in mind—that while the early chiefs were spokesmen and leaders in the simplest sense, possessing no real authority, those who headed their tribes during the transition period were more or less rulers and more or less politicians. It is a singular fact that many of the "chiefs", well known as such to the American public, were not chiefs at all according to the accepted usages of their tribesmen. Their prominence was simply the result of an abnormal situation, in which representatives of the United States Government made use of them for a definite purpose. In a few cases, where a chief met with a violent death, some ambitious man has taken advantage of the confusion to thrust himself upon the tribe and, perhaps with outside help, has succeeded in usurping the leadership.

Practice Set 6: Social Sciences

254 Which of the following terms describes tribal structure prior to interference by the American government?

(A) Matriarchal
(B) Patriarchal
(C) Oligarchal
(D) Egalitarian
(E) Tyrannical

255 What question might be created in the mind of the reader after reading this passage?

(A) How did tribal chiefs get their names?
(B) How many tribes were negotiating with the American government?
(C) What other misconceptions about Native Americans have been perpetuated?
(D) Why did the chiefs meet with violent deaths?
(E) Did early politicians model their behavior after that of tribal chiefs?

256 Which of the following is the best definition for the word "singular" in the context of this passage?

(A) Extraordinary
(B) Unusual or strange
(C) Distinctive; unique
(D) Separate; individual
(E) A form in the singular

PASSAGE 134

Question 257 is based on the following passage.

Malaysia is a destination and, to a lesser extent, a source and transit country for women and children trafficked for the purpose of commercial sexual exploitation, and men, women, and children for forced labor; Malaysia is mainly a destination country for men, women, and children who migrate willingly from South and Southeast Asia to work, some of whom are subjected to conditions of involuntary servitude by Malaysian employers in the domestic, agricultural, construction, plantation, and industrial sectors; to a lesser extent, some Malaysian women, primarily of Chinese ethnicity, are trafficked abroad for commercial sexual exploitation. Malaysia improved from Tier 3 to the Tier 2 Watch List for 2008 when it enacted comprehensive anti-trafficking legislation in July 2007; however, it did not take action against exploitative employers or labor traffickers in 2007; the government has not ratified the 2000 UN TIP Protocol (2008).

257 Which of the following statements most closely reflects the probable conditions that facilitate human trafficking and/or labor exploitation in Malaysia?

(A) There is a lack of employment opportunities in South and Southeast Asia
(B) Malaysia has fewer cultural taboos about sexual activity
(C) The Southeast Asian and Malaysian cultures deem it acceptable for children to work in agriculture and industry
(D) The 2000 UN TIP Protocol is too restrictive
(E) Industrialized nations outsource much of their factory production to Malaysia

PASSAGE 135

Questions 258 and 259 are based on the following passage.

Many scholars hold Karl Marx to be one of the founding fathers of modern-day social science. Karl Marx is and always has been a polemical figure, but his conceptualization of the dialectic that shapes all societal conflicts, class struggle, has fundamentally changed the way that many politicians, academics, and lay people view and analyze global power relationships. The theories of Karl Marx, known as Marxism, are most often employed as methods of critiquing not only capitalism, but also the very political systems that they engendered: socialism and communism. Thus, Marxism can be a highly useful and self-reflexive analytical tool.

258 According to the author, Marxism is a self-reflexive analytical tool because:

(A) It accurately deconstructs power structures within capitalistic societies
(B) It can be used as a method of critically examining its own economic systems
(C) It elucidates important issues related to class conflict
(D) It helps academics set up a dialectical research framework
(E) It enables free-thinking academic exchange

259 The term "dialectic" in the passage is most analogous to:

(A) The scientific method
(B) Reason engendered by discussion
(C) Protest
(D) Political dialogue
(E) Exploitation of workers

PASSAGE 136

Questions 260 to 262 are based on the following passage.

Although it seems hard to imagine, humans originated in one place and then spread across the globe to create the vast network of cultures and nations that constitute our modern world. This phenomenon fascinates many, including scientists who are deeply interested in the Diaspora of modern man from the Horn of Africa to the far-reaching corners of the globe. While it is no longer disputed that modern man originated in northern Africa, many anthropologists debate the area from which human settlers organized and then colonized the rest of the world. Recent research suggests that the first humans out of Africa settled in Arabia and from there staged the global dispersal of modern man. This conclusion was drawn based on DNA comparisons between populations in Europe, North Africa, and the Near East. Scientists were able to determine that all the populations were most closely related with the Arabians samples. Thus, the Arabian settlers are the common denominator in the dispersal of modern man.

260. The primary purpose of this passage is to:

- (A) Discuss the African Diaspora of early humans
- (B) Show how the interests of scientists and laymen intersect
- (C) Discuss the dissemination point of modern man
- (D) Show how DNA analysis can be used in anthropological research
- (E) Start a debate about man's origins in Africa

261. The author's attitude towards DNA analysis as an anthropological research method can best be described as:

- (A) Skeptical
- (B) Leery
- (C) Impartial
- (D) Favoring
- (E) Devoted

262. According to the author, polemics surrounding the dispersal of early humans tend to focus on:

- (A) Whether or not early humans originated in the Horn of Africa
- (B) Whether or not Europe or Arabia were the starting points of modern man's colonization of the globe
- (C) The Near East's role in the dispersal of humans throughout the world
- (D) The point of origin for organized human dispersal across the globe
- (E) Whether or not DNA analysis is an effective way of determining the point of origin of the organized human diaspora

PASSAGE 137

Question 263 is based on the following passage.

These caves were inhabited by man during an immense stretch of time, and, as you dig down, you light upon one layer after another of his leavings. But note in such a case as this how easily you may be baffled by someone having upset the heap of clothes, or, in a word, by rearrangement. Thus, the man whose leavings ought to form the layer half-way up may have seen fit to dig a deep hole in the cave-floor in order to bury a deceased friend, and with him, let us suppose, to bury also an assortment of articles likely to be useful in the life beyond the grave. Consequently, an implement of one age will be found lying cheek by jowl with the implement of a much earlier age, or even, it may be, some feet below it.

263. How do archaeologists reconcile apparent contradictions in the location and age of artifacts uncovered in a dig?

- (A) They examine written records of early inhabitants of the area
- (B) They interview current residents of the area
- (C) They create a scenario that explains the juxtaposition of artifacts from different time periods
- (D) They make note of the level of preservation of the artifacts
- (E) They sort the artifacts according to their function

Practice Set 6: Social Sciences

PASSAGE 138

Questions 264 and 265 are based on the following passage.

Niccolo Machiavelli's seminal work, The Prince, is considered to be one of the first works of modern political philosophy; it is also one of the most controversial. Nonetheless, The Prince has influenced Western thought related to governance ever since its publication in 1532. Machiavelli uses his treatise to outline leadership and success relative to royal (or political) rule. **In today's world it is quite controversial as The Prince negates the importance of personal virtue in leaders and lofty political idealism - realism is the goal of the treatise and the reality of the world is that successful outcomes go to the strongest in the fight for survival and the battle of the wits.** Despite its controversial message, The Prince is written in eloquent, yet simple language that relays its message with surgical precision. **Nearly all English speakers are well-acquainted with the polemical aphorism that lies at the thematic heart of The Prince: The end justifies the means.**

264 The two portions in **boldface** are related to each other in which of the following ways?

Ⓐ The first **boldface** section undermines the conclusion drawn by the second bold-faced section

Ⓑ The first **boldface** section is an extrapolation on the conclusion drawn by the second **boldface** section

Ⓒ Both **boldface** sections challenge the author's position

Ⓓ The first **boldface** section is a position that the author does not agree with; the second **boldface** section is a position that the author does agree with

Ⓔ Both **boldface** sections undermine the goals and objectives of the modern-day political landscape

265 The author most clearly makes a case for the fact that:

Ⓐ Polemical books are often among the most influential

Ⓑ Leadership requires a combination of virtue and vice

Ⓒ Political ideas often evolve

Ⓓ Human nature remains the same as political systems change

Ⓔ Political goals are best achieved by way of a Machiavellian approach

PASSAGE 139

Questions 266 to 268 are based on the following passage.

Let us suppose that a colony of twenty or thirty families establishes itself in a wild district, covered with underbrush and forests; and from which, by agreement, the natives consent to withdraw. Each one of these families possesses a moderate but sufficient amount of capital, of such a nature as a colonist would be apt to choose—animals, seeds, tools, and a little money and food. The land having been divided, each one settles himself as comfortably as possible, and begins to clear away the portion allotted to him. But after a few weeks of fatigue, such as they never before have known, of inconceivable suffering, of ruinous and almost useless labor, our colonists begin to complain of their trade; their condition seems hard to them; they curse their sad existence.

266 Based on the passage, which of the following contributes to the colonists' dissatisfaction with their lot?

Ⓐ A lack of sufficient monetary funds

Ⓑ A lack of cooperation among the settlers

Ⓒ The departure of the native population

Ⓓ Difficult and unproductive land–clearing

Ⓔ The division of land into portions

267 According to the passage, all of the following are true of the colonists EXCEPT

Ⓐ The colonists were divided into family units.

Ⓑ The colonists did not bring the provisions they needed to clear the land.

Ⓒ The colonists did not appreciate some of the difficulties they would face.

Ⓓ The colonists did not suffer in silence.

Ⓔ The colonists brought an appropriate supply of livestock with them.

For the following question, consider each of the three choices separately and select all that apply.

268 The passage implies which of the following about the colonists' experience?

☐ A The experience described is typical of that encountered by most early pioneers.

☐ B The settlers should have sought help from the natives rather than seeking their withdrawal.

☐ C The colonists made reasonable preparations for their endeavor.

Chapter 3: Reading Comprehension

PASSAGE 140

Question 269 is based on the following passage.

Research into the eating habits of women shows that they are mimetic; women tend to want to mirror the way their fellow female diners enjoy their food. Psychologists theorize this has to do with the fact that women are more prone to same-gender imitation than their male counterparts—men seem to be oblivious to the behavior of other eaters in the dining group. Underpinning women's copycat eating habits is likely a stronger need to both belong to and be liked by the group, particularly the other females in the group.

269. All of the following can be inferred from the passage EXCEPT

   (A) Same-gender conformity is a more feminine trait
   (B) Men are the less conventional gender
   (C) Women in a dining group tend to eat the same amount of food
   (D) Women value how they are perceived by others
   (E) Men in a dining group eat disparate amounts of food

PASSAGE 141

Questions 270 and 271 are based on the following passage.

One of the famous events in the American Revolutionary War was George Washington's crossing of the Delaware River on the night of December 25, 1776. The dangerous feat of transporting 2,400 soldiers, horses, and heavy artillery across a frozen river at night became the fodder for artists. In reality, Washington was likely striving for such a dramatic impact. For many months, his forces had not had a major victory, so another defeat would be devastating for morale, which is why he orchestrated a secret attack on some highly trained mercenaries who thought the river protected them. Washington's plans were almost thwarted by a severe storm, but his troops pressed on and won the battle, bolstering confidence in eventually gaining independence.

270. The author of the passage mentions "became the fodder for artists" primarily to

   (A) stress how many paintings have been made about the crossing of the Delaware River
   (B) emphasize the spectacle that Washington may have endeavored to create
   (C) cite a potential justification for why the attack on the mercenaries had to be secret
   (D) explain why the event could have potentially been a disaster for Washington's troops
   (E) discuss conditions that the soldiers endured when crossing the Delaware River

271. Which of the following best describes the overall organization of the passage?

   (A) A historical event is described, then two possible outcomes are analyzed.
   (B) A historical dilemma is discussed, then its modern repercussions are outlined.
   (C) A military maneuver is introduced, then the mechanism of executing it is explored.
   (D) A famous battle is presented, then its artistic benefits are examined.
   (E) A perilous event is described, then the motivation behind it is clarified.

PASSAGE 142

Questions 272 to 274 are based on the following passage.

The future of AI is full of potential. If predictions pan out, AI will soon be capable of everything from picking out people's clothes to printing them out on demand. Yet, as artificial intelligence pundits attest, the ultimate goals of AI—superhuman intelligence, immortality, and the elimination of social evils- can only be reached by stationing a microscopic robot in the human body.

Enter the nanobot. According to computer scientist and technological prognosticator Ray Kurzweil's book, "The Singularity is Nearer," the next decade will see the creation of artificial entities capable of "swimming to the human brain allowing us to expand our intelligence 1 million fold." Other predicted perks of the nanobot include access to virtual worlds, a cure for cancer, and the cessation of human aging.

272. The author of the passage is primarily concerned with

  A. Announcing the release of Ray Kurzweil's book, "The Singularity is Nearer"
  B. Informing readers about a possible new technology
  C. Assuring readers that nanobots will stop aging and cure cancer
  D. Warning readers of the dangers of Artificial Intelligence becoming superior to human intelligence
  E. Encouraging readers to use the new technology as soon as it is available.

For Questions 273 and 274, consider each of the three answer choices separately and select all that apply.

273. With which of the following statements do you think the author would most likely agree?

  A. Nanobots are inevitable; Kurzweil has a track record of accurate predictions.
  B. Nanobots have potential, but there is no guarantee that they will become a reality.
  C. The ultimate goals of AI can only be reached by stationing a robot inside the human body.

274. Which of the following can be inferred about Kurzweil?

  A. He is well respected in his field.
  B. He has not given careful thought to the implications of nanobots.
  C. He believes people should take advantage of nanobots as soon as the technology is accessible.

PASSAGE 143

Question 275 is based on the following passage.

According to recent psychological research published in the British Journal of Psychology, men are more likely to display altruistic behavior in the presence of attractive women. Conversely, women's behavior remains constant regardless of the attractiveness of their male company. Psychologists conclude that male behavior is determined by the need to impress prospective mates, while female behavior is based less on the need to impress and more on the need to be selective and receptive with respect to potential male partners.

275. The author primarily makes his or her point by:

  A. Objectively evaluating the facts
  B. An emotional appeal to the reader
  C. Providing both a view and counterview
  D. Criticizing the opinions of the psychologists
  E. Offering a source of authority

PASSAGE 144

Questions 276 and 277 are based on the following passage.

Our culture is turning into a genuine din of confused crowds. Not only are riots and mob outbursts becoming more frequent, but all forms of interest—patriotic, spiritual, moral, political, and financial—also quickly turn into a jumble of hyperbolic and ostentatious narrow-mindedness and incoherence. No matter how much of an icon one aspires to become, one discovers that the self-cultivation path moves too slowly. People have to turn into destructive power, using a complete army to consume their way to the finish line. The mental level and genuineness of the conventions of democracy are comparable to those of business-related marketing. Although it is impossible to say that the practice of creating crowds is unique to the present, it appears that the propensity to be involved with a crowd has significantly elevated in the last few years.

For the following question, consider each of the three answer choices separately and select all that apply.

276. The passage addresses the issues with gibbering crowds, but it could be inferred that the passage leaves out the positivity of talking crowds because

  A. Crowds usually talk about something important
  B. Sociologists see no use for gibbering crowds
  C. People do not have a desire to learn about themselves

277. The passage's structure of the passage can best be described as

  A. A description of the positive and negative aspects of the crowd culture
  B. The problem and solution of how crowds have taken over society
  C. Lists of events that have occurred in crowds
  D. Characteristics of the context in crowds' conversations
  E. Explanations of the negative effects of people talking in crowds

PASSAGE 145

Questions 278 to 280 are based on the following passage.

The Federal Bureau of Investigation (FBI) and Bureau of Justice Statistics (BJS) are the two sources from which government crime statistics are generated. The FBI publishes data annually that outlines crimes that have been reported to law enforcement. However, this data is certainly limited considering the vast number of crimes committed that remain unreported each year. The data output from the FBI has historically included information on specific violent crimes and property crimes, but has left out other offenses, such as drug crimes. On the other hand, BJS tracks crime by delivering a large survey annually to Americans ages twelve and up. One benefit of this method is its ability to record crimes regardless of whether or not they were formally reported. Nonetheless, this method of collecting data poses serious limitations. For instance, victims of murders obviously cannot complete surveys, so statistics on murders are not gathered from the survey. Despite the imperfections of both crime tracking processes, comparing data from the FBI and BJS can provide a satisfactory overview of crime across the nation.

278. Which of the following best summarizes the author's perspective on crime tracking in the United States?

  A. The author feels that the two methods of tracking crime are sufficient though they both have significant limitations.
  B. The author feels that the two methods of tracking crime are overall insufficient due to the serious limitations outlined in the passage.
  C. The author feels that the BJS's method of tracking crime is superior to the FBI's method because it includes both reported and unreported crimes.
  D. The author feels that the FBI's method of tracking crime is superior to the BJS's method because it includes more violent crimes, such as murders.
  E. The author feels that both methods used for tracking crime are thorough and minor limitations are unavoidable.

279. Which two words from the text have the same meanings in context?

  A. "violent" and "murders"
  B. "imperfections" and "limitations"
  C. "obviously" and "satisfactory"
  D. "tracking" and "statistics"
  E. "annually" and "formally"

280 Which sentence best outlines the two major points from the passage?

(A) The BJS's method of collecting crime data is strong because it includes reported and unreported crimes, but also weak because it fails to capture certain crimes like murders.

(B) Although the methods used for collecting crime data are flawed, they are sufficient overall.

(C) The FBI uses law enforcement reports to determine crime statistics and the BJS uses an annual public survey to determine crime statistics.

(D) Neither the methods of the FBI or the BJS accurately capture the drug crime statistics in the United States.

(E) The FBI publishes data annually and the BJS uses a public survey to analyze crime statistics.

PASSAGE 146

Question 281 is based on the following passage.

It pays to work hard in college. Researchers have concluded that slacker students in college are at the highest risk for credit card debt, unemployment, and hunkering down for a permanent stay in mom and dad's basement. Even more troubling is the fact that these students lack critical job skills—they run the highest risk of not improving their reasoning, writing, and critical thinking skills by the time they walk across the stage to accept their diploma. Many students believe college to be a time of fun and exploration, but if such experiences are not combined with hard work, future success is not a guarantee.

281 The author's claims about slacker students would be weakened by all of the following EXCEPT

(A) Several examples of students who were slackers yet still succeeded after college

(B) Research that demonstrated slacker college students improving their academic skills despite low work ethics

(C) Evidence that slacker college students obtained post-graduation jobs as easily as their hard-working counterparts

(D) Evidence that slacker students do not struggle with financial issues any more than their hard-working counterparts

(E) Evidence that hardworking and slacker college students had similar post-graduation living conditions

PASSAGE 147

For Questions 282 and 283, select only one answer choice.

The scientific study of linguistics is the systematic investigation of the properties and characteristics of languages. Linguistics examines the various effects of phonetic sounds, grammar, and the generation of meaning. However, that is not all linguistics explores. Topics like the history of families of languages, the process of learning language skills, how language is processed by the brain, and how language is connected to social factors are also investigated. Linguistics is complimentary to a range of other disciplines like philosophy, sociology, biology, anthropology, education, and literature. Furthermore, the subfield of applied linguistics dives into the use of linguistic concepts in classrooms in order to promote students' abilities to communicate in native languages and second languages.

282 Which of the following is an accurate conclusion that can be drawn from the passage in relation to the utilization of linguistics in other disciplines?

(A) Anthropologists can learn from linguistics by better understanding concepts such as how people have migrated to different countries throughout history.

(B) Linguists can help teachers by demonstrating the best way to present a lesson to children of various ages.

(C) Biologists and linguists can work together to understand how the mouth works to produce phonetic sounds.

(D) Linguists can collaborate with philosophers to help teach about how social factors impact Americans.

(E) Applied linguistics specialists are the only type of linguists that can collaborate with professionals from other disciplines.

283 Which sentence best summarizes the passage?

(A) Linguistics is the study of features of language and environmental implications of language use as it stretches across a variety of fields.

(B) The study of language, known as linguistics, examines how sounds are learned, formed, and used.

(C) The study of language, called linguistics, can benefit a variety of other disciplines such as biology and education.

(D) Linguistics is the scientific study of language.

(E) Linguistics studies a multitude of topics that are highly applicable to the field of education.

PASSAGE 148

Questions 284 to 286 are based on the following passage.

Many people believe that the traditional religious beliefs of Nordic Vikings have vanished or been overtaken by other belief systems. However, between 500 and 1000 people residing in Denmark still practice worship to Norse gods like Thor and Odin. Even a thousand years after the time of the Vikings, offerings are made, feasts are enjoyed, and drinks are toasted in the exact same way.

The modern believers of the old Nordic religion ("The Old Way") follow the resources handed down through generations, such as poetry called, "The Edda." Followers of The Old Way make offerings to certain gods depending on a specific season and theme. They select sites for sacrifices like Bronze Age burial mounds and Viking Age ship ports. Sacrifices are made by male or female priests while participants watch from a ceremonial circle. Typically, offerings are carried once per season, amounting to about four times per year. However, the traditional Viking calendar was set up much differently than the western calendar is today, with the year beginning around mid-October.

284. Which sentence from the passage best transitions into the discussion of the intricacies of Nordic offerings?

285. Which of the following words or phrases could best replace, "vanished," in the first paragraph without changing the meaning of the sentence?

   (A) Vaporized
   (B) Abscond
   (C) Been taken by storm
   (D) Adapted
   (E) Faded away

286. Which of the following conclusions can most likely be drawn from the passage?

   (A) The rise of Christianity led to the conversion of most people in Norway.
   (B) There are four gods in the old Norse religion and one is celebrated for each season.
   (C) Modern people without Nordic ancestors are unlikely to follow The Old Way.
   (D) Male and female priests do not share the same duties when performing a sacrifice.
   (E) The traditional Viking calendar has been dismissed because it is no longer applicable in today's world.

PASSAGE 149

Question 287 is based on the following passage.

Art is often considered a defining characteristic of civilization, but recent anthropological finds suggest otherwise. The oldest known painting kits were recently unearthed in a South African cave, and anthropologists estimate the artifacts are over 100,000 years old. The painting kits consisted of stone and bone tools for crushing, mixing, and applying paint to cave walls, animal skins and maybe even body parts. The paint was made from red and yellow ochres and housed in sea snail shells. Thus, art predates not only modern man, but also complex human societies.

287. The author suggests that the painting kits found in South Africa are important because:

   (A) They give us insight into the early humans
   (B) They illuminate the kinds of tools available to early humans
   (C) They give us information on the earliest forms of art as body decoration
   (D) They show that art predates civilization
   (E) They help us trace the development of artistic methods in human civilization

PASSAGE 150

Questions 288 and 289 are based on the following passage.

The unconscious mind has long been a topic of interest among psychologists. The term, "unconscious," originally referred only to one's unintentional actions. It has since evolved to encompass the automatic processing of information and how that processing impacts behavior.

Despite centuries of studying and philosophizing the unconscious mind, theories among psychologists remain relatively varied. Cognitive psychologists equate the unconscious processing of information with subliminal processing of information. This perspective leads to the conclusion that the unconscious is very limited. On the other hand, social psychologists believe the unconscious mind is a powerful influence over higher level mental processes.

For Questions 288 and 289, consider each of the choices separately and select all that apply.

288. Based on the passage, which of the following could be possible alternative reasons for psychologists disagreeing on the concept of the unconscious?

   A. Psychologists tend to be highly controversial, so it is easy to find disagreements among theories.

   B. Psychologists have different areas of emphasis in which they work, which skews training and perspectives in a particular way.

   C. Psychologists are not all adequately trained so only some have the correct answers.

289. Which of the following are minor points presented by the author?

   A. Cognitive psychologists equate the unconscious with subliminal information processing.

   B. Social psychologists believe the unconscious has a powerful influence over mental processes.

   C. Theories among psychologists regarding the unconscious are relatively varied.

PASSAGE 151

Questions 290 to 292 are based on the following passage.

Simply memorizing timelines and reading folktales is insufficient in modern classrooms where students are yearning to learn about diversity, cultural history, and so much more. Modern educational standards demand that children gain a deeper understanding of the world and its people. Topics like geography, economics, and civilizations must be explored in-depth. Social studies teachers impart essential knowledge by leading meaningful lessons and discussions in the hope that children can make productive decisions in the future.

A high-quality social studies curriculum serves four important purposes. First, students are taught to become better judges of global affairs, both historically and presently. Second, students develop a more thorough perspective on how modern nations developed and the methods by which major political changes take place. Third, students learn how to participate in a democracy and contribute to their communities. Fourth, students get the chance to think critically about decisions that were made by others throughout history.

290. Which of the following is the greatest weakness in the author's argument that a high-quality social studies education is important?

   A. The author does not give any purposes for a high-quality social studies curriculum.

   B. The author does not outline modern social studies standards of education.

   C. The author provides four concise points to support the idea that a high-quality social studies education is important.

   D. The author uses technical terms that are difficult for common readers to understand.

   E. The author does not provide specific examples of how learning social studies can serve children in the future.

291. How do the first and second paragraphs relate to one another?

   A. The first paragraph focuses on the role of the social studies teacher before the second paragraph explains how students' lives are immediately impacted by understanding social concepts.

   B. The first paragraph focuses on the role of the social studies teacher before the second paragraph outlines four functions that a high-quality social studies curriculum serves.

   C. The first paragraph introduces the topic of modern social studies education and why it is important before the second paragraph explains how students' lives are immediately impacted by understanding social concepts.

   D. The first paragraph introduces the topic of modern social studies education and why it is important before the second paragraph outlines four functions that a high-quality social studies curriculum serves.

   E. The first paragraph focuses on the topics that are involved in a social studies curriculum before the second paragraph outlines four functions that a high-quality social studies curriculum serves.

292. Which of the following assumptions can be made about former social studies education curriculums?

Ⓐ Former social studies curriculums focused heavily on folktales, which modern curriculums are now intentionally avoiding.

Ⓑ Former social studies curriculums included a lot of memorization and disconnected stories, but lacked the ability to deeply transform how students view the world.

Ⓒ Former social studies curriculums did not teach about how modern nations developed.

Ⓓ Former social studies curriculums did a superior job of helping students memorize specific dates and names.

Ⓔ Modern social studies curriculums can contribute to student participation and understanding of other subjects by improving decision-making skills and critical thinking skills.

PASSAGE 152

Question 293 is based on the following passage.

Despite being a social phenomenon, the crowd has become very different from a social group, in general. Without physically being in a crowd, people can still be social in their thoughts and deeds. One representation of this is the family. Again, a mob is an example of a clearly antisocial crowd. Crowd behavior is detrimental to the individual as well as to society. In contemporary times, the increasing tendency of crowd behavior can pose a threat not only to the values of civilization but also to the development of personality and self-awareness.

293. Select the sentence that compares similar conduct between society as a whole and an individual.

PASSAGE 153

Questions 294 and 295 are based on the following passage.

The Amazon, the world's largest rainforest, is one of the few regions on Earth that is home to millions of indigenous people who choose to live in isolation. These people depend fully on the resources from the forest for survival. The territories inhabited by indigenous people remain the best preserved lands in the Amazon, which makes the sustainment of indigenous settlements crucial in efforts for conservation. For this reason, safeguarding the rights of indigenous groups simultaneously works to care for the diverse ecosystems that reside in the Amazon.

There are a variety of strategies in place to advocate for indigenous groups. Efforts have been made to ensure that representation in governance. Additionally, mental health services have been provided to those who need them among indigenous groups.

For the following question, consider each of the three answer choices separately and select all that apply.

294. Which of the following are major points from the passage?

Ⓐ Efforts are made to ensure indigenous peoples are represented in the government.

Ⓑ Mental health support has been provided to indigenous peoples in need.

Ⓒ Protecting indigenous populations simultaneously works to conserve the Amazon.

295. Which of the following points would least likely be included in a summary of this passage?

Ⓐ The Amazon is home to millions of indigenous people.

Ⓑ The lifestyle of indigenous people preserves the Amazon.

Ⓒ Indigenous people in the Amazon choose to live in isolation from more developed towns.

Ⓓ Supporting and protecting indigenous groups works to care for the rainforest.

Ⓔ Indigenous people depend fully on the Amazon for survival.

PASSAGE 154

Questions 296 to 298 are based on the following passage.

Nevada's transition into statehood was rushed on October 31st, 1864, in order to ensure three more electoral votes for Abraham Lincoln's reelection on November 8th. Since Nevada was added to the Union during the Civil War, it earned the nickname, "Battle Born State." The original name of the state came from the Spanish, who were the first Europeans to explore the land. They called it, "Nevada," which means, "snowy" because of the great snow-covered mountains. The United States acquired the territory in 1848 after winning the Mexican American War. However, the region remained relatively calm until the discovery of silver at the Comstock Lode in 1859. After, the population skyrocketed with Americans travelling across the country to mine for precious minerals.

The mining scene in Nevada continued to evolve, but other economic attributes were born as well. In 1931, big time gambling arrived, furthering the possibilities of getting rich quickly in this state. Nevadan industries continued booming, while their relatively few laws kept a "wild west" atmosphere alive.

296 Based on the passage, which of the following aspects of Nevada developed the least from the mid 1800s to the mid 1900s?

- (A) The population
- (B) The mining industry
- (C) The economy
- (D) The amount of restricting legislature
- (E) Desirability of settlers

297 What is the purpose of the first sentence in the second paragraph?

- (A) To transition from discussing mining to talking about other economic attributes
- (B) To provide a thesis about gambling that is then proven throughout the remainder of the paragraph
- (C) To conclude the discussion on mining
- (D) To introduce a new topic of the "wild west" atmosphere in Nevada
- (E) To provide a thesis about mining that is then proven throughout the remainder of the paragraph

298 Which sentence from the passage best expresses the author's perspective on Nevada prior to its induction into statehood?

PASSAGE 155

Question 299 and 300 is based on the following passage.

Social work is an agile field that can deliver services to a wide array of populations. One population served by social workers is older adults. These gerontological social workers strive to empower older individuals to live fulfilling lives and navigate physical, mental, and financial barriers.

Gerontological social workers can work with older adults in long-term care facilities, assisted-living homes, and individual homes. In these settings, social workers collaborate with clients and their families to generate customized solutions to unique problems. Social workers may connect families with community resources, help facilities set up the physical parameters needed to serve the client, and communicate with insurance companies to ensure high-quality therapeutic interventions.

299 Which of the following is the most likely use of this passage?

- (A) To educate social work students about possible careers working with older people
- (B) To tell a true story about social workers changing the lives of older adults
- (C) To educate older individuals and their families about the benefits of working with a gerontological social worker
- (D) To argue for the rights of gerontological social workers in their various workplaces
- (E) To argue for the rights of older adults in residential care facilities

300 Based on the passage, which of the following tasks would least likely be completed by a gerontological social worker?

- (A) Speaking to a family about mental problems the client is facing
- (B) Helping a family set up meal delivery services for a client
- (C) Ordering a ramp for a client who utilizes a wheelchair
- (D) Calling an insurance company to verify therapeutic benefits
- (E) Delivering therapeutic services to a client

Answer Key

Q. No.	Correct Answer	Your Answer
251	C	
252	A	
253	B	
254	D	
255	C	
256	C	
257	A	
258	B	
259	B	
260	C	
261	C	
262	D	
263	C	
264	B	
265	A	
266	D	
267	B	
268	C	
269	B	
270	B	
271	E	
272	B	
273	B	
274	A	
275	E	

Q. No.	Correct Answer	Your Answer
276	B, C	
277	E	
278	A	
279	B	
280	C	
281	A	
282	C	
283	A	
284	Followers...theme.	
285	E	
286	C	
287	D	
288	B	
289	A, B	
290	E	
291	D	
292	B	
293	Crowd...society.	
294	C	
295	C	
296	D	
297	A	
298	However,...1859.	
299	C	
300	E	

Practice Set 6: Answers & Explanations

PASSAGE 131: SUMMARY/PARAPHRASE

The passage is about a previously unknown tribe of indigenous islanders. The main idea of the passage is to summarily characterize the islanders. There are no major points, merely a list of information of the islanders that indicates that they had little exposure to modern life. The purpose of the passage is to describe a previously unknown tribe.

251 **Choice C is correct** because the writer explicitly reveals that the natives eat taro and yams, both vegetables. Because the natives have spears and knives and trade goats and pigs, the reader may conclude that they also kill and eat meat. It would be difficult, with the limited information in this passage, to believe that their diet is either restrictive or inclusive, so answer choices D and E must be eliminated. There is nothing in the passage to suggest that the natives are aggressive, so A is also incorrect. Narcissism is also not evident here, making answer choice B incorrect. Opportunistic describes people who recognize and take advantage of an opportunity, much as these natives do when they paddle around the ship waiting to dive for objects that are thrown overboard. Overt means open or obvious. It was obvious to those on the ship that the natives waited openly for items to be thrown overboard. That the natives exhibit some vanity is revealed by the writer's description of the designs on their canoes and the body ornamentation in the form of goats' beards and shells worn by the natives.

Choice A is incorrect because there is nothing in the passage to suggest that the natives are aggressive. **Choice B is incorrect** because narcissism is not evident in the passage. **Choice D is incorrect** because it would be difficult, with the limited information in this passage, to believe that the natives' diet is restrictive. **Choice E is incorrect** because it would be difficult, with the limited information in this passage, to believe that the natives' diet is inclusive.

PASSAGE 132: SUMMARY/PARAPHRASE

The passage is about the attitude of Japanese officers during World War II. The main idea is that Japanese officers were underprepared for an allied counterattack. There are two main ideas: (a) that many Japanese commanders were overconfident due to the ease of early victories and (b) even those who were more alert to the possibility of an allied counterstrike tended to be ignored by the prevailing opinion. Two minor points amplify and develop the major points: (a) that the Japanese defeat at Midway had gone unpublicized and (b) that Lt. Commander I too had specific intelligence that was ignored. The primary purpose of the passage is to give insight into the prevalent attitudes in the Japanese military that led to their lack of preparedness.

252 **Choice A is correct** because the Japanese were probably optimistic about winning the war, but optimism is not likely to be considered a symptom of disease. Based on previous battle victories, they would feel optimistic when going into battle.

Choice B is incorrect because courage is a positive emotion and, like optimism, not symptomatic of disease. **Choice C is incorrect** because complacency, like satisfaction, suggests a sense of contentment, and it is doubtful that the Japanese would be satisfied until the war ended with their ultimate victory. **Choice D is incorrect** because satisfaction implies a conclusion or fulfillment, which is unlikely given that the war was ongoing. **Choice E is incorrect** because, in this context, overconfidence is the best choice to describe a mindset that could cause the Japanese to overlook warnings that might have changed the outcome of the war.

253 **Choice B is correct** because the writer includes these details to show that Haruki did not make a hasty or rash judgment when warning the Japanese command.

Choice A is incorrect because one example of work by the Naval Intelligence Center is not enough to evaluate the group's overall efficiency. **Choice C is incorrect** because the passage focuses on the discovery of the Allied positions, not on their location specifically. **Choice D is incorrect** because a single investigation by Haruki is insufficient to justify his position within the Japanese military. **Choice E is incorrect** because the passage indicates that despite previous Japanese naval victories, their lack of preparedness was not the reason they ignored Haruki's warning.

PASSAGE 133: SUMMARY/PARAPHRASE

The passage is about American Indian chiefs. The main idea is that the popular understanding of the role of a chief in tribal affairs did not always reflect the actual role of the individuals designated as chiefs. The main ideas are: (a) while chiefs had traditionally been figureheads with little actual power, they were often political leaders during a key transitional period and (b) the political power of chiefs during this transitional period was due to either backing from the US government or power-plays by ambitious tribesmen. The primary purpose of the passage is to disabuse the reader of a widely-held but not entirely correct belief, and to more accurately inform the reader about the facts.

254 **Choice D is correct** because the writer of this passage is careful to downplay the role of so-called chiefs in the tribal structure prior to interference by the American government. They had no real power or authority. Based on the absence of other information, the reader can conclude that the tribal structure was egalitarian, that all members had the opportunity to express their opinions and that all were listened to.

Choice A is incorrect because there is no evidence that the structure was matriarchal—ruled by adult women. **Choice B** is incorrect because there is no evidence that the structure was patriarchal—ruled by adult males. **Choice C** is incorrect because an oligarchy is ruled by a small select group, which does not appear to be the case here. **Choice E** is incorrect because a tyrant rules by fear, which is also not the case with the native tribes described in the passage.

255 **Choice C is correct** because any time that a popularly held belief is shown to be even partially incorrect, one should ask how he or she came to believe it in the first place. The writer of this passage states that the American public's understanding of a tribal chief's function is not correct according to the tribesmen. Now that the reader has a better understanding of the meaning of the title "chief," he or she may wonder what other commonly held ideas about the natives may also be incorrect or inaccurate.

Choice A is incorrect because there is no mention in the passage of any specific chiefs, so curiosity about their names would not arise in this context. **Choice B** is incorrect because the purpose of the passage is to clarify the position of the chief in a tribe, not to discuss the actual negotiations that took place between tribes and the American government; therefore, it is not likely that the reader would have questions about the number of tribes involved in the negotiations. **Choice D** is incorrect because the violent deaths of chiefs are mentioned only as an event that led to Americans taking advantage of the tribes, and the reasons for their deaths are not important in this context. **Choice E** is incorrect because, although the writer mentions that chiefs served "more or less" as politicians, there is no evidence that their behavior influenced the behavior of the Americans.

256 **Choice C is correct** because distinctive or unique means that it stands alone as an example; there is no other like it. This aligns with the intended use of "singular" in the context.

Choice A is incorrect because extraordinary would be used in the sense of an achievement or accomplishment, which does not apply in this context. **Choice B** is incorrect because this "singular" fact is neither unusual nor strange. **Choice D** is incorrect because "singular" in this context does not mean a separate or individual idea. **Choice E** is incorrect because it refers to the use of the word "singular" in grammar, which is not relevant here.

PASSAGE 134: SUMMARY/PARAPHRASE

The passage is about human rights in Malaysia. The main idea is that Malaysia is a notorious hub of human trafficking. The major points are that (a) Malaysia is a destination for people trafficked for both sexual exploitation and for forced labor and (b) that while Malaysia took action to improve its anti-trafficking laws, it has yet to tackle exploitative labor practices. The purpose of the passage is to inform the reader about the status of human trafficking in Malaysia.

257 **Choice A is correct** because the passage reveals that men, women, and children from South and Southeast Asia willingly migrate to Malaysia to work. One can infer that jobs are in short supply in the countries that they have left.

Choice B is incorrect because there is no information in the passage about the cultural beliefs in Malaysia. **Choice C** is incorrect because we cannot infer that the Malaysian culture is more accepting of child labor. **Choice D** is incorrect because there are no details about the 2000 UN TIP Protocol and its restrictions. **Choice E** is incorrect because the passage does not reveal that industrialized nations outsource their labor to Malaysia.

PASSAGE 135: SUMMARY/PARAPHRASE

The passage is about the political philosophy of Karl Marx. The main idea is that Marxist analysis is a highly useful tool in analyzing a variety of social and political systems. There are two major points: (a) that Marxist analysis has changed the way people think about socio-political systems and (b) that while Marxist theories are often used to critique capitalism, they can also be used to critique socialism and communism, systems that are themselves based in Marxism. The purpose of the passage is to inform the reader of an under-publicized aspect of Marxism, namely its usefulness in critiquing its own systems.

258 **Choice B is correct** because, since self-reflexivity means the ability to self-critique and find contradictions and artificialities, it is true that, according to the passage, Marxism is self-reflexive because it critically analyzes its own theories.

Choice A is incorrect because self-reflexivity means the ability of a person (or in this case a theory) to accurately see and assess its own artificialities and contradictions, and merely saying that Marxism deconstructs capitalistic power structures does not account for self-reflexivity at all. **Choice C is incorrect** because self-reflexivity is the ability to self-critique or analyze and is not a way of delineating the specifics of class conflict in general. **Choice D is incorrect** because, while it may be true that self-reflexivity helps academics set up research frameworks, the passage states that self-reflexivity in Marxism is a particularly valuable feature because it allows Marxism to critique its own economic theories. **Choice E is incorrect** because the passage does not indicate that self-reflexivity or engaging in self-critique creates an environment of free-thinking academic exchange.

259 **Choice B is correct** because dialectic means to gather intellectual information or reason by way of discussion and debate.

Choice A is incorrect because dialectic stands in opposition to the scientific method, which gathers information using empirical methods, rather than through discussion and reasoning. **Choice C is incorrect** because dialectic is a method of academic inquiry powered by discussion, while protest means to express an objection—these two terms are not analogous. **Choice D is incorrect** because, although dialectic involves dialogue, it is not limited to the political arena. **Choice E is incorrect** because dialectic is a method of eliciting reason via discussion, not the process of worker exploitation.

PASSAGE 136: SUMMARY/PARAPHRASE

The passage is about the spread of human-kind. The main idea is that while there is a consensus among specialists that humans originated in Africa before spreading outward, there is still debate as to exactly where early humans settled first as they dispersed from northern Africa. The main point is that recent evidence suggests that the initial point of colonization was the Arabian Peninsula. There is a minor point about DNA evidence suggesting genetic similarities between relevant populations that support the major point. The purpose of the passage is to inform and persuade: much of the tone is factual, but the final sentence suggests that the author is trying to get the reader to accept the conclusion that Arabia was the first area of human colonization. The author seems to assume that the evidence cited is conclusive.

260 **Choice C is correct** because the primary purpose of the passage is to discuss the point of origin from which modern man disseminated across the globe; this point was determined to be Arabia by way of DNA analysis.

Choice A is incorrect because, while the African Diaspora is an important aspect of the passage, the primary purpose is to show that scientists have determined the location of modern man's dissemination (Arabia). **Choice B is incorrect** because, although the author mentions that many are fascinated by the spread of human culture—including scientists and possibly laymen—this statement is not developed, and the author never directly references laymen; thus, the primary purpose is not to discuss how the interests of scientists and laymen intersect. **Choice D is incorrect** because, although DNA analysis helps scientists determine the point of origin, discussing the use of DNA analysis in anthropological research is not the main purpose of the passage. **Choice E is incorrect** because there is nothing polemical about the passage; the author does not use the information to instigate a debate.

261 **Choice C is correct** because the author makes use of a tone and style that do not betray any judgments towards the validity of DNA analysis as an anthropological research method; the author's attitude appears cool and detached, thus impartial.

Choice A is incorrect because the author's tone ad style do not indicate skepticism or doubt about the validity of DNA as an anthropological research method; the author seems neutral rather than skeptical. **Choice B is incorrect** because the author's tone and style do not indicate disbelief or wariness (leery) toward anthropological DNA analysis; the attitude is detached and candid. **Choice D is incorrect** because the author's tone does not suggest approval or favorability toward DNA analysis; instead, it is more detached and observational. **Choice E is incorrect** because the author does not show devotion or dedication to anthropological DNA analysis; the tone is detached and impartial rather than devoted.

262 **Choice D is correct** because the author indicates that the focus point of scientific debate is the point of origin of modern man's organized dispersal across the globe.

Choice A is incorrect because the author states that anthropologists are no longer debating whether early humans originated in the Horn of Africa, so the scientific polemics do not focus on this issue. **Choice B is incorrect** because, although the author discusses DNA samples from Europeans and Arabians, there is no suggestion that these two places are the focus of scientific debate. **Choice C is incorrect** because, while the Near East is mentioned as a region subjected to DNA testing, the passage does not specify its role in the human Diaspora or suggest it is central to scientific debate. **Choice E is incorrect** because the author does not indicate that scientists debate the use of DNA analysis in studying the dispersal of modern man.

PASSAGE 137: SUMMARY/PARAPHRASE

The passage is about the archaeology of cave dwellings. The main idea is that the distribution of finds is often counterintuitive. The major points are (a) over centuries of occupation, cave dwellers left behind many layers of leavings (b) the leavings are sometimes found in unexpected layers (c) the occupants of the caves may themselves dug into the layers and buried bodies and implements in a way that disturbed the layering process. The purpose of the passage is to explain how objects from a much older age can often be found alongside much newer objects in archaeological sites.

263 **Choice C is correct** because using earlier discoveries or prior knowledge about human artifacts provides a logical and reliable starting point for dating newly found artifacts.

Choice A is incorrect because, depending on the age of the artifacts, there may be no written records to identify their function or relative age. **Choice B** is incorrect because there may be no residents left in the area who can identify the artifacts through memory or oral tradition. **Choice D** is incorrect because sorting artifacts according to their function only groups them by use and does not help determine their age. **Choice E** is incorrect because the level or degree of preservation depends on many factors and is not a reliable means of dating artifacts.

PASSAGE 138: SUMMARY/PARAPHRASE

The passage is about Machiavelli's The Prince and its influence. The main idea is that The Prince has been both highly controversial and very influential on political thought. There are two main points: (a) that The Prince has been controversial for its cynical view of political life and (b) that its message of "the end justifies the means" has made a lasting impression on many readers. There is a minor point that specifies some of the ways in which The Prince runs contrary to many cherished political ideals contrasting the work's brazen realism with belief in political ideals. The main purpose of the passage is to inform and briefly familiarize the reader with the work and surrounding controversy. The tone is largely factual, and while the author mentions the controversial nature of the work, they do not express an opinion on the controversy.

264 **Choice B is correct** because the first bold-faced section explains in detail why The Prince is controversial, which supports the second section's conclusion that the statement "the end justifies the means" is well-known and controversial.

Choice A is incorrect because both bold-faced sections highlight how The Prince promotes political theories that are controversial today, so the first section does not undermine the second. **Choice C** is incorrect because the author's position is that The Prince is both poignant and controversial, and both sections support this claim. **Choice D** is incorrect because both bold-faced sections reinforce the author's view of The Prince as a controversial yet poignant book. **Choice E** is incorrect because while both sections discuss how The Prince challenges modern political ideas, they do not undermine modern political practices themselves.

265 **Choice A is correct** because the author clearly argues throughout the passage that The Prince remains highly influential despite—or because of—its controversial nature, making a strong case that polemical books tend to be the most influential.

Choice B is incorrect because the author does not discuss leadership as a combination of virtue and vice; rather, the focus is on how The Prince dismisses the importance of personal vice in leaders. **Choice C** is incorrect because although the author implies that political ideas evolve by contrasting modern ideas with Machiavellian ones, this is an inference and not a direct argument made in the passage. **Choice D** is incorrect because the author does not directly address human nature, even though the passage touches on political change and evolution. **Choice E** is incorrect because the author does not argue that the Machiavellian approach works best in practice; no case is made for it being the superior political method.

PASSAGE 139

266 **Choice D is correct** because the passage specifically highlights fatigue, suffering, and "almost useless labor" experienced by the settlers after land clearing began.

Choice A is incorrect because the passage states settlers have "a little money" but does not imply that the amount is insufficient. **Choice B** is incorrect because the passage does not mention any lack of or need for cooperation. **Choice C** is incorrect because the departure of the natives is not described as a problem in the passage. **Choice E** is incorrect because although land division is mentioned, it is not presented as a negative influence on the colonists.

267 **Choice B is correct** because the passage states the settlers brought "sufficient" tools and does not indicate a lack of tools as a problem.

Choice A is incorrect because the passage indicates the settlers were divided into families. **Choice C** is incorrect because the passage mentions new fatigue and "inconceivable suffering" experienced by the settlers. **Choice D** is incorrect because the passage notes that colonists made complaints. **Choice E is incorrect** because the passage mentions there were enough animals available.

268 **Choice C is correct** because the passage clearly states that the colonists brought sufficient livestock, seeds, money, tools, and food, and had an agreement with the native population before starting their work.

Choice A is incorrect because the passage describes a specific group of colonists and does not suggest that their experience is typical. **Choice B** is incorrect because the passage does not indicate that lack of manpower was the colonists' problem, nor does it imply that natives could assist them.

PASSAGE 140: SUMMARY/PARAPHRASE

The passage is about gender differences in imitation of behaviors. The main idea is that women tend to imitate the way other women behave more than men tend to imitate the way other men behave. The main point is that studies show that women tend to imitate other women in their eating habits, where men do not exhibit a similar pattern, lending credence to an existing hypothesis that women exhibit more same-sex imitation than men. There is a minor point that speculates that the reason for this phenomenon is that women have a greater need to fit in to and be liked by groups. The purpose of the passage is to inform and explain, which is indicated by the straightforward and factual language.

269 **Choice B is correct** because the passage specifies that men are less likely than women to conform to group eating behavior, but it does not claim that men are generally the less conventional gender in all contexts.

Choice A is incorrect because, while the passage suggests women have a stronger need to be liked by other females and thus tend to conform more, it does not make this the main point about gender differences overall. **Choice C** is incorrect because, although women copy each other's eating habits, the passage does not explicitly say they eat the same amount of food. **Choice D** is incorrect because the passage mentions women's desire to be liked and accepted but does not directly state that women value how others perceive them in general. **Choice E** is incorrect because the passage indicates men do not pay attention to each other's eating habits, so their food consumption is likely to vary, not be uniform.

PASSAGE 141

270 **Choice B is correct** because "fodder for artists" implies that the scene was painted or used in artwork many times, so it was a dramatic or impressive event; a dramatic event is a "spectacle." The second half of the text indicates that Washington "endeavored" or "tried" to create a memorable event in order to help boost the morale of his troops, since he had "not had a major victory" for a long time.

Choice A is incorrect because there is no indication of the actual number of paintings made of the event, only the implication that many artists have used the event as a theme for their work. **Choice C** is incorrect because, while the artwork could have advertised the attack if done beforehand, the passage implies that the attack was kept secret and it only was celebrated in art later. **Choice D** is incorrect because the storm and dangerous conditions could have rendered the event a disaster; the art produced would not have hurt his plans. **Choice E** is incorrect because the conditions are discussed in the earlier part of the sentence. The quoted words do not explain what the weather or other factors of the crossing were like.

271 **Choice E is correct** because the passage starts with Washington's crossing of the Delaware River, which is described as a "dangerous" or "perilous" feat. The "motivation" or "reason" follows: Washington wanted to boost morale with a successful victory that was impressive. Therefore, he attacked highly trained mercenaries in those dangerous conditions because the mercenaries were unprepared for such a desperate move.

Choice A is incorrect because only one "outcome" or "possible result" is described in the text: the fact that Washington's plans were successful. There is no discussion of what might have happened if the attack had failed. **Choice B** is incorrect because the crossing may be considered a "dilemma" if Washington was balancing his troops' safety against the desire to win a battle, but the "modern repercussions" or "present results" are not mentioned. The text states that the troops received bolstered confidence, but there is no comment, for example, that they won the war and now the country is independent. **Choice C** is incorrect because the "mechanism of executing" an event includes the technical details of a project, but there is no discussion about how Washington managed to get the horses, men, and artillery across the river, nor are there any details about how he surprised the mercenaries. **Choice D** is incorrect because art is mentioned in the passage to show how dramatic the event of crossing the Delaware was. The details included in the text refer to why it was a dangerous but strategically logical ploy under the circumstances. The lack of a victory and bolstering confidence relate to the reasons for the event, not to reasons for it to be artistically pleasing.

PASSAGE 142

272 **Choice B is correct** because it most logically fits the text's discussion of nanobots and their future in artificial intelligence. The author's claim that "the next decade will see the creation of artificial entities swimming to the brain" supports this conclusion.

Choice A is incorrect because the author's book is not the primary focus of the passage. Although the passage mentions the book, it does not speak of its release dates nor does it focus on the book wholly. **Choice C is incorrect** because the author does not guarantee that nanobots will stop aging or cure cancer. **Choice D is incorrect** because there is no warning. The author never implies that nanobots may be dangerous. **Choice E is incorrect** because the text is not persuasive. The author is informing people about the nanobot, not persuading people to use it.

273 **Choice B is correct.** The author uses the words, "If predictions pan out." The word "if" implies uncertainty.

Choice A is incorrect because the author never indicates that Kurzweil's predictions are accurate. **Choice C is incorrect.** This is the opinion of the pundits, not the author.

274 **Choice A is correct.** We know that Kurzweil is respected in his field because he is referred to as a "technological prognosticator" and has published a book on the subject.

Choice B is incorrect because the text does not discuss the extent of thought Kurzweill put into the risks of nanobots. The reader does not know that he has not given it careful consideration. **Choice C is incorrect** because there is no indication of Kurzweill's viewpoint on AI. There is no reason to believe that he is making a persuasive argument.

PASSAGE 143: SUMMARY/PARAPHRASE

The passage is about gender differences in altruistic behaviors. The main idea is that men are more likely than women to change their behavior based on the presence of attractive members of the opposite sex. The two main points are (a) that men are more likely to perform altruistic acts in the presence of attractive women and (b) that this behavior is caused by a need to impress potential mates. The purpose of the passage is to explain gender differences in a particular type of behavior.

275 **Choice E is correct** because the author supports the claims by citing a credible source, the British Journal of Psychology, which strengthens the argument and makes it more convincing.

Choice A is incorrect because, although the author objectively evaluates the facts, the compelling aspect comes primarily from citing the authoritative source rather than just the objective evaluation. **Choice B is incorrect** because the author's approach is deductive and objective, not designed to invoke an emotional response. **Choice C is incorrect** because the author does not present or address any counterview to the claim. **Choice D is incorrect** because the author does not criticize the opinions of other psychologists in the passage.

PASSAGE 144

276 **Choice B is correct** because the author discusses only the negative effects of gibbering crowds as it states in the passage that "Our culture is turning into a genuine din of confused crowds" and that mob and riot outbursts are "becoming more frequent." **Choice C is correct** because the passage states that the people do not want self-culture.

Choice A is incorrect because the author doesn't mention how crowds talk about something important, but that was left out to discuss the negative issues about crowds.

277 **Choice E is correct** because several reasons and examples are provided with the negative effects of talking in crowds when it provides that every topic discussed leads to confusion.

Choice A is incorrect because the passage does provide the negative aspects of crowd culture, but the positive aspects are not provided in the passage. **Choice B is incorrect** because there is a problem with the discussion arising within crowds of people and that is described in the passage, but the solution to this problem is not included. **Choice C is incorrect** because an event or two is listed, but it is only included to support the negative effects of crowd culture. **Choice D is incorrect** because the topics that are usually discussed are provided, including "patriotic, religious, ethical political" but this is merely a detail to support the rest of the structure of the passage.

PASSAGE 145

278 **Choice A is correct** because the author expresses flaws in both the FBI's and BJS's methods. The author states that the method used by the FBI is, "limited considering the vast number of crimes committed that remain unreported each year," and that it does not report certain offenses like drug crimes. The author states that the method used by the BJS, "poses serious limitations," because important vital crimes like murder can't be reported. However, the author concludes, "Despite the imperfections of both crime tracking processes, comparing data from the FBI and BJS can provide a satisfactory overview of crime across the nation." In other words, the author believes the methods are sufficient despite their imperfections.

Choice B is incorrect because the author does feel that there are serious limitations with both methods (and outlines them in the passage), but does not feel that this makes the methods insufficient as evidenced by the sentence, "Despite the imperfections of both crime tracking processes, comparing data from the FBI and BJS can provide a satisfactory overview of crime across the nation." **Choice C** is incorrect because the author presents issues with both the FBI's method and the BJS's method. Although the BJS does account for unreported crimes, the author points out that it fails to track murder rates. The author makes no claims that one is superior to the other. **Choice D** is incorrect because the author presents issues with both the FBI's method and the BJS's method. Although the FBI does track more violent crimes like murders, the author also points out that it fails to track unreported crimes. The author makes no claims that one is superior to the other. **Choice E** is incorrect because the author points out several limitations to both methods of tracking crime and does not describe them as, "thorough," but rather, "satisfactory." Also, the author never indicates that limitations are unavoidable and it cannot be assumed that the author does not go on to discuss other, more thorough suggestions for tracking crime.

279 **Choice B is correct** because the passage says, "Despite the imperfections of both crime tracking processes," suggesting that "imperfections" refers to the flaws of each method. Then, the passage says, "this method of collecting data poses serious limitations," suggesting that "limitations" also refers to the flaws of each method. Therefore, these two words have the same meaning in context.

Choice A is incorrect because the passage states, "from the FBI has historically included information on specific violent crimes," suggesting that "violent" refers to an umbrella term for aggressive crimes. Then, the passage says, "victims of murders obviously cannot complete surveys, so statistics on murders are not gathered from the survey," suggesting that "murders" refers to one specific type of crime. Though related, these two words do not share the same definition in context. **Choice C** is incorrect because the passage says, "victims of murders obviously cannot complete surveys," suggesting that "obviously" means the point is easily understandable and apparent. Then, the passage says, "comparing data from the FBI and BJS can provide a satisfactory overview of crime across the nation," suggesting that "satisfactory" refers to the adequate nature of the crime reports. Therefore, these two words have very different definitions in context. **Choice D** is incorrect because the passage states, "Despite the imperfections of both crime tracking processes," suggesting that "tracking" refers to the gathering of statistics in relation to crime. Then, the passage says, "so statistics on murders are not gathered," suggesting that "statistics" refers to the number of reported crimes.

The process of gathering statistics is different from the resultant number. Therefore, these two words are not equivalent in meaning. **Choice E** is incorrect because the passage states, "The FBI publishes data annually," suggesting that "annually" refers to the amount of time that passes before each FBI publication. Then, the passage says, "record crimes regardless of whether or not they were formally reported," suggesting that "formally" refers to the condition of a crime report. These two definitions are very dissimilar, so the words do not mean the same thing in context.

280 **Choice C is correct** because the point of the passage is to analyze the two methods of gathering crime statistics in the United States. The author introduces the passage, then spends the following three sentences discussing the FBI's method for collecting statistics. Then, the author uses the following four sentences discussing the BJS's method for collecting statistics before concluding the passage.

Choice A is incorrect because it does not include any information about the FBI's method for tracking crime, which is one of the major points. Also, it outlines two of the minor points that elaborate on the BJS's method for tracking crime. **Choice B** is incorrect because it states the main idea of the passage but does not outline the two major points. The two major points are the fact that the FBI uses law enforcement reports to determine crime statistics and the BJS uses an annual public survey to determine crime statistics. **Choice D** is incorrect because the passage only discusses the fact that the FBI's method does not account for drug crimes. The passage does not state that the BJS's method fails to account for drug crimes. Also, the information provided on drug crimes is a minor point that falls under the major point of the FBI's method of data collection. **Choice E** is incorrect because, while it accurately captures the major point that the BJS uses a public survey to analyze crime statistics, it does not accurately state the other major point. It only states that the FBI publishes data annually but does not explain what method the FBI uses.

PASSAGE 146: SUMMARY/PARAPHRASE

The passage is about the longer-term benefits of working hard in college. The main idea is that lazier college students tend to fare significantly worse along several measures than their more industrious peers. There are two main points: (a) that slacker students are at a higher risk of poor economic outcomes and (b) that slacker students often do not improve vital skills such as critical reasoning. The purpose of the passage is to caution students to take college seriously - rhetorical flourishes such as "even more troubling" indicate that the author has a clear bias toward what outcomes are better.

Chapter 3: Reading Comprehension

281 **Choice A is correct** because a few exceptions, such as some slacker students still achieving success, fall within the expected margin of error and do not weaken the author's overall claims.

Choice B is incorrect because evidence showing that slacker students improve their academic skills despite low work ethic would directly contradict the author's claim that poor academic skills hinder future success. **Choice C is incorrect** because if there were no significant difference in job outcomes between students with low and high work ethics, it would undermine the author's argument that slacking harms post-graduation employment prospects. **Choice D is incorrect** because if both hardworking and slacker students had the same financial situation, it would challenge the claim that working hard in college pays off financially. **Choice E is incorrect** because if both groups had the same living situation, it would undermine the author's assertion that slacker students are more likely to live with their parents after graduation due to lack of effort.

PASSAGE 147

282 **Choice C is correct** because the passage expresses that linguistics studies phonetic sounds. It also states that linguistics is complimentary to other disciplines, like biology. Biology is the study of life, including human anatomy. Therefore, both biologists and linguists would be interested in studying how the mouth works to produce sounds.

Choice A is incorrect because linguistics does not study human migration. The only mention of history in the passage is, "Topics like the history of families of languages," are examined in linguistics. **Choice B is incorrect** because, while linguists can help students in a classroom with learning language and communication skills, the passage does not state that linguists can help teachers learn how to teach children of various ages. Teachers would more likely be experts in this area. **Choice D is incorrect** because, while linguistics does examine how language is connected to social factors, linguists are not experts in how social factors impact Americans overall. In addition, philosophers would not be the discipline to collaborate with on this topic. Rather, sociologists would cover this topic. **Choice E is incorrect** because the passage explains that linguistics compliments a variety of other fields. The passage does not indicate that applied linguistics is the only subfield that is complimentary.

283 **Choice A is correct** because it includes all main points from the passage in a concise and understandable way with no unnecessary details. The sentence includes the brief definition of linguistics as well as an overview of what linguistics studies. It also provides brief information on the fact that linguistics overlaps with multiple other disciplines.

Choice B is incorrect because it does not include any information about the broad reach linguistics has and its ability to compliment other disciplines. This sentence only includes a definition of linguistics and what it studies. **Choice C is incorrect** because, although it defines linguistics and expresses that it compliments other fields, it does not provide any information on the features of language that linguistics studies. Therefore, choice A is the better option. **Choice D is incorrect** because it is simply a definition of linguistics and includes no other points from the passage such as what linguistics studies or how it compliments other disciplines. **Choice E is incorrect** because it does not define linguistics or explain the features of language that linguistics studies. It also only discusses the application of linguistics in education and does not mention how it compliments other fields.

PASSAGE 148

284 **"Followers of The Old Way make offerings to certain gods depending on a specific season and theme."** This sentence is correct because most of the previous sentences don't mention offerings. The only one that does is the last sentence of the first paragraph, which mentions offerings in a list with feasts and toasts. This list format suggests that the sentence is providing an overview of the information to come, not transitioning into a specific topic yet. Following, the first sentence of the second paragraph only explains how new believers have learned the ways of old believers.

285 **Choice E is correct** because the word, "vanished," means disappeared. In the context of the sentence one can gather that it has disappeared over time, especially with the presentation of other religions. The phrase, "faded away," means to gradually become less strong and then disappear. The meaning of, "vanished," in context and the meaning of, "faded away," are very similar. Therefore, "faded away," is the best replacement.

Choice A is incorrect because, "vaporized," does mean that something disappeared, but it means that something turned into gas or vapor as it disappeared. Since the item being discussed is religious beliefs, this word would not apply. Therefore, choice E is the better option. **Choice B is incorrect** because, "abscond," means to leave hurriedly and secretly. This does not accurately describe the manner in which the believers of the ancient Norse gods dwindled. Rather, the beliefs would have faded away over time with the introduction of other belief systems. Therefore, choice E is the better option. **Choice C is** incorrect because the phrase, "been taken by storm," means to rapidly become very successful or popular. This is the opposite of what is being described in the sentence. The sentence is expressing that many people think the traditional beliefs of the Vikings went away, not increased immensely. **Choice D is incorrect because,** "adapted," means something was modified for a new purpose. In the sentence, the word, "vanished," means that the beliefs disappeared over time. The beliefs were not changed and no new purpose for the beliefs is discussed. Because these two definitions are so dissimilar, choice E is the better option.

286 **Choice C is correct** because the passage states, "The modern believers of the old Nordic religion ("The Old Way") follow the resources handed down through generations." Therefore, most people who believe in the old Nordic religion had Nordic ancestors to pass on the religion. So, it is unlikely that people without Nordic ancestors would follow this religion, especially with the low number of followers to the religion in modern times.

Choice A is incorrect because this information cannot be inferred based on the passage alone. Although Christianity may have played a large role in converting Vikings, the passage does not make any mention of the specific other religions that played a role. **Choice B is** incorrect because the passage states that sacrifices are made to gods once per season but does not indicate that there are only four gods. The passage says, "Followers of The Old Way make offerings to certain gods depending on a specific season and theme." However, it can be interpreted that there are a variety of gods to choose from, not just four. **Choice D** is incorrect because the passage states, "Sacrifices are made by male or female priests while participants watch from a ceremonial circle." There is no other mention of gender throughout the passage. So, it can be assumed that male and female priests share the same duties when performing sacrifices. **Choice E** is incorrect because it is not clear based on the passage whether the followers of The Old Way follow a western calendar, Viking calendar, or any other type of calendar. One cannot assume that the Viking calendar has been dismissed because, as the passage states, their religious beliefs have not been.

PASSAGE 149: SUMMARY/PARAPHRASE

The passage is about how art relates to civilization. The main idea is that, contrary to popular belief, art predates complex human civilizations. There are two main points: (a) that art is often considered constitutive of civilization and (b) recent archaeological finds suggest that art significantly predates civilization. The purpose of the passage is to debunk a commonly held view that the author views as false. The author of the passage makes an implicit assumption that art is well-defined, and that primitive painting is in fact art.

287 **Choice D is correct** because, according to the author, the significance of the early human painting kits lies in their demonstration that artistic practices existed before the advent of human civilization, challenging the common view that art is a marker of civilization.

Choice A is incorrect because the author emphasizes that the painting kits are important not just as a characteristic of civilization, but specifically because they show art existed among the earliest human ancestors. **Choice B** is incorrect because although the author discusses the tools, the main point is that these tools predate human civilization, not just their specific nature. **Choice C is** incorrect because while the author mentions art used for body decoration, the primary importance is that the painting kits show artistic practices predate civilization. **Choice E** is incorrect because the author focuses more on the fact that art predates civilization, rather than on whether the kits were carried by humans during migrations.

PASSAGE 150

288 **Choice B is correct** because the passage expresses that there are different types of psychologists, like cognitive psychologists and social psychologists. Therefore, their unique training may cause them to view topics through a particular lens.

Choice A is incorrect because the passage does not indicate in any way that psychologists are controversial or that disagreements are expected. There is not sufficient information to make that assumption. **Choice C is** incorrect because the passage does not indicate in any way that psychologists are not all adequately trained or that some are subpar. There is not sufficient information to make that assumption.

289 **Choice A is correct** because this is a minor point working to support the major point that theories among psychologists regarding the unconscious are varied. Choice B is correct because this is a minor point working to support the major point that theories among psychologists regarding the unconscious are varied.

Choice C is incorrect because this is a major point, which is then proven by multiple minor points that follow.

PASSAGE 151

290 **Choice E is correct** because the author does not give any direct reasons as to how learning social studies can be beneficial. The author states that children can become better decision makers, become better judges of global affairs, develop deeper perspectives, learn to participate politically, and think critically. However, not a single example or specific reference is given to support those benefits.

Choice A is incorrect because the second paragraph explicitly states, "A high-quality social studies curriculum serves four important purposes," before listing those four purposes. **Choice B** is incorrect because the author does not need to provide additional information on social studies standards in order to make the point that social studies education is important. Simply stating that modern educational standards demand a deep understanding of the world is sufficient. This section of the passage only serves as a segue to discuss high-quality social studies classes. **Choice C** is incorrect because this is a strength of the author's argument, not a weakness. The author does provide four concise and solid points in support of the argument being made. **Choice D** is incorrect because the author does not use any technical terms in the passage. Contrarily, the passage is written in a casual informative style that most readers would likely be able to understand.

291 **Choice D is correct** because the first paragraph does introduce the topic with a hook, an overview of social studies topics, and a thesis stating the author's argument. Then, the second paragraph lists and describes four purposes that a social studies curriculum serves.

Choice A is incorrect because the first paragraph does not focus on the role of the social studies teacher. It does mention social studies teachers, but that is only one detail in a paragraph that aims to introduce the topic of modern social studies education. Then, the second paragraph does not focus on how students' lives are immediately impacted by understanding social concepts. This would mean that students could apply these social lessons to their own social lives instantaneously. However, the second paragraph simply outlines long term benefits of high-quality social studies curriculums, such as being able to meaningfully participate in a democracy. **Choice B** is incorrect because the first paragraph does not focus on the role of the social studies teacher. It does mention social studies teachers, but that is only one detail in a paragraph that aims to introduce the topic of modern social studies education. Therefore, choice D is the better option. **Choice C** is incorrect because the second paragraph does not focus on how students' lives are immediately impacted by understanding social concepts. This would mean that students could apply these social lessons to their own social lives instantaneously. However, the second paragraph simply outlines long term benefits of high-quality social studies curriculums, such as being able to meaningfully participate in a democracy. Therefore, **choice D is the better option.** Choice E is incorrect because, although the first paragraph does mention the topics involved in social studies, that is not the purpose of the paragraph overall. Rather, the paragraph aims to introduce the topic of modern social studies education.

292 **Choice B is correct** because the passage states, "Simply memorizing timelines and reading folktales is insufficient in modern classrooms." From this sentence, it can be assumed that memorization and folktales have previously been associated with social studies curriculums. Furthermore, the remainder of the passage goes on to express what modern social studies curriculums should include. The passage discusses exploring various topics in depth, building decision making skills, thinking critically, and changing perspectives. In other words, the deep transformation that is now a part of social studies curriculums was not always.

Choice A is incorrect because the text only mentions folktales in a hook that says, "Simply memorizing timelines and reading folktales is insufficient." Although it can be inferred that folktales were a part of former curriculums, it cannot be assumed that they were heavily focused on. Additionally, there is no indication that folktales are now avoided. They may still be included as part of deeper and more transformative modern social studies curriculums. Therefore, choice B is the better option. **Choice C** is incorrect because the passage states, "students develop a more thorough perspective on how modern nations developed." Because it says students develop a more thorough perspective it can be assumed that former curriculums helped develop somewhat of a thorough perspective on how modern nations developed. Therefore, curriculums did teach about how modern nations were developed to some degree. **Choice D** is incorrect because, although the text does say that memorization was an important part of former social studies curriculums, it does not say that memorization is no longer an important part of social studies. Rather, the passage explains how modern social studies curriculums are more thorough, but it cannot be assumed that specific dates and names have been left out. Therefore, choice B is the better option. **Choice E is incorrect** because, while this is an accurate conclusion that can be drawn from the text, the question specifically asks for an assumption about former social studies curriculums. In contrast, this assumption is made about modern social studies curriculums.

PASSAGE 152

293 The sentence "**Crowd behavior is detrimental to the individual as well as to society**" explicitly draws a parallel between the effects of crowd behavior on both the individual and the broader social group. It highlights how the negative consequences of crowd behavior impact not only the personal experiences and development of individuals but also the overall societal structure and values. This comparison illustrates how the actions and influences of crowds can harm both individual identity and community cohesion, thus aligning the conduct of society with that of the individual.

PASSAGE 153

294 **Choice C is correct** because multiple sentences from the passage work to support and explain this idea. For example, the fact that efforts are made to represent indigenous people in government and the fact that mental health services have been provided are two points that contribute to this idea. This is the main idea of the passage, so it would be classified as a major point.

Choice A is incorrect because this is a minor point that elaborates on the idea that indigenous groups are protected and supported in part because it simultaneously preserves the rainforest. Only one sentence from the passage discusses this topic. **Choice B is incorrect because** this is a minor point that elaborates on the idea that indigenous groups are protected and supported in part because it simultaneously preserves the rainforest. Only one sentence from the passage discusses this topic.

295 **Choice C is correct** because this point would be least likely to be included in a summary of the passage. It does not contain necessary information in order to convey the main idea of the passage, which is the fact that supporting indigenous populations simultaneously works to conserve the rainforest. This sentence is more of an explanation of what it means to be an indigenous tribe, which is detailed information that would likely be excluded from a summary.

Choice A is incorrect because this point would likely be included in a summary of the passage. The fact that many indigenous people reside in the Amazon is essential background information to present before making a point that protection of these people is important. Therefore, choice C is the better option. **Choice B is incorrect** because this point would likely be included in a summary of the passage. It is necessary to make this point before conveying the main idea, which is the fact that supporting indigenous groups works simultaneously to care for the rainforest. It would not be clear why the main point is true without an understanding of the fact that the lifestyle of the people preserves the Amazon. **Choice D is incorrect** because this is the main idea of the text, so this point would be required in a summary of the passage. **Choice E is incorrect** because this point would likely be included in a summary of the passage. This point directly relates to the fact that the lifestyle of indigenous people preserves the Amazon. Without an understanding of the fact that people depend on the Amazon for survival, it would be unclear how this population and the preservation of the rainforest relate to one another.

PASSAGE 154

296 **Choice D is correct** because the passage states, "Nevadan industries continued booming, while their relatively few laws kept a "wild west" atmosphere alive." Therefore, there was not a lot of restricting legislature despite the continuous growth and development of the state.

Choice A is incorrect because the passage states that the region was calm until the discover of the Comstock Lode in 1859, at which point the population skyrocketed. As mining continued to evolve and gambling started, it can be assumed that many continued flocking to Nevada throughout this time period. **Choice B is incorrect** because the passage states that the Comstock Lode was discovered in 1859, which led to many more people mining in Nevada. The passage states that mining continued to evolve into the mid1900's. **Choice C is incorrect** because the passage explains that mining evolved during this time and made major changes for the economy of Nevada, such as an increase in population. Additionally, the passage explains that the introduction of gambling to the state made a big impact. Therefore, the economy as a whole developed greatly. **Choice E is incorrect** because the passage states that the region was calm until 1859 when the population skyrocketed. The passage goes on to explain that the possibilities of getting rich quickly in the state continued to draw people from across the nation.

Chapter 3: Reading Comprehension

297 **Choice A is correct** because the sentence mentions the discussion in the previous paragraph about mining by stating, "The mining scene in Nevada continued to evolve." Then, the sentence transitions into the topic of gambling by saying, "but other economic attributes were born as well." This is only an introduction to the topic and is not a clear thesis statement to be proven.

Choice B is incorrect because this sentence acts as a hook to smoothly transition from the topic of mining to the topic of gambling. It does not make a clear argument about gambling to be proven, but simply introduces a new idea. **Choice C** is incorrect because the beginning of a paragraph would not be an appropriate place for a conclusion sentence. Instead, this sentence serves the purpose of transitioning into a new topic, which is gambling. **Choice D** is incorrect because the "wild west" atmosphere of Nevada is not mentioned until later on in the paragraph following a discussion about gambling. This sentence serves as a transition into the topic of gambling. So, choice A is the better option. **Choice E** is incorrect because this sentence acts as a hook to smoothly transition from the topic of mining to the topic of gambling. It does not make a clear argument about mining to be proven, but simply introduces a new idea.

298 **"However, the region remained relatively calm until the discovery of silver at the Comstock Lode in 1859."** This is the correct sentence because it is the only sentence from the text that describes the condition of Nevada prior to its induction into statehood in 1864. The other sentences that talk about Nevada prior to statehood only explain how it was named, who originally explored it, and how it was acquired by the Union.

PASSAGE 155

299 **Choice C is correct** because the passage is written in an informative style. It details the position of a gerontological social worker in particular, but also includes general information about what social work is. Thus, it is likely that this passage is directed to individuals who may not be especially familiar with social work as a field.

Choice A is incorrect because the passage starts by explaining what social work is. If students were already studying social work this information would likely be unnecessary. Therefore, it is more likely that this passage seeks to inform older people looking for services, making choice C the better option. **Choice B** is incorrect because this passage is written in an informative style and makes no indication that a story will be told. Rather, this passage seeks to tell others about what gerontological social workers do. **Choice D** is incorrect because this passage is written in an informative style and does not use any persuasive techniques. It does not seem to be making any arguments and does not discuss the rights of social workers at all. The only mention of the workplace is when explaining that social workers can serve older adults in a variety of settings. **Choice E** is incorrect because this passage is written in an informative style and does not use any persuasive techniques. It does not seem to be making any arguments and does not discuss the rights of older adults at all.

300 **Choice E is correct** because the passage states social workers, "communicate with insurance companies to ensure high-quality therapeutic interventions." The passage does indicate that social workers deliver herapeutic interventions in any way.

Choice A is incorrect because the passage states that social workers help older adults overcome mental barriers and collaborate with families to find solutions. Therefore, this would likely be a task that a gerontological social worker would complete. **Choice B** is incorrect because the passage states that social workers collaborate with families and connect them with community resources. A meal deliver services would qualify as a community resource. Therefore, this would likely be a task that a gerontological social worker would complete. **Choice C** is incorrect because the passage states social workers, "help facilities set up the physical parameters needed to serve the client." Ordering a ramp would be an example of setting up a facility physically. Therefore, this would likely be a task that a gerontological social worker would complete. **Choice D** is incorrect because the passage states social workers, "communicate with insurance companies to ensure high-quality therapeutic interventions." Calling an insurance company to verify benefits would be an example of this. Therefore, this would likely be a task that a gerontological social worker would complete.

Chapter 4
Text Completion

Chapter 4: Text Completion

Text Completion questions are designed to further test your ability to understand what you read. They will also test your vocabulary, particularly your ability to apply sophisticated vocabulary in context. You will be asked to read a short passage of 1-5 sentences. There will be 1-3 blanks in the passage where a crucial word is missing. You will need to fill in each blank using several options provided.

The passages used for Text Completion questions will be drawn from a variety of topics, including the physical, biological, and social sciences; the arts and the humanities; business; and everyday life. As with Reading Comprehension questions, you do not need to be an expert on the topic covered, you only need to read the passage attentively enough to be able to pick the right word for the blank.

All Text Completion questions will be in a multiple-choice format. Each passage will have 1-3 blanks, and you will be given several options to choose from to fill in the blanks. Generally, passages with only one blank will have five options to choose from while those with 2-3 blanks will have only three options per blank.

What Skills Do Text Completion Questions Test?

Text Completion questions test your ability to understand complex sentences and passages. They also test your ability to use sophisticated vocabulary in context and your ability to use reasoning to complete an idea based on incomplete information. Some key skills that are tested include your ability to:

- understand a text holistically and be able to determine the meaning of individual components
- use reasoning to fill in important gaps in information
- understand high level vocabulary
- apply vocabulary in context

What Does a Text Completion Question Look Like?

Text Completion questions will always be based on a short passage of one or more sentences. The passage will have 1-3 blanks. You will be asked to read the passage and get a feel of what words will best complete it using several options given. Below are examples of what Text Completion questions will look like on the GRE General Test:

Introduction to Text Completion

For each blank select one entry from the corresponding column of choices. Fill all blanks in the way that best completes the text.

1. The later Roman Empire was continually (i) _____ invasions of nomadic and semi-nomadic peoples who were often themselves (ii) _____ by marauding tribes from the Central Asian steppes.

Blank (i)	Blank (ii)
Ⓐ delighted	Ⓓ displaced
Ⓑ threatened	Ⓔ dismissed
Ⓒ enthralled	Ⓕ averred

2. Harry's _____ performance on the project both failed to impress his superiors and helped to lose the company an important client.

Ⓐ rapacious
Ⓑ desultory
Ⓒ indomitable
Ⓓ arcane
Ⓔ indefatigable

Answer Key

The correct answers are:

1. **Choice B:** threatened and **Choice D:** displaced
2. **Choice B:** desultory

Strategies for Text Completion Questions

You will have 18 and 23 minutes to complete the Verbal Reasoning sections. While budgeting your time is important, Text Completion questions are different from Reading Comprehension questions and require you to alter your strategies accordingly. In the first place, the passages used for Text Completion questions will generally be much shorter than those used for Reading Comprehension questions. This means that it will take you less time to carefully read a passage for a Text Completion question than it would for you to carefully read a Reading Comprehension passage. Moreover, Text Completion questions are much more focused, and to answer them effectively, you may need to grasp subtle aspects of sentence structure. While you will not want to get hung up on a single Text Completion question, you will generally want to read the passages with more care than those used for Reading Comprehension questions. Do not try to skim through Text Completion questions. If you feel that you are taking too much time on a single question, either make an educated guess or bookmark it (in case you have time later) and then move on.

As with Reading Comprehension, do not let the subject matter of the passage throw you off—your ability to correctly answer these questions will not rely on your expertise in any particular area. When answering Text Completion questions, one of the key skills you will need is the ability to grasp the overall meaning of the passage even with certain words missing. You will then need to apply your understanding of the passage, coupled with your grasp of key transitional words in the passage, to correctly choose the word that best fits with the overall meaning of the passage. Where Reading Comprehension questions test your ability to grasp general meanings, Text Completion questions test your ability to read carefully and understand more subtle cues about the meaning of specific sections of text.

The key skills for Text Completion are reading closely and applying vocabulary in context. You'll need to get a quick idea of what the passage is about, and the general tone, but beyond that, you need to be able to see how specific words fit into the whole passage. Focus most of your attention on the individual meanings of different components of the passage. Often there are overt indications of which words will best complete the passage; either the word you need to complete the passage will be essentially defined in another clause, or the context will strongly suggest that you use a word with the opposite meaning to what has already been said. These contextual indicators are quite valuable, so keep a close eye out for them. Also, because vocabulary is a more important part of Text Completion questions, anything you can do to review or improve your vocabulary will probably be helpful.

 Key Points to Remember

- Read the passage carefully - do not skim
- Focus on significant words to help you grasp precise meanings
- Keep an eye out for sections of the passage that either closely match or negate the definition of one of the word options
- Apply vocabulary in context

What follows are some more specific strategies for answering Text Completion questions. In the next chapter, you'll have a chance to put your skills to the test through several practice questions and learn how to hone them in the answers and explanations that follow.

1. Review Vocabulary

Anything that you can do to strengthen your vocabulary prior to the test will be helpful. Although the GRE General Test does not feature any section that is strictly designed to test vocabulary, the Verbal Reasoning section assumes a fairly high-level vocabulary. Your command of sophisticated vocabulary is especially important for the Text Completion and Sentence Equivalence sections since you will need to identify the right word to fill in a blank. If you are not confident in your vocabulary, do what you can to improve it as part of your preparation for the test (this will serve you well in graduate school as well). Note that in many cases you will not need to know a precise definition of a word, but you do need to have a general sense of what it means. There are several things you can do to improve your vocabulary for the test:

Introduction to Text Completion

- Review lists of common "GRE words" such as the ones included in the *Online Resources*
- Use a vocabulary builder
- Get a sense of key Greek or Latin root words and what they mean—many words in English are based on Greek or Latin words, and knowing the meaning of a few key Greek or Latin words can help you figure out the meanings of numerous English words

2. Get a General Feel of the Passage

Be fore you try to fill in any blanks, get a general sense of what the passage says, and the tone. Doing this will help you get a general feel for whether a particular word fits or not. As you read the passage, pay close attention to words that may signal a shift in tone or perspective. Such words give insight into the meaning of the passage as a whole, and can also tell you something about the particular phrase that you'll need to complete.

3. Pay Special Attention to Significant Words

Certain keywords can give tremendous insight into the meaning of a passage or phrase. Many times your ability to correctly answer Text Completion questions will hinge on whether you are able to detect qualifying words in a passage. Be especially alert for words like "although" and "despite", which suggest that what has been said so far is about to be qualified. Also keep an eye out for words like "therefore", "moreover" and "thus", which suggest summation or additional support for points that have already been made.

4. Don't Assume That You Should Always Fill In the First Blank First

Sometimes the order in which you fill in the blanks won't matter. For some questions, however, it will be difficult to fill in one blank without first correctly filling in another blank. The first blank won't always be the one you should try to fill in first—sometimes you will need to reason backward through the passage. Keep in mind that some Text Completion questions are very straightforward, and others are designed to test your reasoning, so be prepared to use more than just vocabulary to find the correct answer.

5. Come Up With Your Own Words To Fill In the Blanks

As you read through the passage, try to think of words that would fill in the blanks; then, compare the answer options given to the words you have thought of and try to select similar words from among the options. If you are unsure of what some of the words mean and cannot identify similar words, try to eliminate words with opposite meanings to the words you picked.

6. Check Your Work

Always re-read the passage with the answer(s) you have selected and filled in to see whether the passage is grammatical and makes sense with the options you have chosen. Even if your choice seems right, if it does not produce a coherent, grammatically correct passage, it isn't the correct answer.

7. Use Process of Elimination

You can apply the process of elimination to Text Completion questions as well. Sometimes, you may quickly identify the correct answer or answers, but other times you may be uncertain. In cases where you don't find the right answer to be immediately obvious, use the process of elimination to narrow the options. Many times a word with the opposite meaning from the correct answer will appear among the choices—you can immediately dismiss such words. Other times you will find words that simply have nothing to do with the context, and these can be dismissed as well. As with any other multiple-choice question, eliminating obviously wrong answers will always increase your odds of getting the right answer.

Practice Set 1: One Blank

301 The crude tools of human civilizations leave a trail throughout time that _____ even when the written records of events become unclear or seem to be in direct contradiction to one another.

- (A) discontinue
- (B) perdures
- (C) excavates
- (D) derides
- (E) beguiles

302 According to the theory of natural selection, traits that prove particularly _____ have a greater chance of being passed on to future generations, because the individuals that possess these traits are more likely to survive long enough to mate.

- (A) innocuous
- (B) expedient
- (C) salient
- (D) titillating
- (E) prolific

303 Competition is highly desirable in a free market economy—the concentration of market capital in relatively few enterprises can _____ economic health by forcing customers to pay prices they can barely afford.

- (A) attenuate
- (B) consecrate
- (C) commiserate
- (D) alleviate
- (E) fulminate

304 The more loudly and adamantly he denied any involvement with the crime, the less the jury believed him. Clearly his _____ would not pass muster with them, and he had no doubt their deliberations would be short and to the point. guilty!

- (A) dyspepsia
- (B) harangue
- (C) approbation
- (D) peregrination
- (E) gaucherie

305 The combined _____ of scientists present at the time of the launch could not have enabled them to predict the unanticipated events predicated by what should have been a routine display of military prowess.

- (A) demeanor
- (B) heresy
- (C) efficacy
- (D) acumen
- (E) callosity

306 Perhaps the most _____ of any play ever performed, James Carthwaite's rendition of "Born to be Wilde," based on the art and antics of the late Oscar Wilde, took eight hours to perform and was executed over two consecutive nights—or would have been had it not closed down halfway through the first night.

- (A) pedantic
- (B) odious
- (C) onerous
- (D) moribund
- (E) prolix

Chapter 4: Text Completion

307 _____, once thought to be the result of poor motivation or bad genetics and the fault of the released prisoners rather than the institutions that released them, has institutional and social dimensions that are far beyond the control of the ex-offender, and, that unabated, virtually enslave ex-offenders to criminal lifestyles ensuring that they become permanent residents of our penal institutions.

- (A) Gasconade
- (B) Recidivism
- (C) Exfiltration
- (D) Chicanery
- (E) Attenuation

308 An Augustinian monk, Gregor Mendel, studied genetics by conducting experiments on garden peas, and in 1865 was the first scientist to propose the concept of _____ traits and the science of genetics.

- (A) bequeathed
- (B) inbred
- (C) maternal
- (D) acquired
- (E) heritable

309 Perhaps not surprisingly, a recent study suggests that teens in the United States spend a _____ amount of money on clothes; in fact, apparel accounts for roughly 20 percent of all teen spending.

- (A) conspicuous
- (B) temperate
- (C) nebulous
- (D) ignominious
- (E) impecunious

310 At a loss to explain the overwhelming popularity of today's insipid TV reality shows, critics have come to the conclusion that viewers who are obsessed with reality programs are drawn to the _____ lifestyles depicted and allow the radiance of the stars' lives override the spurious dilemmas and dubious coping skills of the so-called stars.

- (A) refulgent
- (B) austere
- (C) laudable
- (D) monotonous
- (E) sanctimonious

311 Contrary to a popular myth, the _____ pinks and oranges of a sunset are at their most brilliant in areas with relatively unpolluted air.

- (A) fervid
- (B) plangent
- (C) crepuscular
- (D) lambent
- (E) winsome

312 Strict laws prohibiting dog fighting aim to reduce the number of dogs injured or killed each year in this heinous but lucrative industry by targeting those truly responsible, not the dogs who are bred and forced to fight, but the depraved owners who perpetuate this _____ of sport for personal glory and financial gain.

- (A) tirade
- (B) artifice
- (C) debauch
- (D) travesty
- (E) apparition

313. While the original conception of rhetoric confined its uses to political discourse, many people now agree that the art of debate _____ every field of study.

- A) permits
- B) permeates
- C) aggrandizes
- D) aggravates
- E) rectifies

314. Even though my sister cleaned the sink and the floor, she was still _____ with the state of the bathroom, and sought to bring it up to her standards of cleanliness.

- A) mystified
- B) unsatisfied
- C) fearful
- D) knowledgeable
- E) unconsidered

315. Henry VIII may have been the most powerful man in the world in his time, but as a monarch he certainly was not fortuitous when it came to producing a male heir to ascend to the throne. His _____ included Prince Edward who died in childhood and the Princesses, Mary and Elizabeth.

- A) progenitors
- B) scions
- C) devisees
- D) lineage
- E) promulgations

316. The various psychosocial variables that constitute the human mind cannot be understood through strict experimentation without also considering the _____ such experiments inherently introduce in the subject.

- A) prejudices
- B) pellucidity
- C) impartiality
- D) riposte
- E) plutocracy

317. Cirrus clouds, which form high in the atmosphere and are known for their wispy, _____ appearance, are actually composed of ice crystals rather than water droplets.

- A) halcyon
- B) sinuous
- C) gossamer
- D) variegated
- E) lambent

318. An example of operant conditioning is a commuter who _____, after several experiences, which route to his or her job takes the least amount of time, and adopts that route as a result of this learning.

- A) assumes
- B) theorizes
- C) ascertains
- D) disputes
- E) validates

319. More people living longer lives due to worldwide improvements in health care and nutrition translates to the need for nursing homes across the country to develop their _____ care capacity to attend to the needs of an ageing population over the long run.

- A) ameliorative
- B) palliative
- C) regressive
- D) salubrious
- E) proprietary

Chapter 4: Text Completion

320. Although Aristotle did not have a high opinion of octopi, calling them "stupid creatures," their reputation as problem solvers and critical thinkers has recently been _____, largely due to the antics of a Delhi zoo octopus named Andy who selects what he wants to eat from a menu of 28 fresh fish choices, regularly ambushes his fellow tank mates just for fun, and has to be kept in a specialized tank because he has learned to pick all traditional tank locks.

- (A) ruminated
- (B) bifurcated
- (C) expedited
- (D) ameliorated
- (E) scintillated

321. The human ability to recognize that the size of an object is _____, even as the distance between the person and object makes it appear to change in size, is called size constancy.

- (A) immutable
- (B) flexible
- (C) stable
- (D) abiding
- (E) uniform

322. Perception differs from sensation and refers not just to the reception of stimuli, but the _____ of those stimuli to determine what information can be gathered and how the information should be used.

- (A) insight
- (B) interpretation
- (C) translation
- (D) elucidation
- (E) adaptation

323. The Romantic notion of "the sublime" has its origins in the eighteenth-century fascination with the natural world in all its forms; the term was used to describe landscapes so awe-inspiring that they simultaneously terrified and _____ those who saw them.

- (A) perturbed
- (B) eviscerated
- (C) transcended
- (D) galvanized
- (E) beguiled

324. It is not just the existence of multiple types of cells, but the _____ between these cells that allow a multicellular organism to function.

- (A) communion
- (B) accord
- (C) synergy
- (D) intimacy
- (E) contention

325. Rather than operate independently, cells in a multicellular organism are arranged into complex _____ of specialized cells that work together to complete complex functions.

- (A) cooperatives
- (B) aggregates
- (C) collectives
- (D) division
- (E) unanimity

326. While the consequences of criminal law cases may exceed those of civil law, especially in terms of financial reparations, the two function _____ to maintain social order.

- (A) perniciously
- (B) superciliously
- (C) redundantly
- (D) intractably
- (E) conjunctly

Practice Set 1: One Blank

327 Genghis Khan is remembered as one of history's most _____ leaders; as founder of the Mongol Empire, he initiated the invasions that would ultimately lead to Mongol control of most of Eurasia.

- (A) rancorous
- (B) timorous
- (C) disingenuous
- (D) erratic
- (E) belligerent

328 The English teacher was impressed by his newest student's _____ observations; on her first day in class, she commented on several aspects of the novel that her classmates had overlooked.

- (A) urbane
- (B) pedantic
- (C) trenchant
- (D) equivocal
- (E) loquacious

329 The jagged peaks and _____ drops of the Himalayas are signs of their relative youth; older mountains tend to be smaller and more rounded as a result of erosion.

- (A) overweening
- (B) notorious
- (C) surreptitious
- (D) precipitous
- (E) nascent

330 The children grew _____ when cold temperatures forced them to remain inside.

- (A) boorish
- (B) phlegmatic
- (C) gregarious
- (D) restive
- (E) feckless

331 It is hardly surprising that questions concerning the nature and behavior of light have _____ some of the most brilliant thinkers throughout history; depending on how it is studied, light exhibits the properties of either a wave or a particle.

- (A) placated
- (B) confounded
- (C) fettered
- (D) implicated
- (E) enervated

332 The average person is likely familiar with only three phases of matter—solid, liquid, and gas—and would no doubt be _____ to learn of the bizarre states of matter, such as super fluids and Bose-Einstein condensates, that can occur at extremely low temperatures.

- (A) contrite
- (B) saturnine
- (C) nonplussed
- (D) dispirited
- (E) livid

333 Blinking is an involuntary movement that occurs many times a day, and most times people are not even _____ of the fact that they do it so often.

- (A) reticent c
- (B) foretold
- (C) cognizant
- (D) belied
- (E) unctuous

334 We were appalled by the waiter's _____; when we complained that our food came cold, he told us that it was our fault for ordering an unusual dish.

- (A) effrontery
- (B) pusillanimity
- (C) dexterity
- (D) circumspection
- (E) asperity

Chapter 4: Text Completion

335 3M is an extremely diversified company, with businesses dealing in health care, office supplies, display and graphics, electronics and communications, industry and transportation, and security and personal protection all falling under its _____.

- (A) aegis
- (B) vagaries
- (C) covenant
- (D) opus
- (E) tutelage

336 Most people in North America are more familiar with grey squirrels, but in some regions and smaller, _____ areas, black squirrels thrive in abundance.

- (A) variegated
- (B) razed
- (C) homogenized
- (D) localized
- (E) denigrated

337 Walt's presentation was very _____; it helped clarify some difficult aspects of our group's goals for the remainder of the project.

- (A) lucid
- (B) malevolent
- (C) meretricious
- (D) obscure
- (E) bewildering

338 Although the majority of urban legends are no doubt _____ their doubtful origins do not seem to have any effect on their ability to captivate listeners.

- (A) hyperbolic
- (B) ephemeral
- (C) judicious
- (D) prurient
- (E) apocryphal

339 The _____ nature of the American automotive industry has led to periods of panic when a foreign producer overtakes it and periods of euphoria when it introduces new models that sweep the world with their popularity.

- (A) baroque
- (B) indulgent
- (C) recurrent
- (D) immutable
- (E) steadfast

340 Mastery of the business cycle has long eluded economists; every bold claim of finally conquering the volatile corporate world seems to be _____ by a subsequent collapse of stock prices.

- (A) attenuated
- (B) elevated
- (C) reinforced
- (D) garnished
- (E) subsumed

341 Years of _____ could not sustain the surgeon's confidence—after his first malpractice lawsuit he didn't trust himself to perform even the simplest of procedures.

- (A) laudation
- (B) censure
- (C) indictment
- (D) suppression
- (E) ingenuity

342 By apparently _____ their status as the eccentrics of the biological sciences, botanists have delivered functional solutions to real-world problems—their latest odd achievement is discovering a genus of mushroom that can break down oil spills.

- (A) mystifying
- (B) denigrating
- (C) reinventing
- (D) abiding
- (E) shirking

Practice Set 1: One Blank

343. When observing the size of other planets, one should appreciate the ability of the telescope to _____ the size of these planets and make them appear bigger than they are to the naked eye.

- A) test
- B) magnify
- C) reduce
- D) impede
- E) capture

344. Judge Gordon was known for his _____ in upholding the law; although his rulings sometimes went against his personal preferences, they were always in keeping with legal precedent.

- A) turpitude
- B) probity
- C) speciousness
- D) torpor
- E) urbanity

345. Astronomers can estimate the distance between earth and another planet through a procedure that is _____ to a bat's sonar—bouncing radio waves off of a distant object and measuring the amount of time it takes to return.

- A) superior
- B) indebted
- C) abhorrent
- D) deleterious
- E) debased

346. By discarding pointe shoes, Isadora Duncan pioneered the era of modern dance, liberating the body from physical restrictions that she felt _____ full expression.

- A) entailed
- B) catered
- C) facilitated
- D) implicated
- E) precluded

347. Because human _____ of light is wavelength-dependent and short wavelength blue light is the most widely scattered in the atmosphere, the sky appears blue to human eyes.

- A) perception
- B) acumen
- C) perspicacity
- D) awareness
- E) conception

348. After Dr. Jonas Salk developed the polio vaccine, he refused to patent his invention or reap any profit from it so that its global distribution was fully maximized. This was a truly _____ action.

- A) autonomous
- B) wasted
- C) altruistic
- D) redundant
- E) meddlesome

349. The appraisal of a work of art typically stands for about a decade, though certain pieces may need to be appraised more or less frequently due to the market _____ for particular artists.

- A) tempo
- B) conditions
- C) perseverance
- D) inspection
- E) waning

350. The artist's painting really _____ the landscape, providing a succinct summary of the landscape's essential features.

- A) enraptures
- B) encapsulates
- C) deviates
- D) obfuscates
- E) expands

Answer Key

Q. No.	Correct Answer	Your Answer
301	B	
302	B	
303	A	
304	B	
305	D	
306	E	
307	B	
308	E	
309	A	
310	A	
311	D	
312	D	
313	B	
314	B	
315	B	
316	A	
317	C	
318	C	
319	B	
320	D	
321	A	
322	B	
323	E	
324	C	
325	A	

Q. No.	Correct Answer	Your Answer
326	E	
327	E	
328	C	
329	D	
330	D	
331	B	
332	C	
333	C	
334	A	
335	A	
336	D	
337	A	
338	E	
339	C	
340	A	
341	A	
342	C	
343	B	
344	B	
345	B	
346	E	
347	A	
348	C	
349	B	
350	B	

Practice Set 1: Answers & Explanations

301 **Choice B is correct** because "perdures" means remaining in existence over time. This word fits in the context of the sentence because it accurately expresses what the trail of crude tools does. In other words, the trail left behind by the crude tools of human civilizations endures over time.

Choice A is incorrect because "discontinue" means an action is ceased or halted. This word does not fit in the context of the sentence because it means the opposite of the intended meaning of the sentence. The sentence is trying to express that the trail left endures over time, not that it stops. **Choice C** is incorrect because "excavates" means making a hole by digging in the earth. This word does not fit in the context of the sentence because it does not accurately describe what the sentence is trying to say about the trail. The sentence is trying to express that the trail lasts throughout time. Nothing is mentioned or implied about digging or moving earth. **Choice D** is incorrect because "derides" means expressing contempt or ridiculing. This word does not fit in the context of the sentence because it does not accurately describe what the sentence is trying to say about the trail. The trail is not ridiculing anything or being ridiculed. Rather, it is lasting throughout time, which makes choice B the best option. **Choice E** is incorrect because "beguiles" means to charm someone in a deceptive way. This word does not fit in the context of the sentence because it does not accurately describe what the sentence is trying to say about the trail. The trail is not charming anyone or being charmed. Rather, it is lasting throughout time, which makes choice B the best option.

302 **Choice B is correct** because "expedient" means convenient and practical. This word fits in the context of the sentence because it describes the type of traits that would be passed on due to their ability to help organisms survive longer. Practical traits would be beneficial to survival.

Choice A is incorrect because "innocuous" means not harmful or offensive. This word does not fit in the context of the sentence because it does not accurately describe the type of traits that would be passed on due to their ability to help organisms survive longer. Traits that are not offensive would not necessarily be more beneficial for survival. Therefore, choice B is the best option. **Choice C** is incorrect because "salient" means standing out prominently. This word does not fit in the context of the sentence because it does not accurately describe the type of traits that would be passed on due to their ability to help organisms survive longer. Traits that are noticeable would not necessarily be more beneficial for survival. Therefore, choice B is the best option. **Choice D** is incorrect because "titillating" means arousing mild sexual interest. This word does not fit in the context of the sentence because it does not accurately describe the type of traits that would be passed on due to their ability to help organisms survive longer. Traits that arouse sexual interest from other organisms would not necessarily be more beneficial for survival. Therefore, choice B is the best option. **Choice E** is incorrect because "prolific" means producing much or being present in a great number. This word does not fit in the context of the sentence because it does not accurately describe the type of traits that would be passed on due to their ability to help organisms survive longer. Traits that are productive or present in great numbers would not necessarily be more beneficial for survival. Therefore, choice B is the best option.

303 **Choice A is correct** because "attenuate" means to reduce the effect or force of. In other words, a lack of competition diminishes economic health and its impacts on the purchasing power of customers.

Choice B is incorrect because "consecrate" means declaring something as sacred. This word does not fit in the context of the sentence because it does not accurately describe what happens to economic health when there is no competition. The passage does not mention or infer that anything is becoming sacred. Rather, the passage is expressing that competition improves economic health thereby positively affecting consumers. **Choice C** is incorrect because "commiserate" means to express or feel empathy or pity for someone. This word does not fit in the context of the sentence because it does not accurately describe what happens to economic health when there is no competition. The passage does not mention or infer that people are feeling pity over economic health. Also, economic health cannot feel pity itself. Rather, the passage is expressing that competition improves economic health thereby positively affecting consumers. **Choice D** is incorrect because "alleviate" means making suffering less severe. This word does not fit in the context of the sentence because it does not accurately describe what happens to economic health when there is no competition. Economic health would not need to be alleviated because it is unlikely to cause suffering. Rather, the passage is expressing that competition improves economic health thereby positively affecting consumers. **Choice E** is incorrect because "fulminate" means expressing strong protest or angry criticism. This word does not fit in the context of the sentence because it does not accurately describe what happens to economic health when there is no competition. The passage does not mention or infer that anyone is angrily protesting. Also, economic health cannot angrily protest itself. Rather, the passage is expressing that competition improves economic health thereby positively affecting consumers.

304 **Choice B is correct** because "harangue" means a public speech that is lengthy and forceful. This word fits in the context of the sentence because it describes the way the man would have passionately denied his involvement in the crime before the jury.

Choice A is incorrect because "dyspepsia" means indigestion. This word does not fit in the context of the sentence because it does not accurately describe what the man would have been doing before the jury. Rather than experiencing indigestion, which is unrelated to the rest of the passage, he would likely be passionately defending himself via speech. Therefore, choice B is the best option. **Choice C** is incorrect because "approbation" means approval or praise. This word does not fit in the context of the sentence because it does not accurately describe the action the man is taking before the jury. Rather than approving of the jury, the man is likely passionately defending himself via speech. Therefore, choice B is the best option. **Choice D** is incorrect because "peregrination" means a long walk or wandering. This word does not fit in the context of the sentence because it does not accurately describe the action the man is taking before the jury. Rather than walking and wandering before the jury, the man is likely passionately defending himself via speech. Therefore, choice B is the best option. **Choice E** is incorrect because "gaucherie" means an awkward and unsophisticated act. This word does not fit in the sentence because it does not accurately describe the action the man is taking before the jury. Based on the passage, he was not necessarily concerned about his politeness or grace. Rather, he was likely passionately defending himself via speech. Therefore, choice B is the best option.

305 **Choice D is correct** because "acumen" means the ability to make good judgements and quick decisions. This word fits in the context of the sentence because it describes a quality of the scientists that, despite possessing, did not allow them to predict a military event. In other words, although the scientists showed quick decision making skills, they could not have anticipated the surprising event.

Choice A is incorrect because "demeanor" means an outward behavior or manner. This word does not fit in the context of the sentence because it does not accurately describe the quality of the scientists that, despite possessing, did not allow them to predict the event. The demeanor of the scientists would be irrelevant when considering their abilities to make accurate predictions. Therefore, choice D is the best option. **Choice B** is incorrect because "heresy" means a belief or opinion contrary to the formal religion. This word does not fit in the context of the sentence because it does not accurately describe the quality of the scientists that, despite possessing, did not allow them to predict the event. The passage does not discuss religious beliefs, formal religions, or opinions contrary to formal religions in any way. **Choice C** is incorrect because "efficacy" means the ability to produce a desired result. This word does not fit in the context of the sentence because it does not accurately describe the quality of the scientists that, despite possessing, did not allow them to predict the event. The efficacy of the scientists, or their ability to get things done, would likely be irrelevant when considering their abilities to make accurate predictions. Therefore, **choice D** is the best option. Choice E is incorrect because "callosity" means the state of being thick or hardened. This word does not fit in the context of the sentence because it does not accurately describe the quality of the scientists that, despite possessing, did not allow them to predict the event. The hardness or thickness of the scientists, whether literally or metaphorically, would likely be irrelevant when considering their abilities to make accurate predictions. Therefore, choice D is the best option.

306 **Choice E is correct** because "prolix" means something is tedious, lengthy, or drawn out. This word fits in the context of the sentence because it accurately describes a play that is eight hours long and requires two nights to perform. The way that the play is portrayed in the remainder of the passage suggests that its lengthiness is its most notable aspect.

Choice A is incorrect because "pedantic" means caring too much about unimportant details and annoys others with tiny corrections. This word does not fit in the context of the sentence because it does not accurately describe the play according to the remainder of the passage. The passage does not suggest that the play included any unimportant details or irrelevant corrections. Therefore, choice E is the best option. **Choice B** is incorrect because "odious" means extremely repulsive and leading to hatred. This word does not fit in the context of the sentence because it does not accurately describe the play according to the remainder of the passage. The passage does not suggest that the play included anything repulsive or deserving of hatred. Therefore, choice E is the best option. **Choice C** is incorrect because "onerous" means involving hardship or burdensome difficulty. This word does not fit in the context of the sentence because it does not accurately describe the play according to the remainder of the passage. The passage does not suggest that the play posed any great burden on anyone. Therefore, choice E is the best option. **Choice D** is incorrect because "moribund" means approaching death. This word does not fit in the context of the sentence because it does not accurately describe the play according to the remainder of the passage. The passage does not suggest that the play was related to death or that it was dying. Therefore, choice E is the best option.

Practice Set 1: Answers & Explanations

307 **Choice B is correct** because "recidivism" means the tendency of a convicted criminal to reoffend. This word fits in the context of the sentence because it accurately names the phenomenon being discussed in the passage. The passage is expressing that criminal lifestyles, or lifestyles of repeated offending, is the result of institutional and social dimensions beyond the control of the offender, not just poor motivation or bad genetics.

Choice A is incorrect because "gasconade" means extravagant boasting. This word does not fit in the context of the sentence because it does not relate to the remainder of the passage. The passage does not discuss the way offenders boast. Rather, it discusses the way offenders continue to commit offenses and why this occurs. Therefore, choice B is the best option. **Choice C** is incorrect because "exfiltration" means removing someone or something from a hostile area. This word does not fit in the context of the sentence because it does not relate to the remainder of the passage. The passage does not discuss war tactics or the removal of criminals from enemy filled areas. Rather, it discusses the way offenders continue to commit offenses and why this occurs. Therefore, choice B is the best option. **Choice D** is incorrect because "chicanery" means the use of trickery or deception to achieve a purpose. This word does not fit in the context of the sentence because the concepts of trickery and deception are not mentioned directly or implied in any way throughout the passage. The passage does not discuss trickery by criminals or deception toward criminals. Rather, it discusses the way offenders continue to commit offenses and why this occurs. Therefore, choice B is the best option. **Choice E** is incorrect because "attenuation" means a reduction of the strength or force of something. This word does not fit in the context of the sentence because nothing in the passage is being weakened or reduced. The passage does not reduce criminals in any way. Rather, it discusses the way offenders continue to commit offenses and why this occurs. Therefore, choice B is the best option

308 **Choice E is correct** because "heritable" means capable of being transmitted to offspring. This word fits in the context of the sentence because it describes the nature of traits and how they relate to the study of genetics. It would make sense that, by experimenting on garden peas, discoveries relating to heritable genes could be made.

Choice A is incorrect because "bequeathed" means passing something on to another person by beneficiary or will. This word does not fit in the context of the sentence because it does not accurately describe traits and how they relate to the science of genetics. Rather than being chosen as a gift for another person, traits are heritable and are transmitted to offspring genetically. Therefore, choice E is the best option. **Choice B** is incorrect because "inbred" means deeply rooted or produced by breeding between relatives. This word does not fit in the context of the sentence because it does not accurately describe the traits being discussed in the passage. Garden peas cannot choose at will who they breed with. Rather, it would make more sense that, by experimenting on garden peas, discoveries relating to heritable genes could be made. Therefore, choice E is the best option. **Choice C** is incorrect because "maternal" means relating to a mother. This word does not fit in the context of the sentence because it does not accurately describe the traits being discussed in the passage. Because garden peas are nonhuman it is unlikely that mother peas would be specifically labeled and analyzed. Rather, it would make more sense that, by experimenting on garden peas, discoveries relating to heritable genes could be made. Therefore, choice E is the best option. **Choice D** is incorrect because "acquired" means buying, obtaining, or learning something. This word does not fit in the context of the sentence because it does not accurately describe traits and how they relate to the science of genetics. Rather than being purchased or learned in some way, traits are heritable and are transmitted to offspring genetically. Therefore, choice E is the best option.

309 **Choice A is correct** because "conspicuous" means standing out as clearly obvious. This word fits in the context of the sentence because it accurately describes the money that teens spend on clothing according to the rest of the passage. In other words, the amount of money that teens spend on clothing is very apparent and notable, as evidenced by the fact that it makes up for 20% of all teen spending.

Choice B is incorrect because "temperate" means relating to a region with mild temperatures. This word does not fit in the context of the sentence because it does not accurately describe the money that teens spend on clothing according to the rest of the passage. The passage does not discuss specific regions, weather patterns, or temperatures in any way. Rather, the passage aims to express that teens spend a notable amount of their money on clothing. Therefore, choice A is the best option. **Choice C** is incorrect because "nebulous" means hazy or in the form of a cloud. This word does not fit in the context of the sentence because it does not accurately describe the money that teens spend on clothing according to the rest of the passage. The passage does not mention anything being hazy or cloudy, either literally or metaphorically. Rather, the passage aims to express that it is very clear that teens spend a notable amount of their money on clothing. Therefore, choice A is the best option. **Choice D** is incorrect because "ignominious" means deserving public disgrace, shame, or humiliation. This word does not fit in the context of the sentence because it does not accurately describe the money that teens spend on clothing according to the rest of the passage. The passage does not indicate that teens spending money on clothing is deserving of shame in any way. Rather, the passage aims to inform the reader that teens spend a notable amount of their money on clothing. Therefore, choice A is the best option. **Choice E** is incorrect because "impecunious" means having little or no money. This word does not fit in the context of the sentence because it does not accurately describe the money that teens spend on clothing according to the rest of the passage. The passage expresses that teens do have money to spend and choose to spend it on clothing in a notable way. Therefore, choice A is the best option.

310 **Choice A is correct** because "refulgent" means radiant or shining brightly. This word fits in the context of the sentence because it describes the nature of the stars' lifestyles that is portrayed in reality TV shows, which captivates viewers to the point of obsession. In other words, these stars are depicted as living brilliantly glowing lives.

Choice B is incorrect because "austere" means a stern, cold, and strict manner. This word does not fit in the context of the sentence because it does not accurately describe the nature of the stars' lifestyles that is portrayed in reality TV shows. The passage suggests that these lifestyles are so captivating and radiant for viewers that they become obsessed. It is unlikely that a lifestyle that comes off cold and severe would be so popular. Therefore, choice A is the best option. **Choice C** is incorrect because "laudable" means efforts to help others that deserve praise and admiration. This word does not fit in the context of the sentence because it does not accurately describe the nature of the stars' lifestyles that is portrayed in reality TV shows. The passage suggests that these lifestyles are captivating because they are radiant to the point of diminishing other characters, which is opposite to the action of helping others. Therefore, choice A is the best option. **Choice D** is incorrect because "monotonous" means tedious and dull. This word does not fit in the context of the sentence because it does not accurately describe the nature of the stars' lifestyles that is portrayed in reality TV shows. The passage suggests that these lifestyles are so captivating and radiant for viewers that they become obsessed. It is unlikely that a lifestyle that comes off boring and repetitive would be so popular. Therefore, choice A is the best option. **Choice E** is incorrect because "sanctimonious" means hypocritical or appearing morally superior to others. This word does not fit in the context of the sentence because it does not accurately describe the nature of the stars' lifestyles that is portrayed in reality TV shows. The passage suggests that these lifestyles are so captivating and radiant for viewers that they become obsessed. It is unlikely that people who are hypocritical and think greater of their own morals would be so popular. Therefore, choice A is the best option.

311 **Choice D is correct** because "lambent" means gleaming with a soft radiance. This word fits in the context of the sentence because it describes the way the beautiful colors in a sunset shine brilliantly. In other words, the pinks and oranges of a sunset gleam the most brilliantly in areas with unpolluted air.

Choice A is incorrect because "fervid" means passionate, emotional, and heated. This word does not fit in the context of the sentence because it does not accurately describe the way pinks and oranges sometimes grace a sunset. Rather than being overpowering and passionate, they can be described as glowing radiantly. Additionally, since sunsets are inanimate, they cannot feel emotions. Therefore, choice D is the better option. **Choice B** is incorrect because "plangent" means a loud, plain, deep sound. This word does not fit in the context of the sentence because the sentence is not describing any sounds taking place during a sunset. Rather, the sentence is discussing the colors that can be visually seen during a sunset. Therefore, choice D is the best option. **Choice C** is incorrect because "crepuscular" means dim lighting related to twilight or dawn. This word does not fit in the context of the sentence because it does not accurately describe the way pinks and oranges sometimes grace a sunset. Rather than being dim or indistinct, they can be described as glowing radiantly. Additionally, this passage specifically relates to sunsets, not dawn. Therefore, choice D is the better option. **Choice E** is incorrect because "winsome" means attractive due to charming and innocence. This word does not fit in the context of the sentence because it does not accurately describe why the sunsets are attractive or pleasing to viewers. Rather than displaying charming and innocence, they are described as showing brilliant colors. Therefore, choice D is the best option.

312 **Choice D is correct** because "travesty" means a crude, grotesque, or shocking thing. This word fits in the context of the sentence because it accurately describes the sport of dog fighting according to the remainder of the passage. In other words, the author feels that this sport is a disgraceful event as evidenced by the statement that it is heinous, depraved, and requires laws to prohibit it.

Choice A is incorrect because "tirade" means a long, angry speech of accusation. This word does not fit in the context of the sentence because it does not accurately describe the sport of dog fighting according to the remainder of the passage. The author expresses that the sport is a disgraceful event as evidenced by the statement that it is heinous, depraved, and requires laws to prohibit it. The passage does not indicate that it has anything to do with speaking or giving speeches. Therefore, choice D is the best option. **Choice B** is incorrect because "artifice" means clever tricks or devices used to deceive others. This word does not fit in the context of the sentence because it does not accurately describe the sport of dog fighting according to the remainder of the passage. The author expresses that the sport is a disgraceful event as evidenced by the statement that it is heinous, depraved, and requires laws to prohibit it. The passage does not indicate that it is deceptive in any way. Therefore, choice D is the best option. **Choice C** is incorrect because "debauch" means to destroy the moral purity of something. This word does not fit in the context of the sentence because it does not accurately describe the sport of dog fighting according to the remainder of the passage. The author expresses that the sport is a disgraceful event as evidenced by the statement that it is heinous, depraved, and requires laws to prohibit it. The passage does not indicate that it was ever morally pure to begin with. Therefore, choice D is the best option. **Choice E** is incorrect because "apparition" means a ghostlike presentation of a person. This word does not fit in the context of the sentence because it does not accurately describe the sport of dog fighting according to the remainder of the passage. The author expresses that the sport is a disgraceful event as evidenced by the statement that it is heinous, depraved, and requires laws to prohibit it. The passage does not mention or infer anything about ghosts or faint representations of people. Therefore, choice D is the best option.

313 **Choice B is correct** because "permeates" means spreading through and becoming present in a wider way. This word fits in the context of the sentence because it accurately describes the way the art of debate has spread throughout many fields of study rather than being confined to politics as it was originally.

Choice A is incorrect because "permits" means giving authorization or consent to something. This word does not fit in the context of the sentence because the art of debate cannot give permission to something. Rather, the art of debate is spreading throughout every field of study, making choice B the best option. **Choice C** is incorrect because "aggrandizes" means increasing the power, status, or wealth of something. This word does not fit in the context of the sentence because the art of debate does not increase the power or financial status of anything according to the passage. Rather, the art of debate is spreading throughout every field of study, making choice B the best option. **Choice D** is incorrect because "aggravates" means making something worse or more serious. This word does not fit in the context of the sentence because the art of debate is not making something worse or more serious according to the remainder of the passage. Rather, the art of debate is spreading throughout every field of study, making choice B the best option. **Choice E** is incorrect because "rectifies" means making something right or correct. This word does not fit in the context of the sentence because the art of debate is not making anything more correct according to the remainder of the passage. Rather, the art of debate is spreading throughout every field of study, making choice B the best option.

314 **Choice B is correct** because unsatisfied is defined as "when one's wishes, expectations, or needs are not fulfilled or met", which aligns with the concept of unmet "standards of cleanliness" described in the passage.

Choice A is incorrect because mystified means "to utterly bewilder or perplex", which does not align with the theme of the passage. **Choice C** is incorrect because fearful means "a state of fear or anxiety" which is not alluded to or discussed in the passage. **Choice D** is incorrect because knowledgeable means "intelligent and well informed", which is not a concept described or alluded to in the passage. **Choice E** is incorrect because unconsidered means an action or remark "not thought of in advance", which would contradict the sister's pre-established "standards of cleanliness".

315 **Choice B is correct** because "scions" means a descendant of a notable family. This word fits in the context of the sentence because it accurately describes the position that the prince and princesses held. They were the offspring, or descendants, of Henry VIII.

Choice A is incorrect because "progenitors" means an ancestor from which an organism descended from. This word does not fit in the context of the sentence because it does not describe the position that the prince and princesses held. Rather than being the source from which Henry VIII descended, they were the offspring that followed. Therefore, choice B is the best option. **Choice C** is incorrect because "devisees" means a person to whom real estate is left by will. This word does not fit in the context of the sentence because it does not describe the position that the prince and princesses held. There is no mention of real estate or anything being passed on to the prince and princesses. Rather, the sentence is expressing that they were simply the descendants of Henry VIII. **Choice D** is incorrect because "lineage" means a descendant from an ancestor. Although the prince and princesses were a part of the lineage of Henry VIII, the word, "scions" refers specifically to descendants of a notable family rather than any common person. This makes choice B a better option. **Choice E** is incorrect because "promulgations" means something is made known to the public. This word does not fit in the context of the sentence because it does not relate to the topic of the sentence. Nothing is being announced or made public. Rather, the sentence is expressing that the prince and princesses were descendants of Henry VIII.

Chapter 4: Text Completion

316 **Choice A is correct** because "prejudices" means a preconceived opinion not based on reason or experience. This word fits in the context of the sentence because it describes the preconceived thoughts that would potentially interfere in a subject's mind during an experiment. In other words, thoughts that were already existent are psychosocial variables that impact experiments on the mind.

Choice B is incorrect because "pellucidity" means the quality of being clear and transparent. This word does not fit in the context of the sentence because it does not describe the preconceived thoughts that would potentially interfere in a subject's mind during an experiment. If the subject were thinking clearly and transparently it would not interfere with an experiment. Rather, if the mind was tainted with prejudices experiments would be impacted. Therefore, choice A is the best option. **Choice C** is incorrect because "impartiality" means an attitude of equality, fairness, and objectivity. This word does not fit in the context of the sentence because it does not describe the preconceived thoughts that would potentially interfere in a subject's mind during an experiment. If the subject were thinking objectively it would not interfere with an experiment. Rather, if the mind was tainted with prejudices experiments would be impacted. Therefore, choice A is the best option. **Choice D** is incorrect because "riposte" means a quick, sharp, and clever response. This word does not fit in the context of the sentence because it does not describe the preconceived thoughts that would potentially interfere in a subject's mind during an experiment. If the subject were giving quick and clever remarks that would not explain how the experiment would be impacted. Rather, if the mind was tainted with prejudices experiments would be impacted. Therefore, choice A is the best option. **Choice E** is incorrect because "plutocracy" means governmental control by the wealthy. This word does not fit in the context of the sentence because it does not describe the preconceived thoughts that would potentially interfere in a subject's mind during an experiment. The passage does not mention or infer anything about governmental control. Rather, the topic of the sentence is on the mind and psychosocial factors.

317 **Choice C is correct** because "gossamer" means a delicate film of cobwebs. This word fits in the context of the sentence because it describes how wispy clouds might look.

Choice A is incorrect because "halcyon" means a past time that was idyllic and peaceful. This word does not fit in the context of the sentence because it does not describe the way wispy clouds would look. Rather than idyllic, wispy clouds might seem like a film of cobwebs, making choice C the best option. **Choice B** is incorrect because "sinuous" means having many curves or turns. This word does not fit in the context of the sentence because it does not describe the way wispy clouds would look. Rather than wavy, wispy clouds might seem like a film of cobwebs, making choice C the best option. **Choice D** is incorrect because "variegated" means patchy or streaked with different colors. This word does not fit in the context of the sentence because it does not describe the way wispy clouds would look. Rather than being colorful, wispy clouds might seem like a film of cobwebs, making choice C the best option. **Choice E** is incorrect because "lambent" means lightly glowing or flickering. This word does not fit in the context of the sentence because it does not describe the way wispy clouds would look. Rather than glowing, wispy clouds might seem like a film of cobwebs, making choice C the best option.

318 **Choice C is correct** because "ascertains" means making sure of something. This word fits in the context of the sentence because it describes the knowledge that is verified after an individual learns which route takes the least amount of time. In other words, the person has made sure that a particular route is the fastest.

Choice A is incorrect because "assumes" means something is supposed to be the case without proof. This word does not fit in the context of the sentence because it does not accurately describe what the individual is doing in relation to the routes to work. The person is testing various routes to make sure that one is the fastest, not simply guessing or making assumptions. Therefore, choice C is the best option. **Choice B** is incorrect because "theorizes" means forming a premise or framework for something. This word does not fit in the context of the sentence because it does not accurately describe what the individual is doing in relation to the routes to work. The person is testing various routes to make sure that one is the fastest, not simply developing a premise or framework. Therefore, choice C is the best option. **Choice D** is incorrect because "disputes" means a disagreement or argument. This word does not fit in the context of the sentence because it does not accurately describe what the individual is doing in relation to the routes to work. The person is testing various routes to make sure that one is the fastest, not arguing about anything. Therefore, choice C is the best option. **Choice E** is incorrect because "validates" means checking or proving the accuracy of something. This word does not fit in the context of the sentence because it does not accurately describe what the individual is doing in relation to the routes to work. The person is testing various routes to make sure that one is the fastest, not verifying the accuracy of a route.

319 **Choice B is correct** because "palliative" means relieving symptoms without treating the condition of cause. This word fits in the sentence because it describes the nature of the care that is provided in nursing homes for the ageing population. In other words, the condition of aging is not being treated or cured. However, the symptoms that come with aging can be minimized.

Choice A is incorrect because "ameliorative" means making something better or more satisfactory. This word does not fit in the context of the sentence because it does not accurately describe the nature of the care that is provided in nursing homes for the aging population. Rather than delivering care that is improving, nursing homes are delivering care that helps with symptoms of aging without curing the condition. Therefore, choice B is the best option. **Choice C** is incorrect because "regressive" means becoming less advanced or worsening. This word does not fit in the context of the sentence because it does not accurately describe the nature of the care that is provided in nursing homes for the aging population. Rather than delivering care that is getting worse or less advanced, nursing homes are delivering care that helps with symptoms of aging without curing the condition. Therefore, choice B is the best option. **Choice D** is incorrect because "salubrious" means wholesome and promoting health. This word does not fit in the context of the sentence because it does not accurately describe the nature of the care that is provided in nursing homes for the aging population. While the care given in nursing homes may indeed promote health, it is more likely to be described as, "palliative" which refers to relieving symptoms of aging. Therefore, choice B is the better option. **Choice E** is incorrect because "proprietary" means owned by someone or being exclusively held by someone. This word does not fit in the context of the sentence because it does not accurately describe the nature of the care that is provided in nursing homes for the aging population. Rather than delivering care that is owned by someone, nursing homes are delivering care that helps with symptoms of aging without curing the condition. Therefore, choice B is the best option.

320 **Choice D is correct** because "ameliorated" means making something better. This word fits in the context of the sentence because it describes the way the reputation of octopi has improved due to a seemingly intelligent octopus named Andy that is described in the remainder of the passage. In other words, the problem of considering octopi as stupid creatures has been made better recently.

Choice A is incorrect because "ruminated" means thinking deeply about something. This word does not fit in the context of the sentence because it does not accurately describe how the reputation of octopi has changed in recent times. Rather than being deeply thought about, the reputation of octopi has been made better due to a seemingly intelligent octopus named Andy that is described in the remainder of the passage. Therefore, choice D is the best option. **Choice B** is incorrect because "bifurcated" means dividing something into two branches. This word does not fit in the context of the sentence because it does not accurately describe how the reputation of octopi has changed in recent times. Rather than being divided into two branches, the reputation of octopi has been made better due to a seemingly intelligent octopus named Andy that is described in the remainder of the passage. Therefore, choice D is the best option. **Choice C** is incorrect because "expedited" means making something happen more quickly. This word does not fit in the context of the sentence because it does not accurately describe how the reputation of octopi has changed in recent times. Rather than happening more quickly, the reputation of octopi has been made better due to a seemingly intelligent octopus named Andy that is described in the remainder of the passage. In addition, since a reputation is a noun and not an action, it is unable to happen more quickly. Therefore, choice D is the best option. **Choice E** is incorrect because "scintillated" means to emit flashes of light or sparkles. This word does not fit in the context of the sentence because it does not accurately describe how the reputation of octopi has changed in recent times. Rather than emitting light or sparkles, the reputation of octopi has been made better due to a seemingly intelligent octopus named Andy that is described in the remainder of the passage. Additionally, a reputation is an intangible thing that is unable to emit light or sparkles. Therefore, choice D is the best option.

321 **Choice A is correct** because "immutable" means incapable of changing. This word fits in the context of the sentence because it accurately describes the way humans can recognize the size of an object regardless of the changes in proximity to the object. In other words, this skill is unwavering even when external factors are altered.

Choice B is incorrect because "flexible" means capable of bending without breaking. This word does not fit in the context of the sentence because it does not accurately describe the way humans can recognize the size of an object regardless of the changes in proximity to the object. Rather than being able to bend without breaking (which does not apply to something non-tangible, like a skill), this skill is unchanging even when the distance is altered. Therefore, choice A is the best option. **Choice C** is incorrect because "stable" means firmly fixed, durable, and not easily disturbed. This word does not fit in the context of the sentence because it does not accurately describe the way humans can recognize the size of an object regardless of the changes in proximity to the object. Rather than being firmly fixed in a spot, this skill is unchanging even when the distance is altered. Therefore, choice A is the best option. **Choice D** is incorrect because "abiding" means lasting for a long time or enduring. This word does not fit in the context of the sentence because it does not accurately describe the way humans can recognize the size of an object regardless of the changes in proximity to the object. Rather than enduring over a period of time (which is not discussed in the passage at all), this skill is unchanging even when the distance is altered. Therefore, choice A is the best option. **Choice E** is incorrect because "uniform" means having the same arrangement and appearance. This word does not fit in the context of the sentence because it does not accurately describe the way humans can recognize the size of an object regardless of the changes in proximity to the object. Rather than having the same arrangement as something else, this skill is unchanging even when the distance is altered. Therefore, choice A is the best option.

322 **Choice B is correct** because "interpretation" means explaining the meaning of something. This word fits in the context of the sentence because it accurately describes the way that perception involves reasoning and understanding the stimuli received in order to determine what to do with the information.

Choice A is incorrect because "insight" means the power to gain an intuitive understanding into a situation. This word does not fit in the context of the sentence because it does not accurately describe the way that perception involves reasoning and understanding the stimuli received in order to determine what to do with the information. Rather than being intuitively understood, the stimuli are being analyzed and explained. Therefore, choice B is the better option. **Choice C** is incorrect because "translation" means moving something from one place to another or converting a message from one language to another. This word does not fit in the context of the sentence because it does not accurately describe the way that perception involves reasoning and understanding the stimuli received in order to determine what to do with the information. Rather than being moved or changed to another language, the stimuli are being analyzed and explained. Therefore, choice B is the better option. **Choice D** is incorrect because "elucidation" means a clarification of something. This word does not fit in the context of the sentence because it does not accurately describe the way that perception involves reasoning and understanding the stimuli received in order to determine what to do with the information. Rather than being clarified, the stimuli are being analyzed and explained. Therefore, choice B is the better option. **Choice E** is incorrect because "adaptation" means rewritten in a new form to suit different conditions. This word does not fit in the context of the sentence because it does not accurately describe the way that perception involves reasoning and understanding the stimuli received in order to determine what to do with the information. Rather than being changed to fit a new situation, the stimuli are being analyzed and explained. Therefore, choice B is the better option.

323 **Choice E is correct** because "beguiled" means to charm someone in a deceptive way. This word fits in the context of the sentence because it accurately describes the way such beautiful landscapes both terrified and charmed those who viewed them, leading to the concept of "the sublime." In other words, these landscapes were so captivating that people were lost in their allure.

Choice A is incorrect because "perturbed" means feeling unsettled, anxious, or concerned. This word does not fit in the context of the sentence because it does not accurately describe the way such beautiful landscapes both terrified and charmed those who viewed them. Rather than making people feel anxious or unsettled, these landscapes are described as awe-inspiring and leading to the concept of, "the sublime." Therefore, choice E is the best option. **Choice B** is incorrect because "eviscerated" means to disembowel or remove contents. This word does not fit in the context of the sentence because it does not accurately describe the way such beautiful landscapes both terrified and charmed those who viewed them. Rather than making people feel disemboweled or like something had been removed, these landscapes are described as awe-inspiring and leading to the concept of, "the sublime." Therefore, choice E is the best option. **Choice C** is incorrect because "transcended" means to surpass or go beyond the limits. This word does not fit in the context of the sentence because it does not accurately describe the way such beautiful landscapes both terrified and charmed those who viewed them. No limits are discussed, so there is nothing surpassing the boundaries. Rather, the landscapes are described as awe-inspiring and leading to the concept of, "the sublime." Therefore, choice E is the best option. **Choice D** is incorrect because "galvanized" means coating a metal in a specific way or causing someone to take action suddenly. This word does not fit in the context of the sentence because it does not accurately describe the way such beautiful landscapes both terrified and charmed those who viewed them. The passage does not mention or infer anything about metals. Also, no one is being pushed to take sudden action. Rather, these landscapes are described as awe-inspiring and leading to the concept of, "the sublime." Therefore, choice E is the best option.

324 **Choice C is correct** because "synergy" means the cooperation of multiple things to produce a greater effect. This word fits in the context of the sentence because it accurately describes the way single cells of different types must work together well in order for a multicellular organism to function correctly.

Choice A is incorrect because "communion" means sharing deep and personal thoughts and feelings. This word does not fit in the context of the sentence because it does not accurately describe the way cells work together. Cells do not share thoughts and feelings because they are incapable. Rather, they work together harmoniously so that a multicellular organism can function correctly. Therefore, choice C is the best option. **Choice B** is incorrect because "accord" means a formal agreement or granting of something. This word does not fit in the context of the sentence because it does not accurately describe the way cells work together. Cells are simple beings that do not make any sort of formal agreements. Rather, they are genetically programmed to work together harmoniously so that a multicellular organism can function correctly. Therefore, choice C is the best option. **Choice D** is incorrect because "intimacy" means a close familiarity, comfort, or relationship. This word does not fit in the context of the sentence because it does not accurately describe the way cells work together. Cells are simple beings that are incapable of developing intimate relations with each other. Rather, they work together harmoniously so that a multicellular organism can function correctly. Therefore, choice C is the best option. **Choice E** is incorrect because "contention" means a heated disagreement. This word does not fit in the context of the sentence because it does not accurately describe the way cells work together. If cells were in heated disagreement, they would not be working together well. However, this sentence expresses that they work together harmoniously so that a multicellular organism can function correctly. Therefore, choice C is the best option.

325 **Choice A is correct** because "cooperatives" means organizations that are run jointly by members. This word fits in the context of the sentence because it describes the way that cells in a multicellular organism are arranged into groups of specialized cells that work together to complete specific functions. In other words, cells do not operate independently in the body, but join into groups with certain objectives.

Choice B is incorrect because "aggregates" means a mass or whole that is made up of several combined elements. This word does not fit in the context of the sentence because it does not accurately describe the way that cells in a multicellular organism are arranged into groups. The sentence does not discuss the whole body that is made up of many cells. Rather, it is focused on the specific groups that cells are divided into for unique purposes. Therefore, choice A is the best option. **Choice C** is incorrect because "collectives" means organizations that are participated in by a variety of individuals without ownership. This word does not fit in the context of the sentence because it does not accurately describe the way that cells in a multicellular organism are arranged into groups to complete specific purposes. Rather than simply participating in an organization, the cells act as owners over their specialized groups. Therefore, choice A is the better option. **Choice D** is incorrect because "division" means separating something into parts. This word does not fit in the context of the sentence because it does not accurately describe the way that cells in a multicellular organism are arranged into groups to complete specific purposes. Rather than simply being divided, the cells are systematically arranged in groups according to specialized abilities and work in those groups as owners. Therefore, choice A is the better option. **Choice E** is incorrect because "unanimity" means agreement by all people involved. This word does not fit in the context of the sentence because it does not accurately describe the way that cells in a multicellular organism are arranged into groups to complete specific purposes. The sentence is not expressing that they are all in agreement. Rather, the sentence is expressing that they all serve unique purposes according to their specified groups. Therefore, choice A is the best option.

326 **Choice E is correct** answer because "conjunctly" means two things are connected or associated. This word fits in the context of the sentence because it accurately describes the way that criminal law cases and civil law cases relate to one another. In other words, despite their differences in consequences, they are used together to maintain social order.

Choice A is incorrect because "perniciously" means in a way that is harmful. This word does not fit in the context of the sentence because it does not accurately describe the way that criminal law cases and civil law cases relate to one another. The two do not aim to harm social order, but rather to function in a connected way to maintain social order. **Choice B** is incorrect because "superciliously" means in a patronizing or haughty way. This word does not fit in the context of the sentence because it does not accurately describe the way that criminal law cases and civil law cases relate to one another. Neither of the cases discussed is portrayed as being patronizing or belittling to others. Rather, the passage is expressing that the two function in a connected way to maintain social order. **Choice C** is incorrect because "redundantly" means exceeding what is needed to the point of being unnecessary. This word does not fit in the context of the sentence because it does not accurately describe the way that criminal law cases and civil law cases relate to one another. Neither of the cases discussed is described as redundant or excessive. Rather, the passage is expressing that the two function in a connected way to maintain social order. **Choice D** is incorrect because "intractably" means something is difficult to control or govern. This word does not fit in the context of the sentence because it does not accurately describe the way that criminal law cases and civil law cases relate to one another. Neither of the cases discussed is portrayed as difficult to manage. Rather, the passage is expressing that the two function in a connected way to maintain social order.

327 **Choice E is correct** because "belligerent" means hostile and combative. This word fits in the context of the sentence because it accurately describes Genghis Khan's leadership style according to the rest of the passage. The text states that he initiated invasions that lead to great control. Therefore, he was aggressive with taking over areas that were previously ruled by others.

Choice A is incorrect because "rancorous" means bitter

Chapter 4: Text Completion

and resentful. This word does not fit in the context of the sentence because it does not accurately describe Genghis Khan's leadership style according to the rest of the passage. The text does not directly mention or imply that Khan was bitter or resentful about anything, but it does express that he initiated invasions to gain control. Therefore, choice E is the best option. **Choice B is incorrect** because "timorous" means timid and lacking confidence. This word does not fit in the context of the sentence because it does not accurately describe Genghis Khan's leadership style according to the rest of the passage. The text does not directly mention or imply that Khan was nervous or fearful. To the contrary, the text explains that he initiated invasions to gain control. Therefore, choice E is the best option. **Choice C is incorrect** because "disingenuous" means insincere and lacking candor. This word does not fit in the context of the sentence because it does not accurately describe Genghis Khan's leadership style according to the rest of the passage. The text does not directly mention or imply that Khan was dishonest about anything, but it does express that he initiated invasions to gain control. Therefore, choice E is the best option. **Choice D is incorrect** because "erratic" means unpredictable or occurring at an irregular pattern. This word does not fit in the context of the sentence because it does not accurately describe Genghis Khan's leadership style according to the rest of the passage. The text does not suggest that Khan was unpredictable in any way, but it does express that he initiated invasions to gain control. Therefore, choice E is the best option.

328 **Choice C is correct** because "trenchant" means keen or sharp in intellect. This word fits in the context of the sentence because it accurately describes the student's demeanor according to the rest of the passage. The text explains that the teacher was impressed because she easily noticed several aspects of the novel that others overlooked. Therefore, she is presented as smart and quick thinking.

Choice A is incorrect because "urbane" means courteous and socially polished. This word does not fit in the context of the sentence because it does not accurately describe the student's demeanor according to the rest of the passage. The text does not suggest that the teacher was impressed with her manners or politeness. Rather, the teacher was impressed that she easily noticed several aspects of the novel that others overlooked. Therefore, she is presented as smart and quick thinking, making choice C the best option. **Choice B is incorrect** because "pedantic" means annoying others by pointing out small and unimportant errors. This word does not fit in the context of the sentence because it does not accurately describe the student's demeanor according to the rest of the passage. The text does not suggest that the teacher or her fellow students were annoyed with her in any way. The passage does not make any mention of the student pointing out small problems. Rather, the teacher was impressed that she easily noticed several aspects of the novel that others overlooked. Therefore, she is presented as smart and quick thinking, making choice C the best option. **Choice D is incorrect** because "equivocal" means ambiguous or open to multiple interpretations. This word does not fit in the context of the sentence because it does not accurately describe the student's demeanor according to the rest of the passage. The text does not suggest that the student was unclear or vague in her speaking. Rather, the teacher was impressed that she easily noticed several aspects of the novel that others overlooked. Therefore, she is presented as smart and quick thinking, making choice C the best option. **Choice E is incorrect** because "loquacious" means very talkative. This word does not fit in the context of the sentence because it does not accurately describe the student's demeanor according to the rest of the passage. The text does not indicate that the student talked excessively. Rather, the teacher was impressed that she easily noticed several aspects of the novel that others overlooked. Therefore, she is presented as smart and quick thinking, making choice C the best option.

329 **Choice D is correct** because "precipitous" means dangerously high, steep, and inclined. This word fits in the context of the sentence because it accurately describes the nature of the drops in the Himalayas. This is supported by the text as it explains that dissimilar mountains are more rounded. Additionally, it fits alongside the descriptor of having, "jagged peaks."

Choice A is incorrect because "overweening" means showing excessive confidence or pride in yourself. This word does not fit in the context of the sentence because it does not accurately describe the nature of the drops in the Himalayas. Physical aspects of mountain ranges cannot be confident in themselves, as they are inanimate. **Choice B is incorrect** because "notorious" means famous and well known. This word is not the best fit in the context of the sentence because it is not related to the rest of the passage. Although the steep drops in the Himalayas may indeed be notorious, the rest of the passage is discussing the way the drops in the Himalayas contrast with rounded mountains. Therefore, it can be assumed that the sentence is aiming to express how dangerously inclined the drops are, not how famous they are. **Choice C is incorrect** because "surreptitious" means something is kept secret because it would otherwise be disapproved of. This word does not fit in the context of the sentence because it does not accurately describe the nature of the drops in the Himalayas. The text does not suggest that any aspect of the Himalayas is kept secret. Rather, the text aims to express that the drops in the Himalayas are dangerously high and steep. **Choice E is incorrect** because "nascent" means recently coming into existence. This word does not fit in the context of the sentence because it does not accurately describe the appearance of the drops in the Himalayas according to the rest of the text. Although the passage does express that the Himalayas may be young, the purpose of the passage is to express how jagged and steep it is in comparison with more rounded mountains. Therefore, choice D is the better option.

330 **Choice D is correct** because "restive" means unable to keep still or silent. This word fits in the context of the sentence because it accurately describes how children would likely be feeling if they were forced to stay inside all of the time. In other words, the children were growing restless and difficult to control as they could not go outside.

Choice A is incorrect because "boorish" means rude and poor mannered. This word does not fit in the context of the sentence because it does not accurately describe how children would likely be feeling if they had to remain inside all of the time. There is no explanation in the text for why the children would develop poor manners as a result of this. Therefore, choice D is the best option. **Choice B** is incorrect because "phlegmatic" means having an unemotional, calm, and dull disposition. This word does not fit in the context of the sentence because it does not accurately describe how children would likely be feeling if they had to remain inside all of the time. There is no explanation in the text for why the children would develop a calm disposition and this would likely be the opposite of what would happen if they had not been able to run around and play for an extended period of time. Therefore, choice D is the best option. **Choice C** is incorrect because "gregarious" means sociable and fond of company. This word does not fit in the context of the sentence because it does not accurately describe how children would likely be feeling if they had to remain inside all of the time. There is no explanation in the text for why the children would develop to become more social as a result of staying indoors. Rather, they would more likely grow restless and become eager to run around and play. Therefore, choice D is the best option. **Choice E** is incorrect because "feckless" means weak and worthless. This word does not fit in the context of the sentence because it does not accurately describe how children would likely be feeling if they had to remain inside all of the time. There is no explanation in the text for why the children would become weaker or less capable. Rather, they would more likely grow restless and become eager to run around and play. Therefore, choice D is the best option.

331 **Choice B is correct** because "confounded" means confused or perplexed. This word fits in the context of the sentence because it accurately describes the way the complex study of light has stumped even the most brilliant thinkers. The passage explains that light can exhibit properties in two forms, which supports the idea that even very intelligent people are bewildered when studying it.

Choice A is incorrect because "placated" means making someone less angry or hostile. This word does not fit in the context of the sentence because it does not accurately describe the way the complex study of light has stumped even the most brilliant thinkers. No one in the passage is portrayed as being angry or hostile or needing to become less angry or hostile. Rather, the passage aims to express that light is a challenging topic to study. **Choice C** is incorrect because "fettered" means restrained or kept from making progress. This word does not fit in the context of the sentence because it does not accurately describe the way the complex study of light has stumped even the most brilliant thinkers. No one in the passage is described as being restrained. Rather, the passage aims to express that light is a challenging topic to study. **Choice D** is incorrect because "implicated" means showing to be involved. This word does not fit in the context of the sentence because it does not accurately describe the way the complex study of light has stumped even the most brilliant thinkers. The study of light is not implicating brilliant thinkers. Rather, the passage aims to express that light is a challenging topic to study and it bewilders brilliant thinkers. **Choice E** is incorrect because "enervated" means drained of energy or vitality. This word does not fit in the context of the sentence because it does not accurately describe the way the complex study of light has stumped even the most brilliant thinkers. The study of light is not taking vitality from brilliant thinkers. Rather, the passage aims to express that light is a challenging topic to study and it bewilders brilliant thinkers.

332 **Choice C is correct** because "nonplussed" means very surprised and confused. This word fits in the context of the sentence because it accurately describes the way average people would likely feel after learning that there are more phases of matter than the three that are most commonly known. This sentence aims to express that most people are only familiar with solids, liquids, and gases but would be surprised to realize that there are multiple others.

Choice A is incorrect because "contrite" means showing sorrow and expressing remorse. This word does not fit in the context of the sentence because it does not accurately describe the way average people would likely feel after learning about the other phases of matter. The passage aims to express that most people are only familiar with solids, liquids, and gases but would be surprised to realize that there are multiple others. It does not indicate that anything related to this topic should elicit sorrow or remorseful feelings. Therefore, choice C is the best option. **Choice B** is incorrect because "saturnine" means slow, gloomy, and serious. This word does not fit in the context of the sentence because it does not accurately describe the way average people would likely feel after learning about the other phases of matter. The passage aims to express that most people are only familiar with solids, liquids, and gases but would be surprised to realize that there are multiple others. It does not indicate that anything related to this topic should elicit gloominess or seriousness. Therefore, choice C is the best option. **Choice D** is incorrect because "dispirited" means having lost enthusiasm. This word does not fit in the context of the sentence because it does not accurately describe the way average people would likely feel after learning about the other phases of matter. The passage does not suggest that average people are enthusiastic about the states of matter to begin with. The passage aims to express that most people are only familiar with solids, liquids, and gases but would be surprised to realize that there are multiple others. It does not indicate that anything related to this topic should be disheartening. Therefore, choice C is the best option. **Choice E** is incorrect because "livid" means furiously angry. This word does not fit in the context of the sentence because it does not accurately describe the way average people would likely feel after learning about the other phases of matter. The passage aims to express that most people are only familiar with solids, liquids, and gases but would be surprised to realize that there are multiple others. It does not indicate that anything related to this topic should elicit anger or fury. Therefore, choice C is the best option.

333 **Choice C is correct** because "cognizant" means having knowledge or awareness of something. This word fits in the context of the sentence because it makes sense that most people are not aware of blinking because it is involuntary and occurs so many times each day. In other words, the sentence is expressing that many people don't realize they are blinking because it occurs so naturally.

Choice A is incorrect because "reticent" means to reserved thoughts and feelings. This word does not fit in the context of the sentence because it does not make sense that most people would be reserved in relation to blinking. The sentence does not suggest people are shy or unwilling to share feelings. Rather, the sentence is expressing that many people don't realize they are blinking because it occurs so naturally. Therefore, choice C is the best option. **Choice B** is incorrect because "foretold" means predicted beforehand. This word does not fit in the context of the sentence because it does not suggest that anything related to blinking was predicted beforehand. Rather, the sentence is expressing that many people don't realize they are blinking because it occurs so naturally. Therefore, choice C is the best option. **Choice D** is incorrect because "belied" means disguised or revealing to be false. This word does not fit in the context of the sentence because it does not make sense that most people would be disguised in relation to blinking. The sentence does not suggest people are revealing something as false. Rather, the sentence is expressing that many people don't realize they are blinking because it occurs so naturally. Therefore, choice C is the best option. **Choice E** is incorrect because "unctuous" means excessively flattering. This word does not fit in the context of the sentence because it does not make sense that most people would be overly praising in relation to blinking. The sentence does not suggest people are flattering others about anything. Rather, the sentence is expressing that many people don't realize they are blinking because it occurs so naturally. Therefore, choice C is the best option.

334 **Choice A is correct** because "effrontery" means shameless and boldly rude. This word fits in the context of the sentence because it accurately describes the way the waiter behaved according to the rest of the sentence. In other words, the waiter was boldly rude as he accused the customers of being at fault when their food arrived cold.

Choice B is incorrect because "pusillanimity" means timid or lacking courage. This word does not fit in the context of the sentence because it does not accurately describe the way the waiter behaved according to the rest of the sentence. The waiter accused the customers of being at fault when their food arrived cold. Therefore, he was not lacking courage but, rather, was being boldly rude. Thus, choice A is the best option. **Choice C** is incorrect because "dexterity" means skillful in using hands to perform tasks. This word does not fit in the context of the sentence because it does not accurately describe the way the waiter behaved according to the rest of the sentence. The waiter accused the customers of being at fault when their food arrived cold. Therefore, he was not doing anything impressive with his hands but, rather, was being boldly rude. Thus, choice A is the best option. **Choice D** is incorrect because "circumspection" means being careful and unwilling to take risks. This word does not fit in the context of the sentence because it does not accurately describe the way the waiter behaved according to the rest of the sentence. The waiter accused the customers of being at fault when their food arrived cold. Therefore, he was not acting careful but, rather, was being boldly rude. Thus, choice A is the best option. **Choice E** is incorrect because "asperity" means a harshness of tone or manner. This word does not fit in the context of the sentence because it is not the best word that can be used to describe the way the waiter behaved according to the rest of the sentence. The waiter accused the customers of being at fault when their food arrived cold. The sentence does not describe the specific tone of voice that was used. Therefore, he was not necessarily speaking in a harsh tone but, rather, was being boldly rude. Thus, choice A is the best option.

Practice Set 1: Answers & Explanations

335 **Choice A is correct** because "aegis" means the protection or support of a particular organization. This word fits in the context of the sentence because it describes the way that all of the listed businesses fall under its wings. In other words, 3M protects and supports business dealings in all of the listed areas.

Choice B is incorrect because "vagaries" means an unexpected change in someone's behavior. This word does not fit in the context of the sentence because it does not accurately describe the way that all of the listed business dealings are protected and supported by 3M. The text does not mention any changes in behavior for any particular people or the company as a whole. Therefore, choice A is the best option. **Choice C** is incorrect because "covenant" means a binding agreement between two or more people. This word does not fit in the context of the sentence because it does not accurately describe the way that all of the listed business dealings are protected and supported by 3M. The text does not mention any agreements between any particular people or organizations. Therefore, choice A is the best option. **Choice D** is incorrect because "opus" means a musical work. This word does not fit in the context of the sentence because it does not accurately describe the way that all of the listed business dealings are protected and supported by 3M. The text does not mention anything related to music or musical works. Therefore, choice A is the best option. **Choice E** is incorrect because "tutelage" means instruction or guardianship over an individual. This word does not fit in the context of the sentence because it refers to guardianship over people rather than inanimate things like business dealings. Rather than being under the instruction and guidance, these business dealings are under the protection and support of 3M. Therefore, choice A is the best option.

336 **Choice D is correct** because "localized" means restricted to a particular area. This word fits in the context of the sentence because it accurately describes the smaller areas where black squirrels live in contrast to the abundance of grey squirrels across North America. In other words, black squirrels thrive in particular regions.

Choice A is incorrect because "variegated" means exhibiting different colors. This word does not fit in the context of the sentence because it does not accurately describe the smaller areas where black squirrels live in contrast to the abundance of grey squirrels across North America. The passage does not mention anything about the colors of the areas. Rather, the passage aims to express that black squirrels thrive in particular regions. **Choice B** is incorrect because "razed" means completely destroyed or demolished. This word does not fit in the context of the sentence because it does not accurately describe the smaller areas where black squirrels live in contrast to the abundance of grey squirrels across North America. The passage does not mention anything about the areas being destroyed. Rather, the passage aims to express that black squirrels thrive in particular regions. **Choice C** is incorrect because "homogenized" means made uniform or similar. This word does not fit in the context of the sentence because it does not accurately describe the smaller areas where black squirrels live in contrast to the abundance of grey squirrels across North America. The passage does not mention anything about making areas similar to one another. Rather, the passage aims to express that black squirrels thrive in particular regions. **Choice E** is incorrect because "denigrated" means criticized unfairly. This word does not fit in the context of the sentence because it does not accurately describe the smaller areas where black squirrels live in contrast to the abundance of grey squirrels across North America. The passage does not mention anything about the areas being unfairly critiqued. Rather, the passage aims to express that black squirrels thrive in particular regions.

337 **Choice A is correct** because "lucid" means expressed clearly or easy to understand. This word fits in the context of the sentence because it accurately describes Walt's presentation according to the rest of the passage. The sentence explains that the presentation helped clarify difficult aspects of the group's goals. Therefore, the presentation must have been clear and easy to understand.

Choice B is incorrect because "malevolent" means showing a wish to do evil to others. This word does not fit in the context of the sentence because it does not accurately describe Walt's presentation according to the rest of the passage. The sentence explains that the presentation served to clarify the group's goals. There is no indication that the presentation was evil in any way. Therefore, choice A is the best option. **Choice C** is incorrect because "meretricious" means falsely attractive with no substantial value. This word does not fit in the context of the sentence because it does not accurately describe Walt's presentation according to the rest of the passage. The sentence explains that the presentation served to clarify the group's goals. There is no indication that the presentation turned out to have less value than originally thought. The author also does not seem to make any sort of point relating to the attractiveness of the presentation to begin with. Therefore, choice A is the best option. **Choice D** is incorrect because "obscure" means unclear or uncertain. This word does not fit in the context of the sentence because it does not accurately describe Walt's presentation according to the rest of the passage. The sentence explains that the presentation served to clarify the group's goals. If his presentation was unclear, it would not serve to clarify but to confuse listeners about the group's goals even more. Therefore, choice A is the best option. **Choice E** is incorrect because "bewildering" means confusing or perplexing. This word does not fit in the context of the sentence because it does not accurately describe Walt's presentation according to the rest of the passage. The sentence explains that the presentation served to clarify the group's goals. If his presentation was confusing, it would not serve to clarify but to challenge listeners to understand the group's goals even more. Therefore, choice A is the best option.

338 **Choice E is correct** because "apocryphal" means something is widely circulated as true but has doubtful authenticity. This word fits in the context of the sentence because it accurately describes urban legends according to the rest of the passage. The sentence is stating that the origins of such legends are doubtful and have questionable origins, but that this does not seem to impact their ability to engage people.

Choice A is incorrect because "hyperbolic" means exaggeration or overstating the truth. This word does not fit in the context of the sentence because it does not accurately describe urban legends according to the rest of the passage. The sentence is not claiming that urban legends are exaggerative and makes no statement that they stretch the truth. Rather, the sentence aims to express that urban legends are doubtful with questionable origins, though they are very captivating. **Choice B** is incorrect because "ephemeral" means lasting for a short time. This word does not fit in the context of the sentence because it does not accurately describe urban legends according to the rest of the passage. The sentence is not claiming that urban legends only last for a short time. It does not discuss the time that the legends have circulated at all. Rather, the sentence aims to express that urban legends are doubtful with questionable origins, though they are very captivating. **Choice C** is incorrect because "judicious" means using sound decision making skills. This word does not fit in the context of the sentence because it does not accurately describe urban legends according to the rest of the passage. The sentence is not claiming that urban legends are told with good decision making skills or have display decision making skills themselves. Rather, the sentence aims to express that urban legends are doubtful with questionable origins, though they are very captivating. **Choice D** is incorrect because "prurient" means unwholesome and encouraging interest in sexual matters. This word does not fit in the context of the sentence because it does not accurately describe urban legends according to the rest of the passage. The sentence is not claiming that urban legends encourage sexual interest and does not depict them as unwholesome in any way. Rather, the sentence aims to express that urban legends are doubtful with questionable origins, though they are very captivating.

339 **Choice C is correct** because "recurrent" means occurring often or repeatedly. This word fits in the context of the sentence because it accurately describes the way the American automotive industry has followed consistent patterns of panic and euphoria as discussed in the passage. In other words, the nature of the industry is to repeatedly undergo discord when foreign producers excel, followed by bliss when America excels.

Choice A is incorrect because "baroque" means relating to the style of European architecture in the 17th century. This word does not fit in the context of the sentence because it does not accurately describe the nature of the American automotive industry according to the rest of the text. The passage does not mention anything about architecture. In addition, it does not specifically mention Europe or the time period of the 17th century. Since this is unrelated to the topic of the sentence, choice C is the best option. **Choice B** is incorrect because "indulgent" means giving someone excessive generosity or leniency. This word does not fit in the context of the sentence because it does not accurately describe the nature of the American automotive industry according to the rest of the text. The passage does not describe giving generously or being lenient in any way. Rather, the passage is saying that the nature of the industry is to repeatedly undergo discord when foreign producers excel, followed by bliss when America excels. Therefore, choice C is the best option. **Choice D** is incorrect because "immutable" means unchanging over time. This word does not fit in the context of the sentence because it does not accurately describe the nature of the American automotive industry according to the rest of the text. The passage is saying that the nature of the industry is to repeatedly undergo discord when foreign producers excel, followed by bliss when America excels. This is the opposite of being unchanging and steady. Therefore, choice C is the best option. **Choice E** is incorrect because "steadfast" means resolutely firm and unwavering. This word does not fit in the context of the sentence because it does not accurately describe the nature of the American automotive industry according to the rest of the text. The passage is saying that the nature of the industry is to repeatedly undergo discord when foreign producers excel, followed by bliss when America excels. This is the opposite of being firm and unwavering. Therefore, choice C is the best option.

340 **Choice A is correct** because "attenuated" means reduced in force or effect. This word fits in the context of the sentence because it accurately describes the way bold claims are impacted by the collapse of stock prices that follows. In other words, the bold claims about conquering the corporate world are reduced in effect when stock prices go down.

Choice B is incorrect because "elevated" means placed higher than the surrounding areas. This word does not fit in the context of the sentence because it does not accurately describe the way bold claims are impacted by the collapse of stock prices that follows. The sentence is not saying that these bold claims are elevated to be in a higher position. Rather, the sentence is expressing that bold claims are diminished, as evidenced by the statement that the business cycle continues to elude economists. Therefore, choice A is the best option. **Choice C** is incorrect because "reinforced" means strengthened or supported. This word does not fit in the context of the sentence because it does not accurately describe the way bold claims are impacted by the collapse of stock prices that follows. The sentence is not saying that these bold claims are reinforced to become stronger. Rather, the sentence is expressing that bold claims are diminished, as evidenced by the statement that the business cycle continues to elude economists. Therefore, choice A is the best option. **Choice D** is incorrect because "garnished" means decorated or embellished. This word does not fit in the context of the sentence because it does not accurately describe the way bold claims are impacted by the collapse of stock prices that follows. The sentence is not saying that these bold claims are decorated or that any accessories are added to them. Rather, the sentence is expressing that bold claims are diminished, as evidenced by the statement that the business cycle continues to elude economists. Therefore, choice A is the best option. **Choice E** is incorrect because "subsumed" means included or absorbed into something else. This word does not fit in the context of the sentence because it does not accurately describe the way bold claims are impacted by the collapse of stock prices that follows. The sentence is not saying that these bold claims are absorbed into any other claims or that they are adopted by anything else. Rather, the sentence is expressing that bold claims are diminished, as evidenced by the statement that the business cycle continues to elude economists. Therefore, choice A is the best option.

341 **Choice A is correct** because "laudation" means praise and commendation. This word fits in the context of the sentence because it accurately explains the fact that the surgeon's confidence was shaken after his malpractice lawsuit even though he had experienced years of positive feedback.

Choice B is incorrect because "censure" means an expression of severe disapproval. This word does not fit in the context of the sentence because it does not accurately explain why the shaken confidence of the surgeon due to the malpractice lawsuit was in contrast with his previous work. It would not make sense for a malpractice lawsuit to shake the surgeon's confidence if he had already undergone years of severe disapproval for his work. **Choice C** is incorrect because "indictment" means a written legal accusation from a person of authority. This word does not fit in the context of the sentence because it does not accurately explain why the shaken confidence of the surgeon due to the malpractice lawsuit was in contrast with his previous work. It would not make sense for a malpractice lawsuit to shake the surgeon's confidence if he had already undergone years of accusations of legal wrongdoing. **Choice D** is incorrect because "suppression" means preventing something from being seen or operating. This word does not fit in the context of the sentence because it does not accurately explain why the shaken confidence of the surgeon due to the malpractice lawsuit was in contrast with his previous work. It would not make sense for a malpractice lawsuit to shake the surgeon's confidence after years of suppression. The concept of suppressing is not related to the passage at all. **Choice E** is incorrect because "ingenuity" means cleverness and inventiveness. This word does not fit in the context of the sentence because it does not accurately explain why the shaken confidence of the surgeon due to the malpractice lawsuit was in contrast with his previous work. It would not make sense for a malpractice lawsuit to shake the surgeon's confidence after he had previously been inventive. The two states of being are not opposite to one another and inventiveness is not even relevant to the passage.

342 **Choice C is correct** because "reinventing" means changing something so much that it appears to be new. This word fits in the context of the sentence because it explains the way that botanists have re-established their reputation. They have changed their reputation into eccentrics of the biological sciences. This is supported by the subsequent fact about their mushroom discovery.

Choice A is incorrect because "mystifying" means utterly bewildering and mysterious. This word does not fit in the context of the sentence because it does not explain the way that botanists have re-established their reputation as eccentrics. Botanists are not making their status bewildering to others. Rather, they are changing their status as eccentrics. This makes choice C the best option. **Choice B** is incorrect because "denigrating" means criticizing unfairly. This word does not fit in the context of the sentence because it does not explain the way that botanists have re-established their reputation as eccentrics. Nothing in the text suggests that botanists are criticizing their status. Rather, they are changing their status as eccentrics. This makes choice C the best option. **Choice D** is incorrect because "abiding" means enduring for a long time. This word does not fit in the context of the sentence because it does not explain the way that botanists have re-established their reputation as eccentrics. Botanists are not making their status last for a long time. The concept of time is not even mentioned in the passage. Rather, they are changing their status as eccentrics. This makes choice C the best option. **Choice E** is incorrect because "shirking" means avoiding or neglecting a responsibility. This word does not fit in the context of the sentence because it does not explain the way that botanists have re-established their reputation as eccentrics. Botanists are not neglecting their status in any way. Rather, they are changing their status as eccentrics. This makes choice C the best option.

Chapter 4: Text Completion

343 **Choice B is correct** because magnify means to "zoom in or make larger" which is supported by the phrase in the passage "make them appear bigger than they are to the naked eye".

Choice A is incorrect because test means to "establish the quality, performance, or reliability of something" which does not align with the overall meaning of the passage. **Choice C** is incorrect because reduce means to "make smaller or less in amount" which runs contrary to the overall meaning of the passage. **Choice D** is incorrect because impede means to "delay or prevent something or someone by obstructing them" which does not align with the meaning of the passage. **Choice E** is incorrect because capture mans to "take into one's possession or control by force which does not align with the meaning of the passage.

344 **Choice B is correct** because "probity" means honor and integrity. This word fits in the context of the sentence because it accurately describes the reputation Judge Gordon attained for upholding the law. The passage explains that he ruled with legal precedent even if it went against his personal preferences, which is a very integral thing to do.

Choice A is incorrect because "turpitude" means shameful and wicked. This word does not fit in the context of the sentence because it does not accurately describe the reputation that Judge Gordon attained for upholding the law. The passage explains that he ruled with the legal precedent, not that he behaved shamefully or wickedly. Therefore, choice B is the best option. **Choice C** is incorrect because "speciousness" means appearing true when it is really false. This word does not fit in the context of the sentence because it does not accurately describe the reputation that Judge Gordon attained for upholding the law. The passage explains that he ruled with the legal precedent, not that he was secretly dishonest. Therefore, choice B is the best option. **Choice D** is incorrect because "torpor" means inactivity and lethargy. This word does not fit in the context of the sentence because it does not accurately describe the reputation that Judge Gordon attained for upholding the law. The passage explains that he ruled with the legal precedent, not that he was lazy or lacked energy. Therefore, choice B is the best option. **Choice E** is incorrect because "urbanity" means suave and courteous. This word does not fit in the context of the sentence because it does not accurately describe the reputation that Judge Gordon attained for upholding the law. The passage explains that he ruled with the legal precedent, not that he was well-mannered and smooth. Therefore, choice B is the best option.

345 **Choice B is correct** because "indebted" means owing money or gratitude for a favor. This word fits in the context of the sentence because it describes the way that the sonar of bats influenced the procedure used by astronomers. Astronomers are indebted to the sonar of bats for their ability to estimate the distance between earth and other planets.

Choice A is incorrect because "superior" means higher in rank, status, or quality. This word does not fit in the context of the sentence because it does not describe the way that the sonar of bats influenced the procedure used by astronomers. The method used by astronomers is not better than that of a bat, but was inspired by bats. Therefore, choice B is the best option. **Choice C** is incorrect because "abhorrent" means repugnant or inspiring loathing. This word does not fit in the context of the sentence because it does not describe the way that the sonar of bats influenced the procedure used by astronomers. The method used by astronomers is not repugnant, but is useful in determining the distance of different planets. The sentence is expressing that the procedure used by astronomers was inspired by bats. Therefore, choice B is the best option. **Choice D** is incorrect because "deleterious" means causing harm or damage. This word does not fit in the context of the sentence because it does not describe the way that the sonar of bats influenced the procedure used by astronomers. The method used by astronomers is not damaging in any way, but is useful in determining the distance of different planets. The sentence is expressing that the procedure used by astronomers was inspired by bats. Therefore, choice B is the best option. **Choice E** is incorrect because "debased" means reduced in quality or value. This word does not fit in the context of the sentence because it does not describe the way that the sonar of bats influenced the procedure used by astronomers. The method used by astronomers was not getting worse in any way, but is continuing to be useful in determining the distance of different planets. The sentence is expressing that the procedure used by astronomers was inspired by bats. Therefore, choice B is the best option.

346 **Choice E is correct** because the sentence has to do with "discarding pointe shoes," for the purpose of "liberating the body from physical restrictions." Therefore, what goes in the blank must be a word that expresses Duncan's feeling that rigid dance shoes prevented full expression, which is a negative outcome similar to not allowing something to occur, which is captured in "precluded."

Choice A is incorrect because "entailed" means involved and lacks a negative connotation. **Choice B** is incorrect because "catered" suggests allowing and encouraging expression, which is not the intended meaning. **Choice C** is incorrect because "facilitated" has a positive connotation in the sense of allowing for or causing an increase in expression, which is the opposite of the intended meaning. **Choice D** is incorrect because "implicated" means, shown to be responsible for something, which also lacks a negative connotation and does not transmit the desired meaning.

347 **Choice A is correct** because "perception" means seeing and becoming aware of something through the senses. This word fits in the context of the sentence because it explains the way human eyes process light. In other words, human eyes perceive light as described in the passage.

Choice B is incorrect because "acumen" means the ability to make good decisions. This word does not fit in the context of the sentence because it does not explain the way human eyes process light. The passage does not relate to decision making in any way. Rather, the passage aims to explain that human eyes perceive light in a way that makes the sky appear blue. Therefore, choice A is the best option. **Choice C** is incorrect because "perspicacity" means shrewd and discerning. This word does not fit in the context of the sentence because it does not explain the way human eyes process light. The passage does not relate to being clever or cunning in any way. Rather, the passage aims to explain that human eyes perceive light in a way that makes the sky appear blue. Therefore, choice A is the best option. **Choice D** is incorrect because "awareness" means knowledge or understanding of a situation. This word does not fit in the context of the sentence because it does not explain the way human eyes process light. The passage is not discussing human awareness, but human vision. The passage aims to explain that human eyes perceive light in a way that makes the sky appear blue. Therefore, choice A is the best option. **Choice E** is incorrect because "conception" means forming a plan, idea, or child. This word does not fit in the context of the sentence because it does not explain the way human eyes process light. The passage does not relate to creating anything new. Rather, the passage aims to explain that human eyes perceive light in a way that makes the sky appear blue. Therefore, choice A is the best option.

348 **Choice C is correct** because altruistic is defined as "showing a selfless concern for the wellbeing of others", which aligns closely with the actions described in the passage.

Choice A is incorrect because autonomous means "having the freedom to act independently", which does not align with the overall meaning of the passage. **Choice B** is incorrect because wasted means "used or expended carelessly, extravagantly, or without purpose", which does not align with the examples and implications of the passage **Choice D** is incorrect because redundant means "no longer needed or useful", which is not applicable to the context of this passage. **Choice E** is incorrect because meddlesome means "fond of interference", which is not applicable to the examples or context of this passage.

349 **Choice B is correct** because "conditions" best completes the sentence because it is expressing that the state of the market alters how frequently art must be appraised. The word "conditions" means the state of how something is working. Therefore, "conditions" would fit in the sentence and complete the idea that the market operations of specific artists' work affect appraisals.

Choice A is incorrect because "tempo" is incorrect because this word means the rate or speed of a motion. This word would not fit in the sentence because a market does not move. It would not make sense to refer to the speed of a market for a certain artist. **Choice C** is incorrect because "perseverance" means persistence with something difficult. The market is not persevering through anything, so it would not make sense to use this word after "market." **Choice D** is incorrect because "inspection," means a careful examination of something. The market for particular artists is not being examined in this sentence. Rather, the conditions of the market impact how frequently art must be appraised. **Choice E** is incorrect because "waning" means getting progressively smaller. It would not make sense that art needs to be appraised more frequently or less frequently if the market was consistently getting smaller. Instead, it would likely be one or the other. Additionally, the word "waning" is not written in the correct verb tense to match the rest of the sentence.

350 **Choice B is correct** because the sentence is about a painting rendered by an artist that captures the essential qualities and features of a given landscape. Given that the definition of "encapsulates" is to capture the essential features of something succinctly, it is the best choice.

Choice A is incorrect because "enraptures" means to give intense pleasure or joy which does not align with the context and meaning of the sentence. **Choice C** is incorrect because "deviates" means to depart from an established course, which does not align with the context and meaning of the sentence either. **Choice D** is incorrect because "obfuscates" means to render unclear, obscure, or unintelligible, which runs contrary to the meaning of summarization implied by the passage. **Choice E** is incorrect because expands means to broaden or enlarge, which does not align with the context and meaning of the sentence.

Chapter 4: Text Completion

Practice Set 2: Two Blanks

351 In 1915 Niels Bohr proposed a model of an atom that modified an earlier model. Based on quantum mechanics, the Bohr model is called a planetary model, as it shows electrons with a negative charge (i) _____ a nucleus, which has a positive charge. Bohr suggested a(n) (ii) _____ relationship between gravitational forces in the solar system and the electrical force between positively charged nuclei and negatively charged electrons.

Blank (i)	Blank (ii)
(A) envelops	(D) analogous
(B) converges	(E) homologous
(C) orbits	(F) retrogression

352 Due to his many successful (i) _____ on the battlefield, Napoleon was incredibly self-assured as a leader and warfighter. Therefore, his ill-fated decision to invade Russia during its harsh winter could largely be viewed as (ii) _____.

Blank (i)	Blank (ii)
(A) retreats	(D) rational
(B) campaigns	(E) hubristic
(C) articles	(F) well-devised

353 Once cells were (i) _____ from the embryos of deceased frogs and placed into Petri dishes, scientists observed their spontaneous reorganization into multicellular organisms, based on which they (ii) _____ that there is a cellular capacity to adapt even after an organism's death.

Blank (i)	Blank (ii)
(A) vivisected	(D) deduced
(B) extracted	(E) insinuated
(C) dissected	(F) inferred

354 Stephens professes to have no bias, but a discerning analysis of his article "Our Youth Must Work" reveals that the author employs (i) _____ to create an ingenious yet invalid argument aimed at misleading readers into agreeing with a youth service program that penalizes students from the lower socio-economic echelons in favor of their (ii) _____ peers who will simply be able to buy their way out of the proposed two years of community or military service.

Blank (i)	Blank (ii)
(A) dissimulation	(D) erudite
(B) hubris	(E) ostentatious
(C) sophistry	(F) patrician

355 When the experiment (i) _____, the scientists sought to quickly analyze the data and publish their work in an academic journal. Had they not, their discovery could have been (ii) _____ by other academics who might take the credit for solving the same problem at a later date.

Blank (i)	Blank (ii)
(A) concluded	(D) thwarted
(B) began	(E) pilfered
(C) failed	(F) uncertified

356 The newfound money couldn't (i) _____ the sorrow. Tiffany had inherited more money than she would ever be able to spend, but she would rather have had her parents back. She couldn't help but (ii) _____ the comments that her friends made about her situation. They reprimanded her for her sullenness, and told her that she was lucky to be in the situation that she was.

Blank (i)	Blank (ii)
(A) masticate	(D) lionize
(B) interpolate	(E) oblige
(C) alleviate	(F) begrudge

357. Horoscopes are somewhat like fortune cookie fortunes - they sound true, because they are based on human nature and human behavior, both of which are homogenous and therefore fairly predictable. Furthermore, horoscopes are highly generic or shrouded in metaphor whose (i) _____ can easily be changed to meet the (ii) _____ of our lives and can be applied to almost everyone almost anytime.

Blank (i)	Blank (ii)
(A) palpability	(D) exigencies
(B) elucidation	(E) generalizations
(C) omnipotence	(F) generalities

358. The flu of 1918 infected an estimated 500 million people worldwide, killing 3 to 5 percent of the world's population within two years. Although the (i) _____ was entirely unpreventable and particularly deadly, it galvanized leaders world-wide to develop a (ii) _____ strategy for dealing with mass infections, leading ultimately, to the creation of the World Health Organization.

Blank (i)	Blank (ii)
(A) endemic	(D) congruous
(B) pandemic	(E) germane
(C) epidemic	(F) refractory

359. In light of his many (i) _____ with the ladies and his illicit dealings in pornography, the pastor's comments on the on the aberrations of deviate behavior among parishioners was viewed as sanctimonious (ii) _____ and readily dismissed.

Blank (i)	Blank (ii)
(A) adumbrations	(D) chit-chat
(B) dilettantes	(E) invective
(C) peccadilloes	(F) cant

360. Women, though not (i) _____ genetic disorders generally, are far less likely than men to display symptoms of an X-linked hereditary disease such as hemophilia. In the case of hemophilia, for example, the woman's second, X chromosome acts as a kind of buffer; the normal gene is typically able to produce enough clotting factors to (ii) _____ any life-threatening bleeds.

Blank (i)	Blank (ii)
(A) inclined to	(D) mollify
(B) intransigent towards	(E) forestall
(C) impervious to	(F) engender

361. While single-celled organisms can (i) _____ nutrients directly from the environment, multicellular organisms have specialized structures for obtaining and breaking down the food that is the source of necessary nutrients. These digestive systems are composed of multiple functions that (ii) _____ food sources into processable liquid and extract nutrients. The process results in waste, which is expelled from the organism via another, related system.

Blank (i)	Blank (ii)
(A) osmose	(D) flux
(B) exude	(E) deliquesce
(C) cull	(F) coagulate

362. Invasive species constitute a serious threat to (i) _____ plants and animals, whether by preying on them directly or competing with them for resources. The emerald ash borer has had a particularly (ii) _____ effect on the environment; as its name implies, it attacks and kills all varieties of ash trees, and it is spreading throughout the United States at an alarming rate.

Blank (i)	Blank (ii)
(A) inveterate	(D) deleterious
(B) pugnacious	(E) covert
(C) indigenous	(F) perfidious

Chapter 4: Text Completion

363 Gary always resented the way people (i) _____ television. If he ever mentioned a program he had recently watched he was always met with reprimands from others. They told him how television was a waste, how it rotted his brain. The (ii) _____ was staggering. Gary knew that these same people also watched television; they just denied it in public in order to put on airs. And what was so sacrosanct about the other forms of media? There were trashy novels, just like there were trashy television programs.

Blank (i)	Blank (ii)
(A) derided	(D) equanimity
(B) bolstered	(E) duplicity
(C) protracted	(F) sublimity

364 Although folklore regards a green sky as a (i) _____ of tornadoes, the belief is not backed by scientific evidence. In fact, tornadoes are one of the more unpredictable forms of severe weather; although radar can detect signs indicating a possible tornado, such data generally requires eyewitness (ii) _____.

Blank (i)	Blank (ii)
(A) propagation	(D) reciprocity
(B) incursion	(E) approbation
(C) harbinger	(F) corroboration

365 Though we were charmed by the (i) _____ waters of the Mediterranean, the highlight of our trip to Greece was undoubtedly the chance to visit the Parthenon. Photos cannot adequately capture the grandeur of this (ii) _____ relic from ancient times, so we found ourselves stunned into silence when confronted by its stately columns and imposing pediments.

Blank (i)	Blank (ii)
(A) pellucid	(D) portentous
(B) turbid	(E) august
(C) quiescent	(F) irrevocable

366 Howard knew that the story of the musician who trades integrity for money was (i) _____, but it felt new to him. He was being offered the chance to sign a recording contract, but a quick glance at the fine print told him that he would be signing away his dignity. The contract would guarantee him fame and fortune, but it would license his music to the highest bidder and charge (ii) _____ prices to his loyal fans.

Blank (i)	Blank (ii)
(A) cliché	(D) inconsequential
(B) facetious	(E) judicious
(C) metaphorical	(F) appalling

367 An element is a(n) (i) _____ substance. It cannot be broken into other elements and has no component elements. There are 92 elements that occur in nature. When different elements are connected to create a new substance, the result is a compound, which is made of multiple, sometimes (ii) _____ elements, that are otherwise unrelated. Pure elements are rare as most matter exists in the form of compounds.

Blank (i)	Blank (ii)
(A) unalloyed	(D) multifarious
(B) adulterated	(E) homogenous
(C) veritable	(F) conglomerate

368 While the study of viruses is important in and of itself, it must be noted that it also has potential (i) _____ for other areas of medicine. For example, a handful of otherwise innocuous viruses may (ii) _____ the development of certain forms of cancer; the Epstein-Barr virus has so far been linked to Hodgkin's lymphoma, Burkitt's lymphoma, nasopharyngeal carcinoma, and central nervous system lymphomas associated with HIV.

Blank (i)	Blank (ii)
(A) proscriptions	(D) precipitate
(B) exigencies	(E) attenuate
(C) ramifications	(F) truncate

369 Diabetes results from inadequate levels of insulin in the body. When not enough insulin is produced many physiological functions are compromised. The results include vision (i) _____, decreased circulatory function, failures in the nervous system and kidney failure. The second most common cause of blindness in the United States is diabetes, which demonstrates how serious and (ii) _____ .this condition is in the U.S.

Blank (i)	Blank (ii)
(A) diminishing	(D) pervasive
(B) stagnation	(E) circumscribed
(C) impairment	(F) capacious

370 In the human body two systems manage hormone release. The endocrine system is a (i) _____ of glands each of which (ii) _____ different hormones into the bloodstream. Hormones pass through the blood to bring "messages" to different organs, which have hormone-receptors. The exocrine system, which is distinct from the endocrine system, an internal system, releases products outside of the body, including sweat and saliva.

Blank (i)	Blank (ii)
(A) force	(D) disperse
(B) crux	(E) secrete
(C) cadre	(F) beget

371 In a(n) (i) _____ relationship, when one variable increases, the other decreases. The most (ii) _____ obvious example of this involves heating water. When a pan of water is placed over a heat source, as the temperature rises, liquid water begins to vaporize, thus reducing the mass of the water in the pan. In this case, as the variable temperature increases, the variable, mass, decreases.

Blank (i)	Blank (ii)
(A) contradictory	(D) familiar
(B) conforming	(E) proverbial
(C) inverse	(F) mundane

372 Although its desolate landscapes and small population may make South Dakota seem a (i) _____ locale, it is actually one of the best places to start a business. High taxes in eastern states like New York and New Jersey can (ii) _____ even well-planned ventures. In contrast, South Dakota has some of the lowest taxes in the country.

Blank (i)	Blank (ii)
(A) morbid	(D) foil
(B) inhospitable	(E) obviate
(C) germane	(F) lampoon

373 The most successful companies can have humble —even (i) _____ beginnings; that Sony's first product was an ineffective rice cooker surely proves that (ii) _____ is nearly as important as vision when trying to get a business off the ground.

Blank (i)	Blank (ii)
(A) mundane	(D) tenacity
(B) frugal	(E) presumption
(C) bogus	(F) sophistry

374 While most people are aware of the existence of vestigial structures like the appendix, far fewer realize that humans also retain some reflexes and behaviors that, though (i) _____ now, would have proven valuable to the organisms from which we evolved. Goosebumps, for example, cause whatever fur an animal has to stand on end, thereby making it appear larger and a more (ii) _____ opponent when faced with a potential predator.

Blank (i)	Blank (ii)
(A) superfluous	(D) impassive
(B) apocryphal	(E) formidable
(C) exiguous	(F) obsequious

For more practice, visit www.vibrantpublishers.com

Chapter 4: Text Completion

375. Those unfamiliar with her (i) _____ sense of humor tended to take her words at face value, and were sometimes repelled by her apparent inability to speak seriously of any subject. For those in the know, however, her (ii) _____ remarks were endlessly entertaining.

Blank (i)	Blank (ii)
(A) flippant	(D) jocular
(B) raucous	(E) iconoclastic
(C) erudite	(F) equivocal

376. Although the differences are no doubt (i) _____ to the casual listener, various studies have shown that men and women do not use language in precisely the same way. Men, for example, are far more likely to compliment women than vice versa, perhaps due to deeply ingrained cultural attitudes that condemn as (ii) _____ any romantically assertive woman.

Blank (i)	Blank (ii)
(A) pertinent	(D) garish
(B) blatant	(E) brazen
(C) indiscernible	(F) capricious

377. Gazelles are known to be fast as well as (i) _____; this often leads people to (ii) _____ dance and ballet performers with these graceful creatures of the savanna.

Blank (i)	Blank (ii)
(A) erratic	(D) associate
(B) lithe	(E) trivialize
(C) diaphanous	(F) defer

378. "Shooting stars" are meteors, hunks of rocks that (i) _____ through space, that burn up in the Earth's atmosphere in a streak that can often be seen by the naked eye; meteorites are pieces of meteors that aren't completely (ii) _____, and fall all the way to the ground.

Blank (i)	Blank (ii)
(A) hurtle	(D) collated
(B) waft	(E) extirpated
(C) droll	(F) serrated

379. "Monteverdi's L'Orfeo enjoys its (i) _____ reputation in part because it is regarded as the first fully developed opera. Yet due credit must also be given to both the score and the libretto, which retells the (ii) _____ tale of Orpheus's journey to the underworld to restore his beloved Eurydice to life.

Blank (i)	Blank (ii)
(A) renowned	(D) droll
(B) incongruous	(E) poignant
(C) unscathed	(F) maudlin

380. "The former dictator's (i) _____ was legendary, although it was only after he was deposed, the full extent of his wealth became known—huge mansions spread across the country, and a (ii) _____ of luxury goods.

Blank (i)	Blank (ii)
(A) prowess	(D) paucity
(B) cupidity	(E) surfeit
(C) prudishness	(F) postulate

381. "Medieval European rulers often tried to legitimize their rule by (i) _____ ties to the ancient Roman Empire. Although actual ties were tenuous, this strategy engendered the German emperor adopting the (ii) _____ title of "Holy Roman Emperor".

Blank (i)	Blank (ii)
(A) rending	(D) ludicrous
(B) alleviating	(E) grandiose
(C) espousing	(F) gregarious

382. The governor signed the bill into law despite widespread and (i) _____ objections, leading some to question whether he truly had the people's best interests at heart. In response to such criticisms, the governor merely stated that the new laws, however (ii) _____ in the short term, were ultimately necessary.

Blank (i)	Blank (ii)
(A) bombastic	(D) unpalatable
(B) moribund	(E) imminent
(C) vociferous	(F) execrable

383. The meteorologists of the world have recently found themselves working under the (i) _____ of political discourse. With environmental concerns suddenly on everybody's mind, these (ii) _____ scientists have been thrust into the vicious world of political partisanship. Although many of them have stepped up to the challenge admirably, it seems unfair to suddenly demand political insight from people previously focused exclusively on scientific pursuits.

Blank (i)	Blank (ii)
(A) encumbrance	(D) reticent
(B) auspices	(E) ostentatious
(C) insight	(F) conspiratorial

384. When the long, stiff tubes of a Suctoria's tentacle attach to an animal for a feeding, tiny (i)_____ move to the tip of the tentacle, which then (ii)_____ the prey and begin absorbing its cytoplasm.

Blank (i)	Blank (ii)
(A) granules	(D) reinforce
(B) static	(E) immobilize
(C) bulbs	(F) emancipate

385. In spite of the immense intellect, and sometimes outright genius, of the people working within it, the field of physics still faces many factors (i) _____ to its growth. As it turns out, the difficulty of accepting new ideas does not exist solely among the working-class population, but can be found in academia as well. Entrenched logic, petty careerism, and just plain (ii) _____ are all as prevalent in the field of physics as they are in the conventional, nine-to-five world.

Blank (i)	Blank (ii)
(A) correlated	(D) eminence
(B) antagonistic	(E) acquiescence
(C) supplanted	(F) inscience

386. Although we tend to think of our judgments of others as (i) _____ observations, the reality is that a variety of unconscious beliefs and biases affect our opinions. For example, we so expect a person's physical appearance to (ii) _____ his overall intelligence and morality that attractive people are more likely to receive good grades in school and land a well-paying job.

Blank (i)	Blank (ii)
(A) dispassionate	(D) ascribe to
(B) chary	(E) purport to
(C) momentous	(F) jibe with

387. Although the (i) _____ against murder is universal, the definition of the crime is highly (ii) _____. A strict adherence to Buddhist teachings, for example, would most likely lead one to condemn even killing in self-defense, which is generally tolerated in modern society.

Blank (i)	Blank (ii)
(A) litigation	(D) contentious
(B) vituperation	(E) fallacious
(C) proscription	(F) inclusive

388. While Van Gogh's decision to slice off his ear to impress his lover can only be defined as (i)_____, his significant impact on post-impressionistic and neo-impressionistic art can be only described as (ii) _____.

Blank (i)	Blank (ii)
(A) casual	(D) dubious
(B) irrelevant	(E) haggard
(C) quixotic	(F) transcendent

389. When the CEO met his (i)_____, he hailed the lower-ranked workers for their (ii)_____ through the course of the year, which had seen the company generate record profits.

Blank (i)	Blank (ii)
(A) subordinates	(D) gumption
(B) serfs	(E) largesse
(C) colleagues	(F) recalcitrance

Chapter 4: Text Completion

390 Riding my carefree bicycle ride this morning has filled me with (i)_____, however this pleasurable experience will come to an end when I have to (ii)_____ in the yard doing chores later in the days

Blank (i)	Blank (ii)
Ⓐ ecstasy	Ⓓ exercise
Ⓑ fear	Ⓔ frolic
Ⓒ courage	Ⓕ toil

391 While Isaac Newton (i)_____ a number of fundamental laws concerning the exploration of our physical world, his contributions to the fields of mathematics will likely (ii)_____ his contributions to physics.

Blank (i)	Blank (ii)
Ⓐ lambasted	Ⓓ overshadow
Ⓑ received	Ⓔ contrive
Ⓒ conceived	Ⓕ impede

392 By using a Bunsen burner, one can (i)_____ different experimental materials, preventing any bacterial contamination from inadvertently (ii)_____ the purified samples.

Blank (i)	Blank (ii)
Ⓐ distribute	Ⓓ inoculating
Ⓑ limit	Ⓔ marinating
Ⓒ sterilize	Ⓕ exhausting

393 Monarch butterflies have a very long and often (i)_____ migration route that can often take them several months depending on their (ii)_____ in North America.

Blank (i)	Blank (ii)
Ⓐ vicarious	Ⓓ volition
Ⓑ fractious	Ⓔ origin
Ⓒ precarious	Ⓕ polarity

394 Good financial (i)_____ is required to run a small business, and if you are not (ii)_____ in the ways of accounting, you should consider hiring a professional.

Blank (i)	Blank (ii)
Ⓐ vitiate	Ⓓ pliant
Ⓑ acumen	Ⓔ learned
Ⓒ credence	Ⓕ frenetic

395 Martin Luther King Jr. was an advocate for (i)_____. In spite of his non-violent nature, he was (ii)_____ by individuals who viewed him as a threat to their way of life.

Blank (i)	Blank (ii)
Ⓐ recidivism	Ⓓ assassinated
Ⓑ pacifism	Ⓔ promoted
Ⓒ trepidation	Ⓕ conscripted

396 Cyrano de Bergerac, as he is portrayed in Rostand's play, is something of a (i)_____. For all his swagger and (ii)_____ words, he remains a deeply sympathetic character, no doubt because at heart he is simply an insecure man tormented by unrequited love.

Blank (i)	Blank (ii)
Ⓐ archetype	Ⓓ licentious
Ⓑ paradox	Ⓔ iconoclastic
Ⓒ cliché	Ⓕ bombastic

397 Despite the (i)_____ with which it is learned, (ii)_____ exist in the English language which separate speakers who are fluent versus those who are merely proficient.

Blank (i)	Blank (ii)
Ⓐ ease	Ⓓ subtleties
Ⓑ malaise	Ⓔ allegiances
Ⓒ courage	Ⓕ errors

Practice Set 2: Two Blanks

398 In telecommunication systems, broadcast signals can be (i) _____ allowing someone to broadcast over someone else's network. For example, if station A were (ii) _____ a signal to people tuned into their station it would be possible for station B to have their own signal be distributed over station A's network. This signal intrusion is accomplished when station B sends a stronger signal to station A's transponder.

Blank (i)	Blank (ii)
(A) interjected	(D) transcribing
(B) interpolated	(E) simulcasting
(C) appropriated	(F) circulating

399 The novels of Thomas Hardy often (i) _____ the ambitions of the increasingly mobile working classes with the realities of Victorian society. Both The Mayor of Casterbridge and Jude the Obscure are (ii) _____ of this theme, showing the tragic consequences of working-class men (iii) _____ their traditional role through ambition.

Blank (i)	Blank (ii)
(A) erudite	(D) conducive
(B) jubilant	(E) inimical
(C) fatuous	(F) incongruous

400 When the manager (i) _____ the thief red handed, she relieved him from his position at the company (ii) _____.

Blank (i)	Blank (ii)
(A) rebuked	(D) regally
(B) fought	(E) ostentatiously
(C) apprehended	(F) posthaste

Answer Key

Q. No.	Correct Answer	Your Answer
351	C, D	
352	B, E	
353	B, F	
354	C, F	
355	A, E	
356	C, F	
357	B, F	
358	B, D	
359	C, F	
360	C, E	
361	A, E	
362	C, D	
363	A, E	
364	C, F	
365	A, E	
366	A, F	
367	A, D	
368	C, D	
369	C, D	
370	C, E	
371	C, D	
372	B, D	
373	A, D	
374	A, E	
375	A, D	

Q. No.	Correct Answer	Your Answer
376	C, E	
377	B, D	
378	A, E	
379	A, E	
380	B, E	
381	C, E	
382	C, D	
383	A, D	
384	A, E	
385	B, F	
386	A, F	
387	C, D	
388	C, F	
389	A, D	
390	A, F	
391	C, D	
392	C, D	
393	C, E	
394	B, E	
395	B, D	
396	B, F	
397	A, D	
398	C, E	
399	C, F	
400	C, F	

Practice Set 2: Answers & Explanations

351 **Choice C is correct** because "orbits" refers to the spherical path of an object around another object. This word fits the context of the sentence as it describes how electrons, which have a negative charge, revolve around the positively charged nucleus in the Bohr model. In other words, the model proposed by Niels Bohr places the nucleus in the center, with electrons circulating in an orbital fashion around it. **Choice D is correct** because "analogous" means similar or comparable to something else. This word fits the context because it accurately describes the relationship between gravitational forces in the solar system and the electrical force in an atom. Bohr suggested that the two systems were similar in how central forces govern orbiting bodies.

Choice A is incorrect because "envelopes" means covering or surrounding something. This does not describe the relationship in the Bohr model, where electrons revolve around the nucleus rather than enclosing it. There is no indication that the nucleus is covered or wrapped. **Choice B** is incorrect because "converges" means coming together at a point. This is inaccurate in the context of the Bohr model, where electrons do not meet or converge with the nucleus but instead orbit it. There is no point of intersection implied. **Choice E** is incorrect because "homologous" means having the same position or structure, especially in a biological or anatomical context. This word does not fit the sentence because it implies sameness, whereas Bohr described the forces as comparable—not identical. Therefore, "analogous" is more appropriate. **Choice F** is incorrect because "retrogression" means a return to a less advanced state. It is a noun, while the sentence requires an adjective. Furthermore, this term does not describe any similarity or comparison between atomic and astronomical forces. There is no mention of decline or regression in the context.

352 **Choices B and E are correct** because the sentence seeks to highlight how Napoleon's military success and confidence might have been his undoing. Therefore, campaigns, which in this circumstance are defined as a "series of military actions with specific objectives in mind" and hubristic, defined as "exaggerated pride or self-confidence" appropriately fit the message and context of the passage.

Choice A is incorrect because retreats means to "withdraw military forces from the enemy after defeat", which does not align with the theme of the passage. **Choice C** is incorrect because articles means a "particular item or object" which is not aligned with the meaning or context of the passage. **Choice D** is incorrect because rational means "based in accordance with reason or logic", which runs contrary to the meaning of the passage. **Choice F** is incorrect because well-devised means "well planned or crafted", which is antithetical to the context of the passage.

353 **Choice B is correct** because the sentence states that cells were placed into Petri dishes, so the word in the blank needs to convey that they were removed from frog embryos. That is the meaning of "extracted." **Choice F is correct** for the second blank because the sentence describes a "spontaneous reorganization" of cells into "multicellular organisms," which provided evidence for the scientists to conclude that cells are capable of adapting even after an organism's death. The word "inferred" fits best because it means arriving at a conclusion based on evidence.

Choice A is incorrect because "vivisected" refers to the dissection of living organisms. However, the frogs in the sentence are described as "deceased," so this term does not apply. **Choice C** (in the first blank) is incorrect because "dissected" means to cut open a deceased specimen for examination, but it does not imply that cells were removed for further study. The context clearly calls for a word that suggests removal of material, which "extracted" does. **Choice D** is incorrect because "deduced" means arriving at a conclusion through logical or systematic reasoning. While this may be part of the scientific process, the sentence emphasizes drawing a conclusion from evidence—making "inferred" the more precise choice. **Choice E** is incorrect because "insinuated" means to suggest or hint at something, usually negative or subtle. This connotation does not match the sentence, which describes a clear scientific inference based on observation, not a vague suggestion.

354 **Choice C is correct** because "sophistry" means reasoning that appears plausible on a superficial level but is actually flawed or deceptive. This word fits the context of the sentence, which describes how Stephens crafts an argument that seems clever but misleads readers into supporting a biased youth service program. In other words, Stephens presents faulty reasoning that appears sound on the surface. **Choice F is correct** because "patrician" refers to someone of high rank, noble background, or upper social class. This word accurately describes the peers who contrast with students from lower socio-economic classes. The context supports this, particularly the mention of peers being able to "buy their way out of situations," which reflects privilege and wealth.

Choice A is incorrect because "dissimulation" refers to concealing one's thoughts, feelings, or character. The sentence does not suggest that Stephens is hiding his views; rather, he is openly expressing them, albeit in a misleading way. This makes "sophistry" the better choice. **Choice B** is incorrect because "hubris" means excessive pride or self-confidence. The sentence does not suggest that Stephens is arrogant or prideful. It focuses instead on the faulty reasoning of his argument, not on his character.

Chapter 4: Text Completion

Choice D is incorrect because "erudite" means highly educated or knowledgeable. The contrast in the sentence is not about intelligence or education but about socio-economic status. The focus is on financial privilege, as shown by the mention of buying one's way out of trouble. **Choice E** is incorrect because "ostentatious" means showy or overly flashy in a way that attracts attention. While this might suggest wealth, the sentence emphasizes social class and privilege, not behavior or appearance. Therefore, "patrician" is more appropriate.

355 **Choice A is correct** answer for the first blank because the first sentence highlights the actions of scientists subsequent to an experiment, and the justifications for pursuing those actions. As such, "concluded" is the only viable solution for the first blank. **Choice E is correct** because "pilfered" means "to steal" which aligns with the allusion of theft indicated later on in the sentence by "other scientists."

Choice B is incorrect because "began" indicates a state of initiation. The first sentence implies a state of termination was achieved before data analysis and publication. **Choice C** is incorrect because "failed" is the opposite of "solving a problem" as stated in the second sentence. **Choice D** is incorrect because thwarted means "to prevent from accomplishing something" which does not align with the context of the passage. **Choice F** is incorrect because uncertified means "not having official documentation to verify the veracity of something" which does not align with the context of the passage as well.

356 **Choice C is correct** because "alleviate" means to make suffering less severe. This word fits the context of the sentence, as it conveys how the inherited money could not lessen Tiffany's sorrow after the death of her parents. Her friends criticized her for her sorrowful demeanor, but the passage emphasizes that the money had no power to ease her emotional pain. **Choice F is correct** because "begrudge" means to give reluctantly or to feel envious or resentful of someone else's fortune or behavior. This word accurately describes Tiffany's emotional response toward her friends, who made callous remarks about her grief. She resented their lack of empathy and possibly envied their emotional detachment.

Choice A is incorrect because "masticate" means to chew food. This word is unrelated to the emotional content of the passage and does not describe the impact—or lack thereof—of the money on Tiffany's grief. **Choice B** is incorrect because "interpolate" means to insert something between fixed points, often in writing or data. This does not fit the context of emotional suffering or the role of money in Tiffany's mourning process. **Choice D** is incorrect because "lionize" means to publicly praise or treat someone as a celebrity. This is the opposite of how Tiffany feels toward her friends. She does not admire or praise them—instead, she resents their insensitivity. **Choice E** is incorrect because "oblige" means to make someone morally or legally bound to an action. There is no suggestion in the passage that Tiffany feels bound to her friends or that any obligation exists. The better interpretation is that she feels resentful, making "begrudge" the correct choice.

357 **Choice B is correct** because "elucidation" means an explanation that makes something clearer. This word fits the context of the sentence, as it describes how metaphors within horoscopes can be interpreted in various ways to suit the specific circumstances of a reader's life. In other words, horoscopic language is flexible and often clarified through subjective interpretation. **Choice F is correct** because "generalities" refers to vague or broad statements that lack specificity. This word fits the context of the sentence because it explains how horoscopes relate to a wide range of people's lives due to their lack of detailed, personal information. These statements speak to common human experiences, which makes them appear applicable to many.

Choice A is incorrect because "palpability" refers to something that is tangible or perceptible. This does not suit the context, as the passage discusses metaphorical language in horoscopes—not physical qualities. The focus is on interpretability, not physical presence. **Choice C** is incorrect because "omnipotence" means unlimited power. This does not fit the context of metaphors being interpreted in horoscopes. The metaphors are not powerful in themselves, but rather flexible and ambiguous, making "elucidation" a better choice. **Choice D** is incorrect because "exigencies" means urgent needs or demands. This term is irrelevant in the context of horoscope interpretation, where the emphasis is on how vague statements seem personally relevant—not on responding to emergencies or pressing situations. **Choice E** is incorrect because "generalizations" refers to broad claims often derived from limited evidence. While it may seem similar to "generalities," it has a more argumentative or analytical tone. In contrast, "generalities" better captures the vague, non-specific nature of horoscope language, which is meant to feel universally relatable without asserting strong claims.

358 **Choice B is correct** because "pandemic" refers to an international outbreak of a disease that is widespread and difficult to control. This term is appropriate in the context of the sentence, which describes how a massive number of people around the world were affected. **Choice D is correct** because "congruous" means in agreement or harmony. This word fits the context of the sentence, as it describes how leaders worldwide collaborated on a common strategy to help combat the global health crisis.

Choice A is incorrect because "endemic" refers to a disease that is consistently present within a specific area or population. This does not accurately describe the 1918 flu outbreak, which was widespread and global in nature, rather than confined or recurring in a limited area. **Choice C is incorrect** because "epidemic" describes a sudden outbreak of disease in a particular region. While the 1918 flu began as an epidemic, it quickly spread across nations, making "pandemic" the more accurate term. **Choice E is incorrect** because "germane" means relevant or closely related to a subject. While relevance may be implied, this word does not effectively describe the cooperative and unified approach that world leaders took in response to the crisis. "Congruous" better captures the idea of global coordination and agreement. **Choice F is incorrect** because "refractory" means stubborn or resistant to control. This contradicts the intended meaning of the sentence, which emphasizes international cooperation and a unified effort to find a solution.

359 **Choice C is correct** because "peccadilloes" means small, unimportant offenses or sins. This word fits the context of the sentence, as it describes the numerous questionable actions the pastor engaged in—such as involvement with women and dealings in pornography. These actions are portrayed as minor moral failings that nonetheless contradict the church's standards. **Choice F is correct** because "cant" refers to hypocritical or sanctimonious talk, especially of a moral or religious nature. This word is appropriate because the pastor's own sinful behavior made his criticisms of others seem hollow and hypocritical.

Choice A is incorrect because "adumbrations" means vague foreshadowing or outlines. This word does not accurately describe the pastor's inappropriate behavior. He was not subtly predicting future events; rather, he was actively engaging in morally questionable actions. Therefore, Choice C is the best option. **Choice B is incorrect** because "dilettantes" refers to people who take up an art or interest in a superficial way. This word does not describe the pastor's behavior with women and pornography. He was not dabbling in a topic with superficial interest; he was participating in behavior considered sinful. Therefore, Choice C is the best option. **Choice D is incorrect** because "chit-chat" means trivial or casual conversation. This does not reflect the way the pastor's comments on the sins of others were perceived. Given his own immoral actions, his criticisms were viewed as hypocritical, not merely as inconsequential banter. Therefore, Choice F is the best option. **Choice E is incorrect** because "invective" refers to harsh or abusive language. While the pastor's words may have been critical, the focus of the sentence is on the hypocrisy of his moral judgments, not on their severity. Thus, Choice F more accurately captures the tone and meaning.

360 **Choice C is correct** because "impervious" means unable to be affected by or to allow something to pass through. This word fits the context of the sentence because it describes how women are not entirely immune to genetic disorders. In other words, they are not completely unaffected. However, the sentence clarifies that women are less likely than men to experience genetic issues, particularly in relation to X-linked diseases. **Choice E is correct** because "forestall" means to prevent or obstruct something from happening. This word fits the context of the sentence because it describes how women's genes produce clotting factors that prevent life-threatening bleeds. These genetic mechanisms help stop serious bleeding before it becomes dangerous.

Choice A is incorrect because "inclined" means having a tendency toward something. This does not fit the sentence, which discusses how women are affected by genetic disorders. Genetic disorders are not a matter of personal tendency or choice. The sentence emphasizes that women are not completely immune, making Choice C more appropriate. **Choice B is incorrect** because "intransigent" means unwilling to compromise or change one's views. This word does not apply here, as genetic disorders are not subject to personal opinion or negotiation. The sentence is about biological vulnerability, not attitudes or behaviors, so Choice C is the better fit. **Choice D is incorrect** because "mollify" means to calm or soothe someone's anger. This word does not describe the role of clotting factors in preventing serious bleeding. The clotting factors are not soothing anything; they are stopping a biological process. Therefore, Choice E is the most accurate option. **Choice F is incorrect** because "engender" means to cause or give rise to something. This word implies that the clotting factors would initiate bleeding, which is the opposite of their function. The sentence makes it clear that these factors prevent life-threatening bleeds, making Choice E the best choice.

361 **Choice A is correct** because "osmose" refers to diffusion, or the movement of substances—often fluids—through a membrane. This fits the context of the sentence, which describes how single-celled organisms absorb nutrients directly from their environment. In contrast with multi-celled organisms, which must break substances down, single-celled organisms rely on the simple transfer of nutrients through their membranes. **Choice E is correct** because "deliquesce" means to dissolve into a liquid state. This word fits the sentence because it describes how the digestive system in multi-celled organisms transforms food into a liquid form to extract nutrients. In essence, digestion involves breaking food down into a liquid, processable state—making deliquesce the most accurate choice.

Choice B is incorrect because "exude" means to ooze or steadily discharge. This does not fit the sentence because single-celled organisms absorb nutrients—they do not release or discharge them. The passage focuses on intake, not expulsion, so Choice A is the better fit. **Choice C is incorrect** because "cull" means to select or remove from a group. This term does not fit the context because the passage does not describe a selective process. Single-celled organisms do not actively choose nutrients; rather, nutrients diffuse into them directly, making Choice A the best option. **Choice D is incorrect** because "flux" means flow or movement. While related to fluids, it does not capture the transformation process described in the sentence. The passage is about how food is broken down into a liquid for digestion—not simply how it moves—so Choice E is more precise. **Choice F is incorrect** because "coagulate" means to change into a solid or semi-solid state. This is the opposite of what the sentence describes. In digestion, food is transformed into a liquid state to aid in nutrient absorption, making Choice E the correct choice.

362 **Choice C is correct** because "indigenous" means originating naturally in a particular place. This word fits the context of the sentence because it accurately describes the plants and animals that are at risk. The sentence explains that invasive species—those that do not naturally occur in a place—threaten plants and animals that are indigenous, as invasive species can prey on them and compete for necessary resources. **Choice D is correct** because "deleterious" means unexpectedly harmful. This word fits the context because it accurately describes the emerald ash borer. The passage explains that the emerald ash borer has caused significant environmental damage by rapidly spreading across the nation and killing all varieties of ash trees.

Choice A is incorrect because "inveterate" means long established and unlikely to change. This does not fit the context since the sentence is not discussing the habits of the plants and animals but rather their natural presence in an environment. The passage emphasizes that invasive species threaten plants and animals that are indigenous. Therefore, Choice C is the best option. **Choice B** is incorrect because "pugnacious" means quick to argue or combative. This does not fit because the passage is not referring to the behavior of plants and animals in terms of aggressiveness or quarrelsomeness. Instead, it focuses on the threat invasive species pose to indigenous organisms. Thus, Choice C remains the best choice. **Choice E** is incorrect because "covert" means hidden or not openly displayed. This does not fit the sentence since the emerald ash borer's impact has been very visible and widespread, not hidden. The passage clearly states the extensive damage caused by this pest, making Choice D the better option. **Choice F** is incorrect because "perfidious" means deceitful or untrustworthy. This is not appropriate in this context because the passage is about environmental harm, not deception. The damage caused by the emerald ash borer has been obvious and devastating, which supports Choice D as the best answer.

363 **Choice A is correct** because "derided" means to ridicule or laugh at someone or something. This word fits the context of the sentence as it describes the action Gary's peers took according to the passage. The text explains that others reprimanded Gary for watching television, saying it was a waste and that it rotted his brain. Therefore, Gary's peers ridiculed him for watching television. **Choice E is correct** because "duplicity" means contradictory, two-faced, or dishonest behavior. This word fits the context because it describes how Gary's peers behaved in relation to television according to the passage. Although they ridicule Gary for watching television, Gary knew that people also watched television despite denying it in public. In other words, those ridiculing Gary behaved differently at home than in the presence of others.

Choice B is incorrect because "bolstered" means to provide support to something. This word does not fit the context as the others in the passage did not support television; instead, they criticized both television and Gary for watching it. Therefore, Choice A is the best option. **Choice C** is incorrect because "protracted" means lasting longer than expected. This word does not fit the context because it does not describe what others did regarding television in the passage. **Choice D** is incorrect because "equanimity" means mental calmness and composure. This does not fit the context since the passage does not describe Gary's peers as calm or composed. Rather, they ridiculed Gary for watching television, making Choice E the better option. **Choice F** is incorrect because "sublimity" means being extremely good or enjoyable. This does not fit the context as the passage does not indicate Gary's peers were extremely good or enjoyable. Instead, it explains that although they ridiculed Gary, they themselves watched television secretly. Therefore, Choice E is the best option.

364 **Choice C is correct** because "harbinger" means something that foreshadows a future event or signals the approach of another. This word fits the context of the sentence as it describes how folklore interprets a green sky in relation to tornadoes. In other words, folklore suggests that a green sky precedes a tornado, indicating its arrival, although this idea lacks scientific support. **Choice F is correct** because "corroboration" means evidence that supports or confirms a theory or statement. This word fits the context of the sentence because it describes what is needed from eyewitnesses in order to predict a tornado. Simply seeing a green sky is not sufficient; eyewitness confirmation is needed to verify that there are true signs.

Choice A is incorrect because "propagation" means increasing through breeding or spreading something widely. This word does not fit the context because it does not accurately describe the relationship between folklore about green skies and tornadoes. Folklore about green skies is not aiming to spread tornadoes, as nothing in the passage suggests tornadoes are multiplying or covering more ground. Rather, it aims to predict when tornadoes will occur. Therefore, Choice C is the best option. **Choice B is incorrect** because "incursion" means a raid or sudden invasion. This word does not fit the context because it does not accurately describe the relationship between green skies and tornadoes. Tornadoes are not being invaded or attacked by folklore, which would not make sense. Rather, folklore about green skies aims to predict when tornadoes will occur. Therefore, Choice C is the best option. **Choice D is incorrect** because "reciprocity" means mutual dependence or exchanging of things so both parties benefit. This word does not fit the context because it does not describe what is needed from eyewitnesses to predict a tornado. Nothing is being exchanged to or from eyewitnesses. Rather, eyewitnesses are needed to confirm signs of possible oncoming tornadoes. **Choice E is incorrect** because "approbation" means approval or praise. This word does not fit the context because it does not describe what is needed from eyewitnesses to predict a tornado. Nothing in the passage discusses praise or approval of tornadoes or their prediction methods. Rather, the sentence expresses that eyewitness support is needed to confirm signs of possible oncoming tornadoes.

365 **Choice A is correct** because "pellucid" means translucently clear or easily understood. This word fits the context of the sentence because it describes the waters of the Mediterranean, according to the rest of the passage. The passage describes these waters as charming, and water can certainly be described as clear. **Choice E is correct** because "august" means respected and impressive. This word fits the context of the sentence because it describes the Parthenon, according to the rest of the passage. The passage describes the Parthenon as the highlight of the trip due to its grandiosity. Therefore, this monument was respected and impressive.

Choice B is incorrect because "turbid" means cloudy, thick, and obscure. This word does not fit the context of the sentence because it does not describe the waters of the Mediterranean according to the rest of the passage. The passage describes these waters as charming and indicates they were worthy of viewing. If these waters were cloudy and thick, it is unlikely the passage would describe them this way. **Choice C is incorrect** because "quiescent" means in a state of inactivity or dormancy. This word does not fit the context of the sentence because it does not accurately describe the waters of the Mediterranean according to the rest of the passage. The passage does not suggest that the waters are still or inactive in any way.

Rather, the passage expresses that they are charming and worthy of visiting. Therefore, Choice A is the best option. **Choice D is incorrect** because "portentous" means overly serious in an attempt to be important. This word does not fit the context of the sentence because it does not accurately describe the Parthenon according to the rest of the passage. The passage describes the Parthenon as the highlight of the trip, grand, and a stunning relic of ancient times. Therefore, it can be assumed that the author does not feel it is attempting to be important, but that it truly is a cherished monument. **Choice F is incorrect** because "irrevocable" means not able to be changed or reversed. This word does not fit the context of the sentence because it does not accurately describe the Parthenon according to the rest of the passage. The passage does not express anything relating to making changes to the Parthenon or undoing aspects of it. Rather, the passage discusses the grandeur of this ancient relic. Therefore, Choice E is the best option.

366 **Choice A is correct** because "cliché" means a thought that is overused and lacks original perspective. This word fits the context of the sentence because it describes how Howard feels about the story of the musician who trades integrity for money. In other words, this storyline may be overused, but it still felt original to him. **Choice F is correct** because "appalling" means horrific and causing shock. This word fits the context of the sentence because it describes the nature of the prices loyal fans would have to pay if the musician signed the contract. In other words, loyal fans would have to pay terribly high and shocking prices because of a recording contract that ultimately stripped the musician of his dignity.

Choice B is incorrect because "facetious" means treating serious issues with inappropriate humor. This word does not fit the context of the sentence because it does not accurately describe how Howard feels about the story. The story is not humorous and does not appear to use jokes when handling serious situations. Rather, the storyline contrasts with the newness Howard felt toward it, so Choice A is the best option. **Choice C is incorrect** because "metaphorical" means figurative or used symbolically. This word does not fit the context of the sentence because it does not accurately describe how Howard feels about the story. The passage does not indicate that the story is not literal in any way. **Choice D is incorrect** because "inconsequential" means insignificant. This word does not fit the context of the sentence because it does not accurately describe the nature of the prices loyal fans would have to pay if the musician signed the contract. The remainder of the passage suggests the contract would have many negative effects (all but the guaranteed fame). Therefore, it is unlikely the price changes for loyal fans would be unimportant. Rather, it can be assumed the prices would be drastically higher, making Choice F the best option. **Choice E is incorrect** because "judicious" means using sound decision-making skills. This word does not fit the context of the sentence because it does not accurately describe the nature of the prices loyal fans would have to pay if the musician signed the contract. Prices cannot make decisions or show sound judgment because they are inanimate. Rather, it can be assumed that prices for loyal fans would be drastically higher along with all other negative effects mentioned, making Choice F the best option.

367 **Choice A is correct** because "unalloyed" means unmixed or pure. This word fits the context of the sentence because it accurately describes elements according to the rest of the passage. The passage explains that elements can't be broken down and have no components. Therefore, they are pure substances. **Choice D is correct** because "multifarious" means having many of various types. This word fits the context of the sentence because it describes the nature of the elements that come together to make a compound. The passage explains that compounds are composed of multiple elements that are sometimes unrelated. Therefore, these elements may come in many different types.

Choice B is incorrect because "adulterated" means poorer in quality because it is contaminated with other substances. This word does not fit the context of the sentence because it does not accurately describe elements according to the rest of the passage. The passage explains that elements can't be broken down and have no components. In other words, they are pure substances and are not contaminated. **Choice C** is incorrect because "veritable" means worthy of emphasis. This word does not fit the context of the sentence because it does not accurately describe elements according to the rest of the passage. The sentence is not aiming to emphasize the word "substance" or make it especially exciting that anything is a substance. Rather, the passage explains the substance by saying it can't be broken down and has no components. In other words, elements are pure. **Choice E** is incorrect because "homogenous" means of similar kind. This word does not fit the context of the sentence because it does not describe the nature of the elements that come together to make a compound. The passage explains that compounds are composed of multiple elements that are sometimes unrelated, not elements that are all of a similar kind. **Choice F** is incorrect because "conglomerate" means many different things gathered together to make a whole. This word does not fit the context of the sentence because it does not accurately describe the nature of the elements that form compounds. While many elements do gather together to make a compound, this sentence expresses that these elements are made up of multiple unrelated types. This makes Choice D the best option.

368 **Choice C is correct** because "ramifications" means consequences or results. This word fits in the context of the sentence because it labels the possible effects that can come from studying viruses according to the rest of the passage. The passage explains that studying viruses can impact the development of other diseases. Therefore, these impacts are consequences. **Choice D is correct** because "precipitate" means causing something undesirable to happen suddenly or prematurely. This word fits in the context of the sentence because it describes what can happen to the development of other diseases such as cancers. In other words, the diseases can progress more rapidly than they otherwise would have.

Choice A is incorrect because "proscriptions" means forbidding or banning something. This word does not fit in the context of the sentence because it does not accurately label the possible effects that can come from studying viruses according to the rest of the passage. The passage does not discuss forbidding or banning anything. Rather, it explains that studying viruses can have consequences for other areas of medicine, making Choice C the best option. **Choice B** is incorrect because "exigencies" means urgent needs or demands. This word does not fit in the context of the sentence because it does not accurately label the possible effects that can come from studying viruses according to the rest of the passage. The passage does not discuss any immediate needs or emergencies. Rather, the passage explains how studying viruses can have consequences for other areas of medicine, making Choice C the best option. **Choice E** is incorrect because "attenuate" means reducing the force or effect of something. This word does not fit in the context of the sentence because it does not accurately describe what can happen to the development of other diseases. The sentence is not claiming that studying viruses can make other diseases less forceful or impactful. Rather, the passage explains that the diseases can progress more rapidly than they otherwise would have. **Choice F** is incorrect because "truncate" means shortening the duration or extent of something. This word does not fit in the context of the sentence because it does not accurately describe what can happen to the development of other diseases. The sentence is not claiming that studying viruses can make other diseases last for a shorter duration. Rather, the passage explains that the diseases can progress more rapidly than they otherwise would have.

369 **Choice C is correct** because "impairment" means an aspect that is weakened or damaged. This word fits in the context of the sentence because it describes the effect on vision that diabetes can have on the body according to the rest of the passage. The text explains that insufficient insulin production causes many physiological issues and lists several negative effects. Therefore, it can be assumed that vision is also weakened or damaged. **Choice D is correct** because "pervasive" means spreading widely.

This word fits in the context of the sentence because it describes how prevalent diabetes is in the U.S. In other words, since the passage states the second most common cause of blindness in the United States is diabetes, it can be concluded that this condition is widespread across the nation.

Choice A is incorrect because "diminishing" means becoming less impressive or valuable. This word does not fit in the context of the sentence because the other items in the list are stated as nouns, and this word is a verb. Also, it does not accurately describe the effect on vision according to the rest of the passage. Vision is not just less impressive when insulin production is insufficient; it is weakened or damaged. Therefore, Choice C is the better option. **Choice B** is incorrect because "stagnation" means the state of not flowing or moving. This word does not fit in the context of the sentence because it does not accurately describe the effect on vision according to the rest of the passage. Vision does not flow to begin with, so discussing stagnation is irrelevant. Rather, vision can be weakened or damaged, making Choice C the best option. **Choice E** is incorrect because "circumscribed" means to restrict within limits. This word does not fit in the context of the sentence because it does not describe the prevalence of diabetes in the U.S. according to the rest of the passage. The passage states the second most common cause of blindness in the United States is diabetes, so it can be concluded that this condition is widespread across the nation. The condition is not restricted or limited. **Choice F** is incorrect because "capacious" means having a lot of space inside. This word does not fit in the context of the sentence because it does not describe the prevalence of diabetes in the U.S. according to the rest of the passage. The passage states the second most common cause of blindness in the United States is diabetes, so it can be concluded that this condition is widespread across the nation, not that it is roomy. Also, it does not make sense for a condition to be roomy inside since it is not a tangible item.

370 **Choice C is correct** because "cadre" means a small group with very particular training. This word fits in the context of the sentence because it accurately describes the glands that make up the endocrine system. The glands join together as a group to complete specific tasks. **Choice E is correct** because "secrete" means producing or discharging a substance. This word fits in the context of the sentence because it describes the action that takes place with the hormones and the bloodstream. In other words, the endocrine system works by the glands discharging hormones into the bloodstream.

Choice A is incorrect because "force" means a strength, energy, or compulsion. This word does not fit in the context of the sentence because it does not accurately describe the glands that make up the endocrine system. They are not described as a strength or force, but are joined together in a group to carry out a specific purpose. Therefore, Choice C is the best option. **Choice B** is incorrect because "crux" means the most important point of an issue. This word does not fit in the context of the sentence because it does not accurately describe the glands that make up the endocrine system. There is no issue being discussed, and it would not make sense to describe glands using this word. Rather, the sentence is explaining that glands are joined together in a group to carry out a specific purpose, making Choice C the best option. **Choice D** is incorrect because "disperse" means to distribute or spread over a wide area. This word does not fit in the context of the sentence because it does not accurately describe the action that takes place with the hormones and the bloodstream. Hormones are not being spread over a wide area; rather, they are being discharged into a specific place. Therefore, Choice E is the best option. **Choice F** is incorrect because "beget" means to give rise to or bring about. This word does not fit in the context of the sentence because it does not accurately describe the action that takes place with the hormones and the bloodstream. Hormones are not being created by the glands; rather, they are being discharged into the bloodstream. Therefore, Choice E is the best option.

371 **Choice C is correct** because "inverse" means opposite in position. This word fits in the context of the sentence because it describes the nature of the relationship being explained throughout the remainder of the passage. The text explains that in this particular type of relationship, one variable increases while the other does the opposite, or decreases. Increasing and decreasing are inverse of one another. **Choice D is correct** because "familiar" means known from association. This word fits in the context of the sentence because it describes the example presented in the second half of the passage. The text discusses heating water, which is something that most people have experienced or associated with. Therefore, this example is both familiar and obvious.

Choice A is incorrect because "contradictory" means inconsistent or mutually opposed. This word does not fit in the context of the sentence because it does not describe the nature of the relationship being explained throughout the remainder of the passage. The text explains that in this particular type of relationship, one variable increases while the other does the opposite, or decreases. The text does not indicate that these relationships are inconsistent or undermine themselves in any way. **Choice B** is incorrect because "conforming" means complying with rules, standards, or laws. This word does not fit in the context of the sentence because it does not describe the nature of the relationship being explained throughout the remainder of the passage. The text explains that in this particular type of relationship, one variable increases while the other does the opposite, or decreases. This could metaphorically be considered the opposite of conforming with one another. The text does not indicate that they are complying with any rules or laws, as no rules or laws are even mentioned in the passage. **Choice E is incorrect** because "proverbial" means commonly known or spoken of. This word does not fit in the context of the sentence because it does not describe the example presented in the second half of the passage. The text discusses heating water, which is something most people have experienced or associated with but is not necessarily something discussed regularly. Therefore, this example is familiar but not stereotypical, making Choice D the best option. **Choice F is incorrect** because "mundane" means dull and lacking excitement. This word does not fit in the context of the sentence because it does not describe the example presented in the second half of the passage. The text discusses heating water, which is something most people have experienced or associated with, but it is not necessarily boring or dull. Therefore, this example is better described as familiar.

372 **Choice B is correct** because "inhospitable" means harsh and difficult to live in. This word fits in the context of the sentence because it describes how South Dakota seems in terms of living conditions. In other words, because of its desolate landscapes and small population, it appears to be a harsh environment to live in. **Choice D is correct** because "foil" means preventing something from succeeding. This word fits in the context of the sentence because it describes how the high taxes of eastern states can ruin businesses. This contrasts with the low taxes of South Dakota, which means businesses there are more likely to succeed.

Choice A is incorrect because "morbid" means disturbing, unpleasant, and often related to death. This word does not fit in the context of the sentence because it does not accurately describe how South Dakota seems in terms of living conditions. The passage describes South Dakota as having desolate landscapes and a small population. While these may be difficult to live with, they are not disturbing or related to death. Therefore, Choice B is the better option. **Choice C is incorrect** because "germane" means pertinent or relevant to a subject being considered. This word does not fit in the context of the sentence because it does not accurately describe how South Dakota seems in terms of living conditions. The passage describes South Dakota as having desolate landscapes and a small population. It does not make sense to describe South Dakota as relevant, since no other topic is being discussed for it to relate to. Rather, the living conditions could be described as difficult, making Choice B the best option. **Choice E is incorrect** because "obviate" means to avoid a difficulty. This word does not fit in the context of the sentence because it does not accurately describe the way the high taxes of eastern states impact businesses. These states with high taxes are not avoiding difficulties; instead, they are destroying and preventing businesses from succeeding. Therefore, Choice D is the best option. **Choice F is incorrect** because "lampoon" means to publicly ridicule using harsh satire. This word does not fit in the context of the sentence because it does not accurately describe how the high taxes of eastern states impact businesses. These states are not ridiculing business ventures; rather, they are preventing their success. Therefore, Choice D is the best option.

373 **Choice A is correct** because "mundane" means dull or lacking excitement. This word fits in the context of the sentence because it describes the nature of the beginnings of many successful companies. In other words, many strong companies can have very boring starts. This is illustrated by the example given about Sony's first product. **Choice D is correct** because "tenacity" means very determined. This word fits in the context of the sentence because it describes one of the most important values of a successful company according to the rest of the passage. The text explains that determination is equally important as vision when starting a company, as shown by the fact that the successful technology company Sony originally started with a rice cooker.

Choice B is incorrect because "frugal" means careful in the use of money or resources. This word does not fit in the context of the sentence because it does not accurately describe the nature of the beginnings of many successful companies according to the passage. The text explains that strong companies often have humble starts and gives the example of Sony originally selling a rice cooker. The passage does not discuss spending habits. Therefore, it aims to explain that simplicity is often a characteristic of successful business beginnings, not frugality. **Choice C is incorrect** because "bogus" means not genuine. This word does not fit in the context of the sentence because it does not accurately describe the beginnings of many successful companies according to the passage. The text explains that strong companies often have humble starts and cites Sony's first product. The passage does not imply companies are fake or false. Thus, simplicity, not fakeness, is the key idea. **Choice E is incorrect** because "presumption" means an idea taken as true without certainty. This word does not fit in the context of the sentence because it does not describe one of the values of a successful company according to the passage. The text does not suggest that companies act on assumptions. Instead, it explains that determination is as important as vision in starting a company. **Choice F is incorrect** because "sophistry" means reasoning that seems plausible but is actually unsound. This word does not fit in the context of the sentence because it does not describe one of the values of a successful company according to the passage. The text does not imply companies present false arguments. Rather, it explains that determination is crucial, as demonstrated by Sony's humble beginnings.

374 **Choice A is correct** because "superfluous" means unnecessarily excessive. This word fits in the context of the sentence because it describes the way vestigial structures appear in modern human bodies. The passage explains that, although these structures seem unnecessary now, they once served an important purpose in ancient organisms. **Choice E is correct** because "formidable" means inspiring fear through impressive largeness. This word fits in the context of the sentence because it describes how animals appeared to predators when their fur stood out straight instead of lying flat. In other words, ancient organisms looked more dangerous and intimidating to potential threats:

Choice B is incorrect because "apocryphal" means something circulated as true but of doubtful authenticity. This word does not fit in the context of the sentence because it does not accurately describe vestigial structures in modern humans. Structures like the appendix are not myths or doubtful; they are real body parts that no longer serve the same function they once did. **Choice C is incorrect** because "exiguous" means very small. This word does not fit in the context of the sentence because vestigial structures vary in size and shape and are not all very small. The key idea is that these structures no longer serve their original purpose, not that they are small. **Choice D is incorrect** because "impassive" means not feeling or showing emotion. This word does not fit the context because the feature of fur standing out straight was meant to intimidate predators, not to appear unemotional or indifferent. **Choice F is incorrect** because "obsequious" means showing excessive attentiveness and obedience. This word does not fit the context because the fur standing out was not intended to make animals appear obedient, but rather to make them look more threatening to predators.

375 **Choice A is correct** because "flippant" means a failure to show a serious and respectful attitude. This word fits the context of the sentence because it describes the girl's sense of humor in the passage. The text expresses that her humor involved an inability to speak seriously and was sometimes repelling to those who did not know her. Therefore, it can be assumed that her sense of humor was disrespectful and she was not often serious. **Choice D is correct** because "jocular" means characterized by joking and playfulness. This word fits the context of the sentence because it describes the nature of the remarks the girl was endlessly making. In other words, the others listening were entertained by her lack of seriousness.

Choice B is incorrect because "raucous" means a disturbingly harsh noise. This word does not fit the context because it does not accurately describe the girl's sense of humor. The passage does not express that she is very loud or noisy. Rather, it emphasizes that her humor lacks seriousness and can be repelling. Therefore, Choice A is better. **Choice C is incorrect** because "erudite" means having or showing great knowledge. This word does not fit the context because the passage does not suggest she is particularly knowledgeable. Rather, her humor is described as lacking seriousness and sometimes repelling. Therefore, Choice A is better. **Choice E is incorrect** because "iconoclastic" means attacking cherished beliefs or institutions. This word does not fit because the girl's remarks, though sometimes repelling, are better described as flippant—entertaining but not necessarily attacking anything. **Choice F is incorrect** because "equivocal" means ambiguous or open to multiple interpretations. This word does not fit because the text does not suggest the girl was unclear when she spoke. Instead, her humor was entertaining but sometimes repelling, fitting better with Choice D.

376 **Choice C is correct** because "indiscernible" means very difficult to see clearly. This word fits the context of the sentence because it describes the nature of the differences in the way men and women use language according to the rest of the passage. In other words, to the casual listener, these differences are hard to distinguish. However, studies show that there are differences, such as the example provided about compliments. **Choice E is correct** because "brazen" means bold and shameless. This word fits the context of the sentence because it describes the way romantically assertive women can be condemned by cultural attitudes. In other words, women may be less likely to compliment men because they do not want to appear bold and shameless in pursuing romance so as to avoid criticism.

Choice A is incorrect because "pertinent" means applicable to a certain matter. This word does not fit the context of the sentence because it does not accurately describe the nature of the differences in the way men and women use language. These differences are not applicable to anything, as there is no other topic being discussed. Rather, these differences are hard to distinguish for a casual listener despite the fact that studies do reveal their existence. **Choice B is incorrect** because "blatant" means done openly and unashamedly. This word does not fit the context of the sentence because it does not accurately describe the nature of the differences in the way men and women use language. These differences are not open and unashamed, but hard to distinguish. These differences are challenging to notice for a casual listener despite the fact that studies do reveal their existence. **Choice D is incorrect** because "garish" means offensively bright and showy. This word does not fit the context of the sentence because it does not accurately describe the way romantically assertive women can be condemned by cultural attitudes. Women are not condemned as being too bright or vivid for being romantically assertive, as their color and clothing do not change. Rather, they may be condemned as being too bold in their pursuit of romance, making Choice E the best option. **Choice F is incorrect** because "capricious" means impulsive, unpredictable, and inconsistent. This word does not fit the context of the sentence because it does not accurately describe the way romantically assertive women can be condemned by cultural attitudes. Women are not necessarily condemned as being impulsive for being romantically assertive or giving a compliment, as this can be done with much thought or in a predictable manner. Rather, they may be condemned as being too bold in their pursuit of romance, making Choice E the best option.

377 **Choice B is correct** because "lithe" means thin, supple, and graceful. This word fits the context of the sentence because it describes the nature of a gazelle's body, since gazelles are often thought of as slender and elegant creatures. This is supported by the following statement that relates gazelles with ballet performers and calls them graceful creatures. **Choice D is correct** because "associate" means connecting one thing with something else. This word fits the context of the sentence because it describes the relation between ballet performers and gazelles. Both ballet performers and gazelles are considered graceful, slender, and elegant. Therefore, these two things are likely to be associated with one another.

Choice A is incorrect because "erratic" means moving unpredictably and with no pattern. This word does not fit the context of the sentence because it does not accurately describe gazelles according to the rest of the passage. The text explains that gazelles are fast, graceful, and related to ballet performers. Therefore, it can be assumed that they do not move randomly or impulsively, but in an elegant way. So, Choice B is the better option. **Choice C is incorrect** because "diaphanous" means light, delicate, and translucent. This word does not fit the context of the sentence because it does not accurately describe gazelles according to the rest of the passage. The text does not mention anything about gazelles being fragile or people being able to see through them. Rather, the text explains that gazelles are fast, graceful, and related to ballet performers. Therefore, Choice B is the better option. **Choice E is incorrect** because "trivialize" means making something less important or complex than it really is. This word does not fit the context of the sentence because it does not accurately describe what people do in relation to gazelles and ballet performers. The text does not indicate that people make ballet performers seem less important. Rather, it suggests that people relate ballet performers to gazelles because of their similarities in the way they move. Therefore, Choice D is the better option. **Choice F is incorrect** because "defer" means postpone or suspend. This word does not fit the context of the sentence because it does not accurately describe what people do in relation to gazelles and ballet performers. The text does not indicate that people make ballet performers do anything later. Rather, it suggests that people relate ballet performers to gazelles because of their similarities in the way they move. Therefore, Choice D is the better option.

378 **Choice A is correct** because "hurtle" means to move rapidly and forcefully. This word fits the context of the sentence because it describes the action that hunks of rock go through to be seen as shooting stars. In other words, the passage explains that rocks are forced through space at a high speed, then burn up in the Earth's atmosphere, leaving behind a streak that appears as a shooting star. **Choice E is correct** because "extirpated" means to extinguish or destroy completely. This word fits the context of the sentence because it describes the pieces of meteors being discussed. The passage explains that some meteors leave behind meteorites which then fall to the ground. Therefore, it can be assumed that meteorites are pieces of meteors left behind after the rest of the meteor has been destroyed.

Choice B is incorrect because "waft" means to float or pass gently through the air. This word does not fit the context of the sentence because it does not accurately describe the action that hunks of rock go through to be seen as shooting stars. The passage does not describe meteorites as simply drifting through the air. Rather, they move rapidly through space and fall to the ground after breaking off from a larger meteor. Their movement is better described as rapid and forceful, making Choice A the better option. **Choice C is incorrect** because "droll" means having a curious or funny quality. This word can be used as an adjective or noun, but not as a verb, as the blank requires. Additionally, it does not describe the action of hunks of rock moving through space. The passage does not imply that meteorites have any humorous qualities. Therefore, Choice A is the better option. **Choice D is incorrect** because "collated" means collected, arranged, or assembled. This word does not fit the context of the sentence because it does not describe the pieces of meteors being discussed. The passage does not say that meteors are collected or organized. Rather, it explains that some meteors leave behind meteorites which fall to the ground. Thus, Choice E is the better option. **Choice F is incorrect** because "serrated" means saw-like or having jagged edges. This word does not fit the context of the sentence because it does not describe the pieces of meteors being discussed. The passage does not provide any physical description of meteorites. Therefore, Choice E is the better option.

379 **Choice A is correct** because "renowned" means famous and known by many people. This word fits the context of the sentence because it accurately describes the reputation of the first fully developed opera. The passage explains that the opera is credited for both its score and libretto, supporting the fact that it is well-known and respected. **Choice E is correct** because "poignant" means

evoking sadness or regret. This word fits the context of the sentence because it accurately describes the tale of Orpheus's journey according to the passage. In other words, his journey to the underworld to restore his beloved to life is emotional and serious.

Choice B is incorrect because "incongruous" means not in harmony with its surroundings. This word does not fit the context of the sentence because it does not accurately describe the reputation of the opera. Nothing in the passage suggests that the opera is out of harmony with other performances or with itself. Instead, the text emphasizes the opera's impressive composition and status as the first fully developed opera, making Choice A the better option. **Choice C is incorrect** because "unscathed" means without damage or injury. This word does not fit the context of the sentence because it does not describe the reputation of the opera. The passage does not mention the opera being harmed or in danger. Rather, it highlights the opera's impressive achievements, making Choice A the best option. **Choice D is incorrect** because "droll" means humorous and unusual. This word does not fit the context of the sentence because it does not describe the tale of Orpheus's journey. The passage explains that this tale involves a serious trip to the underworld to restore his beloved, which is emotional rather than funny. Therefore, Choice E is the better option. **Choice F is incorrect** because "maudlin" means drunkenly emotional and silly. This word does not fit the context of the sentence because it does not accurately describe the tale of Orpheus's journey. The passage indicates the tale is serious and sad, not overly sentimental or silly. Therefore, Choice E is the best opt

380 **Choice B is correct** because "cupidity" means greed for money and possessions. This word fits the context of the sentence because it accurately describes the legendary wealth of the dictator mentioned in the passage. The text explains that the dictator had great wealth, including huge mansions and luxury goods. Therefore, it can be assumed that he had a strong desire for material belongings. **Choice E is correct** because "surfeit" means an excessive amount of something. This word fits the context of the sentence because it accurately describes the quantity of luxury goods that the dictator possessed according to the passage. The text states he was extremely wealthy and owned huge mansions, which implies he also had an excessive amount of luxury goods.

Choice A is incorrect because "prowess" means expertise in a particular area. This word does not fit the context of the sentence because it does not describe the dictator's legendary wealth. The passage does not suggest that the dictator was an expert in anything; rather, it highlights his great wealth. Therefore, Choice B is the better option. **Choice C is incorrect** because "prudishness" means being overly concerned with morals and offended by rude things. This word does not fit the context because the passage does not indicate the dictator was morally offended or concerned. Instead, it focuses on his great wealth, making Choice B the better option. **Choice D is incorrect** because "paucity" means a small quantity of something. This word does not fit the context because the passage emphasizes the dictator's extreme wealth, not a lack of luxury goods. It can be assumed he had many luxury goods, so Choice E is the better option. **Choice F is incorrect** because "postulate" means to assume something as true without proof. This word does not fit the context because the passage does not discuss any assumptions or beliefs about the dictator's possessions. It clearly states he was extremely wealthy, implying an abundance of luxury goods, making Choice E the best option.

381 **Choice C is correct** because "espousing" means to adopt or become attached to a way of life. This word fits the context of the sentence as it describes what the Medieval European rulers tried to do to legitimize their rule. The passage explains that there were only tenuous, or weak, ties between their rule and that of the ancient Roman Empire. However, they forced a connection by adopting the related title of "Holy Roman Emperor." In other words, the connection between the two empires was a forced attachment. **Choice E is correct** because "grandiose" means excessively impressive in appearance. This word fits the context because it describes the nature of the title "Holy Roman Emperor," which the German emperor adopted. Using this title was a flashy way of forcing a connection to the ancient Roman Empire, with the goal of making their rule appear more legitimate.

Choice A is incorrect because "rending" means tearing something into pieces. This word does not fit the context because the passage does not suggest that anything was torn apart. Rather, it explains there were weak ties with the ancient Roman Empire, but a connection was forced. Therefore, Choice C is the best option. **Choice B is incorrect** because "alleviating" means to make something less severe. This word does not fit the context because the passage does not express that the rulers tried to reduce suffering. Instead, it describes how they forced a connection to legitimize their rule. Therefore, Choice C is the best option. **Choice D is incorrect** because "ludicrous" means foolish and unreasonable to the point of amusement. This word does not fit the context because the title "Holy Roman Emperor" is not depicted as foolish or funny. Rather, it is showy to legitimize their rule and make it appear impressive. **Choice F is incorrect** because "gregarious" means sociable and fond of company. This word does not fit the context because the title "Holy Roman Emperor" is not a sociable entity. Rather, it is described as showy and meant to make the rule appear

382 **Choice C is correct** because "vociferous" means insistent complaining and loud voicing of opinions. This word fits the context of the sentence as it describes the nature of the people's objections according to the passage. The text explains that the people widely opposed the law and criticized the governor for signing it into existence. Therefore, it can be assumed that their objections were persistent and forcefully expressed. **Choice D is correct** because "unpalatable" means difficult to tolerate or accept. This word fits the context because it accurately describes how the governor described the laws in the short term. The sentence structure suggests that this word contrasts with the fact that the laws were ultimately necessary. Thus, the laws were described as challenging to accept initially, though needed in the long term.

Choice A is incorrect because "bombastic" means something that sounds important but actually has little meaning. This word does not fit the context because it does not accurately describe the nature of the people's objections. The passage does not suggest the objections are pompous or meaningless. Rather, the objections are widespread and serious. Therefore, the complaints are likely insistent and opinionated, making Choice C the best option. **Choice B** is incorrect because "moribund" means in terminal decline. This word does not fit the context because it does not accurately describe the people's objections. The passage does not suggest the objections are fading away; instead, they are widespread and vocal. Therefore, Choice C remains the best option. **Choice E** is incorrect because "imminent" means something about to happen. This word does not fit the context because it does not accurately describe how the governor portrayed the laws. The sentence implies a contrast between short-term difficulty and long-term necessity, and imminence is not an opposite or contrast to necessity. **Choice F** is incorrect because "execrable" means extremely bad or unpleasant. This word does not fit the context because the governor supports the laws and is unlikely to describe them in such a strongly negative way. Instead, he would characterize them as difficult but necessary, making Choice D

383 **Choice A is correct** because "encumbrance" means a burden or impediment. This word fits the context of the sentence because it describes the obstacle meteorologists now face according to the passage. The text explains that, because of rising environmental concerns, meteorologists have been forced to provide political insight on the topic without having any background or training in navigating politics. Therefore, this acts as a challenge for meteorologists. **Choice D is correct** because "reticent" means not revealing one's thoughts or feelings easily. This word fits the context of the sentence because it describes the demeanor of meteorologists based on the passage. The text suggests that meteorologists have had to adapt and accept this change in the requirements of their position.

Nothing in the text suggests that meteorologists have complained or resisted despite being suddenly thrust into politics.

Choice B is incorrect because "auspices" means guidance, support, or prophecy. This word does not fit the context because it does not describe the obstacle meteorologists face according to the passage. The text does not suggest any prophetic guidance was given to or by meteorologists. Rather, meteorologists face the challenge of providing political insight without training. Therefore, Choice A is the best option. **Choice C** is incorrect because "insight" means gaining an accurate and deep understanding. This word does not fit the context because it does not describe the obstacle meteorologists face. The text does not suggest that political discourse has given meteorologists a deeper understanding. Rather, they are challenged by having to provide political insight without relevant training. Therefore, Choice A is the best option. **Choice E** is incorrect because "ostentatious" means something done to seek attention. This word does not fit the context because it does not describe meteorologists' demeanor. The passage suggests that meteorologists have adapted and accepted the new demands, not that they sought attention. **Choice F** is incorrect because "conspiratorial" means relating to a secretive plan to do something unlawful. This word does not fit the context because it does not describe meteorologists' demeanor. The passage indicates meteorologists adapted without conspiracy or illegal intent.

384 **Choice A is correct** because "granules" are small particles. Since the sentence states that something tiny is moving to the tip of the tentacle, it would make sense for those tiny particles to be granules. **Choice E is correct** because "immobilize" means preventing something from moving, which would be what a predator would likely want to do to an animal of prey before eating it or, in this case, absorbing its cytoplasm.

Choice B is incorrect because "static" means something is lacking movement. Since the sentence explains that these tiny particles are moving to the tip of the tentacle, it would not make sense for "static" to be in the blank. **Choice C** is incorrect because "bulbs" are rounded storage organs, such as plating bulbs and lightbulbs. They are not typically tiny, which would make choice A the better option. **Choice D** is incorrect because "reinforce" means to strengthen or support. A predator would not likely want to reinforce its prey before eating it. Rather, it would want to immobilize the prey, making Choice E the better option. **Choice F** is incorrect because "emancipate" means to free. A predator would not want to free its prey but eat it. Therefore, this word would not make sense in the context of the sentence.

Practice Set 2: Answers & Explanations

385 **Choice B is correct** because "antagonistic" means feeling hostility or opposition toward someone or something. This word fits the context of the sentence because it accurately describes the factors impeding the growth of the field of physics according to the passage. The text explains that acceptance of new ideas is a challenge in physics, along with entrenched logic and petty careerism. Therefore, the growth of the field is likely being met with opposition or resistance. **Choice F is correct** because "inscience" means a lack of knowledge or awareness. This word fits the context of the sentence because it accurately describes the "just plain," or simple attitude that is prevalent in the field of physics that inhibits its growth. The passage explains that acceptance of new ideas is a challenge in physics, along with entrenched logic and petty careerism. A lack of knowledge and awareness fits on this list as it would also contribute to opposition to the growth of the field.

Choice A is incorrect because "correlated" means having a mutual relationship or connection. This word does not fit the context because it does not describe the factors impeding the growth of physics. The factors described are resisting the growth rather than being related to it. Choice B is a better option. **Choice C is incorrect** because "supplanted" means taking the place of something else. This word does not fit the context because the factors are not replacing growth but impeding it. Choice B is a better option. **Choice D is incorrect** because "eminence" means being important, superior, or respected. This word does not fit the context because it does not describe the simple attitude that inhibits growth. The passage discusses challenges to acceptance and resistance, not respect or prominence. **Choice E is incorrect** because "acquiescence" means a reluctant and passive agreement. This word does not fit the context because the passage does not describe physics as being passively accepted, but rather met with resistance and lack of awareness.

386 **Choice A is correct** because "dispassionate" means impartial and not influenced by strong emotion. This word fits the context of the sentence because it describes how we perceive our own judgments of others according to the passage. In other words, we consider our judgments to be objective and free of emotion, but in reality, they are influenced by many unconscious beliefs and biases. **Choice F is correct** because "jibe with" means to be in accord or agreement. This word fits the context of the sentence because it accurately describes how a person's physical appearance matches their intelligence and morality according to our expectations. The passage explains that we make judgments about people assuming that more attractive individuals will also have better intelligence or moral character.

Choice B is incorrect because "chary" means cautiously reluctant to do something. This word does not fit the context because it does not describe how we think of our own judgments. The passage suggests our judgments are biased yet seem unemotional, not hesitant or reluctant. There is no indication that we hesitate to judge. **Choice C is incorrect** because "momentous" means of great importance or significance. This word does not fit the context because it does not describe how we think of our judgments. The passage does not suggest we see our judgments as highly significant events, but rather as impartial. **Choice D is incorrect** because "ascribe to" means to attribute to a specific cause. This word does not fit the context because the passage does not say a person's appearance is caused by their intelligence or morality, but that it aligns or agrees with these traits. **Choice E is incorrect** because "purport to" means to pretend or claim falsely to be something. This word does not fit the context because the passage does not suggest that the appearance falsely claims to reflect intelligence or morality, but that it is perceived to agree with them.

387 **Choice C is correct** because "proscription" means forbidding or banning something. This word fits the context of the sentence because it describes the universal attitude and legality against murder. In other words, the fact that murder is forbidden is a universally accepted concept. **Choice D is correct** because "contentious" means causing an argument or controversy. This word fits the context of the sentence because it describes how murder is treated differently across belief systems. Although murder is universally forbidden, different cultures regard killing in unique ways, making it a controversial topic. This is supported by the example given regarding Buddhist teachings.

Choice A is incorrect because "litigation" means settling a dispute in a court of law. This word does not fit the context because it does not describe the universal attitude against murder. The text explains that murder is universally forbidden, not that legal processes are the same everywhere. **Choice B is incorrect** because "vituperation" means bitter and abusive language. This word does not fit the context because it does not describe the universal attitude against murder. The passage is about the prohibition of murder, not about the tone of language used against it. **Choice E is incorrect** because "fallacious" means based on a mistaken belief. This word does not fit the context because the text does not suggest that the concept of crime is based on mistaken views. Rather, it explains that killing is a controversial topic due to different cultural perspectives. **Choice F is incorrect** because "inclusive" means involving all parties or aspects. This word does not fit the context because the passage does not suggest that the definition of crime includes everyone or all aspects. Instead, it highlights the varying cultural perspectives on killing, making it contentious.

388 **Choices C and F are correct** because the passage aims to juxtapose Van Gogh's curious personal decisions with his significant contribution to the field of art. Given quixotic means "exceedingly idealistic and impractical" and transcendent means "exceptional or surpassing the ordinary" in this context, both serve to deliver the general message of the passage clearly and succinctly.

Choice A is incorrect because casual means "lacking a high degree of interest or devotion", which runs contrary to the considered rationale which was stated to be behind Van Gogh's actions. **Choice B** is incorrect because irrelevant means "not connected to something", which does not align with Van Gogh's stated motive in the passage. **Choice D** is incorrect because dubious means "suspect or not to be relied upon", which does not coincide with the "significant impact" Van Gogh is stated to have made. **Choice E** is incorrect because haggard means "looking exhausted or unwell", which fails to fit within the context of the passage.

389 **Choices A and D are correct** because the passage aims to describe the praise being bestowed by the highest ranking member of the company on all other members of the company, a praise which was generated through positive qualities of those lower ranked workers. Therefore, subordinates, which is defined as "those under the authority of others within an organization" along with gumption, defined as "shrewd and spirited initiative and resourcefulness" satisfy this aim of the passage.

Choice B is incorrect because serfs are defined as "[typically] medieval workers bound to work on plots of feudal land", which does not align with description or remit of a company in present day. **Choice C** is incorrect because while colleagues, defined as "coworkers in a profession, often of similar rank" might satisfy part of the passage, it does not account for the difference in worker rank later described in the passage. **Choice E** is incorrect because largesse means "laziness", which is antithetical to the meaning of the passage **Choice F** is incorrect because recalcitrance means "unwilling to obey rules or follow instructions", which does not align with the theme of the passage.

390 **Choices A and F are correct** because the sentence seeks to highlight the contrast in sentiment evoked from a bicycle ride compared to that of doing yard work. Given that ecstasy is defined "as an overwhelming feeling of happiness" and toil means "to work incessantly" they help to highlight this contrast at play.

Choice B is incorrect because fear is an "unpleasant emotion caused by the belief that something is a threat", which does not align with the sentiment of "carefree" stated in the earlier part of the passage with respect to the bicycle ride. **Choice C** is incorrect because courage is "strength in the face of pain or grief" in the context of the passage, and runs contrary to the "carefree" nature of the bicycle ride. **Choice D** is incorrect because exercise means "an activity which requires physical effort", which satisfies the basic structure of the clause, however, does not address the notion of a "pleasurable experience coming to an end" as well the word toil. **Choice E** is incorrect because frolic is "playful action or merriment", which does not align with the drab tone struck by the passage in describing an end to a pleasurable experience

391 **Choices C and D are correct** because the passage aims to highlight different degrees of impact the contributions of Newton in different fields of academia. Conceived, with a meaning of "formed or devised" and overshadow with a definition of "appearing more prominent or important than an alternative" serve to most effectively convey the key notion of the passage.

Choice A is incorrect because lambasted means to "harshly criticize", which does not fit with the structure of the passage. **Choice B** is incorrect because received in the context of the passage would mean "to consent to be given or presented with" which does not align with the overall aim of the passage. **Choice E** is incorrect because contrive mean to "bring about by deliberate use of skill and artifice", which does not align with the overall meaning of the passage. **Choice F** is incorrect because impede means "to hinder something", does not align with the overall meaning of the passage.

392 **Choices C and D are correct** because the passage aims to highlight the utility of Bunsen burners in reducing contamination of samples. The use of "sterilize", which means "to make something free of bacteria or other microorganisms" and "inoculating", which means "the introduction of pathogens or microorganisms into a body" allow the meaning of this passage to be most explicitly conveyed.

Choice A is incorrect because distribute means "to give shares of something", which does not effectively convey the meaning of the passage. **Choice B** is incorrect because limit means "a restriction or threshold beyond which something may not pass", which does not best convey the meaning of the passage. **Choice E** is incorrect because marinating "means to let sit and soak for an extended period of time", which does not align with the meaning of the passage. **Choice F** is incorrect because exhausting means either "to make tired" or "to have used up completely", which does not effectively convey the meaning of the passage.

393 **Choice C is correct** because "precarious" means uncertain or dangerously likely to fall. This word fits the context of the sentence because it describes the nature of the migration route monarch butterflies take according to the rest of the text. The sentence explains that this route is long and can take several months. It makes sense that the route is not necessarily easy or guaranteed. **Choice E is correct** because "origin" means the point where something is derived. This word fits the context of the sentence because it describes the position in North America where monarch butterflies begin their route of migration.

Choice A is incorrect because "vicarious" means experienced through imagination or the experience of another person. This word does not fit the context because it does not accurately describe the nature of the migration route of monarch butterflies. The passage does not suggest the butterflies are experiencing anything through others; they are actually migrating. **Choice B is incorrect** because "fractious" means irritable and quarrelsome. This word does not fit the context because it does not describe the nature of the migration route of monarch butterflies. The passage does not suggest the butterflies are moody or argumentative. **Choice D is incorrect** because "volition" means the power of using one's will. This word does not fit the context because it does not describe the position in North America where the butterflies begin their route. The passage focuses on the location as the starting point, not on the butterflies' willpower. **Choice F is incorrect** because "polarity" means having two opposite or contradictory aspects. This word does not fit the context because it does not describe the starting position of the butterflies in North America. The passage refers to various starting points, not poles or opposites.

394 **Choice B is correct** because "acumen" means the ability to make good judgments and quick decisions. This word fits in the context of the sentence because it describes the necessary skill set in managing finances when running a small business. In other words, small business owners should be able to make sound financial decisions quickly. **Choice E is correct** because "learned" means having much knowledge by study. This word fits in the context of the sentence because it describes being formally educated in accounting, which the passage suggests is important. The passage explains that if no formal education and training has been attained, someone should be hired.

Choice A is incorrect because "vitiate" means to spoil or impair the quality of something. This word does not fit in the context of the sentence because it does not accurately describe the necessary skill set for managing finances. The passage is not saying finances should be ruined by owners, but that good financial judgment is needed. **Choice C is incorrect** because "credence" means belief that something is true. This word does not fit in the context of the sentence because it does not accurately describe the necessary skill set for managing finances. The passage emphasizes good judgment, not just belief. **Choice D is incorrect** because "pliant" means flexible and easily influenced. This word does not fit the context because it does not describe being formally educated in accounting. The passage focuses on knowledge and training, not flexibility. **Choice F is incorrect** because "frenetic" means fast, energetic, and wild. This word does not fit the context because it does not describe being formally educated in accounting. The passage suggests the need for knowledgeable expertise, not wild energy.

395 **Choices B and D are correct** because the sentence aims to highlight MLK Jr.'s peaceful nature while also highlighting the rationale his killers used to perpetrate their murderous actions. Pacifism, which is "the belief that violence is untenable and that disputes should be settled through peaceful means" along with assassinated, which means "to murder a (usually important) person for political or religious means" most effectively conveys the meaning of the passage.

Choice A is incorrect because recidivism is "the likelihood of falling back into criminal habits after the ending of incarceration", which does not align with the theme of the passage. **Choice C is incorrect** because trepidation means "a feeling of fear or agitation", which does not align with the theme of the passage. **Choice E is incorrect** because promoted means "advanced or raised to a higher position or rank", which does not align with the overall context of the passage. **Choice F is incorrect** because conscripted means "compelled to enlist in an endeavor", which does not align with the theme of the passage.

396 **Choice B is correct** because "paradox" means something that is self-contradictory. This word fits in the context of the sentence because it describes the nature of Cyrano de Bergerac according to the rest of the passage. The text describes him as both having swagger and being deeply sympathetic and insecure. Since these two traits are not often displayed together, the character is seen as paradoxical. **Choice F is correct** because "bombastic" means something is given exaggerated importance. This word fits in the context of the sentence because it describes the words of the character Cyrano de Bergerac, who has a lot of swagger. In other words, his words seem more significant than they actually are.

Choice A is incorrect because "archetype" means a typical example of something. This word does not fit in the context of the sentence because it does not describe the unique nature of the character. The text does not express that Cyrano is typical or overused. Rather, it describes him as both having swagger and being deeply sympathetic and insecure—traits that are rarely seen together. This makes him paradoxical, not archetypal. **Choice C is incorrect** because "cliché" means something that is overused and lacks original thought. This word does not fit the context because the passage does not suggest that Cyrano is typical or unoriginal. Instead, it highlights the unusual combination of traits—swagger and deep insecurity—that make the character paradoxical. **Choice D is incorrect** because "licentious" means promiscuous and unprincipled in sexual matters. This word does not fit the context because it does not describe Cyrano's way of speaking. The passage does not imply he is vulgar or sexually assertive. Rather, it suggests his speech is exaggerated and self-important—more fittingly described as bombastic. **Choice E is incorrect** because "iconoclastic" means attacking cherished beliefs or institutions. This word does not fit the context because it does not describe Cyrano's speech. The passage does not suggest he is attacking established beliefs. Instead, it describes his words as exaggerated and grand, making "bombastic" the more accurate choice.

397 **Choices A and D are correct** because the passage looks to express how there is a small but important distinction between proficient and fluent speakers of the English language. As ease is defined as "absence or difficulty of effort" and subtleties is defined as "small but important distinctions or features", they serve as best answers to convey the passage's meaning.

Choice B is incorrect because malaise means "a general feeling of discomfort or uneasiness that is difficult to identify", which does not align with the intent of the passage. **Choice C is incorrect** because courage is defined as "the ability to do something in the face of pain or grief", which does not align with the syntax or meaning of the passage. **Choice E is incorrect** because allegiances means "loyalty or commitment of subordinates to their superiors or to a group or cause", which fails to align with the meaning of the passage. **Choice F is incorrect** because errors means "mistakes", which does not allow logically complete the meaning of the passage.

398 **Choice C is correct** because "appropriated" means taken for one's own use, often without permission. In the context of broadcast signals, it fits well to describe unauthorized use or takeover of someone else's signal network **Choice E is correct** because "simulcasting" refers to simultaneously broadcasting the same signal across multiple platforms or locations. This makes sense in the context of a station trying to transmit a signal to its audience, which is then hijacked or overridden by another signal.

Choice A is incorrect because "interjected" means to insert abruptly, usually in speech or conversation, and doesn't fit the technical context of broadcasting systems. **Choice B is incorrect** because "interpolated" means to insert something into something else, often in a textual or numerical sense, and doesn't fit the context of signal hijacking or network takeover. **Choice D is incorrect** because "transcribing" refers to writing down or converting speech to text, which is unrelated to the act of broadcasting a signal. **Choice F is incorrect** because "circulating" generally refers to something moving around within a system or area, and doesn't carry the specific meaning of broadcasting a signal over a network.

399 **Choice C is correct** because "fatuous" means silly or pointless. In this context, Hardy's novels portray the ambitions of the working class as ultimately futile or misguided in the face of rigid Victorian societal structures. This word aligns with the tragic tone and message of the novels mentioned. **Choice F is correct** because "incongruous" means not in harmony or out of place. This fits well because The Mayor of Casterbridge and Jude the Obscure both illustrate how working-class aspirations clash with societal expectations, highlighting the inconsistency or conflict between ambition and social reality.

Choice A is incorrect because "erudite" means scholarly or well-educated. This describes a tone or level of learning, not the nature of working-class ambitions in conflict with society. **Choice B is incorrect** because "jubilant" means showing great joy or triumph. This tone does not match the tragic outcomes or the critical portrayal of the working-class struggle in Hardy's novels. **Choice D is incorrect** because "conducive" means making a situation more likely or possible. The novels do not encourage or support the success of ambition; instead, they depict its failure. **Choice E is incorrect** because "inimical" means hostile or harmful. While society might be seen as inimical to ambition, the sentence is describing the novels and their thematic content, not something actively opposing ambition.

400 **Choices C and F are correct** because the passage aims to convey the actions of a manager subsequent to catching a thieving employee. Apprehended means "caught or arrest for a crime" and posthaste means "with great speed or immediacy", which effectively convey the theme of the passage.

Choice A is incorrect because rebuked means to "express sharp disapproval or criticism because of behavior or actions", which does not logically align with the structure of the passage. **Choice B is incorrect** because fought means "to battle with", which does not align with the theme of the passage, particularly the words "red handed". **Choice D is incorrect** because regally means "in a royal or monarchical fashion", which does not align with the meaning of the passage. **Choice E is incorrect** because ostentatiously means "in a pretentious or showy way which is designed to impress", which does not best align with the intent of the passage.

Practice Set 3: Three Blanks

401 Although he took great pains as an educator to (i) _____ a love of reasoning and virtue in his students, Athenian (ii) _____ of the day considered Socrates to be a/an (iii) _____, intent on destroying their authority and subverting the youth of Athens.

Blank (i)	Blank (ii)	Blank (iii)
Ⓐ ingurgitate	Ⓓ portents	Ⓖ centurion
Ⓑ importune	Ⓔ potentates	Ⓗ iconoclast
Ⓒ inculcate	Ⓕ profligates	Ⓘ neophyte

402 Although the problems identified with the SR7 (i) _____ Rover, designed to collect data and soil samples from the surface of Mars have been publicized extensively over the past few weeks, they are not of much consequence when considered individually. However, the cumulative effect of the myriad of (ii) _____ must be factored into scientists' decision to launch the Rover or (iii) _____.

Blank (i)	Blank (ii)	Blank (iii)
Ⓐ Canard	Ⓓ gimmicks	Ⓖ take the bull by the horns
Ⓑ Reconn-aissance	Ⓔ gimcracks	Ⓗ throw the baby out with the bath water
Ⓒ Alliance	Ⓕ glitches	Ⓘ go back to the drawing board

403 Growing a vegetable garden may seem difficult, but anyone can do it. Home-grown (i) _____ is tastier, healthier, and cheaper than what you find in grocery stores. It is important to plan out your (ii) _____ – research what plants grow best in your region, find out how much sun the plants require, and make sure you have the tools you need. After planting your vegetables, tend them daily. Watering and weeding are a must. Once your (iii) _____ is ripe, harvest and enjoy the fruits of your labor!

Blank (i)	Blank (ii)	Blank (iii)
Ⓐ calumny	Ⓓ acreage	Ⓖ concurrence
Ⓑ produce	Ⓔ nadir	Ⓗ fruitage
Ⓒ morasses	Ⓕ quagmire	Ⓘ exculpation

404 A series of intense storms and rising water levels over the last several years has resulted in (i) _____ in erosion on beaches across the country. As a result, many states are considering beach nourishment projects: replacing the large amounts of lost sediment with similar material either transported from other locations or manufactured. This new sand is usually (ii) _____ as a result of the processing methods used to manufacture it and therefore erodes faster, creating (iii) _____ cycle of erosion and replacement.

Blank (i)	Blank (ii)	Blank (iii)
Ⓐ an escalation	Ⓓ darker	Ⓖ an accelerated and expensive
Ⓑ a depletion	Ⓔ smaller-grained	Ⓗ an ineffective and unhygienic
Ⓒ an altercation	Ⓕ foul-smelling	Ⓘ a never-ending and inexplicable

405 The Abkhazian uprisings against the Russian Empire were unsuccessful, but had a lasting impact on the (i) _____ of the region. Some Abkhaz fled of their own accord – mostly those who were (ii) _____ to the anti-Russian revolts. Others left involuntarily, as victims of the ethnic cleansings in the North Caucasus. During the late 1800s the Russian Army forced the Abkhaz, Adyghe, Ubykh, and Abaza peoples from their homelands. The majority of these (iii) _____ populations settled in the Ottoman Empire.

Blank (i)	Blank (ii)	Blank (iii)
Ⓐ demographics	Ⓓ copasetic	Ⓖ complacent
Ⓑ recidivism	Ⓔ sympathetic	Ⓗ appeased
Ⓒ raiment	Ⓕ phlegmatic	Ⓘ dispossessed

Chapter 4: Text Completion

406 Locating the (i) _____ organisms of the ocean has proven a daunting task. The ocean has more than 250 times the habitable volume as the land, leaving (ii) _____ amounts of space to cover. Even being able to locate viruses and phytoplankton, let alone being able to study their relationship to the environment, is a tremendous undertaking. But (iii) _____ understanding of marine life cannot be attained without knowing the role that microscopic organisms play in it.

Blank (i)	Blank (ii)	Blank (iii)
(A) haughty	(D) exorbitant	(G) exhaustive
(B) vituperative	(E) coquettish	(H) diminutive
(C) enigmatic	(F) ardent	(I) reticent

407 Prior to the nineteenth century, female ballet dancers were effectively barred from lead roles due to their (i) _____ corsets, hoops, and high heels. With the invention of the pointed shoe, however, all of this changed; ballet dancers came to be seen as ethereal creatures capable of floating effortlessly across the stage. Ballets consequently began to feature stories of nymphs and spirits that showcased the (ii) _____ costumes and (iii) _____ bodies of nineteenth-century ballerinas.

Blank (i)	Blank (ii)	Blank (iii)
(A) cumbersome	(D) dulcet	(G) brittle
(B) maladroit	(E) meretricious	(H) supine
(C) disheveled	(F) diaphanous	(I) lithe

408 An eye for seemingly (i) _____ details can make all the difference in marketing a product. Color, for example, can have (ii) _____ but powerful effects on a person's mood if not used carefully. Yellow runs the risk of being overpowering, but its undeniably eye-catching intensity can be an effective tool for a (iii) _____ businessman; Harry N. Allan, who first brought the taxicab to the United States, painted his cars yellow for precisely this reason.

Blank (i)	Blank (ii)	Blank (iii)
(A) disparate	(D) inadvertent	(G) sagacious
(B) spurious	(E) nugatory	(H) impecunious
(C) trifling	(F) salutary	(I) officious

409 It did not take the new members long to see that the group was (i) _____ its leadership was disorganized and (ii) _____ and virtually all efforts at community outreach had ceased. They hoped, however, that their own enthusiasm would not only revive the organization but also (iii) _____ renewed outside interest in its cause.

Blank (i)	Blank (ii)	Blank (iii)
(A) chimerical	(D) frowzy	(G) perpetrate
(B) superannuated	(E) torpid	(H) foster
(C) moribund	(F) stringent	(I) convoke

410 If the candidate's speech was intended to stir up (i) _____ feeling, he must have been sorely disappointed by the almost (ii) _____ effect it had on the audience. Although it was refreshing to see a politician (iii) _____ inflammatory taglines in favor of reasoned argument, his speech was simply too long to hold the audience's attention.

Blank (i)	Blank (ii)	Blank (iii)
(A) rancorous	(D) incendiary	(G) eschew
(B) partisan	(E) noxious	(H) preclude
(C) indigenous	(F) soporific	(I) abhor

411 His decision to become a middle-school drama teacher surprised those who were familiar with his considerable talent and (i) _____ interest in performing. In response to the queries of his friends, he said that felt it was (ii) _____ him to do something about the (iii) _____ state of arts education in the public schools.

Blank (i)	Blank (ii)	Blank (iii)
(A) manifest	(D) inimical to	(G) banal
(B) inordinate	(E) munificent of	(H) abysmal
(C) perfunctory	(F) incumbent upon	(I) odious

Practice Set 3: Three Blanks

412 The (i) _____ nature of the sloth is well documented; its very name is a reference to the Biblical sin of spiritual and physical apathy. Unlike the average (ii) _____, however, the sloth has a compelling reason to (iii) _____ physical activity; the sloth's diet consists almost entirely of leaves, which provide little in the way of energy or nutrition, forcing the sloth to conserve its strength.

Blank (i)	Blank (ii)	Blank (iii)
(A) fulsome	(D) virago	(G) abstain from
(B) lugubrious	(E) libertine	(H) inveigh against
(C) phlegmatic	(F) sluggard	(I) wean themselves off

413 (i) _____ criminals are an increasing threat to both private companies and the world economic system. Not only were five computer programmers recently arrested for hacking into the servers of several American companies and stealing 160,000,000 credit card numbers, but their leader was also caught hacking into the Nasdaq stock exchange. The America's stock exchange is far from alone in its (ii) _____. 53 percent of the world's exchanges have fallen victim to the (iii) _____ of hackers in the last year.

Blank (i)	Blank (ii)	Blank (iii)
(A) Cyber	(D) aversion	(G) puissance
(B) Cryptic	(E) perfidy	(H) nostrum
(C) Captious	(F) vulnerability	(I) cynosure

414 Although their (i) _____ beauty suggests extreme fragility, butterflies have developed a number of practical defenses against predators and other dangers. Some species advertise their (ii) _____ taste with bright colors and memorable patterns in the hopes that a predator will not make the same mistake twice, while others attempt to (iii) _____ their enemies with misleading eye-shaped spots on their wings.

Blank (i)	Blank (ii)	Blank (iii)
(A) tremulous	(D) insidious	(G) maim
(B) inordinate	(E) elusive	(H) placate
(C) mincing	(F) fulsome	(I) confound

415 Although all parents expect some degree of (i) _____ obedience, those that carry their demands may inadvertently hinder their child's development. Children who grow up in a household where absolute (ii) _____ parental authority is the norm are often not given a chance to exercise their own judgment, and may therefore have low-self-esteem and a (iii) _____ sense of self.

Blank (i)	Blank (ii)	Blank (iii)
(A) filial	(D) propensity for	(G) tenuous
(B) reciprocal	(E) intransigence towards	(H) mercurial
(C) scrupulous	(F) deference to	(I) dissolute

416 General Motors saw a 19 percent fall in net income due to a (i) _____ drop in profits in Asia. Recently poor economic conditions have made Europe the largest trouble spot for the company, but GM narrowed losses in Europe while registering higher than normal losses in Asia. A rise in (ii) _____ from the Japanese, Korean, and Australian automobile markets contributed to losses in the region. Despite a 4 percent gain in North America, GM is in trouble if it does not come up with strategies to perform more (iii) _____.

Blank (i)	Blank (ii)	Blank (iii)
(A) propitious	(D) competitors	(G) erratically
(B) precipitous	(E) assailant	(H) consistently
(C) promontory	(F) hindrances	(I) pedantically

417 Some scholars (i) _____ that the works of William Shakespeare were in fact written by a(n) (ii) _____ of authors, rather than a single man. But, they have a difficult time identifying any possible suspects, figuring out how many there were or explaining how so many people could write in such a(n) (iii) _____.

Blank (i)	Blank (ii)	Blank (iii)
(A) declaim	(D) coterie	(G) cohesive style
(B) assume	(E) menagerie	(H) flamboyant -manner
(C) contend	(F) gild	(I) complicated time

Chapter 4: Text Completion

418 Much to the (i) _____ of consumers, modern technology has allowed businesses to advertise more effectively - and more (ii) _____ than ever; the average city-dweller is now exposed to somewhere between 3,000 and 5,000 ads every day. The constant (iii) _____ of marketing is so frustrating that 43 percent of cell phone users say they would willingly pay more for a cell phone service that blocks such messages.

Blank (i)	Blank (ii)	Blank (iii)
(A) edification	(D) consummately	(G) dearth
(B) trepidation	(E) obtrusively	(H) parlance
(C) disgruntlement	(F) nefariously	(I) barrage

419 To combat the fears of Russification, Christianization, and general assimilation, Tatar reformers had to (i) _____ the importance of strengthening Tatar cultural identity. This, along with a more flexible (and therefore in many ways more durable) (ii) _____ of Islam, helped the Tatar community retain their ethnic identity while developing a modernized secular relationship with Russia. To this end, writers like Amirkhan highlighted the capability of Tatars to embrace reforms and secular education while still (iii) _____ their Tatar identity.

Blank (i)	Blank (ii)	Blank (iii)
(A) desiccate	(D) aesthetic	(G) abdicating
(B) accentuate	(E) indoctrination	(H) perpetuating
(C) abrogate	(F) apperception	(I) gainsaying

420 Proposed solutions to the conflict take the form of the packaged and phased approaches – addressing all the (i) _____ of the conflict in one fell swoop versus creating a schedule to deal with each question one at a time. The first allows for resolution in a single document and enables everyone to focus immediately on (ii) _____ action. Unfortunately, it is less politically viable and less flexible. The second (iii) _____ immediate pressures making leadership able to engage in substantive conversation, but risks derailing due to changes in external circumstance and inertia.

Blank (i)	Blank (ii)	Blank (iii)
(A) inaccuracies	(D) tangible	(G) alleviates
(B) perquisites	(E) ephemeral	(H) exterminating
(C) components	(F) amorphous	(I) implicates

421 Wildflowers are faithful to their bumblebee "sweethearts." In a recent study, (i) _____ found that wildflowers produce fewer seeds when a single bumblebee species is removed. Apparently, the plant/pollinator relationship is (ii) _____. Each bee species focuses on a single plant variety until it finishes blooming, thus increasing the fidelity of the species. The result is a rise in seed production. The study underlined the importance of (iii) _____ in the conservation of ecosystems as the removal of a bee species resulted in decreased plant reproduction.

Blank (i)	Blank (ii)	Blank (iii)
(A) cryptologists	(D) monogamous	(G) anathemas
(B) geologists	(E) polygamous	(H) surfeit
(C) ecologists	(F) hypergamous	(I) biodiversity

422 Researchers have discovered (i) _____ method for targeting and manipulating any gene in the human genome. An RNA-guided enzyme found in the Streptococcus bacteria could (ii) _____ be used to cure many genetic diseases as well as to reprogram stem and adult cells. The (iii) _____ of this discovery are far-reaching, but scientists are not yet sure what all the possibilities are. Using the RNA-guided enzyme is relatively simple, which makes the scientific community hopeful in regard to its real-world applications.

Blank (i)	Blank (ii)	Blank (iii)
(A) a superfluous	(D) abstractly	(G) impositions
(B) an expedient	(E) presumptively	(H) implications
(C) an imprudent	(F) dubiously	(I) inhibitions

423 Scientists have long been fascinated by superfluids, such as liquid helium, since they seem to defy the laws of (i) _____. Moving without the (ii) _____ of gravity or surface tension, superfluids have zero viscosity and can squeeze through holes the size of a molecule or climb up the side of a glass. They have been (iii) _____ to remain in motion for years after the centrifuge containing them has stopped spinning.

Blank (i)	Blank (ii)	Blank (iii)
(A) geology	(D) opprobrium	(G) observed
(B) physics	(E) celerity	(H) obliterated
(C) biology	(F) interference	(I) envisioned

Practice Set 3: Three Blanks

424 Although The Picture of Dorian Gray was (i) _____ at the time of its publication as a (ii) _____ account of a man's descent into moral depravity, it is now regarded as a classic work of English literature. In fact, the book's history underscores how the current social climate can (iii) _____ the true value of a piece of art.

Blank (i)	Blank (ii)	Blank (iii)
Ⓐ vaunted	Ⓓ histrionic	Ⓖ obfuscate
Ⓑ reviled	Ⓔ insipid	Ⓗ emblazon
Ⓒ expunged	Ⓕ lurid	Ⓘ atrophy

425 Automobiles sold in the United States have either a manual or automatic transmission. If the car is a manual, that means the driver has to shift through a (i) _____ of gears to accelerate, while an automatic car will shift on its own with no (ii) _____ from the driver. It is fair to say driving an automatic takes (iii) _____, but most people can learn to drive a manual with little trouble.

Blank (i)	Blank (ii)	Blank (iii)
Ⓐ gamut	Ⓓ contrivance	Ⓖ less coordination
Ⓑ sequence	Ⓔ assistance	Ⓗ a long time
Ⓒ filigree	Ⓕ reliance	Ⓘ more stability

426 The first world war has been overshadowed in the popular imagination by World War II, but its length, violence, and the widespread changes it brought shocked people who lived through it. A war that everyone thought would be over within months turned into a (i) _____ stalemate of four long years; the (ii) _____ waste of life in the trenches was unprecedented in its bloodiness; and the war led directly to the (iii) _____ of four great empires.

Blank (i)	Blank (ii)	Blank (iii)
Ⓐ recalcitrant	Ⓓ querulous	Ⓖ accretion
Ⓑ protracted	Ⓔ anachronistic	Ⓗ demise
Ⓒ divergent	Ⓕ wanton	Ⓘ disparity

427 Analysis of content consumption on social media is a useful method to (i) _____ viewer preferences and thereby prevailing social interests. The undeniable popularity of videos with endearing and mischievous pets in their most (ii) _____ moments (iii) _____ the claim that most viewers are attracted to gratuitous violence and other demoralizing themes.

Blank (i)	Blank (ii)	Blank (iii)
Ⓐ expound	Ⓓ beguiling	Ⓖ proves immaterial
Ⓑ gauge	Ⓔ quixotic	Ⓗ merely obviates
Ⓒ challenge	Ⓕ odious	Ⓘ serves to corroborate

428 The House of Representatives (i) _____ passed the bill; however, the passage of the bill in the Senate was (ii) _____ by a filibuster, which was enacted in an effort to help make the legislation more (iii) _____, thereby ensuring different perspectives were considered.

Blank (i)	Blank (ii)	Blank (iii)
Ⓐ swiftly	Ⓓ ringfenced	Ⓖ bipartisan
Ⓑ stubbornly	Ⓔ impeded	Ⓗ controlling
Ⓒ salaciously	Ⓕ recalled	Ⓘ uncommon

429 All vertebrate cardiovascular systems include a heart, a muscular pump that contracts to (i) _____. blood through the blood vessels. The upper chamber of the heart is the atrium, and is where blood enters the muscle. The lower chamber is the ventricle. When the ventricle (ii) _____, blood is forced from the heart via an artery. The aorta is the main artery leaving the heart and bringing nutrients and oxygen out to the other organs. The pulmonary artery returns the oxygen-(iii) _____.blood to the heart so that it can be enriched with nutrients and sent back out into the body.

Blank (i)	Blank (ii)	Blank (iii)
Ⓐ pitch	Ⓓ constricts	Ⓖ squandered
Ⓑ propel	Ⓔ compresses	Ⓗ augmented
Ⓒ project	Ⓕ cinches	Ⓘ depleted

Chapter 4: Text Completion

430. Research on the psychological impacts of color, such as red (i)_____ captivating attention, enhancing athletic (ii)_____, impeding cognitive skills, increasing aggressivity, and building sexual attraction in certain circumstances, is a great topic of interest to the public, although it is still in an (iii)_____ empirical stage.

Blank (i)	Blank (ii)	Blank (iii)
Ⓐ audio	Ⓓ performance	Ⓖ mature
Ⓑ stimuli	Ⓔ awards	Ⓗ inceptive
Ⓒ hue	Ⓕ incompetency	Ⓘ experimental

431. When assessing the (i)_____ of a home for purchase, the (ii)_____ of the property is often emphasized, however the home's zip code must be (iii)_____ against a number of other considerations, including size, cleanliness, and quirkiness.

Blank (i)	Blank (ii)	Blank (iii)
Ⓐ quality	Ⓓ geography	Ⓖ juxtaposed
Ⓑ piety	Ⓔ viscosity	Ⓗ reassured
Ⓒ scandalousness	Ⓕ liability	Ⓘ outlasted

432. The (i)_____ of fields like quantum mechanics can (ii)_____ students from pursuing further education in them. However, if the harder concepts in these fields are introduced (iii)_____, students are less likely to flee to simpler topics.

Blank (i)	Blank (ii)	Blank (iii)
Ⓐ abrogation	Ⓓ contrive	Ⓖ empirically
Ⓑ relatability	Ⓔ inundate	Ⓗ swiftly
Ⓒ complexity	Ⓕ dissuade	Ⓘ gradually

433. While health is often attributed to the absence of disease, it is (i)_____ a far more nuanced condition that is better (ii)_____ in the ancient Chinese phrase, "maintaining life." However, rather than implementing one-size-fits-all lifestyle changes, experts recommend introducing a (iii)_____ exercise routine, along with a customized dietary plan, in order to match the specific profile of each individual.

Blank (i)	Blank (ii)	Blank (iii)
Ⓐ arguably	Ⓓ encapsulated	Ⓖ proscribed
Ⓑ ostensibly	Ⓔ extolled	Ⓗ bespoke
Ⓒ conspicuously	Ⓕ abrogated	Ⓘ preordained

434. Gene editing technologies have (i)_____ the treatment of several diseases. Instead of merely treating the (ii)_____ of these diseases, gene therapies modify (iii)_____ constituents of a person's genetic code, thereby addressing the diseases at their source.

Blank (i)	Blank (ii)	Blank (iii)
Ⓐ revolutionized	Ⓓ repechages	Ⓖ relational
Ⓑ vilified	Ⓔ symptoms	Ⓗ educational
Ⓒ indemnified	Ⓕ foibles	Ⓘ foundational

435. When installing a hardwood floor the color and durability of the wood are only as (i)_____ as the quality of underlayment, which is an umbrella term that describes the (ii)_____ that is (iii)_____ between the primary floor and subfloor in order to promote stability, insulation, and moisture protection.

Blank (i)	Blank (ii)	Blank (iii)
Ⓐ subordinate	Ⓓ substance	Ⓖ layered
Ⓑ impeccable	Ⓔ epidermis	Ⓗ superimposed
Ⓒ paramount	Ⓕ dispense	Ⓘ imprinted

Practice Set 3: Three Blanks

436. The findings of multiple social psychology studies suggest that humans are much more (i)_____ than we like to admit. Although we tend to think of our opinions and beliefs as highly personal and deeply-rooted, the truth is that they are greatly influenced by our surroundings. In some cases, we are even willing to (ii)_____ the evidence of our own senses in the interests of conformity; in the Asch experiments, participants routinely misjudged the length of a line in order to (iii)_____ the majority judgment.

Blank (i)	Blank (ii)	Blank (iii)
Ⓐ tractable	Ⓓ vituperate	Ⓖ abide by
Ⓑ fatuous	Ⓔ repudiate	Ⓗ preclude
Ⓒ dogmatic	Ⓕ garner	Ⓘ quibble with

437. The death of Hu Yaobang, a Party leader committed to economic and social reforms, was the (i)_____ that caused the now famous Tiananmen Square protests. The demonstrations, which lasted seven weeks and were primarily non-violent, culminated in the government's brutal massacre of hundreds, if not thousands, of protestors - a (ii)_____ abuse of government power that resulted in widespread (iii)_____.

Blank (i)	Blank (ii)	Blank (iii)
Ⓐ catalyst	Ⓓ redoubtable	Ⓖ encomium
Ⓑ imbroglio	Ⓔ heinous	Ⓗ sanctimony
Ⓒ antidote	Ⓕ dubious	Ⓘ opprobrium

438. The palace of Versailles was the (i)_____ of Louis the XIV of France. During his (ii)_____, France experienced a degree of (iii)_____ prosperity that became the domain of only a privileged few a century later.

Blank (i)	Blank (ii)	Blank (iii)
Ⓐ abode	Ⓓ reign	Ⓖ lavish
Ⓑ cavalcade	Ⓔ recital	Ⓗ jejune
Ⓒ retort	Ⓕ arbor	Ⓘ esoteric

439. After the dancers finished their (i)_____ and basked in the adulation of the crowd, they (ii)_____ to the (iii)_____ of their everyday lives.

Blank (i)	Blank (ii)	Blank (iii)
Ⓐ conversation	Ⓓ adorned	Ⓖ rowdiness
Ⓑ waltz	Ⓔ adjourned	Ⓗ anonymity
Ⓒ milling	Ⓕ allayed	Ⓘ consanguinity

440. Some Wall Street traders (i)_____ their investments by shorting stocks and buying options. The practice can (ii)_____ massive profits by helping to effectively (iii)_____ risk.

Blank (i)	Blank (ii)	Blank (iii)
Ⓐ revolutionized	Ⓓ abet	Ⓖ marginalize
Ⓑ relatability	Ⓔ yield	Ⓗ masquerade
Ⓒ hedge	Ⓕ penalize	Ⓘ inundate

441. Drinking water helps to (i)_____ key (ii)_____ of the body, thereby ensuring all aspects of your body maintain (iii)_____, helping to ensure all the various endogenous processes are appropriately balanced.

Blank (i)	Blank (ii)	Blank (iii)
Ⓐ revitalize	Ⓓ constituents	Ⓖ equilibrium
Ⓑ atomize	Ⓔ harbingers	Ⓗ salvation
Ⓒ parallelize	Ⓕ orbitals	Ⓘ regurgitation

442. While we have known that atoms are composed of protons, electrons, and (i)_____ for a long time, the ability to (ii)_____ them has only recently been discovered. This innovation in microscopy set off an (iii)_____ revolution in new subatomic inquiry.

Blank (i)	Blank (ii)	Blank (iii)
Ⓐ exomes	Ⓓ migrate	Ⓖ tepid
Ⓑ neutrons	Ⓔ avoid	Ⓗ regulated
Ⓒ mandibles	Ⓕ visualize	Ⓘ unparalleled

443. Those who are familiar with Shakespeare's plays no doubt see Richard III as a murderous (i) _____ who killed his two young nephews in order to claim the throne for himself. Some modern historians, however, believe that the evidence against Richard is (ii) _____ at best, and suggest that Shakespeare may have had politically compelling reasons for (iii) _____ his character.

Blank (i)	Blank (ii)	Blank (iii)
(A) iconoclast	(D) quotidian	(G) renovating
(B) mendicant	(E) tenuous	(H) commemorating
(C) reprobate	(F) whimsical	(I) maligning

444. It is important to listen to the (i) _____ of your grandparents. While their bodies may be (ii) _____ and ailing, their minds are often (iii) _____ of knowledge gained from years of experience.

Blank (i)	Blank (ii)	Blank (iii)
(A) sagacity	(D) doddery	(G) delinquent
(B) salutations	(E) agitated	(H) cornucopias
(C) animations	(F) virile	(I) abrasions

445. When the scientist realized what he had discovered, he shouted (i) _____! It was only after the fact that the (ii) _____ impact of his once (iii) _____ discovery would later be identified.

Blank (i)	Blank (ii)	Blank (iii)
(A) Blunderbuss	(D) deleterious	(G) loquacious
(B) Eureka	(E) stupendous	(H) celebrated
(C) Glasnost	(F) magnificent	(I) unintelligible

446. Victimology at times ventures into highly (i) _____ areas, such as victim precipitation, which occurs when a victim attracts the attention of an attacker through (ii) _____ behavior of some sort. Although studies that center on the victim's identity and habits ultimately aim to reduce crime, to some, the terminology used in such research does little besides blame the victim and implicitly (iii) _____ the crime.

Blank (i)	Blank (ii)	Blank (iii)
(A) salacious	(D) timorous	(G) condone
(B) propitious	(E) brash	(H) provoke
(C) contentious	(F) fulsome	(I) rescind

447. Many of the troops returning from Vietnam experienced (i) _____. Those that escaped these psychological effects of battle often became (ii) _____ anti-war advocates, (iii) _____ around the country for an end to the conflict.

Blank (i)	Blank (ii)	Blank (iii)
(A) shellshock	(D) ardent	(G) campaigning
(B) rickets	(E) muted	(H) admiring
(C) impetigo	(F) malleable	(I) snarling

448. When the (i) _____ finished his (ii) _____ and the band walked off stage, the crowd roared with chants of "(iii) _____!", begging them to return to the stage.

Blank (i)	Blank (ii)	Blank (iii)
(A) jingoist	(D) dimunation	(G) Pinochle
(B) abolitionist	(E) revelation	(H) Flabbergast
(C) pianist	(F) solo	(I) Encore

Practice Set 3: Three Blanks

449 Although incest is now (i) _____ to many, if not most, societies, a surprisingly large number of cultures have at one time or another permitted it. Indeed, brother-sister marriage was virtually (ii) _____ within the ancient Egyptian royal family, where it was used to ensure that the bloodline remained (iii) _____.

Blank (i)	Blank (ii)	Blank (iii)
Ⓐ venial	Ⓓ condoned	Ⓖ omnipotent
Ⓑ abhorred	Ⓔ mandated	Ⓗ immaculate
Ⓒ ancillary	Ⓕ rectified	Ⓘ empyreal

450 In 2010, California approved a cap-and-trade program that aims to reduce the greenhouse gas emissions of California-based businesses. But while most people agree that action must be taken to (i) _____ the worst effects of climate change, some companies feel these particular demands are too (ii) _____ to meet. Makers of concrete are particularly (iii) _____ of the new regulations; because the release of carbon dioxide is central to the production of concrete, the new law could have devastating effects for businesses that specialize in this.

Blank (i)	Blank (ii)	Blank (iii)
Ⓐ forestall	Ⓓ onerous	Ⓖ cognizant
Ⓑ descry	Ⓔ meretricious	Ⓗ wary
Ⓒ propitiate	Ⓕ amorphous	Ⓘ devoid

Answer Key

Q. No.	Correct Answer	Your Answer	Q. No.	Correct Answer	Your Answer
401	C, E, H		426	B, F, H	
402	B, F, G		427	B, D, G	
403	B, D, H		428	A, E, G	
404	A, E, G		429	B, D, I	
405	A, E, I		430	B, D, H	
406	C, D, G		431	A, D, G	
407	A, F, I		432	C, F, I	
408	C, D, G		433	A, D, H	
409	C, E, H		434	A, E, I	
410	B, F, G		435	C, D, G	
411	A, F, H		436	A, E, G	
412	C, F, G		437	A, E, I	
413	A, F, G		438	A, D, G	
414	A, F, I		439	B, E, H	
415	A, F, G		440	C, E, G	
416	B, D, H		441	A, D, G	
417	C, D, G		442	B, F, I	
418	C, E, I		443	C, E, I	
419	B, E, H		444	A, D, H	
420	C, D, G		445	B, D, H	
421	C, D, I		446	C, F, G	
422	B, E, H		447	A, D, G	
423	B, F, G		448	C, F, I	
424	B, F, G		449	B, E, H	
425	B, E, G		450	A, D, H	

Practice Set 3: Answers & Explanations

401 **Choice C, Choice E, and Choice H are correct** because we can teach logic, but values such as love or reason and virtue must be instilled. The love of reasoning and virtue is an abstract quality and something we attempt to inculcate (C) in students, making C the correct answer. Those who have authority can be referred to as potentates (E) or autocratic rulers. Athenian potentates may well have perceived Socrates as an iconoclast (H). Iconoclasts attack or otherwise undermine cherished ideas and institutions including social structures and authorities of the day.

Choice A is incorrect because Socrates did not ingurgitate (A) or gulp his students. **Choice B** is incorrect because Socrates did not importune (B), meaning inconvenience, his students with a love of reasoning and virtue. **Choice D** is incorrect because those who have authority are not portents (D), as portents are omens or premonitions. **Choice F** is incorrect because those who have authority would not be profligates (F), or recklessly wasteful individuals. **Choice G** is incorrect because Socrates cannot be considered a centurion (G) or leader of a unit of 100 soldiers. **Choice I** is incorrect because neophyte means novice and implies inchoate knowledge and skills; this certainly would not describe a teacher charged with educating the patrician Athenian youth

402 **Choice B, Choice F, and Choice G are correct** because the SR7 Rover was designed to go out into space and gather intelligence. The SR7 is going out on a reconnaissance (B) mission to conduct an on-the-ground search/ investigation with the aim of bringing back information for the superiors, in this case, the scientists. Clearly the SR7 suffers from a number of small problems or glitches (F) that are not significant on their own, but when taken together have the potential to delay the launch of the Rover. Taking the bull by the horns is synonymous with taking action, and taking action, in this case amounts to launching the SR7, so (G) would be correct in this circumstance.

Choice A is incorrect because canard means a derogatory story, report or rumor. Option A certainly does not imply the exploratory nature of the mission but rather raises questions about its legitimacy. **Choice C** is incorrect because alliance (C) would imply a pact between organizations or nations that is not supported by the passage. **Choice D** is incorrect because gimmicks (D), or ingenious and novel stratagems to attract attention and increase appeal, there probably would be no threat to the launch. **Choice E** is incorrect because gimcracks (E) being showy, insignificant trifles such as one might pick up at a country fair, are not the issue here **Choice H** is incorrect because throwing the baby out with the bathwater would make the sentence repetitive and nonsensical, suggesting that scientists "...launch the SR7 or launch the SR7." **Choice I** is incorrect because going back to the drawing board means to scrap the entire SR7 because of a few glitches, which would once again not make sense in the context of the passage.

403 **Choice B, Choice D, and Choice H are correct** because produce (as a noun) is a product, usually agricultural. Acreage means an amount of land, which makes sense in the context of planning a garden. The last blank requires a word that means vegetables that have grown. As fruitage means harvest or yield, usually from an agricultural endeavor, this would be correct.

Choice A is incorrect because calumny is a misrepresentation or slander which does not align with the context of the passage. **Choice C** is incorrect because morass is a marsh or a confusing and difficult situation. which does not align with the context of the passage. **Choice E** is incorrect because nadir means the lowest point, which does not align with the context of the passage. **Choice F** is incorrect because a quagmire is a situation that is difficult to extract oneself from which does not align with the context of the passage. **Choice G** is incorrect because concurrence is a convergence or simultaneous occurrence, which does not align with the context of the passage. **Choice I** is incorrect because exculpation is an acquittal, which does not align with the context of the passage.

404 **Choice A, Choice E, and Choice G are correct** because erosion (wearing away of rocks and other deposits on the earth's surface) is substantial because of the phrase "large amounts of lost sediment." To escalate means to intensify or accelerate, and thus A is the correct answer. While all options could be viable, the only one which aligns with the topic of erosion is smaller-grained. Given the information we have that beach nourishment causes fast erosion. It is safe to assume that having to replace the sand would require rapid action (acceleration) and would be expensive, so G is the best choice.

Choice B is incorrect because depletion is a reduction in, which does not best align with the context of the passage. **Choice C** is incorrect because an altercation means a conflict or fight, which does not align with the context of the passage. **Choice D** is incorrect because darker means a reduction in the amount of available light, which does not align with the context of the passage. **Choice F** is incorrect because foul-smelling means odious in nature, which does not align with the context of the passage. **Choice I** is incorrect because inexplicable is unable to be explained, which does not align with the context of the passage. **Choice H** is incorrect because unhygienic, which means unsanitary in nature, which does not align with the context of the passage.

Chapter 4: Text Completion

405 **Choice A, Choice E, and Choice I are correct** because the first blank is about changing ethnic make-up of Abkhazia, or its demographics. If the Abkhazians were leaving after revolts against the Russians failed, then they probably were also somewhat anti-Russian, or at least were sympathetic to (agreed with, looked on with favor) anti-Russian activity. For the last blank, we know that the groups, or peoples, were moved from their homes – they were expelled, kicked out, which is what dispossessed means.

Choice B is incorrect because recidivism is the act of a person repeating criminal behaviour after being convicted of a crime. This does not align with the context of the passage. **Choice C** is incorrect because raiment means clothing, which does not align with the context of the passage. **Choice D** is incorrect because copasetic means "in excellent order", which does not align with the context of the passage. **Choice F** is incorrect because phlegmatic means having an unemotional and stolidly calm disposition, which does not align with the context of the passage. **Choice H** is incorrect because appeased means to pacify or placate by ascending to demands **Choice G** is incorrect because complacent means showing smug or uncritical satisfaction with oneself or ones achievements, which does not align with the context of the passage.

406 **Choice C, Choice D, and Choice G are correct** because the paragraph says that it is difficult to locate the many organisms living in the ocean because of the space they have to live in. Our lack of experience with them gives the organisms a secretive quality. "Enigmatic" means "mysterious." This accurately describes how aquatic life would appear to humans if we've rarely or never seen them before. The second sentence stresses the sheer size of the ocean and describes how this size is perceived in terms of searching for marine life. It must be considered excessively large for that purpose. "Exorbitant." means "excessive." This describes exactly how one would feel about the size of the ocean when searching it for life. The last sentence stresses how understanding every aspect of marine life is necessary in order to attain a certain type of understanding about the ocean. This "certain type" of understanding must be complete understanding if it requires understanding everything, including microscopic organisms." "Exhaustive" means "complete." This makes sense. A complete understanding of marine life would require knowing how everything, including microscopic organisms, function within the ocean.

Choice A is incorrect because "Haughty" means "proud." Being rarely seen would not cause aquatic life to be "proud." **Choice B** is incorrect because "Vituperative" means "offensive." Being rarely seen would not make aquatic life offensive. **Choice E** is incorrect because "Coquettish" means "demure." This personality trait does not explain how the size of the ocean would be perceived by those looking for life within it. **Choice F** is incorrect because "Ardent" means "zealous." This word does not describe how the ocean would be perceived by those trying to find life within it. **Choice H** is incorrect because "Diminutive" means "small." A small understanding would not require knowing how every microscopic organism functions within the ocean. **Choice I** is incorrect because "Reticent" means "shy." A "shy" understanding does not make sense.

407 **Choice A, Choice F, and Choice I are correct** because in the first sentence, we learn that female dancers' corsets, hoops, and high heels prevented them from taking center stage - probably because the costumes were simply too difficult to move in. Cumbersome (burdensome or unwieldy) is the correct answer. For the last two blanks, the answers must mesh with notions about ballet dancers, in particular how they act the part of nymphs and spirits, they float effortlessly, and they are ethereal. Diaphanous is correct because it means very sheer and light and fits in well with the passage's depiction of ballet dancers. Lithe, which means supple or limber, is best for the final blank for the same reason.

Choice B is incorrect because Maladroit is not a good fit because it usually describes people or their actions, not clothing; it means inept or awkward. **Choice C** is incorrect because Disheveled does not make very much sense; there is no indication that the dancers' costumes were routinely untidy or disordered, and even if they were, couldn't they simply fix them? **Choice D** is incorrect because Dulcet means soothing or melodious; it usually refers to sound, so it is probably not the best description of costumes. **Choice E** is incorrect because Meretricious (tawdry or based on pretense) is too negative a word. **Choice G** is incorrect because Brittle (easily damaged or destroyed) will not work well for the last blank; dancers' bodies may seem fragile, but the connotations of brittle are too negative for a passage that otherwise describes the dancers in flattering terms. **Choice H** is incorrect because Supine does not make sense; a dancer could hardly remain inactive or lying on her back.

408 **Choice C, Choice D, and Choice G are correct** because the use of the word seemingly suggests that the details that make all the difference do not seem particularly important, so you should look for a word that means something like insignificant. As trifling means trivial or insignificant, it is the best answer for the first blank. To fill in the second blank, we need a word that in some way contrasts with powerful, and that describes the effects of color on a person's mood. Inadvertent, which works well with the notion that color could be written off as a trifling detail; it means unintentional, would be best here. Finally, the last blank requires a word that describes the kind of businessman who uses color effectively - savvy or something similar, perhaps. Sagacious, which means "shrewd" is most appropriate.

Choice A is incorrect because disparate, which means distinct or dissimilar, does not align with the context of the passage. **Choice B** is incorrect because spurious means not genuine, authentic, or true. It does not make sense in this context, particularly given the later discussion of color; color can't be inauthentic. **Choice E** is incorrect because nugatory means of no real value. It does somewhat contrast with powerful, but it also makes no sense in this sentence; if color can be an effective tool in marketing, clearly it does have value. **Choice F** is incorrect because salutary is too specific; it means healthful or wholesome, and one can easily imagine a situation in which color could have a negative effect on one's mood. **Choice H** is incorrect because impecunious means penniless, which is more or less irrelevant to this sentence, unless the businessman is so poor that he can't afford a bucket of paint. **Choice I** is incorrect because officious (meddlesome or aggressive in offering one's services) does not make sense either; the businessman in question is presumably looking out for himself rather than offering to help others.

409 **Choice C, Choice E, and Choice H are correct** because if virtually all efforts at community outreach had ceased, the group is probably not doing well. The best answer is moribund, which means in a dying state or stagnant for the first blank. To fill in the next blank, we need to look for a word that could conceivably describe the leadership of such a group. Torpid (inactive or slow) fits in well with moribund and is the correct answer. Finally, the last sentence implies that the new recruits hope to stir up new interest in the group, so we need a word that means something like elicit or incite. The best answer for this blank is foster (to promote the growth of or to encourage).

Choice A is incorrect because chimerical means unreal. Since the group definitely exists because new members have joined it and are making plans to rehabilitate it, this answer would be incorrect. **Choice B** is incorrect because while the group may be superannuated (antiquated or too old for use), the fact that it is experiencing difficult times does not in and of itself imply that it is very old or obsolete. **Choice D** is incorrect because frowzy means slovenly or musty, which has no bearing on how well the group is functioning. **Choice F** is incorrect because stringent is slightly more plausible, but would not necessarily cause problems for the group; strict or exacting leadership could be harmful if taken too far. **Choice G** is incorrect because perpetuate means to commit or to execute and has generally negative connotations (as in, perpetrate a crime) - it is out of place here. **Choice I** is incorrect because convoke means to call together, which does not fit best with the context of the passage.

410 **Choice B, Choice F, and Choice G are correct** because given the political context, partisan (partial to a particular person or party) makes the most sense. We are then told that the candidate was probably disappointed by the speech's effect. If his goal was in fact to stir up partisan feelings, soporific, which means tending to cause sleep, is the best answer. In the final sentence, we are told that the candidate's speech was characterized by reasoned argument. To fill in the final blank, then, we need to find a word that will make the sentence read something like the politician avoided inflammatory taglines in favor of reasoned arguments. To eschew means to abstain or to avoid and is the correct answer.

Choice A is incorrect because rancorous, or spiteful, is a bit extreme; in the absence of further information, we should give even a politician the benefit of the doubt and assume he doesn't want to elicit actual hostility. **Choice C** is incorrect because indigenous is not a very good choice either; it means originating in a particular region. **Choice D** is incorrect because incendiary (tending to arouse or inflame) does not align with the context of the passage. **Choice E** is incorrect because noxious is probably too strong a word to be warranted in this context; it means harmful or corrupting. **Choice I** is incorrect because abhor (to loathe or to detest utterly) is too strong a word, and does not really work with the sentence structure - one does not generally abhor something in favor of something else. **Choice H** is incorrect because preclude is also not quite what we need; it means to make impossible.

411 **Choice A, Choice F, and Choice H are correct** because if people were surprised by this man's decision to teach, he must have had at least a passing interest in performing, so look for a word that reflects this. Manifest (evident or obvious) achieves this. Given that he decided to teach in spite of this, he must have felt it was important in some way - keep this in mind when filling in the second blank. The correct answer is incumbent upon (obligatory). As for the last blank, try to think of why he might feel obligated to teach - presumably because he feels that the state of arts education in the public schools needs improving. The best answer is abysmal, which means extremely bad or severe.

Choice B is incorrect because inordinate (not within proper or reasonable limits) is too strong, given that it implies his interest was excessive and unhealthy. **Choice C** is incorrect because if his interest were merely perfunctory, however, it is unlikely anyone would be surprised; it means hasty and superficial or indifferent. **Choice D** is incorrect because inimical to is certainly not the correct answer; he would surely not choose to do something that was harmful or hostile to him. **Choice E** is incorrect because on the other hand, he would have to have a fairly high opinion of himself to say that his decision was munificent of (very generous of) him.

Chapter 4: Text Completion

Choice G is incorrect because to say that arts education is banal would be a bit harsh; the purpose of elementary and secondary arts programs isn't really innovation, so it would be unfair to criticize them as hackneyed or trite. **Choice I** is incorrect because odious is also too strong a word, though for different reasons. It means hateful or detestable, which implies some degree of moral condemnation.

412 Choice C, Choice F, and Choice G are correct because as this passage implies, the sloth has a reputation for being slow and lazy, and the first missing word will reflect that. Phlegmatic, which means not easily excited to action or display of emotion and is the correct answer. phlegmatic, which means not easily excited to action or display of emotion and is the correct answer. Sluggard fits perfectly; it refers to a person who is habitually inactive or lazy. Finally, we know from the rest of the passage that sloths do not move frequently, so they must avoid physical activity. The best answer is abstain from, which means to hold oneself back voluntarily.

Choice A is incorrect because fulsome is too negative for the neutral and descriptive tone of the passage; it means offensive to good taste or sickening. **Choice B** is incorrect because lugubrious means mournful or gloomy and has nothing to do with the subject of the passage. **Choice D** is incorrect because virago means an ill-tempered, scolding woman, which should be eliminated. **Choice E** is incorrect because libertine is similarly irrelevant; it means a person who is morally or sexually unrestrained. **Choice H** is incorrect because inveigh against does not make sense; sloths do not protest strongly against physical activity, they simply refrain from it. **Choice I** is incorrect because there is also no indication that sloths go through an active period, so it cannot be that they wean themselves off (withdraw from) physical activity.

413 Choice A, Choice F, and Choice G are correct because the passage is talking about hackers and computer programmers and cyber criminals working online and with technology. Also, the Nasdaq is an American stock exchange and it was hacked, so the second blank must mean something similar to being open to an attack by hackers. Vulnerability (how capable something is of being attacked or how susceptible it is to danger) means exactly that. Finally, puissance means force or strength, and thus makes it the best choice for the third blank, rather than nostrum (a panacea or a sham cure) or cynosure (a thing that attracts notice because of its beauty or brilliance).

Choice B is incorrect because cryptic means difficult to decipher, which does not align with the context of the passage. **Choice C** is incorrect because captious means tending to find fault or raise petty objections, which does not align with the context of the passage. **Choice D** is incorrect because aversion means a strong dislike or disinclination, which does not align with the context of the passage. **Choice E** is incorrect because perfidy means deceitfulness or untrustworthiness, which does not align with the context of the passage. **Choice H** is incorrect because nostrum means a medicine, especially one that is not considered effective that is prepared by an unqualified individual. **Choice I** is incorrect because cynosure is a person or thing that is the center of attention or admiration, which does not align with the context of the passage.

414 Choice A, Choice F, and Choice I are correct because for the first blank, we are looking for a word to describe a kind of beauty that would suggest extreme fragility. Tremulous, which means timid or quivering, is the best answer. As for the second blank, we know from the passage that some butterflies advertise their taste in the hopes that a predator will not make the same mistake twice. The best answer in this regard is fulsome (offensive or sickening). Finally, we are told that some butterflies deal with predators by sporting eye-shaped spots on their wings; these spots probably either frighten or confuse predators. Confound, which means to perplex and is the correct answer for the final blank as a result.

Choice B is incorrect because inordinate (excessive) beauty would not necessarily imply fragility, so this could not be correct. **Choice C** is incorrect because mincing is too negative a word for the neutral, even respectful, tone of this passage; it means affectedly dainty or elegant. **Choice D** is incorrect because an insidious taste is not obvious enough to deter a predator; it means stealthily treacherous or operating in an inconspicuous way but actually with grave effect. **Choice E** is incorrect because predators might actually seek out an elusive (hard to express or define) taste, provided it was a pleasant one. **Choice H** is incorrect because it is not clear how the spots could placate (appease or conciliate) a predator; it is not as if the butterflies are offering up their wings for consumption. **Choice G** is incorrect because it is unlikely that the spots could maim (mutilate or impair) a predator.

415 Choice A, Choice F, and Choice G are correct because to fill in the first blank, we need a word that describes the kind of obedience that all parents expect. The correct answer is filial, which simply means of, pertaining to, or befitting a son or daughter. To fill in the second blank, think about what kind of parenting doesn't give children a chance to exercise their own judgment - presumably, one where the parents make all of the decisions. The best answer is deference to (respectful submission or yielding to). Finally, we need a word to describe the sense of self possessed by children who grow up in authoritarian households. Tenuous (thin or weak), would be the correct answer.

Practice Set 3: Answers & Explanations

Choice B is incorrect because reciprocal (corresponding or given or felt by each toward the other, mutual) makes no sense, as it implies that all parents expect to obey their children, at least in some circumstances. **Choice C** is incorrect because scrupulous means minutely careful or exact obedience, and in any case, it makes no sense to speak of degrees of exact obedience. **Choice E** is incorrect because intransigence towards (inflexibility towards) will not work, because it implies that the children are doing whatever they want, regardless of their parents' orders. **Choice D** is incorrect because propensity for (natural tendency toward) we do not normally speak of absolute propensities - it is somewhat like saying absolute leanings. In any case, the phrase propensity for parental authority is awkward and unclear; does it imply, for example, that the parents are naturally skilled at giving orders? If you cannot make sense of a sentence once you have tried out a word, that word is almost certainly incorrect. **Choice H** is incorrect because mercurial (volatile or animated) it connotes too much positivity for this context; the author clearly disapproves of this parenting style and feels it has negative consequences. **Choice I** is incorrect because dissolute (indifferent to moral restraints or licentious) is too judgmental; the author obviously does not regard these children as in any way immoral.

416 **Choice B, Choice D, and Choice H are correct** first because precipitous (meaning dangerously high or steep), fits well with the context of the passage (which describes an extreme depreciation in net income). For the second blank competitors is best because in Asia it makes sense for these other countries to have companies competing for the same business. The last sentence logically must be making the point that GM will be in trouble if it does not perform better and performing consistently, steadily or evenly, is a positive thing that GM would want to do.

Choice A is incorrect because propitious means favorable or auspicious, which does not align with the context of the passage. **Choice C** is incorrect because promontory, which means an outcropping or peninsula, does not align with the context of the passage. **Choice E** is incorrect because assailant is an attacker, which does not align with the context of the passage. **Choice F** is incorrect because hindrances, which means impediments to, is too vague compared to other options. **Choice G** is incorrect because erratically, or unstable and unpredictable, is not a positive thing when talking about a business's performance. **Choice I** is incorrect because pedantically, didactically and pompously, does not make sense in this context either.

417 **Choice C, Choice D, and Choice G are correct** because contend reflects that there is a debate that exists among scholars. The best answer for the second blank is coterie, because coterie is a group of people, which fits with the context of the passage. Finally, cohesive style fits best for the third blank, as it refers to the seamless collaboration between writers, rather than a particular tone within the writing.

Choice A is incorrect because declaimed means to utter or deliver words in a rhetorical or impassioned way, which does not best align with the context of the passage. **Choice B** is incorrect because assume means to make a supposition without proof, which goes against the content of the passage. **Choice E** is incorrect because menagerie is a diverse and strange collection of people or things, which does not align with the context of the passage. **Choice F** is incorrect because gild means to cover in gold, which does not align with the context of the passage. **Choice H** is incorrect because flamboyant manner means boisterous or over the top, which does not align with the context of the passage. **Choice I** is incorrect because complicated time highlights difficulties associated with the current status quo, which runs contrary to the intent of the passage.

418 **Choice C, Choice E, and Choice I are correct** because most people don't like advertisements, and if they are seeing/hearing 3,000to 5,000 of them per day, they are probably fairly upset - the first missing word should reflect this. Disgruntlement, which means discontent or sulky dissatisfaction, achieves this end. The second missing word probably also focuses on the frustration of consumers - irritatingly, perhaps. Obtrusively (meddlesome or blatant), makes sense in the context of the passage without being repetitive. Finally, we need to find a word to describe the kind of marketing we are exposed to - most likely one that once more draws attention to its prevalence or frequency. The correct answer is barrage, which means an overwhelming quantity or explosion, and therefore best conveys the notion that we are constantly subjected to ads of one kind or another.

Choice A is incorrect because although some commercials might be edifying (instructive or beneficial), this passage clearly focuses on the downsides of advertising rather than the positives hence eliminating edification. **Choice B** is incorrect because trepidation is too strong a word; consumers are irritated by advertising, but they do not experience tremulous fear or agitation. **Choice D** is incorrect because consummately does not continue with this theme, and it would in any case be redundant coming directly after effectively (it means completely or perfectly). **Choice F** is incorrect because nefariously (wickedly or heinously) is probably an overstatement; it is better to avoid such strongly condemnatory words unless you have a very compelling reason to believe the passage requires one. **Choice G** is incorrect because dearth means inadequate supply or lack, which does not align with the context of the passage.

Chapter 4: **Text Completion**

Choice H is incorrect because parlance (a way of speaking or an idiom) is not particularly relevant to this passage, which focuses on the quantity of ads we are exposed to, not on the kind of language they use.

419 **Choice B, Choice E, and Choice H are correct** because the text is about the attempt to both embrace modernizing reforms and maintain a Tatar identity, so the first blank must be accentuate (give importance to or stress). If the Tatars are developing a secular approach, then they must find a new apperception, or understanding, of Islam. Since the entire passage has been about how Tatars continued to maintain, or perpetuated, their identity, H is the only reasonable choice for the third blank

Choice A is incorrect because desiccate means to remove the water from a substance, which does not align with the context of the passage. **Choice C is incorrect** because abrogate means to repeal or do away with, which does not align with the context of the passage. **Choice D is incorrect** because aesthetic means the external appearance of something, which does not align with the context of the passage. **Choice F is incorrect** because apperception means fully conscious perception, which does not best align with the context of the passage. **Choice G is incorrect** because abdicating means stepping down from a throne, which does not align with the context of the passage. **Choice I is incorrect** because gainsaying means to deny or contradict a fact or statement, which does not align with the context of the passage.

420 **Choice C, Choice D, and Choice G are correct** because the first blank is part of a comparison. The second half – dealing with each question one at a time – tells us that the first half must mean the opposite of that, or dealing with all the parts at once. Components means pieces or parts, and therefore is the only acceptable choice. The second blank is also a comparison. Ephemeral and amorphous mean not concrete or lacking form, while tangible means the opposite. In this comparison concrete action is the more logical opposition to continued negotiations, so tangible is the best choice. Finally, for the last blank, both alleviate and exterminate could work logically in the last sentence – the phased approach could lessen (alleviate) or destroy/get rid of (exterminate) the immediate pressures. However, grammatically and stylistically only alleviate fits.

Choice A is incorrect because inaccuracies means incorrect aspects or errors. This does not align with the context of the passage. **Choice B is incorrect** because perquisite is defined as a special right or privilege enjoyed as a result of one's position, which does not align with the context of the passage. **Choice E is incorrect** because ephemeral means lasting for only a short period of time, which does not align with the context of the passage.

Choice F is incorrect because amorphous means lacking defined geometry, which does not align with the context of the passage. **Choice H is incorrect** because exterminating means to eradicate, which does not align with the context of the passage. **Choice I is incorrect** because implicates means to demonstrate the involvement of someone through indirect means, which does not align with the context of the passage.

421 **Choice C, Choice D, and Choice I are correct** because this text is about plants and animals and their relationship, and ecologists study the interaction between organisms and their environment. The bees stay with a single flower, so the second blank needs to describe a relationship where you are with only one person – monogamous. Finally, the passage claims that it is important for an ecosystem to have a larger number of species (in this case bee species), or biodiversity.

Choice A is incorrect because cryptologists are those who study codes and ciphers which does not align with the context of the passage. **Choice B is incorrect** because geologists are those who study earth and its composition which does not align with the context of the passage. **Choice E is incorrect** because polygamous means a relationship between several parties, which does not align with the context of the passage. **Choice F is incorrect** because hypergamous means a relationship with someone of higher status or more wealth, which does not align with the context of the passage. **Choice G is incorrect** because anathemas means despised or repugnant, which does not align with the context of the passage. **Choice H is incorrect** because surfeit, which means an overabundance of something, does not align with the context of the passage.

422 **Choice B, Choice E, and Choice H are correct** because expedient (suitable or advantageous) is the only valid choice for the first blank given that the method is also described as simple and useful. For the second blank the best choice is E – since the scientists are hopeful for the future of the enzyme, presumptively (in all likelihood, presumably) is the best fit. Finally, the last blank has to be a word that is similar to possibilities or repercussions. implications.

Choice C is incorrect because imprudent means a bad idea, which does not align with the context of the passage. **Choice A is incorrect** because superfluous means unnecessary, which does not align with the context of the passage. **Choice D is incorrect** because abstractly means intangible, which does not align with the context of the passage. **Choice F is incorrect** because dubious means unlikely, which does not align with the context of the passage. **Choice G is incorrect** because impositions means to be put upon in an undesired fashion, which does not align with the context of the passage. **Choice I is incorrect** because inhibitions means limiting factors, which does not align with the context of the passage.

423 **Choice B, Choice F, and Choice G are correct** because gravity and surface tension refer to laws of physics, not biology or geology. Second, being able to slide through a tiny hole or climb up the side of a glass implies that these laws are not in effect, or are not interfering with the movement of the superfluid. Finally, while envisioned could possibly work for the final blank, observed is much more appropriate, especially considering that scientists rarely make assumptions without experimenting and observing to check their validity.

Choice A is incorrect because geology is the study of rocks and minerals, which does not align with the context of the passage. **Choice C** is incorrect because biology is the study of life, which does not align with the context of the passage. **Choice D** is incorrect because opprobrium is defined as a harsh criticism or censure, which does not align with the context of the passage. **Choice E** is incorrect because celerity means swiftness of movement, which does not align with the context of the passage. **Choice H** is incorrect because obliterated means completely destroyed, which does not align with the context of the passage. **Choice I** is incorrect because envisioned means imagined, which does not align with the context of the passage.

424 **Choice B, Choice F, and Choice G are correct** because we know from the word though that the first half of the first sentence is meant to contrast with the second half, so if The Picture of Dorian Gray is now an acclaimed work, it must have been ignored or even criticized at the time it was published. The best answer is reviled, which means vilified or disparaged. We don't have much to go on for the second blank, except that the novel was taken as an account of moral depravity; we can assume, at least, that the missing adjective is nothing complimentary. However, lurid, ties in with the book's perceived immorality and is therefore the best choice; it means gruesome, shocking, or terrible in intensity. The final blank clearly deals with the effect of social climate on the reception of a piece of art. The correct answer is obfuscate, which means to make obscure or unclear.

Choice A is incorrect because vaunted, which means boasted of, is close to the opposite of what we are looking for. **Choice C** is incorrect because expunged is better, but still not a good choice; it means erased or wiped out, which the novel clearly was not, given that it is still in existence today. **Choice D** is incorrect because histrionic, which means deliberately affected or overly dramatic, is somewhat plausible, but cant be picked if all the choices have been read. **Choice E** is incorrect because insipid is probably not correct; it means vapid or bland, which just doesn't seem a strong enough description for a supposedly immoral story. **Choice H** is incorrect because emblazon does not seem like a very good choice; it means to decorate with brilliant colors or to proclaim, whereas this passage is about the lack of recognition Dorian Gray received as a result of its social context. **Choice I** is incorrect because atrophy (to affect with atrophy, which means degeneration, decline, or disuse) will not work either, unless you believe that social climate can affect the actual value (i.e. not the perceived value) of something.

425 **Choice B, Choice E, and Choice G are correct.** For the first sentence, there are several gears to be shifted through, as in a sequence. For the second blank, the entry must reflect the lack of action required from the driver. Assistance is the only suitable option to that end. Finally, a driver must shift a manual but do nothing in an automatic which suggests less coordination is needed in an automatic.

Choice A is incorrect because gamut means the complete range or scope of something, which does not align with the context of the passage. **Choice C** is incorrect because filigree refers to a delicate art form of intricate metal work that involves twisting, curling, or plaiting fine metal threads into ornamental designs, which does not align with the context of the passage. **Choice D** is incorrect because contrivance means to use skill to bring something about or create something, which does not align with the context of the passage. **Choice F** is incorrect because reliance speaks to a dependence on or trust in someone or something, which does not align with the context of the passage. **Choice H** is incorrect because a long time refers to an extended temporal period, which does not align with the context of the passage. **Choice I** is incorrect because more stability refers to the establishment of a sturdier foundation, which does not align with the context of the passage.

426 **Choice B, Choice F, and Choice H are correct** because "protracted" (B) means prolonged or extended in time, which aligns with the passage's description of a war that lasted four years instead of ending quickly. The "wanton" (F) waste of life in the trenches describes the senseless and excessive bloodshed, making it the most appropriate word for that blank. Finally, "demise" (H) refers to the collapse or end of something, which accurately fits the context of the fall of four great empires as a result of the war.

Choice A is incorrect because "recalcitrant" means stubborn or resistant to authority, which does not logically describe a prolonged war stalemate. **Choice C** is incorrect because "divergent" means differing or deviating, which does not clearly describe the waste of life in the trenches. **Choice D** is incorrect because "querulous" means complaining or whining, and is not appropriate for describing loss of life. **Choice E** is incorrect because "anachronistic" refers to something out of place in time, which doesn't make sense when describing the nature of war casualties. **Choice G** is incorrect because "accretion" means growth or accumulation, the opposite of the collapse described in the passage. **Choice I** is incorrect because "disparity" means inequality or difference, which does not fit the context of the fall of empires.

427 **Choice B, Choice D, and Choice G are correct** because the sentence is about analyzing social media content consumption to understand viewer preferences, making gauge (B) the most suitable word—it means to measure or assess. Pet videos described as "endearing and mischievous" are best captured by beguiling (D), meaning charming or enchanting, especially in a playful way. The phrase referencing the "undeniable popularity" of pet videos contradicting the preference for violence is best completed with proves immaterial (G), which means to show something is irrelevant or not valid.

Choice A is incorrect because expound means to explain in detail, which does not match the context of evaluating data. **Choice C** is incorrect because challenge implies opposition or dispute, but there is no contrary stance being addressed in the first blank. **Choice E** is incorrect because quixotic refers to unrealistic or impractical ideals, which doesn't apply to pet videos generally. **Choice F** is incorrect because odious means repulsive or hateful, which contradicts the positive and playful tone of the pet videos. **Choice H** is incorrect because merely obviates means to make something unnecessary, not to disprove or invalidate a claim. **Choice I** is incorrect because serves to corroborate would mean the pet videos support the claim that people prefer violent content, which the passage argues against.

428 **Choice A, Choice E, and Choice G are correct** because swiftly (A) highlights the contrast in the passage between the fast pace of legislative action in the House and the slower pace in the Senate. Impeded (E), meaning delayed or obstructed, emphasizes the Senate's slower processing of legislation, reinforcing this contrast. Bipartisan (G) accurately reflects the Senate's role in ensuring different viewpoints are considered, which aligns with the idea of cooperation between opposing political parties.

Choice B is incorrect because stubbornly implies resistance or inflexibility, which doesn't clearly relate to legislative pacing or support the contrast with "swiftly." **Choice C** is incorrect because salaciously refers to inappropriate or lewd interest in sexual matters, which is irrelevant to the context of government processes. **Choice D** is incorrect because ringfenced refers to the protection or isolation of funds, which doesn't fit the passage's theme about legislative procedure or pace. **Choice F** is incorrect because recalled refers to memory or retrieval of information, which is unrelated to how bills move through legislative bodies. **Choice H** is incorrect because controlling implies dominance or supervision, which contradicts the passage's tone of inclusiveness and cooperation in decision-making. **Choice I** is incorrect because uncommon merely means rare or unusual, which doesn't contribute meaningfully to the discussion of legislative timing or processes.

429 **Choice B, Choice D, and Choice I are correct** because to propel is to cause something to move forward. The contraction of the heart muscle moves blood forward and out of the muscle. To constrict is to squeeze from all sides. Constricts is the correct choice as it refers to the pressure exerted to send blood out of the heart. Depleted means seriously decreased or exhausted. Blood depleted of oxygen must be enriched. As the blood travels the circulatory system different organs and systems use the oxygen. By the time the blood returns to the heart, the oxygen has been depleted making it the best choice.

Choice A is incorrect because pitch means "to throw", which does not apply to liquid moved through a closed system. **Choice C** is incorrect because project is similar to pitch as it refers to throwing or casting something out, which does not apply to the movement of a liquid through a closed system. **Choice E** is incorrect because to compress is to press together to create a solid mass, which does not best fit the context of the passage. **Choice F** is incorrect because to cinch is to circle something with a tight grip, which does not best fit the context of the passage. **Choice G** is incorrect because squandered means wasted, which does not fit the context of the passage. **Choice H** is incorrect because augmented is an antonym, which means added to, and does not fit the meaning of the passage.

430 **Choice B, Choice D, and Choice H are correct** because stimuli (B) refers to things that elicit a response—in this case, colors triggering psychological reactions, which is the core idea of the sentence. Performance (D) fits the context of the sentence, which discusses how red can enhance athletic outcomes—something directly related to the execution of tasks or actions, i.e., performance. Inceptive (H), meaning in the early or beginning stage, accurately reflects the passage's point that color research is still in its infancy, despite public interest.

Choice A is incorrect because audio refers to sound, which has no relevance in a sentence focused on visual stimuli like color. **Choice C** is incorrect because hue, while related to color, is singular and would be repetitive and grammatically inconsistent with the plural noun needed for the sentence. **Choice E** is incorrect because awards are the outcomes of performance, not the subject of enhancement by color stimuli—thus the focus should be on performance itself, not what it may earn. **Choice F** is incorrect because incompetency is the opposite of enhancement, contradicting the sentence's point that red improves athletic ability. **Choice G** is incorrect because mature, meaning fully developed, does not contrast with public dissatisfaction. The sentence structure requires a word that implies the research is still insufficient. **Choice I** is incorrect because experimental is nearly synonymous with empirical, making it redundant and stylistically inappropriate in this sentence.

431 **Choices A, D, and G are correct** because the passage aims to highlight the importance of location associated with buying a home, while at the same time considering other factors which could influence the assessment. To that end, quality, defined as "the standard of something as measured against other things of similar kind", geography, defined as "the nature and arrangement of places, things, and features", and juxtaposed, which means "contrasted against" most effectively conveys the intent of the passage.

Choice B is incorrect because piety means "the quality of being religious or reverent", which does not align with the theme of the passage. **Choice C** is incorrect because scandalousness means "disgracefulness that offends public morality", which does not align with the theme of the passage. **Choice E** is incorrect because viscosity is "a quantity describing the magnitude of internal friction of a substance", which does not align with the meaning of the passage. **Choice F** is incorrect because liability means "the state of being responsible for something". While the clause might be suitable syntactically, it fails to align with the meaning of the passage due to the reference of "zip code" in a later clause. **Choice H** is incorrect because reassured means "to say or do something to remove fears or doubts", which does not align with the theme of the passage. **Choice I** is incorrect because outlasted means "lived or lasted longer than" which does not align with the theme of the clause or passage.

432 **Choices C, F, and I are correct** because the passage aims to highlight the stepwise approach which encourages students to not discontinue the pursuit of complex subjects such as quantum mechanics. Complexity, defined as "the state or quality of being intricate or complicated", dissuade, defined as "persuasion to not take a particular course of action", and gradually, defined as "occurring bit by bit over a period of time" serve to effectively convey the meaning of the passage.

Choice A is incorrect because abrogation is defined as "the abolition of a law, right, or agreement", which does not align with the meaning of the passage. **Choice B** is incorrect because relatability is defined as "the quality of being easy to understand or feel sympathy for", which does not align with the meaning of the passage. **Choice D** is incorrect because contrive is defined as "to bring about by deliberate use of skill or artifice", which does not align with the context of the passage. **Choice E** is incorrect because inundate, defined as "overwhelm with things or people to be dealt with", does not align with the context of the clause within which it resides. **Choice G** is incorrect because empirically is defined as "by means of experience or observation rather than theory or pure logic", which does not align with the meaning of the passage. **Choice H** is incorrect because swiftly means quickly, which would likely lead to more confusion or discouragement, not less.

433 **Choice A, Choice D, and Choice H are correct** because arguably (A) introduces a defensible but possibly debatable claim that health is more than just the absence of disease. This fits the tone and structure of a statement presenting a nuanced perspective. Encapsulates (D) is appropriate because it means "to express the essential features of something succinctly," which matches the idea of a more complex definition of health including the act of maintaining life. Bespoke (H), meaning custom-made or personalized, contrasts effectively with "one-size-fits-all," supporting the idea that wellness routines should be tailored to individual needs.

Choice B is incorrect because ostensibly implies something that only appears to be true, which would undermine the argument being made, rather than support it. **Choice C** is incorrect because conspicuously, meaning clearly visible or noticeable, does not relate to the logical structure or message of the sentence. **Choice E** is incorrect because extolled means praised highly, which does not logically fit with the idea of describing what health includes. **Choice F** is incorrect because abrogated, meaning to abolish or do away with (usually a law), carries a legal and negative connotation irrelevant to the subject of health. **Choice G** is incorrect because proscribed, meaning forbidden or prohibited, does not match the context of encouraging personalized health solutions. **Choice I** is incorrect because preordained implies fate or inevitability, not customization or individual adaptation.

434 **Choices A, E, and I are correct** because the sentence aims to highlight how gene editing technologies have presented an exciting development to treat underlying causes of certain diseases rather than the symptoms. To that end, revolutionized, defined as "changing something radically or fundamentally", symptoms defined as "a physical sign of the existence of a disease", and foundational, defined as "denoting an underlying basis or principle" all combine to convey this sentiment in the most effective manner possible.

Choice B is incorrect because vilified is defined as "to speak or write about in an abusive or disparaging manner", which does not align with the context of the passage. **Choice C** is incorrect because indemnified is defined as "to secure someone against legal liability or harm", which does not align with the context of the passage. **Choice D** is incorrect because repechages is defined as "a contest in which those who failed to win heats of a regatta compete to win a place in the final",

Chapter 4: Text Completion

which does not align with the context of the passage. **Choice F** is incorrect because foibles are defined as "minor weaknesses or eccentricities", which does not fit with the context of the passage. **Choice G** is incorrect because relational is defined as "concerning the way in which two people or things are connected", which does not align with the context of the passage. **Choice H** is incorrect because educational is defined as "of or relating to an approach to learning", which does not align with the context of the passage.

435 **Choice C, Choice D, and Choice G are correct** because paramount (C) means "more important than anything else," which correctly emphasizes that the color and durability of the wood are just as significant as the underlayment. Substance (D) fits the second blank because it refers to a material of a particular kind—here, the underlayment used in flooring. Layered (G) is appropriate for the third blank because the sentence describes how the underlayment is placed between the subfloor and the hardwood, implying a stacking or layering process.

Choice A is incorrect because subordinate implies that the color and durability are less important than the underlayment, contradicting the sentence's claim of equal importance. **Choice B** is incorrect because impeccable, meaning flawless or perfect, suggests the quality of the underlayment determines the color and durability, which is not the logical structure of the sentence. **Choice E** is incorrect because epidermis refers to the outer layer of skin and is biologically specific, making it ill-suited for describing a construction material between layers of flooring. **Choice F** is incorrect because dispense is a verb meaning "to distribute" or "do without," which does not match the noun form required by the sentence. **Choice H** is incorrect because superimposed implies one item is placed over another but both remain visible, which doesn't align with the function of an underlayment hidden between two layers. **Choice I** is incorrect because imprinted means to press a mark into a surface, which doesn't describe the purpose or position of the underlayment in the flooring structure.

436 **Choice A, Choice E, and Choice G are correct** because we are told that we like to think of ourselves as firm in our beliefs, when in truth those beliefs are easily swayed. The first blank, therefore, must refer to this susceptibility to external suggestion. Tractable, which means easily managed or yielding, best completes the first blank. In order to fill in the last two blanks, you need to have some sense of what the sentence as a whole is saying; the gist seems to be that participants in the Asch study misjudged the length of a line in the interests of conformity. To repudiate works well; it means to reject or to refuse to acknowledge. Finally, we need a word that means something like agree with to fill in the last blank. Abide by (to act in accord with or to submit to) is the correct answer.

Choice B is incorrect because fatuous (foolish) is a bit too judgmental. **Choice C** is incorrect because the first blank, therefore, must refer to this susceptibility to external suggestion. Dogmatic is nearly the opposite; it means opinionated or asserting opinions in a doctrinaire manner. **Choice D** is incorrect because vituperate (vilify or berate) makes no sense in this context; there is no suggestion that the participants actively criticized their sensory perceptions. **Choice F** is incorrect because to garner means to gather, which does not align with the context of the passage. **Choice H** is incorrect because preclude means to make possible, which does not align with the context of the passage. **Choice I** is incorrect because quibble with means "to make trivial objections", which does not make sense in the context of the passage.

437 **Choice A, Choice E, and Choice I are correct** because the first sentence informs us that the death of Hu Yaobang caused the protests, so we are looking for a word that describes something that causes something else. The correct answering this context is catalyst, which means a thing that precipitates an event or change. As for the final two blanks, you should be able to glean from the rest of the passage that the government responded to the protests in a particularly savage way that was probably not received well in other countries, so you should be looking for words in keeping with this. Heinous (hateful or totally reprehensible) is best fit for the second blank as a result, and opprobrium (reproach or censure) seems a quite likely reaction, and should be suitable for the third blank.

Choice C is incorrect because an antidote (something that prevents or counteracts injurious or unwanted effects) causes improvement, but that clearly will not work in this sentence, which describes events culminating in a massacre. **Choice B** is incorrect because imbroglio will also not work; it means a misunderstanding or an intricate and perplexing affair, and better describes the circumstances following Hu Yaobang's death than the death itself. **Choice D** is incorrect because redoubtable means formidable, and it often implies respect, which is clearly not appropriate here in this context. **Choice F** is incorrect because dubious means questionable and is also not a good choice; there is no question that the government's actions were unethical. **Choice G** is incorrect because encomium would certainly not be an appropriate response; it means a formal expression of high praise. **Choice H** is incorrect because sanctimony is also a bad fit; it means pretended, affected, or hypocritical religious devotion, righteousness, etc.

Practice Set 3: Answers & Explanations

438 **Choices A, D, and G are correct** because the sentence aims to highlight the opulence of the palace home of Louis XIV, and how France prospered under his reign, and how that prosperity ebbed after his reign. As a result, abode, defined as "a place of residence", reign, defined as "a period of rule", and lavish, defined as "sumptuously rich, elaborate or luxurious" satisfy the aims of the passage.

Choice B is incorrect because cavalcade is defined as "a formal procession of people walking, on horseback, or riding vehicles", which does not align with the context of the passage. **Choice C** is incorrect because retort is defined as "something said in response to a remark or accusation", which does not align with the context of the passage. **Choice E** is incorrect because recital is defined as "a performance of a program of music by a solo instrumentalist or singer or by a small group", however this definition does not align with the context of the passage. **Choice F** is incorrect because arbor is defined as "a shady garden alcove with sides and a roof formed by trees or plants over a wooden frame", which does not align with the context of the passage. **Choice H** is incorrect because jejune is defined as "naive, simplistic, and superficial", which does not align with the context of the passage. **Choice I** is incorrect because esoteric is defined as "something understood by only a small number of people with specialized knowledge of a subject", which does not align with the context of the passage.

439 **Choices B, E, and H are correct** because the passage seeks to contrast the spotlight and adulation dancers achieve, and contrast it against the rather unfamous existence off of the stage. Waltz, defined as "a dance in triple time performed by a couple as they turn rhythmically around the dance floor", adjourned, defined as "displacement to another locale", and anonymity, defined as "lack of distinctive features" serves to best convey the meaning of the passage.

Choice A is incorrect because conversation is defined as "a discussion between different parties", which does not align within the full context of the passage. **Choice C** is incorrect because milling is defined as "idealing about", which does not align with the context of the passage. **Choice D** is incorrect because adorned is defined as "decorated to make beautiful or attractive", which does not align with the context of the passage. **Choice F** is incorrect because allayed is defined as "diminished or put to rest", which does not align with the context of the passage. **Choice G** is incorrect because rowdiness is defined as "behavior which is noisy and possibly violent", which does align with the context of the passage. **Choice I** is incorrect because consanguinity is defined as "being descended from the same ancestor", which does not align with the context of the passage.

440 **Choices C, E, and G are correct** because the passage aims to highlight strategies that would reduce risk and increase profits. Hedge, defined as "protecting oneself by making contrasting bets on a particular opportunity", yield, defined as "to produce or provide", and marginalize, defined as "to reduce the standard of something or someone" effectively convey the aims of the passage.

Choice A is incorrect because revolutionized is defined as "changed radically or fundamentally", which does not align with the context of the passage. **Choice B** is incorrect because relatability is defined as "the quality of being easily understood or feeling sympathy for", which does not align with the context of the passage. **Choice D** is incorrect because abet is defined as "encouraging or assisting someone to do something wrong", which does not align with the context of the passage. **Choice F** is incorrect because penalize is defined as "subject to a form of punishment", which does not align with the context of the passage. **Choice H** is incorrect because masquerade is defined as "a false show or pretense", which does not align with the context of the passage. **Choice I** is incorrect because inundate is defined as "overwhelmed with things or people to be dealt with", which does not align with the context of the passage.

441 **Choices A, D, and G are correct** because the intent of the passage is to highlight water's ability to bring recharge and maintain balance within the body. The words revitalize, defined as "to imbue new life and vitality", constituents, defined as "components which make up part of a whole", and equilibrium, defined as "balance" best serve to deliver on the aims of the passage.

Choice B is incorrect because atomize is defined as "conversion to very fine particles or droplets", which does not align with the context of the passage. **Choice C** is incorrect because parallelize is defined as "the adaptation of a software program to run in concert with another", which does not align with the context of the passage. **Choice E** is incorrect because harbingers is defined as "a person or thing that foreshadows the approach of another", which does not align with the context of the passage. **Choice F** is incorrect because orbitals are defined as "the dynamic paths that planets follow with respect to time", which does not align with the context of the passage. **Choice H** is incorrect because salvation is defined as "the state of being protected from harm or a dire situation", which does not align with the context of the passage. **Choice I** is incorrect because regurgitation is defined as "the repetition of information without information or comprehension", which does not align with the context of the passage.

Chapter 4: Text Completion

442 **Choices B, F, and I are correct** because the passage seeks to highlight the impact which innovations in subatomic microscopy had on new discoveries. Neutrons, defined as "an uncharged subatomic particles in the nucleus of most atoms", visualize, defined as "to make something visible to the eye", and unparalleled, defined as "being unequaled", all serve to best convey the meaning of the passage.

Choice A is incorrect because exomes is defined as "the sequence of all exons in a genome", which does not align with the context of the passage. **Choice C** is incorrect because mandibles are defined as "the jaws of something or someone, usually in relation to insects", which does not align with the context of the passage. **Choice D** is incorrect because migrate is defined as "moving from one location to another", which does not align with the context of the passage. **Choice E** is incorrect because avoid is defined as "to stay away from", which does not align with the context of the passage. **Choice G** is incorrect because tepid is defined as "showing little enthusiasm for", which does not align with the context of the passage. **Choice H** is incorrect because regulated is defined as "controlled or supervised", which does not align with the context of the passage.

443 **Choice C, Choice E, and Choice I are correct** because the first sentence describes Richard III, at least in Shakespeare, as murderous. Clearly we need a word that implies condemnation of some sort. Reprobate (a depraved or unprincipled person) is the correct answer in this context. For the second blank, we know from the use of however that the historians mentioned in the sentence must doubt Shakespeare's portrayal of Richard; they presumably believe that the evidence against him is weak. Tenuous means thin or unsubstantiated and is the best answer in this context. Finally, for the last blank, we need to find a word that deals with Shakespeare's handling of Richard's character. Maligning (slandering or speaking ill of) is the correct answer to that end.

Choice A is incorrect because an iconoclast is a person who attacks traditional beliefs or institutions, and the passage gives us no reason to suspect Richard of subversive activities; regardless of whether or not he killed his nephews, he presumably did not attack the monarchy as an institution. **Choice B** is incorrect because mendicant won't work; it simply means beggar, which a king is unlikely to be in any case. **Choice D** is incorrect because quotidian means ordinary or commonplace - something that would presumably have no effect on the veracity of the evidence. **Choice F** is incorrect because whimsical means fanciful or given to fanciful notions; it is not normally used in the context of something as serious as evidence. **Choice G** is incorrect because renovating describes someone who renovates a person's reputation would be restoring it to good condition. **Choice H** is incorrect because commemorating also has connotations that are too positive for this context; to commemorate means to honor the memory of.

444 **Choice A, Choice D, and Choice H are correct** because sagacity (A) means wisdom, which directly reflects the idea of "knowledge gained from years of experience" as stated in the passage. Doddery (D) refers to physical frailty due to age, which fits with the description of the grandparent as "ailing," reinforcing the contrast between physical weakness and mental strength. Cornucopias (H), meaning "an abundant supply of good things," complements the idea that the grandparent, though physically weak, is rich in wisdom and experience—drawing attention to the contrast between a failing body and a fruitful mind.

Choice B is incorrect because salutations means "greetings", which does not align with the context of the passage. **Choice C** is incorrect because animations means "the state of being full of life and vigor" which is the opposite of the passage's meaning. **Choice E** is incorrect because agitated means "feeling or appearing troubled or nervous", which does not align with the implications of the context of the passage. **Choice F** is incorrect because virile means "having or characterized by strength and energy", which runs contrary to the context of the passage. **Choice G** is incorrect because delinquent means "late for something", which does not align with the context and meaning of the passage. **Choice I** is incorrect because abrasions means the process of scraping or wearing something away, which does not align with the context and meaning of the passage.

445 **Choices B, D, and H are correct** because the passage aims to highlight the diminished prospects of a previously praised discovery, and how it contrasts with the initial sentiments of the scientist that made the discovery. To that end, Eureka, defined as a "cry of joy or satisfaction when one discovers something", deleterious, defined as "causing harm or damage", and celebrated, meaning "to be praised for achievement or accomplishment" best satisfy the aim of the passage.

Choice A is incorrect because Blunderbuss is defined as "a muzzle loading firearm with a short barrel and a flaring muzzle", which does not align with the context of the passage. **Choice C** is incorrect because Glasnost is defined as "the policy of more open or consultative government", which does not align with the context of passage. **Choice E** is incorrect because stupendous is defined as "extremely impressive", which does not align with the context of the passage. **Choice F** is incorrect because magnificent is defined as "very good or excellent", which does not align with the context of the passage. **Choice G** is incorrect because loquacious is defined as "tending to talk a great deal", which does not align with the context of the passage. **Choice I** is incorrect because unintelligible is defined as "indecipherable", which does not align with the context of the passage.

446 **Choice C, Choice E, and Choice G are correct** because for the first blank, the key information here is that some people believe that the language used in victimology risks blaming the victim. It would seem, then, that victimology sometimes deals with controversial or touchy subjects, and we need a word that reflects this. The best answer is contentious, which means characterized by argument or controversy. Where the second blank is concerned, we are looking for a word describing behavior that might catch the attention of a criminal. The correct answer is brash, which means impertinent or, in this case, impetuous. Finally, we need a word that means something like excuse for the final blank - excusing the crime is the natural consequence of blaming the victim. You are left with condone, which means to disregard or to give tacit approval to.

Choice A is incorrect because salacious is not a good choice; although some people might take a salacious (lustful or obscene) interest in certain crimes, this passage does not deal with that. **Choice B** is incorrect because propitious means favorable or auspicious, which does not align with the context of the passage. **Choice D** is incorrect because timorous seems unlikely. While it is not out of the question that a criminal might target someone, who seems fearful or timid, such is surely not the case in most crimes. **Choice F** is incorrect because fulsome is too strong a word, even given the controversial nature of the term victim precipitation; it means offensive to good taste or sickening. **Choice H** is incorrect because to provoke (to anger or to induce) might describe what, according to the theory of victim precipitation, the victim does, but it is not a good fit here. **Choice I** is incorrect because rescind is too formal a word for this context; implicitly excusing the crime is not the same as officially invalidating or revoking it.

447 **Choices A, D, and G are correct** because the passage aims to describe the effects of war on Vietnam veterans, and how the events of war directed them towards pacifism. Shellshock, defined as "a form of post-traumatic stress disorder brought on by exposure to intense combat", ardent, defined as "enthusiastic or passionate", and campaigning, defined as "working in an organized or active way towards a particular goal" best convey the intent of this passage.

Choice B is incorrect because rickets is defined as "a disease of children driven by vitamin D deficiency", which does not align with the context of the passage. **Choice C** is incorrect because impetigo is defined as "a type of highly contagious skin infection", which does not align with the context of the passage. **Choice E** is incorrect because muted is defined as "quietly or subtly", which does not align with the context of the passage. **Choice F** is incorrect because malleable is defined as "easily influenced and pliable", which does not align with the context of the passage. **Choice H** is incorrect because admiring is defined as "expressive of admiration or warm approval", which does not align with the context of the passage. **Choice I** is incorrect because snarling is defined as "making an aggressive growl with barred teeth", which does not align with the context of the passage.

448 **Choices C, F, and I are correct** because the passage aims to highlight the impact a band had on a crowd made them desirous for an extension of the performance. Pianist, defined as "one who plays the piano", solo, defined as "a portion of a musical event dominated by a single performer", and Encore, defined as "a call by the audience to extend a performance" all serve as best answers to convey the meaning of this passage.

Choice A is incorrect because jingoist is defined as "extreme chauvinism or nationalism which is marked by especially belligerent foreign policy", which does not align with the context of the passage. **Choice B** is incorrect because abolitionist is defined as "one who fought to outlaw slavery", which does not align with the context of the passage. **Choice D** is incorrect because diminution is defined as "the reduction of size, extent, or importance of something", which does not align with the context of the passage. **Choice E** is incorrect because revelation is defined as "a surprising or previously unknown fact", which does not align with the context of the passage. **Choice G** is incorrect because Pinochle is defined as "a type of card game", which does not align with the context of the passage. **Choice H** is incorrect because Flabbergast is defined as "to greatly surprise or astonish", which does not align with the context of the passage.

449 **Choice B, Choice E, and Choice H are correct** because incest is taboo in many contemporary cultures, so you should look for a word that expresses strong censure or disapproval. Abhorred, which means detested, achieves this for the first blank. By contrast, the second blank requires a word that means something stronger than tolerated; if brother-sister marriages were actually used by the royal family for a specific purpose, they must have been approved of or even required. Mandated, which means authorized or required, achieves this end. To fill in the last blank, you will need to think about what the purpose of marrying within the royal family might have been. You can probably guess that the Egyptian royal family, like most royalty throughout history, wanted their line to remain untainted by inferior blood, so the missing word probably means something like pure. The correct answer is immaculate, or free from spot or stain, as it achieves this end.

Choice A is incorrect because venial means not seriously wrong or excusable and is a near antonym, which does not align with the context of the passage. **Choice C** is incorrect because ancillary means subordinate or auxiliary and would imply that society approved of, or at least tolerated, incest. **Choice D** is incorrect because condoned (to overlook or to excuse) does not align with the context of the passage. **Choice F** is incorrect because rectified (remedied or righted) will not work in this sentence either, as it implies that brother-sister marriages were seen as a problem to be fixed. **Choice G** is incorrect because omnipotent does not modify bloodline rather than family; the family almost certainly wished to remain unlimited in power, but it does not make much sense to refer to the bloodline in this way. **Choice I** is incorrect because empyreal is also slightly off the mark; it means pertaining to the sky or celestial. As a matter of fact, the Egyptian royals were considered divine, but since this information is not provided in the passage itself, it is best to eliminate this answer.

450 **Choice A, Choice D, and Choice H are correct** because most people would probably want something done about the worst effects of climate change - or any other problem, for that matter. To fill in the first blank, therefore, we need a word that means something like address or mitigate. Forestall, meaning to prevent or anticipate, best achieves this end. For the second blank, we need a word that explains why the companies mentioned in the passage feel they cannot comply with the law. The final sentence should tell you that onerous (burdensome) is a suitable choice as concrete companies feel that cutting emissions is essentially impracticable. The final blank requires a word that describes the relationship between concrete makers and the new law. Wary, meaning cautious towards or leery of, is the best answer in this regard.

Choice B is incorrect because it is not enough to discern or perceive the worst effects (the definition of descry), and it is not clear how reducing emissions would accomplish this in any case. **Choice C** is incorrect because it is also hard to imagine how one could propitiate (appease or conciliate) climate change - generally speaking, only people are capable of being appeased. **Choice E** is incorrect because meretricious does not make sense; surely even a law that is tawdry or based on pretense can be followed, and in any case, there is nothing in the passage suggesting that the program is simply for show. **Choice F** is incorrect because amorphous (lacking in shape or structure) is less suitable for the final sentence than onerous (burdensome). Concrete companies feel that cutting emissions is essentially impracticable. **Choice G** is incorrect because there is no reason, based on this passage, to think that concrete makers are more cognizant (aware) of the law than any other company affected by it. **Choice I** is incorrect because devoid simply does not make sense in this sentence; it means not possessing, and laws are not generally things that can be possessed.

Chapter 5
Sentence Equivalence

Chapter 5: Sentence Equivalence

Sentence Equivalence questions test your ability to interpret and understand what you read, and also your ability to use vocabulary in context. Each Sentence Equivalence question will consist of a sentence with a single blank. You will be asked to choose two words from among six that produce complete sentences with the most similar meanings.

The passages used for Sentence Equivalence questions will be drawn from a variety of topics, including the physical, biological, and social sciences, the arts and the humanities, business, and everyday life. As with other types of questions for the Verbal Reasoning component of the GRE, you need not be an expert on the topics covered in Sentence Equivalence questions too. You will, however, need to read the passage carefully enough to understand what is being said and be able to complete the sentence grammatically. All Sentence Equivalence questions will follow the same multiple-choice format. You will be given a sentence with a single blank and will be given 6 options to fill in the blank.

What Skills Do Sentence Equivalence Questions Test?

Like Text Completion questions, Sentence Equivalence questions test your ability to understand what you are reading and reason from incomplete information. However, Sentence Equivalence questions focus more on the meaning of a single sentence, so you'll need to be able to differentiate how different words complete the sentence. Some key skills that are tested include your ability to:

- reason based on incomplete information
- understand the meaning of sentences
- understand high level vocabulary
- apply vocabulary in context

What Does a Sentence Equivalence Question Look Like?

Sentence Equivalence questions will always be based on a single sentence. The sentence will have a single blank. You will be asked to read the sentence and get a feel for what two words from among the six given will produce sentences with the most similar meaning. Below is an example of what a Sentence Equivalence question will look like on the GRE General Test:

Select the two answer choices that, when used to complete the sentence, fit the meaning of the sentence as a whole and produce completed sentences that are alike in meaning.

1. Under Stalin, the Soviet state showed many of the same _____ tendencies of the Tsarist government it had replaced; dissent of any kind was stifled and political authority was centralized.

   A liberalizing
   B despotic
   C vicious
   D corrupt
   E oligarchic
   F autocratic

Answer Key

The answers to the above question are **Choice B** despotic and **Choice F** autocratic.

Strategies for Sentence Equivalence Questions

Sentence Equivalence questions are the least time-intensive question type you will see on the Verbal Reasoning component. Time budgeting is important for every component of the test, however, assuming that you have managed your time well for other types of questions, you should have plenty of time to give the necessary attention to Sentence Equivalence questions. Like Text Completion questions, it is important to read Sentence Equivalence questions with care. Do not skim Sentence Equivalence questions, since it is important that you understand exactly what the sentence means. Missing a keyword in a Sentence Equivalence can spell disaster since the focus of these questions is very narrow. Given that each question is based on a single sentence, even a careful reading should not take very long. If you find yourself taking any more than a minute or so on a Sentence Equivalence question, you should skip to another question and come back to it later if you have time.

As with the other types of questions on the Verbal Reasoning portion, do not let the subject matter of the passage throw you off—your ability to correctly answer these questions is independent of any expertise you may possess in the subject area of the passage. When answering Sentence Equivalence questions, you need to be able to quickly assess the meaning of a sentence based on incomplete information and have enough command of vocabulary to choose the words that will be the best fit to complete the sentence. You will not need to make any judgment about whether the passage is true or false.

The key skills for Sentence Equivalence questions are understanding the meaning of specific sentences and how individual words shape meaning. As you read the sentence, don't give the topic too much thought—focus on what the sentence means. Be sure to attend to important words that signal emphasis or qualification as these will help you decide which words will be the best fit for the blank. As with Text Completion, your vocabulary will play a role in your ability to do well on Sentence Equivalence questions. However, keep in mind that you will always be using words in context, so you won't necessarily need to know their exact meaning or dictionary definition. Also, remember that your task is to produce two sentences with the most similar meaning, not to find the two words with the most similar meaning.

 Key Points to Remember

- Read the sentence carefully - do not skim
- Keep an eye out for sections of the passage that either closely match or negate the definition of one of the word options
- Apply vocabulary in context

What follows are some more specific strategies for answering Sentence Equivalence questions. In the next chapter, you'll have a chance to put your skills to the test through several practice questions and learn how to hone them in the answers and explanations that follow.

1. Review Vocabulary

Previous versions of the GRE featured sections that were specifically geared toward vocabulary. The GRE General Test no longer features these sections, but as has been noted previously, vocabulary is still very important. This is especially so for Text Completion and Sentence Equivalence questions, where you will need to have some idea of what some "big" words mean in order to fill in the appropriate blanks. Note that Sentence Equivalence questions focus on the meaning of the completed sentence more than on the meaning of any individual word, so you can often get away with having a general understanding of what a word means. Nonetheless, anything that you can do to strengthen your vocabulary prior to the test will be helpful, since the test assumes a fairly high-level vocabulary. If you are not confident in your vocabulary, do what you can to improve it as part of your preparation for the test (this will serve you well in graduate school as well). Again, there are many cases when you will not need to know a precise definition of a word, but you will need to have a general sense of what it means. There are several things you can do to improve your vocabulary for the test:

- Review lists of common "GRE words" such as the one included in the *Online Resources*
- Use a vocabulary builder
- Get a sense of key Greek or Latin root words and what they mean - many words in English are based on Greek or Latin words, and knowing the meaning of a few key Greek or Latin words can help you figure out the meanings of numerous English words

2. Read the Sentence Carefully

Before you try to fill in any blank, read the sentence carefully. Sentence Equivalence questions focus on the meaning of sentences, so you'll need to get a clear sense of what the sentence means without the blank filled in to understand what words will effectively complete it.

3. Pay Special Attention to Significant Words

As with Text Completion questions, you should pay close attention to pivotal words in the sentence in Sentence Equivalence questions too. Keywords can give tremendous insight into the meaning of the sentence and provide strong indicators of what word you will need to choose to complete the sentence correctly. Words like "although", "despite", "moreover" or "therefore" which either emphasize or qualify something that has been said are often especially significant, so look out for them and be sensitive to how they modify the meaning of the sentence.

4. Be Careful Not to Make Your Choice Solely on the Meaning of Words

It may sound counter-intuitive, but sometimes two words with very similar meanings will not necessarily produce sentences of similar meanings. When answering Sentence Completion questions, you might be tempted to simply select the two words from among the options that have the most similar meaning, and use them to answer the question. This is a bad strategy for two reasons. In the first place, sometimes there will be more than one pair of words that have similar meanings. Without focusing on the meaning of the sentence, you might choose the wrong pair since you need to produce two grammatically correct, coherent sentences with similar meanings and not just find words that have similar meanings. The second reason is more counter-intuitive; however, sometimes the two words with the most similar meanings will not produce the two sentences with the most similar meanings. Keep this in mind and always focus on the meaning of the sentence, rather than on the meaning of the words you are choosing to complete it.

5. Come Up With Your Own Words To Fill In the Blanks

As with Text Completion questions, you can try to think of words that will fill in the blank to complete the sentence and then compare them to the options given to see if you can find any similar words. Sometimes you'll be able to see words that obviously correspond to those you have already thought of to fill in the blanks; other times, you'll be able to eliminate words with opposite meanings. Either of these options will be helpful to you as you try to answer the question.

6. Check Your Work

As with Text Completion questions, be sure that you always fill in the options that you choose to complete the sentence to make certain that your choices produce coherent, grammatically correct sentences with similar meanings. Remember that you need to satisfy all of these requirements in your answer.

7. Use Process of Elimination

The process of elimination is always useful in answering any type of multiple-choice question, and Sentence Equivalence is no exception. Unless the answer is immediately obvious to you, you should always be looking to narrow your choices by getting rid of potential answers that don't fit or don't make sense. When using the process of elimination for Sentence Equivalence questions, always keep in mind what the goals of the question are. You need to find the two words that will produce two distinct sentences that are coherent, grammatically correct, and have similar meanings. If a word doesn't make sense in context, you can dismiss it. If a word doesn't fit grammatically into the sentence, you can dismiss it. Keep this in mind as you answer Sentence Equivalence questions since it will help you eliminate inappropriate answer choices.

Chapter 5: Sentence Equivalence

Practice Questions

451. Rows of breathtakingly beautiful and _____ marble columns stretched the length of the basilica, watching over the 15th-century church's exceptional mosaic floor.

   A. clement
   B. ornate
   C. embroidered
   D. baroque
   E. dowdy
   F. garish

452. He watched the peripheral artery bypass through the observation window and marveled at the doctor's _____, which justified the already tremendous amounts of audaciousness necessary to perform such a procedure.

   A. aggression
   B. reticence
   C. proficiency
   D. contempt
   E. delusion
   F. expertise

453. It is known that many firms engage in misleading and often _____ accounting practices to inflate their short-term profits.

   A. counterfeit
   B. infamous
   C. fraudulent
   D. villainess
   E. dubious
   F. slanderous

454. I asked her to stop _____ me all the time about fixing the faucet in the spare room bathroom.

   A. hounding
   B. bearing
   C. ferreting
   D. badgering
   E. weaseling
   F. remonstrating

455. Due to recession, companies have learnt to be _____ with their marketing budgets and not spend outlandishly.

   A. gluttonous
   B. frugal
   C. altruistic
   D. lavish
   E. parsimonious
   F. miserly

456. The scent of freshly baked bread _____ into the room from the bakery below.

   A. drifted
   B. wafted
   C. coasted
   D. transmitted
   E. poised
   F. inured

457. The evening's _____ rays were enchanting to behold as they lit the horizon with their amazing display of colour.

   A. twilight
   B. diurnal
   C. crepuscular
   D. noontide
   E. enlightened
   F. modicum

458. In spite of his apparent knowledge of historical figures, Henry was a/an _____ when it came to well-known French Impressionists.

   A. dilettante
   B. unskilled
   C. amateur
   D. dabbling
   E. connoisseur
   F. proficient

258 | GRE Verbal Practice Questions

459. You could see why Annette was his muse; she had a healthy complexion and a/an _____ mane of golden tresses that cascaded down her back.

- A. barren
- B. profuse
- C. elaborate
- D. plenteous
- E. pretentious
- F. luxuriant

460. Archaeologists have found evidence that _____ tribes made baskets for collecting and storing food.

- A. old-fashioned
- B. primitive
- C. obsolete
- D. trampled
- E. antiquated
- F. archaic

461. Despite its _____ dimensions, the office space was still undersized for our needs.

- A. capacious
- B. abundance
- C. expansive
- D. brimming
- E. minute
- F. discrepant

462. Brazil and Argentina discussed the importance of gathering genetic information from the _____ tribes that live in the Amazonas region.

- A. homegrown
- B. inherited
- C. alien
- D. indigenous
- E. aboriginal
- F. inbred

463. Gang related crime was _____ in that area; even the police were wary about entering after dark.

- A. epidemic
- B. endemic
- C. curtailed
- D. governable
- E. exuberant
- F. prevalent

464. Though both protons and neutrons are housed in the nucleus of an atom, the protons but not the neutrons define the electric charge of the nucleus; neutrons contribute to the mass of the nucleus, but they have no electric charge to _____ to the nucleus.

- A. extenuate
- B. impart
- C. bestow
- D. remit
- E. bequeath
- F. ossify

465. Though a significant number of countries are governed as democracies, the government structures that exist around the world are far from _____; along with democracies, an assortment of ruling systems including theocracies, technocracies, constitutional monarchies, absolute monarchies, and dictatorships are in use today.

- A. bilious
- B. lachrymose
- C. homogenous
- D. undifferentiated
- E. discrete
- F. disjointed

Chapter 5: Sentence Equivalence

466. The marketing team _____ a new campaign to boost sales.
- [A] connived
- [B] contrived
- [C] devised
- [D] schemed
- [E] blueprints
- [F] casted

467. There was great public outrage when the _____ publication appeared in the media talking about the existence of child slavery in first world countries.
- [A] quarrelsome
- [B] controversial
- [C] metaphysical
- [D] doubtful
- [E] polemic
- [F] cantankerous

468. European imperialism redrew the borders of many African nations from the ones that existed before the colonizers arrived; many groups that were _____ before the Europeans' arrival found themselves, as a result of conquest, part of new nations that contained historically unacquainted ethnic groups by the time European rule ended.
- [A] sequestered
- [B] parochial
- [C] insular
- [D] sectarian
- [E] illiberal
- [F] catholic

469. Socialists often decry the _____ excesses of most capitalist societies.
- [A] materialistic
- [B] nonconforming
- [C] indolent
- [D] capitalism
- [E] victorian
- [F] bourgeois

470. The economic _____ between first world countries and third world countries have increased since the 1950s.
- [A] disparities
- [B] burrow
- [C] disagreeable
- [D] hole
- [E] animosity
- [F] discrepancies

471. The exact timing of hurricane season depends on the part of the world under _____, but meteorologists have determined that on average the month of May is the most active month for hurricane activity worldwide while the month of September usually has the least hurricane activity.
- [A] cogitation
- [B] consideration
- [C] circumlocution
- [D] introspection
- [E] expatiation
- [F] rumination

472. Media are some of the most effective tools cultural influencers can use to spread their messages to the widest possible audience; some use media to influence others in _____ ways, forwarding fashion and hairstyle trends for example, while others employ media to incite dissension and societal upheaval.
- [A] innocuous
- [B] aberrant
- [C] injurious
- [D] banal
- [E] equivocal
- [F] exorbitant

Practice Questions

473 After the fall of the Iron Curtain, multinational corporations acquired companies in countries that had been part of the Soviet Bloc and _____ problems at every level of their new possessions.

- A encountered
- B took on
- C happened upon
- D affronted
- E emulated
- F studied

474 America's founding fathers used compromise to _____ disagreements that arose when assaying the emerging government; for example, the founders determined the best solution would be to create a two-house legislative body in order to suppress conflicts that arose between two factions over how citizens would be represented in the national government.

- A quell
- B castigate
- C emulate
- D exacerbate
- E obviate
- F precipitate

475 The social stigma associated with a conviction for a serious crime can present nearly _____ obstacles for someone attempting to re-enter society and contribute to the citizenry after completing a period of incarceration; a criminal record can prevent a person from finding employment or even voting in certain jurisdictions.

- A culpable
- B dogmatic
- C intransigent
- D emollient
- E recalcitrant
- F florid

476 Except for the _____ example of "The Necklace," Maupassant's short stories are not known for surprise endings, most of his work emphasizes characterization and the exploration of sexuality.

- A famous
- B great
- C ignominious
- D infamous
- E notorious
- F preeminent

477 In response to negative attention in the press following a public performance of his opera, Shostakovich subtitled his next work "An artistic response to just criticism," although many _____ listeners heard sarcasm coming through the seemingly happy moments of the music.

- A discriminative
- B intensive
- C intelligent
- D perceptive
- E sharp-witted
- F veteran

478 When the Japanese attacked Pearl Harbor on 7 December 1941, their ultimate aim was not to totally defeat the United States, but to win a war of attrition so they could eventually have _____ over the peoples and products of the Eastern Pacific Rim, an outcome the United States would never have accepted.

- A ascendance
- B clout
- C hegemony
- D privileges
- E management
- F reign

Chapter 5: Sentence Equivalence

479. Although it might not seem apparent to the _____ observer, a watch has more mass when it is wound up than when it is not because when its spring is put into tension, that is, when it is wound up, it experiences an increase in the potential energy it bears and thus it increases in mass.

   - [A] casual
   - [B] concerned
   - [C] curious
   - [D] dispassionate
   - [E] heedless
   - [F] interested

480. At the beginning of the twentieth century, it appeared that Russia was going to become the center of the musical and literary world, but instability in the country and the 1917 October Revolution put an end to any _____ Russia might have enjoyed.

   - [A] clout
   - [B] importance
   - [C] place
   - [D] privilege
   - [E] superintendence
   - [F] sway

481. After World War Two, many were _____ by the contrast between the unprecedented technological progress of the preceding years and the inability of human societies to get along with each other.

   - [A] addled
   - [B] agitated
   - [C] cozened
   - [D] deluded
   - [E] graveled
   - [F] stunned

482. Because the military, economic and social life of any society is _____ by that of other countries, few things take place in any nation that are not related to events in bordering countries.

   - [A] accommodated
   - [B] conditioned
   - [C] habituated
   - [D] inured
   - [E] primed
   - [F] recast

483. After such a lengthy illness, her complexion was still _____; she obviously needed a few more days of repose.

   - [A] hearty
   - [B] salubrious
   - [C] bilious
   - [D] albino
   - [E] vigorous
   - [F] sallow

484. Although in the past biologists kept the subfields of biology separate, in recent years the emphasis has been on the study of the biological phenomena that living things have in common, a search for _____, characteristic of twentieth-century scientific inquiry.

   - [A] universals
   - [B] specifics
   - [C] details
   - [D] circumscription
   - [E] generality
   - [F] precision

485. The effects of urban gentrification is an ongoing tale of winners and losers; some residents benefit from the _____ of business investment and improved school quality that come with the improvements in neighborhoods, but other residents are displaced as rents increase and property taxes rise.

- [A] profusion
- [B] abridgement
- [C] ardor
- [D] parapet
- [E] accretion
- [F] culmination

486. Belief in evolution is based on evidence, otherwise it would be _____.

- [A] inconceivable
- [B] implausible
- [C] questionable
- [D] incontestable
- [E] probable
- [F] cogitable

487. Males and females can have different management styles, leading sometimes to misunderstandings and when the misunderstandings are not resolved, they can result in decreases in a company's _____.

- [A] creativity
- [B] edge
- [C] effectiveness
- [D] productivity
- [E] potency
- [F] adaptability

488. Although the human body has been studied intensively for centuries, it should not be thought that there is nothing more to learn; scientists will be making _____ discoveries about the body for as long as there are scientists.

- [A] germinal
- [B] innovative
- [C] ingenious
- [D] novel
- [E] original
- [F] primal

489. Although spontaneous generation was debunked in 1688, belief in it persisted for two more centuries until the 1870's, when Louis Pasteur definitively _____ that it could not occur.

- [A] adduced
- [B] disconfirmed
- [C] divulged
- [D] evinced
- [E] publicized
- [F] substantiated

490. Mendel's study of heredity and his imaginative deductions based on the work were completed in the 1860's, but his discoveries did not become widely known until after 1900, largely because an influential botanist of the 1860's failed to see the _____ of Mendel's work and did not lend Mendel his support.

- [A] preeminence
- [B] prominence
- [C] renown
- [D] significance
- [E] substantiveness
- [F] worth

Chapter 5: Sentence Equivalence

491. When asked where he had been, the suspect _____ spinning an elaborate story but failing to provide any evidence of his whereabouts.

- A) fawned
- B) equivocated
- C) quaffed
- D) prevaricated
- E) transgressed
- F) palpitated

492. Although one-third of the world's population is thought to be infected with tuberculosis, the disease may remain _____ for several years; in many cases, it never becomes active at all.

- A) restive
- B) inimical
- C) latent
- D) fulsome
- E) quiescent
- F) discreet

493. Affirmative action programs aimed at increasing the number of women and minorities in upper management can sometimes lead to the white males in the company feeling _____.

- A) boorish
- B) apprehensive
- C) unassertive
- D) unfazed
- E) uneasy
- F) worrisome

494. The Internet provides a window into cultures that may be unfamiliar from the ones in which we live; a quick Internet search can provide _____ into how people from other cultures live, how they interact with one another, and what is important to them.

- A) perspicacity
- B) erudition
- C) sagacity
- D) sapience
- E) apotheosis
- F) proclivity

495. In nineteenth-century Europe, female behavior was subject to the most stringent of social rules; women who _____ convention and had children out of wedlock were often treated as outcasts.

- A) wafted
- B) extolled
- C) flouted
- D) spurned
- E) disinterred
- F) condoned

496. More so than other types of cells, animal cells are fragile and remain _____ to changes in their immediate environment.

- A) receptive
- B) sensible
- C) sensitive
- D) sensual
- E) sensorial
- F) subject

497. Although Galileo maintained that his theory of heliocentrism was compatible with Christian belief, Church leaders did not agree, and ultimately brought him before the Inquisition where he was forced to _____ his beliefs.

- A) repudiate
- B) beatify
- C) preclude
- D) foment
- E) accrue
- F) abjure

498. The mother _____ her child for stealing money from his sister's piggy bank.

- A) placated
- B) castigated
- C) flustered
- D) vilified
- E) upbraided
- F) descried

Practice Questions

499 When a company's name becomes synonymous with the product it sells, the company loses its distinctive _____ and other companies can sell similar products as if they were selling the same product as the original company.

- [A] ability
- [B] advantage
- [C] dominance
- [D] edge
- [E] stranglehold
- [F] superiority

500 When workers are invited to use their own individual ingenuity and imagination to solve problems confronting the company, they get a chance to believe that they are _____ to the company and the company is frequently able to become stronger.

- [A] fundamental
- [B] indispensable
- [C] integral
- [D] intrinsic
- [E] significant
- [F] vital

501 The rich and, to some people, strident sound of bagpipes is a far cry from the more _____ tones of so many other instruments.

- [A] mellifluous
- [B] dulcet
- [C] lithe
- [D] obstreperous
- [E] abstruse
- [F] stentorian

502 Bruegel's paintings are _____ for their vivid colors and realistic representations of peasant scenes such as vomiting and brawling at inns.

- [A] eye-catching
- [B] famous
- [C] glaring
- [D] notable
- [E] remarkable
- [F] tawdry

503 The audience was unimpressed with the lecture; despite the speaker's dazzling rhetoric and considerable charisma, it was clear that his claims were _____.

- [A] fervid
- [B] specious
- [C] picaresque
- [D] fallacious
- [E] officious
- [F] feckless

504 Technology has led to many changes in the time spent on household responsibilities; with the adoption of appliances such as microwaves, washing machines, and vacuum cleaners into the home, the time spent on household tasks have _____ tremendously compared to the substantial time spent on household duties a century ago.

- [A] bated
- [B] minified
- [C] masticated
- [D] attenuated
- [E] impinged
- [F] augmented

505 Efforts to address the so-called "glass ceiling" have met with only _____ success; although women are twice as likely as men to startup businesses, only 3 percent of these female-owned businesses generate revenue of over $1 million.

- [A] middling
- [B] halcyon
- [C] equivocal
- [D] ecumenical
- [E] sophomoric
- [F] garrulous

Chapter 5: **Sentence Equivalence**

506. The human body's immune system is a powerful biological process that is responsible for fighting off thousands of harmful organisms; when the immune system is working properly, the body is protected from dangerous bacteria, but when it is impaired the body is vulnerable to a _____ of dangerous, disease-carrying microbes.

   A. plethora
   B. surfeit
   C. legion
   D. consanguinity
   E. peculation
   F. extolment

507. A microscope contains one or more lenses that magnify the image of the organism placed on its focal plane; depending on the power of the lens, the microscope can allow people to _____ view the cells of organisms with little to no effort.

   A. mendaciously
   B. salubriously
   C. adventitiously
   D. fastidiously
   E. punctiliously
   F. exiguously

508. To make identifying one animal from another more _____, scientists from different societies have devised various classification systems, but now some scientists are advocating the creation of a single, universal animal classification system for all cultures across the globe to adopt.

   A. tamable
   B. vociferous
   C. resplendent
   D. quiescent
   E. glib
   F. tractable

509. The nucleus is the most _____ part of an atom; a nucleus's significance lies in that the majority of the atom's mass is located in the nucleus, and, in living organisms, the nucleus is the site where DNA lives and begins to be interpreted by the cell.

   A. effulgent
   B. substantive
   C. epochal
   D. indispensable
   E. recondite
   F. evidentiary

510. Research suggests that those with a _____ for math may have inherited their skills from their parents; a 2009 study revealed that the development of the part of the brain used in calculations is overwhelmingly governed by genetics.

   A. mendacity
   B. aptitude
   C. recidivism
   D. eloquence
   E. dereliction
   F. propensity

511. Metabolism is a word that is often _____ with weight loss, but metabolism is associated with many more processes than regulating a person's ability to convert fat to energy; it can refer to all of the chemical reactions that occur inside the cells of living organisms.

   A. affiliated
   B. colligated
   C. caviled
   D. distended
   E. ensconced
   F. abrogated

512. As anthropologists know, certain practices and beliefs unite the _____ cultures of the world; every known civilization, for example, has practiced some form of religion.

- [A] inimitable
- [B] profligate
- [C] disparate
- [D] palatial
- [E] myriad
- [F] prolix

513. Totalitarian governments usually feel threatened by any individual voice that becomes _____ they do what they can to silence such potential problems.

- [A] eminent
- [B] noteworthy
- [C] recognizable
- [D] salient
- [E] significant
- [F] visible

514. Even during his lifetime, Caligula had a reputation for moral _____; one account had him ordering his guards to throw a group of innocent spectators into the Colosseum's arena to be devoured by wild animals.

- [A] desuetude
- [B] finesse
- [C] probity
- [D] degeneracy
- [E] insularity
- [F] turpitude

515. Faberge eggs are known for the incredibly _____ designs; the first one ever made opened to reveal a gold yolk, which itself concealed a gold hen and a miniature diamond replica of the Russian Imperial Crown.

- [A] sumptuous
- [B] ubiquitous
- [C] ostentatious
- [D] incipient
- [E] prudish
- [F] lugubrious

516. Ann Rand wrote that copyrights and patents are a way of _____ a most basic property right, the right to profit from the product of one's own mind.

- [A] effectuating
- [B] legislating
- [C] observing
- [D] promulgating
- [E] protecting
- [F] validating

517. The components that make up a culture vary depending on the group in question; shared language, experiences, history, food, and language are some of the delineating elements distinguishing one culture from another, but a powerful, albeit intangible, aspect of what defines a culture is an _____ bond members feel for one another.

- [A] irascible
- [B] execrable
- [C] inextirpable
- [D] illustrious
- [E] opprobrious
- [F] indelible

Chapter 5: Sentence Equivalence

518. The world's oceans are home to many bizarre and fascinating creatures, but few are more _____ than the octopus, which has three hearts, no bones, and an intelligence level that far exceeds that of other invertebrates.

   A. prosaic
   B. extant
   C. inscrutable
   D. enigmatic
   E. nascent
   F. incredulous

519. In his "Letter from Birmingham Jail," Martin Luther King catalogued the multitude of abuses experienced by African Americans living in the 1960's in the United States and _____ a course for change.

   A. calculated
   B. drafted
   C. framed
   D. organized
   E. prepared
   F. schemed

520. Study after study has _____ that when women and men have similar levels of education, similar jobs, and similar work histories, men earn more than women. Even when they are children, women tend to see themselves earning less money than men when they become adults.

   A. manifested
   B. projected
   C. publicized
   D. revealed
   E. uncloaked
   F. unveiled

521. As Franz Liszt said, the _____ influence on the musicians of the late 19th century that is, the musicians of the Romantic Period, was the work and towering legacy of Ludwig van Beethoven, the late classical composer who died in 1827.

   A. ancillary
   B. distinguished
   C. notable
   D. preponderant
   E. sovereign
   F. auxiliary

522. Karl Popper's most important contribution is his statement that if a hypothesis is to have scientific _____ it must be testable, that is, there must be a way that can potentially show that the theory is wrong.

   A. condition
   B. capacity
   C. position
   D. rank
   E. standing
   F. status

523. Rather than putting so much _____ in definitions, Karl Popper wrote that it would be better to carefully phrase one's sentences so that the various meanings of the words used would not matter and people would argue less about words.

   A. credit
   B. dubiety
   C. force
   D. hope
   E. progeny
   F. stock

524 It is quite remarkable to see a book in such _____ condition; I've never seen a 17th-century first edition of that high standard before.

- [A] sanitary
- [B] untarnished
- [C] purified
- [D] pristine
- [E] immaculate
- [F] adulterated

525 Most substances exist as solids at room temperature, but _____ substances exist as gases, such as oxygen, or liquids, such as water.

- [A] certain
- [B] majority
- [C] gaseous
- [D] naught
- [E] various
- [F] all

526 Quarks and gluons, the primary building blocks of matter, are theorized to have formed during the _____ moments of the universe just microseconds after the Big Bang.

- [A] anticipated
- [B] nascent
- [C] reticent
- [D] antiquated
- [E] astute
- [F] inchoate

527 Through mechanisms such as nerve signaling, acupuncture has been proven to be an effective medical practice, particularly in _____ pain and inflammation.

- [A] mitigating
- [B] assuaging
- [C] embellishing
- [D] bilking
- [E] extenuating
- [F] rectifying

528 Accessibility to relief benefits after the hurricane was hindered in some cases by policy instructions written in _____ terms that few could decipher.

- [A] verbose
- [B] arcane
- [C] prosaic
- [D] laconic
- [E] obscure
- [F] dissenting

529 There is a/an _____ similarity between a 1929 picture of frightened citizens crowding the streets around the New York Stock exchange on the first day of the October Stock Market crash that ushered in the Great Depression and pictures taken seventy-two years later of New Yorkers looking up at the World Trade Center towers on September 11, 2001.

- [A] eerie
- [B] curious
- [C] interesting
- [D] striking
- [E] surprising
- [F] uncanny

530 When purified sodium comes into contact with water, it forms an _____ reaction. The powerful exothermic forces generated mean that this substance should always be handled with care.

- [A] explosive
- [B] muted
- [C] incendiary
- [D] endogenous
- [E] incredible

Chapter 5: Sentence Equivalence

531. The infamous persecution of so-called heretics during the Spanish Inquisition resulted in the forced _____ of any religious or scientific views that were not in line with the Catholic faith, often under conditions of torture.

- [A] reiteration
- [B] submission
- [C] altercation
- [D] atonement
- [E] recantation
- [F] rescinding

532. Predatory loans were implicated in the wave of home evictions, which had a particularly _____ impact on low-income families.

- [A] subordinate
- [B] tawdry
- [C] injurious
- [D] pernicious
- [E] naive
- [F] pretentious

533. Extensive liberal arts study was once considered an integral component of a quality education, but as societies have become more technologically, dedicating years to studies in classic literature or philosophy are more often perceived as _____ endeavors that should be set aside for training in more practical study in the sciences or in medicine.

- [A] erudite
- [B] lofty
- [C] asinine
- [D] obtuse
- [E] chary
- [F] fetid

534. The lack of social integration programs and adequate rehab programs upon release from prison has been shown to correlate with higher _____ rates.

- [A] dissolution
- [B] recidivism
- [C] diatribe
- [D] eccentricity
- [E] relapse
- [F] initiation

535. The music of the ballet and its composer were _____ in the government-run media and the composer was forced to repudiate his work or risk losing his livelihood.

- [A] aspersed
- [B] degraded
- [C] disgraced
- [D] exculpated
- [E] repudiated
- [F] traduced

536. The fact that all living cells come from pre-existing living cells and all living cells use the same _____ to transmit DNA from one generation to another, pose problems for those who seek to determine the origin of the first living cell.

- [A] determinant
- [B] impetus
- [C] ingredient
- [D] means
- [E] mechanism
- [F] median

537. Animals that deal with the seasonal shortage of food by hibernating typically _____ themselves beforehand in order to store up enough energy for the winter months.

- [A] incense
- [B] preen
- [C] glut
- [D] recast
- [E] enervate
- [F] gorge

Practice Questions

538 Putting an end to considerable debate, the samples taken from the Martian atmosphere revealed _____ that oxygen molecules were present on the red planet, albeit in minuscule amounts.

- [A] perennially
- [B] indubitably
- [C] conversely
- [D] indisputably
- [E] abundantly
- [F] unconscionably

539 Wildlife populations have _____ at alarming rates in the past 50 years alone, threatening the biodiversity of the planet, as well as our place in it.

- [A] decimated
- [B] arbitrated
- [C] plummeted
- [D] attenuated
- [E] exacerbated
- [F] plunged

540 Children with undiagnosed special needs are particularly prone to develop low self-esteem when _____ for a conduct they cannot control.

- [A] chastised
- [B] applauded
- [C] revoked
- [D] berated
- [E] annealed
- [F] appeased

541 Virginia Woolf was known as a complex writer who suffered from depression and _____ mood swings, which bore an influence on her novels that explored themes of despair, isolation, and human connection.

- [A] incontrovertible
- [B] deferential
- [C] erratic
- [D] reminiscent
- [E] volatile
- [F] entrenched

542 A number of companies have pledged to hire refugees following the start of the war in a _____ effort to provide opportunities to the less fortunate, as well as strengthen their workforce through diversity and innovation.

- [A] utilitarian
- [B] philanthropic
- [C] meticulous
- [D] fastidious
- [E] benevolent
- [F] devious

543 Growing public demand for more sustainable manufacturing based on renewable energy has resulted in a gamut of products with fewer _____ effects on the environment.

- [A] detrimental
- [B] arbitrary
- [C] elusive
- [D] adverse
- [E] transient
- [F] mitigating

544 Martin Luther King's justly famous "Letter from Birmingham Jail," was written in response to a/an _____ statement by "Eight Alabama Clergymen" that had been published in newspapers throughout the United States.

- [A] disreputable
- [B] famous
- [C] oppugnant
- [D] opprobrious
- [E] shoddy
- [F] vicious

545 Modern texting has evolved into a simple and _____ form of communication that replaces the lengthier forms of expression used in letters or even emails.

- [A] pithy
- [B] grandiloquent
- [C] abstruse
- [D] exorbitant
- [E] succinct
- [F] exhaustive

Chapter 5: Sentence Equivalence

546 The unique and sometimes visionary premises of independent films are proof of what writers and directors can achieve when not _____ by concerns of money and popularity.

- A fettered
- B emaciated
- C obviated
- D macerated
- E satiated
- F constrained

547 Several _____ play a role in the rising of sea levels, such as the melting rate of glaciers, thermal expansion, and sinking land mass.

- A correlations
- B contingencies
- C entities
- D determinants
- E variables
- F endeavors

548 Garlic has been shown to be a/an _____ immune booster, with antimicrobial properties in some cases similar to those of penicillin.

- A generic
- B deciduous
- C potent
- D resilient
- E notorious
- F efficacious

549 Although the Chinese economy has been growing rapidly for three decades, there is some concern that this expansion will slow as more and more people obtain college degrees; those with a university education will no doubt be _____ to accept the low-paying factory jobs that have contributed to China's success.

- A crass
- B nonplussed
- C disinclined
- D loath
- E urbane
- F frantic

550 One effect of public education is to eliminate the idiosyncrasies that make each person a one of a kind, so that what was once a unique snowflake gets _____ into a drop of water little different from all the other drops of water in the world.

- A commuted
- B deformed
- C disfigured
- D exchanged
- E reduced
- F rendered

551 Engaging in social work in conflictive regions requires a certain level of tolerance for abruptly changing, potentially violent situations, which typically dissuades the more _____.

- A adulterous
- B venturesome
- C ostentatious
- D faint-hearted
- E intrepid
- F timorous

552 While many business decisions have been altered by the likes of A.I. and machine learning in the past 10 years, the _____ of most business decisions are still built on trust.

- A foundations
- B profits
- C underpinnings
- D trajectories
- E operations
- F outcome

553 Improvisation is the art of creating sharp-witted and _____ dialogue on the spot, resulting in a live performance without scripts or rehearsal.

- A laborious
- B impromptu
- C implicit
- D ad-lib
- E aberrant
- F tacit

Practice Questions

554. When Joseph Stalin attended the premier of Shostakovich's opera "The Nose," he left early, apparently offended by the _____ plot and shocked by the progressive music of the score.

- [A] ebullient
- [B] gamey
- [C] impish
- [D] phlegmatic
- [E] puckish
- [F] ribald

555. Astrophysicists are testing the theory of primordial black holes making up dark matter in the universe by trying to detect any_____ wobbling in the orbit of nearby planets like Mars, which might be caused by their minute gravitational pull.

- [A] unforeseen
- [B] irregular
- [C] unstable
- [D] idiosyncratic
- [E] precarious
- [F] anomalous

556. Charles Dickens is known for the clearly defined characters he creates, his vivid descriptions of settings, and for his efforts to use his work to raise public consciousness about the _____ practices of privileged groups in British society of his time.

- [A] beneficial
- [B] benignant
- [C] co-optive
- [D] deceptive
- [E] deleterious
- [F] exploitive

557. In 2010, an electrician who had worked for Pablo Picasso revealed that he had in his possession a/an _____ of Picasso's work spanning the entire creative career of the artist.

- [A] argosy
- [B] collection
- [C] cornucopia
- [D] repository
- [E] stockpile
- [F] wellspring

558. The Trinidadian author, V. S. Naipaul, won the Nobel Prize for literature in 2001, but is widely _____ by Caribbeanists for his allegedly negative portrayals and views of the Caribbean and its people.

- [A] chided
- [B] excoriated
- [C] exculpated
- [D] sanctioned
- [E] libeled
- [F] slandered

559. Two developments that greatly aided advancement in biology in the 17th century were the growth of scientific societies and the further development of the microscope; one aided individual discovery and the other aided _____ among professionals of what had been discovered.

- [A] dispersal
- [B] dissipation
- [C] collection
- [D] concentration
- [E] dissemination
- [F] propagation

Chapter 5: Sentence Equivalence

560. Several European states, such as the UK and Spain, have recently started _____ a tax on non-reusable plastic, in an effort to curb environmental contamination.

- A imposing
- B lodging
- C levying
- D abetting
- E inflicting
- F soliciting

561. _____ dreams of wealth will do you little good as an entrepreneur; research suggests that those with a concrete business plan are twice as likely to succeed as those without.

- A Nebulous
- B Sagacious
- C Craven
- D Cogent
- E Dubious
- F Fervid

562. Rescue vehicles were not able to reach the areas affected by the flash floods until the storm winds _____, leaving thousands stranded and in need of aid.

- A surged
- B plummeted
- C abated
- D abstained
- E deferred
- F subsided

563. The fearsome crashing of thunder, which makes so many children _____ and seek their parents, has a surprisingly simple explanation; each bolt of lightning heats the surrounding air, causing it to expand so rapidly that it breaks the sound barrier.

- A clinch
- B quail
- C demur
- D rebuff
- E cower
- F simper

564. The movement of glacial ice across a territory often results in the depositing of landforms, called moraines, composed of _____ transported from another location.

- A gusts
- B eddies
- C sediment
- D crags
- E gales
- F debris

565. As global temperatures rise, doctors warn of the dangers of heat exposure, which can cause a rapid pulse and _____ sweating, potentially leading to heatstroke and even death.

- A copious
- B bilious
- C constricted
- D evocative
- E satiated
- F profuse

566. A Chief Financial Officer, or CFO, of a company ensures a business's financial _____ by developing financial strategies, managing cash flow, and working toward sustainable economic growth via the authoritative oversight of fundraising, investments, and debt.

- A state
- B dishevelment
- C health
- D prosperity
- E reverie
- F side

567. Edgar Allan Poe's _____ tales of crumbling mansions and dying women are perennial favorites among those with a taste for horror and mystery.

- A whimsical
- B morbid
- C saturnine
- D sublime
- E droll
- F esoteric

Practice Questions

568 The Milgram experiments conducted at Yale University in 1961 revealed insight into the _____ of most individuals to follow orders given by an authority figure, even when it resulted in harming others.

- A abhorrence
- B propensity
- C readiness
- D euphoria
- E tirade
- F temerity

569 Because they can go for several years without erupting, it can be difficult to determine which volcanoes are extinct and which are merely dormant - a _____ state of affairs.

- A disconcerting
- B extenuating
- C trenchant
- D ominous
- E inimitable
- F luculent

570 Given that they account for roughly half of America's GDP, it would be a mistake to _____ the importance of small businesses.

- A broach
- B denigrate
- C glean
- D sanction
- E lionize
- F disparage

571 After having fraudulently sold the Eiffel Tower on two occasions, con artist Lustig was finally captured in an operation of exchanging _____ banknotes.

- A tenuous
- B authentic
- C counterfeit
- D genuine
- E aboriginal
- F forged

572 The Fear and Greed Index was developed in order to _____ the emotions that motivate behavior on the stock market, as a predictor of more optimistic or restrained investment activity.

- A entice
- B gauge
- C influence
- D ascertain
- E undermine
- F orchestrate

573 The act of petting a cat or a dog has been shown to have _____ effects on health, such as lowering blood pressure and improving mental well-being.

- A beneficial
- B adverse
- C favorable
- D ambivalent
- E transient
- F abysmal

574 Astronomers who have recently caught an impressive glimpse of the supernova Pa 30 have commented that its exterior protrusions of dust and gas are _____ of a dandelion seed.

- A implosive
- B reminiscent
- C reverent
- D expulsive
- E suggestive
- F coercive

575 Turmeric has been found to possess remarkable anti-inflammatory and antioxidative properties, which make it a/an _____ herb for arthritis sufferers to incorporate into their diet.

- A temperate
- B exemplary
- C sporadic
- D secular
- E salubrious
- F flimsy

Chapter 5: Sentence Equivalence

576. The addictive quality of social media "likes" has been linked with a rise in feelings of _____, as well as other negative health impacts, especially among young users.

- [A] despondency
- [B] entitlement
- [C] fidelity
- [D] torpor
- [E] dejection
- [F] paucity

577. As entry fees are often _____ for low-income families, several museums have started offering free entrance on certain days of the week.

- [A] adorning
- [B] prohibitive
- [C] whimsical
- [D] liberal
- [E] intractable
- [F] exorbitant

578. In contrast to the high cost of leading brands in operating systems, open-source alternatives, such as Linux, provide not only customizable interfaces and _____ features, but are also available free to download.

- [A] incognizant
- [B] manifold
- [C] indelible
- [D] myriad
- [E] specious
- [F] defective

579. Certain shades of pink have been found to have a tranquilizing effect on their viewer, reducing muscle strength, and _____ hostility, making it the color of choice in various psychiatric wards and holding cells.

- [A] eliciting
- [B] inspiring
- [C] provoking
- [D] diminishing
- [E] entailing
- [F] curtailing

580. Although many people assume that research and development tax credits are only available to large companies with money to invest in on-site laboratories and the like, the truth is that even small businesses can be eligible for tax benefits, provided that their work is innovative and their management _____.

- [A] shrewd
- [B] supine
- [C] adroit
- [D] dogmatic
- [E] ineluctable
- [F] meretricious

581. In certain autoimmune diseases, inflammation becomes a chronic condition that results from immune cells essentially _____ the body's own tissue, as if it were a foreign pathogen.

- [A] safeguarding
- [B] lambasting
- [C] assailing
- [D] engendering
- [E] espousing
- [F] assaulting

582. Extracurricular activities, such as the debate club or theater arts, have been known to boost self-esteem, particularly in more _____ students who struggle to participate in class activities.

- [A] diffident
- [B] bellicose
- [C] listless
- [D] reticent
- [E] despondent
- [F] apathetic

583. Ernest Shackleton became famous for his _____ efforts to ensure the survival of his team during the Endurance Expedition; after months of coping with the harsh Antarctic conditions, Shackleton made an 800-mile open-boat voyage in the hopes of seeing his companions rescued.

- A erudite
- B dogged
- C phlegmatic
- D desultory
- E preternatural
- F indefatigable

584. The viola, a slightly larger version of the violin with a deeper, richer sound, may be less renowned, but no less melodically expressive than its more _____ counterpart.

- A ornate
- B heralded
- C quiescent
- D insipid
- E taciturn
- F acclaimed

585. In the musical Camelot, Mordred exposes Lancelot and Guinevere's _____ love affair in his efforts to overthrow King Arthur, Guinevere's husband.

- A inchoate
- B noisome
- C clandestine
- D discrete
- E illicit
- F gauche

586. The movement of gas molecules is rather _____; particles move quickly and more or less randomly.

- A belligerent
- B turgid
- C volatile
- D irrevocable
- E frenetic
- F malleable

587. First time business owners often encounter financial challenges as a result of _____ their initial funds on trivial expenditures, while undervaluing the importance of investing in competent and reliable personnel.

- A economizing
- B inducing
- C misallocating
- D withholding
- E rationing
- F squandering

588. Mindfulness, the practice of being present in everyday tasks, leads to more focused activity and has been shown to reduce anxiety and _____ well-being.

- A exacerbate
- B bolster
- C deplete
- D enhance
- E pander
- F appease

589. Innovative musicians have demonstrated that the _____ of compressed air waves to generate exquisite sounds and tone can be achieved using a range of unconventional materials from carved-out vegetables to soda cans.

- A dissipation
- B propagation
- C entreaty
- D embellishment
- E transmission
- F exception

Chapter 5: Sentence Equivalence

590. New discoveries in neuroscience suggest electrical (or "ephaptic") fields produced by neurons may be responsible for cognition and perhaps even consciousness, _____ previous theories based solely on neural firing.

- A entailing
- B abdicating
- C upending
- D supplanting
- E adulating
- F emulating

591. Although originally a holiday for the Celtic New Year's Eve, Halloween has undergone tremendous cultural _____ and is currently observed in many countries around the globe.

- A retribution
- B intrusion
- C epiphany
- D diffusion
- E exclusion
- F dissemination

592. The concept of yin and yang, as presented in the Dao De Jing, challenges the Western model of opposing dualities by _____ the focus onto changing qualities, and how they relate throughout transitioning states.

- A reorienting
- B indulging
- C ascertaining
- D shifting
- E deducting
- F extenuating

593. The first trade unions formed to _____ workers rights to safer working conditions and fair compensation, often confronting management with a list of demands and a unified front.

- A adulterate
- B condone
- C advocate
- D deflect
- E champion
- F discern

594. For scientists concerned about climate change, the recent prevalence of "extreme weather" - hurricanes, droughts, and the like - is an alarming _____ of things to come.

- A portent
- B vagary
- C harbinger
- D antithesis
- E enigma
- F imbroglio

595. In response to a culture of mounting debt as a result of impulse buys and frivolous purchases, specialists advise _____ spending that is limited to essential needs and otherwise shopping at thrift stores or second-hand shops.

- A parsimonious
- B redolent
- C lavish
- D frugal
- E extravagant
- F ascetic

596. One of the _____ of flood water entering a city is the overflow of sewage canals, which can transport potentially infectious "black water," containing human waste and other toxins.

- [A] sanctions
- [B] hazards
- [C] improprieties
- [D] impediments
- [E] perils
- [F] expositions

597. Bioengineers working on cancer treatments have recently created cyborgs, bacteria infused with pre-programmed DNA material, in order to develop target-specific attackers that would _____ tumor cells.

- [A] fulminate
- [B] incorporate
- [C] annihilate
- [D] procreate
- [E] obliterate
- [F] promulgate

598. Gender-based wage inequalities typically stem from the socially prescribed _____ of females to be more likely to take on the role of caretaker for children and elderly parents, and thereby earn less on average than their male counterparts.

- [A] consternation
- [B] tirade
- [C] proclivity
- [D] derision
- [E] disdain
- [F] predisposition

599. Aspiring actors often seek out stable, part-time work to make ends meet, as they struggle in the _____ world of minor roles and short-term contracts.

- [A] callous
- [B] belligerent
- [C] apprehensive
- [D] precarious
- [E] insecure
- [F] anomalous

600. Although undocumented workers provide labor for thousands of businesses, resulting in billions of dollars in tax revenue annually, they are _____ of their rights and often tolerate substandard conditions and treatment in turn for a steady paycheck.

- [A] assimilated
- [B] deprived
- [C] rendered
- [D] stripped
- [E] endorsed
- [F] enrolled

Answer Key

Q. No.	Correct Answer	Your Answer	Q. No.	Correct Answer	Your Answer	Q. No.	Correct Answer	Your Answer
451	B, D		476	A, F		501	A, B	
452	C, F		477	D, E		502	D, E	
453	C, E		478	A, C		503	B, D	
454	A, D		479	A, D		504	B, D	
455	B, E		480	A, F		505	A, C	
456	A, B		481	A, F		506	A, C	
457	A, C		482	B, F		507	D, E	
458	A, C		483	C, F		508	A, F	
459	B, F		484	A, E		509	B, D	
460	B, F		485	A, E		510	B, F	
461	A, C		486	B, C		511	A, B	
462	D, E		487	C, D		512	C, E	
463	B, F		488	D, E		513	D, E	
464	B, C		489	D, F		514	D, F	
465	C, D		490	D, F		515	A, C	
466	B, C		491	B, D		516	A, E	
467	B, E		492	C, E		517	C, F	
468	A, C		493	B, E		518	C, D	
469	A, F		494	A, C		519	B, C	
470	A, F		495	C, D		520	A, D	
471	B, E		496	C, F		521	D, E	
472	A, D		497	A, F		522	E, F	
473	A, C		498	B, E		523	A, F	
474	A, E		499	B, D		524	D, E	
475	C, E		500	B, C		525	A, E	

Answer Key

Q. No.	Correct Answer	Your Answer	Q. No.	Correct Answer	Your Answer	Q. No.	Correct Answer	Your Answer
526	B, F		551	D, F		576	A, E	
527	A, B		552	A, C		577	B, F	
528	B, E		553	B, D		578	B, D	
529	A, F		554	B, F		579	D, F	
530	A, C		555	B, F		580	A, C	
531	E, F		556	D, F		581	C, F	
532	C, D		557	B, D		582	A, D	
533	A, B		558	A, B		583	B, F	
534	B, E		559	E, F		584	B, E	
535	A, F		560	A, C		585	C, E	
536	D, E		561	A, E		586	C, E	
537	C, F		562	C, F		587	C, F	
538	B, D		563	B, E		588	B, D	
539	C, F		564	C, F		589	B, E	
540	A, D		565	A, F		590	C, D	
541	C, E		566	C, D		591	C, F	
542	B, E		567	B, C		592	A, D	
543	A, D		568	B, C		593	C, E	
544	C, D		569	A, D		594	A, C	
545	A, E		570	B, F		595	A, D	
546	A, F		571	C, F		596	B, E	
547	D, E		572	B, D		597	C, E	
548	C, F		573	A, C		598	C, F	
549	C, D		574	B, E		599	D, E	
550	E, F		575	B, E		600	B, D	

Chapter 5: Sentence Equivalence

Answers & Explanations

451 **Choice B is correct** because "ornate" means elaborately or highly decorated, which fits well with the description of the marble columns being part of a breathtakingly beautiful basilica. "Ornate" is often used to describe intricate architectural or artistic details, especially in grand historical settings. **Choice D is correct** because "baroque" refers to a highly decorative and elaborate style, especially in architecture and art, associated with grandeur and richness—an appropriate description for the marble columns in a 15th-century church with an exceptional mosaic floor.

Choice A is incorrect because "clement" means mild or merciful, usually used to describe weather or a person's temperament—not physical features like marble columns. **Choice C** is incorrect because "embroidered" refers specifically to needlework on fabric, not a description appropriate for stone or architectural features like marble columns. **Choice E** is incorrect because "dowdy" means unfashionable or drab in appearance, which contradicts the idea of something "breathtakingly beautiful." **Choice F** is incorrect because "garish" means overly bright and showy in a tasteless way, which also clashes with the tone of elegance and reverence in the sentence.

452 **Choice C is correct** because "proficiency" means a high degree of skill or competence. In the context of a complex medical procedure like a peripheral artery bypass, the doctor's skill is what the observer is marveling at, especially given the audacity required for such surgery. **Choice F is correct** because "expertise" also means advanced knowledge or skill in a particular field. This word appropriately conveys the doctor's mastery of the procedure, aligning with the sentence's focus on justified confidence.

Choice A is incorrect because "aggression" implies hostility or forcefulness, which doesn't suit the context of professional skill during a surgical operation. **Choice B** is incorrect because "reticence" means reluctance to speak or act, which contrasts with the "audaciousness" required and observed during the surgery. **Choice D** is incorrect because "contempt" means disdain or disrespect, which doesn't describe a positive quality or skill in the context of surgery. **Choice E** is incorrect because "delusion" suggests a false belief, which would undermine the competence and boldness implied in the sentence.

453 **Choice C is correct** because "fraudulent" refers to deceitful or dishonest behavior, especially for financial gain. This fits the context of accounting practices that are used to mislead and artificially inflate profits. **Choice E is correct** because "dubious" means questionable or suspicious. In this context, it appropriately describes accounting methods that may not be illegal but are ethically or professionally questionable.

Choice A is incorrect because "counterfeit" refers specifically to fake physical items like money or documents, not practices. **Choice B** is incorrect because "infamous" describes a reputation, not an action or method. Accounting practices themselves aren't "infamous." **Choice D** is incorrect because "villainess" refers to a female villain and doesn't logically apply to accounting practices. **Choice F** is incorrect because "slanderous" means defamatory in speech or writing, which does not relate to financial accounting practices.

454 **Choice A is correct** because "hounding" means persistently harassing or nagging someone. It fits the context of being repeatedly asked to fix the faucet. **Choice D is correct** because "badgering" also means persistently annoying or nagging someone with repeated requests or questions—exactly what's happening in the sentence.

Choice B is incorrect because "bearing" means carrying or enduring something; it doesn't relate to nagging or pestering. **Choice C** is incorrect because "ferreting" means searching for something persistently or uncovering hidden information—not repeatedly asking someone. **Choice E** is incorrect because "weaseling" usually refers to avoiding something or being sneaky, not persistently asking or nagging. **Choice F** is incorrect because "remonstrating" means protesting or expressing opposition, often in a reasoned way—not pestering or harassing.

455 **Choice B is correct** because "frugal" means being economical or careful with spending, especially to avoid waste—this directly aligns with companies cutting back on marketing budgets during a recession. **Choice E is correct** because "parsimonious" also means extremely unwilling to spend money—fitting the idea of being highly cautious or stingy with marketing budgets.

Choice A is incorrect because "gluttonous" means excessively greedy, especially with food—not relevant to budget restraint. **Choice C** is incorrect because "altruistic" means selflessly concerned for the well-being of others, which doesn't relate to marketing budgets or spending habits. **Choice D** is incorrect because "lavish" means extravagant or overly generous, which is the opposite of what the sentence is describing. **Choice F** is incorrect because "miserly" implies an unpleasant level of stinginess or meanness in spending. While close in meaning to parsimonious, it carries a more negative tone than the sentence implies, which seems more practical than mean-spirited.

456 **Choice A is correct** because "drifted" means to move or be carried along smoothly and slowly through air or water. It appropriately describes how the scent of bread enters the room gently and naturally. **Choice B is correct** because "wafted" means to pass or cause to pass easily or gently through the air, often used to describe smells or sounds. It fits perfectly in the context of the scent rising from a bakery.

Choice C is incorrect because "coasted" generally refers to moving easily without using power, typically used for physical motion—not for smells. **Choice D** is incorrect because "transmitted" is too technical or mechanical, typically referring to signals, diseases, or messages, not smells. **Choice E** is incorrect because "poised" means balanced or ready, which does not describe the movement of scent. **Choice F** is incorrect because "inured" means desensitized to something, often unpleasant. It's not relevant to the scent's movement.

457 **Choice A is correct** because "twilight" refers to the soft, glowing light from the sky when the sun is below the horizon, especially at dawn or dusk. It fits the context of enchanting evening rays beautifully. **Choice C is correct** because "crepuscular" means related to twilight or active during twilight. It precisely captures the idea of evening light described in the sentence.

Choice B is incorrect because "diurnal" means active during the daytime or occurring every day, which doesn't emphasize evening light. **Choice D** is incorrect because "noontide" refers to noon or midday, not the evening. **Choice E** is incorrect because "enlightened" refers to being spiritually or intellectually aware and doesn't describe rays of light in a literal sense. **Choice F** is incorrect because "modicum" means a small amount of something and is unrelated to light or the evening.

458 **Choice A is correct** because "dilettante" refers to someone who dabbles in a field, such as the arts, without serious commitment or deep knowledge. It fits the context well since Henry lacks expertise in French Impressionists despite appearing knowledgeable in other areas. **Choice C is correct** because "amateur" refers to someone who engages in an activity without professional skill or knowledge. It supports the contrast with Henry's apparent historical knowledge.

Choice B is incorrect because "unskilled" is too generic and lacks the nuance to describe someone who simply lacks depth in a specific area of knowledge. **Choice D** is incorrect because "dabbling" is a verb or present participle, and the sentence calls for a noun to fit grammatically. **Choice E** is incorrect because "connoisseur" means an expert, especially in matters of taste or the arts, which contradicts the context of Henry's lack of knowledge. **Choice F** is incorrect because "proficient" means skilled or competent, again contradicting the sentence's implication.

459 **Choice B is correct** because "profuse" means plentiful or abundant, which also fits well in describing an abundant amount of hair cascading down her back. **Choice F is correct** because "luxuriant" means rich, abundant, and healthy growth, which fits perfectly to describe a thick, beautiful mane of golden hair.

Choice A is incorrect because "barren" means lacking growth or empty, which contradicts the description of abundant hair. **Choice C** is incorrect because "elaborate" means detailed or complicated, which does not fit describing hair. **Choice D** is incorrect because "plenteous" is less commonly used, though similar to "profuse," but it is stylistically awkward here compared to "profuse" or "luxuriant." **Choice E** is incorrect because "pretentious" means attempting to impress by affecting greater importance, which is irrelevant to describing hair.

460 **Choice B is correct** because "primitive" means relating to early stages of development or ancient times, which fits well describing early tribes making baskets. **Choice F is correct** because "archaic" means very old or old-fashioned, especially belonging to an earlier period, which also fits the context of ancient tribes.

Choice A is incorrect because "old-fashioned" suggests outdated by current standards but is less appropriate when referring specifically to ancient tribes. **Choice C** is incorrect because "obsolete" means no longer in use or out of date, which does not fit since the tribes are ancient, not just outmoded. **Choice D** is incorrect because "trampled" means crushed or stepped on, which is irrelevant here. **Choice E** is incorrect because "antiquated" means old-fashioned or outdated but is typically used to describe ideas or objects, less so people or tribes.

461 **Choice A is correct** because "capacious" means having a lot of space or room, which fits the idea that despite the office being roomy, it was still too small for the needs. **Choice C is correct** because "expansive" means wide or extensive in size, fitting the context of large office dimensions.

Choice B is incorrect because "abundance" is a noun, not an adjective, so it doesn't grammatically fit describing dimensions. **Choice D** is incorrect because "brimming" usually describes something filled to the top, and it doesn't fit describing dimensions. **Choice E is incorrect** because "minute" means very small, which contradicts the sentence context about large dimensions. **Choice F is incorrect** because "discrepant" means inconsistent or conflicting, which does not describe physical size.

462 **Choice D is correct** because "indigenous" means native to a particular region, fitting the context of tribes living in the Amazonas region. **Choice E is correct** because "aboriginal" also means original or earliest known inhabitants of a region, which suits the context well.

Choice A is incorrect because "homegrown" typically refers to something cultivated or developed locally, often used for plants or products, not for describing native tribes. **Choice B is incorrect** because "inherited" relates to something passed down genetically or by tradition, not to describing tribes as native. **Choice C is incorrect** because "alien" means foreign or unfamiliar, which contradicts the context. **Choice F is incorrect** because "inbred" refers to breeding within a restricted group and has a negative connotation, not appropriate here.

463 **Choice B is correct** because "endemic" means regularly found or native to a particular area, which fits the context of gang-related crime being common there. **Choice F is correct** because "prevalent" means widespread or commonly occurring, which also suits the context well.

Choice A is incorrect because "epidemic" usually refers to a sudden outbreak of disease, which is too strong and specific for the context of ongoing crime. **Choice C is incorrect** because "curtailed" means reduced or cut short, which contradicts the meaning of crime being widespread. **Choice D is incorrect** because "governable" means able to be controlled or governed, which does not fit the description of crime levels. **Choice E is incorrect** because "exuberant" means energetic or enthusiastic, which is unrelated to crime prevalence.

464 **Choice B is correct** because "impart" means to give or convey, which fits the context of electric charge being given to the nucleus. **Choice C is correct** because "bestow" means to present or give, also fitting the idea of electric charge being given to the nucleus.

Choice A is incorrect because "extenuate" means to lessen the seriousness of something, which does not fit the context. **Choice D is incorrect** because "remit" means to send back or forgive, which is unrelated here. **Choice E is incorrect** because "bequeath" means to leave something in a will after death, which does not suit the scientific context. **Choice F is incorrect** because "ossify" means to turn into bone or become rigid, which is unrelated.

465 **Choice C is correct** because "homogeneous" means uniform or of the same kind, which fits the context indicating that government structures are not uniform worldwide. **Choice D is correct** because "undifferentiated" means not distinct or lacking differences, which fits the idea that government systems are varied rather than undifferentiated.

Choice A is incorrect because "bilious" means bad-tempered or spiteful, which does not fit the context. **Choice B is incorrect** because "lachrymose" means tearful or sad, which is unrelated here. **Choice E is incorrect** because "discrete" means separate or distinct, which contradicts the idea that governments are not uniform. **Choice F is incorrect** because "disjointed" means lacking coherence or disconnected, which does not best describe the variety of government systems here.

466 **Choice B is correct** because "contrived" means to plan or devise something, often with some ingenuity, which fits the context of creating a new marketing campaign. **Choice C is correct** because "devised" means to come up with a plan or strategy, which accurately describes the act of creating a new campaign.

Choice A is incorrect because "connived" means to secretly cooperate or plot, often with negative connotations, which does not fit the neutral or positive context here. **Choice D is incorrect** because "schemed" implies plotting, usually with a negative or secretive intent, so it's less appropriate here. **Choice E is incorrect** because "blueprints" is a noun and does not fit grammatically as a verb here. **Choice F is incorrect** because "casted" is an incorrect past tense of "cast"; the correct past tense is "cast." Also, "cast" does not fit the context of creating a campaign.

467 **Choice B is correct** because "controversial" means causing public disagreement or debate, which fits the context of a publication provoking public outrage. **Choice E is correct** because "polemic" means a strong verbal or written attack on a particular topic, which suits a publication discussing a sensitive issue like child slavery.

Choice A is incorrect because "quarrelsome" describes a person who tends to argue, not a publication. **Choice C is incorrect** because "metaphysical" relates to abstract philosophical concepts, unrelated to public outrage or media. **Choice D is incorrect** because "doubtful" means uncertain or unlikely, which doesn't match the idea of a publication causing outrage.

Choice F is incorrect because "cantankerous" describes a bad-tempered or argumentative person, not a publication.

468 **Choice A is correct** because "sequestered" means kept away or isolated, which also suits the description of groups being separate before colonial borders were redrawn. **Choice C is correct** because "insular" means isolated or detached, which fits the context of groups being separated before European colonization.

Choice B is incorrect because "parochial" means having a limited or narrow outlook, which does not specifically imply geographic or social isolation. **Choice D** is incorrect because "sectarian" relates to religious sects and conflicts, which is not the focus of the sentence. **Choice E** is incorrect because "illiberal" means intolerant or opposed to liberal principles, which is unrelated here. **Choice F** is incorrect because "catholic" means universal or inclusive, the opposite of isolated or separated.

469 **Choice A is correct** because "materialistic" refers to an excessive focus on material wealth and possessions, which fits the criticism socialists often have about capitalist societies. **Choice F is correct** because "bourgeois" relates to the middle/upper class values, often associated with capitalist excesses, making it a suitable description of societal excesses socialists criticize.

Choice B is incorrect because "nonconforming" means not conforming to established norms, which does not specifically describe excesses in capitalist societies. **Choice C** is incorrect because "indolent" means lazy or avoiding activity, which is unrelated to societal excesses. **Choice D** is incorrect because "capitalism" is a noun and does not describe excesses; the sentence requires an adjective. **Choice E** is incorrect because "Victorian" refers to the period or style from Queen Victoria's reign, which is unrelated to the excesses of capitalist societies.

470 **Choice A is correct** because "disparities" means significant differences or inequalities, which appropriately describes the growing economic gaps between first world and third world countries. **Choice F is correct** because "discrepancies" means differences or inconsistencies, which also fits the context of economic differences increasing over time.

Choice B is incorrect because "burrow" means to dig or tunnel, which is unrelated to economic differences. **Choice C** is incorrect because "disagreeable" is an adjective meaning unpleasant, and does not function as a noun describing economic gaps. **Choice D** is incorrect because "hole" is informal and vague, and does not suitably describe economic disparities.

Choice E is incorrect because "animosity" means hostility or resentment, which is unrelated to economic differences.

471 **Choice B is correct** because "consideration" refers to the act of carefully thinking about or analyzing something. In this context, meteorologists are determining hurricane activity timing by considering different parts of the world — which directly relates to thoughtful analysis. **Choice E is correct** because "expatiation" means a detailed discussion or elaboration on a topic. While more commonly used in speech or writing, it fits here by suggesting an in-depth treatment or exploration of the subject (hurricane activity across different parts of the world).

Choice A is incorrect because "cogitation" refers to deep thought, often abstract or philosophical, rather than practical analysis or scientific study. **Choice D** is incorrect because "introspection" refers specifically to self-reflection, which is irrelevant in the context of meteorological studies. **Choice F** is incorrect because "rumination" also leans toward contemplative or reflective thought rather than structured scientific analysis. **Choice C** is incorrect because "circumlocution" refers to speaking in a roundabout way and is unrelated to analysis or study.

472 **Choice A is correct** because "innocuous" means harmless or not likely to offend or injure. This fits the context of the sentence since forwarding fashion and hairstyle trends are light and generally safe uses of media. **Choice D is correct** because "banal" means lacking originality or being dull and trite. This aligns with the examples given, as promoting common trends can be seen as unoriginal or superficial, indicating a less impactful form of influence.

Choice B is incorrect because "aberrant" means deviating from the norm. This does not fit the context since fashion and hairstyle trends are mainstream and not abnormal. **Choice C** is incorrect because "injurious" means harmful. This contradicts the intended meaning of harmless influence in the sentence. **Choice E** is incorrect because "equivocal" means ambiguous or unclear. This does not describe the clear and light-hearted use of media exemplified by fashion trends. **Choice F** is incorrect because "exorbitant" means excessive, usually in price or amount, which is irrelevant to the context of media influence.

473 **Choice A is correct** because "encountered" means to come across or face problems, which fits the context of multinational corporations coming into contact with difficulties at various levels of their new possessions. **Choice C is correct** because "happened upon" means to find something by chance, which also fits the idea that the corporations came across problems without implying any specific action taken.

Choice B is incorrect because "took on" implies the corporations actively assumed responsibility or took steps to solve the problems, which is not indicated in the passage. **Choice D** is incorrect because "affronted" means insulted or offended, which does not fit the context. **Choice E** is incorrect because "emulated" means to imitate, which is irrelevant here. **Choice F** is incorrect because "studied" means to examine carefully, which does not convey merely coming into contact with problems.

474 **Choice A is correct** because "quell" means to suppress or put an end to something, which fits the context of resolving disagreements through compromise. **Choice E is correct** because "obviate" means to remove a difficulty or prevent a problem, which aligns with the idea of using compromise to avoid or eliminate conflicts.

Choice B is incorrect because "castigate" means to reprimand or criticize severely, which does not fit the context of resolving disagreements. **Choice C** is incorrect because "emulate" means to imitate, which is not relevant to resolving conflicts. **Choice D** is incorrect because "exacerbate" means to make a problem worse, which is the opposite of what the sentence conveys. **Choice F** is incorrect because "precipitate" means to cause something to happen suddenly or prematurely, which does not match the idea of resolving disagreements through compromise.

475 **Choice C is correct** because "intransigent" means unwilling to change or compromise, which fits the context of obstacles that are very difficult or impossible to overcome. **Choice E is correct** because "recalcitrant" means stubbornly resistant to authority or control, which can describe obstacles that refuse to be overcome.

Choice A is incorrect because "culpable" means deserving blame, which does not fit the context of describing obstacles. **Choice B** is incorrect because "dogmatic" means strongly opinionated in an arrogant manner, which is unrelated to obstacles. **Choice D** is incorrect because "emollient" means soothing or softening, which contradicts the idea of difficult obstacles. **Choice F** is incorrect because "florid" means excessively ornate or flowery, which does not describe obstacles.

476 **Choice A is correct** because "famous" means well-known or widely recognized, which fits the context of an example that stands out for its surprise ending compared to Maupassant's usual style. **Choice F is correct** because "preeminent" means outstanding or superior in quality, which also fits the idea of "The Necklace" being an exceptional or notable example among his works.

Choice B is incorrect because "great" is vague and does not specifically highlight the uniqueness or recognized status of the example in relation to the context of surprise endings. **Choice C** is incorrect because "ignominious" means deserving or causing public disgrace or shame, which does not fit the context of a well-known literary example. **Choice D** is incorrect because "infamous" means well known for a bad quality or deed, which implies a negative connotation not suggested by the sentence. **Choice E** is incorrect because "notorious" also carries a negative connotation of being famous for something bad, which is not appropriate in this context.

477 **Choice D is correct** because "perceptive" means having or showing sensitive insight or understanding, which fits well with listeners who can detect sarcasm beneath the surface of the music. **Choice E is correct** because "sharp-witted" means quick to notice or understand things, especially subtle or hidden meanings, which also suits listeners who perceive sarcasm in the music.

Choice A is incorrect because "discriminative" generally refers to making distinctions, often in a neutral or technical sense, and doesn't specifically imply insight into subtle emotional cues like sarcasm. **Choice C** is incorrect because "intelligent" simply means having high cognitive ability but doesn't necessarily imply sensitivity to emotional nuance or sarcasm. **Choice B** is incorrect because "intensive" relates to something being concentrated or thorough, which is unrelated to perceiving sarcasm. **Choice F** is incorrect because "veteran" means experienced or long-practiced, but experience alone doesn't guarantee perception of sarcasm in music.

478 **Choice A is correct** because "ascendance" means the state of rising to power or dominance, which also fits the context of gaining control. **Choice C is correct** because "hegemony" means leadership or dominance, especially by one country or group over others, which fits perfectly with the idea of control over peoples and products in the Eastern Pacific Rim.

Choice B is incorrect because "clout" refers to influence or power but is more informal and less precise in a geopolitical or military context. **Choice D** is incorrect because "privileges" refers to special rights or advantages, which doesn't capture the broad dominance implied in the sentence. **Choice E** is incorrect because "management" suggests administrative control, which is narrower and less forceful than the intended meaning. **Choice F** is incorrect because "reign" usually refers to the period during which a sovereign rules and does not directly convey the idea of dominance over regions or peoples.

479 **Choice A is correct** because "casual" means an observer who is not deeply engaged or attentive, fitting the idea of someone who might not notice the subtle increase in mass when the watch is wound. **Choice D is correct** because "dispassionate" means impartial or unemotional, implying a detached observer who might not find the mass difference apparent.

Choice E is incorrect because "heedless" implies a reckless or careless attitude, which adds a negative connotation not supported by the sentence. **Choice B is incorrect** because "concerned" suggests the observer is attentive or worried, which contradicts the idea of missing the detail. **Choice C is incorrect** because "curious" implies active interest and attention, making it unlikely such an observer would miss the mass change. **Choice F is incorrect** because "interested" also suggests awareness and attention, which does not fit the context.

480 **Choice A is correct** because "clout" conveys the idea of influence or power, fitting the sentence's context about Russia's potential dominance in the cultural world before the revolution. **Choice F is also correct** because "sway" specifically implies a controlling or leading influence, which aligns well with the idea of Russia's anticipated central role.

Choice B is incorrect because "importance" suggests significance but lacks the connotation of control or leadership implied in the sentence. **Choice C is incorrect** because "place" refers to status or position but does not clearly express influence or control. **Choice D is incorrect** because "privilege" refers to special rights or advantages, not influence or control in this context. **Choice E is incorrect** because "superintendence" means oversight or management, which is unrelated here.

481 **Choice A is correct** because "addled" means confused or bewildered, which also suits the reaction of many people facing this paradoxical situation. **Choice F is correct** because "stunned" captures the sense of being shocked or overwhelmed, which fits the emotional impact of the contrast between technological progress and social failure after World War Two.

Choice B is incorrect because "agitated" suggests nervousness or restlessness, which is not the primary tone implied by the context of contemplation and shock. **Choice C is incorrect** because "cozened" means deceived or tricked, which doesn't align with the idea of emotional or cognitive dissonance caused by historical events. **Choice D is incorrect** because "deluded" implies being misled or believing something false, whereas the sentence is about genuine confusion or shock, not false beliefs. **Choice E is incorrect** because "graveled" is a rare and old-fashioned word for being perplexed, but it is not commonly used and would sound awkward or unclear in this context.

482 **Choice B is correct** because "conditioned" means influenced or determined by something else, which fits the sentence's idea that a country's military, economic, and social life is shaped by that of other nations. **Choice F is correct** because "recast" means to reshape or alter, and in this context, it implies that the aspects of a nation's life are reshaped due to external (international) influences, which aligns well with the sentence's theme of interdependence among nations.

Choice A is incorrect because "accommodated" usually means adapted or made suitable, which doesn't clearly convey the idea of being shaped or influenced by external forces. **Choice C is incorrect** because "habituated" means accustomed or used to something, which focuses more on internal familiarity rather than external influence. **Choice D is incorrect** because "inured" means made accustomed to something unpleasant, which carries a connotation of desensitization rather than systemic influence. **Choice E is incorrect** because "primed" means prepared or made ready, which is unrelated to the idea of being shaped or determined by other countries.

483 **Choice C is correct** because "bilious" refers to a sickly, greenish or yellowish complexion, which accurately conveys the appearance of someone recovering from a lengthy illness. It implies she still looked unwell. **Choice F is correct** because "sallow" means having a yellowish or unhealthy pale complexion, also appropriate for describing someone who has not fully recovered and still needs rest.

Choice A is incorrect because "hearty" suggests robust health and energy, which contradicts the description of her still needing repose. **Choice B is incorrect** because "salubrious" means health-giving or healthy, again not fitting with the idea of someone who still appears ill. **Choice D is incorrect** because "albino" is a genetic condition involving lack of pigmentation and is not related to illness or recovery, making it inappropriate in this context. **Choice E is incorrect** because "vigorous" implies strong and energetic, which contradicts the idea of a person still weak from illness.

Chapter 5: Sentence Equivalence

484 **Choice A is correct** because "universals" refers to principles or traits that apply broadly across all living things. This aligns perfectly with the sentence's idea of studying what living things have in common, a central aim of twentieth-century biology. **Choice E is correct** because "generality" denotes the quality of being widespread or common to many cases. In the context of scientific inquiry focused on broad biological patterns, this term appropriately captures the shift from specialization to commonalities.

Choice B is incorrect because "specifics" implies focusing on particular or narrow details, which contradicts the passage's focus on shared biological phenomena. **Choice C is incorrect** because "details" also suggests close attention to individual elements rather than the broader search for common patterns across life forms. **Choice D is incorrect** because "circumscription" refers to restriction or limitation, which is inconsistent with the broader, more integrative approach described in the passage. **Choice F is incorrect** because "precision" typically refers to exactness or accuracy, but the context here emphasizes general traits rather than finely tuned measurements.

485 **Choice A is correct** because "profusion" refers to an abundance or large quantity of something. This fits the context of business investment and improved school quality—beneficial outcomes that come in large amounts with gentrification. **Choice E is correct** because "accretion" means a gradual accumulation or growth, especially in terms of benefits or positive development. It fits well with the idea of increasing investment and educational quality.

Choice B is incorrect because "abridgement" implies a reduction or shortening, which contradicts the notion of increased benefits due to gentrification. **Choice C is incorrect** because "ardor" refers to enthusiasm or passion, which is unrelated to the material improvements like investment or school quality mentioned in the sentence. **Choice D is incorrect because** "parapet" is a protective wall or barrier, typically on rooftops or balconies, and has no relevance to the context of neighborhood development or investment. **Choice F is incorrect** because "culmination" refers to the climax or final stage of something. The sentence is about ongoing benefits, not a final result, so this word does not fit the context.

486 **Choice B is correct** because "implausible" means not seeming reasonable or probable; failing to convince. The sentence suggests that without evidence, belief in evolution would lack credibility, making "implausible" an appropriate choice. **Choice C is correct** because "questionable" means open to doubt or suspicion. If belief in evolution were not supported by evidence, it would logically be considered doubtful or questionable.

Choice A is incorrect because "inconceivable" means impossible to imagine or grasp mentally. The sentence implies that belief without evidence would be unreasonable, not unimaginable. **Choice D is incorrect** because "incontestable" means unable to be disputed. This contradicts the sentence logic; the point is that belief would be disputable without evidence. **Choice E is incorrect** because "probable" implies likelihood or reasonableness, which is the opposite of what the sentence is asserting about belief without evidence. **Choice F is incorrect** because "cogitable" means thinkable or conceivable. The sentence critiques the validity of belief without evidence, not whether it can be thought of.

487 **Choice C is correct** because "effectiveness" refers to the degree to which something is successful in producing a desired result. If misunderstandings from differing management styles are unresolved, the company's ability to function efficiently and reach goals may decline. **Choice D is correct** because "productivity" directly relates to output and performance. Miscommunications and unresolved differences can reduce teamwork and efficiency, thereby lowering the productivity of the company.

Choice A is incorrect because "creativity" refers to the ability to generate new ideas, which may not necessarily be impacted by misunderstandings in management styles. **Choice B is incorrect** because "edge" suggests a competitive advantage, which is more abstract and could be affected by a range of factors beyond internal misunderstandings. **Choice E is incorrect** because "potency" typically refers to strength or power in a more general or physical sense, and doesn't fit the corporate context as precisely as "effectiveness" or "productivity." **Choice F is incorrect** because "adaptability" refers to the ability to adjust to new conditions, which could actually be enhanced, not diminished, in a diverse leadership environment.

488 **Choice D is correct** because "novel" means new or unfamiliar, which fits the idea of scientists continuing to make new discoveries about the human body. **Choice E is correct** because "original" refers to something new and unique, emphasizing that future discoveries will be fresh and not derived from previous knowledge.

Choice B is incorrect because "innovative" implies creativity and practical invention, which is not the primary focus here; the sentence emphasizes newness rather than innovation. **Choice C is incorrect** because "ingenious" suggests cleverness or creativity, which relates more to how something is done rather than the fact that discoveries are new. **Choice A** is incorrect because "germinal" means in an early developmental stage, which doesn't fit the context of ongoing, continuous discoveries. **Choice F** is incorrect because "primal" means primitive or fundamental, not new or emerging, and therefore doesn't match the idea of continued novel discoveries.

489 **Choice D is correct** because "evinced" means to show clearly or make evident. In this context, it suggests that Louis Pasteur clearly demonstrated that spontaneous generation could not occur, which aligns with the use of "definitively" in the sentence. **Choice F is correct** because "substantiated" means to provide evidence to support or prove the truth of something. Pasteur substantiated the idea that spontaneous generation was false, meaning he provided definitive proof against it.

Choice A is incorrect because "adduced" means to cite as evidence, which is more appropriate in an argumentative or legal context. It doesn't convey the conclusive demonstration implied by "definitively." **Choice B** is incorrect because "disconfirmed" means to prove to be false, which seems like a good fit, but it lacks the definitive and evidentiary strength that "evinced" and "substantiated" offer. **Choice C** is incorrect because "divulged" means to reveal or disclose something secret, which doesn't fit the scientific tone or the idea of disproving a theory. **Choice E** is incorrect because "publicized" means to make known publicly, which relates to spreading information, not to demonstrating or proving a scientific point.

490 **Choice D is correct** because "significance" refers to the importance or meaning of something. The sentence implies that Mendel's work was overlooked because the botanist did not recognize how important or meaningful it was. **Choice F is correct** because "worth" means value or merit. It fits the context well, suggesting that the botanist failed to recognize the value or merit of Mendel's discoveries, which is why he did not support them.

Choice A is incorrect because "preeminence" refers to being superior or distinguished above others. While Mendel's work later became preeminent, the botanist wouldn't necessarily have been expected to recognize its superiority at the time—just its value or significance. **Choice B** is incorrect because "prominence" refers to being well-known or easily noticeable, which is more about visibility than intrinsic value. The botanist didn't fail to recognize how famous it was (it wasn't yet); he failed to see its importance. **Choice C** is incorrect because "renown" means fame or acclaim. Mendel's work wasn't famous yet, so this word doesn't suit the context. **Choice E** is incorrect because "substantiveness" is an awkward and uncommon form. While it can mean meaningfulness or importance, it is not as idiomatic or precise in this context as "significance" or "worth."

491 **Choice B is correct** because "equivocated" means to speak ambiguously or evasively, especially in order to mislead or avoid giving a clear answer. This fits the context where the suspect spins an elaborate story without giving real proof. **Choice D is correct** because "prevaricated" means to lie or speak in a misleading way. This is appropriate because the suspect is telling a detailed story but not providing evidence—suggesting deception.

Choice A is incorrect because "fawned" means to flatter excessively or show servile deference, which has nothing to do with telling a deceptive story. **Choice C** is incorrect because "quaffed" means to drink something (especially alcohol) heartily, which is irrelevant here. **Choice E** is incorrect because "transgressed" means to violate a law or moral code. While the suspect may have committed a crime, this word doesn't fit the context of answering a question with a story. **Choice F** is incorrect because "palpitated" means to beat rapidly, often in reference to the heart. It describes a physical reaction, not storytelling or deception.

492 **Choice C is correct** because "latent" refers to something that is present but not currently active or visible. In the context of tuberculosis, this accurately describes the state in which the infection exists in the body without causing active disease. **Choice E is correct** because "quiescent" also means inactive or dormant. Like "latent," it fits well with the idea of a disease that exists without showing symptoms or becoming active for a long time.

Choice A is incorrect because "restive" means restless or hard to control, which is the opposite of what the sentence conveys about the dormant state of tuberculosis. **Choice B** is incorrect because "inimical" means harmful or hostile, which doesn't describe a dormant condition—TB may become harmful later, but the sentence focuses on its inactive phase. **Choice D** is incorrect because "fulsome" typically means excessively flattering or insincere; it does not relate to disease or inactivity. **Choice F** is incorrect because "discreet" means careful or tactful, especially in speech or action. It doesn't describe the state of a disease.

493 **Choice B is correct** because "apprehensive" means anxious or fearful that something bad or unpleasant will happen. In the context of the sentence, white males might feel uncertain or fearful about how affirmative action policies could affect their opportunities, making "apprehensive" a suitable choice. **Choice E is correct** because "uneasy" refers to a feeling of discomfort or worry. This matches the emotional response described — a reaction to perceived changes in workplace dynamics or opportunities due to affirmative action policies.

Choice A is incorrect because "boorish" means rude or ill-mannered, which describes behavior, not feelings. The sentence is about how the individuals feel, not how they act. **Choice C is incorrect** because "unassertive" means lacking confidence or unwilling to stand up for oneself, which is unrelated to the emotional tension or discomfort suggested by the sentence. **Choice D is incorrect** because "unfazed" means not disturbed or affected, which directly contradicts the idea of someone feeling negatively impacted. **Choice F is incorrect** because "worrisome" describes something that causes worry, not the feeling itself. The sentence is about how the white males feel, not about what is causing the worry.

494 **Choice A is correct** because "perspicacity" refers to keen insight and the ability to understand things quickly and clearly. In the context of the sentence, the Internet offers quick and meaningful understanding into other cultures, making "perspicacity" an appropriate choice. **Choice C is correct** because "sagacity" means wisdom or shrewdness, particularly in understanding and judging complex situations. Since the sentence emphasizes gaining cultural understanding, "sagacity" fits well as it implies a deep and thoughtful comprehension of different ways of life.

Choice B is incorrect because "erudition" refers to extensive academic learning or scholarly knowledge, which is not the same as the kind of practical or intuitive insight the sentence implies. **Choice D is incorrect** because "sapience" also refers to wisdom, but it often has a broader or more philosophical connotation. While not completely wrong, "sagacity" better matches the idea of understanding social and cultural behaviors. **Choice E is incorrect** because "apotheosis" means the highest point in the development of something or elevation to divine status, which is unrelated to gaining insight into cultures. **Choice F is incorrect** because "proclivity" means a natural tendency or inclination toward something, which does not fit the idea of gaining insight or understanding from an Internet search.

495 **Choice C is correct** because "flouted" means openly disregarded or showed contempt for rules or conventions. In the sentence, women who flouted social norms by having children out of wedlock were severely judged, making this the best fit. **Choice D is correct** because "spurned" means rejected with disdain or contempt. Women who spurned (i.e., rejected) societal conventions were likewise subject to social exclusion, aligning well with the idea of becoming outcasts.

Choice A is incorrect because "wafted" means to float or drift through the air, which is unrelated to rejecting or defying social rules. **Choice B is incorrect** because "extolled" means to praise highly, which contradicts the context of defiance or disobedience. **Choice E is incorrect** because "disinterred" means to dig up something that has been buried, especially a body, and has no relevance to defying social conventions. **Choice F is incorrect** because "condoned" means to accept or allow behavior that is morally wrong or offensive, which doesn't fit the subject of the sentence — women being punished for their own actions, not tolerating the actions of others.

496 **Choice C is correct** because "sensitive" means easily affected by external factors, which fits the context of animal cells being fragile and reacting to environmental changes. **Choice F is correct** because "subject" means being liable or exposed to something. Animal cells being subject to changes in their environment implies they are vulnerable to such changes, aligning well with the sentence.

Choice A is incorrect because "receptive" means willing to accept new ideas or suggestions, which is more about mental openness than physical vulnerability. **Choice B is incorrect** because "sensible" means showing good sense or judgment, which is irrelevant to the physical fragility of cells. **Choice D is incorrect** because "sensual" relates to physical pleasure or the senses, which is unrelated to cellular sensitivity. **Choice E is incorrect** because "sensorial" also pertains to the senses, often used in relation to perception or experiences, not cellular fragility or environmental susceptibility.

497 **Choice A is correct** because "repudiate" means to reject or disavow a belief, especially publicly. In the context of Galileo being forced by the Inquisition to abandon his support of heliocentrism, "repudiate" fits perfectly — he had to deny and renounce his beliefs under pressure. **Choice F is correct** because "abjure" means to formally renounce a belief or cause, especially under oath. This word is often used in historical or legal contexts, making it highly appropriate for Galileo's forced retraction before the Inquisition.

Choice B is incorrect because "beatify" means to declare someone blessed, especially in a religious context — it is unrelated to rejecting beliefs. **Choice C is incorrect** because "preclude" means to prevent something from happening, which doesn't fit the idea of Galileo being forced to give up his beliefs. **Choice D is incorrect** because "foment" means to stir up or instigate, especially something negative like rebellion — the opposite of what Galileo was forced to do. **Choice E is incorrect** because "accrue" means to accumulate or receive over time, which is irrelevant to the context of being forced to give up beliefs.

498 **Choice B is correct** because "castigated" means to severely scold or reprimand someone, especially for wrongdoing. In this context, the mother is reacting strongly to her child's act of stealing, which justifies a harsh verbal rebuke. **Choice E is correct** because "upbraided" also means to criticize or scold sharply. It fits the context of a parent disciplining a child for bad behavior, such as stealing money.

Choice A is incorrect because "placated" means to calm or pacify someone, which is the opposite of what a mother would do when reprimanding a child for stealing. **Choice C is incorrect** because "flustered" means to make someone nervous or confused, and does not imply punishment or reprimand. **Choice D is incorrect** because "vilified" means to slander or speak ill of someone, often publicly or unfairly — too strong and inappropriate for a parent's disciplinary scolding. **Choice F is incorrect** because "descried" means to catch sight of or notice something — unrelated to scolding or punishment.

499 **Choice B is correct** because "advantage" also captures the idea of a beneficial position in competition, which aligns with the loss of uniqueness implied in the sentence. **Choice D is correct** because "edge" refers to a competitive advantage or unique quality that distinguishes the company in the market. When the company's name becomes generic, it loses this distinctiveness.

Choice A is incorrect because "ability" does not fit the context, as the company is not losing a skill or capability but rather its unique market position. **Choice C is incorrect** because "dominance" suggests control over the market, which is stronger than mere distinctiveness and not implied here. **Choice E is incorrect** because "stranglehold" indicates a firm grip or control, conflicting with the loss of distinctiveness described. **Choice F is incorrect** because "superiority" suggests being better than others, implying control or dominance rather than just uniqueness or distinctiveness.

500 **Choice C is correct** because "integral" means being an essential part of something. When workers feel integral to the company, they see themselves as important components contributing directly to the company's success. **Choice B is correct** because "indispensable" means absolutely necessary or essential. Feeling indispensable suggests that workers believe the company cannot do without them, which fits the idea of personal contribution motivating employees.

Choice A is incorrect because "fundamental" refers more to a basic or foundational element, which is less personal than feeling connected or essential as part of the company. **Choice D is incorrect** because "intrinsic" means inherent or natural to something, but it doesn't clearly convey the idea of personal involvement or connection to the company's success. **Choice E is incorrect** because "significant" means important, but it lacks the stronger connotation of being essential or a core part of the company. **Choice F is incorrect** because "vital" means necessary for life or existence, but it is often used more in general or urgent contexts rather than to express a personal connection or sense of belonging to the company.

501 **Choice A is correct** because "mellifluous" means sweet or smoothly flowing sound, which contrasts well with the "strident" (harsh, loud) sound of bagpipes mentioned in the sentence. **Choice B is correct** because "dulcet" means pleasing to the ear, especially melodious and soothing, which also contrasts with the harshness of bagpipes.

Choice C is incorrect because "lithe" refers to flexibility or gracefulness, usually describing movement, not sound. **Choice D is incorrect** because "obstreperous" means noisy and difficult to control, which is similar to "strident" and thus does not provide a contrast. **Choice E is incorrect** because "abstruse" means difficult to understand, which is unrelated to sound quality. **Choice F is incorrect** because "stentorian" means very loud and powerful, which aligns more closely with "strident" and doesn't contrast with it.

502 **Choice D is correct** because "notable" means worthy of notice or attention. This fits the context well, as the sentence highlights distinctive and meaningful aspects of Bruegel's work—vivid colors and realism—without requiring the paintings to be universally famous. **Choice E is correct** because "remarkable" implies something that stands out and is extraordinary. This matches the tone of appreciation for Bruegel's realistic and vibrant depictions, making it an appropriate and strong fit.

Choice A is incorrect because "eye-catching" tends to emphasize surface-level visual appeal. While Bruegel's art is visually striking, the phrase lacks the depth or seriousness expected in a discussion of art history. **Choice B is incorrect** because "famous" implies widespread recognition, which may be accurate, but the sentence doesn't emphasize fame—it emphasizes the qualities of the work. "Famous" also overlaps too much with general reputation rather than the merit of the paintings. **Choice C is incorrect** because "glaring" typically carries a negative connotation, suggesting something overly bright or harsh, which doesn't fit the positive tone of the sentence. **Choice F** is incorrect because "tawdry" means cheap or gaudy, often with moral judgment, and would misrepresent Bruegel's respected artistic contributions.

503 **Choice B is correct** because "specious" means something that appears to be true or plausible on the surface but is actually false or misleading. This fits the sentence well—the speaker's rhetorical flair might make his claims seem convincing at first, but the audience ultimately found them unconvincing and deceptive. **Choice D is correct** because "fallacious" directly refers to logical errors or false reasoning. The context of the sentence—"it was clear that his claims were…"—implies the speaker's arguments were flawed despite his engaging style, which is exactly what "fallacious" conveys.

Choice A is incorrect because "fervid" means intensely passionate or enthusiastic. While the speaker may have been fervid in delivery, the word does not describe the truth or falsity of the claims themselves. **Choice C** is incorrect because "picaresque" refers to a genre of literature involving roguish protagonists in adventurous plots. This literary term has no relevance to the truth value or logic of the speaker's arguments. **Choice E** is incorrect because "officious" describes someone who is overly eager to offer unwanted help or advice. It refers to behavior or personality, not to the quality of claims. **Choice F** is incorrect because "feckless" means ineffective or irresponsible. Although negative, it doesn't capture the idea of false or logically flawed claims, which is central to the sentence.

504 **Choice B is correct** because "minified" means made smaller or reduced. In the context of the sentence, which discusses how household technology has reduced the time spent on chores compared to the past, "minified" accurately reflects the effect of such advancements. **Choice D is correct** because "attenuated" means reduced in force, effect, or value. Applied to the sentence, it properly conveys that the amount of time required for household tasks has diminished due to modern appliances.

Choice A is incorrect because "bated" is most commonly used in the phrase "with bated breath," meaning in anxious anticipation. It does not relate to reduction in time or quantity. **Choice C** is incorrect because "masticated" means to chew food, which is irrelevant to the context of household duties or time spent. **Choice E** is incorrect because "impinged" means to have a negative effect or impact on something or to encroach upon. It doesn't suggest a reduction in time or effort. **Choice F** is incorrect because "augmented" means increased. This contradicts the sentence, which clearly states that the time spent on household tasks has decreased, not increased.

505 **Choice A is correct** because "middling" means average or moderate in quality or success. The sentence describes how efforts to break the glass ceiling have had limited results, with only a small percentage of female-owned businesses generating substantial revenue—an outcome that reflects modest or moderate success. **Choice C is correct** because "equivocal" means ambiguous or uncertain. In this context, it indicates that while some progress may have been made in addressing gender inequality in business, the overall results are unclear or not definitively successful, aligning with the statistics mentioned.

Choice B is incorrect because "halcyon" refers to a peaceful, prosperous, or idyllic time. This doesn't align with the sentence, which emphasizes limited or disappointing success, not prosperity. **Choice D** is incorrect because "ecumenical" refers to promoting unity among different religions or groups. It has no relevance to gender dynamics or business success. **Choice E** is incorrect because "sophomoric" means immature or lacking in maturity. While it could describe poor thinking or planning, it doesn't accurately describe the degree of success mentioned in the sentence. **Choice F** is incorrect because "garrulous" means excessively talkative. It is irrelevant to the context of business success or statistical outcomes.

506 **Choice A is correct** because "plethora" refers to a large or excessive amount of something. In this context, it implies that when the immune system is impaired, the body becomes vulnerable to a great number of harmful microbes, which fits the idea of widespread risk. **Choice C is correct** because "legion" also means a vast number or multitude. It suggests an overwhelming quantity of disease-carrying organisms, which effectively communicates the danger posed to a weakened immune system.

Choice B is incorrect because "surfeit" means an excessive amount, often with a negative connotation related to overindulgence (e.g., in food or drink). While it can technically refer to excess, it's less precise in the context of describing numerous threats or enemies like microbes. **Choice D** is incorrect because "consanguinity" refers to kinship or blood relation, which is irrelevant to the context of harmful microbes and immune defense. **Choice E** is incorrect because "peculation" refers to embezzlement or theft of public funds—completely unrelated to biology or the immune system. **Choice F** is incorrect because "extolment" means praise or glorification, which has no connection to disease or immunity in this context.

507 **Choice D is correct** because "fastidiously" means with great attention to detail or care. In this context, it implies that the microscope enables people to observe cells in a precise and careful manner, aligning with the function of magnification and detailed viewing. **Choice E is correct** because "punctiliously" refers to showing great attention to detail, often in terms of correctness or precision. Here, it effectively conveys the idea that microscopes allow users to observe cellular structures with a high degree of meticulousness and accuracy.

Choice A is incorrect because "mendaciously" means deceitfully or dishonestly. This has no relevance to the process of viewing cells through a microscope, which is a factual and visual activity, not a deceptive one. **Choice B** is incorrect because "salubriously" means healthfully or in a way that promotes well-being. While microscopes may help promote health indirectly by aiding diagnosis, the context here is about viewing cells, not about healthfulness. **Choice C** is incorrect because "adventitiously" means accidentally or occurring by chance. Microscopes are designed to allow purposeful, precise observation—not accidental viewing. **Choice F** is incorrect because "exiguously" means scantily or meagerly. This contradicts the intended meaning of enhanced viewing through a microscope, which allows detailed and clear observation, not limited or scant viewing.

508 **Choice A is correct** because "tamable" means able to be tamed or controlled, which aligns with the goal of making animal identification simpler and more manageable across different classification systems. **Choice F is correct** because "tractable" means easily managed or controlled, which fits the idea of making it easier to identify and classify animals.

Choice B is incorrect because "vociferous" means loud or noisy, which does not relate to ease of identification. **Choice C** is incorrect because "resplendent" means shining or dazzling, which is irrelevant to classification or identification. **Choice D** is incorrect because "quiescent" means inactive or dormant, which does not fit the context of making identification easier. **Choice E** is incorrect because "glib" means superficial or insincere, which is unrelated to the clarity or manageability of classification systems.

509 **Choice B is correct** because "substantive" means having a firm basis in reality and being important or meaningful, which fits the nucleus as a major part of the atom with significant mass and biological importance. **Choice D is correct** because "indispensable" means absolutely necessary, which suits the nucleus's essential role in housing DNA and initiating its interpretation in living cells.

Choice A is incorrect because "effulgent" means shining brightly, which is not relevant to the nucleus's role. **Choice C** is incorrect because "epochal" means highly significant or momentous, which is more abstract and less precise in this scientific context. **Choice E** is incorrect because "recondite" means little known or obscure, which does not apply here since the nucleus is well understood. **Choice F** is incorrect because "evidentiary" relates to evidence, which does not directly describe the nucleus's importance or nature.

510 **Choice B is correct** because "aptitude" means a natural ability or talent, which fits perfectly with having an inherited skill for math. **Choice F is correct** because "propensity" means a natural tendency or inclination, which also makes sense in the context of having an inherited tendency toward math skills.

Choice A is incorrect because "mendacity" means untruthfulness or lying, which is unrelated to skills or genetics. **Choice C** is incorrect because "recidivism" means a tendency to relapse into bad behavior, which does not apply to math skills. **Choice D** is incorrect because "eloquence" means fluent or persuasive speaking, which is unrelated to mathematical ability. **Choice E** is incorrect because "dereliction" means neglect of duty, which does not fit the context of inherited math skills.

511 **Choice A is correct** because "affiliated" means closely associated or connected with something, which fits the idea that metabolism is often linked with weight loss. **Choice B is correct** because "colligated" means bound or connected together, which also fits the context of metabolism being connected to weight loss.

Choice C is incorrect because "caviled" means to raise trivial objections, which is unrelated to the connection described. **Choice D** is incorrect because "distended" means swollen or expanded, which does not fit the context of association. **Choice E** is incorrect because "ensconced" means settled securely or comfortably, which does not apply here. **Choice F** is incorrect because "abrogated" means abolished or repealed, which is unrelated to the context of metabolism being connected to weight loss.

512 **Choice C is correct** because "disparate" means fundamentally different or distinct, which fits the idea that certain practices unite cultures that are otherwise very different. **Choice E is correct** because "myriad" means countless or very many, which also makes sense when referring to a large number of diverse cultures.

Choice A is incorrect because "inimitable" means impossible to imitate, which does not fit the context of uniting cultures. Choice B is incorrect because "profligate" means recklessly extravagant or wasteful, which is irrelevant here. Choice D is incorrect because "palatial" means relating to a palace or grand, which doesn't describe cultures. Choice F is incorrect because "prolix" means tediously wordy, which is unrelated to the idea of uniting cultures.

513 **Choice D is correct** because "salient" means most noticeable or important, which fits the idea of an individual voice that stands out and threatens a totalitarian government. **Choice E is correct** because "significant" means important or meaningful, which also fits the context of a voice that could challenge authority.

Choice A is incorrect because "eminent" means famous or respected, which does not specifically imply a threatening or noticeable voice. Choice B is incorrect because "noteworthy" means deserving attention but is less strong than "salient" or "significant" in this context. Choice C is incorrect because "recognizable" means able to be identified, which does not necessarily imply a threat. Choice F is incorrect because "visible" means able to be seen, but doesn't carry the meaning of importance or threat implied here.

514 **Choice D is correct** because "degeneracy" means moral decline or corruption, which fits the description of Caligula's immoral actions. **Choice F is correct** because "turpitude" means depraved or wicked behavior, which also aligns perfectly with Caligula's notorious reputation for immorality.

Choice A is incorrect because "desuetude" means disuse, which doesn't relate to morality. Choice B is incorrect because "finesse" means skill or delicacy in handling situations, which is unrelated to moral character. Choice C is incorrect because "probity" means honesty and integrity, which is the opposite of what the sentence implies. Choice E is incorrect because "insularity" means being isolated or narrow-minded, which doesn't fit the context of moral behavior.

515 **Choice A is correct** because "sumptuous" means rich, luxurious, and elaborate, which fits the description of the intricate and lavish Fabergé egg designs. **Choice C is correct** because "ostentatious" means showy or designed to impress, which also aligns with the highly decorative and elaborate nature of Fabergé eggs.

Choice B is incorrect because "ubiquitous" means found everywhere, which doesn't relate to the design quality. Choice D is incorrect because "incipient" means just beginning or emerging, which doesn't fit the context. Choice E is incorrect because "prudish" means excessively proper or modest, which is unrelated. Choice F is incorrect because "lugubrious" means mournful or gloomy, which does not match the ornate and luxurious description.

516 **Choice A is correct** because "effectuating" means putting a right into effect or practice, which aligns with the idea that copyrights and patents actively implement the basic property right to profit from one's own ideas. **Choice E is correct** because "protecting" means safeguarding or defending a right, which also fits the role of copyrights and patents in maintaining and securing this fundamental property right.

Choice F is incorrect because "validating" means confirming or establishing legality but does not directly imply putting the right into practical effect. Choice B is incorrect because "legislating" means making laws, which refers to creating rules rather than applying or enforcing the right. Choice C is incorrect because "observing" means complying with or noticing something, which is unrelated to the active role of copyrights and patents. Choice D is incorrect because "promulgating" means formally announcing or declaring, which is about spreading information rather than implementing the right.

517 **Choice C is correct** because "inextirpable" means impossible to remove or eradicate, which fits the idea of a deep, lasting bond that defines a culture. **Choice F is correct** because "indelible" means unforgettable or impossible to erase, which also aligns with the concept of a strong, enduring cultural bond.

Choice A is incorrect because "irascible" means easily angered, which does not fit the context of a unifying bond. Choice B is incorrect because "execrable" means extremely bad or unpleasant, which is unrelated. Choice D is incorrect because "illustrious" means famous or well-known, which does not describe a bond. Choice E is incorrect because "opprobrious" means expressing scorn or disgrace, which contradicts the idea of a positive cultural bond.

518 **Choice C is correct** because "inscrutable" means impossible to understand or interpret, which aligns with the mysterious nature of the octopus. **Choice D is correct** because "enigmatic" means mysterious or difficult to understand, fitting the description of the octopus as a fascinating and unusual creature.

Choice A is incorrect because "prosaic" means ordinary or dull, which contradicts the idea of the octopus being bizarre and fascinating. Choice B is incorrect because "extant" means still existing, which is neutral and doesn't capture the unusual nature described. Choice E is incorrect because "nascent" means just coming into existence, which doesn't fit the context. **Choice F** is incorrect because "incredulous" means unwilling or unable to believe something, which doesn't describe the octopus itself.

519 **Choice B is correct** because "drafted" means to compose or write a preliminary version, which fits the idea of Martin Luther King outlining a plan for change. **Choice C is correct** because "framed" means to construct or formulate something carefully, which aligns with King shaping or defining a course for change.

Choice A is incorrect because "calculated" means to determine mathematically or to plan with caution, which is less precise in this context. **Choice D** is incorrect because "organized" means to arrange systematically, but does not specifically imply outlining a plan. **Choice E** is incorrect because "prepared" means made ready, which is too general here. **Choice F** is incorrect because "schemed" means to plot secretly, which carries a negative connotation not fitting King's intentions.

520 **Choice A is correct** because manifested means "made evident or clear." In the context of the sentence, this suggests that repeated studies have clearly demonstrated the existence of gender wage disparities, aligning with the idea of discovering or showing a consistent finding. **Choice D is correct** because revealed means "disclosed or made known," which fits perfectly with the sentence's focus on studies that have uncovered information about pay inequality and perceptions of future earnings.

Choice B is incorrect because projected implies forecasting or estimating future outcomes, which does not match the idea of reporting findings based on current or past data. **Choice C** is incorrect because publicized means making something widely known to the public, which focuses on dissemination rather than the act of discovering the information. **Choice E** is incorrect because uncloaked suggests that the information was deliberately hidden and then exposed, which is not implied in the sentence. **Choice F** is incorrect because unveiled also suggests a dramatic or formal revealing of previously concealed information, which goes beyond the neutral tone of simply discovering facts through research.

521 **Choice D is correct** because preponderant means "dominant or having superior influence." In the context of the sentence, it conveys that Beethoven's legacy had the greatest impact on Romantic-era musicians, aligning with the idea of a strong and prevailing influence. **Choice E is correct** because sovereign means "supreme in power or influence." This fits the sentence's portrayal of Beethoven's legacy as towering and unmatched, making it the most authoritative and influential force on musicians of the time.

Choice A is incorrect because ancillary means "providing support or help," which implies a secondary or subordinate influence, not the primary one described in the sentence. **Choice B** is incorrect because distinguished means "well-respected or recognized," which describes Beethoven's reputation but not the extent or dominance of his influence. **Choice C** is incorrect because notable means "worthy of notice," which is too weak to convey the idea of Beethoven being the most influential figure. **Choice F** is incorrect because auxiliary means "offering supplementary help or support," which again suggests a supporting role rather than a central or dominant influence.

522 **Choice E is correct** because standing means "reputation or position in a particular context," and in this case, it refers to the credibility or legitimacy of a hypothesis within science. If a hypothesis is to have scientific standing, it must meet the criteria of testability. **Choice F is correct** because status also refers to a hypothesis's level of recognition or acceptance in the scientific community. For a theory to achieve the status of being scientific, it must be testable and falsifiable, as Karl Popper argued.

Choice A is incorrect because condition refers to a state or requirement, which doesn't directly reflect the recognized legitimacy of a scientific hypothesis. **Choice B** is incorrect because capacity means ability or potential, which is too vague in this context and doesn't refer specifically to scientific credibility. **Choice C** is incorrect because position could theoretically work, but it's more ambiguous and doesn't clearly refer to scientific legitimacy or recognition the way standing or status do. **Choice D** is incorrect because rank refe

523 **Choice A is correct** because credit can mean belief or trust in the truth or value of something. In this context, placing too much credit in definitions means relying too heavily on them as if they are unquestionably authoritative, which Popper advises against. **Choice F is correct** because stock (as in the phrase "putting stock in something") directly means placing faith, confidence, or trust in it. This fits Popper's point about people overvaluing the exactness of definitions.

Choice B is incorrect because dubiety means doubt or uncertainty, which is the opposite of placing trust in something. **Choice C** is incorrect because while force can imply emphasis or intensity, it doesn't clearly carry the idea of belief or trust, which is central to the sentence's meaning. **Choice D** is incorrect because hope means a desire or wish for something to happen, not belief in the value or correctness of definitions. **Choice E is incorrect** because progeny means offspring or descendants, which is unrelated to the idea of intellectual trust or belief.

524 **Choice D is correct** because pristine means "in its original, unspoiled condition," which perfectly fits the description of a remarkably well-preserved 17th-century book. **Choice E is correct** because immaculate means "perfectly clean or flawless," which also aligns with the idea of an exceptionally well-maintained book.

Choice A is incorrect because sanitary relates to cleanliness in a health context, which is not relevant to the condition of a book. **Choice B is incorrect** because untarnished means "not spoiled or stained," but is usually used metaphorically for reputation rather than physical condition. **Choice C is incorrect** because purified means "freed from impurities," which doesn't apply to the physical state of a book. **Choice F is incorrect** because adulterated means "made impure or inferior," which is the opposite of the intended meaning.

525 **Choice A is correct** because the text explains that most substances exist as solids, then provides an exception as indicated by the word "but." The word "certain" completes the thought that not all substances exist as solids. Instead, particular ones exist in other states of matter. **Choice E is correct** because the text explains that most substances exist as solids, then provides an exception as indicated by the word "but." The word "various" means several. This completes the thought that not all substances exist as solids, but several exist in other states of matter.

Choice B is incorrect because "majority" means most of something. The sentence is expressing that most substances exist as solids, then provides an exception as indicated by the word "but." Saying that majority exist as other forms of matter would contradict what was initially stated. **Choice C is incorrect** because "gaseous" describes being in the physical state of gas. The sentence would not repeat this descriptor by saying that "gaseous substances exist as gases," because it is both obvious and repetitive. **Choice D is incorrect** because "naught" refers to nothing or the number zero. There are clearly at least two (not zero) substances that exist in other states at room temperature because the sentence lists oxygen and water. **Choice F is incorrect** because "all" means that every substance exists as a gas or liquid at room temperature. This is not true because the first half of the sentence explains that most substances are solids at room temperature. So, this sentence would be contradicting itself.

526 **Choice B is correct** because "nascent" means very new or recently appeared, which is an apt description for the universe that came into being just "microseconds after the Big Bang." **Choice F is correct** because "inchoate" means not fully formed yet, which is a suitable description for the universe that came into existence shortly after the Big Bang.

Choice A is incorrect because "anticipated" refers to something that was expected to happen, which is not in line with the meaning conveyed in the sentence. **Choice C is incorrect** because "reticent" describes a person who is reserved in expressing themselves, which is not related to the sentence. **Choice D is incorrect** because "antiquated" refers to something that is very old, whereas the universe in the sentence is still new, having just appeared. **Choice E is incorrect** because "astute" means able to provide accurate assessments, which is not in line with the intended meaning of the sentence.

527 **Choice A is correct** because "mitigating" means reducing severity, which fits here in the sense of alleviating pain. **Choice B is correct** because "assuaging" means soothing or putting an end to something unpleasant, which is appropriate here in terms of reducing the intensity or eliminating pain and inflammation, making acupuncture an "effective medical practice."

Choice C is incorrect because "embellishing" means adding details to enhance an appearance, however, the meaning intended in the sentence has to do with pain alleviation. **Choice D is incorrect** because "bilking" means cheating someone out of money, which is not in line with the subject matter of the sentence. **Choice E is incorrect** because "extenuating" describes factors that lessen the severity of an offense, which is not related to the subject of pain management. **Choice F is incorrect** because "rectifying" means correcting a mistake, which is not related to the subject of effective medical treatments.

528 **Choice B is correct** because "arcane" refers to something difficult to understand except by a few, which is apt here in terms of the legal terminology used to explain relief benefits that "few could decipher." **Choice E is correct** because "obscure" means something that is unknown to most people, which is true given the usage of legal terms in a relief benefits document.

Choice A is incorrect because "verbose" means using an excess of words, which would not necessarily imply the instructions are difficult to "decipher" or understand. **Choice C is incorrect** because "prosaic" means dull and unimaginative, which does not mean it is difficult to understand. **Choice D is incorrect**

because "laconic" means using very few words, which does not necessarily mean difficult to understand. **Choice F is incorrect** because "dissenting" means expressing disagreement, which is not expressed in the passage and it does not capture the nature of the writing being difficult to understand.

529 **Choice A is correct** because eerie means strange or frightening, especially in a way that evokes unease. In the sentence, the author is drawing a parallel between two distressing historical events—the 1929 Stock Market Crash and the 9/11 attacks—both involving frightened citizens. Describing the similarity as eerie captures the unsettling emotional resonance of those scenes. **Choice F is correct** because uncanny means something that is mysterious, unsettling, or eerily similar. The use of uncanny highlights how disturbingly alike the two moments appear, reinforcing the emotional and visual impact referenced in the sentence.

Choice B is incorrect because curious implies mild interest or oddness without the emotional depth required by the context of frightened citizens. **Choice C is incorrect** because interesting is too neutral and lacks the sense of emotional disturbance the sentence conveys. **Choice D is incorrect** because striking means very noticeable or impressive, which does not reflect the eerie and fearful tone of the sentence. **Choice E is incorrect** because surprising emphasizes unexpectedness, which is not the main focus; the sentence emphasizes emotional eeriness rather than surprise.

530 **Choice A is correct** because explosive describes a reaction that is sudden, violent, and releases a large amount of energy. This fits precisely with the highly reactive and dangerous nature of sodium's interaction with water, which can result in loud, forceful eruptions. **Choice C is correct** because incendiary means capable of causing fire or combustion. The reaction between sodium and water is exothermic and can ignite flammable materials, making incendiary a fitting descriptor for the fiery potential of the reaction.

Choice B is incorrect because muted means subdued or quiet, which directly contradicts the idea of a powerful and dangerous reaction. **Choice D is incorrect** because endogenous means originating from within, typically in biological contexts, and does not describe the nature of a chemical reaction between sodium and water. **Choice E is incorrect** because tertiary refers to something third in order or level, which is unrelated to chemical intensity or danger. **Choice F is incorrect** because incredible means hard to believe or astonishing, which reflects an emotional response rather than the physical characteristics of a reaction.

531 **Choice E is correct** because the blank requires a word meaning the withdrawal of a point of view, as in, a "recantation," the taking back of something previously expressed. **Choice F is correct** because "rescinding" similarly means to revoke a previously established position, which corresponds to the intended meaning of a forced withdrawal of certain religious or scientific views.

Choice A is incorrect because "reiteration" means to express again, which is contrary to the meaning of withdrawing one's position. **Choice B** is incorrect because "submission" means yielding to force or the delivery of a document. Neither of these meanings corresponds to withdrawing a previously held view. **Choice C** is incorrect because an "altercation" is a kind of noisy dispute, typically one that is in public, which does not fit into the meaning of the sentence. **Choice D** is incorrect because "atonement" means the making of amends for past wrongdoings, which is not the intended meaning of the sentence.

532 **Choice C is correct** because "injurious" means harmful and it captures the negative effect that such loans had on low-income families. **Choice D is correct** because "pernicious" means very negative and detrimental, which reflects the effects of predatory loans.

Choice A is incorrect because "subordinate" means having a secondary or less important position in a ranking, which does not capture the intended meaning of adverse effects. **Choice B** is incorrect because "tawdry" describes things that are showy but low in quality, which does not convey the meaning of an adverse effect. **Choice E** is incorrect because "naive" describes a person who is gullible and inexperienced in life, which does not fit the meaning of the sentence. **Choice F** is incorrect because "pretentious" describes a person appearing or trying to appear more important or more valuable than is the case, which does not correspond to the situation presented.

533 **Choice A is correct** because erudite means scholarly or deeply learned. In the sentence, liberal arts studies are described as intellectually rich pursuits. The word erudite captures how these studies are seen as academically impressive but increasingly viewed as impractical compared to technical or scientific education. **Choice B is correct** because lofty means elevated or noble in ideas, but it can also imply being impractically idealistic or disconnected from practical concerns. This fits the sentence's contrast between the idealized nature of liberal arts and the demand for practical, technical training in modern society.

Choice C is incorrect because asinine means foolish or unintelligent, which is too harsh and does not align with the sentence's more nuanced critique of liberal arts as less practical rather than simply foolish. **Choice D** is incorrect because obtuse means slow to understand or dull, which is overly negative and does not reflect the intended contrast with practicality. **Choice E** is incorrect because chary means cautious or wary, which is unrelated to the intellectual value or practicality of liberal arts education. **Choice F** is incorrect because fetid means foul-smelling, which is irrelevant to the context of education and perception.

534 **Choice B is correct** because "recidivism" refers to returning to prison for another conviction after having been released, which is a rate that "correlates" with a lack of "social integration programs." **Choice E is correct** because "relapse" means a return to a previous state or condition, particularly a negative one, which is a fitting term for a return to prison.

Choice A is incorrect because "dissolution" refers to the rupture of an agreement, which is not the subject matter in the sentence. **Choice C** is incorrect because a "diatribe" is a speech that is abusive and accusatory, the incidence of which cannot be correlated with the lack of social programs for former prisoners. **Choice D** is incorrect because "eccentricity" refers to the quality of being strange and different, which is not relevant to the statement on social programs for ex-prisoners. **Choice F** is incorrect because "initiation" refers to the start or entry into a program or group, whereas the sentence discusses the return of ex-prisoners to prison.

535 **Choice A is correct** because aspersed means to slander or speak falsely and maliciously about someone. In the sentence, the government-run media attacked the composer's reputation unfairly, which aligns with the meaning of aspersed. **Choice F is correct** because traduced also means to speak maliciously and falsely about someone's character or work. This fits the context of the sentence where the composer's music and reputation were unfairly maligned by the media.

Choice B is incorrect because degraded means to lower in status or quality but does not specifically imply false or malicious attack. **Choice C** is incorrect because disgraced describes someone who has lost honor or respect, but it does not capture the act of media slander. **Choice D** is incorrect because exculpated means cleared of blame, which is the opposite of the negative media attack described. **Choice E** is incorrect because repudiated means to reject or disown, and the sentence says the composer was forced to repudiate his own work, not the media.

536 **Choice D is correct** because means refers to the method or way something is done. In the sentence, it highlights the process by which DNA is transmitted, fitting well with the idea of how living cells pass genetic information. **Choice E is correct** because mechanism means the system or process by which something occurs. This word aligns perfectly with the biological process of DNA transmission from one generation to another.

Choice A is incorrect because determinant means a factor that decisively affects the nature or outcome of something, which is broader and less precise than the specific process implied here. **Choice B** is incorrect because impetus means a driving force or motivation, which does not fit the scientific context of transmission. **Choice C** is incorrect because ingredient means a component or element, which is too general and does not specifically imply a method or process. **Choice F** is incorrect because median means the middle value in a data set and is unrelated to the context of DNA transmission.

537 **Choice C is correct** because glut means to fill or supply to excess. In the context of animals storing energy for winter, glut appropriately conveys the idea of consuming or storing an abundance of food. **Choice F is correct** because gorge means to eat greedily or to excess. Animals preparing for hibernation need to consume large amounts of food to build energy reserves, so gorge fits perfectly in this context.

Choice A is incorrect because incense means to make angry, which is unrelated to eating or preparation for hibernation. **Choice B** is incorrect because preen means to groom oneself, which doesn't relate to eating or energy storage. **Choice D** is incorrect because recast means to change or reorganize, which doesn't fit the context. **Choice E** is incorrect because enervate means to weaken or drain energy, which is the opposite of what animals do before hibernation.

538 **Choice B is correct** because "indubitably" means without a doubt, which corresponds to the findings "putting an end to considerable debate." **Choice D is correct** because "indisputably" refers to something that cannot be disputed or argued, which is appropriate for findings that are based on the evidence of "samples."

Choice A is incorrect because "perennially" refers to something that persists or reappears year after year, which is not appropriate for the sentence. **Choice C** is incorrect because "conversely" indicates a contrast to a previously expressed view, which is not the case in the sentence, given there was "debate" over the presence of oxygen. **Choice E** is incorrect because "abundantly" means generously or in large amounts, whereas the blank needs to be filled with a term meaning "putting an end" to a debate. **Choice F is incorrect** because "unconscionably" conveys the meaning of something morally reprehensible, which is not in line with the subject or nature of the sentence.

539 **Choice C is correct** because the blank requires a word that means that wildlife populations have decreased considerably, which is the meaning of "plummeted." **Choice F is correct** because "plunged" means something has gone down drastically, which is appropriate in reference to wildlife populations decreasing to the extent of threatening "biodiversity."

Choice A is incorrect because although "decimated" means reduced severely, it would have to be in the passive voice to work in the sentence. Otherwise, it would imply that wildlife populations decimated other populations, which is not the case. **Choice B is incorrect** because "arbitrated" means to have made an official judgment or settled a dispute, which is not related to the subject matter of the sentence. **Choice D is incorrect** because "attenuated" means reduced in effect or value, which is not an adequate fit for the sentence stating that "biodiversity" is "threatened" and even humanity's "place in it." In addition, the verb would have to be in the passive, not active voice. **Choice E is incorrect** because "exacerbated" means a negative situation has worsened. While this is true for the sentence in general, it does not apply to animal populations, which are a quantity and hence require a verb that implies "be reduced."

540 **Choice A is correct** because to be "chastised" means to be reprimanded, which involves receiving a negative reaction. In the case of children with special needs who are unaware of misbehavior or are "unable to control" it, this could lead to issues of "low self-esteem." **Choice D is correct** because "berated" is a strong form of scolding or criticizing, which, when directed at behavior that cannot be modified, can lead to self-esteem issues.

Choice B is incorrect because "applauded" means to congratulate, which would be used to encourage behavior, and is not appropriate for this sentence. **Choice C is incorrect** because "revoked" means to be canceled or withdrawn in an official way, which cannot be applied to a person, as it is in this sentence. **Choice E is incorrect** because "annealed" means strengthened through a process of cooling and heating, as in a piece of iron, which does not apply in this context. **Choice F is incorrect** because "appeased" means to pacify by agreeing to certain demands, which is contrary to the meaning intended in the sentence.

541 **Choice C is correct** because "erratic" means unpredictable and changing, which is an appropriate way to describe "mood swings" that involve "despair and isolation." **Choice E is correct** because "volatile" means unstable and likely to change unexpectedly, which is how "mood swings" affect a person, particularly if they "suffer from depression."

Choice A is incorrect because "incontrovertible" means indisputable, which is not in line with the subject of the sentence describing Woolf and her novels. **Choice B is incorrect** because "deferential" means respectful, which is not a suitable way to describe changing mood swings. **Choice D is incorrect** because "reminiscent" describes something that reminds one of something else, which is not relevant to the statement on Woolf's emotional predisposition. **Choice F is incorrect** because "entrenched" means something is unlikely to change, which is the opposite meaning of "mood swings" that oscillate from one state to another unexpectedly.

542 **Choice B is correct** because "philanthropic" describes an action committed for the benefit of other people, which is a suitable description for initiatives to employ refugees. **Choice E is correct** because "benevolent" means the effort was done with the intention of doing good, which is a suitable description for offering support to people fleeing war.

Choice A is incorrect because "utilitarian" means an action is committed solely for the purpose of maximizing one's well-being. Although, arguably, companies benefit from the employment of refugees ("...strengthen their workforce through diversity and innovation"), the sentence states the effort is "to provide opportunities to the less fortunate," which implies their own benefit was not the primary motive behind the pledge. **Choice C is incorrect** because "meticulous" means paying great attention to detail, which is not in line with the subject matter of the sentence. **Choice D is incorrect** because "fastidious" means very attentive to detail, which is not related to the spirit of the effort discussed. **Choice F is incorrect** because "devious" means deceptive and using indirect tactics to achieve one's goal. While offering employment to refugees does "strengthen [the] workforce" of the companies involved, the sentence does not suggest this effort is carried out deceptively.

543 **Choice A is correct** because detrimental means causing harm or damage. In the context of sustainable manufacturing, products with fewer detrimental effects align with the goal of reducing environmental harm. **Choice D is correct** because adverse means harmful or unfavorable. This fits the sentence's emphasis on reducing negative impacts on the environment.

Chapter 5: Sentence Equivalence

Choice B is incorrect because arbitrary means based on random choice or personal whim, which doesn't relate to environmental effects. **Choice C** is incorrect because elusive means difficult to find or catch, which is unrelated here. **Choice E** is incorrect because transient means temporary or short-lived, which does not describe the nature of environmental effects in this context. **Choice F** is incorrect because mitigating means lessening or alleviating, which is an action rather than a description of effects.

544 **Choice C is correct** because oppugnant means hostile or opposing, which conveys that the statement by the "Eight Alabama Clergymen" was objectionable or offensive—fitting the reason Martin Luther King felt compelled to respond. **Choice D is correct** because opprobrious means expressing harsh criticism or scorn, highlighting the statement's offensive or reproachful nature in the context of King's rebuttal.

Choice A is incorrect because disreputable refers to having a bad reputation but does not specifically imply that the statement itself was offensive or hostile. **Choice B** is incorrect because famous is neutral or positive and does not fit the context of a critical or offensive statement. **Choice E** is incorrect because shoddy means poorly made or inferior in quality, unrelated to the tone or offensiveness of a statement. **Choice F** is incorrect because vicious, although meaning cruel, lacks a close synonym among the options and is less precise than oppugnant and opprobrious for describing the nature of the statement.

545 **Choice A is correct** because "pithy" means using few words to express one's thoughts, which is an appropriate contrast to the "lengthier forms of expression" found in other modes of communication. **Choice E is correct** because "succinct" means expressed in a concise way, which is an apt way of describing text messages that tend to use few words to convey an idea.

Choice B is incorrect because "grandiloquent" describes a style of communicating that uses elaborate wording intended to impress, which is not an apt description of short, concise texts. **Choice C** is incorrect because "abstruse" means difficult to understand and, therefore, is not compatible with the description of text messages being "simple." **Choice D** is incorrect because "exorbitant" means in excess or extravagant, which is contrary to text messaging becoming a "simple" and less "lengthy" way to communicate. **Choice F** is incorrect because "exhaustive" refers to something produced in great depth, which is contrary to the meaning of conciseness in reference to text messages.

546 **Choice A is correct** because fettered means restrained or restricted, which fits the idea of independent filmmakers working freely without being limited by financial or popularity concerns. **Choice F is correct** because constrained means restricted or limited, aligning well with the sentence's context of not being held back by external pressures.

Choice B is incorrect because emaciated means abnormally thin or weak, which doesn't relate to restrictions or limitations. **Choice C** is incorrect because obviated means removed or prevented, which doesn't fit the context of being restricted. **Choice D** is incorrect because macerated means softened by soaking, which is unrelated to the sentence. **Choice E** is incorrect because satiated means fully satisfied, which does not imply restriction or limitation.

547 **Choice D is correct** because "determinants" are factors that play a definitive role in certain processes or outcomes, which is an appropriate way of describing the phenomena that result in rising sea levels. **Choice E is correct** because "variables" are factors that influence an outcome with changing values, which is appropriate for the factors listed, as they can change from year to year.

Choice A is incorrect because "correlations" are relationships that connect phenomena, whereas the sentence lists the independent phenomena that are considered to have a causal effect on rising sea levels. **Choice B** is incorrect because "contingencies" are future events that may be possible, or preparations for such events, which is not appropriate for the sentence discussing events currently taking place. **Choice C** is incorrect because "entities" are things that exist independently, whereas this sentence is discussing processes that are interconnected. **Choice F** is incorrect because "endeavors" refer to purposeful activity, while the processes mentioned describe natural happenings rather than intentional events.

548 **Choice C is correct** because possessing antimicrobial properties en par with penicillin means that garlic is very strong, in other words, "potent," at increasing immune response. **Choice F is correct** because "efficacious" is a way of saying highly effective, which is a suitable way to describe garlic as offering strong immune boosting effects.

Choice A is incorrect because "generic" means ordinary or without outstanding characteristics, which is not a fitting description for garlic when compared to an antibiotic. **Choice B** is incorrect because "deciduous" refers to trees whose leaves fall in the autumn, which has nothing to do with the statement. **Choice D** is incorrect because "resilient" describes something that can withstand disturbances, which is not discussed in the sentence, but rather the relative strength of garlic's effect on the immune system. **Choice E is incorrect** because "notorious" means well-known, which does not describe garlic's effects on the immune system, given it has not been stated if this is known or not.

549 **Choice C is correct** because disinclined means unwilling or having a lack of desire to do something, fitting the idea that university-educated individuals would likely not want low-paying factory jobs. **Choice D is correct** because loath means unwilling or reluctant to do something, which also aligns perfectly with the sentence's suggestion that college graduates would resist taking such jobs.

Choice A is incorrect because crass means insensitive or crude, which does not relate to willingness. **Choice B is incorrect** because nonplussed means confused or surprised, which does not fit the context of job acceptance. **Choice E is incorrect** because urbane means suave or sophisticated, unrelated to job preference. **Choice F is incorrect** because frantic means very anxious or hurried, which is not relevant here.

550 **Choice E is correct** because reduced means made smaller or less significant, which fits the idea of unique traits being diminished to create similarity. **Choice F is correct** because rendered means caused to become or made, which fits the metaphor of transforming a unique snowflake into an ordinary drop of water.

Choice A is incorrect because commuted means substituted or changed, but it doesn't clearly convey the loss of uniqueness implied in the sentence. **Choice B is incorrect** because deformed means distorted in shape, which has a negative physical connotation not fitting the metaphor. **Choice C is incorrect** because disfigured means spoiled in appearance, which is too harsh and unrelated to the idea of standardization. **Choice D is incorrect** because exchanged means swapped or traded, which doesn't convey the transformation or loss of uniqueness.

551 **Choice D is correct** because "faint-hearted" means lacking in courage, which is what situations in conflict areas require to be able to do social work. **Choice F is correct** because "timorous" means possessing a timid disposition, which describes someone likely to be "dissuaded" by work under "abruptly changing, potentially violent" circumstances.

Choice A is incorrect because "adulterous" describes someone who has engaged in an extramarital affair and has nothing to do with the subject matter of the sentence. **Choice B is incorrect** because "venturesome" would describe an individual eager for adventure, whereas the sentence states that conflictive regions "dissuade" those unprepared for changing, unpredictable situations, particularly if they are dangerous. **Choice C is incorrect** because "ostentatious" describes people who show off their achievements or possessions to impress others, which is not in line with the subject matter. **Choice E is incorrect** because "intrepid" means courageous, which is contrary to the kind of people dissuaded by "potentially violent" situations in a conflictive region.

552 **Choice A is correct** because foundations refers to the base or core upon which something is built. In the sentence, it supports the idea that trust is still the essential base of most business decisions, even with the rise of A.I. and machine learning. **Choice C is correct** because underpinnings also refers to the underlying support or basis for something. It reinforces the idea that trust remains a key support structure in decision-making processes.

Choice B is incorrect because profits are outcomes of decisions, not the basis for them. The sentence is focused on what business decisions are built upon, not their results. **Choice D is incorrect** because trajectories refer to paths or directions over time, which is not the focus of the sentence discussing the foundational aspects of decisions. **Choice E is incorrect** because operations refer to the day-to-day activities of a business, not the core basis of decision-making. **Choice F is incorrect** because outcome refers to the result of a decision, not the basis it's built on.

553 **Choice B is correct** because "impromptu" refers to something produced spontaneously, which accurately describes the performances that are done "without scripts or rehearsal." **Choice D is correct** because "ad-lib" means performing without previous preparation, which is what "improvisation" is about.

Choice A is incorrect because "laborious" describes something that is difficult to do and requires a lot of time and effort, which is not the intended meaning of dialogue produced instantaneously. **Choice C is incorrect** because "implicit" describes something that is not made explicit, which does not apply to a dialogue expressed in a performance. **Choice E is incorrect** because "aberrant" refers to something that is unusual in a displeasing way, which is not the case for an art form that engages in "sharp-witted" dialogue. **Choice F is incorrect** because "tacit" describes something that is understood without being verbally expressed, which is not suitable for the description of a dialogue.

554 **Choice B is correct** because gamey means slightly indecent or risqué, often in a sexual way. In the context of the sentence, Stalin was apparently offended by the content of the opera, and a gamey plot would certainly have included material that could provoke such a reaction, especially from someone with strict cultural expectations. **Choice F is correct** because ribald refers to something that is vulgar or indecent in speech or content, usually in a coarse or humorous way. A ribald plot would likely contain sexually explicit or offensive material, making it believable that Stalin would walk out in disapproval.

Choice A is incorrect because ebullient means lively and enthusiastic, which is not inherently offensive and does not explain Stalin's reaction. **Choice C is incorrect** because impish means mischievous in a playful, harmless way—not something that would normally shock or offend. **Choice D is incorrect** because phlegmatic means calm or unemotional, which doesn't make sense in the context of a plot that would cause offense. **Choice E is incorrect** because puckish, like impish, means playfully mischievous, not offensive or inappropriate enough to cause someone to leave in protest.

555 **Choice B is correct** because irregular means not consistent or even, which fits the context of planetary motion being disrupted in a way that doesn't follow its normal path. Astrophysicists looking for evidence of black holes would be searching for such unusual deviations. **Choice F is correct** because anomalous means deviating from what is standard, normal, or expected. In the sentence, any anomalous wobbling in a planet's orbit could indicate the influence of an external force—possibly a primordial black hole—making this word a perfect fit.

Choice A is incorrect because "unforeseen" means unpredicted, whereas the detection of the wobble would be in line with theories on primordial black holes. **Choice C is incorrect** because "unstable" means that the wobble is possibly losing control, which is not the intended meaning. **Choice D is incorrect** because "idiosyncratic" refers to a unique occurrence, which does not fit as the unusual wobbling, if it exists, should be present on other planets as well. **Choice E is incorrect** because "precarious" means changing in an unexpected way, similar to a lack of stability, which does not match with the possible extra wobble the astrophysicists hope to see.

556 **Choice D is correct** because deceptive means misleading or dishonest, especially to gain an unfair advantage. This fits the sentence's tone, which critiques the unethical practices of privileged groups that Dickens sought to expose. **Choice F is correct** because exploitive means taking unfair advantage of others, particularly those who are vulnerable. Dickens was known for portraying how the rich exploited the poor, especially children and workers, so this word directly aligns with the context.

Choice A is incorrect because beneficial means good or helpful, which contradicts the critical tone of the sentence. **Choice B is incorrect** because benignant means kind and benevolent—again, the opposite of what Dickens was criticizing. **Choice C is incorrect** because co-optive means to absorb or assimilate, especially for a different purpose. While it might sound slightly manipulative, it lacks the moral weight of exploitation or deception. **Choice E is incorrect** because deleterious means harmful, which is close in tone, but it's more about general harm rather than intentional wrongdoing or unethical behavior, which is central to Dickens's critique.

557 **Choice B is correct** because collection refers to an assembled group of works or objects, which fits the context of possessing a body of Picasso's art spanning his career. **Choice D is correct** because repository means a place or store of valuable items, implying the electrician had a significant and organized holding of Picasso's works, consistent with the sentence.

Choice A is incorrect because argosy suggests a treasure trove or rich supply of items. While it implies value, it is an archaic term that is less neutral and not commonly used in this context. **Choice C is incorrect** because cornucopia also implies an abundant and overflowing supply, emphasizing richness and variety. Although positive, it doesn't convey the straightforward sense of a collection or storage of artworks. **Choice E is incorrect** because stockpile implies an amassed supply usually for practical use, lacking the refined nuance needed for describing art. **Choice F is incorrect** because wellspring means an original source that can be replenished, which incorrectly suggests that Picasso's works are endlessly renewable rather than a fixed body of work.

558 **Choice A is correct** because chided means to scold or express disapproval, which fits the context of criticism directed at Naipaul for his negative portrayals. **Choice B is correct** because excoriated means to severely criticize or denounce, matching the strong disapproval Caribbeanists reportedly have toward Naipaul's views.

Answers & Explanations

Choice C is incorrect because exculpated means to clear from blame or fault, which contradicts the negative criticism implied. **Choice D** is incorrect because sanctioned can mean either to approve or to penalize, but it doesn't clearly convey criticism here. **Choice E** is incorrect because libeled means to defame someone in writing, implying false statements, which is not necessarily suggested by the sentence. **Choice F** is incorrect because slandered means to make false spoken statements damaging to someone's reputation, which doesn't fit since the criticism seems based on his actual work.

559 **Choice E is correct** because dissemination means the act of spreading or distributing information widely, which fits perfectly with the idea of sharing discoveries among professionals. **Choice F is correct** because propagation means the spreading or promoting of ideas or knowledge, also aligning with the sharing of scientific discoveries.

Choice A is incorrect because dispersal implies scattering or spreading out but lacks the sense of purposeful sharing of knowledge. **Choice B** is incorrect because dissipation means wasting or scattering in a way that leads to loss, which does not fit the context of sharing knowledge. **Choice C** is incorrect because collection refers to gathering, not spreading information. **Choice D** is incorrect because concentration implies focusing or gathering in one place, which contrasts with the idea of distributing knowledge.

560 **Choice A is correct** because "imposing" means establishing in an official way, which is an appropriate way to express the introduction of a new tax. **Choice C is correct** because "levying" means collecting in an obligatory way, as in taxes or fines, which is precisely what is being done with the new tax.

Choice B is incorrect because "lodging" means submitting or providing in an official capacity, which is contrary to enforcing a law in order to receive taxes. **Choice D** is incorrect because "abetting" means aiding a person in criminal activity, which does not apply in the issuance of a tax law. **Choice E** is incorrect because "inflicting" is used with a negative emotional charge, in the sense of causing pain or suffering, and is not suitable in the context of implementing a new tax. **Choice F** is incorrect because "soliciting" means asking for something in a persuasive way, which is not appropriate in the context of making it a legal requirement to pay a tax.

561 **Choice A is correct** because nebulous means vague or unclear, which contrasts with the concrete business plans mentioned later in the sentence. The sentence suggests that unclear or indistinct dreams of wealth won't help an entrepreneur succeed. **Choice E is correct** because dubious means doubtful or questionable, conveying that uncertain or unreliable dreams are unlikely to lead to success, reinforcing the contrast with solid plans.

Choice B is incorrect because sagacious means wise, which would help rather than hinder success. **Choice C** is incorrect because craven means cowardly, which doesn't relate to the idea of useful or useless dreams. **Choice D** is incorrect because cogent means convincing or clear, which is opposite to the intended meaning. **Choice F** is incorrect because fervid means passionate or intense, which does not imply that the dreams are unhelpful.

562 **Choice C is correct** because "abated" means reduced in severity, which is an appropriate reference for winds that have calmed down. **Choice F is correct** because "subsided" means decreased in intensity, which is apt for the calming down of storm winds.

Choice A is incorrect because "surged" means something has increased greatly which is contrary to the intended meaning of storm winds calming down sufficiently to allow rescue vehicles to pass. **Choice B** is incorrect because "plummeted" means dropped severely, which is not the best description for the quieting down of winds, as they cease to blow rather than descend. **Choice D** is incorrect because "abstained" means not engaged in a certain practice, which is not relevant to the situation. **Choice E** is incorrect because "deferred" means delayed, which does not apply to the context of quieting weather conditions.

563 **Choice B is correct** because quail means to feel or show fear or apprehension. It fits the sentence, which describes children reacting fearfully to thunder by seeking their parents. **Choice E is also correct** because cower means to crouch or shrink down in fear. This directly matches the image of frightened children reacting to loud thunder.

Choice A is incorrect because clinch means to grab or secure something tightly (often in triumph or victory), which does not imply fear. **Choice C** is incorrect because demur means to raise doubts or objections—not to show fear. **Choice D** is incorrect because rebuff means to reject or snub, which is unrelated to the fearful response described. **Choice F** is incorrect because simper means to smile in a silly or self-conscious way, which is completely inconsistent with the fear described in the sentence.

For more practice, visit www.vibrantpublishers.com

Chapter 5: Sentence Equivalence

564 **Choice C is correct** because the blank requires a word referring to the material collected and transported by glaciers, such as "sediment," which includes particles like dirt, sand, and rocks that later settle to create a new "landform." **Choice F is correct** because "debris" means the remaining or leftover pieces of larger conglomerates, which is what glaciers carry to create "landforms" in new regions as their ice melts.

Choice A is incorrect because "gusts" are strong bursts of wind, which would not remain within glacial ice and create "landforms" upon melting. **Choice B** is incorrect because "eddies" are circular movements of water or otherwise movement against the main current, which would not leave deposits capable of creating "landforms." **Choice D** is incorrect because "crags" are large rocks perched high and protruding from the mass around them, which is not a fitting description for the material that creates "landforms" after being transported by glacial ice. **Choice E** is incorrect because "gales" are strong winds, typically encountered at sea, which would not be carried by glacial ice or result in "landforms."

565 **Choice A is correct** because "copious" means in large amounts, which is an accurate description of the kind of heavy sweating brought about by heat. **Choice F is correct** because "profuse" means abundant or excessive in quantity, which is also a way to describe a lot of sweating as a reaction to heat.

Choice B is incorrect because "bilious" describes an unpleasant disposition, which is not related to sweating. **Choice C** is incorrect because "constricted" describes something that has been restrained in some way, which is not in line with the extensive sweating one expects under conditions of extreme heat. **Choice D** is incorrect because "evocative" describes something that makes one imagine something pleasant, which is not suitable for an increased level of sweating. **Choice E** is incorrect because "satiated" means fully satisfied, which is not an appropriate description of severe sweating.

566 **Choice C is correct** because "health" means being in good condition. The sentence is expressing that a CFO keeps business finances in good condition for long-term success. Therefore, "health" completes the sentence. **Choice D is correct** because "prosperity" means the state of being successful. The sentence is expressing that a CFO maintains business finances to support long-term success. Therefore, "prosperity" completes the sentence.

Choice A is incorrect because "state" simply means the condition something is in. The CFO does not merely want to ensure the business's financial state,

as that state might be negative. Rather, the CFO works to ensure the business's financial success. Thus, Choices C and D are better options. **Choice B** is incorrect because "dishevelment" means a state of being out of order. The sentence expresses that the CFO works toward the financial success of the company. Therefore, the CFO would not aim to maintain disorder but rather resolve it and lead the company to financial health. **Choice E** is incorrect because "reverie" is the state of being lost in a daydream. By contrast, the sentence emphasizes the deliberate actions CFOs take to achieve financial success. They do not simply dream about finances—they actively manage and sustain them. **Choice F** is incorrect because a "side" of a business refers to a specific section or part. However, the sentence states that the CFO is ensuring something—meaning they are making an outcome certain. One cannot ensure a side, since a side is not an outcome. Rather, the CFO works to ensure a state of health and prosperity, making Choices C and D the better options.

567 **Choice B is correct** because morbid means having an abnormal or unhealthy interest in disturbing and unpleasant subjects, especially death. Poe's stories frequently explore death, decay, and the macabre, making morbid the best fit for describing his gothic tales. **Choice C is correct** because saturnine means gloomy, dark, or melancholic—traits often associated with Poe's tone and the atmosphere in his stories of crumbling mansions and dying women. It aligns well with the somber and eerie mood he creates.

Choice A is incorrect because whimsical suggests playfulness or fanciful notions, which contrasts sharply with the dark and serious nature of Poe's work. **Choice D** is incorrect because sublime means grand or awe-inspiring, which may apply to the effect of some of Poe's writing, but does not directly describe the tales themselves, especially in the context of horror and dying characters. **Choice E** is incorrect because droll means amusing in an odd or whimsical way, which is not consistent with the grim tone of Poe's stories. **Choice F** is incorrect because esoteric means understood by only a select few with specialized knowledge. While Poe's stories are rich and layered, they are not esoteric in subject matter—they are widely appreciated for their accessible horror themes.

568 **Choice B is correct** because "propensity" refers to the inclination or willingness to commit an action, which is what the subjects of the study had towards following orders, "even" if it meant causing harm. **Choice C is correct** because "readiness" also means a willingness to commit an act, which is what the study explored in terms of following orders from an authority figure, despite consequences.

Choice A is incorrect because "abhorrence" means the feeling of hatred or rejection of something, whereas the sentence states that subjects followed orders "even" under conditions of causing harm, which means subjects were not unwilling to do so. **Choice D** is incorrect because "euphoria" is a feeling of great happiness, which would not be a correct characterization of subjects following orders, as no indication was given that the act provided them with pleasure. **Choice E** is incorrect because "tirade" refers to a long and critical speech, which is not a suitable fit in the sentence on social behavior and authority. **Choice F** is incorrect because "temerity" means courage, particularly in the face of danger or opposition, which would be contrary to the subjects following orders even when it involved harming others.

569 **Choice A is correct** because disconcerting means unsettling or disturbing. The sentence discusses the difficulty in distinguishing between extinct and dormant volcanoes—something that could have dangerous consequences. This uncertainty makes the situation disconcerting. **Choice D is also correct** because ominous means giving the impression that something bad or dangerous is going to happen. The inability to know whether a volcano is merely dormant suggests the potential for sudden eruptions, which is clearly ominous.

Choice B is incorrect because extenuating refers to circumstances that lessen the severity of an action, usually in the context of guilt or blame. That does not apply here. **Choice C** is incorrect because trenchant means sharp or incisive, often used to describe commentary or critique—not a state of affairs like the one described. **Choice E** is incorrect because inimitable means unique or impossible to imitate. While volcanoes may be unique, this does not address the unsettling ambiguity described. **Choice F** is incorrect because luculent means clear or lucid, which contradicts the confusion and uncertainty implied in the sentence.

570 **Choice B is correct** because denigrate means to unfairly criticize or belittle something. The sentence argues that small businesses are highly important (contributing about half of America's GDP), so it would be a mistake to minimize or undervalue them. Thus, denigrate fits perfectly. **Choice F is also correct** because disparage means to regard or represent something as being of little worth. Like denigrate, it conveys the idea of undervaluing or belittling, which would indeed be a mistake given the economic importance of small businesses.

Choice A is incorrect because broach means to bring up a topic for discussion, which doesn't relate to minimizing importance. **Choice C** is incorrect because glean means to gather information or learn gradually—again, unrelated to the idea of downplaying importance. **Choice D** is incorrect because sanction can mean either to approve or penalize, but neither meaning fits the idea of undervaluing something. **Choice E** is incorrect because lionize means to treat someone or something as a hero or celebrity, which is the opposite of diminishing importance.

571 **Choice C is correct** because "counterfeit" refers to something that is not authentic, whose exchange, in terms of banknotes, is considered a crime. **Choice F is correct** because "forged" refers to something that has been produced in a false way, which is an appropriate way to describe fake banknotes exchanged by a "con artist."

Choice A is incorrect because "tenuous" refers to something that has little strength or an idea that is doubtful, which is not a suitable way to describe false banknotes. **Choice B** is incorrect because "authentic" indicates the opposite of false, meaning true and original, which would not describe false bills. **Choice D** is incorrect because "genuine" means honest and without deceit, which does not apply to false banknotes. **Choice E** is incorrect because "aboriginal" describes a person or group of people that has lived in a region before colonization, and as such, cannot be applied to describe false money.

572 **Choice B is correct** because "gauge" means to determine or assess the state of people's emotions as they engage in the stock market to understand what "motivates behavior." **Choice D is correct** because "ascertain" means to determine the state of something to a degree of certainty, which is what the index aims to do with the emotions of investors on the stock market to then use as a "predictor" of future activity.

Choice A is incorrect because "entice" means persuade by offering an attractive reward, which is not suitable for an index that evaluates emotions rather than directs them. **Choice C** is incorrect because "influence" means to cause something to change, whereas the index assesses the prevalent emotions at play rather than affecting them. **Choice E** is incorrect because "undermine" means to weaken a person's authority or sense of self, which is not related to the examination of emotions involved in the stock market. **Choice F** is incorrect because "orchestrate" means to organize, which is not in line with the observation of emotions driving market activity.

Chapter 5: Sentence Equivalence

573 **Choice A is correct** because "beneficial" means the effects are positive, which is a fitting description for outcomes that include "lowering blood pressure and improving mental well-being." **Choice C is correct** because "favorable" is another way of saying positive or desirable, which would be suitable for any effects that led to improvement.

Choice B is incorrect because "adverse" means negative, which would not suitably describe effects that improve one's health. **Choice D** is incorrect because "ambivalent" means having uncertain feelings, which does not fit in the context of health benefits. **Choice E** is incorrect because "transient" means temporary, which may be the case with the lowering of blood pressure, however, the example of improved well-being places emphasis on the positivity of the effects, rather than their duration. **Choice F** is incorrect because "abysmal" means extremely low or negative, which is in contrast to the positive outcomes in health improvements.

574 **Choice B is correct** because "reminiscent" means it reminds one of something else, which in the case of the supernova, reminded the astronomers of a "dandelion seed." **Choice E is correct** because "suggestive" means that it brings something else to mind, which is what the supernova does in terms of its appearance having the shape of a "dandelion seed."

Choice A is incorrect because "implosive" means rushing towards the center, which does not fit the sentence about the protrusions of a supernova resembling a dandelion seed. **Choice C** is incorrect because "reverent" means respectful, which is not a suitable way to describe a celestial body. **Choice D** is incorrect because "expulsive" describes something expelled or banned, which is not the case with the image of a supernova. **Choice F** is incorrect because "coercive" means forceful and imposing, which is not relevant to the visual of a supernova being compared to a dandelion seed.

575 **Choice B is correct** because "exemplary" means having excellent qualities, which is an apt description of turmeric for its health benefits. **Choice E is correct** because "salubrious" means healthy or boosting health, which is an appropriate adjective for a herb with "anti-inflammatory and antioxidative properties."

Choice A is incorrect because "temperate" means mild or not extreme in temperature or behavior, which is not fitting to describe an herb with "remarkable" qualities. **Choice C** is incorrect because "sporadic" means without regularity, which is not an appropriate term to describe an herb. **Choice D** is incorrect because "secular" means not affiliated with a religion, which is not fitting for a description of an herb. **Choice F** is incorrect because "flimsy" means weak and unreliable, which does not suitably describe an herb with "remarkable" properties.

576 **Choice A is correct** because "despondency" refers to the negative state of feeling low or without hope, which is a "negative health impact." **Choice E is correct** because "dejection" expresses a state of sadness or discouragement, which also conveys a possible "negative" outcome of social media use.

Choice B is incorrect because "entitlement" means a sense of superiority with the belief that one is deserving of certain privileges, which is not appropriate to describe the "negative health effects" of social media. **Choice C** is incorrect because "fidelity" means loyalty and authentic dependability, which is a positive quality and does not fit the meaning of the sentence about "negative effects." **Choice D** is incorrect because "torpor" refers to a physical state without energy rather than an emotional state, which is what is referenced in terms of a "rise in feelings." **Choice F** is incorrect because "paucity" refers to a shortage or a small, inadequate amount, which is not a suitable description for a "rise in feelings."

577 **Choice B is correct** because "prohibitive" means so excessive as to prevent action, which is what certain "entry fees" are for "low-income families." **Choice F is correct** because "exorbitant" also means so excessively high as to discourage a low-income family from visiting a museum.

Choice A is incorrect because "adorning" means decorative, which is a positive description rather than the negative connotation of excessive entry fees affecting "low-income families" and causing museums to offer "free entrance" on certain days. **Choice C** is incorrect because "whimsical" means imaginative in an unusual way, which is a positive quality that does not fit the negative meaning intended in the sentence. **Choice D** is incorrect because "liberal" means generous or permissive, which is typically a positive quality that would not impact "low-income families" in an adverse way. **Choice E** is incorrect because "intractable" means difficult to control or resolve, which is not a suitable way of describing entry fees.

578 **Choice B is correct** because "manifold" means numerous, which is a suitable way of describing "features" that are comparable to "brand-name operating systems." **Choice D is correct** because "myriad" means countless or having a high number, which is an appropriate way to refer to the many "features" offered by "alternatives."

Choice A is incorrect because "incognizant" describes a person who is unaware of something, which is not a fitting description of "features" in an operating system. **Choice C is incorrect** because "indelible" means impossible to wash away or forget, which is not a relevant description of "features" provided by an operating system. **Choice E is incorrect** because "specious" describes something that appears true while being false, which does not fit the intended meaning of numerous to describe the features offered by Linux in comparison to "leading brands" in operating systems. **Choice F is incorrect** because "defective" means faulty, which is a negative quality and not fitting to describe alternatives being comparable to "leading brands."

579 **Choice D is correct** because "diminishing" means reducing, which is in line with the "tranquilizing" effect that pink shades have on viewers. **Choice F is correct** because "curtailing" means bringing down, which fits well with the results of lowered "hostility" expected from the "tranquilizing" effects of certain pink shades.

Choice A is incorrect because "eliciting" means producing a reaction, which is the opposite of the intended meaning of having a "tranquilizing effect" and thereby reducing hostility. **Choice B is incorrect** because "inspiring" means encouraging something to happen, which is contrary to the intended meaning of suppressing hostility. **Choice C is incorrect** because "provoking" means stimulating a response, which is unfitting in the sentence that describes certain shades of pink reducing hostility. **Choice E is incorrect** because "entailing" means involving, which does not convey the intended meaning of reducing hostility by having a "tranquilizing effect."

580 **Choice A is correct** because shrewd means having sharp judgment or practical intelligence, especially in business matters. The sentence emphasizes that even small businesses can qualify for tax credits if their work is innovative and their management is savvy enough to navigate the requirements. Shrewd fits this idea of being clever or astute. **Choice C is also correct** because adroit means skillful and clever, particularly in managing situations or handling problems. Like shrewd, it reinforces the idea that small business management must be capable and competent to take advantage of the tax credits.

Choice B is incorrect because supine means inactive or passive, which contradicts the idea of being proactive enough to claim tax benefits. **Choice D is incorrect** because dogmatic means rigid or inflexible in beliefs, which doesn't relate to navigating tax benefits successfully. **Choice E is incorrect** because ineluctable means unavoidable or inevitable, which is unrelated to management skill or decision-making. **Choice F is incorrect** because meretricious means flashy or superficially attractive but lacking real value—an unfit description for effective management.

581 **Choice C is correct** because "assailing" fits the meaning of attacking (in this case, the "body's own tissue"), which is the typical cause of inflammation in autoimmune diseases. **Choice F is correct** because "assaulting" is also a way to say attacking, fitting the meaning of the immune system acting against the "body's own tissue."

Choice A is incorrect because "safeguarding" refers to the action of protecting, rather than attacking and therefore conveys the opposite meaning of the one intended. **Choice B is incorrect** because "lambasting" means criticizing severely, typically verbally, which does not fit the context of immune system activity. **Choice D is incorrect** because "engendering" means causing something to happen, which lacks the negative connotation inferred by the immune system acting against the body's own tissue in autoimmune diseases. **Choice E is incorrect** because "espousing" means standing behind and supporting a cause or idea, which does not fit in the context of immune system behavior.

582 **Choice A is correct** because "diffident" describes someone who lacks self-confidence, which is fitting for students who "struggle to participate in class activities" or need support to "boost self-esteem." **Choice D is correct** because "reticent" refers to someone being very reserved and reluctant to express themselves, which aptly describes students who "struggle to participate in class activities" for lack of "self-esteem."

Choice B is incorrect because "bellicose" describes someone who tends to get into fights, which is not the intended meaning here for students who are too shy to "participate in class activities." **Choice C is incorrect** because "listless" describes somebody who lacks energy or interest, whereas the intended meaning has more to do with a lack of "self-esteem." **Choice E is incorrect** because "despondent" describes somebody who is very sad or feeling hopeless, which is not necessarily the case for students who are simply lacking in self-confidence. **Choice F is incorrect** because "apathetic" means indifferent and lacking an interest, which is not the intended meaning of lacking self-confidence or self-esteem.

Chapter 5: Sentence Equivalence

583 **Choice B is correct** because dogged means showing tenacity and grim persistence. Shackleton's sustained and determined efforts to save his team despite extreme hardship align perfectly with this word. **Choice F is also correct** because indefatigable means never showing signs of tiring or giving up, even in the face of great difficulty. This describes Shackleton's relentless journey and leadership under harsh conditions.

Choice A is incorrect because erudite means scholarly or well-educated, which is unrelated to perseverance or survival efforts. **Choice C** is incorrect because phlegmatic means unemotional or calm, which doesn't reflect the active struggle described. **Choice D** is incorrect because desultory means lacking a plan or enthusiasm, which is the opposite of Shackleton's focused efforts. **Choice E** is incorrect because preternatural means beyond what is normal or natural. While his journey may seem extraordinary, the sentence emphasizes determination and endurance more than the supernatural.

584 **Choice B is correct** because "heralded" refers to something being talked about with appreciation and in high terms, which accurately describes the violin, a more "renowned" instrument than the viola. **Choice F is correct** because "acclaimed" means something is celebrated and recognized as worthy of high praise, which is true for the violin in comparison to the "less renowned" viola.

Choice A is incorrect because "ornate" means something that has been decorated very elaborately, which is not a suitable term to describe musical instruments in this context. **Choice C** is incorrect because "quiescent" means that something is still or not showing any visible activity, which is not a fitting description for musical instruments in terms of their "sound" and being "melodically expressive." **Choice D** is incorrect because "insipid" means dull or uninteresting, which fails to convey the positive connotation needed to describe the more "renowned" violin. **Choice E** is incorrect because "taciturn" has the meaning of speaking very little or in a reserved way, whereas the viola is stated to be as "expressive" as the violin.

585 **Choice C is correct** because clandestine means secret or concealed, especially for illicit purposes. Lancelot and Guinevere's affair is hidden from King Arthur, making this word a fitting description. **Choice E is also correct** because illicit means forbidden by law, rules, or custom—often used to describe morally or legally wrong relationships. Given that Guinevere is married to King Arthur, the affair is clearly considered inappropriate and unauthorized.

Choice A is incorrect because inchoate means just beginning or not fully formed, which doesn't align with an already ongoing affair. **Choice B** is incorrect because noisome means offensive, especially to the senses, typically referring to smell—not applicable to a love affair in this context. **Choice D** is incorrect because discrete means separate or distinct, which does not describe a love affair. **Choice F** is incorrect because gauche means socially awkward or lacking grace, which doesn't fit the context of a secretive romantic affair.

586 **Choice C is correct** because volatile means prone to rapid and unpredictable change, especially in a violent or unstable way. In the context of gas molecules, it captures the quick, random movement typical of particles in a gas state. **Choice E is also correct** because frenetic means fast and energetic in a rather wild or uncontrolled way. This fits well with the description of gas molecules moving "quickly and more or less randomly."

Choice A is incorrect because belligerent means hostile or aggressive, which does not accurately describe molecular movement. **Choice B** is incorrect because turgid means swollen or bloated, and when used figuratively, overly complex or pompous—neither of which fits the physical motion of particles. **Choice D** is incorrect because irrevocable means unchangeable or final, which has no relevance to molecular motion. **Choice F** is incorrect because malleable means able to be shaped or molded, usually describing materials or personalities—not the movement of gas particles.

587 **Choice C is correct** because "misallocating" means spending funds on wasteful purchases, such as on "trivial expenditures." **Choice F is correct** because "squandering" similarly means misusing resources in ways that are not prudent or beneficial, in contrast to "investing in competent and reliable personnel."

Choice A is incorrect because "economizing" means saving money and investing funds wisely, which is contrary to the intended meaning of wasting funds on "trivial expenditures." **Choice B** is incorrect because "inducing" has the meaning of making something happen, which does not fit the intended meaning of wasting funds. **Choice D** is incorrect because "withholding" refers to the action of not giving or not spending, which is contrary to the intended meaning of spending wastefully. **Choice E** is incorrect because "rationing" means dividing resources very carefully, which is contrary to the intended meaning of careless spending.

588 **Choice B is correct** because "bolster" means to boost or improve, which is fitting for practices that "reduce anxiety" in terms of their effect on well-being. **Choice D is correct** because "enhance" means to improve and make better, which is also a fitting way to describe the effects of mindfulness on well-being.

Choice A is incorrect because "exacerbate" means to make a bad situation worse, which is contrary to the intended meaning of benefiting well-being. **Choice C** is incorrect because "deplete" means to exhaust any remaining resources, which transmits a negative connotation contrary to the positive effects of mindfulness. **Choice E** is incorrect because "pander" means to cater to the needs or desires of someone, usually in an insincere way, which does not fit the intended meaning of improving well-being. **Choice F** is incorrect because "appease" means to agree to certain terms in order to avoid conflict, whereas the intended meaning has to do with providing a benefit to well-being.

589 **Choice B is correct** because "propagation" refers to the spreading or reproducing of something, as would be the case of compressed air passing through materials to produce sound. **Choice E is correct** because "transmission" refers to the transfer of something, passing it from one place to another, which is fitting to describe the transfer of sound waves using materials as instruments.

Choice A is incorrect because "dissipation" refers to the loss of energy or a change to a less useful state, which is not fitting in the context of producing sound waves to create music. **Choice C** is incorrect because an "entreaty" is a serious or formal request, which is not appropriate in this context of generating music. **Choice D** is incorrect because "embellishment" refers to an exaggeration that makes something look or sound better, which is not the intended meaning here, as the "compressed air" itself is not improved, but produced in such a way as to make sound. **Choice F** is incorrect because "exception" refers to a situation where a rule is not followed, which is not fitting in this sentence regarding the production of sound on different materials.

590 **Choice C is correct** because "upending" refers to the refuting of a theory or altering its fundamentally, which is what the new findings on ephaptic fields do to previous theories on neural firing. **Choice D is correct** because "supplanting" refers to something winning over or replacing previously established conditions, which is in line with a new theory on electrical fields replacing the former theory of neural firing.

Choice A is incorrect because "entailing" refers to one thing involving another as a possible consequence, which is not a fitting description of a new theory challenging or replacing a previous one. **Choice B** is incorrect because "abdicating" refers to formally renouncing one's position, often as a ruler, which is not fitting in the context of new findings in the field of neuroscience. **Choice E** is incorrect because "adulating" means showing praise or fondness excessively, often blindly, which is not an appropriate term for advances in neuroscience. **Choice F** is incorrect because "emulating" conveys the meaning of mirroring someone or something, in terms of standards or behavior, which is not in line with the new findings challenging a previously established theory.

591 **Choice C is correct** because the blank requires a word that means spreading and reaching wider audiences, as would be the "diffusion" of a cultural tradition or holiday. **Choice F is correct** because "dissemination" means the spreading or distributing of information or beliefs, which, in this case, is the Celtic holiday of Halloween.

Choice A is incorrect because "retribution" refers to punishment for some harm that had been committed, which is not fitting in this context of Halloween as a cultural celebration. **Choice B** is incorrect because an "intrusion" refers to a forceful entry into the territory or personal space of another, which is contrary to the intended meaning of a cultural holiday spreading to other countries who willingly adopt it. **Choice C** is incorrect because an "epiphany" is a revelation or a great new idea, which is not in line with the context of Halloween spreading as a holiday, as it is not a novel idea but rather the extension of a pre-existing tradition. **Choice E** is incorrect because "exclusion" refers to the denying of access, which is contrary to the concept of Halloween crossing borders and being celebrated in new countries.

592 **Choice A is correct** because "reorienting" means establishing a different way to perceive things, which is fitting in the context of the Yin Yang Theory placing focus on relationships and change over the Western model based on "opposing" qualities. **Choice D is correct** because "shifting" means changing or altering, which is apt in terms of changing the "focus" from "opposing dualities" to a different perspective, as presented in Yin Yang Theory.

Choice B is incorrect because "indulging" means permitting oneself to enjoy something, which is not fitting in the context of comparing Yin Yang Theory to Western approaches. **Choice C** is incorrect because "ascertaining" refers to determining something to be true with certainty, which is not the case of changing perspectives from a view of "opposing dualities" to one of relationships and change. **Choice E is incorrect** because "deducting" refers to the subtraction of an amount or value from a total, which is not in line with the meaning of the sentence as it compares perspectives. **Choice F is incorrect** because "extenuating" means providing reasons or circumstances that lessen the severity of an offense committed, which is not fitting in the context of comparing Western perspectives with those of Yin Yang Theory.

593 **Choice C is correct** because "advocate" means to promote ideas or to speak on behalf of a cause, which is fitting in the context of trade unions standing up for the "rights" of workers and "confronting management." **Choice E is correct** because "champion" means to support or defend a cause, which is appropriate in terms of trade unions acting to achieve "safer working conditions" and "fair compensation."

Choice A is incorrect because "adulterate" means to decrease the quality of something, often by adding elements of inferior quality, which is not fitting in the context of the first trade unions acting in the interests of the workers with a "unified front." **Choice B is incorrect** because "condone" refers to allowing behavior that is considered morally unacceptable, which is not in line with the first trade unions standing up for "workers rights." **Choice D is incorrect** because "deflect" refers to changing direction or shifting attention away from a topic that is unpleasant, which is not the case with trade unions speaking up for "workers rights" and "confronting management." **Choice F is incorrect** because "discern" means to observe carefully and distinguish nuances or differences, which is not fitting in the context of trade unions acting on behalf of workers rights.

594 **Choice A is correct** because portent means a sign or warning that something (especially something momentous or calamitous) is likely to happen. In the context of climate change and "extreme weather," it accurately captures the idea of these events being ominous indications of future problems. **Choice C is also correct** because harbinger means a forerunner or something that signals the approach of another. Here, it suggests that current extreme weather events are warning signs of more severe environmental consequences ahead.

Choice B is incorrect because vagary refers to an unpredictable or erratic action or occurrence. While weather can be unpredictable, the sentence empha-

sizes a pattern (a prevalence) of extreme events, not randomness. **Choice D is incorrect** because antithesis means the direct opposite, which doesn't logically fit the context of future continuation or worsening of current trends. **Choice E is incorrect** because enigma means something mysterious or difficult to understand. While climate change is complex, the sentence conveys concern over clear, alarming trends—not mystery. **Choice F is incorrect** because imbroglio refers to a confusing or complicated situation, usually involving conflict. This doesn't match the intended tone of prediction and warning.

595 **Choice A is correct** because "parsimonious" describes a person or behavior that minimizes spending, which is precisely what specialists advise in response to "mounting debt." **Choice D is correct** because "frugal" means wise and careful in terms of spending, which is an appropriate way to describe spending that is "limited to essential needs" and shopping at "thrift stores or second-hand shops."

Choice B is incorrect because "redolent" means strongly fragrant or suggestive, which is not fitting in terms of describing spending that counters the accumulation of debt. **Choice C is incorrect** because "lavish" means excessive, in a luxurious way, which is contrary to the purpose of limiting spending to "essential needs." **Choice E is incorrect** because "extravagant" also means excessive and does not provide the intended meaning of careful and "limited" spending. **Choice F is incorrect** because "ascetic" describes a way of life that rejects any pleasure or indulgence, which is too severe for the recommendations that permit "shopping at thrift stores or second-hand shops" when one cannot be limited to the basic necessities only (as indicated by "otherwise…").

596 **Choice B is correct** because "hazards" mean dangers, as in things that can cause harm to public health, such as "infectious" waters entering cities as a result of flooding. **Choice E is correct** because "perils" also refer to dangerous consequences, as would be "black water" entering the city containing toxins.

Choice A is incorrect because "sanctions" are measures taken for a punitive purpose, often in an international context, which is not fitting in the situation of flood waters posing a risk to public health. **Choice C is incorrect** because "improprieties" are behaviors or actions that are deemed morally unacceptable, which is not a fitting description for flood waters. **Choice D is incorrect** because "impediments" are things that are obstructive and get in the way of moving forward, which is not fitting for flood waters causing the "overflow of sewage canals." **Choice F is incorrect** because "expositions" refers to presentations, displays, or explanations, often in the literary or art world, which is not relevant to the situation described of flood waters entering cities.

597 **Choice C is correct** because "annihilate" means to destroy completely, which is the purpose of creating cyborgs for "cancer treatment." **Choice E is correct** because "obliterate" also means to attack and destroy, which is what "attackers" in the form of cyborgs would potentially do to "tumor cells."

Choice A is incorrect because "fulminate" means to criticize or protest intensely, which is not what cyborgs are programmed to do to tumor cells if they are to be used for cancer treatment. **Choice B is incorrect** because "incorporate" means to integrate into a group or an idea, which would be contrary to the purpose of attacking and eliminating tumor cells. **Choice D is incorrect** because "procreate" means to generate more life, which is contrary to the purpose of destroying tumor cells. **Choice F is incorrect** because "promulgate" means to announce publicly new policy or law, which is not fitting to describe the action of cyborgs attacking tumor cells.

598 **Choice C is correct** because "proclivity" means an inclination towards an activity or view, which suitably describes the social tendency of women being "more likely" to take on the role of caretaker, thereby working fewer hours on average than their male counterparts. **Choice F is correct** because "predisposition" is a characteristic that occurs almost naturally, as in the "social-prescribed" expectation of women playing the role of caretaker.

Choice A is incorrect because "consternation" refers to a state of anxiety or confusion, which is not fitting in the context of a "socially-prescribed" expectation of women to become caretakers. **Choice B is incorrect** because "tirade" refers to an angry verbal attack, which does not fit the context of analyzing "[g]ender-based wage inequalities" based on women being more likely to take on caretaking roles. **Choice D is incorrect** because "derision" means the expression of contempt or ridicule, which is not fitting in the context of society "prescribing" certain unequal expectations of women. **Choice E is incorrect** because "disdain" refers to a feeling of disrespect, often with a sense of superiority over another person, which, although may be present in some cases, would not fit the statement as to why women are more likely to become caretakers as a "socially prescribed" tendency.

599 **Choice D is correct** because "precarious" means unsteady and able to change unexpectedly, which is fitting in the context of work that is "minor" and "short-term." **Choice E is correct** because "insecure" describes something that cannot be relied upon, which is fitting for work that is not a dependable source of income, preventing actors from "mak[ing] ends meet."

Choice A is incorrect because "callous" describes someone who is insensitive and able to commit heartless acts, which does not fit the context of unsteady work for aspiring actors. **Choice B is incorrect** because "belligerent" describes someone or policy that is likely to cause conflict or war, which is not fitting in the context of actors trying to make a living. **Choice C is incorrect** because "apprehensive" describes someone who is nervous about future outcomes, which may be suitable to describe the actors, but not their work. **Choice F is incorrect** because "anomalous" means something is out of place or does not fit or belong in a set of data, which is not suitable to describe the type of work that prevents aspiring actors from "mak[ing] ends meet."

600 **Choice B is correct** because "deprived" means being denied or lacking something essential or desirable, which is fitting in terms of undocumented workers lacking basic rights despite working and paying taxes. **Choice D is correct** because "stripped" means something has been taken away or not provided, which is fitting in terms of a lack of rights that results in "substandard" working conditions.

Choice A is incorrect because "assimilated" means someone has become part of a culture, having adopted its norms, which is not fitting in the context of undocumented workers lacking rights while paying taxes. **Choice C is incorrect** because "rendered" means something has been provided or changed in some way, whereas the lack of rights holds the contrary meaning of something not provided. **Choice E is incorrect** because "endorsed" means something or someone is given support, which is not the case in the context of undocumented workers lacking basic rights. **Choice F is incorrect** because "enrolled" means that someone has signed up for an activity or program, which is contrary to the situation of denial and exclusion expressed in the sentence.

Before You Begin the Test

Please Read the Instructions Carefully

This practice test is designed to mirror the structure and rigor of the GRE Verbal Reasoning section. Treat it as a formal simulation. The more seriously you take this exercise, the more accurately it will reflect your current preparedness—and guide your next steps.

The number of questions and the time limits in each section are aligned with those on the actual GRE, providing you with a realistic and reliable measure of your readiness.

Once you complete the test, refer to the answer key to check your responses. You'll also find detailed instructions for calculating your Verbal Reasoning score, along with explanations for each question. Be sure to review these explanations thoroughly—especially for the questions you got wrong—to gain insight into the reasoning behind the correct answers and to sharpen your test-taking strategies.

Set Up Your Testing Environment

To replicate real testing conditions:

- Choose a quiet, uninterrupted space to work in.
- Have the following materials at hand:
    - ❏ Rough paper
    - ❏ A few sharpened pencils
    - ❏ A timer, stopwatch, or clock to track your time (if you are simulating test-day pacing)
- Ensure that you remain free of distractions throughout the session.
- Avoid checking your phone, notes, or external resources during the test.

Why This Matters

Your performance on this test is more than just a score—it's a diagnostic tool. It will help you identify question types you excel at and those that need reinforcement. The explanations provided are a valuable resource—use them to deepen your understanding and refine your test-taking strategy.

Chapter 6
Practice Test #1

IMPORTANT
READ THE INSTRUCTIONS BEFORE BEGINNING THE TEST

1. Take this test under real-like testing conditions. Put away any distractions and sit in a quiet place with no disturbances. Keep a rough paper, some pencils, and a calculator beside you.
2. Begin with **Section 1** of the Verbal Reasoning test.
3. Refer to the **Answer Key** on page 324 and note down the number of questions you got right.
4. Based on your score:
   - ❏ If you answered fewer than 7 questions correctly, proceed to **Section 2 (Easy)** on page 317.
   - ❏ If you answered 7 or more questions correctly, proceed to **Section 2 (Hard)** on page 321.
5. Note down the number of correct answers you got right on **Section 2**.
6. Calculate your **Scaled Score** on page 356 for the test.
7. Review the **detailed explanations** for all questions beginning on page 325.

Chapter 6: Practice Test #1

SECTION 1 | 18 MINUTES

For Questions 1 to 3, select one entry for each blank from the corresponding column of choices. Fill all blanks in the way that best completes the text.

1. After taking Prof. Wilson's class, Alex found that he had _____ chemistry—he loved the topic and quickly grasped even advanced concepts.

Ⓐ an aversion to
Ⓑ an affinity for
Ⓒ an adherence to
Ⓓ a censure for
Ⓔ a forum for

2. Rather than create energy, electrical power plants convert other forms of energy into electricity for transmission and use in homes, business, and industry. For example, fuel (i) _____ from petroleum is burned and the heat from that chemical reaction is converted via generators into electricity. Energy (ii) _____, but is never really "used up." Certain sources of energy, like coal, oil, and natural gas, may become scarce, but energy is present in many different forms, and using all of the potential energy on the planet is an impossibility.

Blank (i)	Blank (ii)
Ⓐ cleaved	Ⓓ suppresses
Ⓑ derived	Ⓔ dissipates
Ⓒ aggregated	Ⓕ saps

3. The following paper studies the intonation of native and non-native Russian speakers when reciting Blok's poem Neznakomka. After analyzing the intonation of "standard" Russian poetry (i) _____, it examines how non-native speakers consciously and subconsciously (ii) _____ the intonation of native speakers when reading poetry. The resulting data shows that the use of rising intonation is closely mirrored among participants with a range of familiarity with Russian poetry. The author looks at cultural and societal conditions to (iii) _____ how this poetic intonation is learned.

Blank (i)	Blank (ii)	Blank (iii)
Ⓐ reticence	Ⓓ eschew	Ⓖ exculpate
Ⓑ incantation	Ⓔ obviate	Ⓗ explicate
Ⓒ recitation	Ⓕ mimic	Ⓘ excoriate

Question 4 is based on the following passage.

It is a fact of <u>the current state of cosmology</u> that the greatest set of evidence for dark matter comes from this galactic gravitational data. Scientists have even made galactic curves describing the rotational properties of stars versus the distance from the galactic center. When the gravitational data is plotted it can be shown that only a small portion of the observed speeds are explicable by classical computations. In other words, there is <u>a scarcity of visible mass in the observed galaxies</u> to attribute the sum total of gravitational effects to visibly observable stars, planets and galaxies. Thus, the simplest way to explain this galactic mystery of insufficient mass is to <u>hypothesize a non-detectable type of mass</u> known as dark matter which can be the cause for the gravitational effects.

4. In the paragraph given, the three underlined portions play which of the following roles?

   Ⓐ theorem and axioms
   Ⓑ cause and effect
   Ⓒ point and counterpoint
   Ⓓ problem and solution
   Ⓔ procedural order of events

Section 1

Question 5 is based on the following passage.

Many experts are very concerned about the bee decline, known as Colony Collapse Disorder, or CCD. The notable scientist Albert Einstein once said, "If the bee disappears from the surface of the earth, man would have no more than four years to live. No more bees, no more pollination... no more men!" When he said this over fifty years ago, many people quickly dismissed it. However, it is now generally accepted that, without the bees, mankind would have a difficult time living. Many experts today agree with Einstein's prediction, or believe that mankind would not be able to survive. With most people scared of bees, or unable to see their true value, it is becoming important to spread the word before it is too late.

5. The author of this passage uses a quote from Albert Einstein for which of the following purposes?

   A. To show that scientists have known about the importance of bees for more than fifty years
   B. To demonstrate that, just because Einstein was highly regarded in math and physics, he was not considered an expert in biology
   C. To show that experts eventually came to agree with Einstein
   D. To use an outside authority to lend support to his position
   E. To demonstrate Einstein's ability to make accurate predictions outside of his area of expertise

For Questions 6 to 9, select the two answer choices that, when used to complete the sentence, fit the meaning of the sentence as a whole and produce completed sentences that are alike in meaning.

6. Many organisms have symbiotic relationships with one another, but the particular nature of the long-term relationship varies depending on the organisms; in some cases, one or both of the members are harmed by the relationship while in other instances the relationship is _____ to both parties.

   A. propitious
   B. pusillanimous
   C. fulsome
   D. maudlin
   E. tenuous
   F. opportune

7. The wide array of diversity among the human species is observable through examining internal and external traits; externally, human diversity can be seen through the vast differences in hair color, height, eye color, and body structure present, but diversity also presents itself in less _____ ways such as blood type and disease susceptibility.

   A. macroscopic
   B. ocular
   C. purblind
   D. telescopic
   E. risible
   F. viscid

8. In many ancient cultures, comets were infamous _____ of doom.

   A. foreseers
   B. oracles
   C. improvidences
   D. harbingers
   E. omens
   F. outriders

9. The poetry of Robert Frost and the music of Mozart are similar in that beneath an apparently _____ surface there is a world of meaning that to some may seem inaccessible.

   A idiosyncratic
   B prosaic
   C recherche
   D unrefined
   E unremarkable
   F transcendent

Questions 10 to 12 are based on the following passage.

Because the gravitational field created by the Moon weakens with distance from the Moon, it exerts a slightly harder tidal force on the side of the Earth facing the Moon than on the opposite side. The Moon thus tends to <u>stretch</u> the Earth slightly along the line connecting the two bodies. The solid Earth deforms a bit, but ocean water, being fluid, is free to move much more in response to the tidal force, particularly horizontally. As the Earth rotates, the magnitude and direction of the tidal force at any particular point on the Earth's surface change constantly; although the ocean never reaches equilibrium—there is never time for the fluid to <u>catch up</u> to the state it would eventually reach if the tidal force were constant—the changing tidal force nonetheless causes rhythmic changes in sea surface height.

10. Select the sentence that explains why the force of the moon's gravitational pull on the Earth is different from its force on the ocean.

11. In the context of this passage, the two underlined words play which of the following roles?

    A They provide ideas that are tangential to the main idea of the passage.
    B They contribute to the progression of ideas in the passage.
    C They provide clarity and unity for the ideas expressed in the passage.
    D They help the layman to more clearly understand the effects of the moon's gravitational pull on the Earth and the oceans.
    E They provide a balanced perspective on the topic.

12. For which of the following commercial enterprises would the information in the passage be more useful?

    A A meteorologist predicting the weather
    B A fishing fleet launching its boats
    C A scientist compiling research
    D A high school student presenting a project
    E An oil company building a drilling platform

SECTION 2 (EASY) | 23 MINUTES

For Questions 1 to 4, select one entry for each blank from the corresponding column of choices. Fill all blanks in the way that best completes the text.

1. The press secretary's _____ answers to probing questions about policy satisfied the journalists without actually revealing any new information.

A	abject
B	interminable
C	candid
D	adroit
E	diligent

2. I found the novel's hero _____ - he seemed like a dull mixture of literary cliches, almost totally devoid of life and originality.

A	desultory
B	recondite
C	insipid
D	variegated
E	venal

3. When the waters (i) _____, they were able to assess the devastation caused by the flooding. The town had been completely (ii) _____ - no building had escaped extensive and costly damage.

Blank (i)	Blank (ii)
A diverged	D expunged
B abated	E decimated
C coalesced	F assimilated

4. At the opera, I was surrounded by people who would not be considered members of an (i) _____ group, but they enjoyed the performance more than the sequin-clad women who came to participate in the high-society ritual. In the cheap seats there was enthusiastic applause and a lack of (ii) _____ movement compared with the fidgeting evident in the orchestra seats below. Surely this is indicative of the (iii) _____ masses' interest in listening to the opera rather than participating in a social ritual that has little to do with the music itself.

Blank (i)	Blank (ii)	Blank (iii)
A elite	D overwrought	G turgid
B opulent	E tacit	H impecunious
C verdant	F restive	I torpid

Questions 5 and 6 are based on the following passage.

Vitz makes the case that selfism is simply bad science and a warped philosophy. The little clinical evidence that does exist is mostly based on empirical observations and doesn't stand the test of solid scientific problem solving. He exposes flaws in each step of the process, from stating the problem, forming and testing the hypothesis, to testing the conclusion. He also identifies several philosophical contradictions and, in some cases, actual misrepresentations. The spread of this bad science and faulty philosophy is believed by the author to have contributed to the destruction of families. Additionally, the entire recovery group mentality convinces the person with "low self-esteem" that their ills are due to trauma inflicted on them in the past. Recovery group therapy strokes the patient with self-pity thereby convincing the clients that they are victims. Once labeled, the "victim" now assumes the attitude of victimhood.

5. If clinical means applying objective or standardized methods to the description, evaluation, and modification of human behavior, which of the following definitions most clearly explains the use of the word "empirical" in this passage?

   (A) pragmatic
   (B) relating to medical quackery
   (C) provable or verifiable by experience or experiment.
   (D) depending upon experience or observation alone
   (E) theoretical

For the following question, consider each of the three choices separately and select all that apply.

6. Identify the idea in the passage that lacks any support.

   [A] The spread of this faulty science has destroyed families.
   [B] Evidence to support the science was gathered in a subjective manner.
   [C] Self-pity leads to an attitude of victimhood.

Questions 7 to 9 are based on the following passage.

The little boxfish is quite a speedy fellow, jetting through water at speeds of six body lengths per second. This isn't just a feat of strength though; the fish's cube-like shape is an important contributor to its aerodynamic qualities. Engineers who tested its abilities were stunned to find a boxfish replica able to slip through air far more efficiently than the most compact cars around. This, they concluded, was due to the fish's bony outer skin, which provided maximum strength while maintaining minimum weight. Tiny vortexes form in the water around the fish providing stability and outstanding maneuverability.

7. Select the sentence that contradicts the generally accepted idea that parabolic curves allow for more efficient flow of air over and under surfaces in motion.

8. Understanding that the boxfish's structure provides maximum strength while maintaining minimum weight one should be able to observe the practical use of this principle in which of the following projects?

   (A) Building a log cabin
   (B) Erecting a skyscraper
   (C) Laying railroad tracks
   (D) Designing a bridge
   (E) Flying a kite

9. The author's word choices in the first sentence of the passage are intended to have what effect?

   (A) To prepare the reader for the technical information to follow
   (B) To set a light-hearted tone for the remainder of the passage
   (C) To set a formal tone for the remainder of the passage
   (D) To create a question in the mind of the reader
   (E) To enable the reader to call to mind similar scenarios

For Questions 10 to 12, select the two answer choices that, when used to complete the sentence, fit the meaning of the sentence as a whole and produce completed sentences that are alike in meaning.

10. Reducing the nation's dependence on fossil fuels is an important _____ in the platforms of the major political parties.

    A plank
    B detriment
    C component
    D goal
    E deterrent
    F theme

11. Rembrandt was extremely _____; his paintings are so lifelike that many say they feel that the people in his portraits are watching them.

    A dexterous
    B conventional
    C adroit
    D ineffectual
    E feckless
    F beneficial

12. Each atom's position in a molecule is _____ by the nature of the chemical bonds attaching it to other atoms in the molecule.

    A governed
    B conjectured
    C negotiated
    D prefigured
    E influenced
    F determined

Question 13 is based on the following passage.

A variant of the observer's paradox is named for the Hawthorne Works, a factory built by Western Electric, where efficiency engineers in the 1920s and 1930s were trying to determine if improved working conditions such as better lighting improved the performance of production workers. The engineers noted that when they provided better working conditions in the production line, efficiency increased. But when the engineers returned the production line to its original conditions and observed the workers, their efficiency increased again. The engineers determined that it was merely the observation of the factory workers, not the changes in the conditions in the production line that increased the measured efficiency.

13. In the context of this passage, which of the following is the best definition of paradox?

    A an instance of a paradoxical phenomenon or reaction
    B an opinion that conflicts with common belief
    C a statement or proposition that seems self-contradictory or absurd but in reality expresses a possible truth
    D any person, thing, or situation exhibiting an apparently contradictory nature
    E a self-contradictory and false proposition

Questions 14 and 15 are based on the following passage.

Though all cotton has a large carbon footprint for its cultivation and production, organic cotton is considered a more sustainable choice for fabric, as it is completely free of destructive toxic pesticides and chemical fertilizers. Many designers have begun experimenting with bamboo fibre, which absorbs greenhouse gases during its life cycle and grows quickly and plentifully without pesticides. Even with this, bamboo fabric can cause environmental harm in production due to the chemicals used to create a soft viscose from hard bamboo. Some believe hemp is one of the best choices for eco fabrics due to its ease of growth, though it remains illegal to grow in some countries. These facts make recycled, reclaimed, surplus, and vintage fabric arguably the most sustainable choice, as the raw material requires no agriculture and no manufacturing to produce.

14. In the context of this passage, what is the best definition for the word "vintage"?

    (A) old-fashioned; dated

    (B) representative of the best and most typical

    (C) of lasting interest and importance; venerable; classic

    (D) a time of origin

    (E) a group of people or objects of the same period

15. How do the facts in this passage provide support for the position stated in the last sentence?

    (A) The facts list all of the other choices available, leaving only those listed in the last sentence as suitable alternatives.

    (B) The facts effectively recognize both points of view regarding each choice, preventing the reader from making objections to the statements.

    (C) The facts are based on scientific research, and, as such, provide proven support for the author's position.

    (D) The author uses the rhetorical technique of part-to-whole to show how all of the facts are related, establishing a solid base for his position.

    (E) The author uses emotionally-charged words like destructive and harm to sway the reader to his point of view.

SECTION 2 (HARD) | 23 MINUTES

For Questions 1 to 4, select one entry for each blank from the corresponding column of choices. Fill all blanks in the way that best completes the text.

1. The atmosphere at the party was _____; everyone was sociable and in good spirits.

   - (A) dour
   - (B) convivial
   - (C) frenetic
   - (D) quotidian
   - (E) placid

2. Bixby loved to (i) _____ his own virtue for supporting numerous charities, but many who knew him as the most ruthless businessman in the community believed he was merely attempting to conceal his (ii) _____.

Blank (i)	Blank (ii)
(A) disseminate	(D) avarice
(B) extol	(E) magnanimity
(C) foment	(F) penury

3. The (i) _____ of Good King Gustav may indeed have been (ii) _____ by the notoriety of his brother, Bad King George, whose reign was characterized by lavish parties for the aristocracy and (iii) _____ taxes on the poor. Over time these onerous taxes caused widespread poverty and starvation, and were subsequently rescinded by King Gustav when he reassumed the throne.

Blank (i)	Blank (ii)	Blank (iii)
(A) beneficence	(D) obfuscated	(G) exorbitant
(B) reticence	(E) apotheosized	(H) inchoate
(C) insouciance	(F) bolstered	(I) antediluvian

4. (i) _____ in his field and hailed as the Father of modern psychology, Dr. Sigmund Freud was not without his fair share of (ii) _____ including an addiction to cocaine and a/an (iii) _____ affair with his wife's sister that spanned decades.

Blank (i)	Blank (ii)	Blank (iii)
(A) Tacit	(D) aberrations	(G) unctuous
(B) Preeminent	(E) foibles	(H) poignant
(C) Ignominious	(F) extremities	(I) inveterate

Questions 5 and 6 are based on the following passage.

The idea behind the concept of cream skimming in business is that the "cream" - high value or low-cost customers, who are more profitable to serve - would be captured by some suppliers (typically by charging less than the previous higher prices, but still making a profit), leaving the more expensive or harder to service customers without the desired product or service at all or "dumping" them on some default provider, who is left with fewer of the higher value customers who, in some cases, would have provided extra revenue to subsidize or reduce the cost to service the higher-cost customers, and the loss of the higher value customers might actually require the default provider to have to raise prices to cover the lost revenue, thus making things worse.

5. Consider the information in the passage and select the scenario that would be considered cream skimming.

   - (A) Colleges refusing to accept high-school students with low GPA's.
   - (B) A retail outlet conducting a private sale
   - (C) Health insurance companies rejecting applications from people with pre-existing conditions
   - (D) A company's decision to hire the handicapped
   - (E) A school district's freezing wages for its highest-paid employees.

Chapter 6: Practice Test #1

For the following question, consider each of the three choices separately and select all that apply.

6. Some states use school vouchers which allow parents to select the school they want to attend. How might this be considered cream skimming?

   A. Parents can choose to send their children to schools where all of the students are high performing.

   B. Lower performing schools are left with underachieving or learning-disabled students who may need more expensive services, putting a strain on their budgets.

   C. Removing high-achieving students from a school will reduce its success in athletic competition.

Questions 7 to 9 are based on the following passage.

Author George Leonard discusses in his book Mastery how homeostasis affects our behavior and who we are. He states that homeostasis will prevent our body from making drastic changes and maintain stability in our lives even if it is detrimental to us. Examples include when an obese person starts exercising, homeostasis in the body resists the activity to maintain stability. Another example Leonard uses is an unstable family where the father has been a raging alcoholic and suddenly stops and the son starts up a drug habit to maintain stability in the family. Homeostasis is the main factor that stops people changing their habits because our bodies view change as dangerous unless it is very slow. Leonard discusses this dilemma as the media today only encourages fast change and quick results.

7. Select the sentence that best states the reason for the frequency with which people with drug and alcohol addictions return to rehabilitation facilities for further treatment.

8. What purpose is served in this passage by the author's including the example of the unstable family in the fourth sentence?

   A. To introduce emotional homeostasis in addition to physical homeostasis

   B. To show how homeostasis is maintained in a dysfunctional family

   C. To show how the media today influence family dynamics

   D. To argue that sons are more likely than daughters to replace a father's negative behavior with negative behavior of their own

   E. To demonstrate the family dynamic that has resulted from today's fast-paced lifestyle

9. Which of the following, if true, undermines the premise of the passage?

   A. Parents have cochlear implants provided for their deaf child.

   B. Dieters who lose ten pounds generally reward themselves with food.

   C. Families eat dinner at the same time every day.

   D. Children of alcoholics marry alcoholics.

   E. Twelve-step programs are successful.

For Questions 10 to 12, select the two answer choices that, when used to complete the sentence, fit the meaning of the sentence as a whole and produce completed sentences that are alike in meaning.

10. The electoral candidates were not allowed to _____ contributions for their political campaigns.

    A. hawk
    B. scope
    C. seek
    D. solicit
    E. sequester
    F. drum

Section 2: (Hard)

11. Due to stricter security measures, all factory workers are required to sign an agreement stating that they will _____ safety guidelines.

    A. concede
    B. abide
    C. dissolve
    D. evanesce
    E. repudiate
    F. acquiesce

12. _____ the laws governing a given system is facilitated by considering the energy and entropy of the system.

    A. Assimilating
    B. Articulating
    C. Describing
    D. Comprehending
    E. Uncovering
    F. Understanding

Question 13 is based on the following passage.

A good logo works in the simplest form. It is a memorable representation of your brand and inspires confidence in your customers. It should be fresh and original—without visual cliches or amateur effects. A logo is well-designed when it looks as good on a business card as it does on a web page or a billboard. To be functional, a good logo must reduce well to simple black & white or grayscale for use on faxes or in newspaper ads. The best logos are elegantly simple.

13. After reading this passage, decide which of the following is the best advice for people who are creating a logo for their business.

    A. In order to get the viewer's attention, use eye-catching colors in the design.
    B. Because it is a visual representation of your company, invest in a professionally designed logo.
    C. To inform the viewer, list all of your products and/or services on your logo.
    D. To inspire confidence in your clients, list endorsements and/or awards on your logo.
    E. To demonstrate that your company works in partnership with its clients, include an image of a handshake in the logo.

Questions 14 and 15 are based on the following passage.

An antioxidant is a molecule capable of inhibiting the oxidation of other molecules. Oxidation is a chemical reaction that transfers electrons from a substance to an oxidizing agent. Oxidation reactions can produce free radicals. In turn, these radicals can start chain reactions. When the chain reaction occurs in a cell, it can cause damage or death. When the chain reaction occurs in a purified monomer, it produces a polymer resin, such as a plastic, a synthetic fiber, or an oil paint film. Antioxidants terminate these chain reactions by removing free radical intermediates, and inhibit other oxidation reactions. They do this by being oxidized themselves, so antioxidants are often reducing agents such as thiols, ascorbic acid or polyphenols.

14. In the context of this passage, which is the best definition of the word, "reducing"?

    A. to correct (as a fracture or a herniated mass) by bringing displaced or broken parts back into their normal positions
    B. to become diminished or lessened
    C. to be turned into or made to equal something
    D. to change (an element or ion) from a higher to a lower oxidation state
    E. to lower in degree, intensity, etc

For the following question, consider each of the three choices separately and select all that apply.

15. According to the passage, which of the following is true about free radicals?

    A. Understanding the action of free radicals on a purified monomer has enabled scientists to help in the design of numerous products that enhance the lifestyle of humans.
    B. Understanding the action of free radicals on cells can lead scientists to create products that will inhibit ageing and prolong life.
    C. Understanding the action of free radicals on cells has led scientists to conclude that the production of free radicals should be avoided.

Answer Key

Section 1			Section 2 (Easy)			Section 2 (Hard)		
Q. No.	Correct Answer	Your Answer	Q. No.	Correct Answer	Your Answer	Q. No.	Correct Answer	Your Answer
1	B		1	D		1	B	
2	B, E		2	C		2	B, D	
3	C, F, H		3	B, E		3	A, F, G	
4	B		4	A, F, H		4	B, D, I	
5	D		5	C		5	C	
6	A, F		6	A		6	A, B	
7	A, B		7	Engineers… around.		7	Homeostasis… slow.	
8	D, E		8	E		8	A	
9	B, E		9	B		9	A	
10	The… horizontally.		10	A, F		10	D, F	
11	D		11	A, C		11	B, F	
12	B		12	A, F		12	D, F	
			13	D		13	B	
			14	A		14	D	
			15	B		15	A, B	

SECTION 1: Answers & Explanations

1 **Choice B is correct** because "an affinity for" means a natural liking or attraction to something. This aligns perfectly with the sentence, which indicates that Alex both enjoyed chemistry and excelled at it. **Choice A is incorrect** because "an aversion to" means a strong dislike, which contradicts the idea that Alex loved the subject.

Choice C is incorrect because "an adherence to" implies strict commitment or loyalty, typically to rules or principles, not personal interest or enjoyment. **Choice D** is incorrect because "a censure for" suggests strong disapproval or criticism, which does not fit the sentence's positive tone. **Choice E** is incorrect because "a forum for" refers to a setting or opportunity for discussion, which is irrelevant to describing someone's feelings about a subject.

2 **Choice B is correct** because "derived" means obtained from a source. Fuel is often derived from petroleum, which accurately describes the process of converting crude oil into usable fuel. **Choice E is correct** because "dissipates" means to spread out or scatter (often in the form of heat or energy), which matches the scientific principle that energy changes form and spreads, but isn't destroyed or used up.

Choice A is incorrect because "cleaved" usually means split or cut, which does not accurately describe how fuel is obtained from petroleum. **Choice C** is incorrect because "aggregated" means collected or gathered into a whole, which doesn't fit the context of refining or processing fuel. **Choice D** is incorrect because "suppresses" implies holding back or restraining, which contradicts the idea of energy dispersing. **Choice F** is incorrect because "saps" means to drain or weaken something, which inaccurately suggests energy is depleted or lost, rather than transformed.

3 **Choice C, Choice F, and Choice H are correct** because they logically and academically support the flow and meaning of the sentence, which discusses the analysis of poetic speech and the imitation of native patterns by non-native speakers. "Recitation" refers to reading poetry aloud, which directly relates to the study of intonation. The paper begins by analyzing how standard Russian poetry is spoken, making this a natural fit. "Mimic" means to imitate, which aligns with the idea that non-native speakers both consciously and subconsciously mirror the speech patterns of native speakers when reading poetry. "Explicate" means to explain or analyze in depth. Since the author investigates how poetic intonation is learned, they aim to clarify or explain this process, especially in light of cultural and societal influences.

Choice A is incorrect because reticence means reluctance or silence, which contradicts the idea of studying spoken intonation. **Choice B** is incorrect because incantation implies a chant with magical or ritual overtones, which is inappropriate in the context of academic analysis. **Choice D** is incorrect because eschew means to avoid, which does not make sense in a sentence about imitating or following native speakers' patterns. **Choice E** is incorrect because obviate means to prevent or eliminate, which doesn't align with the idea of imitation or comparison. **Choice G** is incorrect because exculpate means to clear from blame, a concept unrelated to learning or intonation analysis. **Choice I** is incorrect because excoriate means to harshly criticize, which is too strong and misaligned with the intent to understand how poetic speech is learned.

4 **Choice B is correct** because the passage presents a cause-and-effect relationship: the current state of cosmology and the scarcity of visible mass (cause) lead scientists to hypothesize about a non-detectable type of mass (effect). There is no argument with points and counterpoints, but rather an explanation of why the hypothesis was created.

Choice A is incorrect because there is no argument presented, so there is no point and counterpoint structure. **Choice C** is incorrect because although there is a problem with explaining gravitational effects, a hypothesis is not a solution but rather an attempt to explain the problem. **Choice D** is incorrect because a procedural order of events is typically used to explain how to do something, which does not match the content of the passage. **Choice E** is incorrect because a theorem is a mathematical statement whose truth can be proved based on axioms or assumptions, which is unrelated to the passage's focus.

5 **Choice D is correct** because the author uses a quote from Albert Einstein, a widely respected authority, to lend support and credibility to the claim about the importance of bees. This appeals to the reader's trust in Einstein's authority.

Choice A is incorrect because the passage does not primarily aim to show that scientists have known about bees' importance for more than fifty years. **Choice B** is incorrect because the passage does not attempt to argue that Einstein was not an expert in biology. **Choice C** is incorrect because the author does not discuss whether experts eventually agreed with Einstein. **Choice E is incorrect** because the passage does not seek to demonstrate Einstein's ability to make accurate predictions outside his field.

6 **Choice A is correct** because "propitious" means favorable or beneficial, which fits the context of a symbiotic relationship that benefits both parties. The sentence contrasts harmful relationships with ones that are helpful, making "propitious" an appropriate choice. **Choice F is correct** because "opportune" means well-timed or advantageous. Although it often refers to timing, it can also describe conditions that are favorable or mutually beneficial, making it suitable for a context where both organisms gain from the relationship.

Choice B is incorrect because "pusillanimous" means cowardly or lacking courage, which has no relevance to the nature of symbiotic relationships. **Choice C is incorrect** because "fulsome" often means excessive or insincere, especially in praise, and does not relate to biological interactions or mutual benefit. **Choice D is incorrect** because "maudlin" means overly sentimental or tearfully emotional, which is unrelated to the scientific or biological tone of the sentence. **Choice E is incorrect** because "tenuous" means weak or insubstantial, which contradicts the idea of a mutually beneficial and strong relationship.

7 **Choice A is correct** because "macroscopic" means visible to the naked eye or large enough to be seen without a microscope. The sentence contrasts external traits (which are visible) with internal traits (which are not as easily observed), so "less macroscopic" effectively describes those internal features such as blood type and disease susceptibility. **Choice B is correct** because "ocular" pertains to vision or the eyes. Saying that internal diversity presents itself in ways that are "less ocular" means they are less visible or less apparent to the eye, which aligns with the contrast being drawn in the sentence between external (visible) and internal (not visible) traits.

Choice C is incorrect because "purblind" means having impaired vision or being slow to understand. This word describes a person, not a trait or characteristic, so it doesn't logically complete the sentence. **Choice D is incorrect** because "telescopic" refers to something seen at a great distance or magnified with a telescope. While it relates to vision, it doesn't fit the contrast of visible vs. not readily visible in a biological context. **Choice E is incorrect** because "risible" means laughable or provoking laughter. It has no relation to visibility or physical traits. **Choice F is incorrect** because "viscid" means sticky or thick, often describing liquids. It is unrelated to the concept of visibility or the context of human diversity.

8 **Choice D is correct** because "harbingers" are signs or forerunners of something to come, often something bad. In ancient cultures, comets were frequently interpreted as harbingers of doom, making this word a precise and idiomatic fit. **Choice E is correct** because "omens" are prophetic signs or warnings, often of evil or misfortune. Comets being seen as omens of doom is a historically accurate and contextually appropriate phrase.

Choice A is incorrect because "foreseers" refers to people who predict the future, not events or objects like comets. The sentence calls for a symbol, not a person. **Choice B is incorrect** because "oracles" also refers to people (or sources) that deliver prophecies, especially in ancient cultures, not the prophetic signs themselves. **Choice C is incorrect** because "improvidences" means lack of foresight or care for the future, which doesn't make sense in this context. **Choice F is incorrect** because "outriders" usually refers to people who ride ahead of a group (such as messengers or guards), often in a literal or military sense—not symbolic signs of future disaster.

9 **Choice B is correct** because "prosaic" means ordinary, straightforward, or lacking poetic beauty. The sentence suggests that Frost's and Mozart's works appear simple or plain on the surface, but contain deeper, less obvious meanings. "Prosaic surface" contrasts effectively with the "world of meaning" beneath. **Choice E is also correct** because "unremarkable" means not particularly interesting or distinctive. This fits the idea of a deceptively plain or simple exterior that hides a deeper significance.

Choice A is incorrect because "idiosyncratic" means peculiar or highly individualistic, which contradicts the idea of an apparently simple or plain surface. **Choice C is incorrect** because "recherché" means rare, exotic, or obscure. That would suggest the surface is already complex, which contradicts the sentence's implication of deceptive simplicity. **Choice D is incorrect** because "unrefined" implies crudeness or lack of sophistication, which doesn't align with the respectful tone toward Frost and Mozart. **Choice F is incorrect** because "transcendent" means going beyond ordinary limits or being sublime. That would suggest depth is obvious, not hidden beneath the surface.

10 The correct answer is **"The solid Earth deforms a bit, but ocean water, being fluid, is free to move much more in response to the tidal force, particularly horizontally"** because the earth is solid and, therefore, more rigid, it has less flexibility in its reaction to the moon's gravitational pull. The fluid water is able to react with more flexibility to the moon's gravitational pull.

11 **Choice D is correct** because the author of the passage uses terms that help the average reader understand what happens as the moon exerts its gravitational pull on the Earth. The phrase "catch up" is used to explain the idea of equilibrium in a more accessible way.

Choice A is incorrect because the words do not merely express ideas, and they are not tangential to the meaning of the passage. **Choice B** is incorrect because the progression of ideas in the passage is logical and does not rely on the use of these words for development. **Choice C** is incorrect because while the words may add clarity, they do not unify the ideas in the passage; that role is fulfilled by transitions. **Choice E** is incorrect because balance involves presenting more than one idea equally. Since the passage conveys a single idea, a balanced perspective is not the author's goal.

12 **Choice B is correct** because a fishing fleet relies on daily reports of high and low tides to time the launching of its boats. That timing is affected by the position of the Earth relative to the moon.

Choice A is incorrect because a meteorologist is not likely to be engaging in a commercial enterprise. **Choice C** is incorrect because a scientist would also not typically be involved in a commercial activity affected by daily tidal reports. **Choice D** is incorrect because a student is not a commercial operator and would have no use for this information in that context. **Choice E** is incorrect because although an oil company is a commercial enterprise, the construction of a drilling platform takes a considerable amount of time, and the cycle of tides would not significantly impact such a prolonged process.

SECTION 2 (EASY): Answers & Explanations

1 **Choice D is correct** because adroit means skillful or clever, especially in the use of words or strategies. The sentence states that the press secretary answered in a way that satisfied journalists without revealing any new information, suggesting a clever or tactful way of speaking—exactly what adroit implies.

Choice A is incorrect because abject means miserable or hopeless, which doesn't fit the context of skillfully managing press questions. **Choice B** is incorrect because interminable means endless or seemingly without end. While long answers might hide information, the sentence emphasizes the effectiveness of the responses, not their length. **Choice C** is incorrect because candid means honest and straightforward, which contradicts the idea that nothing new was revealed. **Choice E** is incorrect because diligent means hardworking or careful, which doesn't convey the strategic or clever element implied in the sentence.

2 **Choice C is correct** because insipid means lacking flavor, interest, or originality, which fits perfectly with the description of the novel's hero as dull and cliché-ridden.

Choice A is incorrect because desultory means lacking a plan or purpose, which doesn't directly describe a dull or unoriginal character. **Choice B** is incorrect because recondite means obscure or difficult to understand, which does not fit the context of dullness or lack of originality. **Choice D** is incorrect because variegated means having many different colors or varieties, which contradicts the idea of dullness. **Choice E** is incorrect because venal means corrupt or willing to sell one's influence, which is unrelated to the character's dullness or lack of originality.

3 **Choice B is correct** because "abated" means to lessen or reduce, which fits perfectly with the waters receding after flooding, allowing people to assess the damage. **Choice E is correct** because "decimated" means severely damaged or destroyed, which accurately describes the extent of devastation to the town where no building escaped significant harm.

Choice A is incorrect because "diverged" means to separate or move apart, which does not apply to the context of water receding. **Choice C** is incorrect because "coalesced" means to come together or unite, which contradicts the idea of water levels going down. **Choice D** is incorrect because "expunged"

For more practice, visit www.vibrantpublishers.com

means completely erased or removed, which is too absolute and does not appropriately describe damage to buildings. **Choice F** is incorrect because "assimilated" means absorbed or integrated, which is unrelated to the destruction described.

4 **Choice A, Choice F, and Choice H are correct** because they establish a clear, parallel contrast between two groups of opera-goers—those in the cheap seats and those in the orchestra section—while supporting the overall theme of genuine appreciation versus performative attendance. "Elite" refers to a privileged, high-status social group. The sentence states that the people in the cheap seats "would not be considered members of an elite group," contrasting them with the "sequin-clad women" participating in a high-society ritual, highlighting the class divide. "Restive" means impatient, uneasy, or fidgety. The sentence describes "a lack of restive movement" in the cheap seats, directly contrasting the "fidgeting evident in the orchestra seats." This maintains parallel structure and emphasizes the attentiveness of the less privileged group. "Impecunious" means having little or no money. This perfectly aligns with the reference to "cheap seats" and underscores the idea that those with fewer financial resources showed more genuine appreciation for the music than the wealthier attendees, who were more interested in social performance.

Choice B is incorrect because opulent means richly luxurious or lavish, which doesn't apply to the people in the cheap seats. **Choice C** is incorrect because verdant means green or inexperienced, which is unrelated to social status or cultural engagement. **Choice D** is incorrect because overwrought means excessively nervous or agitated, and the sentence is not describing the audience's emotional state in such terms. **Choice E** is incorrect because tacit means unspoken or implied, and tacit movement is not a meaningful or coherent phrase in this context. **Choice G** is incorrect because turgid means pompous or swollen, which does not sensibly describe the "masses" or their interest in the opera. **Choice I** is incorrect because torpid means sluggish or inactive, which contradicts the idea of "enthusiastic applause" and active engagement by the less privileged audience.

5 **Choice C is correct** because the author reveals that he examined each step of the process and listed the elements of the experiment conducted concerning selfism. It is the only choice that includes the word experiment in its definition, aligning with the passage's focus.

Choice A is incorrect because pragmatic means practical and does not suit the context of this passage, which deals with experimental validation rather than practical application. **Choice B** is incorrect because quackery refers to charlatanism or fakery, which does not apply since the author used legitimate scientific techniques. **Choice D** is incorrect because although clinical evidence based on empirical observation is mentioned, the author criticizes the steps taken to arrive at that data, emphasizing instead that actual experiments were conducted. **Choice E** is incorrect because the author was not merely being theoretical; he was examining experimental procedures, making this choice inappropriate.

6 **Choice A is correct** because the claim that "the spread of this faulty science has destroyed families" is presented without any concrete evidence or examples in the passage. While the author states this belief, no supporting data, studies, or specific cases are provided to validate such a significant claim.

Choice B is incorrect because the passage clearly supports this idea by stating that the little clinical evidence that exists is "mostly based on empirical observations" and then goes on to criticize the scientific methodology used, including flaws in stating the problem and testing the hypothesis. **Choice C** is incorrect because the passage provides a logical progression of how recovery group therapy leads from self-pity to victim labeling and finally to an attitude of victimhood. While some may argue it is an opinion, the author does provide a rationale, making it more supported than Choice A.

7 The correct answer is **"Engineers who tested its abilities were stunned to find a boxfish replica able to slip through air far more efficiently than the most compact cars around."** This sentence explicitly states that the boxfish, despite its lack of curved surfaces, is able to slip through air far more efficiently than most compact cars, the majority of which have curved shapes.

8 **Choice E is correct** because a well-designed kite has a lightweight, rigid framework and is affected by air currents in much the same way that the boxfish is affected by water currents, making it the most analogous in both structure and function.

Choice A is incorrect because the log cabin's structure is extremely heavy and rigid, with great weight concentrated on the exterior, which makes it dissimilar to the boxfish, whose structure is lightweight and streamlined for movement. **Choice B** is incorrect because although modern skyscrapers may have a visually similar exterior, their core structure and reinforced concrete beams bear the building's weight, making the similarity to the boxfish superficial. **Choice C is incorrect because** railroad tracks lack a visible three-dimensional structure and do not share any aerodynamic or hydrodynamic interaction like the boxfish does with its environment. **Choice D is incorrect because** the structure of a bridge is dense and heavy, which is opposite to the light, maneuverable design of the boxfish.

9 **Choice B is correct** because the author's use of phrases like "quite a speedy fellow" and "jetting through water" introduces the boxfish in a light-hearted and playful tone, which makes the scientific discussion more engaging and accessible to a general audience. This tone contrasts with a purely technical or formal style and sets the stage for a lively exploration of the boxfish's abilities.

Choice A is incorrect because although technical information does follow, the first sentence does not function as a preparatory introduction to that information. Instead, it captures interest through whimsical language. **Choice C is incorrect because** the use of casual, animated language like "speedy fellow" is the opposite of formal and doesn't establish a scholarly tone. **Choice D is incorrect because** the first sentence does not pose or imply a question. It presents an observation in a definitive, descriptive way. **Choice E is incorrect because** the description of the boxfish's speed is specific and unusual, not a common or relatable scenario the reader would likely recall from personal experience.

10 **Choice A is correct** because "plank" refers specifically to a principal part or item in a political party's platform, making it the most precise term for a key issue or policy position. **Choice F is also correct** because "theme" means a recurring or central topic or idea, which fits well as a significant focus within political platforms.

Choice B is incorrect because "detriment" means harm or damage, which does not fit the context of an important political issue. **Choice C is incorrect because** "component" means a part of something, but it is more general and less specific to political platforms than "plank" or "theme." **Choice D is incorrect because** "goal" refers to an objective or aim, but the sentence focuses on an issue included in platforms, not just a general aim. **Choice E is incorrect because** "deterrent" means something that discourages or prevents an action, which does not fit the sentence's meaning.

11 **Choice A is correct** because "dexterous" means skillful, especially with the hands, which fits Rembrandt's renowned painting technique. **Choice C is correct** because "adroit" also means skillful and clever, particularly in using the hands or mind, aptly describing Rembrandt's artistic ability.

Choice B is incorrect because "conventional" means ordinary or traditional, which does not capture Rembrandt's exceptional skill. **Choice D is incorrect because** "ineffectual" means lacking the ability to produce an effect, which contradicts Rembrandt's mastery. **Choice E is incorrect because** "feckless" means irresponsible or ineffective, not fitting for an accomplished artist. **Choice F is incorrect because** "beneficial" means helpful or advantageous, which is not the best descriptor of artistic skill.

12 **Choice A is correct** because "governed" means controlled or regulated by something, which fits the idea that an atom's position is controlled by chemical bonds. **Choice F is correct** because "determined" means decided or fixed by something, which also suits the context of atomic positions being fixed by chemical bonds.

Choice B is incorrect because "conjectured" means guessed or speculated, which does not imply certainty or control. **Choice C is incorrect because** "negotiated" implies a mutual discussion or compromise, which doesn't apply to atomic positions. **Choice D is incorrect because** "prefigured" means predicted or indicated beforehand, which doesn't directly relate to positioning by bonds. **Choice E is incorrect because** "influenced" is too vague and less definitive compared to "governed" or "determined."

13 **Choice D is correct** because the situation involving the factory workers describes a paradoxical outcome—where both the addition and removal of improvements led to increased productivity. This contradiction in expected cause-and-effect illustrates a paradoxical result, aligning directly with the meaning of a paradoxical outcome.

Choice A is incorrect because the passage does not describe a paradoxical phenomenon or reaction, but rather a result that contradicts expectations. **Choice B is incorrect because** the example given is not an opinion but a description of actual outcomes observed in a workplace setting. **Choice C is incorrect because** there is no proposition or assertion being made that is paradoxical—just the results themselves. **Choice E is incorrect because** the passage lacks a statement or logical assertion that would qualify as a paradoxical proposition.

Chapter 6: Practice Test #1

14 **Choice A is correct** because vintage fabric refers to fabric that was designed and manufactured in an earlier time. The term "vintage" generally means something from a previous era, making this the most straightforward and accurate definition in the context provided.

Choice B is incorrect because while vintage fabric could represent the best creations of a well-known designer, this is not a requirement for fabric to be considered vintage. It may or may not be the "best" of its kind. **Choice C is incorrect** because not all vintage fabric is of lasting importance or considered a classic. It simply needs to be from an earlier time period, regardless of significance. **Choice D is incorrect** because although the term "vintage" can be associated with a specific era, the definition of vintage fabric does not require identification by year or era unless specifically stated (e.g., "1970s vintage"). **Choice E is incorrect** because this usage of "vintage" is specific to wine, where it refers to the year a wine was produced. It does not directly apply to fabric unless analogously stretched, which is not the case here.

15 **Choice B is correct** because recognizing the opposition's point of view helps prevent the reader from forming objections and encourages them to focus on the author's argument. This technique strengthens the author's persuasive position by addressing potential counterarguments upfront.

Choice A is incorrect because the passage does not simply list and eliminate alternatives. Instead, it evaluates each option's pros and cons, leading logically to the final position rather than excluding choices outright. **Choice C is incorrect because,** although scientific evidence likely exists to support the claims, the passage does not rely primarily on presenting or emphasizing scientific proof to persuade readers. **Choice D is incorrect** because the passage does not use a part-to-whole rhetorical strategy. The facts are presented as separate points rather than components of a larger conceptual framework. **Choice E is incorrect** because, although emotionally charged words appear in the passage, the author's main persuasive technique is logical reasoning and balanced evaluation rather than appealing primarily to emotion.

SECTION 2 (HARD): Answers & Explanations

1 **Choice B is correct** because convivial means friendly, lively, and enjoyable—perfectly describing an atmosphere where everyone is sociable and in good spirits.

Choice A is incorrect because dour means stern or gloomy, which contradicts the positive mood described. **Choice C is incorrect** because frenetic means wildly excited or frantic, which doesn't match the calm, happy social vibe. **Choice D is incorrect** because quotidian means ordinary or everyday, which doesn't capture the lively atmosphere. **Choice E is incorrect** because placid means calm or peaceful, which is less fitting for a lively, sociable party atmosphere.

2 **Choice B is correct** for Blank (i) because extol means to praise highly, which fits the idea of Bixby praising his own virtue. **Choice D is correct** for Blank (ii) because avarice means extreme greed, which contrasts with the virtue he claims and fits the perception of him as a ruthless businessman.

Choice A is incorrect because disseminate means to spread or scatter, which does not fit with praising virtue. **Choice C is incorrect** because foment means to instigate or stir up, which doesn't fit the context of praising virtue. **Choice E is incorrect** because magnanimity means generosity, which would contradict the idea of something negative being concealed. **Choice F is incorrect** because penury means extreme poverty, which is less fitting given the context of ruthlessness and greed.

3 **Choice A, Choice F, and Choice G are correct** because they logically fit the context of the passage about contrasting two kings' behaviors and reputations. "Beneficence" means kindness or charity, which fits the positive actions associated with Good King Gustav. "Bolstered" means supported or strengthened, which fits the cause-effect relationship where the notoriety of Bad King George supports or emphasizes the goodness of King Gustav. "Exorbitant" means excessively high, which suits the description of the harsh taxes imposed by Bad King George on the poor.

Choice B is incorrect because reticence means reluctance to speak or act, which does not fit the description of King Gustav's qualities. **Choice C is incorrect** because insouciance means casual lack of concern, which does not match the idea of the king's positive character. **Choice D is incorrect** because

Section 2 (Hard): Answers & Explanations

obfuscated means made unclear or overshadowed, which contradicts the idea that Gustav's beneficence was supported rather than obscured. **Choice E** is incorrect because apotheosized means glorified or idealized, which does not fit the subject of beneficence here. **Choice H** is incorrect because inchoate means not fully formed or developed, which does not apply to the taxes described. **Choice I** is incorrect because antediluvian means extremely old or outdated, which is not relevant to the description of taxes.

4 **Choice B, Choice D, and Choice I are correct** because they best fit the context of the passage describing Freud's status, personal issues, and a long-lasting affair. "Preeminent" means foremost or highly distinguished, which fits Freud's reputation as the Father of modern psychology. "Aberrations" means deviations from the norm or abnormalities, which aptly describes Freud's serious issues like addiction and an unusual affair. "Inveterate" means long-lasting or habitual, which matches the description of the decades-long affair with his wife's sister.

Choice A is incorrect because tacit means silently understood, which does not describe a renowned figure like Freud. **Choice C** is incorrect because ignominious means shameful or discreditable, which contradicts the positive portrayal in this part of the passage. **Choice E** is incorrect because foibles means minor faults, which understates Freud's serious personal problems. **Choice F** is incorrect because extremities refers to the limbs of the body and is irrelevant here. **Choice G** is incorrect because unctuous means excessively flattering or sycophantic, which does not apply to the affair. **Choice H** is incorrect because poignant means emotionally touching or distressing, which the passage does not support as the intended meaning.

5 **Choice C is correct** because insurance companies reject applicants with pre-existing conditions due to an unfavorable cost-to-benefit ratio. They rely on premiums from healthy subscribers to cover claims, which affects their profitability. This financial reasoning clearly supports why they make such decisions.

Choice A is incorrect because although colleges accept the best students ("cream of the crop"), this does not provide them with financial benefit since the cost of educating each student remains the same. **Choice B** is incorrect because retail stores conducting private sales reduce prices on goods, resulting in no financial benefit despite the sale. **Choice D** is incorrect because while hiring handicapped employees might have long-term benefits, it initially incurs additional costs in training and accommodations, which might deter companies from doing so purely for financial reasons. **Choice E** is incorrect because freezing wages at the highest levels may save costs initially, but there is no guaranteed benefit since employees might leave and the savings are uncertain.

6 **Choice A is correct** because parents selecting schools with mostly high-performing students mirrors the idea of "cream skimming." These schools attract the "high-value" students who are easier or less costly to educate, leaving other schools with fewer resources. **Choice B is correct** because lower-performing schools are left with students who may require more support and resources, similar to the "harder to service" customers in cream skimming. This strains the budgets of those schools.

Choice C is incorrect because reducing a school's success in athletic competition is not directly related to the financial or service-cost aspects of cream skimming. The concept focuses on resource allocation and profitability, not athletic outcomes.

7 The correct answer is **"Homeostasis is the main factor that stops people changing their habits because our bodies view change as dangerous unless it is very slow."** This sentence explains that the body's natural tendency to maintain stability (homeostasis) resists sudden changes, making it difficult for individuals to break addictive habits quickly, which often leads to relapse and repeated rehabilitation.

8 **Choice A is correct** because, just as a dieter's body reacts negatively to a reduced intake of food, the dysfunctional family reacts emotionally to a drastic change. This example illustrates how emotional homeostasis, like physical homeostasis, works to maintain balance despite harmful circumstances.

Choice B is incorrect because the author's purpose is to show emotional instability caused by change, not to show how homeostasis maintains stability in a dysfunctional family. **Choice C** is incorrect because although the author mentions the media's influence on expectations of change, this is not directly connected to family dynamics. **Choice D** is incorrect because the passage does not argue that sons are more likely than daughters to replace negative behaviors. **Choice E** is incorrect because the passage does not focus on fast-paced lifestyles or their effects on family dynamics.

9 **Choice A is correct** because if parents have cochlear implants provided for their deaf child, it challenges the passage's implied premise that hearing parents do not need to change their means of communication to maintain stability. This would suggest the family does change communication methods, undermining the idea that cochlear implants maintain stability by allowing communication to remain the same.

Choice B is incorrect because dieters rewarding themselves with food does not directly challenge or undermine the passage's premise about family stability and communication. **Choice C** is incorrect because families eating dinner at the same time every day supports the idea of routine and stability rather than undermining it. **Choice D** is incorrect because children of alcoholics marrying alcoholics supports the idea of learned behavior and comfort with familiar patterns, which aligns with the passage's themes. **Choice E** is incorrect because the success of twelve-step programs supports the idea that people can change behavior, consistent with the passage's point that change is possible and does not undermine the premise.

10 **Choice D is correct** because "solicit" means to ask for or try to obtain something, especially contributions or support, which fits the context of political campaign fundraising. **Choice F is correct** because "drum" (up) means to actively seek or encourage support or contributions, also appropriate for the context of raising campaign funds.

Choice A is incorrect because "hawk" means to sell aggressively, which is not the usual term for requesting contributions in a political context. **Choice B** is incorrect because "scope" means to look or examine, which doesn't fit here. **Choice C** is incorrect because "seek" is close but less precise than "solicit" or "drum" in this formal fundraising context. **Choice E** is incorrect because "sequester" means to isolate or confiscate, unrelated to asking for contributions.

11 **Choice B is correct** because "abide" means to follow or comply with rules or guidelines, which fits perfectly in the context of signing an agreement to follow safety rules **Choice F is correct** because "acquiesce" means to accept or agree to something reluctantly but without protest, which also fits the context of agreeing to safety guidelines.

Choice A is incorrect because "concede" means to admit or yield, which doesn't fit the idea of following rules. **Choice C** is incorrect because "dissolve" means to end or disappear, which is unrelated here. **Choice D** is incorrect because "evanesce" means to vanish or fade away, not applicable to following rules. **Choice E** is incorrect because "repudiate" means to reject or refuse to accept, the opposite of what the sentence requires.

12 **Choice D is correct** because "Comprehending" means grasping or fully understanding the laws governing the system, fitting perfectly with gaining knowledge of those laws. **Choice F is correct** because "Understanding" also means having a clear grasp or knowledge of the laws, synonymous with comprehending.

Choice A is incorrect because "Assimilating" means integrating or absorbing the laws into one's knowledge or practice, which is slightly different from simply knowing or grasping the laws. **Choice B** is incorrect because "Articulating" means expressing or stating clearly, which is about communication rather than knowledge. **Choice C** is incorrect because "Describing" means explaining or detailing the laws, rather than understanding them. **Choice E** is incorrect because "Uncovering" means discovering or finding out the laws, not necessarily understanding or comprehending them.

13 **Choice B is correct** because the passage emphasizes the importance of a logo being a memorable, fresh, and original representation of a brand. Investing in a professionally designed logo increases the likelihood that it will meet these criteria and function well across various formats and sizes.

Choice A is incorrect because the passage stresses simplicity and avoiding visual clichés or amateur effects, rather than using eye-catching colors to get attention. **Choice C** is incorrect because the passage does not suggest including a list of products or services on a logo, which would clutter and complicate the design. **Choice D** is incorrect because the passage does not mention listing endorsements or awards on a logo to inspire confidence. **Choice E** is incorrect because the passage warns against clichéd imagery and amateur effects, so including a handshake image would not align with the advice for originality and simplicity.

Section 2 (Hard): Answers & Explanations

⑭ **Choice D is correct** because in the context of the passage, "reducing agents" are substances that donate electrons and thereby reduce another substance by changing its oxidation state. This matches the scientific definition of "reducing" as changing an element or ion from a higher to a lower oxidation state, which is precisely what antioxidants do when they inhibit oxidation reactions.

Choice A is incorrect because it refers to a medical procedure for realigning bones or tissues, which is unrelated to the chemical context of the passage.
Choice B is incorrect because "to become diminished or lessened" is too vague and does not capture the chemical meaning relevant to oxidation-reduction.
Choice C is incorrect because "to be turned into or made to equal something" is not a standard definition of "reducing" and doesn't fit the chemistry context.
Choice E is incorrect because while "to lower in degree or intensity" may apply to everyday usage, it does not accurately describe what a reducing agent does in a chemical reaction.

⑮ **Choice A is correct** because the author mentions that the reaction involving free radicals produces useful materials such as plastic and paint film, which contribute positively to modern life. **Choice B is correct** because the reaction can cause cell damage and death; understanding how this works can help prevent such damage and potentially slow the ageing process.

Choice C is incorrect because the passage describes beneficial outcomes when free radicals act on a purified monomer, highlighting their constructive applications rather than harmful effects in that context.

Before You Begin the Test

Please Read the Instructions Carefully

This practice test is designed to mirror the structure and rigor of the GRE Verbal Reasoning section. Treat it as a formal simulation. The more seriously you take this exercise, the more accurately it will reflect your current preparedness—and guide your next steps.

The number of questions and the time limits in each section are aligned with those on the actual GRE, providing you with a realistic and reliable measure of your readiness.

Once you complete the test, refer to the answer key to check your responses. You'll also find detailed instructions for calculating your Verbal Reasoning score, along with explanations for each question. Be sure to review these explanations thoroughly—especially for the questions you got wrong—to gain insight into the reasoning behind the correct answers and to sharpen your test-taking strategies.

Set Up Your Testing Environment

To replicate real testing conditions:

- Choose a quiet, uninterrupted space to work in.
- Have the following materials at hand:
    - ❑ Rough paper
    - ❑ A few sharpened pencils
    - ❑ A timer, stopwatch, or clock to track your time (if you are simulating test-day pacing)
- Ensure that you remain free of distractions throughout the session.
- Avoid checking your phone, notes, or external resources during the test.

Why This Matters

Your performance on this test is more than just a score—it's a diagnostic tool. It will help you identify question types you excel at and those that need reinforcement. The explanations provided are a valuable resource—use them to deepen your understanding and refine your test-taking strategy.

Chapter 7
Practice Test #2

IMPORTANT
READ THE INSTRUCTIONS BEFORE BEGINNING THE TEST

1. Take this test under real-like testing conditions. Put away any distractions and sit in a quiet place with no disturbances. Keep a rough paper, some pencils, and a calculator beside you.
2. Begin with **Section 1** of the Verbal Reasoning test.
3. Refer to the **Answer Key** on page 345 and note down the number of questions you got right.
4. Based on your score:
   - ❏ If you answered fewer than 7 questions correctly, proceed to **Section 2 (Easy)** on page 338.
   - ❏ If you answered 7 or more questions correctly, proceed to **Section 2 (Hard)** on page 341.
5. Note down the number of correct answers you got right on **Section 2**.
6. Calculate your **Scaled Score** on page 356 for the test.
7. Review the **detailed explanations** for all questions beginning on page 346.

Chapter 7: Practice Test #2

SECTION 1 | 18 MINUTES

For Questions 1 to 3, select one entry for each blank from the corresponding column of choices. Fill all blanks in the way that best completes the text.

1. Susie showed the classic symptoms of seasonal depression. In the spring and summer, she always had a smile on her face and loved to spend time with her friends, but in the winter months she became _____ and withdrawn.

   - (A) jubilant
   - (B) fulminating
   - (C) forlorn
   - (D) morbid
   - (E) rueful

2. David loved to (i) _____ his knowledge of mathematics, even going so far as to offer tutoring to other students. Despite this, his grasp of the field was actually quite (ii) _____ and he was often unable to recall important rules or solve difficult problems.

   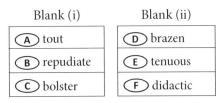

Blank (i)	Blank (ii)
(A) tout	(D) brazen
(B) repudiate	(E) tenuous
(C) bolster	(F) didactic

3. Although Tom tried to (i) _____ Mary by taking her out to her favorite restaurant, she remained (ii) _____ in her anger.

   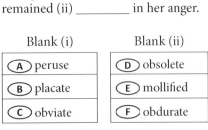

Blank (i)	Blank (ii)
(A) peruse	(D) obsolete
(B) placate	(E) mollified
(C) obviate	(F) obdurate

Question 4 is based on the following passage.

Psychodynamics is another type of covariation information that is important in the effort of understanding the causes of social behavior. Distinctiveness refers to how unique the psychodynamics is to the particular situation. There is a low distinctiveness if an individual behaves similarly in all situations, and there exists a high distinctiveness when the person only shows the behavior in particular situations. If the distinctiveness is high, one will attribute this behavior more to the context instead of personal characteristics.

4. Based on the information in this passage, select the situation below that portrays high distinctiveness.

   - (A) A generally garrulous woman speaks to everyone she meets at the supermarket.
   - (B) A generally laconic man avoids greeting everyone he meets at church.
   - (C) A generally lugubrious best man smiles at everyone in the receiving line at a wedding.
   - (D) A generally confident detective provides unequivocal answers while testifying in a criminal case.
   - (E) A generally enigmatic undercover agent provides polysemous responses while under interrogation.

Question 5 is based on the following passage.

Bacterial and viral infections are caused by two different types of microorganisms. The bacteria are very small unicellular organisms that can be found everywhere around us: in the air, in the food that we eat, in the soil, and millions of them are on the surface of our skin and in our bodies. The bacteria are so small that a single glass of drinking water contains millions of them. Most bacteria are harmless and are kept in control by our immune system. Some of them are even useful and help us absorb vitamins and aid digestion as well. The pathogenic bacteria are the "bad bacteria" as they are the ones causing infections that kill millions of people every year. Bacterial infections that can damage our health considerably are cholera, tuberculosis, bubonic plague and anthrax.

Section 1

For the following question, consider each of the three choices separately and select all that apply.

5. Based on the information in this passage, what might logically be the topic of the subsequent paragraph?

   [A] How viruses interact with humans
   [B] How the use of antibacterial cleansers affect human interaction with bacteria
   [C] How bacterial infections are treated

For Questions 6 to 9, select the two answer choices that, when used to complete the sentence, fit the meaning of the sentence as a whole and produce completed sentences that are alike in meaning.

6. Belief in evolution is based on evidence, otherwise it would be _____.

   [A] inconceivable
   [B] implausible
   [C] questionable
   [D] incontestable
   [E] probable
   [F] cogitable

7. At first the new employee approached his job with vigor, but his enthusiasm soon _____ and now he risks losing his position.

   [A] alleviated
   [B] vanished
   [C] burgeoned
   [D] dwindled
   [E] waned
   [F] elongated

8. That strange _____ was built using a very simple but innovative architectural design method.

   [A] disassemble
   [B] chassis
   [C] dwelling
   [D] groundwork
   [E] edifice
   [F] habitant

9. Whether to go to Cancun or to Rio was a _____ for Helen since she had never been abroad before.

   [A] vacillation
   [B] plight
   [C] impasse
   [D] quandary
   [E] certitude
   [F] conundrum

Questions 10 to 12 are based on the following passage.

Wetter climates brought upon by ice ages starting 2 million years ago greatly increased excavation of the Grand Canyon, which was nearly as deep as it is now by 1.2 million years ago. Volcanic activity deposited lava over the area 1.8 million to 500,000 years ago. At least 13 lava dams blocked the Colorado River, forming lakes that were up to 2,000 feet (610 m) deep. The end of the last ice age and subsequent human activity has greatly reduced the ability of the Colorado River to excavate the canyon. Dams in particular have upset patterns of sediment transport and deposition. Controlled floods from Glen Canyon Dam upstream have been conducted to see if they have a restorative effect. Earthquakes and mass wasting erosive events still affect the region.

10. The primary purpose of this passage is to

    (A) Provide a timeline of events that shaped the Grand Canyon
    (B) Reveal when the last ice age ended
    (C) Show the scope of the Grand Canyon
    (D) How wetter climates are preferable to dry ones
    (E) Tell the reader that deep lakes once existed in the area

11. The author includes information about man made dams primarily to

   (A) Show how human intervention has affected the Grand Canyon
   (B) Demonstrate how engineers can control natural forces
   (C) Demonstrate the progress of human achievement
   (D) Show how water is supplied to towns in the area
   (E) Compare them to lava dams

12. A person most likely to find this information helpful would be

   (A) Someone writing a doctoral thesis
   (B) A park ranger preparing a presentation for a group of students
   (C) A family planning a vacation
   (D) The native people living on the floor of the Grand Canyon
   (E) Engineers planning to build a new dam

SECTION 2 (EASY) | 23 MINUTES

For Questions 1 to 4, select one entry for each blank from the corresponding column of choices. Fill all blanks in the way that best completes the text.

1. Many consider the reign of Louis the XIV to be the _____ of absolutism in France. During his long rule, power was centralized under his direct author0.111ity to an unprecedented degree.

   (A) substantiation
   (B) vindication
   (C) nadir
   (D) apogee
   (E) prototype

2. Ron's (i) _____ remarks about the economy were (ii) _____ to productive discussion. Although he showed no understanding of the subject, his attitude was smug and overbearing.

Blank (i)	Blank (ii)
(A) erudite	(D) conducive
(B) jubilant	(E) inimical
(C) fatuous	(F) incongruous

3. Millions of visitors travel every year to see the (i) _____ natural beauty of Yellowstone National Park in Wyoming. However, this peaceful landscape belies the (ii) _____ nature of our world's geology. 640, 000 years ago, Yellowstone was the scene of a (iii) _____ volcanic eruption and the geysers that draw tourists are themselves the result of continued volcanism.

Blank (i)	Blank (ii)	Blank (iii)
(A) grandiose	(D) tangential	(G) surreptitious
(B) lackadaisical	(E) mercurial	(H) cataclysmic
(C) idyllic	(F) rudimentary	(I) quotidian

Section 2: (Easy)

4. The story of Kaspar Hauser has captured the popular imagination for generations. After his mysterious appearance on the streets of Nuremberg in 1828, some speculated that he was the legitimate heir to the House of Baden who had been robbed of his inheritance as part of a (i) _____ plot. Although popular media has continued to lend credence to the theory that Hauser was the (ii) _____ of the House of Baden, professional historians have tended to (iii) _____ this claim.

Blank (i)	Blank (ii)	Blank (iii)
(A) utilitarian	(D) scion	(G) debunk
(B) beneficent	(E) predecessor	(H) corroborate
(C) nefarious	(F) prelate	(I) repudiate

Questions 5 to 7 are based on the following passage.

Edward III (1312–1377) was king of England from 1327 until his death, and is noted for his military success. Restoring royal authority after the disastrous reign of his father, Edward II, Edward III went on to transform the Kingdom of England into one of the most formidable military powers in Europe. His reign saw vital developments in legislation and government—in particular the evolution of the English parliament—as well as the ravages of the Black Death. Edward was crowned at the age of fourteen, following the deposition of his father. When he was only seventeen years old, he led a coup against his regent, Roger Mortimer, and began his personal reign. After a successful campaign in Scotland in 1333, he declared himself rightful heir to the French throne in 1337, starting what would become known as the Hundred Years' War.

5. In the context of this passage, which of the following best describes the function of Roger Mortimer?

   (A) He served as the guardian of Edward III.
   (B) He was the leader of the parliament.
   (C) He was responsible for deposing Edward II.
   (D) He ruled the country.
   (E) He wrote important pieces of legislation.

6. Based on the information in the passage, which of the following is likely a characteristic of the reign of Edward II?

   (A) Lack of effective leadership
   (B) Repression of the citizenry
   (C) Failure to expand the British Empire
   (D) Failure to prevent the Black Plague
   (E) Living in debauchery

7. Considering that the Hundred Years War was being waged during the last forty years of Edward III's life and reign, which of the following might be an accurate statement?

   (A) The number and scope of King Edward's military successes may have reduced or weakened his troops sufficiently to prevent a quick closure to the war with France.
   (B) The French military had sufficient numbers of troops and weapons to hold off the English for a protracted amount of time.
   (C) Because wartime is generally a time of prosperity, Edward deliberately prolonged the war in order to fill the coffers of the royal treasury
   (D) Rebels from Scotland provided the French with secret information to aid their cause.
   (E) His father, Edward II, was so hated by the French that they were determined to prevent his son's victory.

For Questions 8 and 10, select the two answer choices that, when used to complete the sentence, fit the meaning of the sentence as a whole and produce completed sentences that are alike in meaning.

8. Although the company grew from $16+ billion in revenue in 1990 to $126+ billion in 2005, recent managerial decisions have _____ affected its finances and its long-term stability is threatened.

   [A] ultimately
   [B] negatively
   [C] positively
   [D] significantly
   [E] adversely
   [F] especially

9. The "Trail of Tears" owes its _____ name to the thousands of Cherokees who suffered and often died during their forced relocation westward.

   A. petrous
   B. imperious
   C. pugnacious
   D. evocative
   E. doleful
   F. salubrious

10. It is clear that Mozart, who wrote his first opera at the age of eleven, displayed _____ musical abilities from his earliest years.

    A. prodigious
    B. grandiloquent
    C. preternatural
    D. epicurean
    E. refractory
    F. brazen

Question 11 is based on the following passage.

In society, you will not find health, but you will find it in nature. Unless our feet at least stood in the midst of nature, all our faces would be pale and livid. Society is always diseased, and the best part of it is the most so. There is no scent in it as wholesome as that of the pines, nor any fragrance so penetrating and restorative as the life-everlasting in high pastures. I would keep some book of natural history always by me as a sort of elixir, the reading of which should restore the tone of the system.

11. Which of the following, if true, would most effectively strengthen the author's argument?

    A. Full immersion in a natural surrounding is essential for avoiding ill health.
    B. Nature has restorative qualities that far surpass any medical treatment.
    C. Reading about nature is an inadequate form of restoring health to the mind and body.
    D. Every person reacts to nature in a similar way, and its benefits affect everyone in the same way regardless of personal perspective.
    E. Thriving cities are healthier than other cities, yet their inhabitants still require the benefits that nature can provide.

Questions 12 and 13 are based on the following passage.

The CSI effect is any of several ways in which the exaggerated portrayal of forensic science on crime shows such as *CSI: Crime Scene Investigation* influences its public perception. The term most often refers to the belief that jurors have come to demand more forensic evidence in criminal trials, thereby raising the standard of proof for prosecutors. Although this belief is widely held among American legal professionals, several studies have shown that crime shows are unlikely to cause such an effect. There are several other manifestations of the CSI effect. Greater public awareness of forensic science has increased the demand for forensic evidence in police investigations, which in turn has significantly increased workloads for crime laboratories.

12. The author's use of the underlined word "belief" has what effect on the reader's perception of the information in the passage?

    A. The reader understands the validity of the portrayals of forensic technicians in television shows.
    B. The reader understands the contrast between the belief on the part of the viewing public and the reality of the impact of forensic evidence in an actual trial.
    C. The reader understands the influence of the public on court proceedings.
    D. The reader understands that crime show producers have done extensive research to increase the reality of their shows.
    E. The reader understands the influence that television shows have on events in real life.

13. Increased awareness of forensic techniques as a result of popular television shows may have had what impact on the behavior of criminals?

    A. They have committed fewer crimes because of the increased likelihood of discovery.
    B. They have committed more crimes for which the use of forensic evidence is less important.
    C. They have become more skilled in concealing evidence in the commission of a crime.
    D. They commit fewer crimes of passion.
    E. They are more likely to work alone.

Questions 14 and 15 are based on the following passage.

The age of the internet has led to drastic transformations in the development of marketing strategies around the world. Prior to the widespread use of the internet, advertising was commonly done through newspaper articles in which text and images promoting products were printed for mass audiences. Nowadays, advertising in the newspaper is not nearly as effective. A company may be selling an impeccable product, but without the right means of advertising to a specific clientele, the advertisement will likely be unsuccessful. Choosing the correct medium to communicate is the most critical step for any aspiring marketer. If the right platform for advertising is not selected carefully, the entire message might fail to reach the desired consumer. With the internet being so universally used, promoting must now be done using an inbound marketing strategy rather than an outbound marketing strategy.

14. Based on the context what is the most likely difference between outbound marketing and inbound marketing?

   A) Outbound marketing is a more modern way of communicating a message while inbound marking has been done for centuries.

   B) Outbound marketing makes less of an effort to capture the attention of the consumer while inbound marketing makes a great effort to capture the attention of the consumer.

   C) Outbound marketing involves the use of the internet while inbound marketing involves printed methods of marketing.

   D) Outbound marketing is a traditional way of trying to reach a broad audience while inbound marketing can target individuals more specifically.

   E) Outbound marketing involves promoting certain goods while inbound marketing promotes certain services.

15. What would be the most appropriate title for this passage?

   A) The History of Marketing

   B) Choosing the Right Vehicle for Your Message

   C) Biggest Mistakes in Marketing

   D) Using the Internet to Reach Mass Markets

   E) A Trip Back in Time: Marketing

SECTION 2 (HARD) | 23 MINUTES

For Questions 1 to 4, select one entry for each blank from the corresponding column of choices. Fill all blanks in the way that best completes the text.

1. Subconsciously, humans tend to fear the worst, often in defiance of solid facts and empirical evidence to the contrary. Without realizing it, we all tend to give more credence to the negative than the positive, and we tend to hear and believe _____ predictions, no matter how outlandish, over predictions that tomorrow is going to be pretty much like today.

   A) labyrinthine
   B) abstruse
   C) fustian
   D) grandiloquent
   E) pernicious

2. The first order of business in any mediation is to (i) _____ tensions between conflicting parties by projecting an aura of calm impartiality and demonstrating (ii) _____ interest in the claims of both sides without becoming overwhelmed by the dispute.

   Blank (i)
   A) mollify
   B) diffuse
   C) deprecate

   Blank (ii)
   D) ostensible
   E) categorical
   F) specious

3. Despite their perennial popularity, romance novels are often labeled (i) _____ by those who pride themselves on their (ii) _____ tastes. These critics cite these stories formulaic plots and effusive—even (iii) _____—language. However, it is unlikely that such condemnations will resonate with romance novel enthusiasts, some of whom might argue that the genre's raison d'être is emotional satisfaction rather than intellectual fulfillment.

Blank (i)	Blank (ii)	Blank (iii)
(A) banal	(D) erudite	(G) opaque
(B) aberrant	(E) labyrinthine	(H) piquant
(C) specious	(F) sententious	(I) florid

4. Scientists have long sought a single theory to explain all physical (i) _____. One such theory is string theory, which would, if true, (ii) _____ quantum mechanics and general relativity. However, despite its promise as a complete "theory of everything", string theory has been criticized by detractors for failing to provide (iii) _____ support for its claims.

Blank (i)	Blank (ii)	Blank (iii)
(A) phenomena	(D) interpolate	(G) vitriolic
(B) matter	(E) reconcile	(H) coherent
(C) fecundity	(F) reify	(I) empirical

Questions 5 and 6 are based on the following passage.

Artists like Bill Haley and the Comets adapted the work of the Black artists to come up with their own sound. The music's solid rhythm and heavy back beat inspired new forms of dancing. Soon there were stars —Chuck Berry, Jerry Lee Lewis, Little Richard, and Carl Perkins. Due to the prejudices of the times, Disc Jockey Alan Freed coined the name "rock and roll," ironically using a term that was slang for sex in the Black community at that time. Its initial appeal was to middle class white teenagers who soon came to feel it was their own. In this era, so-called 'race music' was largely censured by America's white establishment as being too rebellious, sexual and anti-social to be acceptable.

For the following question, consider each of the three choices separately and select all that apply.

5. What can the reader infer about the culture of the period discussed in this passage?

   A. Considerable levels of discrimination prevailed.
   B. Numerous genres of music were evolving.
   C. Middle class white teenagers defied their parents.

6. Which of the following is a structural weakness of this passage?

   A. There is too little evidence to support the claim.
   B. The use of indefinite pronouns without sufficient references leads to some confusion while reading the passage.
   C. The comparative nature of the passage is not evident.
   D. Too little information is provided about the people identified in the passage.
   E. The tone of the piece is not consistent from beginning to end.

Questions 7 to 9 are based on the following passage.

Perhaps one of the most fascinating defense mechanisms among reptiles is a lizard's ability to dismember its own tail. While not all species of lizard have this unique skill, iguanas, salamanders, geckos, and many other well-known types of lizards do. A lizard will "lose" its tail if it feels severely threatened or if it has been grabbed by a predator. This feature is imperative to the survival of lizards because of the many other animals that eat them such as birds, snakes, and small mammals.

Once a lizard's tail has been self-amputated, it continues to wiggle for several minutes due to the nerves in the tail continuing to fire. This acts as a distraction to predators and allows lizards to escape from harm, though much more clumsily. The regrowth process will begin within one week. However, the tail will not be fully regrown for a couple of months.

Section 2: (Hard)

7 Which of the following statements best summarizes the second paragraph of the passage?

- Ⓐ Most lizards can detach their tails when under attack in order to escape the many predators that pursue them.
- Ⓑ Tails continue wiggling after being detached to allow lizards to get away and begin the multiple-month process of tail regrowth.
- Ⓒ Many lizards can willingly lose their tails, which continue to wiggle for several minutes, in order to distract predators that have grabbed them.
- Ⓓ The process of regrowing a tail begins shortly after losing it but lasts for several weeks.
- Ⓔ After a lizard loses its tail it is still able to move because of the nerves that continue firing.

For Questions 8 and 9, consider each of the three choices separately and select all that apply.

8 Which of the following accurately explains the author's purpose in writing this passage?

- Ⓐ To educate the reader about a unique defense mechanism seen in lizards
- Ⓑ To persuade the reader to believe that lizards are more interesting than they appear
- Ⓒ To inform the reader about what happens after a lizard loses its tail

9 What does the following quotation from the passage most likely suggest?
"This acts as a distraction to predators and allows lizards to escape from harm, though much more clumsily."

- Ⓐ Tails can become temporarily unnecessary for lizards, but rapid regrowth is essential for survival.
- Ⓑ Tails help a lizard balance and move with agility.
- Ⓒ Tails are not necessary for lizards to survive.

For Questions 10 and 12, select the two answer choices that, when used to complete the sentence, fit the meaning of the sentence as a whole and produce completed sentences that are alike in meaning.

10 As its name suggests, the "corpse flower" emits a strong and _____ odor that is highly unpleasant to humans.

- Ⓐ pusillanimous
- Ⓑ effete
- Ⓒ fetid
- Ⓓ hirsute
- Ⓔ noisome
- Ⓕ florid

11 Joan of Arc, a peasant girl with no military training and with only her religious convictions to guide her, showed great _____ in asking the Dauphin to entrust her with the French army.

- Ⓐ temperance
- Ⓑ temerity
- Ⓒ mettle
- Ⓓ recreancy
- Ⓔ paean
- Ⓕ fecklessness

12 The relatively _____ weather of northern Europe is in large part due to the Gulf Stream, a warm ocean current originating in the waters off of Florida.

- Ⓐ provident
- Ⓑ torpid
- Ⓒ aseptic
- Ⓓ benign
- Ⓔ inveterate
- Ⓕ propitious

Question 13 is based on the following passage.

A value chain is a chain of activities for a firm operating in a specific industry. Products pass through all activities of the chain in order, and at each activity the product gains some value. The chain of activities gives the products more added value than the sum of the independent activities' value. It is important not to mix the concept of the value chain with the costs occurring throughout the activities. A diamond cutter, as a profession, can be used to illustrate the difference of cost and the value chain. <u>The cutting activity may have a low cost, but the activity adds much of the value to the end product,</u> since a rough diamond is significantly less valuable than a cut diamond.

13. Based on the underlined portion of the text, which of the following statements is accurate?

    Ⓐ The value of an item is in direct proportion to the cost of the activities completed to produce it.

    Ⓑ Not all of the activities in a value chain add the same amount of value to the finished product.

    Ⓒ The first step in a chain of activities adds the most value to the finished product.

    Ⓓ Only low-cost activities add high value to the item being created.

    Ⓔ Although the retailer who sells the manufacturer's finished product may determine the price of the item, he does not contribute to the value of the item.

Questions 14 and 15 are based on the following passage.

Geologists identify estuaries based on their shapes and many possible origins. Drowned river valleys, or rivers that were flooded by rising seas after the melting of the last Ice Age, have created shallow estuaries. In other areas, enormous glaciers have carved deep fjords near coastlines. These deeper estuaries are separated from oceans by small sills, which prevent a significant flow of saltwater into the estuary. Additionally, the sharp movements of tectonic plates can result in estuaries by causing land to sink. Still, other estuaries are formed when sand builds up and shapes barrier beaches leading to small lagoons with little flow of freshwater.

14. Which of the following conclusions can be drawn based on the information in the passage?

    Ⓐ There is evidence that all estuaries have existed since the beginning of recorded history.

    Ⓑ Estuaries are insignificant bodies of water that do not receive much attention from geologists.

    Ⓒ Estuaries are developed in only one specific way.

    Ⓓ Estuaries are bodies of water that can be created and destroyed based on the movement and conditions of the water and land surrounding them.

    Ⓔ Estuaries only contain fresh water.

15. Which of the following purposes could this text serve?

    A Teaching students about the natural creation of estuaries

    B Supporting an argument that bodies of water can form through a variety of events

    C Petitioning a local government official for the protection of estuaries in the area

Answer Key

Section 1		
Q. No.	Correct Answer	Your Answer
1	C	
2	A, E	
3	B, F	
4	C	
5	A, C	
6	A, B	
7	D, E	
8	C, E	
9	D, F	
10	A	
11	A	
12	B	

Section 2 (Easy)		
Q. No.	Correct Answer	Your Answer
1	D	
2	C, E	
3	C, E, H	
4	C, D, I	
5	D	
6	A	
7	A	
8	B, E	
9	D, E	
10	A, C	
11	B	
12	B	
13	C	
14	D	
15	B	

Section 2 (Hard)		
Q. No.	Correct Answer	Your Answer
1	E	
2	A, E	
3	A, D, I	
4	A, E, I	
5	A, C	
6	B	
7	B	
8	A, C	
9	B, C	
10	C, E	
11	B, C	
12	D, F	
13	B	
14	D	
15	A, B	

SECTION 1: Answers & Explanations

1 **Choice C is correct** because forlorn means sad, lonely, or abandoned, which accurately describes Susie's behavior in the winter as described in the sentence. It contrasts effectively with her cheerful spring and summer demeanor and aligns with symptoms of seasonal depression.

Choice A is incorrect because jubilant means extremely joyful, which contradicts the description of Susie becoming withdrawn and depressed in the winter. **Choice B** is incorrect because fulminating means expressing vehement protest or anger, which does not match the passive sadness implied by seasonal depression. **Choice D** is incorrect because morbid relates to an unhealthy interest in death or disturbing topics. While it carries a dark tone, it does not precisely fit the emotional withdrawal described. **Choice E** is incorrect because rueful means feeling regret or sorrow, usually for something one has done. It suggests a specific cause of regret, which is not indicated in the passage about Susie's seasonal change in mood.

2 **Choice A is correct** for Blank (i) because "tout" means to promote or boast about something publicly. David "loved to tout his knowledge of mathematics" fits the context, as he liked to show off by offering tutoring to others. **Choice E is correct** for Blank (ii) because "tenuous" means weak or insubstantial. This contrasts with the first part of the sentence and fits with the idea that David's understanding was actually poor—he couldn't recall important rules or solve hard problems.

Choice B is incorrect because "repudiate" means to reject or deny, which contradicts the idea that David loved to display his math knowledge. **Choice C** is incorrect because "bolster" means to support or strengthen, which doesn't convey the same showy, outward behavior as "tout." **Choice D** is incorrect because "brazen" means shameless or bold, which doesn't describe the quality of his understanding—only his attitude. **Choice F** is incorrect because "didactic" means instructive or overly preachy. While this could describe someone's teaching style, it doesn't make sense as a description of the quality of his knowledge.

3 **Choice B is correct** for Blank (i) because "placate" means to calm or appease someone who is angry. Tom tried to placate Mary by taking her out to her favorite restaurant, which makes sense as a way to try to soothe her. **Choice F is correct** for Blank (ii) because "obdurate" means stubborn or unyielding. Even after Tom's effort, Mary remained firm in her anger, showing that she was not easily swayed.

Choice A is incorrect because "peruse" means to read or examine carefully, which does not fit the context of trying to comfort someone. **Choice C** is incorrect because "obviate" means to eliminate or prevent a problem, which doesn't specifically describe an attempt to soothe or comfort a person. **Choice D** is incorrect because "obsolete" means outdated or no longer in use, which doesn't apply to a person's emotional state. **Choice E** is incorrect because "mollified" means soothed or calmed. Since the sentence says Mary remained in her anger, "mollified" contradicts that idea.

4 **Choice C is correct** because high distinctiveness refers to behavior that is unique to a specific situation. A "generally lugubrious" (sad or gloomy) best man who smiles (a behavior inconsistent with his typical demeanor) only in the specific context of a wedding shows behavior that is situation-specific. This aligns with high distinctiveness as described in the passage.

Choice A is incorrect because the woman is generally garrulous and continues that behavior in the supermarket, suggesting low distinctiveness—she behaves the same in various situations. **Choice B** is incorrect because the man is generally laconic and avoids greetings in church, which is consistent with his usual behavior. Thus, this reflects low distinctiveness. **Choice D** is incorrect because the detective is generally confident and behaves confidently in the courtroom as well. This lack of change across contexts suggests low distinctiveness. **Choice E** is incorrect because the undercover agent remains enigmatic and gives ambiguous (polysemous) responses even under interrogation, again indicating consistent behavior across contexts and therefore low distinctiveness.

5 **Choice A is correct** because the passage begins by stating that bacterial and viral infections are caused by different microorganisms, but only bacteria are discussed. It is logical that the next paragraph would introduce viruses to complete the comparison. **Choice C is correct** because after discussing harmful bacterial infections like cholera and tuberculosis, a logical follow-up would be to explain how such infections are treated, providing continuity and practical application of the information.

Choice B is incorrect because while antibacterial cleansers are related to bacteria, the passage focuses on types of bacteria and their effects, not human practices or hygiene habits. The transition to the impact of antibacterial cleansers would be less direct than continuing with viruses or treatments.

6 **Choice A is correct** because "inconceivable" means unimaginable or unthinkable. The sentence implies that without evidence, belief in evolution would be extremely difficult to accept—it would defy reason, making it inconceivable. **Choice B is correct** because "implausible" means not seeming reasonable or probable; failing to convince. The structure of the sentence sets up a contrast: belief in evolution is based on evidence—otherwise, it would be unreasonable or unconvincing, i.e., implausible.

Choice C is incorrect because "questionable" means doubtful or open to challenge. While it suggests uncertainty, it does not fully capture the strong contrast in the sentence, which implies something more extreme than just doubtful. **Choice D** is incorrect because "incontestable" means undeniable or unquestionably true, which contradicts the sentence's logic. Without evidence, belief would not be undeniably true. **Choice E** is incorrect because "probable" means likely to be true or to happen. The sentence implies the opposite: that belief in evolution wouldn't be likely or credible without evidence. **Choice F** is incorrect because "cogitable" means thinkable or conceivable, which is too neutral. The sentence is discussing whether belief would be reasonable, not merely imaginable.

7 **Choice D is correct** because "dwindled" means gradually becoming smaller or weaker, which fits the idea that the employee's enthusiasm decreased over time. **Choice E is correct** because "waned" means to diminish or fade away, also indicating a reduction in enthusiasm.

Choice A is incorrect because "alleviated" means to lessen or relieve something negative, which does not fit the context of losing enthusiasm. **Choice B** is incorrect because "vanished" means disappeared suddenly, which doesn't match the gradual change implied by the sentence. **Choice C** is incorrect because "burgeoned" means to grow or increase rapidly, which is the opposite of what the sentence describes. **Choice F** is incorrect because "elongated" means made longer in time or space, which doesn't relate to enthusiasm diminishing.

8 **Choice C is correct** because "dwelling" means a place where people live, fitting well with the idea of a structure built using architectural design. **Choice E is correct** because "edifice" refers to a large, usually impressive building, which matches the context of something built with a design method.

Choice A is incorrect because "disassemble" is a verb meaning to take apart, not a noun describing a building. **Choice B** is incorrect because "chassis" refers to the base frame of a vehicle, unrelated to architecture or buildings. **Choice D** is incorrect because "groundwork" refers to preparatory work or foundation, not the building itself. **Choice F** is incorrect because "habitant" means an inhabitant or resident, not a structure.

9 **Choice D is correct** because "quandary" means a state of perplexity or doubt, especially over what to do in a difficult situation. Helen is unsure whether to go to Cancun or Rio, so she's clearly in a quandary. **Choice F is correct** because "conundrum" means a confusing and difficult problem or question. Since Helen had never traveled abroad before, choosing between two exciting destinations presents a difficult decision—a conundrum.

Choice A is incorrect because "vacillation" refers to indecisiveness or wavering, which is the action or symptom of being in a quandary or conundrum, but it doesn't describe the situation Helen is in—it describes how she might behave. **Choice B** is incorrect because "plight" refers to a dangerous, difficult, or otherwise unfortunate situation. Choosing between Cancun and Rio is not a hardship—it's a nice problem to have. **Choice C** is incorrect because "impasse" means a situation where no progress is possible, often due to disagreement. Helen can make a choice, even if it's hard—she's not stuck in an unsolvable deadlock. **Choice E** is incorrect because "certitude" means certainty—the opposite of doubt. Helen is unsure, so this doesn't fit.

10 **Choice A is correct** because the passage presents a chronological sequence of geological and human events (such as wetter climates, lava dams, the end of the ice age, and human activity) that influenced the formation and modification of the Grand Canyon. This timeline-based structure supports the idea that the primary purpose is to outline the events that shaped the canyon over time.

Choice B is incorrect because although the end of the last ice age is mentioned, it is not the main focus or goal of the passage. **Choice C** is incorrect because the passage does not emphasize the size or physical dimensions of the Grand Canyon; rather, it focuses on events that changed it. **Choice D** is incorrect because while the passage mentions wetter climates during the ice ages, it does not argue that wetter climates are preferable in general. **Choice E** is incorrect because the existence of deep lakes due to lava dams is only a supporting detail, not the main focus of the passage.

11 **Choice A is correct** because the passage discusses how human activity, especially the building of man-made dams, has impacted the erosion and sediment transport of the Colorado River, thus affecting the Grand Canyon's natural excavation. The mention of controlled floods from Glen Canyon Dam underscores the attempt to counteract human-caused disruption.

Choice B is incorrect because although engineers conduct controlled floods, the purpose of mentioning the dams is not to show mastery over nature but to highlight how they disrupted natural sediment flow. **Choice C** is incorrect because the tone of the passage is not celebratory of human progress; rather, it is neutral or slightly cautionary, noting negative effects of human interference. **Choice D** is incorrect because there is no mention of water supply to towns; the focus is on geomorphological changes to the canyon. **Choice E** is incorrect because while lava dams are mentioned earlier, there is no direct comparison made between lava dams and man-made dams. The two are discussed in different contexts.

12 **Choice B is correct** because a park ranger preparing a presentation for students would benefit from an accessible yet informative overview of the Grand Canyon's geologic history. This passage provides key events like ice ages, lava dams, and human impact in a summarized and educational format suitable for an audience of students.

Choice A is incorrect because a person writing a doctoral thesis would require much more detailed, technical, and sourced information than what is provided in this general summary. **Choice C** is incorrect because a family planning a vacation would likely be more interested in logistical and recreational information, such as trails, weather, and accommodations, rather than the geologic history. **Choice D** is incorrect because while native people may have a cultural connection to the Grand Canyon, this scientific and geological information is not specifically relevant to daily life on the canyon floor. **Choice E** is incorrect because engineers planning a new dam would require specific structural, environmental, and hydrological data, not a general historical summary of geological events.

SECTION 2 (EASY):
Answers & Explanations

1 **Choice D is correct** because "apogee" means the highest point or peak of something. The sentence emphasizes that during Louis XIV's reign, power was centralized to an unprecedented degree, suggesting this was the height of absolutism in France.

Choice A is incorrect because "substantiation" means proof or evidence, which doesn't relate to the idea of a peak or climax of a historical trend. **Choice B** is incorrect because "vindication" means justification or defense, not the high point or culmination of a system. **Choice C** is incorrect because "nadir" is the opposite of apogee; it means the lowest point, which contradicts the idea of unprecedented centralization. **Choice E** is incorrect because "prototype" means an original model or example, not the most extreme or developed form of something, as implied here.

2 **Choice C is correct** for Blank (i) because "fatuous" means silly or foolish, especially in a smug or self-satisfied way. This aligns with the second sentence, which says Ron had no understanding of the subject but still acted smug and overbearing. **Choice E is correct** for Blank (ii) because "inimical" means harmful or hostile, especially to progress or a productive atmosphere. Ron's unhelpful and arrogant comments would naturally hinder, not help, productive discussion.

Choice A is incorrect because "erudite" means learned or scholarly, which contradicts the statement that Ron showed no understanding of the economy. **Choice B** is incorrect because "jubilant" means joyful or triumphant, which doesn't relate to being smug or ignorant. **Choice D** is incorrect because "conducive" means helpful or favorable, which contradicts the idea that Ron's comments hindered discussion. **Choice F** is incorrect because "incongruous" means not in harmony or inappropriate, which is too vague and less precise than inimical in conveying how damaging his remarks were.

3 **Choice C, Choice E, and Choice H are correct** because they best fit the context of the passage describing Yellowstone's serene beauty, the volatility of its geological features, and the dramatic scale of its past eruption. "Idyllic" means peaceful and picturesque, which matches the description of Yellowstone's natural beauty that draws millions of visitors each year. "Mercurial" means unpredictable or volatile, accurately reflecting the hidden instability of Yellowstone's geology despite its calm appearance.

Section 2 (Easy): Answers & Explanations

"Cataclysmic" means extremely destructive, which aptly characterizes the massive volcanic eruption mentioned in the passage.

Choice A is incorrect because grandiose suggests something overly extravagant or pretentious, which doesn't align with the authentic beauty of a natural landscape like Yellowstone. **Choice B is incorrect** because lackadaisical means lazy or lacking enthusiasm, which is not appropriate for describing majestic scenery. **Choice D is incorrect** because tangential means only loosely related or irrelevant, which does not apply to the inherent nature of Earth's geology as described here. **Choice F is incorrect** because rudimentary means basic or undeveloped, which does not fit the context of describing complex geological activity. **Choice G is incorrect** because surreptitious means secretive or stealthy, which doesn't describe the dramatic, openly destructive nature of a volcanic eruption. **Choice I is incorrect** because quotidian means ordinary or everyday, which contradicts the extraordinary and destructive scale of the eruption described.

4 **Choice C, Choice D, and Choice I are correct** because they best fit the context of the passage involving a dark plot, noble lineage, and a claim that historians reject (but not necessarily disprove conclusively). "Nefarious" means wicked or criminal, which aligns with the idea of a sinister plot to deny Kaspar Hauser his inheritance. "Scion" refers to a descendant of a notable family, which fits the speculation that Hauser was part of the royal House of Baden. "Repudiate" means to reject or refuse to accept, which better fits the passage's phrasing that historians "tended to" dismiss the claim—without asserting it has been conclusively disproved. This is more accurate than debunk, which implies definitive disproof.

Choice A is incorrect because utilitarian refers to a practical approach, not something conspiratorial or malicious. **Choice B is incorrect** because beneficent means kind or charitable—clearly the opposite of the malicious plot described. **Choice E is incorrect** because predecessor means someone who came before, not someone descended from a family line. **Choice F is incorrect** because prelate refers to a senior religious figure and is unrelated to noble inheritance or the House of Baden. **Choice G is incorrect** because debunk implies a claim has been definitively exposed as false, which the passage does not support—historians "tended to" reject it, not disprove it. **Choice H is incorrect** because corroborate means to confirm or support, which is the opposite of what the historians are doing.

5 **Choice D is correct** because the passage states that Edward III "led a coup against his regent, Roger Mortimer," indicating that Mortimer was effectively ruling the country during Edward's minority. As a regent, Mortimer held power on Edward's behalf, which matches the function of someone ruling the country temporarily.

Choice A is incorrect because although Mortimer acted as regent, the passage does not indicate he was Edward's guardian in a personal or custodial sense—rather, he held political power. **Choice B is incorrect** because there is no mention in the passage of Mortimer being leader of the parliament or even having a role in it. **Choice C is incorrect** because the passage mentions that Edward II was deposed but does not credit Mortimer directly with that act. **Choice E is incorrect** because the passage discusses legislative developments during Edward III's reign, but there is no indication that Mortimer was involved in writing legislation.

6 **Choice A is correct** because the passage states that Edward III "restored royal authority after the disastrous reign of his father, Edward II," which implies that Edward II's rule was marked by ineffective leadership and weakened royal control.

Choice B is incorrect because the passage does not mention repression of the citizenry as a feature of Edward II's reign. **Choice C is incorrect** because while the passage discusses Edward III's military expansion, it does not suggest that Edward II failed in expanding the empire—it focuses more on political failure. **Choice D is incorrect** because the Black Death occurred during Edward III's reign, not Edward II's, so it wouldn't characterize his father's reign. **Choice E is incorrect** because there is no reference in the passage to debauchery or any immoral personal conduct by Edward II.

7 **Choice A is correct** because it reasonably infers that although Edward III had many military victories, the prolonged nature of the Hundred Years' War may indicate that those successes came at a cost—likely weakening or overextending his forces, which may have hindered a swift end to the conflict. This interpretation aligns with the historical fact that the war lasted well beyond his lifetime, despite his early gains.

Choice B is incorrect because although the French military strength might have been a factor, the passage does not provide any information about the French military's size or capabilities, so this choice is unsupported by the text. **Choice C is incorrect** because it misrepresents wartime economics—wars, especially long ones, are generally drains on a nation's resources, not periods of prosperity. There is no evidence in the passage to suggest Edward prolonged the war for financial gain. **Choice D** is incorrect because there is no mention of Scottish rebels collaborating with the French, making this answer speculative and unsupported by the passage. **Choice E** is incorrect because the passage notes that Edward II's reign was disastrous, but it does not link that reputation to French attitudes or provide any suggestion that his unpopularity influenced French resistance to Edward III.

8 **Choice B is correct** because "negatively" means in a harmful or unfavorable manner. The sentence notes that the company's "long-term stability is threatened," implying that the managerial decisions had a harmful effect—thus, "negatively" fits the context. **Choice E is correct** because "adversely" means in a way that prevents success or development; harmfully. This word is often used in formal or financial contexts (e.g., "adversely affected"), making it a strong fit with the sentence about financial stability.

Choice A is incorrect because "ultimately" refers to something happening in the end or eventually. While plausible grammatically, it doesn't explain how the decisions affected finances. **Choice C** is incorrect because "positively" suggests a beneficial effect, which contradicts the idea that stability is now "threatened." **Choice D** is incorrect because "significantly" indicates a large effect but does not clarify whether that effect was good or bad—it's too vague for the clear negative tone of the sentence. **Choice F** is incorrect because "especially" implies emphasis or exclusivity but not direction (positive or negative), which makes it an imprecise fit here.

9 **Choice D is correct** because "evocative" means bringing strong images, memories, or feelings to mind. The name "Trail of Tears" powerfully calls to mind the suffering and death endured by the Cherokees, so this word is a strong and appropriate fit. **Choice E is correct** because "doleful" means sorrowful or mournful. Since the sentence describes the suffering and death of thousands, this word captures the emotional tone implied by the name.

Choice A is incorrect because "petrous" means stony or rock-like, which is unrelated to the emotional or historical meaning implied by the name. **Choice B** is incorrect because "imperious" means domineering or arrogantly overbearing, which doesn't describe the nature of the name. **Choice C** is incorrect because "pugnacious" means eager to fight or quarrelsome, which has no relevance to the name or the context of suffering. **Choice F** is incorrect because "salubrious" means health-giving or beneficial, which is the opposite of what the name "Trail of Tears" represents.

10 **Choice A is correct** because "prodigious" means extraordinary or impressively great in extent, size, or degree. Mozart composing an opera at age eleven clearly shows extraordinary musical talent from a young age. **Choice C is correct** because "preternatural" means beyond what is normal or natural. This fits well with the idea of Mozart having unusually advanced musical abilities for his age.

Choice B is incorrect because "grandiloquent" refers to pompous or extravagant language, not talent or ability. **Choice D** is incorrect because "epicurean" relates to indulgence in luxury or fine food and drink, which has no relevance to musical skill. **Choice E** is incorrect because "refractory" means stubborn or resistant to authority or control, which does not describe Mozart's abilities. **Choice F** is incorrect because "brazen" means shamelessly bold or impudent, which does not relate to talent or musical aptitude.

11 **Choice B is correct** because the author emphasizes nature's unique restorative power and bases the argument solely on nature's ability to provide health, without suggesting reliance on medicine or doctors. This aligns directly with the idea that nature's restorative qualities surpass other treatments.

Choice A is incorrect because the author shows that even reading about nature offers benefits, so "full immersion" is not necessary for health, making the idea of needing full immersion too extreme. **Choice C** is incorrect because the author clearly states that reading about nature "should restore the tone of the system," indicating that reading nature is indeed adequate to some degree. **Choice D** is incorrect because the author acknowledges that people perceive nature differently depending on their health, so the reaction is not uniform, refuting the idea that everyone benefits the same way. **Choice E** is incorrect because the author claims "society is always diseased, and the best is the most so," contradicting the idea that thriving or better cities are healthier, so this choice is inconsistent with the passage.

12 **Choice B is correct** because the use of the word "belief" highlights a contrast between what the public and legal professionals think about the CSI effect and what studies have shown about its actual impact, helping the reader see the difference between perception and reality.

Choice A is incorrect because the passage does not suggest that the portrayals of forensic technicians on television are valid or accurate; rather, it questions the assumed effects of those portrayals. **Choice C** is incorrect because although the passage mentions public demand for forensic evidence, the focus of

Section 2 (Easy): Answers & Explanations

"belief" is more on the perception of jurors rather than direct public influence on court proceedings. **Choice D** is incorrect because there is no mention in the passage of crime show producers conducting extensive research to improve realism. **Choice E** is incorrect because the passage indicates that the influence of crime shows on real-life events, specifically juror expectations, is disputed rather than clearly established.

13 **Choice C is correct** because increased public awareness of forensic science from TV shows likely motivates criminals to become more skilled at hiding or destroying evidence to avoid detection.

Choice A is incorrect because the passage does not suggest criminals have committed fewer crimes due to fear of discovery; it only discusses increased demand for forensic evidence, not crime rates. **Choice B** is incorrect because there is no indication that criminals have shifted toward crimes where forensic evidence is less important. **Choice D** is incorrect because the passage does not mention any change in the frequency of crimes of passion. **Choice E** is incorrect because the passage does not address criminals' likelihood to work alone or in groups.

14 **Choice D is correct** because the passage discusses the change from outbound marketing to inbound marketing after explaining that traditional methods of marketing, such as publicly read newspapers, are no longer used as often since the internet was established.

Choice A is incorrect because outbound marketing is described as the former way of advertising, which typically involved newspapers, and inbound marketing is described as more prominent since the internet was established. **Choice B** is incorrect because the author does not make any statements regarding how much effort is being put into marketing strategies. Additionally, both strategies attempt to capture the attention of the consumer in different ways. **Choice C** is incorrect because outbound marketing is described as the traditional way of advertising, primarily through newspapers, while inbound marketing has become more prominent since the development of the internet. **Choice E** is incorrect because the concept of promoting goods versus services is not a part of this passage. The passage discusses different ways of marketing despite what the products are.

15 **Choice B is correct** because the passage states, "The most important choice for any marketer in the cutthroat world of advertising is choosing the appropriate medium to transmit the message." In this instance, another word for, "medium," could be, "vehicle." The remainder of the passage discusses means of transmitting a message including newspapers and the internet.

Choice A is incorrect because the passage does include some content relating to former marketing practices that have been used, but clearly moves in the direction of future marketing practices that should be used to capture the attention of a consumer. This is not written in the style of a historical report. **Choice C** is incorrect because the title, "Biggest Mistakes in Marketing," implies that several mistakes would be discussed. In this passage, one specific mistake is discussed, which is using the wrong means of transmitting a message. **Choice D** is incorrect because it contradicts the point of the passage. The author discusses moving toward internet marketing but suggests that the concept of reaching mass markets (such as when advertising in newspapers) is outdated. **Choice E** is incorrect because the passage does include some content relating to older marketing approaches that have been used, but clearly moves in the direction of future marketing approaches using the internet.

For more practice, visit www.vibrantpublishers.com

Chapter 7: Practice Test #2

SECTION 2 (HARD): Answers & Explanations

1 **Choice E is correct** because "pernicious" means harmful or damaging, which fits the context of negative predictions that humans tend to believe despite evidence. The passage discusses a bias toward fearing the worst, so harmful or dangerous predictions align well with this idea.

Choice C is incorrect because "fustian" means pompous or inflated language, which does not specifically convey harmfulness or negativity. **Choice D is incorrect** because "grandiloquent" means using extravagant or pompous language, which again focuses on style rather than harmful content. **Choice A is incorrect** because "labyrinthine" means complex or intricate, which doesn't relate directly to the nature of predictions being feared. **Choice B is incorrect** because "abstruse" means difficult to understand, which doesn't fit the idea of negative predictions that are easily believed.

2 **Choice A is correct** because "mollify" means to soften or mitigate tensions, which fits the context of easing conflict during mediation. Candidates often mistakenly choose "diffuse," confusing it with "defuse," but "mollify" more accurately describes calming tensions. **Choice E is correct** because "categorical" means unconditional or absolute, indicating sincere and clear interest in the claims of both sides—an essential quality for an effective mediator.

Choice B is incorrect because "diffuse" means to scatter or spread out, which is not the same as calming or softening tensions and therefore is less appropriate here. **Choice C is incorrect** because "deprecate" means to express disapproval, which would exacerbate tensions rather than reduce them. **Choice D is incorrect** because "ostensible" means seeming or apparent but not necessarily genuine, which contradicts the need for sincere interest. **Choice F is incorrect** because "specious" means superficially plausible but actually misleading, implying insincerity rather than genuine concern.

3 **Choice A, Choice D, and Choice I are correct** because they best fit the context of critics dismissing romance novels for being overly familiar, while valuing intellectual depth, and criticizing the writing style as overly elaborate. "Banal" means trite or unoriginal, which matches the common criticism of romance novels. "Erudite" means having or showing great knowledge, which fits critics who pride themselves on intellectual tastes. "Florid" means excessively intricate or elaborate in style, which aligns with the description of "effusive—even florid—language."

Choice B is incorrect because aberrant means deviating from the norm, which does not fit the context of romance novels being predictable or formulaic. **Choice C is incorrect** because specious means superficially plausible but actually wrong, which does not capture the criticism of the novels' plot or language here. **Choice E is incorrect** because labyrinthine means complex and convoluted, which contradicts the criticism of formulaic plots. **Choice F is incorrect** because sententious means overly moralizing, which does not apply to the language described. **Choice G is incorrect** because opaque means unclear or difficult to understand, which is not the criticism given. **Choice H is incorrect** because piquant means stimulating or provocative, which contradicts the idea of excessive or overly emotional language.

4 **Choice A, Choice E, and Choice I are correct** because they best fit the context of scientific theories explaining physical events, aiming to unify existing theories, and needing evidence-based support. "Phenomena" refers to observable events or occurrences in nature, which fits the context of explaining physical phenomena. "Reconcile" means to bring into agreement or harmony, which aligns with the idea of uniting quantum mechanics and general relativity. "Empirical" means based on observation or experiment, which is essential for supporting scientific claims.

Choice B is incorrect because matter refers to physical substance, not the broad range of physical events the theory seeks to explain. **Choice C is incorrect** because fecundity means fertility or productivity, which is unrelated to physical events or theories. **Choice D is incorrect** because interpolate means to insert or estimate values, which does not fit the context of unifying theories. **Choice F is incorrect** because reify means to make something abstract more concrete, which does not capture the concept of uniting two theories. **Choice G is incorrect** because vitriolic means harsh or bitter, which does not describe the support for claims. **Choice H is incorrect** because coherent means logical and consistent, but the criticism mentioned is about lack of support, making empirical a better fit.

5 **Choice A is correct** because the passage clearly references the "prejudices of the times" and the censure of "race music" by the white establishment, indicating that considerable discrimination prevailed. **Choice C is correct** because middle class white

352 | *GRE Verbal Practice Questions*

teenagers embraced rock and roll, which was censured by the older generation, showing they defied their parents' cultural beliefs.

Choice B is incorrect because the passage focuses specifically on the evolution of rock and roll and does not discuss multiple genres evolving during that period.

6 **Choice B is correct** because the passage contains several indefinite pronouns like "soon there were stars," "its initial appeal," and "their own," without clear or specific antecedents. This lack of clarity may confuse the reader about exactly who or what is being referred to, which is a structural weakness.

Choice A is incorrect because the passage does provide examples and historical context to support its claims, such as naming specific artists and the origin of the term "rock and roll." **Choice C** is incorrect because the passage is not meant to be comparative in nature; it's a brief historical overview, not a comparison between styles, people, or time periods. **Choice D** is incorrect because while more information about the individuals mentioned might be helpful, the passage's intent is to summarize the cultural emergence of rock and roll, not provide detailed biographies. **Choice E** is incorrect because the tone remains consistent throughout—factual and historical with a slightly critical undertone regarding cultural appropriation and censorship.

7 **Choice B is correct** because it includes information from each of the four sentences in the second paragraph in a concise format.

Choice A is incorrect because it accurately summarizes only the first paragraph of the passage. **Choice C** is incorrect because it accurately summarizes information from both the first and second paragraphs of the passage. **Choice D** is incorrect because it summarizes the information given in the last two sentences of paragraph two, but does not include information from the first two sentences. It fails to mention the tail's ability to wiggle after amputation and the way that this distracts predators so that lizards can escape. **Choice E** is incorrect because it only rewords the first sentence of the second paragraph and does not summarize any other ideas in the paragraph.

8 **Choice A is correct** because the author wrote a factual piece that provided an overall summary of the defense mechanism. **Choice C is correct** because the author did include information that describes what happens to the tail and the lizard after amputation. Additionally, the author wrote about the regrowth process.

Choice B is incorrect because the author does not use any persuasive techniques and does not make any statements about lizards seeming uninteresting in the first place.

9 **Choice B is correct** because the statement shows that when a tail is lost, so is the lizard's coordination. **Choice C is correct** because the statement shows lizards are capable of living without a tail although it causes them to move awkwardly and inelegantly.

Choice A is incorrect because the quotation does not suggest at any point that a lizard will die from tail loss.

10 **Choice C is correct** because "fetid" means having a strong, unpleasant smell. This fits perfectly with the sentence, which emphasizes the flower's strong and unpleasant odor. **Choice E is correct** because "noisome" means offensive to the senses, especially the sense of smell. It reinforces the idea that the odor is highly unpleasant to humans.

Choice A is incorrect because "pusillanimous" means cowardly or lacking courage, which is unrelated to smell. **Choice B** is incorrect because "effete" means worn out or lacking strength or vitality, and does not relate to odor. **Choice D** is incorrect because "hirsute" means hairy, which does not pertain to the idea of a smell. **Choice F** is incorrect because "florid" means excessively ornate or flowery in style, or having a flushed complexion—neither of which describes a smell.

11 **Choice B is correct** because "temerity" means boldness or audacity, especially when considered reckless. Joan of Arc, a young peasant girl with no military background, asking the heir to the French throne to entrust her with an army shows extreme boldness — the very definition of temerity. **Choice C is correct** because "mettle" means courage, spirit, or resilience. The sentence highlights Joan's brave initiative based on conviction alone, showing her inner strength and courage, which is well expressed by "mettle."

Choice A is incorrect because "temperance" means self-restraint or moderation, which does not align with the boldness Joan displayed. **Choice D** is incorrect because "recreancy" means cowardice or betrayal, which is the opposite of Joan's courageous action. **Choice E** is incorrect because "paean" is a song of praise or triumph, and does not describe a personal trait like courage or boldness. **Choice F** is incorrect because "fecklessness" refers to irresponsibility or ineffectiveness, which contrasts sharply with Joan's determination and action.

12 **Choice D is correct** because "benign" means gentle or mild, especially in reference to climate or weather. The sentence refers to the relatively mild weather of northern Europe due to the warm Gulf Stream, so "benign" fits the context well. **Choice F is correct** because "propitious" means favorable or indicating good conditions. When describing weather, "propitious" suggests that the weather is mild and agreeable, which aligns with the sentence's meaning.

Choice A is incorrect because "provident" means showing foresight or being prudent, especially with money. It doesn't apply to weather. **Choice B** is incorrect because "torpid" means sluggish or inactive, usually referring to people or animals, not weather. **Choice C** is incorrect because "aseptic" means free from contamination, usually in a medical or scientific context. It doesn't make sense applied to weather. **Choice E** is incorrect because "inveterate" means long-established and unlikely to change, usually used to describe habits or people, not weather conditions.

13 **Choice B is correct** because the passage explains that not all activities in the value chain contribute equally to the final value. It specifically uses the example of a diamond cutter: while cutting may be a low-cost activity, it adds substantial value to the final product. This implies that each activity contributes differently to value creation, making B an accurate statement.

Choice A is incorrect because the passage clearly distinguishes between cost and value. It states that "it is important not to mix the concept of the value chain with the costs," and gives the example of a low-cost activity (cutting) that adds high value, directly refuting the idea of value being in proportion to cost. **Choice C** is incorrect because the passage does not indicate which step in the chain adds the most value; it only emphasizes that value is added progressively and differently at each stage. **Choice D** is incorrect because while the example involves a low-cost activity adding high value, the passage does not claim that only low-cost activities add high value. It avoids generalizations of this sort. **Choice E** is incorrect because the role of the retailer is not discussed at all in the passage, so there is no basis in the text to evaluate their contribution to the value chain.

14 **Choice D is correct** because the passage describes several ways that estuaries are created and altered because of surrounding water and land including drowned river valleys, glacial movement, shifting tectonic plates, and sand accumulation.

Choice A is incorrect because the passage states that there is evidence that estuaries were created because of the last Ice Age ending. Also, the passage focuses on ways that estuaries can be created, meaning that they have not always existed. **Choice B** is incorrect because the passage does not call estuaries insignificant or imply that they are unimportant in any way. Also, estuaries are described in geological terms in the first sentence. There is no other mention of geology or geologists. **Choice C** is incorrect because the passage details several ways that estuaries can be created including drowned river valleys, glacial movement, shifting tectonic plates, and sand accumulation. **Choice E** is incorrect because the passage states, "bar-built estuaries often have a protected lagoon with little freshwater flow," implying that there is also salt water involved. The passage also states, "These estuaries are separated from the ocean by a shallow sill that prevents extensive movement of saltwater."

15 **Choice A is correct** because this text is written in an informative style and focuses on ways that estuaries form in nature. **Choice B is correct** because this text could serve as the informative piece of an argument. If the author was making an argument that bodies of water can form through a variety of events, the author would need to provide specific examples to support that claim.

Choice C is incorrect because the author does not use any persuasive techniques or discuss protection of the estuaries. If the author were petitioning for protection of the estuaries, the many detailed examples of how estuaries form would not be necessary.

Know Your Scaled Score

This table can be used to calculate your scaled score. Use a pencil to note down your scores for Section 1 and Section 2 (Easy or Hard).

Input the number of questions you got right for both sections and add them in the adjacent columns. To get your scaled score for each section, refer to the table on page 356. Lastly, add both sections' scaled scores to get your total score for all tests.

If you attempted the Easy Section, check your scaled scores in the Verbal (Easy) column.

If you attempted the Hard Section, check your scaled scores in the Verbal (Hard) column.

Section 1 (Number of correct answers)	Section 2 (Number of correct answers)	Total (Section 1 + Section 2)	Scaled Score

SCALED SCORE TABLE

Raw Score	Verbal (Easy)	Verbal (Hard)
27	160	170
26	159	170
25	158	168
24	157	166
23	156	165
22	155	163
21	154	162
20	153	161
19	153	160
18	152	159
17	151	158
16	150	157
15	149	156
14	148	155
13	147	154
12	146	153
11	145	153
10	143	152
9	142	151
8	141	150
7	139	
6	137	
5	135	
4	133	
3	130	
2	130	
1	130	
0	130	

Made in United States
Orlando, FL
19 September 2025